CRACKING THE REGENTS
GLOBAL STUDIES

THE PRINCETON REVIEW

1999–2000

CRACKING THE REGENTS

GLOBAL STUDIES

DAVID DANIEL

1999–2000 Edition

Random House, Inc.
New York

Princeton Review Publishing
2315 Broadway
New York, NY 10024
E-mail: info@review.com

Published in the United States by Random House, Inc., New York, and
simultaneously in Canada by Random House of Canada Limited, Toronto.

ISBN 0-375-75277-3

Editor: Lesly Atlas
Production Coordinator: Stephanie Martin
Production Editor: Kristen Azzara

Manufactured in the United States of America.

9   8   7   6   5   4   3   2   1

1999–2000 Edition

ACKNOWLEDGMENTS

This book would not have been possible without a lot of love and support. Tons of thanks to my family. To my brothers, I say thank you John (for your financial support) and thank you Bob (for your computer support). As for my sisters, I need to thank Linda for always telling me that I should write a book, Judy for introducing our family to Trivial Pursuit years ago (an occurrence which made me, well . . . want to pursue trivia!), Debra, whose eight years in Europe helped me realize that I needed to see the world, and especially Becky, Sarah and Stephanie, whose emotional support kept my head on straight when I felt overwhelmed. And of course, I want to thank my parents, who have always loved and supported me no matter what path I've chosen.

Shouts of thanks to Todd Epperley for keeping me sane, and Aspen for keeping me company.

And then there are all the folks at The Princeton Review. I want to thank Paul Edelblut and David Stewart for their encouragement and support (and for talking me into writing this book in the first place). I also owe special thanks to: Lesly Atlas, my editor, for her patience, persistence and editing skills; and my production editor, Kristen Azzara. Finally, I'd like to thank all of the students I have taught over the years at The Princeton Review, who in many ways have taught me more than I have taught them.

Special thanks to all of the New York State Global Studies teachers who lent their extremely valuable assistance reviewing this project including: Bob Carlina, Charles Cross, Ellen Rutsky, Charles Stein & Moses Weintraub.

TABLE OF CONTENTS

INTRODUCTION

WHAT IS THE PRINCETON REVIEW?

The Princeton Review is an international test preparation company with branches in all the major U.S. cities and several cities abroad. In 1981 John Katzman starting teaching an SAT prep course in his parents' living room. Within five years, Katzman (in partnership with fellow test guru Adam Robinson) had established the largest SAT coaching program in the country.

The Princeton Review's phenomenal success in improving students' scores on standardized tests was (and continues to be) the result of a simple, innovative, and radically effective approach: study the test itself, not what the test *claims* to test. This approach has led to the development of techniques for taking standardized tests based on the principles the test writers themselves use to write them.

The Princeton Review has found that its methods work not just for cracking the SAT, but for any standardized test. We've successfully applied our system to the SAT II, AP, ACT, GMAT, GRE, and LSAT, to name just a few. As a result of hundreds of hours of exhaustive study, we are now applying that system to the New York State Regents exam. This book uses our time-tested principle: figure out what the test-givers want, then teach that to the test-takers in a comprehensive and fun way.

We also publish books and CD-ROMs on an enormous variety of education and career-related topics. If you're interested, check out our web site at www.review.com.

WHAT IS THE GLOBAL STUDIES REGENTS EXAM?

The Global Studies Regents exam consists of two parts. Part One contains multiple choice questions. Most tests have 48 questions, but a couple of them have had 47 or 49 questions. You'll probably want to spend about an hour of your time on this part, maybe a little more, depending on how much time you think you'll need for the essays. Each question is followed by four answer choices. One of them is the Regents favorite. All you have to do is identify it.

You should *never* leave any question blank, because there is no penalty for guessing. It's better to have a twenty-five percent chance of getting the question right than no chance at all. Later, you'll read about some process of elimination techniques that will help you make better guesses. In the meantime, click your heels together and repeat after me: I will not leave any questions blank, I will not leave any questions blank, I will not leave any questions blank.

Part Two contains the essays. The bad news is that you have to write in a well-organized manner. There's no guessing involved, just thinking, organizing, and writing. Even worse news is that each essay question will have several parts. However, the good news is that you will be prepared with the help of this book. Even better news is that you get to select which three essays you want to write from a list of seven, which means you can totally ignore four of them.

Always remember, *you* have the power to decide. You say you're just not in the mood to write an essay about the impact of geography on various cultures around the world? No problem. Ditch it. Just pick a different essay.

PART I

HOW TO CRACK
THE SYSTEM

CHAPTER ONE—CRACKING THE REGENTS: AN OVERVIEW

HEY YOU! WHY ARE YOU FLIPPING THROUGH THE PAGES SO QUICKLY? LEARN SOME PATIENCE! READ THIS CHAPTER FIRST.

You've probably noticed that this book is kinda big. Don't worry. This book isn't crammed with everything that has ever happened on the globe. That would be a waste of time. It's big because it has so many practice tests. Practicing *isn't* a waste of time.

Here's the deal: The more you practice, the better you will do. Not only will you learn how the test is organized and how the test writers think, but you'll also notice something that works even more to your advantage: Rather than creating original questions for every single test, the test writers sometimes use the same questions again. Often, they switch the words around a bit, but it's still pretty much the same thing. Your home isn't new just because you switch the furniture around a little.

SO, WHAT ARE YOU TRYING TO SAY?

What we're saying is that when you decided to buy this book, you bought the best tool available to help you crack the Global Studies Regents exam. There are two big things you need to do: Learn how the test writers think (that's the point of the first three chapters) and then practice what you've learned (that's where the practice tests come in). All of the practice tests in this book are actual Regents Global Studies Exams. These tests are followed by detailed explanations for both the correct and incorrect answer choices. The explanations are designed not just to help you understand the Global Studies material, but to help you think through the answer choices even when you *don't* fully understand the material. If you take all or even most of the practice tests in this book, and if you read the explanations for the questions that you missed, you won't be very surprised by the questions you get on test day.

IS THIS TEST GOING TO TAKE A LONG TIME? I HAVE PLANS, YOU KNOW.

The Global Studies Examination is three hours long. That may sound like a lot of time, but since you have to answer approximately forty-eight multiple choice questions and write three essays, the time will pass quickly. One reason there are so many practice tests in this book is that you need to learn to pace yourself. Every time you take a test, time yourself. Make sure you develop a pacing strategy that allows you to answer all of the multiple choice questions and write three essays. Some students need a lot of time for the essays. Others like to organize and write, but hate thinking through multiple choice questions. Taking a bunch of practice tests will allow you to figure out which kind of test-taker you are. Once you've figured this out, you'll need to make pacing adjustments accordingly.

HOW DO THEY PLAN ON SCORING THIS THING, ANYWAY?

You would think that since the multiple choice section usually contains 48 questions, Part One would be worth 48 points. It just makes sense, right? Well, life in the land of the Regents doesn't always make sense. It's a Global Studies test, after all, not a math test. Instead, Part One is worth 55 points. The Regents use a scaled scoring system. Therefore, if you answer 35 questions correctly, you probably won't receive 35 points. More likely, you'll receive about 43 or 44 points, give or take. Not a bad deal! The scaled system works in your favor, so don't complain. You just need to remember that the more questions you answer correctly, the higher your score will be. Are you still clicking your heels together? Remember, don't leave any questions blank.

In Part Two of the exam, you'll answer three essay questions worth 15 points each. If you read this book carefully and practice a lot, you'll perform well, but how will your grader know how to score it?

The graders are given a set of grading guidelines. They're told to look for things like factual accuracy, logical development, whether or not you answered the question asked, the use of examples, and so on. All of this is discussed in greater detail in Chapter Three. For now, you simply need to understand that each essay is worth 15 points. Since you will write three of them (you'd *better* write three), you can receive a maximum of 45 points on Part Two.

So, it actually all works out kind of well, because the two parts add up to a maximum of 100 points.

ARE THE RUMORS TRUE? DO I REALLY NEED TO REVIEW EVERYTHING FROM MY GLOBAL STUDIES COURSE? SAY IT AIN'T SO!

It ain't so.

Now, don't get *too* excited! If you expect to do well, you need to be familiar with many of the major topics, themes, people, and organizations discussed in your Global Studies course. However, that doesn't mean that every topic is equally important. Instead, some topics and themes are tested much more frequently (and in much greater detail) than others. This book will help you determine where you will need to focus your efforts.

First things first. Take a complete Global Studies exam. There are a bunch of practice tests in this book, so you may as well take the first one. Go ahead. No time like the present.

Time yourself. Take the exam in one sitting. Don't stop for an hour and eat a bowl of ice cream. Disconnect the phone. Turn off the TV. And the radio . . . yes . . . *the radio*! We don't care if you study better when music is playing, the point is you won't get to listen to music when you take the *real* test. Make sure you follow the directions.

When you're finished, score the exam and compare your answers with the answers and explanations in this book. If you received a perfect score on Part One and wrote flawless essays on Part Two, go stand in front of a mirror and dance, dance, dance. If your performance was less than perfect, you need to start figuring out your strengths and weaknesses. You need to develop a study plan.

EXCUSE ME, DID YOU SAY A STUDY PLAN? PUH-LEASE!

Yes. A study plan. Don't worry. All this means is that it makes a lot of sense to figure out how much you know (and how strong a test-taker you are) *before* you waste your time reviewing stuff that you don't need to review, or only need to review a little bit.

If you purchased this book at least two months before the exam, you will have plenty of time to review the strategies in this book and take all of the practice tests. Go to the mirror. Remind yourself how cool you are.

If you purchased this book only a few weeks before the exam, you'll still have enough time, but you might have to cancel a couple of dates or cut down on the channel-surfing. Run to the mirror. Remind yourself how determined you are.

If you purchased this book only a few days before the exam, we hope you did well on your first practice test. If not, you should read the first three chapters several times and then take a couple more practice exams. You'll be surprised how much you can learn in just a few days! Run to the mirror. Tell yourself how lucky you are that you found The Princeton Review.

OKAY, OKAY . . . TIME'S A WASTING. TELL ME MORE ABOUT THE STUDY PLAN.

There are two ways to study: You can review tons of material that may or may not be tested, or you can do things The Princeton Review way. This book is designed to help you determine which themes and famous figures are tested most frequently. The point is, you need to focus your time on things worth focusing on. You probably already know that you need to sift through the tons of global studies materials your teachers have given you. That's probably why you bought this book—you want to become test-wise! To do this, you need to concentrate on major themes, eliminate answer choices that are inconsistent with those themes, and refuse to get freaked out about the stuff that hardly ever gets tested, especially if you're running short on time. That's why you need to plan.

For example, if you say "Confucius" when somebody sneezes and think that Mandela is a trendy new restaurant in Manhattan, you'd better plan on spending a lot of time reviewing the material and the glossary. You might want to obtain a copy of The Princeton Review's course review book, *High School Global Studies Review*. Why? Because Confucius and Mandela are part of the regular cast of characters on the exam. Other people, like Kemal Atatürk and David Ben-Gurion make occasional appearances, but you can still do well on the test even if you remember little about them, or nothing at all.

This does not mean that you have to read the entire biography of regular cast members like Nelson Mandela. There's no need to put a picture of him in your locker, although we're sure he'd be touched if you did. It simply means that if you're really fuzzy on stuff that this book tells you is really important, you should plan on reviewing it.

SO YOU'RE SAYING I NEED TO BE ORGANIZED?

Yes! Go get a calendar. Put a big circle around the day of the actual test (I hope it's not tomorrow!). Depending on how much time you have before the test, you need to plan on taking at least one practice test every week. The more you practice, the better you will do, especially since you'll start to notice that the Regents ask many of the same questions from test to test. After you take each test, you'll need to grade it and review your mistakes.

HOW DO I KNOW IF MY MISTAKES ARE DUE TO A LACK OF PRACTICE AND STRATEGIES AS OPPOSED TO A LACK OF KNOWLEDGE?

You'll know after you take just a couple of practice tests. Keep a list of the questions that you miss. Make sure you read the explanations for both the correct answer choices and the incorrect answer choices. You're going to be able to tell if you missed the question because you were clueless as opposed to being careless. If you were clueless on a question, you need to pay particular attention to how frequently the information in that question is tested. If, for example, the advice in the explanation of a question tells you to review major world religions because they are frequently tested, that's exactly what you should do. If something is really important, we'll tell you so.

Finally, sometimes you'll *think* you know about a certain topic, but in fact you don't. Be consciously aware when you're surprised with an answer. Try to determine the reason for your surprise. There's a big difference between being surprised with an explanation because you thought the answer you picked was correct, and being surprised with your answer because you can't believe you were tricked or careless. In the first situation, you need to review your materials more extensively and straighten out information that might have been twisted around in your mind. In the second situation, you need to slow down and learn test strategies.

OKAY, SO TELL ME WHAT I SHOULD DO NEXT.

Practice, practice, practice! And continue to review according to your study plan. Remember to keep a list of the types of questions that you consistently miss. Also, keep a list of terms and people that you keep forgetting, or just don't quite understand. Finally, make sure to time and consciously pace yourself.

CHAPTER TWO—CRACKING THE MULTIPLE-CHOICE QUESTIONS

SOMETIMES I KNOW THE ANSWER. OTHER TIMES, I GUESS. I THINK IT'S IMPORTANT TO BE FLEXIBLE.

Part One has about forty-eight multiple choice questions. On some, you'll know the correct answer immediately, especially after you prepare with the help of this book. On others, you'll be uncertain, and you'll have to make your best guess. On a few, you might have no idea at all. You might even think there's been some sort of mistake. A misprint or typo in the question, maybe.

The thing to keep in mind is that since there isn't a guessing penalty, there is absolutely no reason to leave any questions blank. Therefore, since you're going to be answering all of the questions, and since some of the questions are going to be easier for you than others, it's important that you learn how to be flexible with yourself. The test writers create a variety of different types of questions and then use a variety of different types of distractions in the incorrect answer choices. It shouldn't be surprising, then, that you need to learn a variety of different ways to find the right answer.

DID YOU EVER HEAR THE ONE ABOUT THE SCULPTOR AND THE ELEPHANT?

A popular children's joke goes something like this: How did the sculptor carve the elephant out of a block of marble? He chopped away everything that didn't look like an elephant.

It's the same deal on the test. It doesn't matter if you get the question right because you know what the right answer is supposed to look like, or because you know what the right answer isn't supposed to look like. In both cases, you get credit for the right answer.

On the pages that follow, you will learn how to approach Regents Global Studies multiple-choice questions from two different angles. The first group of techniques will help you to anticipate the right answer choice after you read the question but before you read the answer choices. The second group of techniques will help you to eliminate incorrect answer choices when you're not sure what the right answer is.

CARVING THE ELEPHANT

Deja vú

It's easy to find the right answer when you've seen the question before. Since the Regents often recycle questions from previous exams, some of the questions that you'll see on your actual test day are probably already located in this book. If you do all of the practice tests and thoroughly read all of the explanations, you'll immediately know the answer to some of the questions when you take the real thing.

Recycled relationships

The Regents not only recycle test questions, they recycle themes. In other words, even when they write new questions, they use the same old general ideas. For example, on one exam the Regents tested the idea that culture in India is greatly influenced by Hinduism. On another exam, they tested the idea that culture in Latin America has been greatly influenced by Catholicism. So if you see a question that asks you to identify something that has greatly influenced the culture of the Middle East, or the culture of anywhere else on the globe, it would be a good idea if you think about the dominant religion of the region. In the case of the Middle East, of course, it's Islam.

Therefore, just by doing a few practice exams and organizing the information, you can come to the conclusion that the Regents believe that religion has a big impact on culture.

Remember, one of your goals is to understand how the Regents' test writers think. Paying attention to concepts and relationships that they consistently test is one of the best ways to get inside their brains. If you get good at doing this, you can zero in on the right answer if you simply ask yourself, "What would the Regents think is important?"

As you'll see later, this way of thinking will go a long way when you're writing the essays as well.

The hip bone's connected to the . . . leg bone.

As you take the practice tests, it's a good idea if you pay attention to the words that the Regents consistently group together. For example, *subsistence farming* is often linked with *traditional societies*. Therefore, if you see the term *subsistence farming* in a question, you should look for an answer choice that uses the words *traditional culture,* or something like it. If those exact words aren't in one of the answer choices, pick an answer choice that still refers to traditional cultures.

Word association works for people as well. If you see Karl Marx, the answer choice will likely refer to communism, or describe communism if the word itself isn't used. If you see Adam Smith, the answer choice will probably refer to laissez-faire economics or a free-market system.

The point is, when you learn about a new person or a new word, don't simply memorize a definition. Link the definition to other words that you also need to know for the test. It'll help you learn concepts, and it will help you spot the correct answer choices immediately.

Six topics (try saying it ten times real fast)

The Regents like certain topics. No, they *really* like certain topics. There happen to be six of them, or at least that's the way we've organized them. They include major political philosophies, major world religions, major economic philosophies, sociological terms, environmental/agricultural terms, and geographical terms and places (especially waterways). If you learn the terms that the Regents use in each of these categories, you're going to be able to answer the majority of the questions correctly.

How are you going to learn them? Keep one sheet of paper for each of these six categories. As you take practice tests, add words and people to the lists. And don't just memorize them, try to connect them together. In other words, know which terms are similar to each other, are different from each other, or are a subcategory of one of the other terms.

The lists on the next two pages will help you get started. With the exception of the geographical terms, these words can be found in the glossary. They're in the glossary because they show up pretty often on the test, which is the whole point!

Political Terms and Systems

Absolute Monarchy
Anarchy
Communism
Democracy
Dictatorship
Divine Right Theory
Fascism

Monarchy
Nonalignment
One-Party System
Republic
Theocracy
Totalitarianism

World Religions

Animism
Buddhism
Christianity
Hinduism

Islam
Judaism
Shintoism
Taoism

Economic Terms and Systems

Barter System
Capital
Capitalism
Cash-Crop Economy
Command Economy
Diversification
Free Trade
Gross National Product
Interdependence

Laissez-faire
Market Economy
Marxism
Mercantilism
One Crop Economy
Per Capita Income
Prime Interest Rate
Socialism
Trade Surplus

Sociological Terms

Civil Disobedience
Class System
Cultural Diffusion
Diversity
Empathy
Ethnocentrism

Genocide
Modernization
Nationalism
Social Mobility
Urbanization
Westernization

Environmental/Agricultural Terms

Commercial Farming
Deforestation
Green Revolution

Greenhouse Effect
Subsistence Farming
Strip Mining

Geographical Terms and Locations

Amazon River
Archipelago
Black Sea
Mediterranean Sea
Nile River

Panama Canal
Peninsula
Persian Gulf
Straits of Hormuz
Suez Canal

It will be helpful if you not only learn the meaning of these terms, but also how they are interconnected. If, for example, you not only learn the definition of *market economy*, but that it is the opposite of *command economy*, it will help you to spot right and wrong answer choices much more quickly and effectively.

Finally, if you learn the people who are associated with some of these terms, especially the political and economic philosophies, and the major world religions, you'll really be on your way toward anticipating the answer to the question even before you read the answer choices.

Oh yeah, and another thing that will help you find the right answer from the start: Make sure you know what you know!

The best way to find the right answer is to make sure you know what the question is asking in the first place. Make sure you read the question slowly and carefully. After you take some practice tests, you will, of course, review the questions that you missed. If it turns out that you missed a few questions because you misread them, then you need to slow down a little bit and read more carefully on the next practice test.

If you don't understand something in the question even after rereading it slowly, you can still use some of the process of elimination techniques that we will teach you. A worse situation occurs when you *think* you know something that in fact you don't. Try to correct any misinformation that's floating around in your head. It's better to say "I don't know for sure," than to say "Oh yeah, I know this," when, in reality, you don't. When you're conscious of the fact that you don't know something for sure, you're more likely to be careful when you're evaluating the answer choices.

In the end, if you weren't able to find the answer to the question based on your knowledge and careful reading, then you can at least eliminate incorrect answer choices. That's what the next section is all about.

CHOPPING AWAY EVERYTHING THAT DOESN'T LOOK LIKE AN ELEPHANT

Just because you don't know the answer, doesn't mean you don't know anything.

Okay, so you read the question and you don't know the answer. It refers to the Hwang Ho River Valley. You can't remember anything about the Hwang Ho River Valley. You're not even sure where it is. Or even what's near it! Pull yourself together and ask yourself, "Okay . . . what *do* I know?" Well, for one thing, you know that it's a river valley!

The words in the questions themselves often give you a clue to the right answer, even if you don't understand everything in the question. Therefore, read every part of each question and every answer choice, and look for clue words that can help you.

You should also keep in mind that the questions on the test are often grouped together by region. For example, four questions about Latin America might be grouped together. They might be followed by three questions about China. This can help you. If you know the answer to two of the China questions, but aren't sure of the answer for the third, you can at least use the information from the other two questions to help you think about (and remember) everything that you know about China. If you still don't know the answer choice, at least eliminate answer choices that are inconsistent with what you *do* know.

If it never happened, then get rid of it.

Let's say you encounter a question about Japan. Let's also say that you didn't entirely understand the question and you're very unsure of the answer. You should still read the answer choices and try to eliminate stuff you know never happened.

If the question asks you to identify something or another about Japan's thingamajig, you can eliminate the answer that refers to Japan's alliance with the United States during World War II. Why? Because Japan and the United States fought *against* each other in World War II.

Always eliminate answer choices that describe events that never occurred.

Sounds good, but what if I *don't know* whether or not the stuff in the answer choice actually occurred?

Often, you'll be reading an answer choice and you won't know if the incident described in the answer choice actually occurred. You need to ask yourself the following question: "Even if it *did* occur, would it matter?"

To demonstrate, let's take an example from the life of Dave Daniel (the author of the book you're holding right now), since his life is infinitely more interesting than the information on the global studies exam (according to him anyway).

Why was Dave late for his date?
1 He was wearing a blue shirt.
2 His jeep wouldn't start.
3 The high winds off Lake Michigan blew a tree down on Lake Shore Drive, stopping traffic.
4 His mom called long distance and kept him on the phone for a long time.

Now, you probably don't know Dave at all (if you do, give him a call sometime). You don't know if he was wearing a blue shirt or not, or even if he likes the color blue. Nevertheless, you should eliminate answer choice number one. Why? Because it doesn't *matter* if he was wearing a blue shirt or not. It's irrelevant. You only need to know that if he *was* wearing a blue shirt, it almost certainly would not affect his schedule. With no knowledge of Dave at all, you've eliminated an answer.

Now, let's say you know a little about Dave, but not too much. Let's say you know that he doesn't live in Chicago. You'd then eliminate answer choice number three because Lake Michigan and Lake Shore Drive refer to Chicago. It may be true that there were high winds and that a tree actually fell and stopped traffic, but it doesn't matter because logically, it wouldn't affect his schedule. (Of course he could have gone out on a date while on vacation in Chicago, but we're trying to determine the *most likely* answer choice.)

If you remember that he doesn't own a jeep, you would immediately eliminate answer choice number two. You're left with answer choice number four, which is a logical possibility, and in truth, is the answer. Done!

Is this the way it really works on the test? Of course! Otherwise we wouldn't have spent so much time explaining it.

I like you because you're so hard to disagree with.

Often, the test writers will give you a gift. It's almost like they're trying to see if you're paying attention. When does this happen? It happens when they give you an answer choice that you just can't argue with. If an answer choice has just gotta be true, it is.

If a question refers to a war, it just makes sense that "people's lives are disrupted." If a question refers to a successful independence movement, it just makes sense that "the colonial power has weakened." If the question refers to a nation with mountain ranges and deserts, it just makes sense that "transportation is difficult."

Is this too easy? Yeah, it is. But that's the point. There's no need to make questions harder than they are. Not every question has an answer choice that you just can't argue with, but when you come across one that does, pick it. And if you're guessing, at the very least, choose the answer that is the hardest to argue with, even if you can argue with it a little bit.

Don't be so extreme. Not everybody's the same, you know.

The test writers often throw in an incorrect answer choice which is stated way too strongly: economic opportunities improved for *everyone*; the example shows that *all* nations are committed to the *elimination* of nuclear arms; frustration over taxes was the *only* motivating force behind the revolt.

Correct answer choices usually have much safer, more middle-of-the-road language: economic opportunities improved for *many people*; the example shows that *many* nations are committed to a *reduction* in the production of nuclear arms; frustration over taxes was *one of the main* motivating forces behind the revolt.

This is not to say that every single time you see an extreme word, you should automatically eliminate it, because that action itself would be too extreme. The point is that you need to be very suspicious of extreme language, especially when a safer answer choice exists. However, if the question involves a totalitarian regime, for example, perhaps some of its actions or policies were extreme, in which case extreme language might be justified.

Opposites attract.

If a set of answer choices contains two opposites, one of them is usually the correct answer. Notice that we said "usually" which means "not always." In other words, use the other process of elimination techniques first. But in the end, if you see two opposites, it should attract your attention.

You should also be aware that if a question has two very similar answer choices, many times they are both incorrect for the simple reason that they both can't be correct. You need to be very careful with this technique, though. Make very sure that the two answer choices are, in fact, extremely similar! If there's any difference between them, the correct answer to the question might hinge on that difference. If, however, the difference between them isn't an issue in the question, then they both have to be eliminated because you can't keep them both.

Hey buddy, do you know the time?

One of the most effective elimination techniques involves knowledge of the time period. We're not suggesting that you sit around all evening and memorize dates. We *are* suggesting that you know the major time periods in the world and know what was going on in general during each time period. A review book like The Princeton Review's Review's *High School Global Studies Review* can help a lot.

For example, if you know the general time period of the Middle Ages and if you know the general time period that communism was developed, you'd know that any answer choice attempting to combine the Middle Ages with communism probably isn't correct. This kind of thing happens all the time. If you can identify answer choices that are out of their time periods, you'll be able to eliminate a lot.

Look at the list below. If you know the general time frame in which each era and event occurred, or at the very least, are able to put them in sequence, you are *soooo* ready to start practicing. Remember, these are just some examples. As you go through the practice tests, you can add more eras and events to the list.

The Enlightenment	The Commercial Revolution
The Renaissance	The Bolshevik Revolution
The Russian Revolution	The Crusades
The Protestant Reformation	The Cuban Revolution
The Neolithic Revolution	The Cultural Revolution in China
The Meiji Restoration	The French Revolution
The Byzantine Empire	The Industrial Revolution
The Cold War Era	World Wars I and II

And by the way, where are we anyway?

Just as you need to have a grasp of the time periods, you need to have a grasp of locations. Keep a world map with your practice tests. Try to recognize answer choices that are inconsistent with the developments of regions. If a question refers to Latin America, get rid of the answer choice that mentions Buddhism. If a question refers to Europe, get rid of the answer choice that refers to large petroleum reserves. You get the idea.

Wish for lists

Lots of times you'll get a list of three names, countries, philosophies, religions, or something else. The question will ask you, "What do these three items have in common?"

Students are often intimidated by lists because they think they need to know about three things instead of just one. Don't be intimidated! These questions are actually gifts, because they give you more than one opportunity to find the correct answer.

Here's the deal: You don't necessarily have to know about all three things in the list in order to answer the question correctly. In fact, you usually only have to know about one of them! Sometimes two.

If you are only familiar with one of the items in the list of three, start eliminating answer choices that are not consistent with just that one example. You will be surprised how many answer choices you can eliminate even if you've never even heard of the other items in the list.

Finally, ask yourself, why are the Regents even bothering?

If all else fails and you're guessing, try to figure out why the Regents are even bothering to ask you the question. For example, if a question asks you to identify a characteristic of a society in ancient Asia, you can probably eliminate the answer choice that says "The society had very little impact on the development of Asian culture."

Why can you eliminate it? Because the Regents aren't going to ask a question about a society that didn't have any impact.

Here's another way of looking at it. The Regents developed this test to make sure that you understand Global Studies. Therefore, every culture, every event and every individual on the test must be significant to your understanding of the globe. If you can remember to ask yourself "why is this thing in the question important" instead of "what is the answer to this question," you'll be able to eliminate answer choices that are inconsistent with the goals of the test.

A BIT ABOUT MAPS, CARTOONS, CHARTS AND OTHER STUFF THAT TAKE UP A LOT OF SPACE

You'll notice that each test usually has about five or six questions that refer you to a map, a cartoon, or a chart. Of course, these questions are very similar to all of the other multiple choice questions, but there are a few things in particular that you should keep in mind.

First, never pick an answer choice that is inconsistent with your knowledge of global studies. For example, even if you don't understand the information in a chart, you shouldn't pick an answer choice that claims "world population is declining." Even if a cartoon confuses you, you can still eliminate answer choices that describe things that have never occurred, just like you can on the other multiple choice questions.

Second, after you've eliminated answer choices that just aren't true, stay very focused on the information presented in a map or on a chart. There might be several answer choices that make sense and are consistent with your knowledge of social studies. You need to find the one answer choice that the information in the chart or on the map describes.

Finally, you need to be especially careful with cartoons. In almost every cartoon question, one of the answer choices describes a literal translation of the occurrence in the cartoon. Don't be literal. Cartoons use symbolism. Therefore, while the correct answer choice needs to *represent* the event in the cartoon, it will not describe the scene literally.

THERE'S JUST NO GUESSING ABOUT GUESSING

The reason that this chapter has so many process of elimination techniques should be self-evident: You're going to need them because you're going to be guessing. You've heard it before, but it's worth repeating: **Don't leave any questions blank!**

That said, there's something important to keep in mind. If a particular question is giving you difficulty, you might want to skip it *temporarily*. It's possible that after you answer some other questions, the information in those questions will enable you to evaluate the question that you skipped. Also, you don't want one or two questions to get you all huffy-puffy and throw you off track when you're trying to answer the other 46 questions that aren't as difficult. If you come across a question that is particularly wacky, don't get all wigged out. Instead, move on to something else and go back to it when you've calmed down.

RANDOM THOUGHTS

Keep in mind that these tests have dates. Therefore, if you're taking a test from 1996, the word "currently" means in 1996, not right now. It usually won't affect the answer choice, but there are a couple of answers to questions in this book that are more understandable if you keep the date of the test in mind.

You also need to realize that although it may seem like you have to review a lot, the suggestions for review in this chapter will also help you on the essays. If you study the Six Topics, for example, it will not only help you on Part One, but it will give you the background you need for Part Two as well.

Finally, if you don't have very much time to review, start with the practice tests in the back of the book, they're the most recent. If, however, you do have enough time to take all of the practice exams, start with the first one and progress through chronologically. You'll want to save the most recent exams (which will be the most representative of the test that you'll actually take) for the weeks immediately before your test date. You'll notice that we've provided a bunch of blank answer sheets at the end of this book. They'll come in handy as you practice the exams over and over again.

CHAPTER THREE—
CRACKING THE ESSAYS

Take a quick peek. Go ahead. We won't tell anybody.

Go ahead and turn to one of the practice tests. Look at Part Two (the section with the essay questions). Read the directions. Get a feel for them. Notice that most of the essay questions have several parts. You're going to have to read the directions for each question very carefully so that you do everything that you're supposed to do, and nothing more.

Do you have a feel for the structure of Part Two? If not, go ahead and take a peek at another essay section on a different test. On the day of the real exam, the last thing you want to be is surprised. Take the time *now* to get comfortable with the wording of the questions. You'll also understand the information that follows a lot better if you've already looked at some essay questions.

Decisions, decisions

You might have noticed that every test has seven essay questions. Fortunately, you only have to answer three of them. If you happen to feel confident about exactly three of the questions, then those are the three you should do! But if you can't find three that you like, or if you like *more* than three (*it can happen!*), you're going to have to make some choices.

First, make sure you read through all seven essay questions. If there's one or two that you absolutely know you won't be able to answer fully, put an X through the number. Get them out of the way. Take them outta the running. *Buh-bye!* Conversely, if there are one or two essay questions that you feel pretty good about, circle the number. Hang on to essay questions you think you'll be able to answer well.

At this point, if you have too many circled numbers, you're going to have to narrow them down. If you have too few, you're going to have to decide which are the best of the ones you don't really like. In either case, ask yourself the following questions:

- Can I answer all of the parts of the question? It's better, for example, to write a decent paragraph for all three parts of an essay question than to write a great paragraph for one part, and nothing for the other two parts.

- Can I think of several examples to support my claim? Make sure that you can write about specific examples, especially if the directions tell you to do so.

- Are my thoughts on this topic organized in my mind or are they jumbled? All other things being equal, choose the topics that you think will be easiest for you to organize. Organization is critical. It's not enough that you merely know about something. You actually have to write about it.

Take your time deciding which three essays you want to do. If the three that you choose are truly the ones that best match your knowledge and abilities, you'll save yourself time when you are actually writing the essays. And you'll get more points!

The points are in the details.

The Regents want you to be able to demonstrate sufficient knowledge of whatever they're asking you to write about. The best way to show them you know what you're talking about is to use specific examples and make specific references.

Yet, it's also important to keep in mind that you don't want to go overboard. You don't need to write a really long list of important details, especially if the details aren't directly related to the question. You definitely don't want to risk going off on tangents, or listing a whole lot of examples when one or two would have made your point. To a certain degree, it's *what* you write, not *how much* you write, that's important.

It's nice to be concise.

You'll notice in the explanations to the practice tests that almost all of the sample essays are one paragraph long. Your grader will really appreciate a concise essay, as long as it is also a complete essay. How do you know if it's complete? You need to double-check that you performed all the tasks that the directions required, and that you backed up any claims you made with a reasonable amount of specific information.

However, if it only takes you two sentences to fully answer a question and use a specific example, you should add another example or go into a little more detail. You want your essay to be concise, but you should definitely write a solid paragraph or two.

Use the sample essays behind each practice exam as a yardstick. All of them are representative of the length and amount of detail that you need. Keep in mind that you might want to split a longer paragraph into two paragraphs. That's fine. Also, keep in mind that the essays that follow the practice tests are typed and therefore don't take up a lot of space. Depending on the size of your handwriting, each essay might take up a whole page.

Do unto the Regents as they've done unto you.

Remember back in Chapter Two when you read how important it is to learn how the Regents think? It's important for the essays as well as the multiple choice section of the exam.

You want to use language that the Regents use. First, don't use extreme language. They don't use it on the multiple choice questions, so you should try to avoid using it on the essay questions, unless you're pretty sure it's warranted. Instead of writing an essay using words like *everybody* and *always*, try writing *most people* and *usually*. Again, if a particular essay *requires* the use of extreme language, then use it. Just don't state things strongly unless you have to.

Second, if you're comparing two things, it's a good idea to stay objective, unless the directions ask you to choose which one is better. For example, if you are comparing capitalism and socialism, it's best to just describe each of them and mention differences and similarities between them. There's no need to say one is better than the other unless the directions tell you to take a stand. On the other hand, if you're writing about behavior or a system that the world community definitely condemns, like genocide or fascism, it's okay to use negative words in the description, like *horrors* or *atrocity*. Likewise, if you're talking about something that is described as a problem, like pollution, it's okay to use words like *unfortunately*.

Third, choose words that you know the Regents like. After you look through the glossary and take a couple of practice exams, you'll notice that there are some words that the Regents just can't get enough of. They love the words *nationalism* and *ethnocentric*, for example. Get in the habit of using the same terms that the Regents use in the multiple choice part of the exam. If you do this, you're going to sound just like them, which is a good thing because they're the ones who tell the graders what to look for. But beware! Don't use words that are out of place in the essay in a misconceived attempt to look impressive. It looks really bad when you try to sound knowledgeable about something that you're not. Don't use *polytheism* unless you have a reason to! However, if you're writing that a nation's government has total control of the economy, for example, it will look a lot better if you use the words *command economy* instead. Why? Because that's one of the terms that the Regents use in the multiple choice questions.

Lead your grader by the hand, so that she will understand.

Don't make your grader wonder, or wander. Lead her by the hand! If you have three things to say, tell her so. Use the words *first, second* and *third*. If you are contrasting two different things, make sure she understands. Use the words *in contrast* or *on the other hand*. If you're changing directions on her, don't give her whiplash! Use the words *but* or *however* so that she can anticipate what she's going to be reading next.

Your essays should not be mystery stories. Nor should they be adventure stories. If the reader can anticipate what's coming up next, you've done exactly what you're supposed to do.

The words below are just a few of the transition words that you should consider using. When they are used correctly, they make your essay easier to read and they demonstrate that you are an organized writer and thinker.

Common Transition Words

and	nevertheless	however
but	consequently	therefore
yet	for example	although
also	in other words	moreover
finally	in contrast	ironically
since	because	as a result

Spelling, punctuation and grammar

Your spelling, punctuation and grammar probably won't have an enormous impact on your score if the content of your essay is superior, but a deficiency in any of these categories will be noticed at least a little and may create an overall bad impression. If your spelling, punctuation, grammar or handwriting make the essay *really* hard to follow, it's probably going to hurt you. Conversely, an error-free essay is easier to read and gives the impression that you are on top of things.

So, the point is simple: Be conscious of not only what you are writing, but the way in which you are writing it. To be sure, you need to pay the most attention to the organization and the content of your essay, but there's no reason to be sloppy with the grammar and spelling if you can avoid it. If you have time at the end of the exam, make sure you proofread your essays for mistakes.

Now that you understand *how* to write, let's talk about *what* you should write.

After you've chosen your essays, spend some time brainstorming and outlining. For example, imagine an essay that asks you to write about three political systems from a list of six. For each political system, you have to describe it, identify a nation that operates under that system, and then discuss an effect that the system has had on the development of the nation you chose.

You should start by going through the list of six political systems. Eliminate any of them that you aren't able to describe. There should be at least three systems left over, or else you shouldn't have chosen this essay in the first place. Then, think of nations that correspond to the political systems that you are still considering writing about. Make sure you pay attention to the directions. They will probably tell you to avoid using the United States in your answer and they might tell you to use a *different* nation for each political system that you chose (in this particular case, telling you to use different nations probably wouldn't be necessary).

You might link *parliamentary democracy* with *India*. You might link *totalitarian regime* with *Cuba*. Whatever nations you choose, make sure that you are able to describe the effect of the political system on the development of the nation.

Finally, brainstorm and make a short outline before you actually write your essay. Think of the effects of the system. In Cuba, for example, the system has led to tensions and economic boycotts from democratic capitalist nations, and has thereby made the nation even more dependent on the Soviet Union than it otherwise might have been. You might also add that when the Soviet Union broke apart and abandoned communism, the economic aid to Cuba from the Soviet Union dried up, and Cuba truly became isolated. Finally, you can focus on the direct internal effects of the system on the citizens of Cuba, whether you want to focus on the standard of living or on human rights violations.

Once you have a short outline, it's time to write a complete, but concise, essay.

All's well that starts and ends well.

It's important to convey that you are organized and that you know what you're talking about. A good opening sentence will accomplish both.

Your opening sentence should state, flat out, what your main point is. For example, if the essay asks you to compare the leadership of Gandhi and Hitler, a good opening sentence would be: "The leadership styles of Hitler and Gandhi were different in at least three ways." If the essay asks you to describe the effect of a particular religion on a particular society, a good opening sentence would be: "Hinduism has affected the cultural and political development of India."

There is no need to be fancy. Just make sure you are answering the question that is asked and that the reader can anticipate what's coming next. Also, make sure that you come through with what you promised in the opening sentence. In the examples above, you would want to make sure that you did, in fact, list three differences between Hitler and Gandhi and that you did, in fact, describe how Hinduism has affected *both* the cultural and political development of India.

Finally, make sure you don't leave your grader hanging. End your essay well. Depending on the nature of the essay, you can either conclude by stating the obvious: "Therefore, Hinduism's impact on the development of India has been enormous," or you might discuss the implications of the information in your essay on humanity: "The enormous differences between the leadership of Gandhi and Hitler demonstrate that power and authority are motivated by different desires and can be used to achieve wildly different goals." In any case, make sure that your closing sentence is consistent with the body of your essay.

Recycled essays: The Regents Top Ten

Just like they do with the multiple choice questions, the Regents recycle essay questions from test to test. Therefore, if you do all of the practice tests in this book, it's likely that at least one or two (and usually a lot more) of the seven essay questions that you see on your actual test will be at least a partial repeat of something you've seen before. Since you only have to write three essays, repeats are a big deal!

There are two ways in which the Regents recycle the material. First, they often recycle the same names (Catherine the Great, Vladimir Lenin) or the same strategic waterways (the Suez Canal, the Straits of Hormuz) or the same events (the Protestant Revolution, the Cultural Revolution in China) within an essay question.

Second, the Regents often recycle the same *type* of question. Therefore, if you understand how to organize an essay for a certain type of question, you'll be able to do the exact same thing on the real test if the same type of question appears.

There are ten different types of essay questions that the Regents are addicted to. If you can learn how to approach and organize an answer for all ten types of questions, you'll be super prepared on test day.

Here is a list of the Regents Top Ten:

- *Change Questions*—The Regents ask you to describe events that have led to change or to evaluate how a change in the world (the decline of communism; the role of women) has affected a certain society. Make sure that you use specific examples, and that you remember to describe both the nature of the society before the change as well as after the change.

- *Problem Questions*—The Regents ask you to describe economic problems, or environmental problems, or problems in the distribution of food, or some other type of problem. Often, you have to identify a nation that has experienced the problem and discuss how the nation has attempted to solve it. Make sure that when you describe the problem, you discuss the consequences for specific groups of people. Depending on the question, you might have to discuss the cause of the problem. If so, make sure that you clearly tie together the cause with the effect.

- *Geography Questions*—You are asked to identify a particular geographic feature (deserts, mountains) or specific place (the Suez Canal, the Amazon River), and describe how it has affected the development of a nation, or how it has positively or negatively affected the nation's relationship with other nations, or why it is important to the global community. Make sure you describe the geographic location well. Don't just say that Japan has mountains. Say that it is a small island nation, consisting mostly of mountains, and that as a result, only about thirteen percent of the land is cultivable. You can then go on and discuss how this fact has contributed to crowded conditions in the cities, or how it contributed to an isolationist policy for so many centuries, or how it meant that Japan had to look elsewhere for raw materials once it industrialized.

- *Cause and Effect Questions*—The Regents ask you to describe and explain the cause and effect of a particular event, or of a particular group's actions, or of conflicts between nations. Make sure that the cause that you suggest is truly a cause, and not just an incidental event. If the cause resulted in a chain of effects that eventually led to the effect in the question, make sure you explain each link in the chain.

- *Human Rights Violation Questions*—You are asked to identify particular human rights violations, identify nations in which these violations have occurred, and discuss the effect of these violations on the development of the nation or on the group that has been violated. Sometimes you are also asked to discuss the motivations of the groups that are doing the violating. Make sure that you describe the violation in as much detail as possible.

- *Leadership Questions*—You are asked to identify the beliefs of particular leaders and discuss how their beliefs affected the nations, societies or organizations that they led. Sometimes you are asked to compare or contrast different leaders. Be specific. Mention specific programs that the leaders initiated, or specific decisions that the leader made. If you are comparing leaders, make sure you focus on *major* similarities or differences (the most significant ones you can think of).

- *Religion Questions*—The Regents require you to identify the major beliefs of particular religions and discuss their impact on the development of a nation or a region. Make sure that you describe the religion in as much detail as possible. If you are discussing the impact of the religion, try to mention more than just social or cultural impacts, but economic and political impacts as well, if they exist.

- *Advice Questions*—These questions put you in the position of an advisor. Your job is to write an essay that discusses the particular strengths and weaknesses of different types of economic systems or political systems and then recommend one of the systems to the leader of a nation. Other advice questions ask you to advise a country on how to solve one of its problems. In either case, make sure that you describe both the current situation in the country, and the effect that your advice will have on the country if it is implemented.

- *Opposition Questions*—The Regents require you to discuss two opposing opinions of a policy or a topic. Sometimes they ask you to identify a person who has articulated each of the opinions that you have described. Be sure to point out the most significant differences between the two opinions. Make sure that you give both sides approximately the same amount of attention. Finally, be sure that you use transition words like "In contrast, person X…" or "Unlike person X, person Y…."

- *Art and Architecture Questions*—You are asked to identify several pieces of art or architecture and describe how they represent the culture of the society in which they were created. Make sure that you make reference to specific details within the piece of art or example of architecture. Describe the function or purpose of those details and their impact on the culture of the society.

As you complete the practice tests, you'll come across all of these types of essay questions several times. You might find it easier to organize an essay for some of the question types than for others. Or you might be attracted to the subject matter of particular types of questions (Religion Questions or Art and Architecture Questions, for example). If so, be conscious of the ones you like and the ones you don't. It might help you decide which essays you want to write when you take the actual exam.

Also, you should be aware that not every single essay falls into one of these ten categories. These are the most popular, but don't get too upset if you see a type of question that you've never seen before. Just skip it if it makes you uncomfortable. Or who knows, you might actually like it.

Self-evaluations can be so cruel.

After you take each practice test, compare your essays with the sample essays behind each exam. You won't be able to actually assign yourself a score, of course, but you will be able to determine if you understood the question and conveyed the thoughts or ideas that needed to be conveyed.

Because the essays often allow you to choose the examples that you want to write about, your essay might differ dramatically from the sample essay. Nevertheless, the sample essay will still allow you to evaluate your organization and your understanding of the question.

In the end, evaluate yourself in two different ways. Congratulate yourself on the things that you did well, and then determine to work on those which you can still improve.

Okay, enough of this. It's time to review and practice. Go ahead and take a look at the glossary if you haven't already. Then, get cracking on the practice tests.

CHAPTER FOUR—
THE HIT PARADE

A glossary of the Regents' favorite terms, people, and organizations

If you know most of the terms, people, and organizations on this list, you're probably scoring fairly well already. If you don't, you can at least take some comfort in the fact that at least you now know what you don't know—ya know?

We know you didn't ask for it, but here's some advice anyway: First, read the list. Put a check mark next to the words, people, and organizations that you already know. Then, start taking practice exams. After you finish each test, carefully read the explanations for the questions you missed. If the question involves one of the terms below, locate the term on the list, make sure you have a grasp of its meaning or significance, and then put a check mark next to it. Do this after every practice test you take. When you're done taking all of the practice tests, you will have learned the entire list of words!

Every item on this list has appeared on the Regents Global Studies Examinations at least three times during the past five years. You'll notice that some items on the list have asterisks next to them. One asterisk (°) means that the item has appeared at least five times in the past five years, two asterisks (°°) means it has appeared at least ten times, and three asterisks (°°°) means it has appeared at least twenty times. Some words appear more than once per test. *Nationalism*, for example, has shown up twenty-seven times, or an average of more than two times per test! *Communism* has appeared more than thirty times!

Geographical terms (like *savanna* and *archipelago*) and actual places (like *Yangtze River* and *Straits of Hormuz*) are not included on the list, but your studies should definitely include a review of a world topographical map as well as a world political map.

Okay. Grab a pencil and start making check marks!

absolute monarchy *See* monarchy.

absolutism the use of absolute power by the government, usually a single leader; opposition is not tolerated; no rights of the people are recognized by the government. *See also* authoritarianism.

agrarian society a farming or rural society; traditional societies are often agrarian; feudal society is also sometimes described as agrarian.

anarchy the absence of order or of government; chaos; lawlessness and political disorder; nations with organized governments, whether they are representative democracies, communist, or fascist, are not anarchies, but if a significant revolt develops in one of those nations and order is temporarily lost, it can be said that the community has degenerated into anarchy.

Animism the religions of many traditional African societies; a belief system based on the spiritual qualities in all of nature, including plants, rivers and the wind; a belief that all natural objects interact with one another; sometimes the test writers use the term **animist religions**.

apartheid° a policy of racial segregation in South Africa before 1991; blacks were denied civil and human rights as well as the economic and social opportunities given to whites. *See also* Nelson Mandela.

appeasement a policy of concession; an attempt to "buy" peace from aggressors by giving the aggressors something they want; a group that appeases often sacrifices part of their land or some of their rights or principles in the hope of preventing aggression.

Atatürk, Kemal the father of modern Turkey; took control of Turkey in 1923; instituted reforms aimed at modernizing, westernizing, and secularizing the customs, military, and economy of Turkey.

authoritarianism the use of absolute power by the government, usually a single leader; opposition is not tolerated; no rights of the people are recognized. *See also* absolutism.

balance of power the test writers have used this term to describe two different types of situations—usually the phrase refers to a balance of power within government, meaning that there are at least two parts of a government that provide checks and balances on each other (an executive branch, a judicial branch, and a legislative branch, for example); the phrase also has been used to refer to the balance of military or economic power within a region (after the formation of the Triple Alliance upset the balance of power in Europe, the Triple Entente formed in an attempt to restore military and political stability to the region; the European Community formed in order to tilt the balance of economic power toward Europe and away from the United States and Japan).

barter system a system based on the exchange of goods or services for other goods or services; no money changes hands—for example, if you give me your CD, I'll give you my brother's; barter systems were common before the Commercial Revolution.

Begin, Menachem Israeli Prime Minister from 1977–1984; strong supporter of the Zionist movement; signed a peace treaty with Anwar Sadat of Egypt, improving relations dramatically between the two nations.

Ben-Gurion, David leader of the Zionist movement for the establishment of a Jewish homeland in Palestine; when the nation of Israel was established in Palestine in 1948, he became the nation's first prime minister.

Bismarck, Otto von leader of Germany in the nineteenth century; united many small German states into one large and powerful German nation; created Triple Alliance with Austria and Italy in the late nineteenth century; the test writers have made reference to his strong will and use of manipulation.

Bolshevik Revolution *See* Russian Revolution.

Bolívar, Simón* a favorite revolutionary of the Regents; Bolívar led independence movements against the Spanish in South America during the nineteenth century; as a result of his efforts, the independent nations of Colombia, Ecuador, Peru, Venezuela, and of course Bolivia were established; he wanted to create a United Gran Colombia (a nation that would have unified the South American continent), but he failed.

Bonaparte, Napoleon *See* Napoleon.

Buddhism** a dominant religion of central and eastern Asia; developed in India in ancient times and spread eastward (India is now almost entirely Hindu); emphasizes a denial of the physical world and a focus on spiritual discipline; meditation is encouraged to help the soul discard worldly distractions.

Bushido, code of *See* Samurai.

capital* money used for investment; money used to purchase equipment necessary to establish a business or organization; often, the test writers use the term **investment capital,** which means the same thing; as nations develop, a lack of investment capital will hinder growth.

capitalism*** economic system based on private ownership and competition; businesses are owned for profit by individuals or groups of individuals; prices are determined not by government decision-making but by the forces of supply and demand; the test writers also use the terms **free-market economy** and **market system** to refer to the same type of system; a system entirely free of government interference has never been developed, but the term still applies to nations which regulate business in the interest of the health or safety of the people. *See also* laissez-faire *and* Adam Smith; *contrast* command economy.

cash crop an agricultural product intended for sale and/or export as opposed to consumption within the community that grew it; cash crops are characteristic of commercial farming, not subsistence farming; examples are tobacco, coffee and sugar; nations or regions that depend on the export of cash crops are referred to as **cash crop economies**, or, if they rely on the export of a *single* cash crop, they are sometimes referred to as **single-crop economies** or **one-crop economies**; nations or regions that rely on a cash crop are economically devastated if a substantial amount of the harvest is ruined or if demand for the product decreases. *Contrast* diversification.

caste system°° a social system based on the teachings of the Hindu religion; individuals are born into a particular caste and cannot change it during their life; since Hindus believe in reincarnation, the manner in which an individual behaves in his or her current caste will determine his or her caste in the next life; the caste determines an individual's job and social status; individuals are expected to marry within their own caste; there is no social mobility. *See also* class system.

Castro, Fidel leader of the Cuban Revolution in the late 1950s; claimed he would establish a democracy in Cuba, but after the Revolution was successful, he established a communist dictatorship; he still retains power as prime minister *and* president of Cuba and has not abandoned his communist philosophy despite economic sanctions imposed by the United States and the failure of communism in Europe. *See also* Cuban Revolution.

Catherine the Great° a favorite of the Regents on the essay portion of the exam; she was the leader of Russia in the late eighteenth century and continued the westernization and modernization of Russia that Peter the Great had started; although many of her cultural and economic ideas were western, she maintained sole authority, sometimes ruthlessly, despite the move towards democracy in the West.

Catholicism *See* Christianity.

Christianity°° a religion based on the teachings and divinity of Jesus Christ; developed in the Middle East and traveled north and westward (the Middle East is now mostly Muslim, with the exception of Israel, which is Jewish, and Lebanon, which has a significant number of Christians); Christianity is dominant in Europe and the Americas. Its two main divisions are **Catholicism** and **Protestantism,** which both have appeared on the exam several times. *See also* Protestant Reformation *and* Crusades.

civil disobedience° peaceful protest; the practice of refusing to obey unjust or immoral laws, without resorting to violence; utilizes demonstrations, strikes, boycotts, and other forms of peaceful protest; the most significant and consistent example of civil disobedience on the exam is Mohandas Gandhi of India.

class system* a society that is divided into classes, or groups of people, usually determined by birth; class systems usually include a small dominant class, a large subservient class, and possibly several classes in between; typically there is very little interaction among the classes and extremely limited social mobility; most traditional societies have some form of class system; the caste system of India is a favorite of the Regents; sometimes the Regents use the term **class structure** instead; if a society is not structured around classes, such as nations that attempt to follow strict communism, the test writers refer to it as a **classless society**; nations that have social or economic classes, but which also have mobility between them, are not described as class systems by the test writers.

Cold War Era* a period from the end of World War II (mid 1940s) to the fall of communism in the Soviet Union (early 1990s); the Cold War pitted the United States against the Soviet Union; the two superpowers kept each other's power in check; both powers tried to influence the development of most of the nations of the world; the United States encouraged the spread of democracy and capitalism while the Soviet Union encouraged the spread of communism; both superpowers maintained enormous nuclear weapon arsenals aimed directly at one another; the Cold War ended when communism fell in Eastern Europe; today, the Soviet Union and the United States are cautiously supportive of one another.

collectivization *See* communism.

colonialism** a nation's practice of invading another nation by taking control of its government and economy and establishing it as its own territory to do with it as it pleases; the new territory is referred to as a colony of the mother country; European colonialism led to its domination of almost the entire globe; colonialism was an important method by which colonizing nations gained access to raw materials and markets during the Industrial Revolution; colonialism has also been a major cause of European cultural diffusion throughout the globe. *See also* mercantilism.

command economy* an economic system that stems from the policies and decisions of the government as opposed to the laws of supply and demand; communism is a type of command economy. *Contrast* capitalism.

commercial farming large-scale farming that is intended to produce food for sale to others within the society or for export to other nations; essentially, commercial farming refers to farms that are businesses; commercial farms use agricultural technology made possible through the Green Revolution. *Contrast* subsistence farming.

Commercial Revolution° the growth of commercialism during the late Middle Ages in Europe, in which products were sold for profit and land was acquired as an investment; established monetary units, banking systems, and joint stock ventures; began a trend of regional trade that was aimed at the acquisition of wealth through trade surpluses; set the stage for the development of colonialism, mercantilism, and eventually industrialization.

communism°°° an economic and political system developed primarily by Karl Marx; the development of a classless society; as a type of command economy, communism involves government ownership of all the means of production; private ownership of business and farms is strictly limited or forbidden altogether; in practice, Communist nations have suppressed the free flow of ideas, political dissent, and the practice of religion; there are no political parties or democratic institutions; the Regents use the terms **communal farming** and **collectivization** to refer to the government-owned farms in the Soviet Union and China under communism. *See also* Communist Revolution in China, Russian Revolution, Cuban Revolution, Karl Marx, Vladimir Lenin, Mao Zedong, *and* Fidel Castro; *contrast* capitalism *and* democracy.

Communist Revolution in China occurred in 1949 under the leadership of Mao Zedong, who became the president of the People's Republic of China; resulted in collectivization of agriculture, government ownership of all means of production, and significant human rights violations; the Communist Party still controls China today, although there has been significant economic reform. *See also* Mao Zedong *and* communism.

Confucius°° a social philosopher of ancient China who taught that individuals have corresponding responsibilities in their relationships; the peasants should respect and follow authority, while those in power in turn owe justice and fairness to the peasants; people should strive to understand their place in society; sometimes the Regents use the terms **Confucianism** and **Confucian philosophy** to represent the teachings of Confucius; Confucian society was a class-based society; millions of Chinese adhere to Confucian philosophy, even today.

constitutional democracy *See* democracy.

constitutional monarchy *See* monarchy.

Cortes, Hernando Spanish conquistador of the sixteenth century; conquered the Aztec Empire and secured control of present-day Mexico for Spain.

Crusades° a series of wars conducted under the flag of religious intolerance and greed for wealth and power, initiated by Christians in Europe who wanted to regain control of the Holy Land, particularly Jerusalem; lasted from the late eleventh century to the end of the thirteenth century; the Christians successfully captured Jerusalem but were kicked out shortly after; the Crusades led to widespread cultural diffusion between Europeans and Middle Easterners and resentment between Christians and Muslims.

Cuban Revolution led by Fidel Castro, a revolution against the Batista government in Cuba; promised to bring economic prosperity and land reform to the peasants of Cuba; after the revolution successfully toppled the Batista government, Castro did not establish democracy as promised, but instead established a "communist" regime. *See also* communism.

cultural diffusion** the process by which the customs or other cultural characteristics of one culture slowly move (diffuse) into another culture, thereby changing it; often cultural characteristics diffuse from one culture to another because of war, or colonization, or even during times of extensive trading; in modern times, cultural diffusion occurs more frequently and rapidly because of television, the internet, and airplanes; fast food restaurants in Japan and Chinese restaurants in New York are examples of cultural diffusion.

Cultural Revolution* led by Mao Zedong, a movement in China in the 1960s to recommit the nation to Communist Party philosophy; involved aggressive suppression of anything considered anti-communist, and the punishment and even death of those suspected of anti-Communist Party activities; part of the revolution included sending government workers to work alongside the peasants; individuality was not tolerated.

deforestation the act of clearing forests for lumber or for the creation of farmland; deforestation, if widespread, can have a significant impact on the environment by causing soil erosion and possibly contributing to the greenhouse effect; deforestation of the Amazon rain forest in Brazil is currently a hot issue.

democracy*** a system of government in which the people themselves make laws and initiate policy, sometimes directly but usually through elected representatives (**representative democracy**); a **constitutional democracy** is one that is limited by the provisions of a constitution, which often includes a bill of rights that protect minority expression and fundamental rights from being abridged by the majority; a **direct democracy** is one in which the people directly vote on every law and policy of the government; no direct democracies exist although even in representative democracies, sometimes the people directly vote on a law through the use of the referendum procedure; a **parliamentary democracy** is simply a type of representative democracy in which the chief legislative body is known as a parliament; the number of democracies in the world is currently on the rise; democracy began in ancient Greece, but was soon abandoned and didn't return until the Age of Enlightenment in England. *Compare* totalitarianism, theocracy, fascism, communism, dictatorship *and* monarchy.

Deng Xiaoping the leader of China after the death of Mao Zedong; initiated substantial economic reforms by introducing elements of capitalism to the Chinese economy; did not initiate political and social reform, despite the protests of many Chinese citizens; cracked down harshly on Tiananmen Square demonstrators. *See also* westernization.

dictatorship° government by a single person who rules with absolute authority; dictators have little or no regard for human rights; often, they come to power as the result of a military coup; other times they come to power after leading popular revolutions; Hitler was the dictator of Nazi Germany; Stalin was a dictator of the Soviet Union; Castro is the dictator of Cuba. *Contrast* democracy; *compare* fascism *and* totalitarianism.

direct democracy *See* democracy.

diversification spreading things out so that nothing in particular dominates; in economic terms, diversification means establishing a variety of methods of income; for example, agricultural economies diversify when they promote industrialization and tourism; diversification can even occur within a particular sector of the economy; for example, a single-crop economy that totally relies on the export of bananas diversifies when it promotes the growth of sugar cane and cotton, even though all of these industries are within the agricultural sector; an industrial economy that totally relies on the importation of petroleum diversifies when it looks for alternative sources of energy; diversification is extremely important to the stability of economies because it allows a nation to absorb the impact of a disaster within one sector of the economy. *Contrast* one-crop economy.

diversity variety; differences within a culture or society; Russia is an ethnically diverse nation while Japan is not; The United States is artistically diverse, with a variety of art forms from a variety of periods from around the world.

Divine Right Theory the theory that used to be popular among monarchies, especially during the European Middle Ages, that their power came directly from God; therefore, they argued, if you disobey the monarchy you are, in effect, disobeying God; this theory justified the absolute power of monarchies. *See also* absolutism.

economic sanctions a method by which a nation or group of nations tries to influence policy in another nation by refusing to trade with the nation, by withdrawing international funds from the nation or by denying its corporations permission to operate within the nation that is being sanctioned; often, economic sanctions are used during times of serious human rights violations or troublesome political developments; economic sanctions were imposed on South Africa to end apartheid; the United States has imposed economic sanctions on Cuba.

Elizabeth I Queen of England in the late sixteenth century; defeated the Spanish Armada in 1588; expanded England's colonial holdings; England became a major economic and military power under her reign.

empathy the act of trying to understand a person's point of view or how that person is feeling; the ability to put oneself "in the shoes" of another person; nations are often empathetic toward other nations during times of natural disasters. *Contrast* ethnocentrism.

Enlightenment° an intellectual movement of the seventeenth and eighteenth centuries in Europe; celebrated human reason, led to reforms in monarchies allowing for representative forms of government and a recognition of inalienable human rights; increased the rate and scope of scientific inquiry; led to religious toleration; marked by the philosophies of people known as the Enlightenment Writers, such as John Locke, Immanuel Kant, and Jean Jacques Rousseau; John Locke happens to be the favorite Enlightenment writer of the Regents—look him up!

ethnocentrism° the belief that one's own group is superior to others; the inability to see world events or your own culture from another perspective; the inability to empathize; isolationist nations are often ethnocentric, sometimes intentionally, sometimes not; aggressive nations are often ethnocentric, believing that others should be just like them; imperialist nations are often ethnocentric, especially when they destroy the accomplishments of other cultures because they claim they are "barbaric"; the attitude in Britain after the publication of Kipling's "White Man's Burden" was ethnocentric; Nazi Germany was extremely ethnocentric; the list just goes on and on! *Contrast* empathy.

European Community (EC)° the economic alliance and, to a lesser degree, political alliance of many of the European nations to integrate their economies, address common problems in a systematic way, establish a single European currency; eliminate trade barriers between the members, allow free and open travel between member nations, essentially integrating Europe into a more unified economy that can compete with the United States and Japan; the Regents also use the term **European Union** and sometimes the term **common market** to mean the same thing, at least for the purposes of the test; the point is that Western Europe is pulling together its resources and promoting Europeanism at the expense of nationalism.

fascism governments that are led by a dictator, but only certain types of dictatorships are fascist; fascist dictators typically have extremely strong personalities, use nationalism to an obsessive degree, unify the nation by blaming foreigners or a minority group within their own country (whom they hate and try to destroy), and perform all of the functions of leadership in a very militaristic way, often using heavily armed troops as a backdrop during speeches; fascism was a popular term during the late 1920s through the end of World War II; Hitler's Germany and Mussolini's Italy were fascist. *See also* dictatorship, totalitarianism, absolutism; *contrast* democracy.

feudalism° a political, social, and territorial system popular in Europe during the Middle Ages, but also in parts of Asia; the monarchy owned most of the land, but gave it to the nobility to manage for themselves in return for loyalty and military service; in turn, the nobility (the landlords, or lords) allowed the vast majority of the people, the peasants (or serfs) to live on the land and agreed to protect them from common enemies in return for loyalty and subservience to the will of the lord; even though it involved an exchange of obligations, feudalism was a bad deal for the serfs, who were very oppressed; no social mobility existed for the serfs; the Regents use the terms **feudal system** and **manorialism** to mean the same thing. *See also* traditional societies.

free enterprise *See* capitalism.

free trade unrestricted trade between nations; the absence of tariffs and customs duties; products can be sold to another nation just like they can be sold within the nation in which they were produced; free trade is an extension of capitalism, which holds that the people are best served when prices and availability are determined by the law of supply and demand in a competitive society; free trade extends the practice of capitalism to the international community; the refusal of Japan to permit free trade practices with the United States is a sore point in the relationship between the two countries; NAFTA and the European Union are results of the free trade movement.

French Revolution° the overthrow of the French monarchy at the close of the eighteenth century; motivated by writings of the Enlightenment and by middle class and peasant class frustration with excessive taxes without representation in government; led to a Reign of Terror in which thousands of French nobles and others were murdered, which led to the emergence of Napoleon, which eventually led to the establishment of representative government in France; resulted in intense feelings of nationalism; motivated revolutionaries in Latin America to take action against the Spanish monarchy.

fundamentalism° a religious movement which focuses on a literal interpretation of the important religious texts and strict adherence to religious doctrines and customs; currently, Islamic fundamentalists are trying to reverse trends toward westernization and modernization in the Middle East; fundamentalists generally do not believe in change; they believe not only that religious doctrines are unchangeable, but that their understanding of those doctrines is unchangeable; most religions have their fundamentalist factions.

Galilei, Galileo an Italian astronomer and scientist of the late sixteenth and early seventeenth centuries; usually referred to simply as Galileo; his most controversial findings involved his observations of the solar system; he attempted to prove the Copernican theory that the Earth and planets travel around the Sun rather than everything in the universe traveling around the Earth; for his efforts, he was condemned by the Catholic Church, which had established doctrines that ran contrary to Galileo's observations; the Church forced Galileo to recant, but by that time, Galileo had set scientific inquiry in motion and soon the Church and everyone else had to admit that Galileo was correct in his findings.

Gandhi, Mohandas°° leader of nonviolent civil disobedience movement against Britain which led to independence for India in 1947; advocated boycotts, demonstrations, and marches as the best means of gaining international support for independence; totally against violence; wanted the Indian subcontinent to remain united after independence, but instead two nations were created—Muslim Pakistan and secular (but predominately Hindu) India. *See also* civil disobedience.

genocide mass murder, particularly of ethnic groups, racial groups, or nationalities, in an attempt to eliminate the group from the face of the earth; the Holocaust, for example, was an act of genocide by Hitler against the Jewish race.

glasnost literally, glasnost means "openness": the policy of social and political reform instituted by Gorbachev in the Soviet Union during the 1980s; it involved a loosening of government control on information and other aspects of life, even to the point of permitting political dissent; the policy opened a door that couldn't be closed, and the Soviet Union soon disbanded; the entire region abandoned communism and adopted representative forms of governments and constitutions that recognized human and civil rights.

golden age° a period of great cultural achievement, particularly in the arts and sciences; often, the golden age of a culture occurs during times of relative peace, when the society has the time, energy and money to focus inward on cultural development; most great civilizations have golden ages, or else they probably wouldn't be called great civilizations (Nazi Germany, for example, conquered much of Europe, but it didn't have a golden age and wasn't a great civilization); the Islamic Empire, the African Songhai Empire, the Indian Gupta dynasty, and Italy during the Renaissance are among the Regent's favorite cultures that had a golden age.

Gorbachev, Mikhail° leader of the Soviet Union during the late 1980s and early 1990s; initiated policy of *perestroika* to restructure economy with elements of capitalism; initiated policy of *glasnost* to allow increased freedom of expression and political dissent; his reforms led to the downfall of the Communist Party in the Soviet Union and Eastern Europe in the early 1990s; presided over the break-up of the Soviet Union into smaller republics. *See also* westernization.

Green Revolution° the development and application of new, efficient methods of farming that increase the yield per acre of farmland; techniques include the use of natural fertilizers, pest control, modern machinery, irrigation systems, crop rotation, and so on; it has allowed developing nations to develop more rapidly by providing surpluses of food that can actually be exported to other nations for a profit; many traditional societies resist changes under the Green Revolution because the people want to continue to farm as their parents did; Green Revolution techniques often change subsistence farms into commercial farms. *See also* commercial farming.

greenhouse effect global warming due to an increase in the amount of carbon dioxide in the atmosphere; the carbon dioxide forms a ring around the Earth's atmosphere that acts like a greenhouse; it allows heat from the Sun to pass through, but doesn't allow all of it to escape, which slowly warms the temperature of the Earth; the increase in carbon dioxide is credited to the burning of fossil fuels and deforestation, which upset the balance of oxygen and carbon dioxide.

gross national product (GNP)° the total monetary value of all the goods and services produced within a nation within a particular time period, usually a year; it's actually more complicated, because foreign investments have to be taken into consideration, but even this simple definition should give you an idea that GNP is a good indicator of how much a nation produces, which in turn is one indicator of the standard of living within the nation.

Hinduism** the dominant religion of India; it involves a belief in reincarnation and forms the basis of the caste system in India; the traditional culture of India is extremely affected by Hinduism; India's government is secular, which means that Hinduism does not form the basis of official government policy. *See also* caste system.

Hitler, Adolf* dictator of Nazi Germany prior to and during World War II; promoted German nationalism based on his claims of German superiority; suspended the German constitution, ruled as a totalitarian dictator, promoted the superiority of the Aryan race which led to the genocide of millions of Jews during the Holocaust; provoked World War II in Europe by invading neighboring nations; was eventually defeated by the Allies, but he committed suicide before the Allies could get to him. *See also* fascism, totalitarianism, nationalism *and* Holocaust.

Ho Chi Minh communist revolutionary leader in Vietnam; drove the French out of Vietnam, establishing north Vietnam as an independent communist nation; led attacks against South Vietnam to unite all of Vietnam as a communist nation.

Holocaust the deliberate and methodical attempt to destroy the Jewish race in Nazi Germany during World War II; as many as six million Jews were killed by way of the gas chamber, firing lines, and other forms of mass murder; Hitler wanted to establish the Aryan race as the master race and felt that he needed to kill the members of other races to accomplish that goal. *See also* genocide.

humanism a philosophy that developed during the European Renaissance and Enlightenment that focuses on the development of human potential to improve human life; it downplays the importance of an afterlife and salvation. *See also* Enlightenment.

Hussein, Saddam dictator of Iraq throughout 1980s and 1990s; invaded neighboring Kuwait in 1990, provoking Persian Gulf War, which he lost; has violently attacked the Kurds in Northern Iraq, driving many of them to Turkey; remains in power despite his human rights violations and aggression against other nations.

imperialism*** the establishment of colonies or spheres of influence in territories outside the boundaries of the imperialist nation; colonialism is a form of imperialism; European imperialism affected the entire globe; Europe did not respect the cultures of the people it conquered; the Europeans became extremely powerful and wealthy from the sixteenth through the twentieth centuries as a result. *See also* colonialism *and* mercantilism.

industrialization°° the process by which an economy changes from an agrarian economy to one that includes heavy industry, such as factories; often leads to urbanization and a decline in traditional customs; industrialization occurred in Europe and the United States quickly and it is continuing to spread into the developing world; industrialization led to increased imperialism in Europe because the factories needed raw materials to produce their goods and then they needed markets in which they could sell the goods; industrialization is a major cause of pollution; sometimes the Regents use the term **industrial society** to refer to a nation that has already industrialized. *See also* Industrial Revolution *and* mercantilism.

Industrial Revolution° the rapid industrial growth that occurred in Europe during the eighteenth century and into the nineteenth century, and that has been occurring in much of the rest of the world ever since; led to the development of the steam engine, which in turn increased the rate of industrialization; led to an increase of imperialism in Europe. *See also* industrialization.

interdependence° dependence among nations, usually in the economic sense; results from economic development that relies on raw materials that are not available within the nation that is developing; for example, the industrialized world is dependent on the Middle East for petroleum without which industry would be halted; most industrial nations do not have enough petroleum of their own, and yet they built an economy that requires it; in addition, the Middle East has now structured its own economy and development based on the sale of petroleum; therefore, if the industrialized world finds an alternative fuel, development in the Middle East will be brought to a halt; as nations trade more and more, their economies and cultures become dependent on the products received through trade; interdependence has led to foreign intervention, as in the case of the Persian Gulf War; it has also led to global cooperation in many cases. *Contrast* isolationism.

Irish Republican Army (IRA) an organization in Northern Ireland that seeks to unify Northern Ireland with Ireland, thereby breaking it away from the United Kingdom; Ireland is Catholic and the IRA is supported by Catholics who resent being discriminated against in predominately Protestant Northern Ireland; Protestants in Northern Ireland want to remain part of the United Kingdom, where Protestantism is the dominant religion.

Islam°°° a religion based on the teacnings of Muhammad; the dominant religion of the Middle East, many parts of south Asia, southeastern Europe, and northern Africa; followers of Islam are known as Muslims; the religion is monotheistic and holds that Muhammad is the prophet of the one, true

God; Islamic fundamentalism is on the rise in much of the Middle East; the sacred text of Islam is the Koran; the two main divisions of Islam are **Shiite** and **Sunni** sects. *See also* Muhammad *and* fundamentalism.

isolationism** the practice of keeping to one's self; "I won't bother you if you don't bother me;" isolationism can lead to the development of an ethnocentric attitude within the nation; the economies of strictly isolationist countries often suffer since few countries have a wide range of resources that a growing and developing economy needs. *Contrast* interdependence.

Judaism** one of the oldest religions in the world, Judaism is based on the teachings found in the Torah; from Judaism sprang Christianity and Islam; it is a monotheistic religion and holds that Jews are the chosen people of God; Jews believe that Palestine was promised to them by God and have established the Jewish nation of Israel in that place; in addition to Israel, Jews are located primarily in Europe and the United States; as a group, they have suffered from discrimination and acts of genocide perhaps more than members of any other religion. *See also* Holocaust *and* Zionism.

Kenyatta, Jomo nationalist who won independence for Kenya from Britain in 1963; promoted acts of violence; accused by the British of leading the Mau Mau uprising, which had initiated acts of violence against whites in Kenya; became president of the new republic of Kenya in 1964; presided over substantial economic growth in Kenya.

Khomeini, Ayatollah led Islamic Revolution in Iran, resulting in the exile of Shah Pahlavi and the creation of an Islamic state; reversed the trends toward westernization that the Shah had initiated and instead instituted the Islamic code as the law of the land. *See also* fundamentalism.

laissez-faire literally, it means "let the people do as they choose;" it is a strict form of capitalism that opposes any economic regulation by the government except for that which is absolutely necessary for the free-market system to operate; in other words, it is a philosophy which holds that the government should create an environment for capitalism to work, but then should stay out of its way; some capitalists believe government regulation is sometimes necessary or desirable and would not call themselves laissez-fair capitalists, but would still call themselves capitalists. *See also* capitalism *and* Adam Smith.

Lenin, Vladimir* leader of the Bolshevik Revolution which established the Soviet Union as a communist state in 1917; ruled as a dictator, although he initiated a few temporary capitalist economic reforms to boost the economy; died in 1924 and succeeded by Stalin.

limited monarchy *See* monarchy.

Locke, John° a writer during the Enlightenment in Europe; had a tremendous impact on the development of constitutional representative governments; he believed that each individual has inalienable rights that the government does not grant and therefore cannot take away; he believed that the people grant to the government its right to govern, thereby refuting the Divine Right Theory. *See also* Enlightenment *and* Divine Right Theory.

Luther, Martin leader of the Protestant Reformation in Germany in the sixteenth century; argued that the Catholic Church was wrong to sell indulgences to raise money; was excommunicated by the Pope, but not before his reform movement gained a life of its own; translated the Bible into German so that the people could read it for themselves rather than relying on the interpretations of the Church hierarchy. *See also* Protestant Reformation.

Machiavelli author of *The Prince*, a guidebook for aspiring sixteenth century Italian princes; contributed to the idea that the ends justify the means; believed that princes should be judged by the success of their endeavors and not by how they went about achieving those successes; his writings eventually inspired people like Hitler and Mussolini, although they only focused on the parts of his work that justified the use of power.

Mandela, Nelson° leader of the African National Congress (ANC) which campaigned against the policy of apartheid in South Africa; he was sentenced to life imprisonment after some demonstrations led to violence, but was released after twenty-five years in 1990 due to internal and international pressure; elected the president of the ANC again in 1990 and, after the abolishment of the policy of apartheid, was elected the first black president of South Africa in the first free and open elections in South Africa in 1994. *See also* apartheid.

manorialism *See* feudalism.

Mao Zedong°° revolutionary leader who established the People's Republic of China as a communist nation in 1949; led the Cultural Revolution in the 1960s and early 1970s in an attempt to recommit the nation to communist principles while purging the nation of everything and everyone suspected of encouraging anti-communism; died in 1976; in the same league as Marx and Gandhi as the most commonly tested revolutionary figures on the Regents Exam.

market economy° *See* capitalism.

Marx, Karl°° wrote the *Communist Manifesto* (with Friedrich Engels) which described the exploitation of workers by industrial capitalists and encouraged the workers to unite to take control of the means of production;

wrote *Das Kapital* to further develop his theories; inspired communism in Eastern Europe, especially in Russia, where the Bolshevik Revolution attempted to establish the first communist state in 1917. *See also* communism.

Marxism° the practice of the philosophy of Karl Marx. *See also* **Karl Marx** *and* communism.

mercantilism° an imperialist economic policy by which imperial nations make a lot of money; colonies are established by an industrializing imperialist nation to gain inexpensive access to raw materials needed in the factories (basically, the imperialist nations rob the colonies blind); then, the factories convert the raw materials into finished products, which are sold back to the colonies at a profit; the people in the colonies don't have any choice but to buy the finished products since the imperial nation forbids colonial trade with other nations and doesn't allow the colonists to establish their own means of production; therefore, all the raw materials in the empire flow to the mother country and flow back out as finished products; imperial Europe made a fortune at the expense of the rest of the world's resources.

militarism the practice of building up the national military and using it for a variety of purposes in addition to defense; a militaristic nation uses the military to enforce its actions within its own nation; nations that are not militaristic often have militaries, but they only use the military against other nations if all other methods fail; militaristic nations are often led by leaders who were or are part of the military establishment themselves and are much more ready to use the military domestically and internationally.

modernization° the process of discarding traditional methods and adopting methods that have only recently developed; farms modernize when they use new farm machinery and methods of pest control; businesses and militaries modernize when they adopt the latest technologies; people modernize their lives when they use motor vehicles instead of just their feet, electricity instead of just candles and sunlight, and computers instead of typewriters, which were used instead of writing by hand; when a society modernizes in a number of ways, it often has an impact on traditional beliefs, because those beliefs exist within a frame of reference that is beginning to disintegrate due to all the modern changes. *See also* traditional societies.

Muhammad founder of the Islamic faith; moved to Medina after his preaching was unsuccessful in his hometown of Mecca; gained strength in Medina and returned to Mecca, this time victorious; he is not treated as a divinity like Christ is treated by Christians; instead, he is seen as a prophet, as indicated in the First Pillar of Islam "There is only one God and Muhammad is his prophet." *See also* Islam.

monarchy°° a system of government in which the leader (the monarch) inherits his or her right to rule; in an **absolute monarchy**, there are no limitations on the monarch's right to rule; in a **constitutional monarchy,** however, the power of the monarchy is limited by the power of other governmental bodies, such as a parliament; often in a constitutional monarchy, the monarch is the head of state, but not the head of government; sometimes the test writers use the term **limited monarchy,** which is essentially the same thing as a constitutional monarchy; many present-day constitutional monarchies were once absolute monarchies. *See also* Divine Right Theory.

monotheism the belief in one god; Judaism, Christianity, and Islam are all monotheistic. *Contrast* polytheism.

Napoleon° military leader of France after the French Revolution ousted the monarchy; declared himself Emperor and began a quest to conquer Europe; was wildly successful in the beginning; established the Napoleonic Codᵉ in France, a major contribution to modern western civil law; finally defeated in Waterloo by the British and the Prussians, but in the meantime had spread many ideas of the French Revolution to the rest of Europe (even though in many ways he didn't practice those ideas himself) and inspired French nationalism enormously.

nationalism°°° loyalty based on a shared nation, customs, language, and history; nationalism has led to independence movements (such as those in Africa) as well as the combination of smaller nations into one larger one (the reunification of Germany); in its extreme, nationalism leads to a feeling of superiority that is often dangerous; nationalism is a relatively new concept; before the eighteenth century, many people identified themselves with their social class or their religion or their particular location; since the eighteenth century, nationalism has swept the globe; in Africa, national governments are trying to instill nationalism in the hearts of their people because many people are loyal to their tribes, not their nation; in Europe, the European Union is eroding nationalism by trying to get people to think of themselves as Europeans, not as French or German, for example; in any case, nationalism has an enormous impact on the political development within a nation and on its relationship with other nations.

North American Free Trade Agreement (NAFTA) a trade agreement between Canada, the United States, and Mexico to allow free trade among the three nations. *See also* free trade.

North Atlantic Treaty Organization (NATO)° an organization formed after World War II for the mutual defense of its member nations against

Soviet aggression or any other aggression; members included the United States, Canada, and most of Western Europe as well as Greece and Turkey; since the end of the Cold War, many wonder if there is still a need for NATO; traditionally, NATO's primary enemy was the Warsaw Pact. *See also* Warsaw Pact.

Nkrumah, Kwame led independence movement from Britain in Ghana; became president of Ghana after independence was granted in 1957, but was ousted by a military coup in 1966.

nomads groups of people who do not live in one place but rather move from place to place, usually according to the availability of grazing lands; many nomadic groups are herders.

nonalignment* a position taken by a nation that doesn't want to take sides; during the Cold War, many Third World nations remained nonaligned, either because they didn't favor one side over the other or because they wanted to gain economic assistance from both sides simultaneously.

one-crop economy an agricultural economy that is based primarily on the export of a single crop; one-crop economies are very risky because poor weather conditions or decreased worldwide demand for the crop can cause an economic crisis in the nation; nations with one-crop economies are encouraged to diversify so that they have other sources of income in the event of an agricultural downturn. *See* diversification.

Organization of Petroleum Exporting Countries (OPEC) an organization created by many of the nations of the Middle East as well as Nigeria, Algeria, Venezuela, and Indonesia; together, the OPEC nations control three-fourths of the world's petroleum reserves; in the 1970s the organization was strongly united and it managed to cut the supply of petroleum, thereby sending the price per barrel through the roof; the economies of the industrialized nations of the world suffered dramatically while the nations of OPEC became very wealthy; today, OPEC is still around, but it is more loosely organized as individual nations within the group are making more of their own decisions and competing against each other.

Organization of American States (OAS) an organization of most of the nations in North and South America; it is an organized effort to limit aggression from outside the hemisphere and to solve regional problems.

Palestine Liberation Organization (PLO) an organization intent on "liberating" Palestine from the Jews, in effect, abolishing the state of Israel; the organization has traditionally sponsored many acts of terrorism against Israelis but in recent years, the leadership has been willing to discuss terms of peace; nevertheless, extremists within the group continue their assault on

Israel, and Israel continues to react violently; the ultimate goal of the PLO is to establish a Muslim Palestinian State in the region now occupied by Israel.

parliamentary democracy *See* democracy *and* parliamentary systems.

parliamentary systems system of government in which the authority to make and execute laws is held by the parliament, a representative body; these systems usually have a prime minister, who acts as its head; the United States is not a parliamentary system because congress can only make laws, but cannot execute them.

per capita income the total income of a nation divided by the number of people who live there; it is used as a measure of the standard of living within a nation; if a nation has an extremely unequal distribution of wealth, however, it often is not a very good indicator of the incomes of the upper class or the lower class; per capita income is a very valuable indicator of the standard of living in nations that have a substantial middle class.

perestroika the policy of economic restructuring in Russia under the leadership of Gorbachev in the 1980s; Gorbachev wanted to spark the stalling Soviet economy with some elements of capitalism; eventually, the reform movement became more than just a reform and led to the downfall of communism in the Soviet Union and Eastern Europe. *See also* Mikhail Gorbachev *and* communism.

Peter the Great° Emperor of Russia in the late 17th and early 18th centuries who was determined to westernize his nation; he built the new capital of St. Petersburg on the Baltic Sea to serve as a "window to the west;" he westernized many of the social customs of Russians, but his success was generally limited to the cities; the people in the rural areas kept to their traditional ways. *See also* westernization.

Pol Pot the leader of communism in Cambodia; his Khmer Rouge instituted the slaughter of over two million Cambodians; now retired, he remains very influential in Cambodia.

polytheism the worship of many gods; ancient Greece was polytheistic. *Contrast* monotheism.

Protestantism *See* Christianity.

Protestant Reformation° a reform movement in the Catholic Church which led to the creation of Protestantism as a separate Christian denomination; began when Martin Luther protested against practices of the Catholic Church in an attempt to reform it from within; aided by the printing press, his writings spread quickly through northern Europe even as the Catholic Church prepared to excommunicate him; eventually, much of northern Europe broke away from the Catholic Church and formed their own denominations of Christianity; Europe was consequently divided along religious lines, a division that causes conflict today in Northern Ireland among other places; often, the test writers simply refer to the movement as the **Reformation**. *See also* Martin Luther *and* Christianity.

representative democracy *See* democracy.

Reformation° *See* Protestant Reformation.

Renaissance°° a cultural rebirth in Europe from the end of the fourteenth to approximately the middle of the seventeenth centuries; it was based on the rediscovery of the culture of ancient Greece and Rome; during the European Middle Ages, much of the literature of ancient Greece and Rome had made its way to the Islamic Empire; an increase in trade, conquest, and contact between Europe and the Islamic Empire resulted in cultural diffusion, which brought many pieces of literature back to Europe; during this time period, there were major accomplishments in art (Michelangelo, for example), science (Galileo) and literature (Shakespeare).

republic a representative from of government; today, it pretty much means the same thing as a representative democracy; some nations call themselves republics but they really aren't because there is only one political party and no real choice within the society. *See also* democracy.

Russian Revolution°° the communist revolution in Russia under the leadership of Lenin, which overthrew the czar; motivated by the writings of Karl Marx and the extremely unstable economic and political situation within Russia; the revolution is also known as the **Bolshevik Revolution** and the **October Revolution**; the impact on the future of Eastern Europe and the rest of the world was enormous, since the Soviet Union was intent on spreading communism throughout the region and the world well into the early 1980s. *See also* communism *and* Vladimir Lenin.

Sadat, Anwar Egyptian president during the 1970s and early 1980s; best known for signing the Camp David Peace Accords with Israel, which led to an era of peace between the two nations and encouraged other Muslim nations in the region to open talks with Israel; was assassinated by Muslim extremists.

Samurai the high ranking warrior class in medieval Japan; they followed the **Code of Bushido,** which emphasized martial arts skills, loyalty, and a willingness to die for the right cause; the code of Bushido affected militaristic attitudes as recently as World War II, in which Japanese kamikaze fighter pilots were willing to kill themselves out of loyalty to the country.

self-determination the ability to choose one's own course of action; in the group environment, it is the group to have political and economic control over its own society without being dominated by another group; many ethnic groups want the right to self-determination; Eastern Europe is being broken up into smaller and smaller pieces because each group wants to determine its own course; independence movements in Africa, the Americas and Asia were motivated by a desire for self-determination.

self-sufficient the ability to maintain oneself without the help of others; in terms of nations, self-sufficiency means the ability of the nation to maintain itself, provide for its citizens without the help of international aid; isolationist nations might be self-sufficient if, in fact, they have everything they need; nations that trade might also be self-sufficient, if they have a trade surplus. *Compare* interdependence.

serfs peasants; during feudal times, serfs were practical slaves to their landlords, who allowed the serfs to farm the land for the landlord and offered the serfs protection from foreign aggressors; the landlords demanded hard labor and expected the serfs to do as they were told. *See also* feudalism.

Shinto° a popular religion in traditional Japan which involves belief in many gods, a focus on the natural world and the pursuit of harmony within it, and a belief in the divinity of the Emperor; after World War II, the Japanese Emperor was forced by the Allies to publicly deny his divinity, a development that has led to a decline in the number of people who practice the Shinto religion; the religion is at the heart of many of Japan's traditional customs; sometimes the test writers use the term **Shintoism**.

Smith, Adam the father of free-market capitalism; wrote *The Wealth of Nations* in response to government regulation that was occurring in imperialist (and mercantilist) Europe; argued that a nation and the people within it are best served if they observe the economic law of supply and demand and if the government permits free competition; although he believed it is appropriate for a government to regulate the economy when it comes to the health and safety of the people, most people associate his writing with strict laissez-faire philosophy. *See also* capitalism *and* laissez-faire.

socialism°° an economic system in which many of the means of production and distribution are owned by the government, as opposed to private individuals or corporations; socialism is sort of in between capitalism and communism; many nations that are often said to have socialist economies actually permit lots of private ownership, it's just that the *major* industries are government owned or highly regulated; socialized nations usually provide services like health care; taxes are often very high in socialized nations when compared to capitalist nations; many nations use a combination of socialism and capitalism in their economies; socialism has nothing to do with the political arrangement in the nation, only the economic arrangement; communism is the most extreme form of socialism. *Compare* capitalism.

social mobility°° mobility is the ability to move from place A to place B, so social mobility is the ability to move from social status A to social status B; if people can improve their income, change jobs, marry who they want, increase their level of education, get a job promotion, move to a different neighborhood, buy a more expensive house or rent a nicer apartment, they are socially mobile; they might have been raised in a lower class family but as adults became members of the upper class; or they might have lost all their money and had to sell the car and take the bus; social mobility is the result of the creation of opportunities and an increase in the freedom of choice and individual decision-making; democracy and capitalism often, but not always, increase the chances for members of society to become socially mobile; traditional societies are usually characterized by a lack of social mobility; strict communist societies are supposedly "classless," so there's no social mobility because there is nothing to move to and from.

Solidarity an anti-communist labor union in Poland, led by Lech Walesa; the momentum of the Solidarity movement eventually led to the downfall of the Communist Party in Poland, which was one of the triggers to the downfall of communism in the rest of Eastern Europe. *See also* Lech Walesa.

spheres of influence the territorial claims of Europe and Japan in China during the nineteenth century; established after Britain forced China to open its ports to the opium trade; when the other European powers realized how weak China was, they rushed to China to establish their own spheres of influence, wherein they controlled trade and many aspects of the economy, and actually set up establishments and flew their own flags; in other words, spheres of influence were another application of European imperialism—same old story, new location. *See also* imperialism.

Stalin, Joseph°° dictator of the Soviet Union after the death of Lenin; ruled with absolute authority; he was a major violator of human rights; collectivized agriculture and initiated Five Year Plans to build up heavy industry; led the Soviet Union through World War II and developed international policies and acts of aggression that led to the Cold War with the United States. *See also* communism.

strip mining the process of removing minerals from the ground by first removing the earth above it; strip mining is not only ugly, but leads to soil erosion and other environmental problems; it also significantly devalues the land—once the minerals have been removed, the land is a mess, there isn't any topsoil, and it would cost a fortune to prepare it for another use like farming or even a housing development or just a park.

subsistence farming° a method of farming that only provides enough food for the people who work on the farm; common in traditional societies; impedes economic development. *Contrast* commercial farming. *See also* traditional societies.

Sun Yat-sen leader of the Chinese Revolution in the early twentieth century, which brought an end to dynastic rule in China and established a republic; his Three Principles of the People (nationalism, socialism, and democracy) were intended to drive foreign interests out of China while at the same time westernizing it from within; organized and became the leader of the Koumintang (the Chinese Nationalist Party) which, after his death, failed to meet the needs of the Chinese people and was driven all the way to Taiwan by the emergence of Mao Zedong and his Communists.

theocracy a nation in which religious authorities exercise political power; Iran under Ayatollah Khomeini was a theocracy; typically, the main religious texts are used as a basis for the civil law and religious customs become enforced social customs.

totalitarianism° domination by a government (often an individual) over all aspects of life, including the economy, the social and cultural institutions, and of course the military and government; Germany under Hitler was a totalitarian regime; so was the Soviet Union under Stalin; totalitarianism is often associated with dictators or fascists; the regimes violate human rights, suppress dissenters, and often engage in acts of aggression against their neighbors.

trade surplus occurs when a nation exports more than it imports; Japan currently has a trade surplus with the United States because it sells more to the United States than it buys; the United States currently has a **trade deficit** with Japan because it buys more from Japan than it sells.

traditional society°° societies that follow the ways of their ancestors; societies reluctant to change or modernize; typically religion and family are very important; the social structure within these societies is usually class-based; social mobility is extremely limited; traditional societies are often agrarian, relying on subsistence farming; the Regents also use the term **traditional cultures** to refer to the same thing; the caste system, for example, is a very important part of traditional Indian society; modernization and urbanization threaten the maintenance of traditional societies.

United Nations°° an organization that includes almost every country of the world; it has no authority over its members, who retain sovereignty, but it is an increasingly important and powerful body; it was created after World War II as a place where problems could be discussed and worked through in the hopes of preventing future wars; it has many units and independent agencies, such as the World Bank and the World Health Organization; it works to collectively address world issues ranging from the spread of disease to economic development, deforestation, political instability, human rights violations, ethnic violence and so on; it's military forces were instrumental in the Persian Gulf War and its peacekeeping forces are being utilized throughout the globe.

urbanization° the movement of people from rural areas to cities; urbanization is occurring throughout the globe, but at a particularly fast rate in Africa and Latin America, two continents that were mostly rural while the northern hemisphere was urbanizing decades ago; urbanization often results in the weakening of traditional values and in problems associated with overcrowding (like pollution and crime); urbanization is often the result of industrialization, as people move to the cities to find jobs.

Walesa, Lech current president of Poland; opposed to the Communist Party in Poland, he organized workers in a union known as Solidarity; he is chiefly responsible for Poland's rejection of communism in 1989 and adoption of democracy and elements of capitalism.

Warsaw Pact° now disbanded, the Warsaw Pact was a military alliance of the Soviet Union and its East European satellites; during the Cold War, it was countered by NATO, an alliance of the United States and parts of Western and Southern Europe.

westernization° the process by which a nation or territory adopts the customs or practices of the industrialized nations of the west, including western Europe, the United States and Japan; Turkey, for example, "westernized" under Kemal Atatürk because it adopted western customs and economic reform; today, China's economy is "westernizing" as it continues to adopt elements of capitalism, although its political and social systems are not westernizing; Russia's Peter the Great is one of the Regents favorite leaders who westernized a nation; so are Gorbachev of the former Soviet Union and Shah Pahlavi of Iran; essentially, capitalism and democracy are associated with the West, so if any nation adopts elements of either one, they are "westernizing."

Zionism a social and political movement for the establishment of a Jewish homeland in Palestine, the land that Jews believe was promised to them by

God; it successfully resulted in the creation of Israel as an independent state in 1948; since then, Zionism refers to the maintenance of Israel as a Jewish homeland despite efforts by its Muslim neighbors to "liberate it" and form a Muslim state. *See also* Judaism *and* Palestine Liberation Organization.

PART II

EXAMS
AND
EXPLANATIONS

EXAMINATION
JANUARY 1996

Part I (55 credits): Answer all 48 questions in this part.

Directions (1–48): For each statement or question, write on the separate answer sheet the *number* of the word or expression that, of those given, best completes the statement or answers the question.

---

1 Which factor is the best indicator of the wealth of a nation?

  1 gross national product (GNP)
  2 prime interest rate
  3 number of millionaires
  4 defense spending

2 The basic characteristic of the economies of most traditional agrarian societies is

  1 surplus crops
  2 subsistence farming
  3 large reserves of investment capital
  4 a variety of crops for export

3 What is one result of the increasing industrialization and urbanization of developing nations?

  1 Infant mortality rates are increasing.
  2 Average life expectancy is decreasing.
  3 Traditional family patterns are changing.
  4 Education is becoming a less important goal.

4 Even if food production in developing nations meets minimum needs, some citizens of these nations will still experience hunger mainly because
1 religious practices do not allow the people to eat many of the foods grown
2 food delivery systems are inadequate
3 governments are using starvation as a means of population control
4 the foods grown have limited nutritional value

5 Which event was used by Mohandas Gandhi to bring world attention to the injustices of British colonialism?
1 Salt March
2 partition of India
3 Sepoy Mutiny
4 formation of the Indian Parliament

6 "We believe in nonaggression and noninterference by one country in the affairs of another and the growth of tolerance between them and the capacity for peaceful coexistence. We, therefore, endeavor to maintain friendly relations with all countries, even though we may disagree with them in their policies."

—Jawaharlal Nehru,
Prime Minister of India

This statement describes the foreign policy known as

1 imperialism   3 isolationism
2 mercantilism   4 nonalignment

7 Since the 1950's, India has experienced conflict with both Pakistan and China over

1 United Nations peacekeeping efforts in the region
2 India's increasing trade with Korea
3 borders and related territorial issues
4 the interpretation of common religious works

8 One similarity between the ancient African kingdoms of Egypt, Ghana, Mali and Songhai is that all of these kingdoms were located

1 in mountainous terrain
2 in coastal areas
3 on major trading routes
4 in rain forest areas

9 After World War II, which action was taken by many African territories?

1 demanding independence from their colonial rulers
2 refusing to join international organizations
3 rejecting most of the technology offered by Western nations
4 creating a strong, united Africa

Base your answer to question 10 on the time line below and on your knowledge of social studies.

1860	1880	1900	1920

▲1867 Diamonds discovered in Boer republics

▲1869 French company completes Suez Canal

▲1874 Gold Coast becomes British colony

▲1884 Berlin Conference takes place

▲1885 German East Africa established

▲1891 Portugal takes control of Angola

▲1902 Britain defeats Dutch settlers in the Boer War

10 Which would be the best title for this time line?
1 African Independence Movements
2 Mineral Discoveries in Africa
3 European Imperialism in Africa
4 Ethnic Conflict in Africa

11 The stability of many African nations continues to be threatened by the
1 spread of animism among the people
2 ethnic and tribal loyalties of the people
3 use of command economies
4 establishment of labor unions

12 The teachings of Confucius encouraged people to
    1 put their own interests first
    2 reject government authority
    3 believe in reincarnation
    4 follow a code of moral conduct

13 An immediate result of the Cultural Revolution in China was that it
    1 helped to establish democracy in urban centers in China
    2 led to economic cooperation with Japan and South Korea
    3 disrupted China's economic and educational systems
    4 strengthened political ties with the United States

Base your answers to questions 14 and 15 on the passage below and on your knowledge of social studies.

"Yesterday, your Ambassador petitioned my Ministers regarding your trade with China ... Our Celestial Empire possesses all things in great abundance and lacks no product within its own borders. There is, therefore, no need to import any product manufactured by outside barbarians in exchange for our own goods."

—Emperor Ch'ien Lung of China
to King George III of Britain, 1793

14 In the view of the Emperor, which foreign policy action was in the best interest of China in 1793?
1 maintaining economic isolation
2 expanding foreign trade
3 increasing international interdependence
4 developing into a colonial power

15 Based on this passage, which type of attitude does the Emperor display?
1 empathetic   3 imperialistic
2 ethnocentric   4 militaristic

Base your answer to question 16 on the map below and on your knowledge of social studies.

Per Capita Income in China

- more than $766
- $383-$766
- $287-$382
- $191-$286
- less than $191

Sources: International Year Book and Statesmen's Who's Who (per capita income); Asian Development Bank (exchange rate in 1989)

The New York Times (adapted)

16 The map shows that the

1 economies of all the regions of China are developing at the same rate

2 distribution of income in China is unequal

3 economies of the interior provinces of China are developing faster than those of the coastal provinces

4 economic development in China is dependent upon the cash crops of Xinjiang and Tibet

17 The diagram below illustrates the social structure of feudal Japan.

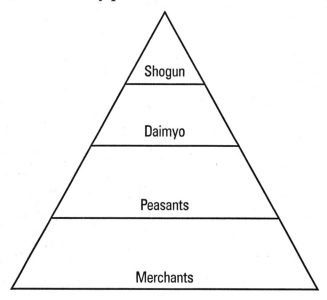

This pyramid shows that feudal Japan had

1 a classless society
2 a growing middle class
3 high social mobility
4 a well-defined class system

18 In Japan, the Meiji Restoration resulted in the

1 division of the nation between the European powers
2 modernization of the nation's industry
3 abolition of the position of emperor
4 government being controlled by the samurai

Base your answer to question 19 on the cartoon below and on your knowledge of social studies.

Source: Arcadio, 1992 Cartoonists & Writers Syndicate

19 The main idea of this cartoon is that Japan

    1 practices free trade
    2 restricts foreign imports
    3 has a policy of balanced trade
    4 imports most of its ships

20 Judaism, Islam, and Christianity share a belief in

    1 the central authority of the Pope
    2 a prohibition on the consumption of pork
    3 reincarnation and the Four Noble Truths
    4 monotheism and ethical conduct

21 A primary purpose of building the Suez Canal was to

1   encourage Jewish settlement in nearby Palestine
2   increase trade between the Middle East, Europe, and Asia
3   reduce the time needed for travel between the Atlantic Ocean and the Caribbean Sea
4   allow Indian merchants to reach the east coast of Africa

22 The actions of most Islamic fundamentalists show that they support

1   the Zionist movement
2   equal rights for women
3   traditional Muslim teachings
4   a renewed attempt at modernization

23 In most of the nations of the Middle East, a major long-term economic concern will be the need for

1   unskilled labor   3   diversified industry
2   imported oil   4   herds of camels

24 A study of Mayas, Aztecs, and Incas would show that these ancient American civilizations

1 produced few cultural achievements
2 lived at peace with their neighbors
3 welcomed the new technology brought by European explorers
4 rivaled the accomplishments of early Middle Eastern cultures

25 Spain's colonial policy of mercantilism affected the development of Latin American nations by promoting

1 the production of raw materials and cash crops
2 free and rapid trade with Asia and Africa
3 respect for the rights of indigenous people
4 isolationism as a response to international political issues

Base your answer to question 26 on the graph below and on your knowledge of social studies.

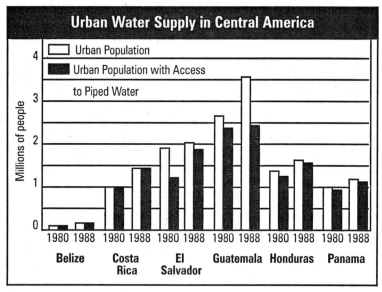

Urban Water Supply in Central America

Source: Frederick S. Mattson, CDM and Associates, Arlington, VA

26 Which statement is best supported by the data in the graph?

1 The urban areas of Honduras and Panama require the largest supply of water in Central America.

2 Belize and Costa Rica are meeting the water needs of their urban population.

3 Urban water supplies are declining in many Central American countries.

4 Most Central American countries experienced a decrease in urban population between 1980 and 1988.

27 Article 27 of the Mexican Constitution of 1917 declares: "Ownership of all minerals belongs to the nation." This phrase was included in the Constitution because

1 Mexicans were importing large quantities of minerals
2 foreign companies were dominating the mining industry
3 Indian peoples controlled most of the land where mineral resources were located
4 large reserves of coal and iron ore had recently been discovered

28 The Protestant Reformation represents a turning point in European history because it

1 allowed religious reformers to escape persecution
2 standardized all religious writings
3 ended religious unity in western Europe
4 forced most of Europe's monarchs to become Protestants

29 The Commercial Revolution in western Europe led directly to the

1 development of a socialist economy
2 establishment of the guild system
3 weakening of the power of the middle class
4 expansion of world trade

Base your answer to question 30 on the cartoon below and on your knowledge of social studies.

KEVIN KALLAUGHER
USA

30 What is the main idea of the 1991 cartoon?

   1 The unification of Germany has been hurt by poor leadership in the country.

   2 The economic differences between East and West Germany have limited the growth of the total German economy.

   3 East Germany's strong economy has strengthened a united Germany.

   4 Both East Germany and West Germany have contributed equally to the new economy of a reunified Germany.

31 The topography and climate of western Europe encouraged

1 the development of communication and transportation systems
2 dependence on a cash-crop economy
3 adoption of the policies of isolationism and neutrality
4 a search for warm-water ports

32 Many of the ideas of Locke, Montesquieu, and Rousseau were associated with

1 the establishment of colonial empires by strong European nations
2 political reforms that ended the absolute monarchy in France
3 the beginnings of the Spanish Inquisition
4 British legislation that improved working conditions in factories

33 The 19th-century term "white man's burden" reflects the idea that

1 Asians and Africans were equal to Europeans
2 Asians and Africans would be grateful for European help
3 imperialism was opposed by most Europeans
4 Europeans had a responsibility to improve the lives of their colonial peoples

34 One of the major goals of the European Union (European Community) has been to

1 remove all trade barriers between member nations

2 open Europe to trade with the United States and Japan

3 block the influence of Latin America in European affairs

4 decrease member nations' military role in the Middle East

35 Since the 1980's, increasing immigration into Western Europe from developing nations has been opposed by Europeans primarily on the grounds that

1 most immigrants have refused to accept employment at the minimum wage

2 immigrants share the same ethnicity and beliefs as their host nation

3 immigrants are believed to be taking jobs needed by citizens

4 unskilled immigrants have refused to settle in urban areas where government benefits are available

36 Which statement describes the situation in Russia during the 200 years when the Mongols ruled?

1 Russia experienced a cultural Renaissance.

2 Russia was isolated and paid tribute to the Khans.

3 Westernization and industrialization began in Russia.

4 Democratic reforms were encouraged in Russian society.

37 The events that led to the overthrow of Czar Nicholas II in 1917 and to the forced resignation of Mikhail Gorbachev in 1991 show that

1 economic crises often lead to political change
2 Russian absolutism continued into the 1990's
3 international conflicts often strengthen the power of leaders
4 Russia is an ethnically unified nation

38 Stalin's Five-Year plans and his decision to form collectives are examples of

1 strategies to modernize the economy of the Soviet Union through forced communism
2 a more friendly foreign policy toward China
3 methods of dealing with the United States during the Cold War
4 programs to westernize, educate, and enlighten the population

39 Since the collapse of the Soviet Union in the early 1990's, Russia has attempted to build an economic system based on

1 a return to feudalism
2 the ideas of Marx and Lenin
3 the writings of Mao Zedong
4 a free-market system

40 Recent events in the former nations of Czechoslovakia and Yugoslavia reflect a nationalist trend of

1 dividing nations along ethnic lines
2 encouraging multi-ethnic cooperation
3 uniting nations with similar interests
4 supporting the development of a command economy

41　The Russian Revolution and the French Revolution both resulted in

　　1　the establishment of direct democracies
　　2　the restoration of old monarchies
　　3　violent political change
　　4　increases in the power of the Catholic Church

42　A person who practices the Shinto faith would be most likely to

　　1　visit a shrine placed on the shore of a lake
　　2　pray five times a day
　　3　bathe in the Ganges River
　　4　make a pilgrimage to Jerusalem

43　Which statement best explains the periods of the Gupta Empire of India, the Golden Age of Greece, and the Renaissance in Italy?

　　1　The winning of a war often inspires scientific and artistic achievement.
　　2　A combination of wealth and a time of relative peace often leads to cultural achievement.
　　3　A dictatorship usually encourages cultural growth and development.
　　4　Periods of censorship are needed for a nation to achieve cultural and scientific greatness.

Base your answer to question 44 on the chart below and on your knowledge of social studies.

Country	Births per 1000	Infant mortality per 1000	Per capita income
Tanzania	48	102.0	$260
Germany	10	5.9	$17,400
Bangladesh	37	116.0	$200
Japan	22	4.4	$34,040
Chile	22	14.6	$2,250

Source: 1995 World Almanac

44 Which conclusion can be drawn from the information in the chart?

1 Developing countries are instituting programs to limit the growth of their populations.
2 Infant mortality is a greater problem in Africa than in Asia.
3 The nations with relatively low birthrates have relatively high per capita incomes.
4 The national birthrate is determined by many different factors.

45 In the 1930's and 1940's, fascist regimes in Japan, Germany, and Italy were similar in that each emphasized

1 empathy toward African nations
2 the protection of human rights
3 imperialism as a foreign policy
4 support for free expression

46 The civil war in Lebanon in the 1970's and 1980's and the fighting in Northern Ireland in the 1960's, 1970's, and 1980's both demonstrate the

1 inability of a command economy to satisfy the needs of the people
2 positive influence of multinational peacekeeping organizations in solving national issues
3 isolation of these countries from international influences
4 inability of the people and government to resolve religious differences

47 With which nation are Pol Pot, the Khmer Rouge, and genocide associated?

1 Korea
2 Japan
3 Myanmar (Burma)
4 Cambodia (Kampuchea)

48 The United Nations has changed over the past decade by

1 increasing its involvement in conflicts within member nations
2 reducing its focus on providing medical care for people in developing nations
3 becoming increasingly deadlocked in the conflicts between the superpowers
4 becoming increasingly anti-Western, as evidenced by the votes in the General Assembly

Answers to the following questions are to be written on paper provided by the school.

Students Please Note:

In developing your answers to Part II, be sure to

(1) include specific factual information and evidence whenever possible

(2) keep to the questions asked; do not go off on tangents

(3) avoid overgeneralizations or sweeping statements without sufficient proof; do not overstate your case

(4) keep these general definitions in mind:

(a) <u>discuss</u> means "to make observations about something using facts, reasoning, and argument; to present in some detail"

(b) <u>describe</u> means "to illustrate something in words or tell about it"

(c) <u>show</u> means "to point out; to set forth clearly a position or idea by stating it and giving data which support it"

(d) <u>explain</u> means "to make plain or understandable; to give reasons for or causes of; to show the logical development or relationships of"

Part II

1 Geographic factors in an area can either aid or hinder the development of a nation or region.

Geographic Factors

Coastline	Rainfall
Mineral resources	Rivers
Mountains	Vegetation

Select *three* geographic factors from the list and for *each* factor selected:

- Identify a specific nation or region where that geographic factor aided or hindered the development of that area [You must use a different nation or region for each factor discussed. Do *not* use the United States in your answer.]

- Discuss how that factor has had either a positive *or* a negative effect on that nation or region [5,5,5]

2 In many nations throughout history, the basic human rights of certain groups have been denied.

Nations

China	Rwanda
Germany	Russia/Soviet Union
Haiti	Turkey
India	

Select *three* of the nations listed and for *each* one selected:

- Identify a specific group within that nation whose basic human rights have been denied

- Explain the historical circumstances that resulted in the denial of human rights for that group [You must use a different group for each nation chosen.]

- Discuss specific actions that have been taken to improve conditions for that group   [5,5,5]

3 Strong leaders use various methods to implement their domestic and foreign policies. These policies have major effects on their own nation or on other nations.

Leaders

Kemal Atatürk   Ho Chi Minh
Otto von Bismarck   Nelson Mandela
Simón Bolívar   Boris Yeltsin
Catherine the Great   Mao Zedong

Select *three* leaders from the list and for *each* one selected:

- Identify the nation with which that leader is associated

- Explain either *one* domestic policy *or one* foreign policy of that leader

- Discuss *one* method used by the leader to put his or her policy into effect   [5,5,5]

4 The values of a society are often reflected in its art and architecture. The pictures on this page and the following page show art or architecture from several cultures.

Select *three* of a the pictures and for *each* one selected:

- Identify the culture that is associated with that specific piece of art or architecture
- Discuss the values and beliefs of the culture that are reflected in that work   [5,5,5]

Mummy Case

Chartres Cathedral

Dome of the Rock

Bronze Sculpture

Ladies with Western Musical Instruments

Bacchus by Michelangelo

5 Historical events are often analyzed in terms of their political, economic, and social effects.

Events

Muhammad flees from Mecca to Medina
Magna Carta signed
Martin Luther posts his ninety-five theses
Aztec Empire defeated by Hernando Cortes
Atomic bomb dropped on Hiroshima
State of Israel created
Communist forces defeat Nationalists in China

Select *three* events listed and for *each* one selected:

- Describe the event
- Discuss a significant political, economic, or social change that resulted from the event   [5,5,5]

6 As a culture changes from a traditional to a modern society, various aspects of the life of the people in that society change.

Aspects of Life

Education
Health care
Marriage choices
Land distribution
Status of elders
Occupations
Roles of women or men

Select *three* aspects of life from the list and for *each* aspect selected:

- Identify a specific nation or region in which a traditional society has undergone change [You may use the same nation or region *or* a different nation or region for each aspect of life selected.]
- Explain how this aspect of life operated in the traditional society
- Describe how this aspect of life has changed [5,5,5]

7 Throughout history, individuals have held differing points of view on the same subject.

Subject — Individuals

Art — Leonardo da Vinci and Pablo Picasso
Economics — Karl Marx and Adam Smith
Independence movements — Mohandas Gandhi and Jomo Kenyatta
Individual rights — Adolf Hitler and John Locke
Scientific investigation — Galileo and Pope Paul V
Westernization — Peter the Great and Ayatollah Khomeini

Select *three* of the subjects from the list and for *each* subject selected, discuss how the points of view of the two individuals differed on the subject with which they are paired. [5,5,5]

ANSWER KEY
JANUARY 1996—PART I

1	1		25	1
2	2		26	2
3	3		27	2
4	2		28	3
5	1		29	4
6	4		30	2
7	3		31	1
8	3		32	2
9	1		33	4
10	3		34	1
11	2		35	3
12	4		36	2
13	3		37	1
14	1		38	1
15	2		39	4
16	2		40	1
17	4		41	3
18	2		42	1
19	2		43	2
20	4		44	3
21	2		45	3
22	3		46	4
23	3		47	4
24	4		48	1

ANSWERS AND EXPLANATIONS
JANUARY 1996—PART I

1   You want the BEST answer, so pick the answer that will tell you the
    MOST about the wealth of a nation, even though it won't tell you
    everything about the nation's wealth.
    **1   In its most simple form, the GNP is the total dollar value of
        products and services produced within a nation over a given
        period of time. It's actually more complicated, because
        foreign investments have to be taken into consideration, but
        the point is that it's a really good indicator of how rich (or
        poor) a nation is.**
    2   The prime interest rate is the rate of interest that banks charge
        customers (usually major corporations) that are considered
        excellent risks. In other words, it's the lowest interest rate you can
        get. If the prime rate rises, interest rates for everybody will rise in
        response. It doesn't indicate how wealthy a nation is, only how
        much it's going to cost to borrow money.
    3   The number of millionaires tells us very little about how rich a
        nation is. Are all of the other citizens poor? Are they middle class?
        How many others are there?
    4   Defense spending tells us how some of the nation's money is spent,
        but it doesn't tell us how much money it has in the first place
        (especially if some of the money spent on defense is borrowed
        money!).

2   Traditional agrarian societies are made up of people who farm their
    own food, and while they may make enough to eat and be satisfied,
    there usually isn't very much extra to sell to others.
    1   Surplus crops are a characteristic of modern commercial farming
        methods, which stress efficiency in land use and harvesting, and
        turn farms into businesses that produce products for sale to others.
    **2   Bingo! Subsistence farming is farming that merely "sustains"
        the farmer and his or her family, with little left for sale or
        trade.**
    3   No. There are no large reserves of capital. We're talking about
        economies that are just getting by.
    4   No exports. The people in these economies eat what they grow.

3   Industrialization and urbanization go hand-in-hand. Industrialization
    means to establish large-scale industries. Urbanization means that the
    cities are growing at the expense of the smaller towns and farms. You
    need to think of countries that are starting to build cities. How will the
    lives of the citizens change?
    1   No. In the cities, there is good medical care. Due to technological
        advancements, infant mortality rates are decreasing in industrial-
        ized nations.
    2   Average life expectancy actually has increased as nations have
        industrialized, again due to medical care and greater access to
        information.
    **3   Family patterns may be getting better; they may be getting
        worse. No matter what your opinion, they certainly are
        changing.**
    4   Education is becoming more important because industrial societies
        need skilled and educated workers.

4   Use your common sense on this one. We know from the question that
    a nation produces enough food for minimum needs. Why would some
    people still be hungry?
    1   Occasionally this might be a problem, but we want the answer that
        tells us the "main" problem. Also, people who practice a religion
        that forbids certain kinds of foods have no reason to grow the
        forbidden foods in the first place.
    **2   This makes sense. Even if there is enough food, if you can't
        distribute it to the people who need it, the food isn't going
        to help them. All too often, this is a serious problem in
        developing nations. Even food that is sent as goodwill gifts
        from other nations sometimes doesn't get delivered to the
        people who need it.**
    3   Ouch! If this were the case, why would they grow the food in the
        first place? Such a government probably wouldn't last very long,
        since if you're going to die, you may as well revolt!
    4   This answer choice doesn't make sense since the question told us that
        the food production meets minimum needs. Therefore, the food must
        have nutritional value or the needs wouldn't be met.

5   Gandhi is important. You had better know that he favored peaceful
    protest. Now, which answer choice sounds like a peaceful protest?
    **1   A march is usually some sort of peaceful protest, which is
        what Gandhi was all about. In the Salt March, he led thou-
        sands of Indians to the sea where they extracted salt from**

the salt water rather than pay the salt tax that the British imposed on them. This was the turning point in bringing world pressure to bear on the British.

2   After independence was won from Britain, the Indian subcontinent was partitioned into Hindu India and Muslim Pakistan. Gandhi wanted one large nation, not two nations.

3   A "mutiny" would certainly have brought attention to the injustices of British colonialism, but Gandhi was a peaceful protester, not a violent one. The Sepoy Mutiny occurred well before Gandhi's time, when some Indian members of the British Navy revolted against their commanders.

4   The formation of the Indian parliament occurred after British colonialism had ended.

6   Jawaharlal Nehru didn't want to get involved in the affairs of other nations. If you don't know what the words in the answer choices mean, you'd better look them up in the glossary. Now would be a better time than later.

1   Imperialism is the practice of forming empires. If you don't want to take sides but rather want to respect all nations, you certainly aren't looking to start an empire.

2   Mercantilism is an economic practice that goes along with forming an empire. Again, respecting all nations means no empire which means no mercantilism.

3   Isolationism means not wanting to have anything to do with anybody else. Nehru isn't saying that India wants to hide itself, but rather that it will strive to respect all other nations.

4   **Nonalignment means "not taking sides." Nehru indicates that India believes in tolerance and the capacity for peaceful coexistence. India wants to get along with everybody, and so it is nonaligned.**

7   If you've reviewed your materials, this question won't be a problem. If you're a bit fuzzy, use your common sense and at least choose the answer that is hardest to argue with. What do most nations that are neighbors fight about? The answer is geographic borders.

1   No. Help from the United Nations is desired in the region. Unfortunately, it hasn't been very helpful in solving the problems.

2   Pakistan and China are not particularly interested in India's trade with Korea. Isn't there something that would cause greater conflict?

3   Land! Territory! Borders! CONFLICT!! India has had disputes with China and Pakistan for decades. Think about it. Two new nations were carved out of the Indian subcontinent. Do you think everybody is going to agree where the lines should be?

4   Since these three nations don't share a common religion, there are no common religious works for there to be a conflict about.

8   Even if you only know about two of these ancient kingdoms, you can still get this right. Start eliminating answer choices that don't apply to the kingdoms you know about.

1   None of the kingdoms were in the mountains. Even if you only know about one of them, strike this answer.

2   Only the ancient Egyptian Kingdom was on the coast.

3   **This is it! The Egyptian Kingdom was on the Nile and on the Mediterranean. The other three were on major land routes going from North and West Africa to eastern and southern Africa. It also makes sense that a kingdom would grow strong because it traded with other kingdoms (and taxed them when it could). Check your textbook for the exact trade routes.**

4   None of the four kingdoms were in rain forest areas.

9   You absolutely have to know that after World War II, European colonialism fell because of independence movements in over fifty African nations. It's essential global studies information at the heart of many correct answer choices.

1   **This is what happened on the continent from top to bottom.**

2   The new African nations eagerly joined international organizations to increase their voice and visibility in world politics and economics.

3   Absolutely not. Most nations have welcomed assistance, especially when it has involved technological innovations.

4   In the years immediately following World War II, creating a unified Africa was a goal of some leaders, but most African nations have turned their concerns inward to solving domestic problems that continue to plague their development.

10 Choose the answer that involves the greatest number of events in the time line.

1   None of these events has to do with independence movements. These events are about European colonialism. The independence movements didn't come along until after World War II.

2   One event is about diamonds. The others are not about minerals at all.

    3 Europe is all over the place in these events: France, Britain, Germany, Portugal...

    4 These events are about European involvement in Africa, not about ethnic conflicts.

11 You need an answer choice that states a problem that is ongoing ("continues") as well as one that threatens "stability."

    1 Animism has declined, not spread. Even if it had spread, it wouldn't necessarily threaten stability.

    2 After African nations won their independence from Europeans, problems persisted from within, especially since the Europeans didn't respect the boundaries of the existing tribes when they drew the new national boundaries. The result was that some tribes were split apart while some rival tribes were enclosed within the same national boundary.

    3 While some African nations have adopted command economies, most are rejecting them and choosing structures that allow market forces to operate.

    4 Labor unions are very limited in Africa.

12 Learn about Confucius. Remember him. He's a permanent cast member of the Global Studies Exam.

    1 Confucius says: Put the group, especially family, before the individual.

    2 Confucius says: Respect authority.

    3 Confucius didn't say anything about religion per se, but was very concerned about how people behaved.

    4 Confucius taught about conduct, specifically the responsibilities that individuals owe to others and to the groups to which they belong.

13 The thing to remember about the Cultural Revolution in China is that it was a state-led effort to reinvigorate Communist Party teachings while actively suppressing everything that opposed it. Why was it needed? Because a lot of people were questioning the legitimacy of the system, which means that the people of China were divided.

    1 The Cultural Revolution most definitely was not a pro-democracy movement. Instead, the Chinese authorities actually attempted to squash pro-democracy literature and people.

    2 No. China was extremely self-involved during this time and didn't go looking for friends.

3 Exactly! Revolutions tend to disrupt a lot of things...that's why they're called revolutions!

4 China didn't regard the United States with a lot of friendliness during this time, nor did the United States regard China well. Even if you only know that the Cultural Revolution was about communism, you should eliminate this answer.

14 Be sure to read the quote carefully. It should be clear that the Emperor of China was not exactly impressed with Britain (notice the use of the word "barbarians"). It should also be clear that he believes that China has everything it needs and therefore has no need for anybody else.

1 The Emperor didn't want to trade with Britain, in effect saying "We don't need you...you barbarians!" When somebody doesn't want to deal with anybody, that somebody wants to be isolated.

2 When he said "there is no need to import any product...," the Emperor was making it pretty clear that he didn't want to trade.

3 Absolutely not. According to the Emperor, China's Celestial Empire wasn't dependent on anyone.

4 Even though the Empire was colonizing in Asia at the time, the practice wasn't the point of the quote. Instead, the quote indicates that the Emperor believed nothing more was needed than what China already possessed.

15 Read carefully. The Emperor was saying "We're cool. We don't need you." What kind of attitude is this?

1 Empathy is the ability to understand and feel what someone else is feeling. It's definitely not what's going on here.

2 If you're ethnocentric, you see things from only your point of view, and you do it with a feeling of superiority. Calling someone else a "barbarian" is a pretty ethnocentric thing to say.

3 The Emperor was imperialistic, but this particular statement is not an imperialistic one. Instead, it is a statement of contentment; a statement that everything is fine as it is and nothing else is needed.

4 This is not a militaristic statement. It is simply a rejection of an offer from Britain, stated in a snobby manner.

16 The first thing to do is review the legend. The map utilizes different shades to show the differing per capita incomes in each province of China.

1 If the economies are developing at the same rate, then why are different provinces shaded differently?

2 Per capita incomes are unequal. That's why some provinces have polka dots and others have stripes.

3 Look at what the different shades mean. The interior provinces are almost all white ones. According to the key, white means only $191-286 per capita. All of the provinces on the coast have higher per capita earnings.

4 What??? This map tells us nothing about the sources of economic development. It only tells us about per capita income in each of the provinces of China.

17 Whenever pyramids are used, it means that the powerful people are at the top (and that there are fewer of them) and that the less powerful people are at the bottom (and that there are more of them).

1 There are definitely classes. That's why there are really dark lines separating the labels (and why there are labels in the first place).

2 There wasn't a significant middle class in feudal Japan. Even if one of these classes were a middle class, though, we wouldn't know if it was growing or diminishing unless we knew how big it was during some previous time.

3 This diagram doesn't tell us if people were actually able to move up the pyramid. In fact, they were not able to do so, but you wouldn't know this from the diagram.

4 There are four groups. There are lines in between them. Groups are ordered from top to bottom. Bingo!

18 The Meiji Restoration eliminated the shogun and restored the emperor to power in 1868. This event occurred because many people in Japan didn't want Japan to be in isolation like it was under the shogun. What do you think happened next?

1 No. That's what happened in China. Japan, however, avoided European colonialism by becoming economically powerful itself. How do you think it became economically powerful? Look at answer choice number two.

2 After the Meiji Restoration, Japan asserted itself in the global marketplace by modernizing quickly. It became economically powerful, reducing the likelihood that it would be overtaken by European colonialists. The Meiji Restoration should automatically be associated with Japan's modernization movement.

3 No. The Meiji Restoration restored the emperor.

4   No. The samurai had some power, but the government was controlled by the emperor.

19   Notice the gigantic ship wanting to import goods into Japan and the door that is much too small for the ship to fit through. What's going on here?
  1   If the cartoonist believed that Japan practices free trade, there wouldn't be a huge wall drawn at the entrance to the country.
  2   Foreign companies want to import more stuff than the door will allow to enter. That's a restriction on imports and that's the point of the cartoon.
  3   If trade were balanced, exports would equal imports, but in the picture, exports is drawn larger than imports.
  4   Cartoons should never be taken this literally. The large ship is carrying a large number of products intended for sale in Japan. The ship itself is probably not intended to be sold. Even if Japan did import the ship itself, it wouldn't fit through the door!

20   This is a good process of elimination question. Start getting rid of answer choices that don't apply to even one or two of the religions in the question.
  1   Only some Christians, namely Catholics, believe in the central authority of the Pope. Non-Catholic Christians, Jews, and Muslims don't.
  2   Judaism and Islam prohibit the consumption of pork, but Christianity does not.
  3   None of these religions espouses reincarnation or the Four Noble Truths. These are tenets of Buddhism.
  4   Strong systems of ethical conduct and the belief in a single supreme being are central to all three religions.

21   If you know your geography, this question is a breeze. If not, you better do a little reading about the Suez Canal (and the Panama Canal, while you're at it).
  1   The building of the canal had nothing to do with encouraging Jewish settlements anywhere.
  2   The purpose of building canals is to make water transportation more efficient. Designed to increase global trade, the Suez Canal links the Mediterranean Sea with the Red Sea, thereby making travel between Europe and Asia much faster (since boats don't have to go around the southern tip of Africa anymore).
  3   The Caribbean Sea and the Atlantic Ocean are already connected, so travel between them doesn't require a canal or anything else.

4 The most efficient way for Indian merchants to reach the eastern coast of Africa is to travel directly across the Arabian Sea, which is what they did before the canal was built and what they continued to do after the canal was built.

22 "Fundamentalism," whether it is Islamic, Jewish, Christian, or anything else, is a belief that the relevant religious documents should be taken literally and that the traditions of the religion should be strictly followed.

1 Zionism is a movement to resettle the Jews in Palestine and is opposed by Islamic fundamentalists.

2 Fundamentalist Islamics oppose equal rights for women because the traditions of Islam require women to be subservient to men.

3 "Fundamentalist" and "traditional" go hand-in-hand. Fundamentalists do not believe in changing the interpretations of religious doctrines or changing the practice of religious customs.

4 Absolutely not. "Modernization" means change. Strict fundamentalists generally try to avoid anything that could lead to a change in religious doctrine or practice, even if it indirectly leads to such a change.

23 The key words in this question are "long-term" and "economic." Right now, many of the nations of the Middle East rely on oil exports. The ones that don't, have agricultural economies. What will they need in the future?

1 They already have plenty of unskilled labor. They will, however, need more skilled labor as the economy modernizes.

2 Most Middle Eastern countries don't need to import oil because they already have plenty. Instead, they export it.

3 What's going to happen when the oil wells run dry? Or when the rest of the world finds another source of energy? The countries of the Middle East will need to make money doing something else. If they diversify their economy, then if something bad happens in one industry, they will have other industries to keep the economy going.

4 Camels are becoming less and less important all the time in the Middle East, and are of no long-term significance for the region's economy.

24 Use your common sense on this one. Even if you don't remember the details of these three civilizations, you should remember that all of them were prosperous, powerful, and productive empires. Remember also, that one of the goals of your Global Studies course (and of this test) is for you to gain an appreciation for a number of different civilizations. With this in mind, which answer choice is the most attractive?

1 The Mayans, Aztecs, and Incas were three extremely significant civilizations in the history of the world. Of course they had cultural achievements.

2 No. Generally, civilizations establish an empire not through friendly means but through war and conquest. The Aztecs and the Incas established huge empires, mostly by fighting and conquering their neighbors.

3 Bad choice. The Europeans almost immediately attacked these civilizations, so there wasn't exactly a welcoming party during which technology and information were exchanged in a neighborly way.

4 This is the perfect Global Studies type of answer. Early Middle Eastern cultures accomplished a lot; early American cultures accomplished a lot too. Different civilizations in different parts of the world have all made significant contributions to our global history. This is the point of the Global Studies course!

25 You must understand "mercantilism" because the concept is on virtually every Global Studies Exam. Look it up now in the glossary if you don't know it yet.

1 The production of raw materials and crops for export back to the mother country (so that the mother country won't have to import the materials from other countries) is a major goal of mercantilism.

2 The goods produced in Latin America usually were sent back to Spain and Portugal, not to Asia and Africa.

3 Definitely not. The Spaniards were very ethnocentric, believing themselves to be superior to the people they conquered.

4 After the region was conquered by Spain, it was never again to become isolated from the rest of the world. Now more than ever, the sovereign nations in the region are immersed in global politics, international organizations, and trade.

26 In the graph, the white line represents the population of each country and the black line represents the part of the population that has access to piped water. Therefore, if the two black and white lines are the

same length, it means that everybody in the country has access to piped water.

1 El Salvador and Guatemala, not Honduras and Panama, have the most people and therefore require the largest supply of water.

2 **Belize and Costa Rica each have black lines that are as long as their white lines. Even when the population of each country grew between 1980 and 1988, the country managed to provide access to piped water for everybody in urban areas.**

3 Look at the difference between the 1980 black lines and the 1988 black lines for each country. In almost all of them, the 1988 lines are longer than the 1980 lines. Therefore, the urban water supplies are increasing, not decreasing.

4 Look at the difference between the 1980 white lines and the 1988 white lines for each country. The 1988 lines are longer. Therefore, the urban population increased in each country between 1980 and 1988.

27 Why do you think the Mexican Constitution would declare that all minerals are owned by the nation? The answer is that they were previously owned by someone else. Otherwise, such a declaration wouldn't be necessary. So, who do you think owned the minerals before Article 27? Remember that Mexico was very much a victim of European imperialism and that the creation of documents of a revolutionary nature such as this one was in reaction to foreign domination.

1 If Mexicans were importing large quantities of minerals, then that would mean that Mexico didn't have very many minerals of its own. But it does. If it didn't have very many minerals of its own, then it's unlikely that ownership of the minerals would have been a big deal.

2 **Yes! Foreign companies owned most of the mines. They would make a profit from Mexico's land by shipping the minerals out of Mexico. The Mexican Constitution was supposed to change this, but it wasn't enforced.**

3 No. After the Europeans took over, the natives never controlled much land at all, whether it had minerals in it or not.

4 No. These deposits were not discovered until much later, but even if they were discovered in 1917, they would likely have been owned by foreigners, so answer choice number 2 would still be the best answer.

28 The thing to remember about the Protestant Reformation is that it was a "protest" which was intended to "reform" the Catholic Church. Since

not everybody agreed with the protest (especially most leaders of the Catholic Church), the protesters eventually left the Catholic Church when they realized they couldn't reform it. The result was that some Christians became what are known as Protestants (like Lutherans and Presbyterians) while others remained loyal to the Catholic Church.

1   The Protestant Reformation was not welcomed by the Catholic Church. Therefore, most protesters were persecuted, some more than others.

2   Absolutely not. The Protestant Reformation (with the aid of the printing press) opened up theological debate and distributed it to the masses. The Bible itself was translated into the languages that the people spoke at home so that each person could read and interpret the Bible for himself or herself.

3   **Bingo! "Protest" usually means an end to unity! Especially the unity created by the Church in the Middle Ages.**

4   The Protestant Reformation did not use force. It was a theological protest, not a military one, and therefore those monarchs that became Protestant did so because they chose to do so.

29 You need to know about the Commercial Revolution, because it shows up on the test a lot. The Commercial Revolution was the start of the modern monetary, banking, and investment system that thrust the western world into capitalism and mercantilism. What do you think happened as a result?

1   No. Socialism didn't become popular until the nineteenth century. Plus, socialism advocates public ownership of property and business, whereas the Commercial Revolution led to private ownership and investment.

2   The Commercial Revolution led to the downfall of the guild system because there was an increase in imports and a decrease in purchases from local craftsmen.

3   No. Generally, the middle class benefited from the Commercial Revolution because the typical business person made more money, increased investments, and thereby became more influential and powerful.

4   **Money is being invested! Western Europe is setting up shop in colonies! Trade, trade, trade!**

30 The key term in the question is the year 1991, representing the uniting of East and West Germany. The man on the bicycle represents Germany. The back wheel is big and modern and represents the western half of the recently reunited country. The front wheel is old

and crumbling and represents the eastern half of the country. Because of the imbalance, the entire country of Germany is slouched.

1 The country hasn't been hurt because of the man on the bike. The country has been hurt because of the front wheel.

2 This is it. All of Germany is slouched because of the crumbling front wheel.

3 The East wheel is crumbling, not strong.

4 The two wheels are not equal, but very different. That's why answer choice number two is so much better.

31 Geography influences a region's development, in this case, the low-lying plains of western Europe. And, remember, if you encounter answer choices that aren't true of western Europe, then you can eliminate them, even if they do have something to do with topography and climate.

1 The relatively mild weather, the flat lands in the north, and the extensive river system in western Europe all have contributed to the development of communication and transportation systems.

2 Cash crops are crops that are intended for export and are the main source of agricultural income for an area, like coffee in Colombia or wheat in Kansas. The farms of western Europe, however, grow a variety of crops, much of which is consumed within western Europe itself, as opposed to being exported to other nations.

3 Western Europe is not isolationist, and even if it were, it would not be due to topography and climate, because the topography and climate of western Europe makes traveling pretty easy.

4 Western Europe has plenty of warm-water ports, so the people there don't have to go searching for them. Russia, however, is an example of a country that has traditionally searched for warm-water ports.

32 Locke, Montesquieu, and Rousseau were political philosophers who believed in democracy and in limiting the power of the government. This is all you need to know to get this question right.

1 The three philosophers wrote about the rights and responsibilities of governments whether they governed large areas or small areas. They were not concerned with the concept of empire.

2 Yes! "Political reform" is what these three philosophers were all about.

3 No. The Spanish Inquisition occurred before these three philosophers were alive and, in any case, was not something that was consistent with their writings.

4 These three philosophers didn't directly affect working conditions. Rather, they were concerned with political reform as opposed to reform in the workplace.

33 Even if you don't know what the term "white man's burden" meant, you should choose an answer choice that explains a position taken by Europeans during the nineteenth century.

1 Europeans ("white men") didn't believe that Asians and Africans were equal to them. If they did, then why in the world would they believe they had a "burden" as a group?

2 Many Europeans did believe that Asians and Africans would be grateful for their "help," but there is a better answer choice that more precisely explains "burden."

3 We can't be sure how many Europeans supported imperialism, but clearly imperialist policies lasted for centuries with general popular support. The middle class in Europe made a considerable amount of money from imperialism, so it shouldn't be too surprising that there was significant popular support.

4 **"Burden" means "responsibility." Many Europeans justified their imperialist ventures by arguing that they had a responsibility to improve the lives of their colonial peoples (which, of course, was a very ethnocentric way of looking at the world).**

34 If you have a basic understanding of the European Union, this question should not be a problem. If you don't, choose the answer that makes sense in describing what a "community" is all about.

1 **The European Union is mostly about economics. The member nations want goods and money to flow easily between them, and so they have removed all trade barriers.**

2 European nations have been trading with the United States and Japan for a long time. But one of the goals of the European Union is actually to increase trade within the Union and to limit imports from the United States and Japan.

3 Latin America is not influential in European affairs, so blocking it is certainly not the goal of the Union.

4 The European Union is mostly about the economy, not the military. If nations want to decrease their military role, they can do it unilaterally, or can limit their participation in the United Nations.

35 Use your common sense on this one. Lots of people are moving to western Europe from less developed places. Why do you think some western Europeans might not be too happy about this?

1　To the contrary, most immigrants moved in order to find work, and so they will accept any job they can get.

2　If this were true, why would this cause some Europeans grief? In fact, many of the immigrants do not share the same ethnicity or religion as most of the others in the host nation.

3　**Yes! If you need a job, and if there are people moving into your city looking for work, you probably won't be happy about the new arrivals.**

4　Unskilled immigrants usually settle in urban areas, so this answer choice doesn't make sense. Because government benefits are more easily available in urban areas, some Europeans have been arguing that the immigrants are "draining" the government by "taking advantage" of the benefits without paying very much into the system. The validity of this claim is an item of intense debate in almost every nation that is experiencing an increase in immigration.

36　The Mongols ruled in Russia during the thirteenth and fourteenth Centuries. If you're clueless about this time period, you need to review your materials.

1　No. The Mongols weren't big fans of the arts.

2　**Yes! The Mongols kept Russia more isolated than it was previously or subsequently.**

3　No. Industrialization hadn't yet occurred anywhere during the time of Mongol rule.

4　No. Democratic reforms hadn't occurred anywhere yet, and they were not encouraged in Russian society until recently.

37　Use your common sense on this one. Think the answer choices through, one step at a time.

1　**Not only does this answer choice make a lot of sense in general, it also describes what happened in the two examples given in the question. In both cases, the leader was ousted because the economy was in shambles (in 1917, due to World War I, and in 1991, due to Gorbachev's *perestroika* program).**

2　If Russian absolutism continued into the 1990s, then how could Gorbachev have been forced to resign? He would have ruled "absolutely."

3　This statement is true in general, but it does not describe what happened in these two examples. The two leaders were ousted primarily because of internal economic problems, not because of international conflicts.

4   Absolutely not. Russia was, and is, extremely diverse.

38   You need to familiarize yourself with "collectivization" because it is frequently on the test. You should also be aware that Stalin was a staunch communist.

1   Yes! Stalin thought that forced communism would modernize the economy. Private ownership of farms and factories was eliminated specifically because Stalin believed communism would enable the country to modernize more quickly.

2   No. This was not the point of the Five-Year Plans, nor were China and Russia friendly.

3   The Cold War hadn't started yet.

4   The plans were mostly economic in nature, and because communism was at their heart, they certainly could not be described as "western."

39   You absolutely need to know that the Soviet Union was a communist nation. Therefore, if communism "collapsed," then the economic system that replaced it would have to be different from communism.

1   Russia is a huge, interconnected country. It is not merely a collection of tiny, feudal kingdoms.

2   Marx and Lenin are related to communism, which is precisely what "collapsed."

3   Mao Zedong is also related to communism (in China, not Russia).

4   Yes! Russia has attempted to build an economy based on a free-market system, where consumer goods are in greater supply to meet Russians' demands. If you don't know this, you need to review your global studies materials. Now!

40   These "former nations" are "former" because they split into parts. If they never divided, they wouldn't be called "former" nations. So which one is the best answer choice?

1   Notice the use of the word "divide." Done.

2   Absolutely not. If they had done this, both nations would still be whole.

3   The two nations didn't combine into one! They divided into more pieces.

4   No way. Both nations embraced a free-market economy, which itself resulted in the two nations splitting into parts.

41   These two revolutions were examples of political change. Even if you just know about one of the two revolutions, you'll get this one right.

Use your common sense and go with the answer choice that is hardest to argue with.

1 No. Neither one did. Plus, be careful of any answer choice that suggests a direct democracy resulted, since there are no nations with direct democracies (but lots and lots of nations with representative democracies).

2 This answer choice has it backwards. In fact, the revolutions occurred to oust the monarchs, not restore them.

3 **Revolutions certainly involve change, or else they would be called "continuations." Often they are violent. The Russian Revolution was violent from the beginning. The French Revolution became violent during the Reign of Terror, after the revolutionists became powerful and began to execute people who disagreed with them.**

4 The power of the Catholic Church decreased in France after the Revolution and was absent both before and after the revolution in Russia.

42 If you know about the Shinto faith, this one is easy. If you don't, eliminate the answer choices that clearly apply to religions that you *do* know about, since those are probably the trap answers.

1 **In Japan, people who practice the Shinto faith believe in ancestor and nature worship. The shrine involves ancestor worship; the shore of a lake involves nature worship.**

2 Muslim worshipers, not Shinto worshipers, pray five times a day.

3 Hindu worshipers, not Shinto worshipers, are more likely to bathe in the Ganges River in India.

4 Christian, Muslim, and Jewish worshipers, not Shinto worshipers, would have the best reasons to make a pilgrimage to Jerusalem.

43 If you know the term "golden age," you should get this right. If you know about any of the three examples mentioned, you should get this right. In other words, you have lots of chances to get this one right. Use the process of elimination.

1 Sometimes the winning of a war does inspire achievement, but the periods in this question were peaceful times.

2 **Absolutely. All three are examples of peaceful prosperity and the cultural achievement that resulted (know the term "golden age," found in the glossary).**

3 No. These three examples did not involve dictators.

4 Guess again. The three examples involve periods of peace and relative freedom. Plus, this answer choice is disputable, since it

would be hard to argue that censorship is a necessary ingredient for cultural and scientific greatness.

44 Look at the information in the chart carefully. Then, start eliminating.
  1 Nothing in the chart tells us about programs designed to limit growth. We only have numbers here, and these numbers are only for one year.
  2 Bangladesh and Japan are both in Asia, and have wildly different infant mortality rates. Tanzania is in *Africa* and its infant mortality rate is between Japan's and Bangladesh's. Plus, we would need to know about ALL of the nations in Africa and Asia in order to properly evaluate this answer choice.
  3 Germany and Japan have the highest per capita incomes on the chart. They also have the lowest birthrates. Done!
  4 Nothing on the chart tells us about the causes of national birth-rates. All we have are numbers.

45 Even if you only know about one of these fascist regimes, you can get this question right. Think about what "fascist" means. Simply knowing what it means won't make you pick the right answer, but it will help you eliminate the wrong ones.
  1 Absolutely not. None of the three regimes expressed empathy toward African nations. Italy actually invaded Ethiopia, which should give you a clue about the correct answer.
  2 Guess again. Fascist regimes are not known for protecting human rights. To the contrary, they are known for the absolute authority of the leader (the fascist).
  3 This is it. Fascist regimes don't necessarily have to be imperialistic, but these three were. All three regimes succeeded in conquering other previously sovereign nations.
  4 None of the fascist regimes supported free expression. To the contrary, they actually punished people who advocated ideas against the interests of the regime.

46 Civil wars are the result of intense, fundamental differences between at least two large groups within a country. Fundamental differences involve characteristics that are basic to a person's existence or philoso-phy, like race and religion.
  1 Neither country has a command economy. Even if they both did, however, if that economy failed to satisfy the needs of the people, it's not likely that the failure of a command economy would result in a civil war. More likely, it would result in political and economic reform.

2   Absolutely not. Even if you don't know that the multinational forces sent to Lebanon failed, the fact that the two conflicts mentioned spanned over a period of decades suggests that these conflicts have not been easy to resolve.

3   No. Even though the international community has not been successful in its efforts to stop violence in these areas, the international community is aware of the problems and has made numerous attempts.

4   The inability of the people and the government to reconcile religious differences (or other fundamental differences) is what civil wars and major internal conflicts are all about. In Lebanon, it's Christians vs. Muslims. In Northern Ireland, it's Catholics vs. Protestants. Both countries remain unstable today due to the lack of meaningful and long-lasting resolutions.

47   You only need to know either Pol Pot or the Khmer Rouge to get this one right. If you don't, review your materials now! If you do, this one is easy.

1   Nuh-uh.

2   Guess again.

3   Not here.

4   Got it! In 1975, Pol Pot led a group known as the Khmer Rouge in Cambodia. They killed hundreds of thousands of people (some estimates are as high as four million) who were suspected of disagreeing with their policies.

48   Use your common sense and knowledge of current events on this one. Think of the UN forces in the Persian Gulf, or the UN peacekeeping force in Somalia, or in the former Yugoslavia, or Cyprus, or anywhere else that you can remember from your reading or the news.

1   Yes! The UN has dramatically increased its involvement in conflicts within member nations over the past decade, though the effectiveness and appropriateness of that involvement is an item of intensifying debate.

2   Absolutely not. One of the least controversial roles of the UN has been its involvement in health issues. Medical care for people in developing nations remains a high priority.

3   This doesn't make sense. The conflicts between the superpowers have been minimal since the end of the Cold War and the collapse of the former Soviet Union.

4   No. The votes have become increasingly western, especially after the fall of communism in Eastern Europe.

PART II

1. GEOGRAPHIC FACTORS

Coastline

For centuries, Russia's only coastline ran along the Arctic ocean in the north and then cut south in the east along the Bering Sea. The southern and western borders were landlocked. Since the Arctic Ocean is almost entirely covered in ice year around, Russia was not able to establish port cities throughout much of its history, except in the east where the population is sparse and thousands of miles away from the population centers of the west. Then, in the eighteenth century, Peter the Great drove the Swedes out of part of the Baltic region and established his new capital city on the Baltic Sea. In addition, both he and, later, Catherine the Great fought wars against the Ottoman Empire in the south to gain access to the Black Sea. Thereafter, Russia's coastline included warm-water ports that it had previously lacked. As a result, Russia's international trade increased dramatically, as did its naval capacity. The limited warm-water coastline of Russia, therefore, dramatically affected its economy and territorial expansion policy for most of its history.

Mineral resources

In the twentieth century, the economy of the Persian Gulf region has been transformed. The Persian Gulf nations of Saudi Arabia, Iraq, Iran, United Arab Emirates, and Kuwait control two thirds of the world's known petroleum reserves. As the world industrialized and motorized, petroleum became an extremely important commodity, and the Persian Gulf region found itself wielding not only increased economic power, but increased political power as well. The region united with a few other oil exporting nations in 1960 in a petroleum cartel known as OPEC. With three quarters of the world's petroleum reserves, OPEC members collectively cut supply dramatically in the 1970s, shooting the price of oil through the roof. Billions of extra dollars flowed into OPEC member nation coffers. Nations like Saudi Arabia used the extra money to modernize their infrastructure and education systems, and spent billions on attempts to improve their agricultural sectors. The presence of petroleum in Kuwait was also the main motivation for Iraqi aggression against it, and the reason the industrialized world mobilized to drive Iraq out. The presence of a single resource, petroleum, has therefore changed the economic and political landscape of the Persian Gulf region.

Mountains

The Himalayas have played an important part in the development of the Indian subcontinent to the south of them and central Asia to the north of them. Geologists believe that the Himalayas were created when India drifted into Asia about forty million years ago. The result was the creation of the highest mountain range in the world. Like most mountain ranges, the Himalayas protect the people on both sides of the range, and yet they also isolate them. The mountains stretch from just northeast of Burma all the way to the northeast corner of Pakistan. In other words, they create a wall between the Indian subcontinent and central Asia. In terms of the weather, the mountains prevent the southern monsoon winds from reaching Russia and cold winter air from reaching India. In terms of military conquest, they have prevented invading armies from going in either direction. But perhaps most importantly, the mountain range led to distinct cultural variations. Politics, religion, and culture on both sides of the range developed separately and then spread east and west along the range rather than through it.

Rainfall

The seasonal rainfalls of Southeast Asia and India are vital to the maintenance of life. The amount of rain that the region receives is dependent on the monsoon winds. While the word *monsoon* could refer to seasonal winds on any part of the globe, it more specifically refers to the seasonal winds in India and Southeast Asia. There, the winds create two seasons: a wet season and a dry season. During summer in the northern hemisphere, hot air rises from the enormous Asian land mass, creating a large area of low pressure. The low pressure pulls winds from the south toward it. These monsoon winds blow over the ocean, collect moisture, and then dump extremely heavy rains on India and Southeast Asia. During winter in the northern hemisphere, the monsoon winds switch direction. Cool air settles over the Asian land mass, sending dry air south toward India and Southeast Asia. The growth of rice, the major staple grain of Southeast Asia, is dependent on the monsoon rains. Rice grows in paddy fields that require hot sun followed by extremely heavy rains. Millions of people rely on the rice for food, and the economies of Southeast Asia rely on rice for export. If the monsoon winds bring too little rain, the result is famine. If the monsoon winds bring too much, the result is devastating flood waters. Most of the nations of Southeast Asia have experienced both.

Rivers

The Nile River has been the lifeblood of Egypt since ancient times. Floodwater from the river created a narrow band of excellent farmland stretching for nearly a thousand miles from the mouth of the river on the Mediterranean Sea. The ancient Egyptians maintained a prosperous kingdom for centuries along its banks. The river provided them not only with food, but with transportation between the villages and cities, all of which were built along or close to the river bank. Although the river sometimes would bring exceptionally high floodwaters, the soil was replenished when the flood waters finally receded. The result was a self-sustaining empire that dominated the entire region for centuries.

2. DENIAL OF BASIC HUMAN RIGHTS

China

In 1989, the Chinese government violated the human rights of over 100,000 peaceful demonstrators in Beijing's Tiananmen Square. University students and others had gathered in the square to push for democratic reforms. Ever since the Communist Revolution, the Chinese people have not had the right to vote or the right to free expression. In recent years, the Communist government has initiated significant free-market economic reforms to create incentives for hard work and innovation and to lure foreign companies into partnerships with the government. The students gathered because they believed that the time had come to push for social and political reform as well. The Chinese government did not agree and reacted violently, cruelly demonstrating the intolerance for freedom of expression that led to the gathering in the first place. Heavily armed government troops converged on the square and dispersed the crowds with open fire. Thousands of people were killed; thousands more were arrested or injured. Although the world community condemned the action, it has continued to increase trade relations with China. Today, the government policies that deny freedom of expression are still in place.

Germany

Although many groups of people were denied basic human rights in Germany during World War II, Jews were singled out and deliberately slaughtered. The rise of Adolf Hitler in post-World War I Germany led to an increase in anti-Semitic propaganda since Hitler's brand of intense nationalism was based on racism as well. Hitler's Nazi party did not merely unite Germans, it united Aryan Germans against virtually everyone else. The millions of Jews who lived in Germany and German-occupied lands were rounded up, blamed for every conceivable problem in society, and methodically killed in gas chambers, firing lines, and ovens. When Nazi Germany was finally destroyed, Germany was split in half and tensions in the region remained high. Many of the surviving Jews fled to Israel and the United States. Though the inhumanity cannot be corrected, many survivors have made it their mission that it never be forgotten so that it is never repeated.

Haiti

Since independence from France in 1804, the people of Haiti have struggled to gain basic human rights such as freedom of expression and the right to vote. A succession of military dictatorships continually violated human rights. In 1957, the Duvalier dictatorship won control of the government and squashed various pro-democracy uprisings. The international community reacted with sanctions and condemnations, and the ruling family finally allowed free elections in 1990. Jean-Bertrand Aristide was elected president, but was overthrown the following year in a military coup. A United Nations embargo in 1993 failed to reinstate Aristide, so a multinational force led by the United States invaded Haiti in 1994. Fortunately, they didn't have to fight very much. The military leaders relinquished their power as the troops came on shore. Since then, UN forces have occupied Haiti to ensure the development of democracy and the recognition of basic human rights, but the future of Haiti remains uncertain.

India

The caste system in India has led to many violations of human rights, especially against members of the lowest caste, the "untouchables." Members of the lowest caste cannot associate with members of higher castes, neither in social situations nor in business partnerships. The untouchables are prevented from marrying, befriending, or even talking to people of higher castes. The government of India has tried to alleviate the situation by outlawing the caste system. However, because the caste system is part of the traditional culture and dominant religion of India, the government's efforts have never been successful, especially in rural areas. In a further effort, the government has taken upon itself to hire many untouchables for government jobs. Nevertheless, because the human rights violations of untouchables are culturally sanctioned by millions of Indians and by the dominant religion, the government can only do so much. If the untouchables are truly to gain human rights in India, a change in culture at a fundamental level will need to occur.

Rwanda

Human rights violations in Rwanda and Burundi stem from conflicts between two groups: the Tutsi (10% of the population in Rwanda and 15%

of the population in Burundi) who traditionally have governed the Hutu (90% of Rwanda, 85% of Burundi). Hutu revolts against Tutsi leadership left hundreds of thousands dead. The Hutu eventually gained control in the 1970s. However, in 1994, the Hutu leaders of Rwanda and Burundi were killed in an airline crash, and thereafter the Tutsi swept through the nations and declared civil war. The crisis has sent millions of Hutu refugees into Zaire. The Hutu are trying to escape torture and death and believe that they cannot safely return to their own country. The United Nations has intervened to aid Zaire in dealing with the onslaught of refugees and has sent a multinational force to restore order to the region. The goal of the UN effort is to create a stable situation in which the Hutu people can safely return to their countries. The problem remains unsettled, however.

Russia/Soviet Union

The former Soviet Union, and Russia before it, consistently violated the human rights of many of their citizens. In czarist Russia, Jews were discriminated against openly, segregated into walled ghettos and denied basic services. As the discrimination became more entrenched in Russian society, the czars even ordered the murder of innocent Jews and the ransacking of their homes and villages. Later, after the formation of the Soviet Union, the government continued its tradition of religious intolerance, especially since the Soviet Union was officially an atheist state. Citizens who openly practiced their religions were discriminated against, especially Muslims in the southern part of the Soviet Union. The international community has spoken out against religious discrimination, but it has not interfered in the internal religious struggles of Russia or the former Soviet Union.

Turkey

Turkey has consistently violated the human rights of one of its fastest growing minorities, the Kurds of southeastern Turkey. The Kurds are a distinct nation of people with a distinct language and yet without a homeland. In addition to Turkey, Kurds live in northern Iraq and northwestern Iran, but want their own nation. Hundreds of thousands of Kurds fled to Turkey when the Iraqi government of Saddam Hussein chased them out with chemical weapons. The Turks responded by increasing their military presence in Kurdish regions and banning the use of Kurdish in schools. Kurds are allowed some representation in government, but they are not allowed to discuss Kurdish issues. In 1995, following terrorist attacks against Turkey by a radical Kurdish group, the Turkish government reacted harshly against all Kurds, not just the extremists. It bombed Kurdish regions in eastern Turkey, hoping to rid itself of the Kurdish "problem" once and for all. With no place to go, Kurds continue to wander around the region hoping to eventually establish a home.

3. STRONG LEADERS

Kemal Atatürk

Atatürk "the Father of the Turks," was the first president of modern Turkey. He earned the adoration of millions of Turks during World War I and then used that loyalty to gain support in his diplomatic career. He successfully secularized the overwhelmingly Muslim nation, introduced western-style dress and customs (abolishing the fez), changed the alphabet from Arabic to Latin, set up a parliamentary system (which he dominated), changed the legal code from Islamic to Western, and set Turkey on a path toward Europe as opposed to the Middle East. However, he instituted these reforms sternly against opposition, and sometimes was ruthless in his determination to institute change. However, he succeeded where so many others would have failed. The economy and opportunities in Turkey are still growing today, despite growing Muslim fundamentalism.

Otto von Bismarck

Otto von Bismarck united the loose collection of independent German states into the single nation of Germany. In the nineteenth century, Germany was still a loose collection of city-states while much of Europe (France, Britain, and Spain, for example) had long been unified under a single government. Bismarck became the chief minister of Prussia, the largest German state, in 1862 and began his quest for unification. Many of the German states, however, were under control of Austria. Thus, he first enlisted the support of Austria (he needed their help) in a war against Denmark in order to gain control of two small German states under its control. After succeeding, Bismarck turned against Austria (he didn't need them anymore) and defeated it soundly, winning control of more German states. The rest of Europe, especially France, became nervous at the prospect of a united Germany. Bismarck provoked France into declaring war on Prussia so that the rest of Europe wouldn't think that Prussia was aggressive. Bismarck then easily crushed the French in the Franco-Prussian War, Germany unified, and Bismarck became its leader. The result was not only the restructuring of the balance of power in Europe, but the development of a strong sense of nationalism in Germany, which proved to be a very dangerous force just decades later in both World Wars.

Simón Bolívar

Simón Bolívar was a nineteenth century revolutionary leader in the Spanish colonies of South America. Inspired by the French and American Revolutions, the people of South America began their revolt against Spanish rule in 1810. Bolívar served competently not only as the military and emotional leader of the revolution, but also as an intelligent and thoughtful strategist. After years of struggle, independence was finally won in 1824 for parts of South America, including Venezuela, Colombia, Ecuador, Peru and, of course, Bolivia, which was named in his honor. Bolívar wanted to establish a United Gran Colombia, essentially a "United States" of South America, but a conference with Jose San Martin, the leader of the revolution in Argentina, failed miserably. Other movements eventually led to the establishment and maintenance of the individual Latin American nations that still exist today. Bolívar died unhappily due to his failure to unite the continent, but his success as a revolutionary is undisputed.

Catherine the Great

Catherine the Great, empress of Russia for over thirty years in the late eighteenth century, continued the two primary traditions of Peter the Great—westernization and territorial expansion. She attacked the declining Ottoman Empire to the south and secured access to the Black Sea for Russia. In addition, she successfully fought wars and negotiated agreements to win parts of Poland, the Ukraine, and Lithuania to the Russian Empire. Domestically, Catherine supported education and development of the arts, granted freedom of religion, but decentralized the power that Peter the Great had worked to amass, returning a considerable amount of power to the landlords. Therefore, although Catherine the Great increased the overall size and military power of Russia, the nation failed to unify under her leadership, even as nationalism was growing in the rest of Europe.

Ho Chi Minh

Ho Chi Minh was the founder of the Socialist Republic of Vietnam. He and his Communist followers drove Japan from Vietnam and then prevented the French from reoccupying the nation after World War II. An accord signed in Geneva in 1954 divided the nation in two. The Communists, under the leadership of Ho Chi Minh, gained control of the land north of the 17th parallel while Ngo Dihn Diem became the president of the democratic south. Under its new constitution, North Vietnam supported reunification of Vietnam as a communist state. Ho Chi Minh supported communist guerrillas in the south, known as the Viet Cong, and soon war broke out.

France and the United States came to the aid of South Vietnam, but Ho Chi Minh's Viet Cong prevented them from securing a victory. A peace agreement eventually led to the reunification of Vietnam as a communist state.

Nelson Mandela

Nelson Mandela, a black South African known for his ability to motivate a crowd, led the anti-apartheid movement in his nation. Apartheid was established in South Africa in 1948 as a policy intent on not just separating black and white South Africans, but denying blacks the same civil rights and opportunities that the white minority enjoyed. Mandela became leader of the African National Congress in the 1950s. At first, he advocated peaceful protest. But after the Sharpeville demonstrations resulted in the massacre of black protesters, the African National Congress supported guerrilla warfare. Mandela was arrested in 1964 for his role in anti-apartheid violence, and sentenced to life imprisonment. After decades of increasing pressure from the black majority and the international community, South Africa finally released Mandela in 1990 and agreed to negotiate on the policy of apartheid. In 1994, after apartheid was abolished, Mandela was elected president in the first free and open elections in South African history.

Boris Yeltsin

Boris Yeltsin was one of the most outspoken voices in favor of reform in the Soviet Union in the late 1980s. As leader of Russia, the largest Soviet republic, he openly criticized the economic and political reform plans of Gorbachev, the president of the Soviet Union. Yeltsin believed that the reform efforts should be initiated at a faster pace, and in a more extensive manner. His ideas won strong support. When the Soviet Union disbanded, Yeltsin remained in power as president of Russia, now an independent state. He cut all ties with the Communist Party and initiated aggressive free-market restructuring of the economy. However, major economic, political, and ethnic problems have developed in Russia under his leadership. Some believe that more extensive reforms are needed, but an increasing number of people attribute the problems to the reforms themselves, and therefore want to abandon them. As a result, Yeltsin has come under intense scrutiny from Communists who want to reassert their power. The future of Yeltsin and Russia, therefore, remains in doubt.

Mao Zedong

Mao Zedong was the leader of the Communist Revolution in China, and after its success, the leader of the Communist Republic of China. Mao collectivized agriculture and industry, instituted sweeping social reform, and, for a time, improved the lives of millions of peasants. His most significant domestic policy was the Cultural Revolution of the late 1960s and early 1970s. Mao believed that parts of Chinese society were straying from the goals of communism. He attributed this problem to the influence of the West and the revisionist forces within the university systems. As a result, culture was truly revolutionized. The universities were shut down for four years. The students and faculty were sent to work in the fields in an effort to change their "elitist" attitudes. When the universities reopened, the curriculum was reorganized to include only communist studies and vocational training. After the Cultural Revolution and Mao's death in 1976, the new leadership quickly changed the education policy and began to focus on restructuring the economic policies. Nevertheless, Mao's Cultural Revolution succeeded in reaffirming communist philosophy at a time when the rest of the communist world was beginning to question itself.

4. ART AND ARCHITECTURE

Mummy case

The mummy case is associated with ancient Egyptian society. The Egyptians believed it was important to mummify the body in the event that the spirit of the dead person (known as the "ka") ever reunited with the body. Mummification and the preparation of the tomb was a long process, sometimes taking as long as three months. But it shows the importance of the afterlife in Egyptian religion. At first, it was only believed that the king would experience life after death, but as Egyptian society developed, it was commonly believed that all men could expect life after death. Only the king was elaborately mummified and entombed in grand places like the pyramids, but the mummy case nevertheless is an important symbol of the religious beliefs of ancient Egypt as a whole.

Dome of the Rock

The Dome of the Rock was built in Jerusalem at the site where Muslims believe Muhammed ascended into heaven. It was not built as a functioning mosque, but rather as a shrine for Muslim pilgrims who were expected to travel to Jerusalem, the third holiest city of Islam. Completed in the late seventh century, it stands as the earliest major example of Islamic architecture. It is beautifully decorated with geometrical patterns, Arabic script, and mosaics. Noticeably lacking, however, are any representations of Muhammed, or any other human figure for that matter. Islam holds that human representations, especially in mosques and other holy places, are a form of idolatry and blasphemy. Muslims believe that only God can create the human body and therefore no attempts should be made to reproduce it. Although this belief has been modified since the construction of the Dome of the Rock, the shrine stands as an excellent reflection of Islamic architecture and beliefs.

Chartres Cathedral

Chartres Cathedral stands as one of the greatest examples of the High Gothic style in Europe and as an excellent reflection of Medieval Christianity. After the first attempt to build the cathedral ended in fire, it was finally completed in 1220, twenty-six years after the second attempt began. Three features of the tremendous Cathedral combined architectural style with Christian theology. First, the alter rests at the intersection of a long nave and two side galleries. In other words, the floor plan is in the shape of the cross, the most important symbol of Christianity. Second, the ceiling in the nave rises to nearly 120 feet, and the towers outside rise much higher than that, focusing the eyes and the spirit upward toward heaven. Third, the walls are dominated by enormous stained glass windows, larger and more intricate than anything that had come before them. Christian symbolism and biblical stories are represented within the designs of the windows. Therefore, the design of Chartres Cathedral was well suited for its purpose.

Bronze sculpture

The bronze sculpture is most likely from the African Kingdom of Benin, a kingdom known for its impressive and unique bronze-work. The bronze sculptures are significant to an understanding of Benin culture because they originated within the culture itself. In other words, the Benin culture developed the bronze-making techniques that they used. The sculptures also give us clues about the dress, customs, and traditions of the Benin Kingdom, which is especially important since there is no written record. Archeologists rely on the sculptures of Benin to give them insight into the rich culture of the civilization.

Ladies with Western Musical Instruments

Ladies with Western Musical Instruments is an important painting because it shows the influence of the West on traditional Japanese culture during and after the Meiji Restoration. Although the ladies are wearing traditional Japanese gowns and are sitting in a traditional Japanese outdoor setting, the instruments and the architecture of the building are clearly Western. Furthermore, it is important to note that the focal points of the painting are people as opposed to objects. Unlike most of the rest of Asia, Japanese art focuses on the people within its society, and their interaction with nature and objects, as opposed to merely focusing on nature and objects themselves. Therefore, in this picture, the focus on people combines with the Western instruments and architecture to suggest that the people of Japan are interacting with the West.

Bacchus by Michelangelo

Bacchus is an important sculpture because it represents the societal and artistic changes that the Renaissance brought to Europe. Unlike the art of the Middle Ages, the sculpture represents the human body realistically and shamelessly. The figure, which is obviously drinking and enjoying itself, is apparently not concerned with salvation, but rather with the satisfaction of human desires. This is not to suggest that people and, more specifically, artists abandoned Christianity altogether and embarked on a quest to fulfill their every desire. To the contrary, Michelangelo's greatest contributions to art and Renaissance society were commissioned by the Catholic Church. Bacchus is important not when it stands by itself, but when it stands among all of the sculptures that were created by Michelangelo and the other Renaissance artists. Together, the sculptures represent the Renaissance's commingling of religion, intellect, aesthetics, and humanity. Even by itself, however, Bacchus represents the desire of Michelangelo to realistically depict the human body in a particularly human experience.

5. HISTORICAL EVENTS

Muhammed flees from Mecca to Medina

When Muhammed was a man in his thirties and forties, he began receiving messages from God. These messages told him idols should be removed from religious places, for example, and that the rich should give more generously to the poor. He began to preach what he had heard to others in Mecca, his hometown, but the religious and civic leaders felt threatened by both the content of his message and the fact that he claimed these messages came from God. He was increasingly harassed and finally fled to Medina. The journey from Mecca to Medina is now known as the *Hegira*. The consequences would change the course of religion throughout much of the world. In Medina, he was immediately accepted as the messenger of God. His following grew dramatically and within just a few years, he returned to Mecca, this time victorious. The entire region revered him as God's messenger, and Islam was born. Although he died only a few years later, in 632, he left behind the Koran which revealed God's revelations to him. As the teachings in the Koran spread, Islam became the dominant religion of the region. Today, Islam has over one billion followers.

Magna Carta signed

As the first document to limit the power of a monarchy, the Magna Carta served as the first step toward modern representative governments and constitutional rights. It was signed by King John of England in 1215, though he didn't sign it willingly. For years, he had ruled as a ruthless and self-serving tyrant, raising taxes on the nobility while restricting their privileges. The nobility organized against him. Endangered, King John fled to Runnymede, where the nobility caught up with him and made him sign the Magna Carta. Although it did not establish representative government or guarantee rights to the peasants, the document revolutionized the monarchy—it limited it. It established rule of law and the beginnings of due process. Eventually, English society built on the ideas of the Magna Carta and established a bill of rights and a representative parliament. Moreover, the Magna Carta has served as the basis for the U.S. Constitution and hundreds of other national documents that recognize inalienable rights.

Martin Luther posts his ninety-five theses

For centuries prior to the rise of Martin Luther, the Roman Catholic Church controlled all religious worship and expression in western Europe. The Church had been engaging in a number of activities that raised the eyebrows of some of the monks and priests, but when the church hierarchy began to sell indulgences, Martin Luther, an Augustinian friar in Germany, could no longer contain his anger. Indulgences were pieces of paper that the church was selling to raise funds for its ambitious construction projects. The church claimed that the purchase of an indulgence would result in a reduction in the amount of time that the purchaser would stay in purgatory. In response to this practice and others, Luther nailed ninety-five theses to a church door in Wittenberg, Germany in 1517, pointing out the theological flaws in the church's practices. Luther's ideas spread quickly, especially with the aid of the printing press. By the time the church was able to excommunicate him in 1520, northern Europe had turned against the Catholic Church and called themselves Protestants. Other Protestant movements gained steam under the direction of John Calvin, Huldrych Zwingli and others. Soon, several Protestant denominations broke away from the Catholic Church. Europe was no longer unified under the Catholic Church, but the Catholic Church that remained became stronger, even more centralized and re-energized. Today, there are millions of Catholics and Protestants throughout the world, but, unfortunately, the unresolved divisions between them can still be seen in places like Northern Ireland.

Aztec Empire defeated by Hernando Cortes

The circumstances leading up to the Aztec defeat were clearly against them from the beginning. The Spanish, who had grand colonization plans for the region, were militarily superior to the Aztecs. They fought with horses, steel swords, and artillery. At first, the Aztecs didn't even fight against the Spanish, since they believed that Cortes, the Spanish explorer who first made contact with the Aztecs, might be a god. This allowed the Spanish to build up their forces with little opposition. When the Spanish began their attack, virtually everything went their way. European diseases, such as smallpox, were introduced to the Aztec population, which dwindled dramatically as a result. Furthermore, the Spaniards used other native groups, which they had previously conquered, to help them destroy the huge Aztec Empire. The Aztec Empire was completely devastated. Spain became the dominant empire on the continent and, eventually, the entire region was remade by the influx of Spanish culture, religion, politics and art.

Atomic Bomb dropped on Hiroshima

Because he believed that dropping an atomic bomb on Japan would end World War II quickly and result in fewer lives being lost, President Truman of the United States ordered an atomic bomb to be dropped on the city of Hiroshima. The event marked the first time such a bomb had been used in warfare. The result was horrendous. Well over 100,000 people were killed or injured and the city was completely leveled for miles. When the Japanese vowed to fight on, President Truman authorized the dropping of a second bomb on Nagasaki, with similar consequences. Japan finally surrendered and World War II was brought to a close. Since the end of the war, the memory of the devastation of the bomb led to the buildup of nuclear weapons, and tremendous fear that they someday might be used. Today, there are enough nuclear weapons to destroy the world several times over. Although the superpowers have agreed to reduce their arsenals, many nations have gained access to nuclear weapons technology and are pursuing military buildups. It is hoped that the horrors of the bomb to humanity, as opposed to the success of the bomb in bringing the war to an end, will prevent their use ever again.

State of Israel created

The state of Israel was created as a Jewish homeland in 1948 under the authority of the United Nations in a small region along the eastern edge of the Mediterranean known as Palestine. For decades prior to the creation of Israel, thousands of Jews had already been moving to the region as part of the Zionist movement, an organized effort by Jews to settle the land that was promised to them by God. When the nation of Israel was formally created, Jews rushed from Europe and the United States to establish the new nation. However, this land was not previously barren. Instead, it was previously occupied by Muslims, who also claimed the land. The Muslim nations that surround Israel refused to recognize it. Soon violence erupted and eventually wars broke out, but Israel held its ground and actually expanded its territory. The Palestinian Liberation Organization formed to liberate the region from the Jews and sponsored violence against Israel. Although recent agreements between Muslims and Jews have offered hope for peace in the region, violence persists. The creation of the state of Israel and the Muslim reaction, therefore, have created a tremendously unstable political, religious, and military environment in the entire Middle East region.

Communist forces defeat Nationalists in China

In 1949, nearly two million Chinese nationalists were forced from mainland China to Taiwan by advancing communist forces. In the years prior to the move, Sun Yat-sen had revolutionized China as a more liberal-minded nation and had created a representative political party in South China known as the Koumintang. His successor, Chiang Kai-shek, unified the northern part of China with the southern part, and kept the nation on track to become a liberal democracy. However, during this time, Imperialist Japan attacked Manchuria in northern China and while the government of Chiang Kai-shek dealt with the invasion, the Communist Party under Mao Zedong gained support. After building up a rural peasant force of over 1 million soldiers, Mao Zedong swept through China and drove the Koumintang off mainland China and over to the nearby island of Taiwan, where the Koumintang created the Republic of China. The impact for mainland China was enormous. It became the largest communist nation in the world under the leadership of Mao Zedong. As for Taiwan, it remained separate from communist mainland China. Taiwan has rejected China's efforts towards reunification, but nevertheless the two nations have grown closer together, especially as the economies of both nations have grown stronger.

6. CHANGE FROM TRADITIONAL TO MODERN SOCIETIES
Education

In traditional China, knowledge and wisdom were greatly respected, but access to education was not available to the masses. Everyone had a role to play in Confucian society. Leaders were often formally educated, elders were knowledgeable from experience, but the millions of peasants often lacked knowledge and diverse experiences. Instead, they worked on the farms, with little need for formal education and little reason to leave their community. Even as recently as the first half of the twentieth century, the literacy rate in China was less than twenty-five percent. But Mao Zedong and the Communist Revolution changed all that. The communists built schools, simplified Chinese writing and even instituted programs of adult education. The result could appropriately be called the Education Revolution. Literacy rates went through the roof, new career opportunities opened up, and of course, everyone learned about their civic responsibilities under communism. Education changed again, however, during Mao Zedong's Cultural Revolution in the late 1960s and early 1970s. Mao believed that the university community was becoming an educated elite, in direct violation of a classless society, and that the faculties were subverting communism by teaching about other systems. Mao shut down the universities for four years and sent the students and teachers to work in the fields. When the schools reopened, only two courses of study were offered: communist studies and vocational studies. Despite this enormous setback, the death of Mao ushered in the end of the Cultural Revolution; the new government, although still communist, immediately redeveloped extensive education programs. Although freedom of thought and speech is not allowed in China, the curricula were expanded significantly, especially in the areas of math, science and even business. As China continues to reform, the educational opportunities for succeeding generations look brighter.

Health care

In the traditional societies of sub-Saharan Africa, health care was not a matter of anatomy and physiology but rather of theology. The sick were taken to shamans, who tried to cure them by driving away the evil spirits that they believed had infested the body. In modern sub-Saharan Africa, health care has been westernized. Unfortunately, however, it is not readily available to some of the people who need it most. Even though they know what needs to be done, many of the nations simply do not have the physical resources, equipment, medicine, or doctors to meet the demands of the population that already exists, much less to keep up with the fastest population growth rate in the world. In addition, geographical barriers such as dense rain forests keep medical personnel from reaching everyone. The medical community has made great progress in vaccinating the public against common diseases, but much more money is needed to address the serious health hazards in sub-Saharan Africa.

Marriage choices

In traditional India, the caste system and family determined which individuals would marry each other. Parents would choose potential spouses for their children from the available families of the same caste. When the parents with a son could reach an agreement with the parents of a daughter, the son and daughter would be married, a dowry would be paid, and the two would stay married for the rest of their lives, giving birth to many children who they, in turn, would marry off to someone of the same caste. When the newly independent government of India outlawed the caste system, many people were encouraged to resist the social pressures of their traditional upbringings and find a spouse for themselves. Today, millions of Indians still choose to follow the caste system, but urbanization has been impacting the lives of millions as well. As Indians become exposed to new ideas and ways of thinking in the cities, they become more willing to follow their individual hearts and minds, rather than the traditions of their parents.

Land distribution

In traditional China, the bulk of the land was owned by landlords who allowed the peasants to farm it, but only so much as to feed themselves. The remainder of the land was individually owned by families, each with a small plot. Each family, however, had many children, so each small plot had to feed a continually increasing number of mouths, and would be split into smaller pieces and distributed to family members upon the death of the owner. The Communist Revolution changed the land distribution of China dramatically. At first, the revolutionaries returned the land owned by the landlords to the peasants, but the policy was swiftly changed when Mao Zedong instituted his enormous collectivization programs. Under his guidance, enormous farms were created on government-owned land, where millions of peasants worked side by side on the fields. Because they did not own the land, however, they lacked the incentive to work hard or to make innovative improvements. The result was disastrous. During the Great Leap Forward, millions of people starved and the government was forced to import wheat from the West. Today, under changing economic policies in China, limited private ownership of land is once again permitted. It is hoped that incentives of private ownership will continue to spur China's burgeoning economy.

Status of elders

In traditional China, elders were respected for their knowledge and experience. Educational opportunities were not available to the vast majority of people. Elders within families and communities were looked to as authorities on a wide variety of topics, both because they were the ones with the most life experience and because of the influence of Confucian philosophy. In addition, they were the spiritual and moral guides of the family, ensuring that the younger generations were true to their responsibilities. However, when the Communist Revolution swept China, the government denounced Confucianism and created a classless society. Loyalty to the family took a back seat to loyalty to the state. The government became the authority on virtually everything and did not tolerate competing ideas. In addition, as the Communist government opened up schools, children became educated for themselves, further reducing the status of the elders. Finally, in recent years, as China has relaxed its control of the economy and invited foreign investment, children are influenced by yet another competing source: the world community. Millions of Chinese still remain loyal to their families and respect their elders, but the status of elders as the providers of knowledge and wisdom and as the protectors of moral obligations has declined significantly.

Occupations

Prior to the Industrial Revolution, millions of Western Europeans worked on farms or as craftsmen in towns and villages. As the forces of industry swept the continent, however, the demographics of the labor force changed dramatically. Millions of people moved to the cities to work in factories or on the trains, docks, piers and warehouses. A much smaller group of people became extremely wealthy and educated. Slowly, however, educational opportunities improved for everyone, and a more broad-based professional class arose. As the developing world industrialized, factory and warehouse jobs in Western Europe were lost, but jobs in the service industries, in health care, in the military, and in the government bureaucracies mushroomed. Today, the occupational landscape of Western Europe is as diverse as it has ever been. Unfortunately, unemployment rates are high in Germany and Italy, for example, but the vast majority of adults are employed in an increasing variety of occupations.

Roles of women and men

While there are a few examples of women who obtained a significant amount of power in traditional China, for the most part, Chinese women were treated as the servants of men. A woman could not divorce her spouse, no matter how cruel he was, nor could she generally remarry even if he died. During times of economic hardship, families sold their daughters into slavery—not only to make money, but so they would have one less mouth to feed. After the Communist Revolution, however, equality was demanded in a classless society. Husbands and wives were treated equally, at least as far as the law was concerned. Women gained the right to divorce their husbands. They obtained property rights. They received equal pay for equal work and were encouraged to pursue professional and vocational careers. Nevertheless, tradition remains an important part of millions of Chinese lives. When the government instituted its one-child-per-family policy, many families killed their infant girls in the hope of gaining a son the next time around. And although the government relaxed its policy, it will take much more than government action or inaction to change the role of women at the family level.

7. INDIVIDUALS WITH DIFFERENT POINTS OF VIEW

Art—Leonardo da Vinci and Pablo Picasso

Leonardo da Vinci and Pablo Picasso approached art from two very different perspectives. Da Vinci believed that artists should represent and build upon nature, and in all cases, the viewer should be able to immediately recognize the scene depicted and its relevance. This art form is known as High Renaissance. Picasso, on the other hand, was an abstractionist, a product of the modern reaction to traditional forms. He developed an art form known as Cubism, a painting style which broke images up into pieces and then recombined them so that several different aspects of the image could be seen side by side. Whereas da Vinci wanted to represent natural images as best he could in his art, Picasso believed that natural images should be distorted in art. According to Picasso, the goal of art should be to provide a perspective of nature that our eyes alone do not give us.

The differences between the two men were likely due as much to the times in which they lived as to their personalities and creative geniuses. The Renaissance's focus on nature, human achievement, and realism contributed to da Vinci's paintings as much as his paintings (and other work) contributed to the culture of the Renaissance. The too real, too industrialized, too mechanical world into which Picasso was born, however, cried out for a perspective from an alternative point of view. While both men were very different, they were both masters of their art forms and remain today the ideal representatives of their times.

Economics—Karl Marx and Adam Smith

Adam Smith and Karl Marx had very different points of view on the subject of economics. Adam Smith wrote in *The Wealth of Nations* that economic prosperity and fairness is best achieved through private ownership. Individuals should own the means of production and sell their products and services on a free and open market, where the demand for their goods and services would determine their prices and availability. Smith argued that needs and desires of individuals would best be met under this type of system. Karl Marx, however, wrote in *The Communist Manifesto* that Smith's system had led to the exploitation of the working class. He argued that private ownership allowed a few people to dominate the economy and exploit the workers and the consumers. Therefore, he concluded that the only way that true fairness and economic prosperity can be achieved is through societal ownership of the means of production. The two men's theories have served as the basis for the economies of many nations. Adam Smith's philosophies served as the basis for capitalism; distortions of Karl Marx's philosophy served as a basis for Communism. Many nations, of course, have combined aspects of both.

Independence Movements—Mohandas Gandhi and Jomo Kenyatta

Independence can be achieved in a variety of different ways. The methods of Gandhi and Kenyatta were nearly polar opposites. Both men led their nations to independence from British rule—Gandhi in India and Kenyatta in Kenya—but that's where the similarity ends. Gandhi believed in civil disobedience; Kenyatta believed in terror. Gandhi led hunger strikes and marches; Kenyatta led the Mau Mau in the killing of both colonists and natives who opposed him. In short, Gandhi believed that you should practice what you preach; Kenyatta believed that the ends justify the means. After independence was won, both men claimed that victory was achieved because of the method of resistance that they endorsed. To their deaths, Kenyatta never denounced the use of violence, and Gandhi never condoned it.

Individual Rights—Adolf Hitler and John Locke

Adolf Hitler and John Locke differed greatly on the idea of individual rights. John Locke believed that governments do not grant individuals their rights, but that individuals possess them by virtue of being individuals. He also believed that the role of government is to protect these rights because governments receive their power from the people. His writings, along with the writings of other Enlightenment writers, began to change the way many educated people in the West thought about the role of government and the natural rights of man, eventually contributing to independence movements in the United States, France and beyond. In contrast, Adolf Hitler didn't even recognize the concept of individual rights. He murdered millions of people during World War II, and treated members of his own Nazi party as pawns in his regime. He did not believe that his regime received its power from the people, nor did he believe that he was obligated to uphold anyone's rights. He simply believed in his own power and authority. Given the number of democratic movements in the world during this century, it seems fair to conclude that the beliefs of John Locke are widely accepted.

Scientific Investigation—Galileo and Pope Paul V

Galileo and Pope Paul V had two very different ideas about the role of scientific investigation in society. Using his telescope, Galileo observed the patterns of the stars and the relationship of the Sun to the Earth and the Moon to conclude that the Earth travels around the Sun. This was in direct contrast to Pope Paul V and the Roman Catholic Church. Pope Paul V defended the church's position that the Earth is at the center of the universe and that the Sun travels around it. Galileo used scientific investigation to reach his conclusions whereas Pope Paul V used the position of the church and his faith to reach his conclusion. Therefore, they not only disagreed on the relationship between the Sun and the Earth, but also on the proper method for the acquisition of knowledge. Pope Paul V brought Galileo to Rome on charges of heresy, and Galileo was forced to recant his findings. But the debate over scientific investigation and the findings that resulted from it continued. Eventually, many people learned to embrace both faith and science simultaneously.

Westernization—Peter the Great and Ayatollah Khomeini

Peter the Great of Russia and Ayatollah Khomeini of Iran took very different approaches to westernization. Peter the Great foresaw the need to modernize and westernize his nation. He traveled to the West, learned western customs and methods of building, and brought many western builders back to Russia with him to transform his society. He even built the new capital of St. Petersburg on the Baltic Sea because it was more accessible to the West than Moscow was. In contrast, Ayatollah Khomeini deplored the westernization of his nation under the Shah Pahlevi. He led an Islamic Revolution which ousted the Shah and established an anti-Western, Islamic fundamentalist regime. He believed that the devout practice of the Muslim faith, as opposed to westernization, would lead his nation to security and prosperity. Even today, both nations are experiencing major economic and social problems due to the consequences of westernizing too quickly, in the case of modern Russia, or reversing trends toward westernization, in the case of modern Iran.

EXAMINATION
JUNE 1996

Part I (55 credits): Answer all 48 questions in this part.

Directions (1–48): For each statement or question, write on a separate answer sheet the *number* of the word or expression that, of those given, best completes the statement or answers the question.

---

1 Censorship, mass arrests, and a secret police force are most characteristic of

1 parliamentary democracies
2 republics
3 totalitarian regimes
4 constitutional monarchies

2 On a map of the world, Asia is to Japan as Europe is to

1 Great Britain   3 Austria
2 the Netherlands   4 Italy

3 Which factor most limited the development of African nationalism?

1 European support of an educational system based on local traditions and language
2 the prior experience of Africans with economic self-sufficiency
3 political boundaries imposed by Europeans that had little relationship to African tribal boundaries
4 the European practice of making decisions based on local customs

4 Which situation would best encourage economic development in most African nations today?

1 increasing the population growth rate
2 attracting investment capital
3 reducing the number of skilled workers
4 depleting their natural resources

5 In the Republic of South Africa, the slogans "Freedom In Our Lifetime" and "New South Africa" changed from promises to reality after

1 Frederick W. de Klerk took over the radical white police force
2 United Nations troops occupied the Transvaal
3 Nelson Mandela was elected President
4 the majority of white South Africans returned to Europe

Base your answer to question 6 on the map below and on your knowledge of social studies.

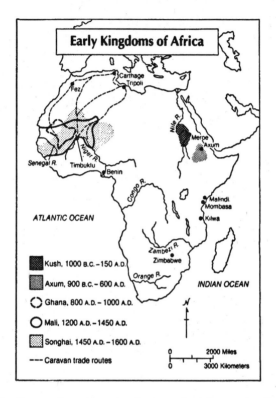

Early Kingdoms of Africa

Carthage
Tripoli
Fez
Nile R.
Meroe
Axum
Senegal R.
Niger R.
Timbuktu
Benin
Congo R.
Malindi
Mombasa
ATLANTIC OCEAN
Kilwa
Zambezi R.
Zimbabwe
Orange R.
INDIAN OCEAN
N

■ Kush, 1000 B.C.–150 A.D.
▨ Axum, 900 B.C.– 600 A.D.
◖ Ghana, 800 A.D.– 1000 A.D.
◯ Mali, 1200 A.D.–1450 A.D.
▦ Songhai, 1450 A.D.–1600 A.D.
– – – Caravan trade routes

0   2000 Miles
0   3000 Kilometers

6 Which conclusion regarding early African trade is supported by the information provided by this map?

1 The kingdom of Zimbabwe grew rich from trade with Egypt.
2 The kingdoms of western Africa traded with the city states of eastern Africa.
3 The Congo and Zambezi Rivers played an important role in Africa's early trade.
4 The west African kingdoms had trading contacts with the cities of the Mediterranean.

7 Which activity is the best example of cultural diffusion in Africa?

1 weaving kente cloth in Ghana
2 using masks in traditional African ceremonies
3 discovering bronze sculptures from Benin
4 practicing of Islam in Nigeria

8 A major problem currently facing the Republic of South Africa is the

1 continuation of attacks from neighboring Zimbabwe
2 move toward the creation of a theocratic state
3 struggle for power between different groups within South Africa's black majority
4 continued international economic embargo against South Africa

9 One result of the European conquest of Latin America was that in Latin America

1 Spanish became the major spoken language
2 Native American cultures flourished
3 the Aztec religion spread
4 many parliamentary democracies were established

10 "The challenges of the Andes helped the Incas develop a thriving civilization."

Based on this statement, what does the author believe?

1 Language and religion are important to national unity.
2 Cultural diversity flourishes in areas of agricultural prosperity.
3 People can overcome the limitations of their environment.
4 Natural resources are necessary for economic independence.

11 In colonial Latin America, the main purpose of the encomienda system was to

1 insure that the Indians were humanely treated
2 provide a steady labor supply for early colonists
3 prevent slavery in Spain's New World colonies
4 build and maintain forts to repel foreign invaders

12 The major reason the Mexican Government strongly supported the North American Free Trade Agreement (NAFTA) was that this agreement would

1 raise tariffs on United States products entering Mexico
2 reduce Mexico's economic dependence on Europe
3 promote investment and economic growth in Mexico
4 stimulate trade between Asia and Latin America

13 A major problem facing many Central American nations is that their nation's wealth is

1 generally invested in consumer industries
2 controlled by a small group of landed elite
3 distributed throughout the large middle class
4 held mainly by government agencies

14 Which statement about India is a fact rather than an opinion?

1 Most Indians are happy with the Hindu practice of arranged marriages.
2 India is fortunate to have a multiparty system of government.
3 The Moguls ruled India for more than 100 years.
4 The partition of British India in 1947 helped India prosper.

Source: Nicolielo, 1992 Cartoonists & Writers Syndicate

15 What is the cartoonist's point of view about events in India since independence?

1 Violence has been the best way to achieve political and social goals.
2 Gandhi's beliefs have resulted in a divided India.
3 The destruction of historic monuments has been the goal of radical groups.
4 Many political activists in India have not followed Gandhi's ideas of nonviolence.

16 The caste system is still practiced in India today primarily because it is

1 encouraged by village customs and traditions
2 enforced by the military
3 supported by Christian and Muslim teachings
4 mandated by law

17 Korea greatly influenced the development of early Japan by

1 acting as a bridge for ideas from China
2 providing Japan with the technology for industrialization
3 serving as a barrier against Chinese aggression
4 protecting Japan from early European exploration

18 A major goal of the Meiji government in Japan was to

1 isolate Japan from other nations
2 achieve political union with China
3 establish Japan as an industrial power
4 encourage colonization of Asia by Western nations

19 After World War I, Japan attempted to solve some of its economic problems by

1 establishing extensive trade with the Soviet Union
2 expanding its influence in Asia
3 practicing the principles of Marxism
4 refusing to rely on Western technology

Base your answers to questions 20 and 21 on the cartoon below and on your knowledge of social studies.

20 In this 1989 cartoon, the cartoonist is expressing the view that

1 students hunger for the writings of Mao, Deng, and Marx
2 China's Government is meeting the needs and wants of its students
3 China's educational system attempts to maintain Communist ideology
4 Communist ideals have eliminated poverty

21 In this cartoon, the student is asking for information about

1 socialism
2 Communism
3 nationalism
4 democracy

22 The outcome of the Opium War showed that in the 19th century,

1 the Chinese Army was the most highly disciplined army in the world

2 China was no longer strong enough to resist Western demands for trading rights

3 the Chinese people were successful in eliminating foreign influence

4 the Chinese Government preferred to continue the opium trade

23 Which statement best explains China's economic shift toward capitalism in the 1980's and early 1990's?

1 China's economic policies were directly influenced by the success of the Soviet economic system.

2 The Tiananmen Square massacre resulted in major economic reforms in China.

3 The success of the Cultural Revolution resulted in the increased westernization of China.

4 Communist economic policies were not meeting the needs of the society.

24 Within the past decade, the decision of the United States Government to grant China "most favored nation" status was important to China because this decision

1 allowed China to join the Southeast Asia Treaty Organization (SEATO)

2 increased China's ability to trade with the United States

3 helped protect China from a possible Japanese invasion

4 eliminated Russian influence in East Asia

25 The ancient civilizations of Mesopotamia and Egypt were similar in that both cultures

  1 developed along rivers
  2 used the ziggurat form for their temples
  3 established trade routes to China
  4 used a hieroglyphic writing system

Base your answer to question 26 on the passage below and on your knowledge of social studies.

The Canal was dug by Egypt's sons and 120,000 of them died while working. The Suez Canal Company in Paris is an imposter company. It usurped our concessions . . . .

Therefore, I have signed today the following law which has been approved by the Cabinet: Article 1 of the decree reads, "The Universal Company of the Suez Maritime Canal — Egyptian Joint-Stock Company — is hereby nationalized. All its assets, rights and obligations are hereby transferred to the Nation."

Source: World History, Prentice Hall

26 This passage describes the decision of the Egyptian Government to

  1 end trade with Mediterranean countries
  2 stop building canals
  3 take control of the Suez Canal
  4 sell the Suez Canal to France

27 Jewish religious and cultural identity has been greatly influenced by

1 Ramadan and the concept of reincarnation
2 the Torah and the Diaspora
3 the New Testament and the Four Noble Truths
4 the Koran and the code of bushido

28 The major goal of many minority groups, such as the Kurds, Tamils, and Sikhs, is to

1 obtain self-rule and economic control of a homeland
2 establish a multicultural state
3 install Christianity as the state religion
4 acquire economic aid from the World Bank

29 A major effect of the decline of the Roman Empire was that western Europe

1 came under the control of the Muslims
2 was absorbed by the Byzantine Empire
3 returned to a republican form of government
4 entered a period of chaos and disorder

30 In Europe, the Crusades resulted in

1 a greater isolation of the region from the world
2 an increased demand for goods from the Middle East and Asia
3 the adoption of Islam as the official religion of many European nations
4 the strengthening of the feudal system

31 Which characteristic was common to the Golden Age of Greece and the Italian Renaissance?

1 A strong military led to national unity.
2 Written constitutions led to the establishment of democratic governments.
3 Prosperity led to the creation of many works of art.
4 Political instability led directly to the formation of unified nation-states.

32 Which system developed as a result of the Commercial Revolution in Europe?

1 manorialism   3 bartering
2 Communism   4 market economy

33 According to the theory of mercantilism, colonies should be

1 acquired as markets and sources of raw materials
2 considered an economic burden for the colonial power
3 granted independence as soon as possible
4 encouraged to develop their own industries

Base your answers to questions 34 and 35 on the map below and on your knowledge of social studies.

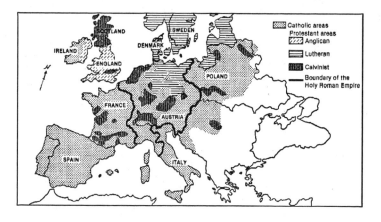

34 Which statement about the Holy Roman Empire is supported by the map?

   1 The religion of the people in the Holy Roman Empire was either Lutheran or Catholic.
   2 The Holy Roman Empire had fewer Protestant areas than the rest of Europe did.
   3 Calvinism was dominant throughout the Holy Roman Empire.
   4 Protestant influences were strongest in the northern areas of the Holy Roman Empire.

35 Which title would be the most appropriate for this map?

   1 "The Impact of the Protestant Reformation"
   2 "The Catholic Counter-Reformation"
   3 "The Fall of the Holy Roman Empire"
   4 "European Religious Unity"

36 "Revolution will occur more and more frequently in the industrialized nations as the proletariat struggles to overcome the abuses of the capitalist system."

This quotation reflects the ideas of

1 Charles Darwin   3 Niccolò Machiavelli
2 Karl Marx   4 John Locke

37 During the 1930's, the Nazi (National Socialist) Party received support from the German people because it promised to

1 abide by the Versailles Treaty
2 improve economic conditions in Germany
3 promote policies that insured ethnic equality
4 utilize international organizations to solve Germany's problems

Base your answer to question 38 on the cartoon below and on your knowledge of social studies.

"EASTERN EUROPE SUBDIVIDED AGAIN TODAY..."

38 What is the main theme of this cartoon from the early 1990's?

1 The fragmentation of Eastern Europe continues.
2 Western Europe is investing heavily in Eastern Europe.
3 Free-enterprise zones continue to be created throughout Eastern Europe.
4 Nation-states no longer exist in Eastern Europe.

39 "Germany Recognizes the Independence of Slovenia"
"United States Establishes Diplomatic Relations with Croatia"
"Latvia Joins the United Nations"

These headlines illustrate the

1 collapse of the governments of these nations
2 strength of the Russian Empire
3 beginning of a united Europe
4 increase in international support for self-determination

40 Since the dissolution of the Soviet Union, the major problems in Eastern Europe and Russia have primarily resulted from the

1 high rate of illiteracy found in most of these nations
2 refusal of government leaders to allow foreign investments
3 switch from a command economy to a free-market economy
4 unwillingness of the industrialized nations to provide advisors

Base your answer to question 41 on the list below and on your knowledge of social studies.

Selected Cold War Events

Berlin blockade (1948–1949)
Premier Khrushchev's visit to the United States (1959)
Cuban missile crisis (1962)
Nuclear Test Ban Treaty (1963)
Joint Apollo-Soyuz space mission (1975)
Russian invasion of Afghanistan (1979)

41 What does this list of events suggest about the Cold War Era?

1 Throughout the period, the United States and the Soviet Union were reluctant to solve conflicts.
2 The level of tension between the United States and the Soviet Union varied.
3 Economics played a key role in causing conflict between the United States and the Soviet Union.
4 The United Nations was instrumental in reducing tensions between the United States and the Soviet Union.

42 The end of the Cold War is best symbolized by the

  1 establishment of the Truman Doctrine and the Marshall Plan
  2 formation of the North Atlantic Treaty Organization (NATO) and the European Common Market
  3 withdrawal of United Nations forces from Somalia and from Kuwait
  4 destruction of the Berlin Wall and the reunification of Germany

43 The French Revolution of 1789, the Chinese Revolution of 1911, and the Bolshevik Revolution of 1917 were similar in that these revolutions

  1 were led by ruthless dictators
  2 were motivated by a desire to overthrow a monarch
  3 led directly to the establishment of Communism
  4 established a higher standard of living for the middle class

44 The amount of carbon dioxide in the atmosphere has increased in recent years. Environmentalists suggest this change is a direct result of the

  1 improper storage of solid and nuclear waste
  2 overcutting of forests and the increased use of fossil fuels
  3 dumping of inorganic material into lakes and rivers
  4 use of herbicides and toxic substances such as asbestos and DDT

45 Which policy shows that appeasement does not always prevent war?

1 British policy toward Germany in Munich during the 1930's
2 French policy in Indochina in the 1950's
3 United States policy toward Cuba in the early 1960's
4 Iraqi policy toward Iran in the 1980's

46 The major goal of the Green Revolution has been to

1 decrease the use of modern farm machinery
2 decrease population growth
3 increase agricultural output
4 increase the number of traditional farms

47 Which factor has most limited the development of national unity in India, Lebanon, and Bosnia-Herzegovina?

1 lack of natural resources
2 inability to end colonialism
3 religious and ethnic differences
4 rapid growth of industry

48 • Japan buys oil from the Middle East.
• Colombia sells coffee to the United States.
• Great Britain joins the European community.
• Poland buys natural gas from Russia.

These statements all relate to the concept of

1 balance of power 3 isolationism
2 interdependence 4 imperialism

Answers to the following questions are to be written on paper provided by the school.

Students Please Note:

In developing your answers to Part II, be sure to

(1) include specific factual information and evidence whenever possible

(2) keep to the questions asked; do not go off on tangents

(3) avoid overgeneralizations or sweeping statements without sufficient proof; do not overstate your case

(4) keep these general definitions in mind:

(a) <u>discuss</u> means "to make observations about something using facts, reasoning, and argument; to present in some detail"

(b) <u>describe</u> means "to illustrate something in words or tell about it"

(c) <u>show</u> means "to point out; to set forth clearly a position or idea by stating it and giving data which support it"

(d) <u>explain</u> means "to make plain or understandable; to give reasons for or causes of; to show the logical development or relationships of"

Part II

ANSWER THREE QUESTIONS FROM THIS PART. [45]

1 In today's world, various global problems affect nations and regions in many different ways

Problems
Environmental pollution
Terrorism
Human rights violations
Refugees
Overpopulation
Religious conflict

Select *three* problems from the list and for *each* one selected:

- Identify a nation or region in which this problem exists today [You must identify a different nation or region for each problem selected. Do *not* use the United States in our answer.]
- Explain *one* specific political, economic, cultural, *or* historical cause of this problem in that nation or region
- Describe *one* action that this nation *or* region *or* the international community has taken to deal with this problem   [5,5,5]

2 Nationalism has played an important role throughout world history. The quotations below express various views about nationalism.

> The young men shall go forth to battle; the married men will make arms and transport food; the women will make tents, uniforms, and will serve in the hospitals; the children will prepare lint from old linen; the old men will gather in public places to rouse the courage of the warriors, to excite hatred of kings and to preach the unity of the Republic.
>
> **_Levee en Masse_, French Revolution, 1793**

> We ardently wish to free Italy from foreign rule. We agree that we must put aside all petty differences in order to gain this most important goal. We wish to drive out the foreigners not only because we want to see our country powerful and glorious, but because we want to elevate the Italian people in intelligence and moral development.
>
> **Count Camillo di Cavor, 1810–1861**

> . . . for the most part . . . the people of China can be spoken of as completely . . . Chinese. With common customs and habits, we are completely of one race . . . . But the Chinese people have only family and clan solidarity; they do not have national spirit. Therefore even though we have . . . people gathered together in one China, in reality they are just a heap of loose sand.
>
> **Sun Yat-sen, 1911**

> . . . the main motive which guided me in my deed was the avenging of the Serbian people . . . . I am a nationalist. I aimed to free the Yugoslavs. For I am a Yugoslav . . . . As far as Serbia is concerned, it is her duty to free us.
>
> **Gavrilo Princip, 1914**

> . . . we insist that in Ghana . . . there should be no reference to Fantis, Ashantis, Ewes, Gas, Dagombas [all names of tribes], "strangers," and so forth but that we should call ourselves Ghanaians — all brothers and sisters, members of the same community — the state of Ghana.
>
> **Kwame Nkrumah, 1961**

> Palestine, the homeland of the Palestinian Arab people, is an inseparable part of the greater Arab homeland, and the Palestinian people are a part of the Arab Nation . . . . The Palestinian Arab people alone have legitimate rights to their homeland, and shall exercise the right of self-determination after the liberation of their homeland . . .
>
> **The Palestinian National Charter, 1968**

Select *three* of the quotations above and for *each* one selected:

- Explain the point of view toward nationalism that is expressed in the quotation
- Discuss *one* way that the attitude expressed affected the history of the society referred to in the quotation   [5,5,5]

3 Religions and/or philosophies greatly influence how people live.

Religion/Philosophy

Animism	Hinduism
Buddhism	Islam
Christianity	Judaism
Confucianism	

Select *three* of the religions or philosophies listed and for *each* one selected:

- Identify a region or nation other than the United States in which the religion or philosophy is practiced by a large number of people
- Explain *one* belief of the religion or philosophy [You must provide a different belief for each religion selected.]
- Describe *one* way the belief has affected the lives of its followers [5,5,5]

4 The European Industrial Revolution had positive and negative effects on certain groups. Several effects of the Industrial Revolution in Europe are shown in the diagram below.

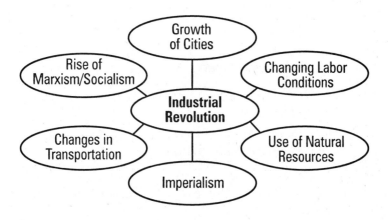

Select *three* of the effects of the European Industrial Revolution shown and for *each* one selected:

- Explain how the Industrial Revolution caused this effect

- Identify *one* specific group that was helped or harmed by this effect of the Industrial Revolution in Europe [You must choose a different group for each effect selected.]
- Describe how this group was helped or harmed by this effect   [5,5,5]

5 Geography has affected civilizations and nations in many ways.

Geographic Features

Arctic Ocean
Gulf Stream/North Atlantic Drift
Himalaya Mountains
Mediterranean Sea
Monsoon
Sahara Desert
Yangtze River

Select *three* of the geographic features listed and for *each* one selected:

- Describe the specific characteristics of the geographic feature
- Explain the effect of that feature on a particular civilization or nation   [5,5,5]

6 Certain individuals have had a major influence on history.

Individuals

Elizabeth I   Joseph Stalin
Galileo Galilei   Ho Chi Minh
Adam Smith   Anwar el Sadat
Napoleon Bonaparte

Select *three* individuals from the list and for *each* one selected:

- Describe a specific contribution or action of this individual
- Discuss a long-term impact of this individual on the course of history   [5,5,5]

7 A newly independent nation is seeking advice from other nations as it establishes its domestic policies on a variety of issues. The nations and the policy being considered are listed below:

Nations—Domestic Policies

Japan—Education
China—Economic reform
Israel—Rights of women
United Kingdom—Health care
Brazil—Land use
India—Population policy

Select *three* nations and the domestic policy with which they are paired. For *each* one selected:

- Explain how that domestic policy was or is being implemented in that nation
- Discuss specific reasons the newly independent nation should or should not follow the example of that nation   [5,5,5]

ANSWER KEY
JUNE 1996—PART I

1	3		25	1
2	1		26	3
3	3		27	2
4	2		28	1
5	3		29	4
6	4		30	2
7	4		31	3
8	3		32	4
9	1		33	1
10	3		34	4
11	2		35	1
12	3		36	2
13	2		37	2
14	3		38	1
15	4		39	4
16	1		40	3
17	1		41	2
18	3		42	4
19	2		43	2
20	3		44	2
21	4		45	1
22	2		46	3
23	4		47	3
24	2		48	2

ANSWERS AND EXPLANATIONS
JUNE 1996—PART I

1 Focus on the words "most characteristic of. . . ." Remember that even though these characteristics may occur in republics or monarchies, the question asks you to identify the type of government in which they *most* often occur.

   1 Democracies, whether parliamentary or not, generally do not conduct mass arrests or utilize a secret police force.

   2 Republics are very diverse and include Germany, the United States, South Africa, and Taiwan. Be careful of categories that are too broad.

   3 Totalitarian regimes attempt to maintain "total" control. In doing so, they censor opinions that run contrary to the opinion of the regime, they frequently arrest hundreds of people who do not conform to the policies of the regime, and they often utilize a secret police force to assist in enforcing it all.

   4 Constitutional monarchies are government arrangements led by a single person (a monarch) who cannot absolutely rule as he or she pleases, but must rule according to the provisions of the constitution (which may be written or simply a matter of custom). Compare to "absolute monarchy," found in the glossary.

2 All four nations in the answer choices are part of Europe. Therefore, you need to look for the answer choice that is unique from the other three in a way that makes it similar to Japan and its relationship to Asia.

   1 Japan is an island nation located off the coast of mainland Asia; Great Britain is an island nation located off the coast of mainland Europe. Bingo!

   2 The Netherlands, while part of Europe, is not an island nation.

   3 Austria, also, is not an island nation. In fact, it's landlocked!

   4 On a map, Italy looks like it's kicking an island (Sicily), but it is not itself an island.

3 This question can be answered correctly through the use of reason and without any knowledge of African nationalism. You don't even need to determine if the events in the answer choices occurred. The three wrong answer choices wouldn't limit African nationalism even if they

occurred (but in reality they did not occur). Therefore, only one answer choice makes sense.

1 The educational system was not based on local traditions and custom, but even if it had been, then African nationalism most likely would have been fostered rather than limited.

2 This answer choice is very unclear, and so, it is not the best answer. To the extent that Africans are economically self-sufficient as a group, this economic independence contributes to African nationalism by making them less dependent on non-African nations. However, to the extent that Africans are self-sufficient as individuals, African nationalism is limited because each individual is less likely to need the assistance or unity of a group.

3 **For nationalism to take hold, a large group of people have to be unified under common customs and traditions. The imposition of political boundaries formed by the colonial power broke up tribes and created Tribalism, thereby limiting the forces that would have allowed nationalist feelings to form and grow. (Note the use of the negative word "imposed.")**

4 Had it occurred, this practice, too, would foster African nationalism, not limit it.

4 This question is specifically asking about Africa, but think about this for a second: Which answer choice makes the most sense in encouraging economic development anywhere on the globe?

1 More people may eventually mean more workers, but the immediate impact of a population growth is going to be more mouths to feed.

2 **For economic development to occur, you need money. Investment capital is money.**

3 Which factory is going to make more money? The one with employees who were trained to operate the equipment, or the one with employees randomly pressing buttons and pulling levers? For economic development to occur, you need skilled workers!

4 Depletion of natural resources might lead to short-term growth if large profits are made from the sale of these resources, but once they're gone, they're gone, and no long-term growth can happen. Economic development requires nations to look far into the future and develop strategies that will lead to long-term growth by actually maintaining and developing the resources, as opposed to depleting them.

5 If you don't know much about South Africa, then choose the answer that at least refers to something or someone that you've heard something good about, since "freedom" is probably going to be a good thing as opposed to a bad thing. If you missed it, review your notes about South Africa!

    1 Frederik W. de Klerk did a lot to put things in motion so that change could occur, but taking over the radical white police force wasn't one of them. Instead, he ended apartheid and supported an election for the presidency, which he lost to Nelson Mandela.

    2 This never happened. The United Nations never sent any troops to South Africa.

    3 When Nelson Mandela was elected as the first black president in 1994, following the end of apartheid, the slogans that had been the battle cry of the black majority in South Africa were finally realized.

    4 This never happened. Besides, most white South Africans didn't move from Europe in the first place, but were born in South Africa (it was their ancestors who originally moved to South Africa). Therefore, it doesn't make much sense to say that the white South Africans "returned" to Europe when, in fact, they had never lived in Europe!

6 The test writers tell you the answer can be determined based on the information on the map. Look at it carefully.

    1 Nothing on the map links Zimbabwe with Egypt and, in fact, Egypt isn't even identified on the map.

    2 Nothing on the map gives us any clues about the West trading with the East.

    3 According to the information on the map, all we know is that the rivers exist. Nothing on the map helps us to determine if the rivers were essential to trading.

    4 Spot the West African kingdoms. Spot the cities of Carthage and Tripoli on the Mediterranean. Spot the dotted lines that connect West Africa to the cities. You got it!

7 This is a question which requires you to know the definition of the term cultural diffusion, which is a process by which the customs, ideas, or beliefs of one culture slowly creep (diffuse) into another culture until they become a regular part of the new culture. English-speaking Americans saying "adios" is one example of cultural diffusion.

1 Kente cloth has never been made anywhere else but in Ghana. Therefore, this is not an example of cultural diffusion. (Even if you don't know anything about kente cloth, look for a better answer.)

2 Many African tribes have used masks in their ceremonies, and many continue to do so. They didn't get this idea from somebody else, but came up with it on their own. No diffusion.

3 The discovery of bronze sculptures from Benin shouldn't surprise anyone since the people in Benin (a major kingdom in Africa from the thirteenth century through the sixteenth century) actually invented many of the techniques for making sculptures from bronze. Since they didn't get help from anybody else, this isn't an example of cultural diffusion.

4 Islam was developed in the Middle East in the seventh century and slowly spread into parts of Africa, including Nigeria. Religion is precisely the type of thing that is both "cultural" and that often "diffuses" into other cultures. The practicing of Islam in Nigeria is a great example of cultural diffusion in Africa.

8 This test was administered in June 1996, so "currently" means in 1996—well after apartheid was abolished and Nelson Mandela took office. Once the black majority gained control of the government, try to think of what might be true.

1 The attacks from South Africa stopped when the African National Congress was recognized as a legal political party. Try to think of something more current.

2 No religious group in South Africa is trying to gain control of the government. Even if there were such a group, would it be proper to label that situation a "problem" if that's what the people of South Africa want? Hmmmmm. . . . look for something that more clearly indicates a "problem."

3 Now that the black majority has gained power, subgroups are struggling with each other to decide who is going to control what and how they are going to do it. This is what often happens: A group unites under a common cause against someone or something, and then after the group wins, its members find out that they have different goals now that they don't have to worry about the original problem they fought so hard to eliminate.

4 Once apartheid ended and Nelson Mandela was elected president, the international economic embargo ceased. Remember, the question asks for something "current."

9 The question tells us that the Europeans took Latin America. Which Europeans? Hopefully, you remember that it was the Spaniards.

1 **When the Spaniards conquered Latin America, they brought with them their language. Had they never come to Latin America, it is doubtful that the majority of people there would suddenly be speaking Spanish! This is an example of cultural diffusion.**

2 Native American cultures flourished before the Europeans arrived, not after. Also, note the use of the word "conquest" in the question, which implies that people were defeated and had things imposed on them. It's more than likely that a culture wouldn't "flourish" under such circumstances.

3 The Europeans were mostly Christian, not Aztec. The Aztec religion spread before the European conquest, not after.

4 It is true that some parliamentary democracies have recently been established in Latin America. However, for centuries after the conquest, Spain controlled the region, and when it did not, military dictators did. Remember, though, that even if you're not certain about the types of government in Latin America, you're supposed to choose the best answer, and answer choice number one is clearly the most direct result of the conquest.

10 This question is a good example of choosing nice, wishy-washy language instead of choosing answer choices with strong, extreme language.

1 Language and religion have very little to do with the challenges of a mountain range. Maybe there's a better answer somewhere down the line.

2 In the mountains it is hard to grow food, not easy. Also, the quote informs us that the Incas developed a "thriving civilization," but it doesn't say anything about that civilization becoming culturally diverse.

3 **What type of thing do you overcome? You overcome a challenge, or a limitation. (Do you see this word in any of the answer choices?) What is the Andes? It is a mountain range and, therefore, it is an environmental challenge. The fact that the Incas were able to overcome the limitations of their environment would surely help them to develop a thriving civilization!**

4   Natural resources might often be important for economic independence, but what does this have to do with the challenges of the
Andes? The fact that some natural resources exist in the Andes is a
benefit of the mountain range, not a challenge.

11   If you don't know what the encomienda system was, look it up in your
Global Studies materials now. It's been on a couple of tests, and it
might be on yours!
1   The Indians were not humanely treated in colonial Latin America
(although some aspects of the system were supposed to protect the
Indians, those provisions weren't enforced). Move on to the next
answer choice.
**2   The main purpose of the system was to reward landowners
by giving them charge of the people who lived on their land.
The system quickly turned Indians into virtual slaves
without any of the rights that were initially intended to help
them gain control of their own small plots of land.**
3   Slavery was widely practiced in Spain's colonies, so the encomienda
system couldn't have been about preventing it (or else it failed
miserably!)
4   Although forts were built and maintained in Latin America, their
existence had nothing to do with the encomienda system.

12   The correct answer must state the "major reason" for the Mexican
government's support of NAFTA.
1   NAFTA does not raise tariffs on U.S. products entering Mexico,
but actually is designed to eventually eliminate those tariffs. Even
if it did raise tariffs, then the goal of raising tariffs would be to
promote economic growth, which is answer choice number three!
2   NAFTA is an agreement signed by the North American nations of
Mexico, the United States, and Canada. While increased trade
among these nations might eventually lead to a decrease in trade
with Europe, certainly the Mexican government's support for
NAFTA had very little to do with possible indirect consequences
for Europe.
**3   Why would the Mexican government support any trade
agreement? The reason would be to promote investment
and economic growth in Mexico. Maybe NAFTA won't result
in long-term economic growth, but clearly the Mexican
government hopes it will.**
4   NAFTA is about trade within North America, not Asia.

13 Remember, we're looking for an answer choice that clearly describes a "problem."

1 Actually, the wealth in Latin America isn't invested in consumer industries, but if it were, it most likely wouldn't be a "problem."

2 This answer choice sounds like it might be a problem and, in fact, it is, since the poor people in these countries don't have much of an opportunity to gain a share of the wealth and thereby improve their standard of living.

3 There isn't a large middle class in Latin America. Rather, there's a small number of wealthy people and a whole lot of poor people. Even if a large middle class did exist, and even if the wealth was distributed among them, this wouldn't be the answer, because it wouldn't describe a "problem."

4 Government agencies don't hold the wealth in Latin America. The small group of landed elite do.

14 This question merely asks you to choose the answer choice that sounds more like a fact than like an opinion. The weird thing is, you don't even have to know if the factual statement in the correct answer choice is actually true or false. You just have to pick the one that sounds like a fact that can be "proven," as opposed to an opinion which is just what somebody thinks and which does not require absolute proof.

1 This statement is only someone's best guess, and therefore it is that person's opinion about reality as opposed to a statement of fact. India is a country with a population of nearly 700 million people. It's almost impossible to talk to all of them and find out what their opinions are. Even if somebody did a poll, it would be hard to prove that everyone polled told the truth or that even if they did, that those who were polled represented the opinions of those who were not.

2 The use of the words "is fortunate" means that somebody is giving an opinion. "India has a multi-party system of government" would be a fact, but the statement that they are fortunate to have one is merely someone's opinion with which someone else might disagree.

3 This is a fact. We can look to history, look at who ruled, count the years, and conclude that this statement is true. If others disagree, you can say, "But it's a fact!" You can then hand them documents showing the dates of Mongol rule and a calculator, and they'll shut up—if they know what's good for them.

4   Whether or not British partition of India helped India to prosper is a matter of opinion, not fact. Sure, it's possible that some historian might come up with some good reasons to support this opinion, but it would still be an opinion as to the cause of Indian prosperity.

15   The only thing we can use to draw conclusions is the cartoon.
1   The cartoon definitely deals with violence, but there's nothing that indicates it is the best way to achieve goals. Also, do you really think the test writers would include a cartoon that gives this kind of message?
2   Gandhi's beliefs have not divided India. Other people's beliefs have. Gandhi wanted Muslims and Hindus to be able to live together. Even if you didn't know this, the cartoon itself doesn't tell us anything about the causes of division, so you need to look for a better answer choice.
3   We don't know if the destruction of monuments is a goal of radical groups, or if it is merely a means to another goal, or even if this destruction was done by a group.
4   **Since the statue has been cracked to pieces, we know that a violent act has been committed. Since the statue happens to be one of Gandhi, the cartoon clearly contrasts the nonviolence message of Gandhi with the violence of the vandalized statue, thereby illustrating that not everyone agrees with Gandhi.**

16   The caste system is based on the Hindu teaching that you must accept the caste into which you are born. Social mobility is not possible under the system. Many people in India continue to practice this system because it is part of their religion.
1   **Tradition and custom are often the reasons people follow a particular system, especially when those traditions and customs are intertwined with religious beliefs. The caste system continues to be practiced for this reason despite the official position of the government of India in favor of equal opportunity.**
2   The caste system doesn't have to be enforced, because many people willingly practice it. If the military were to become involved in the matter, the law would more likely require that the military enforce the abolition of the caste system.
3   The caste system is a Hindu practice, not a Muslim or Christian practice. Both Muslims and Christians are opposed to the system.
4   The caste system is certainly not mandated by law. The Constitution of India requires that individuals be free from discrimination according to caste.

17 Know your geography. Korea and Japan are separated by the Sea of Japan. China is a huge nation that sits to the west and to the north of Korea. Korea is comparatively small.

  1 Korea is big enough to serve as a bridge between Japan and China, but not so big as to protect Japan from China. It just makes sense that ideas from China would flow through Korea on their way to Japan.

  2 The question refers to early Japan (meaning a few thousand years ago). Industrialization didn't hit until the nineteenth century and came mostly from Europe and the United States.

  3 Look again at a map. Korea isn't big enough to serve as a barrier. The Chinese could easily go around Korea and attack Japan, but they usually didn't have to because Korea was under the control of China for a long time. Japan had to protect itself and it did.

  4 Again, Korea is a small nation. How are the Koreans going to protect Japan?

18 If you missed this one, review your Global Studies materials. You simply have to know the facts of the Meiji government in order to get this one right.

  1 The goal of the previous rulers of Japan was to isolate Japan, but the Meiji government wanted to change all of that. It wanted to have a greater influence in Asia, stop European colonialism, and become economically powerful.

  2 This certainly wasn't the case. Japan has never, under any government, wanted to merge with China. In fact, the government wanted to weaken China.

  3 The Meiji government was in power during the late nineteenth century. It wanted to do everything possible to catch up with the Industrial Revolution that had already been occurring in Europe and the United States for decades.

  4 The Meiji government generally wanted to prevent further colonization of Asia by Western nations. Instead, Japan itself wanted to exert greater control of other Asian nations.

19 If you understand some of the basics of modern Japan, you can use your common sense to eliminate some of the answers.

  1 During this time period, Japan was becoming increasingly capitalistic. To the extent that Japan wanted to trade, it did not want to trade with communist nations.

  2 Japan definitely wanted to expand its influence in Asia, mainly so that it could gain access to natural resources that it lacked.

With access to resources, Japan could continue to industrialize and solve some of its economic problems.

3 Again, Japan had no intention of becoming a communist nation. Economically, it was much more tied to the West.

4 A major goal of Japan was to modernize and industrialize. Why would it refuse access to Western technology?

20 Look at the cartoon carefully. Then compare answer choices.

1 The students are hungry for Locke and Jefferson, and are, in effect, telling the man to "hold the Mao."

2 China's government might think that it is meeting the needs of its students, but it certainly doesn't appear to be meeting the wants of its students, since the students want something that isn't even in the government's kettle.

3 **Mao, Deng, and Marx were all communist ideologists. With no alternatives available in the kettle, the cartoon is showing that China's educational system offers nothing but communist ideology to put in the heads of its students, even though the students are specifically asking to try something else.**

4 If the cartoonist believes that communist ideals have eliminated poverty, then why in the world were the children drawn to look like starving outcasts?

21 The question is essentially asking which word best summarizes the theories of Locke and Jefferson. John Locke believed in natural rights of people that the government cannot take away. Thomas Jefferson agreed with Locke and called those rights "inalienable rights" when he wrote the Declaration of Independence. In other words, both men believed in the individuality and the sovereignty of the people.

1 While socialism isn't entirely inconsistent with Locke and Jefferson, there is an answer that represents their theories much more closely.

2 The students definitely don't want communism because they're specifically asking for something else even though communist ideology (Mao, Marx, and Deng) is all that is being served.

3 The students aren't asking about nationalism, which is a love of one's own country and can be just as true of communist nations as of democratic or socialist ones.

4 **By asking for Locke and Jefferson, the students are asking for democracy.**

22 The thing you need to know about the Opium War is that China didn't get what it wanted. It was forced to open up some of its ports for trading with the West.
1 If China couldn't stop the West, then it certainly didn't have the most disciplined army in the world.
2 Yes. This is what the Opium War was all about.
3 Absolutely not. As a result of the War, the West became more influential.
4 No. China wanted to stop the opium trade by closing its ports. That's why there was a war.

23 Don't forget you have a 1989 cartoon on the previous page. Ask yourself which answer choice makes the most sense. Why would any country sometimes have to change its policies?
1 The Soviets weren't capitalists, nor were they successful.
2 The economic reforms started before the Tiananmen Square massacre in 1989. The incident was about political reform, not economic reform.
3 The Cultural Revolution was about decreasing the influence of the West, not increasing it. In addition, the Cultural Revolution was not successful in bringing economic prosperity to China.
4 You know that communist policies were not meeting the desires of the Chinese from the cartoon in question 20. In addition, it just makes sense that if the people's needs are not being met, the government is going to be under enormous pressure to change things.

24 The question tells us that the United States has granted China most favored nation status. Even if you don't know what this means, you can probably see that it is a good thing for China and that it means the United States is on friendly terms with China. What would this type of relationship result in?
1 Logically speaking, since the United States is in North America and not in Southeast Asia, the fact that the United States has granted any kind of status to China probably won't make a difference in China's ability to join SEATO. Factually speaking, SEATO no longer exists, but when it did, it was an organization primarily interested in preventing communist expansion in Southeast Asia.
2 This answer choice links the United States and China in a "favorable" way. Take it!
3 It would be a shock to the world if Japan invaded China since Japan doesn't have the military power to pull it off, but even if they

were planning to do just that, the fact that the United States granted China most favored nation status won't help China, because it's a trade status, not a military status.

4   If the United States could get rid of Russian influence anywhere in the world simply by granting most favored nation status, it would have granted most favored nation status to every single country years ago!

25   If you're guessing, pick the answer that would apply to the greatest number of civilizations even if you're not sure if it applies to these two.
   1   Both civilizations were river valley civilizations, the Mesopotamians in the Tigris and Euphrates river valley, and the Egyptians along the Nile River. This is also the answer that makes the most sense, since without a water supply and a transportation route, the civilization would have had difficulty becoming established.
   2   Only the Mesopotamians used ziggurats.
   3   Neither civilization traded with China.
   4   Only the Egyptians used hieroglyphics.

26   Read the quote carefully. Hopefully, you can glean that everything that the Canal company formerly owned is now owned by the Nation, specifically the nation of Egypt. If you don't understand this, then read the quote again. Now, if everything concerning the canal is owned by Egypt, then what has the Egyptian government done?
   1   Nothing in the quote refers to ending trade.
   2   Since so many people died, maybe they won't build another canal, or maybe they'll just be more careful next time. Isn't there a better answer that will be harder to argue with?
   3   Clearly, the Egyptian government has taken control of the canal. That's what is meant by the words "all its assets, rights and obligations are hereby transferred to the Nation," and by the word "nationalized."
   4   The canal isn't being sold by Egypt, it's being taken over by Egypt. Even if it were being sold, do you think Egypt would sell it to France after it just called a French Company an "imposter?" We think not.

27   If you don't know the items in the answer choices, it's time for you to do a little reviewing of major religions. We want an answer choice that tells us about Jewish faith and culture.
   1   Ramadan is a Muslim holy month. Reincarnation is a Hindu belief.

2   **The Torah is the first five books of the Old Testament and is central to the Jewish faith. The Diaspora (meaning "completely scattered") was the scattering of the Jews in the first century AD throughout Europe and the Middle East. Even if you know only one of these terms, this is the answer you have to pick.**

3   The New Testament is central to Christians and the Four Noble Truths are essential to Buddhists.

4   The Koran is the central book of Islam. The Code of Bushido is the guide for Japanese Samurai warriors.

28   If you don't know very much about the Kurds, Tamils, or Sikhs, choose the answer that is the most general. In other words, choose the answer that you think most minority groups would want as a goal. Remember also that you don't have to know about all three groups to eliminate some answer choices.

1   **All three groups have been trying to establish an independent nation for themselves—the Kurds in the Middle East, the Tamils in Sri Lanka, and the Sikhs in India. So far, none of the three groups has achieved its goal. This is also the answer choice that makes the most sense, since obtaining self-rule and economic control is both an understandable goal as well as a common goal throughout history.**

2   If these three groups liked multicultural states, they would stay where they are already living. The problem is that in the societies where they currently live, they are not respected and are often persecuted.

3   None of these three groups is Christian.

4   None is attempting to acquire economic aid from the World Bank, most probably because they aren't yet recognized as nations!

29   The Roman Empire was huge. It fell due to continuous invasions from the north. Prior to the fall, the empire was organized under one rule. So what do you think happened after the fall?

1   No. The Muslims attempted to take over Southern Europe centuries later, but the Roman Empire declined mostly because of barbarian invasions from the north.

2   No. The Byzantine Empire remained strong in Eastern Europe, but it stayed there.

3   No. We're talking about the beginning of the Middle Ages here. Republican forms of government didn't return until after the Enlightenment.

4 Yes! When large, well-organized bodies fall, there's usually a period of chaos and disorder that follows.

30 If you don't know the basics of the Crusades, you'd better study them now. Once you understand the basics, select the answer choice that makes sense.

1 The Crusades involved thousands of people traveling and fighting, and consequently being exposed to new things. This was hardly a time of isolationism.

2 Yes! As the Europeans traveled to the Middle East and Asia, they became exposed to new things and wanted them for themselves. The Crusades aided in cultural diffusion.

3 Absolutely not. The Crusades were intended to Christianize (or at least weaken) the Muslim world, not the other way around.

4 No way. The Crusades resulted in a weakening of the feudal system because the serfs could do their own thing while their lords were in foreign lands.

31 Familiarize yourself with the term "golden age," if you haven't already. A golden age is a time of prosperity and excellence, usually in the arts or sciences, and marked by a certain genuineness in achievement (art for the sake of art; science for the sake of learning). With this in mind, which answer choice is most attractive?

1 Neither Greece nor Italy were united during their golden ages. A strong military also has little to do with golden ages in the first place.

2 Neither Greece nor Italy had a written constitution during their golden ages. Again, golden ages are about arts and sciences.

3 Yeah! Art! Sounds like a Golden Age characteristic to us.

4 Golden ages are not directly about politics. And Greece and Italy didn't form unified nation-states during this time anyway.

32 You'd better know the definition of "commercial revolution" (which occurred at the end of the Middle Ages) because it shows up a lot. Just remember that it was the start of the modern market system, in which investors and businessmen started buying other people's products and then selling them to third parties for profit, and in which banking and monetary systems got off the ground.

1 No way. Manorialism was a system of self-sufficient manors which involved little trading, much less trading for profit. Manorialism was common before the Commercial Revolution, but not after.

2 Nope. Communism didn't come along until the late nineteenth century. Plus, communism isn't compatible at all with the Commercial Revolution.

3 Bartering is a strict exchange of goods. The Commercial Revolution introduced money as the method of exchange.

4 Yes! Don't forget this: The Commercial Revolution resulted in market economies!

33 "Mercantilism" is a favorite Regents word. Look it up now if you don't know it.

1 You got it! Mercantilist nations established colonies for the primary purpose of gaining wealth for themselves, usually at the expense of the colonies from which they were draining resources.

2 No way! Colonies are a source of free stuff for the colonial power.

3 Absolutely not! If colonies were granted independence as soon as possible, the colonial power wouldn't have unlimited access to the resources of the colonies.

4 No. The colonial power wants the resources of the colonies for its own industries. It doesn't want competition from its own colonies!

34 Look at the map closely and study the key. Now, start eliminating answer choices.

1 If this were true, then why does the map show that there were Calvinist areas?

2 How big is an area? This answer choice is much too ambiguous. We can count people, but we can't count areas unless we know what is meant by the word "area."

3 Just by looking at the map, we can tell that a lot more space is non-Calvinist than Calvinist.

4 In the south, there are a lot of dots (Catholic areas). In the north, there are a lot more stripes and dashes (Protestant areas). Looks like we have ourselves an answer!

35 The map clearly contrasts Catholicism with Protestantism. That's the reason the map makers shaded areas differently, so that you can tell which regions had which types of Christians. Protestantism developed after Catholicism. The areas on the map that are shown as Protestant were formerly Catholic. What's the best title for this map?

1 Yes! That's why the key on the map makes a distinction between Catholic areas and Protestant areas, so that you can see that the Protestant Reformation had an impact on large areas of Europe.

2   This map doesn't tell us anything about the Catholic response to the Protestant Reformation.

3   This map doesn't tell us anything about the loss of territory. It only tells us the dominant religions in certain areas during a specific time.

4   Absolutely not! If there was unity, the entire map would be covered with dots or the same kind of stripe.

36 This person doesn't like capitalism. This person predicts the downfall of capitalism. Do you know the folks in the answer choices? If not, look them up now.

1   Darwin was a scientist, not a philosopher or economist.

2   **Yes! Karl Marx was the leading communist theorist, and advocated communism as a direct alternative to the abuses of capitalism. (Anytime you see the word "proletariat" in a question, you can pretty much guess the correct answer will have something to do with Marx!)**

3   Machiavelli was a political philosopher, but this quote certainly wouldn't have come out of his lips. He authored *The Prince*, which was written to instruct leaders to maintain their power by achieving their political goals through any means necessary.

4   Locke was a political philosopher, not an economic one. While he would agree that people are destined to overcome abuses by their leaders, he was not anti-capitalist. He simply believed in responsible government.

37 First, realize that this question involves the 1930s, a time of worldwide depression. Second, realize that it's asking about the Nazi party, which you should be somewhat familiar with. Put the two together and use your common sense.

1   This treaty officially ended World War I, and it was hated by most Germans, who were humiliated by provisions that severely reduced Germany's ability to develop a strong military or economy. The Nazis advocated ignoring the treaty.

2   **Of course! It was a time of depression, and was especially bad in Germany due to the Treaty of Versailles. The people supported the party that promised to bring economic prosperity.**

3   Absolutely not! If you know only a little about the Nazi party, you must remember that it was not a multicultural group. They believed their own race to be superior to all others.

4 No. The international organizations were against the Nazi Party, mostly because the Nazis advocated ignoring the Treaty of Versailles and then did not respect the borders of other nations.

38 Read the caption to the cartoon carefully. Now take a look at the answer choices.
   1 **"Subdivided" means fragmented. "Again" means continues. Done.**
   2 Nothing in the cartoon tells us this.
   3 There is absolutely nothing about free-enterprise zones in the cartoon.
   4 Sure they do! Look at how many there are on the map! There are more now than there were ten years ago!

39 Read the headlines carefully. Then start eliminating answer choices.
   1 If the government of Croatia collapsed, then how in the world is the United States establishing diplomatic relations with it? If Latvia collapsed, how is it joining the United Nations?
   2 If the Russian Empire were strong, Latvia would not have been able to assert its independence and join the United Nations. Even if you don't know this, look for a better answer choice, since none of the headlines directly refers to the Russian Empire.
   3 All of the countries in the headlines are acting independently. This does not show unity in Europe.
   4 **These nations are supporting (recognizing, establishing diplomatic relations with, joining) other nations. Slovenia, Croatia, and Latvia are all new independent nations carved out of old ones because the people living in these nations wanted to determine their own fate.**

40 Remember, the question is asking you to find the source of the "major problems," so we want something really big.
   1 These nations all have extremely literate populations. If you didn't know this, you do now, but more importantly, look for an even bigger source of problems.
   2 The government leaders are seeking, not refusing, foreign investments so that they can modernize their infrastructure and factories.
   3 **Yes! Communism (a command economy) was abandoned for a free-market economy, and this has caused all sorts of problems, including high inflation and shortages, quite possibly because the economy switched over too quickly. Even if you don't know the details of the dissolution of the**

former Soviet Union, you should know that communism was abandoned for a free-market economy.

4 The industrialized nations have provided and are providing advisors. Why would the industrialized nations not want to help? If Eastern Europe is successful, the industrialized nations will have new markets to sell their products to.

41 Pick the answer choice that is hardest to disagree with. Read the list carefully and then start eliminating answer choices.

1 Eliminate this one. It doesn't explain the treaty and the joint space mission.

2 **How can you disagree with this answer? You can't. There were bad things like a blockade, an invasion, and a crisis. There were good things like a treaty and a visit. Sounds like the tension between the two superpowers varied.**

3 Nothing about this list refers to economics, except maybe the blockade.

4 The United Nations is nowhere to be seen on the list.

42 We want something that puts a dagger in the heart of what the Cold War was about (because of the use of the word "symbolized").

1 No. These occurred at the beginning of the Cold War, not at the end. They represent the Cold War, not the end of it.

2 No. Again, these were near the beginning of the Cold War, not the end.

3 This happened after the Cold War was over, and has nothing to do with it.

4 **Yes! The construction of the Berlin Wall was due to the Cold War, so its destruction best symbolizes the end of the Cold War.**

43 You need to know some facts in order to get this one right, but you can still use your general knowledge to eliminate a few answers.

1 No. The only revolution of the three that was led by a dictator was the Bolshevik Revolution, in which Lenin established himself as the dictator.

2 **Yes! All three revolts overthrew a monarchy. It's also the most attractive answer choice since a whole lot of revolutions were motivated by this desire.**

3 No. All you need to know is that France has never been a communist nation. China eventually became one, but not until 1949.

4 No. Only in France did the middle class establish a higher standard of living in the years following the revolution.

44 We want the answer choice that would have the most harmful effect on the quality of the air, specifically by increasing the amount of carbon dioxide.

1 This problem does not have an immediate impact on air quality (as opposed to water and soil quality), nor does it increase the amount of carbon dioxide.

2 Trees take carbon dioxide and turn it into oxygen. The production of fossil fuels involves the creation of carbon dioxide. Even if you didn't know this for sure, you should like this answer because trees and fuels are things that seem likely to affect air quality.

3 Again, we want something that affects air quality, not water quality.

4 This is an environmental hazard, but does not increase the amount of carbon dioxide.

45 "Appeasement" means giving in to the demands of others in the hopes of preventing something like a war. And you already know what a war is. So what we want in the correct answer choice is an example that involves an appeasement but that also involves a war.

1 Held to deal with the advancements of Hitler, the Munich Conference resulted in a policy of appeasement. The British appeased Germany. But after the Germans invaded Poland, war broke out. We have appeasement. We have a war. We have an answer.

2 Although there was a War in Vietnam (Indochina), there was no appeasement by the French. Instead, they fought.

3 There was no appeasement by the United States. There was also no war.

4 There was definitely a war between Iraq and Iran in the 1980's, but there was no appeasement.

46 The Green Revolution is all about efficient farming. Look it up in the glossary. Memorize it. It shows up a lot.

1 No. The Green Revolution advocates increasing the use of productive, modern farm machinery.

2 No. The Green Revolution is not about population control. It's about increasing food production for a growing population, so that food supply meets demand.

3 Bingo! By increasing agricultural output per acre (through technological advancements and science), the Green Revolution seeks to feed more without having to use more.

4   No. Traditional farms are inefficient and often sustain only the people who work on the farm.

47   Use your common sense on this one. We want something that limits the development of unity.

1   These nations, especially India, have natural resources. Even to the extent that they lack resources, this lack has not been a factor in limiting unity. Isn't there a better answer?

2   Colonialism has ended in India and Lebanon and yet they are still divided. Besides, nations tend to unite, not divide, against foreign enemies, which is why colonialism has so often been defeated.

3   **Yes! Differences tend to limit unity, especially religious and ethnic differences. This just makes sense, even if you don't know the details of the three nations involved in the question.**

4   Rapid growth of industry usually helps to unite a country as opposed to dividing it, though sometimes it pits the people living in the cities against the people living in the countryside. In any case, it's not a factor in these three cases.

48   Three examples involve one nation buying a basic product from another country. The fourth example involves Great Britain joining forces with other nations. If you know the definitions of the words in the answer choices, you're set.

1   Balance of power refers to the political power of the branches of government within one nation. These examples involve relations between at least two nations.

2   **Interdependence is a concept involving the economic reliance that nations have on each other, primarily because they cannot be as prosperous as they would like to be if they did not interact and trade with each other.**

3   These nations definitely are not isolating themselves. They are involving themselves in the global economic community.

4   These nations are not making colonies of each other, but just trading with each other for mutual benefit.

PART II

1. GLOBAL PROBLEMS

Environmental pollution

In 1986, an explosion at a nuclear reactor in Chernobyl in the former Soviet Union sent tons of radioactive debris into the atmosphere. The land around the nuclear reactor was severely affected. Thousands of people were evacuated as their crops and livestock were ruined by contact with radioactive particles. Much of the land in the immediate area still cannot be farmed and since the overall effects of the explosion are still being monitored, access to the region has been restricted. Since the Soviet Union tended to downplay incidents within its own nation, the nation attempted to solve the problem on its own. The reactor was immediately shut down and an investigation was conducted. It was determined that the reactor's design was flawed. Therefore, the government has inspected its other reactors and has planned to shut down those with similar flaws. In the meantime, the land around Chernobyl remains contaminated and the clean-up is slow.

Terrorism

The Palestine Liberation Organization has traditionally sponsored terrorist attacks against Israel, which it wants to liberate from Jewish control and then replace with the Muslim state of Palestine. Since its creation in 1964, the PLO has placed terrorist bombs in Israeli government buildings, shopping centers and small businesses. Israel has usually responded aggressively, often in the form of occupying more territory and brutal military attacks against Palestinians. The number of terrorist attacks have waxed and waned depending on the political developments within the region, but in the late 1980's and early 1990's, the number of terrorist attacks increased as part of the Islamic fundamentalist intifada movement. In 1993, Israel and the PLO agreed to recognize each other and attempt to agree on measures that would lead to peace, but the process angered radical members of the PLO who did not want to negotiate with Israel. Terrorist acts in Hebron followed, though as the result of individual motivations. Today, the terrorism in Israel continues. The world community has condemned acts of terrorism and has made efforts to bring peace to the region, but terrorism will likely continue until Israel and its Muslim neighbors can learn to share the Middle East.

Human rights violations

After the success of the Islamic Revolution in Iran in 1979, the new fundamentalist government reversed the human rights progress made by Shah Pahlavi and strictly monitored Iranians with views opposed to the goals of the new regime. In direct violation of basic human rights, the new government arrested, tortured, and even killed people who it believed represented a threat to the social, political, and religious goals of the government. Much of the world was stunned by the success of a religiously motivated revolution, but the world has not been quick to act on behalf of the people whose religious and political rights are being violated. The United States enacted a trade embargo against Iran, but its decision was due to Iran's support of terrorism, not to Iran's suppression of freedoms within its own country. Instead, reform in Iran has come from within. Many Iranians have become increasingly dissatisfied with the state of the economy and general society since the Islamic Revolution. They have been urging the government to relax its restrictions and protect human rights, and they have begun to have limited success.

Refugees

The refugee crisis in Rwanda and Burundi stems from conflicts between two groups: the Tutsi (10% of the population in Rwanda and 15% of the population in Burundi) who traditionally have governed the Hutu (90% in Rwanda, 85% in Burundi). Hutu revolts against Tutsi leadership left hundreds of thousands dead. The Hutu eventually gained control in the 1970s. However, in 1994, the Hutu leaders of Rwanda and Burundi were killed in an airline crash, and thereafter the Tutsi swept through the nations and declared civil war, resulting in a torrent of two million refugees looking for safety in Zaire. The Hutu are trying to escape torture and death and believe that they cannot safely return to their own country. The United Nations has intervened to aid Zaire in dealing with the onslaught of refugees and has sent a multinational force to restore order to the region. The goal of the UN effort is to create a stable situation in which the Hutu people can safely return to their countries. The problem remains unsettled, however, and unless the political situation can be resolved to the satisfaction of both the Tutsi and the Hutu, it is unlikely that the violence will end.

Overpopulation

Overpopulation has increasingly become a problem in India. India is the world's second largest nation, and is gaining ground fast on the world's largest, China. Perhaps the main reason India has a faster rate of growth than China is that the Chinese government has adopted stricter population control measures. India encourages parents to limit the size of their families through public announcements and government-run clinics that distribute free birth control devices. The government has not passed any population control legislation, however, beyond making funds available for voluntary family planning. Public support for population control is simply too sporadic. Most Indians cling to their traditional way of life, which stresses the importance of large families. Nevertheless, the Indian government is becoming increasingly concerned with the population growth rate.

Religious conflict

Religious conflict between Catholics and Protestants in Northern Ireland has resulted in the deaths of thousands, and the conflict still remains unsettled. When Britain granted Ireland independence, it maintained control of six northern provinces known as Northern Ireland. This seemed to be a good idea at the time, because Ireland was predominantly Catholic while Northern Ireland was predominantly Protestant, just like Britain. However, the government of Northern Ireland discriminated against the Catholic minority, and eventually the Irish Republican Army (IRA) was created to combat the discrimination. The IRA wants to join Ireland, while the Protestant majority wants to remain part of the United Kingdom. The protests quickly led to violence, including bombings, and soon both sides inflicted violence against each other. The consequence of the IRA insurrections is not yet known. We do know that the conflict has raged for decades and that thousands have died. We also know that both sides have been willing to enter into peaceful negotiations in recent years. Both the British and Irish governments have attempted to influence negotiations in Northern Ireland. But since the dispute remains unsettled, and since the Catholic population of Northern Ireland is quickly increasing in proportion to the Protestant population, the future of Northern Ireland is still in question.

2. NATIONALISM

Levee en Masse, French Revolution

This quotation represents the view that nationalism can be a motivating force in arousing the masses to defend the principles under which they want to live. Each person of France—man, woman, and child—was given a part to play, thereby uniting them under the common cause of "hatred of kings . . . and unity of the Republic." The French Revolution began as an anti-monarchy campaign but soon took on a nationalistic fervor when other European monarchies threatened action against the French to suppress their popular uprising. The other monarchies were worried that the ideas of the French Revolution would spread to their own countries. By 1793, the French had not only murdered the members of the monarchy, but were successfully preventing invasions from neighboring monarchies. Eventually, the French revolutionists became aggressive themselves, especially under the leadership of Napoleon. In the decades that followed, commitment to representative forms of government that recognize individual rights swept the continent of Europe. But perhaps just as importantly, the concept of nationalism also spread across Europe. People began to identify themselves with their fellow national citizens, as opposed to with members of their locality or social class. Later, nationalism united people in many European nations and played a principal role in all the major wars to follow.

Count Camillo di Cavour

This quotation represents an extremely nationalist viewpoint. It does not stop at suggesting that the people should identify themselves first as Italians (instead of as members of a particular subgroup), but encourages them to establish themselves as a superior nationality. This viewpoint shouldn't be too surprising, given that Napoleon was forcing his way through Europe under a nationalistic banner at the time. In fact, it was Napoleon that helped Count Camillo di Cavour drive Austria out of Sardinia, a kingdom in Northern Italy. Cavour then aroused nationalism on the entire Italian peninsula, telling them to "put aside all petty differences" and unite. Eventually, the small kingdoms of Italy were united as one nation. Nationalistic fervor continued to grow until the world wars of the following century gave it reason to explode outside its boundaries.

Sun Yat-sen

Previous to Sun Yat-sen's Chinese Revolution of 1911, the Chinese identified themselves with their family, clan, and particular locality. Sun Yat-sen believed that this lack of nationalism led directly to the success of foreign invasions in China and the establishment of European spheres of influence. The Chinese were simply not united as one, even though they shared similar customs and habits. Sun Yat-sen expressed his frustration in the quote, but then he set out to bring the Chinese together under a common national identity with his Three Principles of the People—nationalism, socialism and democracy. Eventually China ridded itself of foreign interests when the Communist Revolution took advantage of the growth of nationalist ideas in the peasant class.

Gavrilo Princip

This quotation of Gavrilo Princip shows that he believed that nationalism is a proper motive for murder. He justified his assassination of Archduke Ferdinand in Sarajevo as a necessary step to the attainment of self-determination for Serbian Slavs. His action did, in fact, result in its intended effect: war. No one could have predicted that the entire continent of Europe would be engulfed by World War I within a matter of months, but a series of alignments and rivalries were triggered by the assassination, and millions of people died as a result. At the end of the war, Serbia and Bosnia united as Yugoslavia, but nationalist differences within the nation persisted, leading to the recent division of Yugoslavia and war along ethnic lines. The region represents an unfortunate example of a place where political line-drawing does not correspond to the nationalistic sentiments of many of the people caught within the lines.

Kwame Nkrumah

Kwame Nkrumah's plea for nationalism was necessary in the new nation of Ghana because it had no natural identity of its own. As they did in most of Africa, the Europeans (in particular the British) drew national boundaries of newly independent nations according to their own political motivations. No consideration was given to the identities of the people within the boundaries. Tribes that were formerly united were split into two, while two rival tribes were grouped together within the same nation. Kwame Nkrumah recognized this problem immediately. As the first president of Ghana, he attempted to unite the nation under common goals, but divided public opinion and mounting national debt made him assume even more centralized authority in an attempt to enforce his plans. He was eventually overthrown in a 1966 military coup. Nationalism has never taken root in Ghana, nor has it in many African nations where tribalism is the source of identity. Ghana's divisions have continued to result in frequent coups and political changeovers.

The Palestinian National Charter

The Palestinian National Charter raises nationalist fervor throughout the Arab world to gain support for its goal: the liberation of Israel as an Islamic Palestinian state. It calls upon the "Arab nation" to unite, referring to Palestine as part of the "greater Arab homeland." While Israel remains a Jewish state, the charter has been successful in organizing regional opposition to it. The PLO has sponsored terrorism against Israel, and numerous skirmishes and even wars have broken out between the two sides. While many Arab nationalists have not become personally involved in aggression against Israel, most of the Arab world is united under the more general nationalist goals of the PLO. Among extremists, the PLO has been so successful in arousing nationalism, it has taken on a life of its own. Even when the PLO was willing to take a more moderate stand and negotiate with Israel in 1993, extremists were furious with the leadership's "sell-out" and some of them independently continued acts of violence against Israel. The situation in the Middle East remains unsettled, but one thing is clear: Nationalism may be initiated by leadership to obtain certain goals, but once nationalistic motives are adopted by the people themselves, where it stops, nobody knows.

3. RELIGIONS AND PHILOSOPHIES

Animism

Animism is not an organized, definable religion in the same way that Islam or Catholicism are. Instead, Animism is the label given to the hundreds of religions that have developed in sub-Saharan Africa. Animist religions do share some common bonds. They generally share a belief in a supreme being that regulates nature, but they also share a belief in thousands of lesser spirits found in all natural things. The religious leaders of the tribes in Africa communicate with the spirits in trees, rocks, water, and even storms, pleading with them to meet the needs of the tribes and listening to them for messages to give to their followers. The idea of the importance of nature has long made Africa more resistant to materialism and industrialization. The traditional African religions require people to love the positive forces of nature while fearing and respecting the negative forces. The predominant role of nature in Animist religions has affected the art, rituals, and even the economic development of sub-Saharan Africa.

Buddhism

Buddhism might be better described as a life philosophy than a religion, since the practitioners do not believe in an all-powerful god or gods that can grant them salvation. Instead, Buddhists generally believe that it is up to the individual to acquire wisdom and to break free of materialism, eventually achieving the state of nirvana, a desire-free life. Buddhism is predominant in East and Southeast Asia and has affected the cultural and social development of the region. Buddhism focuses on proper behavior, realized through the Four Noble Truths and the Eightfold Way. In general, this behavior is centered on meditation and a denial of materialism. The belief contributed to the region's relative isolation and general subsistence living for centuries. Even as the region industrializes, many people in the region do not desire many of the material gains that industrialization and modernization promise them.

Christianity

Christianity has greatly affected the development of Latin America. Christians believe that Christ was the son of God and that belief in him will lead to eternal life. Roman Catholicism, one branch of Christianity, has been the dominant religion of Latin America ever since Europe, most notably Spain, conquered the region. Roman Catholics are Christian, but can be distinguished from Protestants. Roman Catholics believe in the divinity of Christ and also the Virgin Mary, and believe that the Church hierarchy of priests, Pope, and Saints serve as intermediaries between the faithful and God. Unlike most Protestants, Roman Catholics believe in the authority of their local priest to interpret the Bible for them and are much less likely to challenge Church doctrines.

Because it is the dominant religion of Latin America, Catholicism has affected the region enormously. It has served as a dominant unifying force, linking the cultures of Latin America by a common thread. Family life and social life have been greatly affected by the policies of the Church, but this is not to say that all Catholics agree. Liberal Catholic priests have attempted to raise the standard of living of the poor for moral reasons, while conservative Catholic priests have argued that individuals should remain faithful to the policies of their authorities. This dispute, however, only serves to show that the Catholic religion is an extremely important force in the social and political lives of Latin America.

Confucianism

Confucianism is not a religion as much as it is a moral philosophy, since its primary concern is human behavior in the here and now. Widely practiced in traditional China, Confucianism still claims over 150 million followers in China and beyond. The philosophy focuses on proper conduct in relationships and lifestyle. Individuals are expected to understand their role in society and family and perform that role respectfully and consciously. Dead ancestors and the elderly are highly revered. Parents, especially fathers, demand respect from their children, but are also encouraged to treat their children with kindness and fairness. The relationship between rulers and the peasants is similar, with responsibilities assigned to each role. For centuries, Confucianism encouraged a class-based society in which each class had its own code of conduct assigned to it. Subsequently, when the Communist Revolution swept through China, the government officially discouraged any religious or philosophical practice that conflicted with its own authority. Nevertheless, Confucianism has remained an important force on human behavior in China, regulating the nature of the relationships within millions of families even in spite of official government policies.

Hinduism

Hinduism is a traditional religion is the strictest definition. In other words, it has been passed down from generation to generation, not through an all-important written text or by a central religious authority, but simply as a matter of custom and tradition. Hindus believe that who you are in this life was determined by who you were in a past life. And how you conduct yourself in your assigned role in this life will later determine the role (caste) you get in a future life. This belief has affected the social, political, and economic development of India enormously. The caste system in India is based on the Hindu religion. It was outlawed when India became an independent nation, but millions still practice it as part of their religion. The people of the lowest caste (the untouchables) cannot socially mingle or even work side-by-side with the people of the highest caste. This has led not only to widespread social discrimination, but widespread employment discrimination as well. The untouchables do all the dirty jobs that nobody else will do. Many Hindus do not challenge discrimination, because they want to be rewarded with a higher caste in a later life. Social mobility is therefore greatly hindered. Nevertheless, as more people have moved to the cities, they have begun to disassociate themselves from the caste system. In fact, recently untouchables have risen to positions of political authority. However, Hinduism remains a tremendous influence in the lives of millions of Indians.

Islam

Islam means "submission," or in the religious context, "submission to the will of God." Muslims do not believe that Muhammed was the son of God, but rather that he was God's prophet. This belief is best expressed in the first of the Five Pillars of Islam: "There is but one God and Muhammed is his messenger." The other four Pillars reveal proper Islamic conduct, as does the Koran, the most important text of the religion.

The Koran is extremely important since Muslims are focused on submitting to the will of Allah, and the Koran gives them an understanding of what that will is. As a result, the religion nurtures fundamentalism. In other words, many Muslims want to follow the teachings of the Koran as closely as possible. This fact has greatly influenced culture in the Middle East, where Islam is the dominant religion. Not only have many of the people resisted change and westernization because it is often incompatible with the Koran, but they have created state religions so that the governments follow and enforce the teachings of the Koran as well. Most notably, Iran reversed its westernization attempts after the fundamentalist Islamic Revolution of

1979 made the Koran the law of the land. Throughout the Middle East, Islamic fundamentalism is on the rise, precisely because so many Muslims do not want societal changes to result in their failure to practice their understanding of the will of Allah.

Judaism

Judaism is an ancient religion of the Middle East, specifically Palestine. Jews are monotheistic and believe that life should be spent living the will of God, as told to Moses. There are many subgroups within Judaism, but the belief that they are the chosen people of God is central to the faith. It is this belief that has bonded them together even as they were dispersed around the world during the Diaspora. Throughout the Middle Ages and since, Jews have been persecuted and separated from primarily Christian groups in Europe, North America, and North Africa. Yet, many of them never lost touch with their faith. If anything, the persecution and atrocities like the Holocaust made them stronger in their faith and determined that they should have a homeland of their own where they can be reunited with all Jews. The Zionist movement built on the idea that Jews are the chosen people of God and advocated the creation of a Jewish homeland in Palestine, the land that was promised to Moses by God. As a result, the modern nation of Israel was established in 1947 as a Jewish state surrounded by hostile Muslim nations. The creation of the state of Israel has led to persistent violence. Violence and hatred are things that the Jewish community is accustomed to enduring. Their faith that they are the chosen people of God and that Israel is the Promised Land sustains them, like it always has, in the face of opposition.

4. INDUSTRIAL REVOLUTION

Growth of Cities

During the Industrial Revolution, the cities of Europe grew dramatically. Factory jobs lured hundreds of thousands of farmers and rural dwellers into the crowded cities. As the cities became commercial hubs of trade, thousands more were needed to work in warehouses, rail yards, and harbors. Although the industrialization made products more readily available to the lower classes, these classes suffered from extremely dangerous working conditions, overcrowding, pollution, disease, and crime. For millions, city life was very different from the rural life they had previously lived. And while eventually their employment, educational, personal, and cultural opportunities increased due to the growth of the cities, their daily quality of life in terms of space, disease, and crime was adversely affected.

Rise of Marxism/Socialism

The Industrial Revolution created an enormous working class, unlike any class of people that had ever come before it. Factory employees worked long hours in cramped, dirty, and often dangerous environments while the owners of the factories became extremely wealthy. Yet, unlike many other classes of people who have been forced into labor conditions, the factory workers were told that this was their best opportunity and that they, too, could rise to the top. Karl Marx did not believe that the factory workers had opportunities. Instead, he believed that they were being exploited, and that this exploitation was an inevitable consequence of capitalist industrialization. He wrote that the working class must eventually revolt and take control of the means of production, and while many workers attempted to do just that in the nations of Western Europe, a communist revolution did not occur until 1917 in Russia. However, throughout the rest of Europe, social legislation was passed to improve the working conditions in the factories and establish minimum wages.

Changes in Transportation

Two developments in the Industrial Revolution changed transportation, and therefore European economies, dramatically. The first was the invention of the steam engine. The second was the development of improved methods of smelting iron ore. Together, these two developments resulted in the invention of the railroad, and Europe and the rest of the world would never be the same again. Raw materials were easily sent to a thousand locations. Finished products radiated out of factories in all directions. But perhaps most significantly of all, people were suddenly on the move as never before. And with them, their ideas and cultures spread, en masse, to new areas. The development of the railroad aided cultural diffusion more than any other invention up until that point in time (the invention of the radio, television, and the internet have probably outdone it).

Imperialism

Prior to the Industrial Revolution, the nations of Europe began exploring the parts of the world that remained unknown to them. They conquered and colonized the Americas and searched for routes to India, where they could do some trading. Essentially, imperialism during this time was about the acquisition of land, precious metals such as gold, and agricultural products, like spices and tobacco, that weren't available in Europe. Then, the Industrial Revolution swept Europe and imperialism took on a whole new meaning. Slowly, imperialism transformed itself into a quest for raw materials to supply factories. This quest led to the policy of mercantilism. Mercantilist nations acquired incredible wealth by colonizing regions with natural resources and then taking those resources without compensating the natives, and sending the resources back to Europe where they were used to make finished products in the factories. Then, the mercantilist nations sent those finished products back to the colonies, who had to purchase them because the colonial power wouldn't let them trade with anyone else. In short, the colonial powers became rich at the expense of the colonies. The more colonies a nation had, the richer it became. Soon, Europe was colonizing nations on every other continent of the globe. Europe became a clearinghouse for raw materials from around the world while the rest of the world increasingly became exposed to Europe and European ideas.

Use of Natural Resources

The factories of the Industrial Revolution had the capacity to make wonderful products, but first they needed the natural resources from which the products would be made. Europe had its share of coal and iron ore which was used to provide power and equipment for the factories, but raw materials such as cotton and rubber had to be imported because they didn't grow in the climates of Western Europe. As a result, the imperialist and industrial powers of Europe colonized regions of the world that could provide them with the raw materials they needed. It was much cheaper for them to colonize the nations of Africa and Asia than to trade with them, since they could force the natives to harvest or mine the materials, take them back to Europe at cost, and then sell the finished products back to the natives at a grossly inflated price. The need for raw materials transformed the landscape of the conquered regions. Limited raw materials were being depleted faster than at any time in history. Cotton plantations were spread across previously unfarmed land and after a few years, depleted the soil of its nutrients. Therefore, the unprecedented use of natural resources during the Industrial Revolution not only changed the lives of people on every continent, but the environment as well.

Changing Labor Conditions

Prior to the Industrial Revolution, most European families worked on the farms. They worked long hours, especially during the planting and harvesting seasons, but they worked together as families. Roles were clearly defined. Everyone knew what was expected of them—men, women, and children. Although education was becoming increasingly available, the school schedule reflected farming seasons so that children would be able to help their parents. The Industrial Revolution, however, sent millions of families to the cities where both parents had to work to make enough money to support the family, but unlike life on the farms, the parents often worked in different factories. Children often worked in factories as well, separating the family unit in all directions. Whereas the farms provided exposure to clean air and sunshine, the factories exposed the workers to air pollution, hazardous materials, and machinery. Whereas the farms provided seasonal adjustments to the work pattern, the factories monotonously spat out the same finished products day after day, all year long. All of this eventually led to the development of unions and major changes in government policy and economic theory. Thus, as the Industrial Revolution changed the labor conditions of Europe, it also changed the social, political, and economic structure of Europe.

5. GEOGRAPHIC FEATURES

Arctic Ocean

The Arctic Ocean, which is roughly an oval shape around the North Pole, is covered in ice. If the Ocean were warm, travel from Asia and Europe to North America could be easily accomplished by traveling north across the Ocean and then south again to the particular North American destination. But because the water is frozen and the climate and topography in general are inhospitable, travel across the Arctic is rare, and was virtually nonexistent before modern times. Most of Russia's northern coast runs along the Arctic Ocean, while its southern and western borders were landlocked for centuries. Since the ocean is frozen, Russia was not able to establish port cities throughout much of its history, except in the east where the population is sparse and thousands of miles away from the population centers of the West. Then, in the eighteenth century, Peter the Great drove the Swedes out of part of the Baltic region and established his new capital city on the Baltic Sea. In addition, he fought wars against the Ottoman Empire in the south to gain access to the Black Sea. Thus, the nature of the Arctic Ocean affected Russian policy, and thereby the rest of the world, because it stood against Russian penetration more effectively than the empires of Western and Southern Europe.

Gulf Stream/North Atlantic Drift

The Gulf Stream and North Atlantic Drift are warm ocean currents. Largely driven by winds, the currents keep the water moving, thereby stabilizing the climate on much of the earth. Without them, the tropical regions would continue to become hotter and hotter while the polar regions would continue to grow colder and colder. The streams interlock into a huge network of moving water. The Gulf Stream is fed by the South Equatorial Current, which runs along the northeastern coast of South America, bringing with it extremely warm water. The Gulf Stream then carries this water around the eastern edge of Central America and then up along the eastern seaboard of the United States. The waters of the Gulf Stream then head out over the North Atlantic toward Europe, where the waters are now called the North Atlantic Drift. In turn, the North Atlantic Drift, now cooler, flows into the Irminger Current, which clashes with cold waters of the Arctic Ocean. The Gulf Stream and North Atlantic Drift help to moderate the temperatures of Great Britain, Iceland, and Norway. Without them, these nations would be much colder and much less habitable. Instead, Great Britain, for example, enjoys temperatures more similar to those of Philadelphia than those of Moscow, even though nearly half of the nation is as far north as Moscow. The moderate temperatures of course have influenced the agricultural and commercial development of the region.

Himalaya Mountains

Geologists believe that the Himalayas were created when India drifted into Asia about forty million years ago. The result was the creation of the highest mountain range in the world. Like most mountain ranges, the Himalayas protect the people on both sides of the range, and yet they also isolate them. The mountains stretch from just northeast of Burma all the way to the northeast corner of Pakistan. In other words, they create a wall between the Indian subcontinent and central Asia. In terms of weather, the mountains prevent the southern monsoon winds from reaching Russia and cold winter air from reaching India. In terms of military conquest, they have prevented invading armies from going in either direction. But perhaps most importantly, the mountain range led to distinct cultural variations. Politics, religion, and culture on both sides of the range developed separately and then spread east and west along the range rather than through it.

Mediterranean Sea

The Mediterranean Sea lies at the convergence of three continents. Almost entirely surrounded by land, the sea is bounded on the north by Europe, on the south by Africa and on the east by Asia (specifically, the Middle East). It is connected to the waterways of the world in the West through the narrow Strait of Gibraltar (which connects it to the Atlantic Ocean) and on the west by the man-made Suez Canal (which connects it to the Red Sea). The Mediterranean Sea has served as the centerpiece for ancient civilizations, particularly Greece and Rome. However, in more modern times, it has taken on a more global significance. Ever since the opening of the Suez

Canal in Egypt, the Mediterranean Sea has been at the center of world trade as opposed to regional trade. Ships carrying goods and raw materials from North America, Europe, North Africa, the Middle East, and the Indian subcontinent all regularly travel through the Mediterranean Sea on their journeys to the opposite side of the globe. Before the Suez Canal, those same ships had to travel around the tip of Africa. As a result, Egypt has become strategically important to the rest of the world and its economy has become dependent on travel through the Canal. While it can be said that the Suez Canal has made modern Egypt what it is today, the truth is that the Mediterranean Sea has. Without the sea, the Canal would be meaningless. And without the Canal, the sea would not be nearly as globally significant.

Monsoon

Monsoon winds are seasonal winds. While the word monsoon could refer to seasonal winds on any part of the globe, it more specifically refers to the seasonal winds in India and Southeast Asia. There, the winds create two seasons: a wet season and a dry season. During summer in the northern hemisphere, hot air rises from the enormous Asian land mass, creating a large area of low pressure. The low pressure pulls winds from the south toward it. These monsoon winds blow over the ocean, collect moisture, and then dump extremely heavy rains on India and Southeast Asia. During winter in the northern hemisphere, the monsoon winds switch direction. Cool air settles over the Asian land mass, sending dry air south toward India and Southeast Asia. Rice, the major staple grain of Southeast Asia, is dependent on the seasons created by the monsoon rains. Rice grows in paddy fields that require hot sun followed by extremely heavy rains. Millions of people rely on the rice for food, and the economies of Southeast Asia rely on rice for export. If the monsoon winds bring too little rain, the result is famine. If the monsoon winds bring too much, the result is devastating flood waters. Nations such as Vietnam have experienced both.

Sahara Desert

The Sahara Desert dominates northern Africa, stretching in a thousand-mile-wide path from Western Sahara and Mauritania on the Atlantic Ocean, to Egypt and northern Sudan on the Red Sea. With the exception of the coastal communities along the Mediterranean Sea and along the Nile River, North Africa has been virtually swallowed up by the ever-expanding desert. Traditionally, the desert served as a barrier between the Mediterranean, Middle Eastern, and Egyptian Empires and those of sub-Saharan Africa. To be sure, the desert was not impenetrable. The empires of Mali and Ghana sent traders on caravans through the desert to trade with the Middle

East, and they successfully exchanged ideas and resources such as gold. Furthermore, the Islamic religion managed to spread through the region despite the desert. Yet, for the most part, sub-Saharan Africa remained largely unknown to the Middle East and Europe (and thereby the rest of world) for most of its great history. During the Age of Exploration, European ships became familiar with the coastal regions of sub-Saharan Africa, but the interior remained a mystery. It was not until the African slave trade and then later during European colonization of Africa that the rest of the world came into contact with interior sub-Saharan Africa. And by then, the industrialized world was more interested in conquering the region than learning about it. Therefore, the past greatness of sub-Saharan cultures, mostly isolated because of the Sahara Desert, has only recently become known on a worldwide scale.

Yangtze River

The Yangtze River is the longest and most significant river in China. From its tributaries in the Himalayas, the river flows mostly from west to east all the way to the coast of China, where it empties into the East China Sea just north of Shanghai. Because the river is navigable well into the nation's interior, some of China's largest cities have been built along its banks, including Nanjing, Wuhan, and Chongqing. These cities serve as trade centers for the nation's growing industrial and agricultural output. Traditionally, the river has been the lifeblood of the region, providing water to feed the farmlands along its banks. The river, therefore, has sustained life, carried travelers and traders, and unified the interior of southern China more than any other geographical feature in the region.

6. INDIVIDUALS' INFLUENCE ON HISTORY

Elizabeth I

At the same time that Shakespeare was securing Britain's position as a leader in world literature, Elizabeth I was securing Britain's position as a great world power. She sponsored explorations, executed her sister Mary I (the former queen), and increased trade with other nations. When Spain threatened to invade and establish England as a Catholic nation once and for all, she defeated the Spanish Armada, thereby securing Britain as the world's greatest naval power. Elizabeth's reign set the stage for British imperialism. Under her leadership, Britain developed the military and commercial capacities that were later used to colonize much of the world.

Galileo Galilei

Galileo, an Italian scientist, changed the way people understand the world they live in. He started by making careful observations of the way in which chandeliers swung in a cathedral in Pisa, Italy. His observations led him to develop a pendulum clock. Later, he used the scientific method to prove that all objects, no matter how heavy, fall at the same rate and then went on to make scientific conclusions about the universe with the aid of the refracting telescope that he perfected. Perhaps his most significant contribution was his diligent record-keeping in an effort to prove the theory of Copernicus that the Sun, not the Earth, is at the center of our solar system. When the Catholic Church objected to his findings as heresy, it imprisoned him, but by that time Galileo had ignited scientific inquiry beyond the Church's ability to suppress it. Galileo not only influenced the scientific community in practical ways, but influenced the development of skepticism, an ingredient necessary to pursue the scientific method in the first place.

Adam Smith

Adam Smith was an economic philosopher whose ideas transformed nations and still impact much of the world. In *The Wealth of Nations*, Smith outlined his economic theories concerning government's role in a prosperous economy. Essentially, Smith advocated strict laissez-faire economics, or in other words, an extremely limited role for government. Instead of government regulation, Smith argued, the people are best served by the laws which govern free markets. Price and availability of products should be determined by the law of supply and demand. If a business overcharges consumers or does not provide the quality of product that they desire, another business will come along and provide a better or less expensive product, or both. In addition, business owners and employees will be motivated to work hard if they are able to financially gain from their endeavors. Therefore, private ownership, the law of supply and demand, and free competition are essential elements of Smith's theory. Nations that have followed his advice have generally become prosperous. Although certain products and services are regulated or controlled by many nations that are generally capitalist (often in the interest of public safety), virtually every nation has incorporated some of Smith's theories into their economic systems. Even Communist nations such as China and Vietnam have introduced elements of free-market capitalism to spur economic growth.

Napoleon Bonaparte

After the French Revolution unseated the monarchy, a new form of government known as The Directory attempted to establish order in the new French republic. The Directory was overrun by a powerful general, Napoleon, who declared himself Emperor of France and set out to conquer Europe in the name of the French Revolution, even though he himself was a dictator who did not practice what was preached by the revolutionaries. Nevertheless, the ideas of the French Revolution were carried to most of the people of Europe by way of the Napoleonic Wars. These ideas included constitutional government, rule of law, abolition of the feudal system, and (perhaps most importantly) nationalism. These ideas influenced the development of stable democracies in much of Western Europe long after Napoleon was defeated. Although he was a dictator, Napoleon's civil code and educational reforms were copied in much of Europe as ways of maintaining order while increasing opportunities.

Joseph Stalin

Stalin became dictator of the Soviet Union after Lenin's death in 1924. He imposed his will ruthlessly. Those who opposed him often were killed. After collectivizing agriculture, Stalin built up the nation's heavy industry under his Five Year Plans. The Soviet people went without many of the consumer products that the rest of the industrial world was enjoying while the Soviet Union built up its military and industry. Nevertheless, the build-up came just in time to allow the Soviet Union to prevent occupation by Germany in World War II. Under Stalin's leadership, the Soviet Union emerged from World War II one of the world's two superpowers. The long-range result of Soviet industrial and military strength was the pursuit of the Cold War with the United States. Without Stalin's leadership, the Soviet Union would not have been capable of counterbalancing the power of the United States. For decades after Stalin's death in 1953, the Soviet Union built on his industrial and military programs, attempting to expand communism in virtually every direction. Although the Soviet Union collapsed in the early 1990s, Stalin's Soviet Union impacted the course of history in virtually every region of the globe.

Ho Chi Minh

Ho Chi Minh was the founder of the Socialist Republic of Vietnam. He and his communist followers drove Japan from Vietnam occupation and then prevented the French from reoccupying the nation after World War II. An accord signed in Geneva in 1954 divided the nation in two. The communists, under the leadership of Ho Chi Minh, gained control of the land north of the 17th parallel while Ngo Dihn Diem became the president of the democratic south. Under its new constitution, North Vietnam supported reunification of Vietnam as a communist state. Ho Chi Minh supported communist guerrillas in the South, and soon war broke out. France and the United States came to the aid of South Vietnam, but Ho Chi Minh prevented them from securing a victory. A peace agreement eventually led to the reunification of Vietnam as a communist state. The long-range impact was significant for the region, the world and the United States. The world witnessed the defeat of a superpower by a small but determined nation. Communism took a major step forward in the region, but in the decades since, has been discredited in much of the world. For the United States, the defeat affected foreign policy for decades. Even as late as the Persian Gulf War in the 1990's, the American public remained fearful of involving itself in another Vietnam. Therefore, the policies of Ho Chi Minh truly had a global impact.

Anwar el Sadat

Anwar el Sadat was an Egyptian nationalist who served as Vice President under Nasser, who himself asserted Egypt as a major power in the region by nationalizing the Suez Canal and taking an aggressive stand against Israel. When Sadat became president in 1970, he continued many of the policies of Nasser. In 1973, for example, he launched a surprise attack on the Israeli forces in the Sinai, who had occupied the region since the 1967 Six-Day War. Nevertheless, as it became clear that Israel was more than capable of holding its own ground, Sadat began to reform his foreign policy. Most significantly, he agreed to attend peace talks with Israeli Prime Minister Menachem Begin at the invitation of U.S. President Carter. The result stunned the Islamic community, as well as the rest of the world. Sadat signed a peace treaty with Israel, opened the Suez Canal to Israeli shipping, monitored the withdrawal of Israeli troops from the Sinai and recognized Israel as a Jewish homeland. The long-term impact has been crucial to the relative stability of the region. The two nations have not experienced any significant conflict since, and the peace agreement served as an example for Jordan, which signed a peace agreement with Israel the following year, and other Muslim nations, which have since attempted to improve their relations with Israel. Still, Sadat paid the price for his decision. He was assassinated by Muslim fundamentalists because of his foreign and economic policies. The region, however, made an important step toward peace under his leadership.

7. ADVICE BASED ON DOMESTIC POLICIES OF EXISTING NATIONS

Japan—Education

Japan is one of the few nations that has valued education throughout the course of its entire history. To be sure, for most of Japan's history, formal education was available only to the upper class, but knowledge and wisdom have traditionally been highly respected, even by those who couldn't obtain them. It's no surprise, then, that modern Japan also places great value on education, and now, public education is much more available. Over 99 percent of the adult population is literate, and a significant majority of students remain in school for at least twelve years. Academic requirements and examinations are difficult and are led by strict, well-qualified teachers. Perhaps even more significantly, the family culture of Japan supports education. Parents typically monitor their children's progress carefully, helping them with their homework and insisting that they respect their teachers and complete all of their duties. An increasing problem, however, is that many students experience high levels of stress as they feel pressure from teachers, parents, and the general society to constantly perform well. In addition, because Japanese society does not offer a variety of different types of educational programs, students who are more creative or who do not learn according to the norm often fall through the cracks and infuriate their parents and teachers.

A newly independent nation would be well served by adopting many of the education policies of Japan. However, it should be noted that the government cannot necessarily create a successful educational system if the culture of the nation does not support it. Strong education systems result not only from government policy, but also from the skills of excellent teachers and the commitment of students and their families.

China—Economic Reform

Under the leadership of Deng Xiaoping, China's economy has been transformed from a strict communist command economy to one that includes elements of free-market capitalism. The changes were made primarily for two reasons. First, under the command system, foreign investment was extremely limited. Thus, the nation lacked investment capital needed to spur the economy. Second, the command economy lacked incentives for people to work hard and to develop new products and services. To correct these problems, Deng Xiaoping's government entered into joint ventures with foreign companies, in which the profits and business decisions are shared by both. In addition, Deng allowed for limited business and property ownership to stimulate hard work and innovation. The reforms have been wildly successful. China's economy is expanding faster than most of the economies of the world, and reforms continue to be introduced slowly, which gives the economy time to adjust to the changes.

Like China, a new nation should consider implementing economic reform in stages, especially if the previous economy in the region was a command economy. However, because China has not implemented social and political reform to match its economic reform, the new nation should be careful when following China's lead.

Israel—Rights of Women

Israel's constitution has guaranteed equal rights for women since the nation was founded in 1948. Women enjoy equal opportunities with regard to education, property ownership, employment, and political power. In fact, Israel elected a woman, Golda Meir, as Prime Minister in 1969. Women also must serve in the military, though not in the same capacities as their male counterparts, who are sent into combat. Daughters are encouraged to pursue careers in the professions and academia, just as sons are. And while many traditional families separate the roles of men and women to some degree, these roles are not a matter of public policy.

A new nation should consider structuring its approach to equal rights and opportunity on the Israeli model. As the new nation develops economically, politically, and culturally, it will benefit greatly if all of its citizens can make a contribution to that development.

United Kingdom—Health Care

The United Kingdom has been extremely successful in providing access to health care for all of its citizens. The system is not free to British citizens, of course, because they have to pay taxes which, in turn, are used to fund the enormous health budget of the government. However, no cost is incurred by individuals when they visit a doctor or hospital, except to the extent that they have to pay for individual prescriptions. As a result, the health of the overall population in Britain has improved since 1948, when the current system of socialized medicine was enacted by the government. Nevertheless, the quality of the care and the efficiency of its administration often have been brought into question, especially when compared to the quality of care in developed countries that do not have a system of social- ized medicine, such as the United States.

A new nation may want to consider using the British model as it develops its health policy, but it should be aware of the drain that such a policy causes on the national budget. If it intends to pursue socialized health care, it should also make sure that it has the resources to build an appropriate number of medical facilities, staff them with well-qualified doctors and support personnel, and fill them with sufficient medical equipment. If it cannot, the nation will not be able to meet its commitments under a system of socialized health care.

Brazil—Land Use

At first glance, the use of land in Brazil seems to make sense. The bulk of the population is concentrated in the south-central region along the coast in large cities. This region also has good farm land, which is used precisely for that purpose. In the north and western part of the nation, the Amazon basin dominates the landscape. Its tropical rain forests support incredibly diverse species of plants and animals. This area has traditionally been sparsely populated, mostly by traditional tribes. Nevertheless it is this region of the nation where land use has become controversial. The problem is that the Brazilian government is allowing the rain forests to be cut down at a rate that many claim is alarming. Mostly the land is being cleared by logging companies, but as the government has expanded the Trans-Amazon highway, it is becoming increasingly populated and industrialized as well. The destruction of the rain forest may have a significant global impact because it could upset the balance of carbon dioxide and oxygen in the Earth's atmosphere, potentially leading to global warming. In 1989, the government unveiled a comprehensive environmental program to limit the destruction of the rain forest. In addition, the nation hosted the 1992 Earth Summit to improve its public image as an environmentally conscious nation. Despite these efforts, the rain forest continues to be chopped down.

When developing its land use policies, a new nation should consider adopting stricter guidelines than those adopted by Brazil. It should consider the impact of its land use decisions on the regional and global environment. If disruption to the natural terrain is allowed, as some inevitably will be, the new nation should consider using methods that will allow the natural environment to absorb the shock of change (slashing-and-burning, for example, should be avoided). Land use policy can, and should, balance economic growth with environmental responsibility.

India—Population Policy

India is the world's second largest nation, and is quickly gaining ground on the world's largest, China. Perhaps the main reason India has a faster rate of growth than China is that the Chinese government has adopted stricter population control measures. India encourages parents to limit the size of their families through public announcements and government-run clinics that distribute free birth control devices. The government has not passed any population control legislation, however, beyond making funds available for voluntary family planning. Public support for population control is simply too sporadic. Most Indians cling to their traditional way of life, which stresses the importance of large families. Nevertheless, the Indian government is becoming increasingly concerned with the population growth rate.

A new nation would need to evaluate the social culture within its boundaries and determine whether large families are promoted. If they are, the government could adopt India's policy of voluntary birth control, but if the traditions of the culture will resist voluntary measures, the new nation might want to either adopt stricter measures, or else find ways for the economy and environment to shoulder an ever-increasing population.

EXAMINATION
JANUARY 1997

Part I (55 credits): Answer all 48 questions in this part.

Directions (1–48): For each statement or question, write on the separate answer sheet the *number* of the word or expression that, of those given, best completes the statement or answers the question.

---

1 Which statement is an opinion?

  1 Russian athletes are successful because their nation has a superior culture.

  2 The gross domestic product (GDP) of Japan is greater than that of Thailand.

  3 China and India are the two most populous nations in the world.

  4 The majority of people in the Republic of South Africa are black.

2 Which conclusion can be drawn from a study of the early civilizations of Axum, Kush, Mali, and Songhai?

  1 These African societies flourished at the same time.

  2 Farming was more extensive in the Nile River Valley than it was in the Fertile Crescent.

  3 The Neolithic Revolution first occurred in Africa.

  4 These societies had a long and rich history before their first contact with Europeans.

3 "Today you won't find a single African head of state who stands on a podium and declares: 'I am a Marxist.' Instead all the talk is about ... currency, private enterprise, and getting hold of capital."

— Tei Mante of Ghana

Which statement about the economies of African nations is best supported by the information in this quotation?

1 African nations remain heavily dependent on China and North Korea for trade, capital, and food.
2 African nations are more concerned with obtaining investment capital than with discussing political philosophies.
3 African nations realize they must cooperate with each other to improve their economies.
4 The failure of capitalism in Africa has helped the communists grow in strength.

Base your answer to question 4 on the cartoon below and on your knowledge of social studies.

4 What is the main idea of this 1994 cartoon?

  1 White South Africans can no longer vote in their own country.
  2 People who fail to vote in South Africa's elections may be arrested.
  3 Free elections are the key to true democracy in South Africa.
  4 Blacks can control elections in South Africa by casting multiple votes.

5 Many African nations changed their names after gaining independence. The Gold Coast became Ghana, Rhodesia became Zimbabwe, and the Belgian Congo became Zaire. These changes most closely reflect the idea of

1 nationalism 3 mercantilism
2 pan-Africanism 4 capitalism

6 In India, the people have resisted changing their attitudes toward the caste system because

1 national Muslim leaders have supported the caste system
2 the government is unwilling to end the caste system
3 continued religious conflict prevents changes in the caste system
4 the Hindu beliefs of karma and dharma reinforce the caste system

7 One reason India gained its independence from Great Britain in 1947 was that

1 Great Britain was defeated in World War II
2 the Treaty of Versailles required Great Britain to give up its colonies
3 Great Britain did not have the resources to maintain an empire after World War II
4 India had supported the Axis Powers during World War II

8 One result of British colonialism in India was that India

1 adopted a parliamentary system of government
2 developed religious unity
3 supported Western foreign policies in the United Nations
4 created programs to increase its population

9 The Buddhist religion teaches that salvation is earned by

1 following the Ten Commandments
2 worshiping Allah as the one true god
3 learning to give up selfish desire
4 being baptized and confirmed

10 In 1991, Pakistan amended its constitution and made the Koran the basis of all its laws. Which group was responsible for this action?

1 Kashmir separatists
2 Palestine Liberation Organization (PLO)
3 Buddhist monks
4 Islamic fundamentalists

11 One important similarity between Indira Gandhi of India and Benazir Bhutto of Pakistan is that both

1 are Hindu leaders of Islamic nations
2 became important national leaders in nations in which women have not traditionally had equal opportunities
3 came into power as a result of the breakup of the Soviet Union
4 became leaders of the Asian bloc of nations at the United Nations

12 Confucianism in traditional China served to

1 maintain social order
2 create ethnic unrest
3 emphasize material wealth
4 support democratic government

13 During the 1840's, China signed "unequal treaties" with Western nations mainly because

1 China had won the Opium War
2 Western nations had superior military technology
3 leaders in China favored expansion
4 China had requested economic assistance from the West

14 Sun Yat-sen's "Three Principles of the People" (1911) and the demonstrations in Tiananmen Square (1989) were similar in that they both demanded that the Chinese Government

1 achieve global interdependence
2 restore dynastic rule
3 introduce democratic reforms
4 end foreign influences in China

15 Deng Xiaoping's economic reforms in China differ from the previous economic policies of Mao Zedong in that Deng's reforms

1 discourage private ownership of businesses
2 promote further collectivization
3 include elements of capitalism
4 decrease trade with the United States

16 A major effect of geography on Japan is that the

    1 export of oil has helped Japan maintain a favorable balance of trade

    2 fertile plains have enabled Japan to keep food prices low

    3 mountains have prevented invasions by foreign nations

    4 scarcity of natural resources has forced Japan to obtain raw materials from other nations

17 An immediate result of Commodore Matthew Perry's visit to Japan in 1853 was

    1 an alliance between Japan and Russia

    2 the development of trade between Japan and the West

    3 a war between Japan and the United States

    4 the continued isolation of Japan

Base your answer to question 18 on the cartoon below and on your knowledge of social studies.

Bruce Beattie
Daytona Beach News-Journal
Copley News Service

18 What is the main idea of the cartoon?

1 By 2000, American-grown rice will most likely become the largest export from the United States to Japan.

2 Japanese farmers have lost their influence in Japanese politics.

3 The Japanese Government continues to protect its domestic industry and products.

4 American technology has finally been introduced into Japanese factories.

19 Which factor was most important in the development of regionalism in Latin America?

   1 geographic conditions that limited contact between people
   2 presence of different religious groups
   3 Dutch policies of colonization
   4 rapid growth of many different political parties

20 "I will never allow my hands to be idle nor my soul to rest until I have broken the chains laid upon us by Spain."

This statement was most likely made by

   1 a Latin American nationalist
   2 a Portuguese explorer
   3 a Roman Catholic bishop
   4 a Spanish conquistador

Base your answer to question 21 on the diagram below and on our knowledge of social studies.

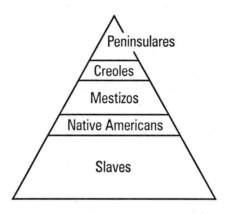

21 Which characteristic of colonial Latin American society is best illustrated in this diagram?

1 social mobility   3 interdependence
2 rigid class system   4 cultural diffusion

22 The Native American population of Mexico in 1492 has been estimated at 25 million; the population in 1608 has been estimated at 1.7 million. This decrease in population was mainly a result of

1 crop failures brought on by poor weather conditions
2 emigration of Native Americans to Europe and Africa
3 wars between various native groups
4 diseases introduced by the Spanish

23 One reason for the development of an early civilization in the Tigris-Euphrates river valleys was that

1 the location protected the people from land invasion
2 periodic flooding left rich soil, which was ideal for farming
3 these rivers provided a direct trade route between Europe and Asia
4 these rivers flowed into the Mediterranean Sea

24 Which activity is an example of an Islamic practice?

1 a bishop conducting a Mass in a church
2 a muezzin calling the faithful to prayer five times a day
3 a rabbi reading from the Torah
4 a monk meditating and praying in a temple

25 Both the French and the British were interested in controlling Egypt in the mid-19th century because Egypt had

1 control of the spice trade
2 an industrial-based economy
3 vital mineral resources
4 a strategic location

26 One way in which the Middle Eastern leaders Kemal Atatürk, Shah Reza Pahlavi, and Gamal Nasser were similar is that they all

1 tried to achieve Arab unity
2 founded the Organization of Petroleum Exporting Countries (OPEC)
3 attempted to modernize their nations
4 demanded the establishment of Islamic fundamentalism

27 Which statement best describes a change that occurred during both the Renaissance and the Enlightenment?

1 Feudalism became the dominant political system.
2 The use of reason and logic was discouraged.
3 Technology and science were considered unimportant.
4 A new questioning spirit and attitude emerged.

28 "God hath power to create or destroy, make or unmake, at his pleasure; to give life or send death; to judge ... and to be judged [by] none.... And the like power have kings ...."

Which idea is described by this passage?

1 theory of divine right
2 enlightened despotism
3 Social Darwinism
4 constitutional monarchy

29 Throughout the 1800's, an increased need for both raw materials and new markets for manufactured goods led various European nations to pursue policies of

1 imperialism
2 socialism
3 isolationism
4 Communism

30 "The proletarians have nothing to lose but their chains ... Workers of the world, unite!"

This statement was made in response to conditions resulting from the

1 Protestant Reformation
2 Counter-Reformation
3 Commercial Revolution
4 Industrial Revolution

31 Which idea was included in the provisions of the Treaty of Versailles to show the intent of the Allies to punish the Central Powers for their role in World War I?

1 All nations shall maintain open covenants of peace.
2 Freedom of the seas will be maintained.
3 Germany will accept full responsibility for causing the war.
4 Territorial settlements shall be made along clearly recognizable lines of nationality.

Base your answer to question 32 on the cartoon below and on your knowledge of social studies.

WONDER HOW LONG THE HONEYMOON WILL LAST?

Culver Pictures

32 Why were the leaders of Western Europe surprised by the event addressed in this cartoon?

1 The Soviet Union and Nazi Germany were both democratic regimes.
2 The ideologies of these two nations were at opposite ends of the political spectrum.
3 The Soviet Union had a long history of close relations with Great Britain.
4 Since 1935, the official government policy of the Soviet Union had supported isolationism.

33 Fascism in Europe during the 1920's and 1930's is best described as a

1 demonstration of laissez-faire capitalism that promoted free enterprise
2 form of totalitarianism that glorified the state above the individual
3 type of economic system that stressed a classless society
4 set of humanist ideas that emphasized the dignity and worth of the individual

34 Which geographic factor has most strongly influenced Russia's foreign policies and economic development?

1 lack of natural resources
2 vast desert regions
3 limited access to warm-water ports
4 extensive mountain ranges

35 Under Joseph Stalin, life in the Soviet Union was characterized by

1 an abundance of consumer goods
2 political instability and numerous civil wars
3 support for small family-run farms
4 the use of censorship and the secret police

36 In both the former Yugoslavia and the former Soviet Union, the desire for self-determination is resulting in increased

1 collectivization
2 ethnic conflict
3 economic equality
4 educational opportunities

37 One reason for the collapse of the Communist economic system in Eastern Europe during the early 1990's was that this system

1 lacked adequate incentives to maintain high productivity
2 used the principles of mercantilism
3 encouraged laissez-faire practices and policies
4 relied on the outdated law of supply and demand

38 In developing countries, the use of wood, charcoal, and dung as major sources of energy has created an increase in

1 economic dependence on industrialized nations
2 sales and profits for international oil corporations
3 deforestation and other environmental problems
4 nuclear waste products

39 Increased educational opportunities, higher levels of air pollution, and the loss of traditional beliefs are changes that are associated with

1 urbanization   3 cultural diffusion
2 nationalism   4 colonialism

40 Traditional animistic beliefs in Africa, Asia, and Latin America are based on

1 a desire for wealth
2 a written tradition
3 an appreciation for the forces of nature
4 a willingness to accept Christianity

41 The Great Leap Forward in China and the five-year plans in the Soviet Union were attempts to increase

1 private capital investment
2 religious tolerance
3 individual ownership of land
4 industrial productivity

42 The accusations of witchcraft in 17th-century England and the practice of foot-binding in 19th-century China are examples of the

1 discrimination against women in various cultures
2 negative aspects of a matriarchal society
3 gradual improvement of women's rights around the world
4 respect given to mothers in traditional cultures

43 During the 18th and 19th centuries, increased contact between Europe and the continents of Africa, Asia, and South America resulted in

1 closer cultural cooperation between Europe and these continents
2 the exploitation of the labor and resources of these continents
3 a return to the political and economic systems of feudal Europe
4 preservation of the rights of the indigenous peoples

44 One reason for both the French Revolution (1789) and the Cuban Revolution (1959) was that

1 people often rebel when they are governed by a foreign power
2 the monarchs did not meet the needs of culturally diverse populations
3 the writings of Karl Marx encouraged workers and the industrialists to unite
4 existing governments failed to address the major economic differences between social classes

45 The Tamils in Sri Lanka, the Sikhs in India, and the Zulus in South Africa have all attempted to

1 establish colonies in Asia
2 practice passive resistance
3 achieve political separatism
4 encourage mercantilism

46 One similarity between the Sepoys in India, the Boxers in China, and the Mau Mau in Kenya is that these groups

1 tried to drive Europeans out of their countries
2 depended on Western support for their success
3 adopted Marxist economic and political principles
4 sought independence through nonviolence

Base your answers to questions 47 and 48 on the chart below and on your knowledge of social studies.

Nations	Birthrate (per 1,000 females)	Infant Mortality Rate (per 1,000 births)
Uganda	51	104
Somalia	50	122
Angola	47	137
Cambodia	46	112
Ethiopia	46	110
Pakistan	40	109
Canada	14	6.8
France	13	6.7
Denmark	13	6.6
Italy	10	8.3
Germany	10	5.9
Japan	10	4.4

Source: Information Please Almanac, 1995 (est. mid-1994)

47 Which is a valid generalization based on the information in the chart?

1 In developing nations, the infant mortality rate decreases as the birthrate increases.
2 Industrialized nations have lower birthrates and infant mortality rates than developing nations do.
3 Decreasing the infant mortality rate will limit population growth in developing nations.
4 Industrialized nations have higher population densities than developing nations do.

48 According to the chart, the lowest birthrates are mostly found in

1 Western Europe   3 North America
2 Southeast Asia   4 Africa

Answers to the following questions are to be written on paper provided by the school.

Students Please Note:

In developing your answers to Part II, be sure to

(1) include specific factual information and evidence whenever possible

(2) keep to the questions asked; do not go off on tangents

(3) avoid overgeneralizations or sweeping statements without sufficient proof; do not overstate your case

(4) keep these general definitions in mind:

    (a) <u>discuss</u> means "to make observations about something using facts, reasoning, and argument; to present in some detail"

    (b) <u>describe</u> means "to illustrate something in words or tell about it"

    (c) <u>show</u> means "to point out; to set forth clearly a position or idea by stating it and giving data which support it"

    (d) <u>explain</u> means "to make plain or understandable; to give reasons for or causes of; to show the logical development or relationships of"

Part II

ANSWER THREE QUESTIONS FROM THIS PART. [45]

1 The economic characteristics of a culture are often influenced by the geography of the region. Several economic characteristics are paired with a specific world region in the list below.

Economic Characteristics — Regions

Choice and use of building material — Middle East
Dependence on staple grains — South Asia
Industrialization — Europe
Intensive farming — East Asia
Nomadic herding — Africa
Single-crop economy — Latin America

Choose *three* economic characteristics from the list and for *each* one chosen:

- Identify a specific nation or civilization in the region with which it is paired
- Explain how the geography of that specific nation or civilization influenced the economic characteristic found in that region
- Describe how the economic characteristic influenced the economic development of that nation or civilization [5,5,5]

2 Organizations are often formed to deal with certain situations.

Organizations

Amnesty International
European Union (EU)
Greenpeace
North Atlantic Treaty Organization (NATO)
Organization of Petroleum Exporting Countries (OPEC)
Palestine Liberation Organization (PLO)
United Nations

Choose *three* organizations from the list and for *each* one chosen:

- Explain the reasons for the formation of the organization
- Identify *one* action taken by the organization
- Discuss the effectiveness of the organization in this action [5,5,5]

3 Powerful political, religious, and economic forces often caused groups of people to move.

Groups of People

Crusaders (1096–1204)
Africans (1500's–1800's)
Jews (1930's–1940's)
Hindus and Muslims in South Asia (1947)
Chinese (1949)
Peasants in Latin America (1980's–1990's)

Choose *three* groups of people from the list and for *each* one chosen:

- Describe a political, religious, *or* economic reason that caused this group of people to move
- Explain the impact of this group's movement on other people, other areas, *or* later events {5,5,5}

4 The values and philosophy of a civilization are often reflected in its art and architecture.

Art/Architecture

Gothic cathedrals   Palace at Versailles
Tea ceremony (*Cha-no-yu*) Oral literature of Africa
Roman roads   Orthodox icons
Great Mosque of Mecca   Maya calendar

Choose *three* forms of art or architecture from the list and for *each* one chosen:

- Describe the purpose and use of the art form
- Explain how the art form reflected the values or philosophy of the civilization [5,5,5]

5 The family is the building block of all cultures. In recent years, the traditional family structure in many areas has been changing.

Areas

India   Latin America
China   Middle East
Japan   Russia
Sub-Saharan Africa

Choose *one* area from the list and for that area:

- Describe the structure of a traditional family

- Discuss the recent changes that are occurring in the traditional family structure in that specific area
- Explain the reason for these changes   [15]

6 Events have shaped history and greatly influenced the lives of many people.

Events

Moors conquer Spain (early 700's)
Aztecs lose control of capital, Tenochtitlán (1520)
Glorious Revolution occurs (1688)
Archduke Franz Ferdinand is assassinated (1914)
Berlin Wall is taken down (1989)
Iraq invades Kuwait (1990)

Choose *three* events from the list and for *each* one chosen:

- Describe the circumstances that led to the event
- Discuss an immediate impact of this event
- Discuss a long-range impact of this event   [5,5,5]

7 You have just been appointed to a committee to gather advice on the best types of leadership and governing styles. You will be investigating individuals with important opinions and experience on these subjects.

Individuals

Ayatollah Khomeini   John Locke
Catherine the Great   Niccolò Machiavelli
V.I. Lenin   Nelson Mandela

a Choose *three* individuals from the list and for *each* individual chosen, discuss the advice you would expect this individual to give on governing styles and leadership. [4,4,4]

b For *one* of the individuals chosen in part *a*, choose a modern national or international crisis and explain how the governing style and leadership of this individual could be applied in the resolution of this crisis. [3]

ANSWER KEY
JANUARY 1997—PART I

1	1	25	4
2	4	26	3
3	2	27	4
4	3	28	1
5	1	29	1
6	4	30	4
7	3	31	3
8	1	32	2
9	3	33	2
10	4	34	3
11	2	35	4
12	4	36	2
13	2	37	1
14	3	38	3
15	3	39	1
16	4	40	3
17	2	41	4
18	3	42	1
19	1	43	2
20	1	44	4
21	2	45	3
22	4	46	1
23	2	47	2
24	2	48	1

ANSWERS AND EXPLANATIONS
JANUARY 1997—PART I

1 An opinion is something that can be disagreed with. It is a personal conclusion that may be based on an observation or a set of facts. A fact, on the other hand, can be proven.

   1 **This is an opinion. In fact, there are several opinions offered in this statement. First, people often have different criteria for defining success, so here is one clue. In addition, the conclusions that Russian culture is superior, and that this superiority is due to the success of its athletes are also opinions. Neither supposition can be proven.**

   2 This is a fact. It can be proven. The gross national product has a definition that everybody agrees on. All we have to do is measure the GNP of the two nations and then determine which is greater. The people who thought Thailand's GNP was greater would then be proven wrong.

   3 This is a fact. It can be proven. We can count the number of people in every single country on earth. It might take a while, but it can be done. Then all we have to do is figure out which two nations have the greatest number of people. It turns out that they're China and India.

   4 This is a fact. It can be proven. We can count the number of black people. We can count the number of people who are not black. We can compare the two numbers and determine which number is larger.

2 First, eliminate answer choices that just aren't true. If you don't know very much about these civilizations, choose the answer choice that is hardest to argue with. Think of the reason that the test writers would have included the question on the exam. By the way, there's a really nice map of these kingdoms on the June 1996 exam (question number 6).

   1 Actually these cultures did *not* flourish at the same time. Besides, why would this be the point of a Global Studies Exam question? Lots of things flourish at the same time. That doesn't tell us much about the world unless we connect that idea to something else.

   2 Farming was actually more extensive in the Fertile Crescent, largely because the Fertile Crescent constitutes a much larger area of arable land, whereas farming on the Nile occurred in a very

narrow band along the river. Nevertheless, you should eliminate this answer choice because none of these civilizations was located in the Fertile Crescent in the first place (the Fertile Crescent is in the Middle East, extending out from the Tigris and Euphrates River valley in a semi-circle to the Mediterranean). Instead, all were located in Africa, with only the Kush along the Nile River. Therefore, just by an examination of these four cultures, we wouldn't be able to compare the Nile river valley to the Fertile Crescent.

3 No. It is believed that the Neolithic Revolution first occurred in the Fertile Crescent. In any case, it occurred long before the time of any of these civilizations.

4 **This is the best answer choice for a variety of reasons. First, by definition, *every* civilization has or has had a long and rich history or else it would not have earned the label "civilization." Second, there is no way that the test writers are going to suggest that civilizations in non-European parts of the world were not rich until the Europeans visited them! Third, this answer choice uses nice, general, hard-to-argue-with language. Fourth, the other three answer choices are just wrong. Need any more reasons?**

3 You should understand after you read the quote that no African head of state talks about Marxism (communism). Of greater importance are money, things that make money, and how to get a hold of money. What can we conclude from this? Look for an answer choice that basically restates what the quote says.

1 China and North Korea are communist. This answer choice doesn't make sense. Plus, China and North Korea are never mentioned in the quote at all.

2 **This is the best answer of the lot. Since all of the talk is about money, that doesn't leave much room for a discussion about politics. Investment capital, by the way, *is* money.**

3 Nothing in the quote indicates cooperation or a lack of cooperation. The quote mentions the stuff that African heads of state are interested in getting, but it doesn't mention how they are going about getting it.

4 Capitalism has not failed in Africa. If it had, why would all the heads of state be talking about private enterprise and getting hold of capital? Plus, communists have not grown in strength, which you should know since the quote tells us that no head of state says "I am a Marxist."

4 You don't even need to look at the cartoon to answer this question. You should be able to answer it just based on your knowledge of South Africa, or even based on your best guess of what makes the most sense. But let's look at the cartoon anyway. It shows a black hand that is breaking free of the chains and casting a vote in a South African election. What can we conclude from this?

1 Nothing in the cartoon tells us about white South Africans, so we should immediately eliminate this answer. You should also realize that this answer choice not only is not true, but doesn't make much sense. Just because one group of people gains rights, doesn't mean that other groups lose rights. The total number of people who have rights in the world can continue to increase.

2 This person's chains aren't falling off because he's voting; he's voting because his chains are falling off him. Plus, is this answer choice consistent with anything you know about the world? No. No society arrests people who don't vote. If that happened in the United States, over half of our population would be in jail!

3 This is the best answer. The chains falling off the arm is representative of the word "free." It makes sense that free elections are the key to "true" democracy, because if the elections aren't free, then a democracy doesn't truly exist.

4 The black person in the cartoon is only casting one vote, so this answer choice has nothing to do with the cartoon. You should also know that this statement is simply untrue.

5 The key phase in this question is "gaining independence." The question gives you several examples, but you don't even need them. If you don't know the words in the answer choices, you need to, so look them up now in the glossary. Which answer choice reflects the desire to change the name of your country after you've won independence?

1 Nationalism is a motivating force behind an independence movement. In these situations, the native people wanted to reassert their own culture and wipe away the remnants of colonization. Changing the names from British names to African names was a symbolic way of reclaiming their African heritage.

2 The name changes were not the result of Pan-Africanism. The name changes occurred independently by each nation.

3 The independence movements wiped the policy of mercantilism from the face of Africa. Mercantilism is closely associated with colonialism.

4 The name changes have nothing to do with economics, or with an economic philosophy, whether it be capitalism or something else.

6　You should definitely learn about the caste system if you haven't already. It shows up on the test a lot. If you don't know anything about it, or only know a little bit about it, you can still eliminate an answer choice or two.

1　The caste system is based on Hinduism, not on Islam. Plus, Muslims are a small minority in India who do not support the caste system.

2　The government of India has officially outlawed the caste system, but it persists nevertheless. Even if you didn't know that the government has outlawed the caste system, this answer choice doesn't make much sense because a government policy to not end something probably wouldn't have a huge impact on people opposed to changing their attitudes about that something.

3　Religious conflict hasn't prevented changes in the caste system. Conflict often causes change, but usually doesn't prevent it. Plus, there isn't any religious conflict over the caste system within the Hindu religion. There is only political and social conflict.

4　The caste system stems from the beliefs of the Hindu religion. The Indian government outlawed the caste system, but not the Hindu religion. Many of the Hindus, who comprise the vast majority of Indians, don't want to give up something that is part of their religion and a part of their tradition. So, many people haven't changed their attitudes about the caste system.

7　Even if you can't think of a single reason that India gained its independence, use your knowledge of global studies to eliminate answer choices that you know are just plain wrong.

1　Great Britain was not defeated in World War II.

2　The Treaty of Versailles did not require Great Britain to give up its colonies. The treaty punished Germany, not Great Britain, because Great Britain was victorious. If it *had* required Great Britain to give up its colonies, then Great Britain would have given up India long before 1947, because the Treaty of Versailles was signed at the end of World War I, not the end of World War II.

3　World War II was very costly to Great Britain and all of Europe. One reason for India's independence, though certainly not the only reason, is that Great Britain simply did not have the resources to withstand an independence movement.

4　India did not support the Axis Powers during World War II. India was under the control of Great Britain. Great Britain may have done a lot of things during World War II, but it didn't fight against itself!

8   Eliminate answer choices that are not true at all. Eliminate answer
    choices that are too extreme. Eliminate answer choices that would not
    logically be caused by British colonialism. Eliminate! Eliminate!
    Eliminate! (Or just know the answer.)

    **1   Yes. India has a parliamentary system of government mainly
        because India became very familiar with that system while
        Britain (which also has a parliamentary system of govern-
        ment) was running the show in India.**

    2   This answer choice is far too extreme. India does not have religious
        unity. Even after Pakistan was created as a Muslim nation, thereby
        making India mostly a Hindu nation, there was not religious unity
        in India because India officially practices freedom of religion (over
        80 percent are Hindu, but a full 10 percent are Muslim). Finally,
        eliminate this answer choice because even if the *entire* nation of
        India were united as a Hindu nation, it wouldn't be due to British
        imperialism, because the British are mostly Christian.

    3   India has not supported Western foreign policies in the United
        Nations. Nor has it supported many other nations' foreign policies.
        Ever since its independence, India has been rather isolationist,
        attempting to respect all other nations while hoping other nations
        stay out of its affairs.

    4   India hasn't created programs to increase its population. Instead, its
        population is increasing due to the traditional beliefs and customs of
        many of its people. Even if it had created programs to increase
        population, that probably wouldn't be due to the influence of
        Britain, whose own population has grown at a slow rate this century.

9   If you know about Buddhism, which you should, then you can simply
    pick the correct answer choice. If you don't, then you should eliminate
    answer choices that relate to religions that you *do* know about since
    there probably isn't going to be an overlap between religions on this
    issue (or else they might as well be the same religion).

    1   Salvation earned by following the Ten Commandments is central to
        Judaism. The Ten Commandments are also important to Chris-
        tians, but they do not believe that salvation is earned through
        practicing them.

    2   Worshipping Allah as the one true god is central to Islam.

    **3   Buddhists believe that complete peace can be reached if one
        frees oneself from the distractions of the physical world and
        focuses on spiritual self-discipline. Salvation is not earned
        through any means other than the commitment to spiritual
        self-discipline.**

4   Baptism and confirmation are central to Christianity. According to Christian doctrine, however, baptism and confirmation are not a way of earning salvation, since Christians believe that salvation is granted only through the grace of God.

10   If you know what the Koran is, you're done. If you know the basic history of Pakistan at all, you're done. If you don't know either, you should. Review your global studies materials.

1   Kashmir is located between India and Pakistan and is claimed by both. Kashmir is only partially controlled by Pakistan, and is very small in relation to the entire nation of Pakistan. Therefore, even though Kashmir is predominantly Muslim, Kashmir separatists are not responsible for the amendment to the Pakistani constitution. Plus, Pakistan is already Muslim, so the fact that Kashmir is Muslim also doesn't have much of an impact.

2   The PLO is not involved in Pakistan.

3   Buddhist monks do not believe in the Koran. Nor are they in Pakistan.

4   Islamic fundamentalists not only believe in the Koran, but they believe that the government should function as an Islamic state. Islamic fundamentalists were successful in amending the constitution of Pakistan to reflect their beliefs.

11   If you only know one of these women, you can still answer this question correctly. If you don't know either of these women, you can still guess well. Eliminate answer choices that do not apply to India or Pakistan in general, or that don't sound like important similarities.

1   India is not an Islamic nation, it is a predominantly Hindu nation, so eliminate this answer choice immediately.

2   This is it. Even if you only know one of these women, this is the only answer that works. If you don't know either of these women, this answer still makes a lot of sense, since it describes something that, if true, is important since India and Pakistan are nations in which women have not traditionally had equal opportunities.

3   Neither the policies of India nor of Pakistan were dependent on the policies of the former Soviet Union, nor is their leadership determined by the existence or the breakup of the former Soviet Union. Neither Pakistan nor India is or was a Communist nation, nor were they part of the Soviet Bloc.

4   It doesn't make sense that a question on the Global Studies Regents exam would expect you to know the identity of a leader of a certain bloc of nations at the United Nations. It simply is not an important enough fact. There are too many other important things to ask about, like women overcoming traditional barriers.

12 You need to know about Confucius because he's one of the Regents' favorites. However, even if you don't know very much about him, you can still guess the right answer if you focus on the word "traditional." Look for an answer choice that is true of most traditional societies.

   1 **Traditional societies are definitely interested in maintaining order. Confucius taught about the social obligations that individuals have towards one another. Central to these social obligations was the idea that authority is to be respected and followed at all times, and that in return, authority owes fairness and justice to the citizenry. Therefore, the teachings of Confucius most definitely served to maintain social order.**

   2 No. Confucian philosophy is all about maintaining order and peace, not creating unrest.

   3 Confucian philosophy focuses on individual relationships and responsibilities. It does not emphasize material wealth. Nor do many traditional societies.

   4 Confucius lived in China, a nation that has never been a democracy. Traditional societies are generally not compatible with democracy.

13 If you know the basics of China during the nineteenth century, you should be able to eliminate at least one or two of the incorrect answer choices, even without specific knowledge of the unequal treaties. Also, focus on the word "unequal."

   1 China lost the Opium War. That was the reason China had to sign the unequal treaties.

   2 **This is the best answer. European powers forced their way into Chinese ports and China retaliated. China lost, though, due to the superior military technology of the Europeans. As a result, China signed the unequal treaties which gave Europe spheres of influence where it could sell its goods and obtain raw materials.**

   3 Leaders in China favored isolationism.

   4 No. Again, China favored isolationism.

14 You only need to know about one of these examples in order to answer this question correctly. Eliminate answer choices that don't make sense or that are too extreme.

1 Few governments want to be dependent on other nations. Interdependence is becoming a reality in the world, but nothing about either of these examples demands that the Chinese government become dependent on other nations. Plus, the decisions of one government cannot achieve global interdependence! China can decide what China wants to do, but it does not have the authority to make all nations dependent on one another.

2 Both of these movements were forward-thinking. They attempted to change China, not restore it to past traditions.

3 **This is the best answer. Both Sun Yat-sen and the demonstrators in Tiananmen Square demanded that the government introduce democratic reforms. Sun Yat-sen was successful in instituting change for a while, but the Tiananmen Square demonstrators were met with severe resistance.**

4 This answer choice is not only extreme ("end" as opposed to "limit") but it is completely false. Both Sun Yat-sen and the student demonstrators in China were motivated by the influences of Western culture.

15 You should definitely know about the general economic policies of Mao Zedong because he shows up on the test frequently. Mao Zedong was an ardent communist and led the Cultural Revolution in China. The question tells you that Deng Xiaoping's economic *reforms* differed from the policies of Mao Zedong. Therefore, you need to find the answer choice that *reforms* communism.

1 Communism discourages private ownership. Deng Xiaoping reformed this policy and allowed some private ownership.

2 Collectivization is a communist principle. Deng Xiaoping reformed this policy and allowed some private ownership.

3 **Bingo! Deng Xiaoping included some elements of capitalism in his economic reforms in order to create incentives and to encourage foreign investment. This was a turnaround from the policies of Mao Zedong.**

4 Deng Xiaoping's economic policies actually increased trade with the United States and many other nations. Western nations were pleased with the economic reforms in China. Although China did not change its social and political structure to the satisfaction of the West, Western nations nevertheless began to trade extensively with China. The United States currently has an enormous trade deficit with China.

16 Japan is a mountainous island nation. Think of everything that you know about Japan's policies throughout the years. Eliminate answer choices that are not consistent with the geography of Japan or that are too extreme.

1   Japan has to import oil because it hardly has any. It is a small nation with a large consumer population. Japan has to import most of its energy resources and the raw materials needed for production.

2   Japan is a mountainous nation. It has managed to cultivate what little land is available for cultivation (13 percent of its land), but it does not have extensive plains, nor are its food prices low. Although Japan has an extensive fishing industry, it still must import some of its food.

3   Japan definitely has mountains, but this answer choice is too extreme. Mountains don't stop ships and airplanes from attacking. Japan was devastated by air raids during World War II and by the hydrogen bombs which were dropped by the United States on Hiroshima and Nagasaki.

4   This is the best answer. Japan lacks many of the natural resources needed for its factories and for sources of energy. As a result, Japan began to colonize parts of Asia in the nineteenth and twentieth centuries in order to gain access to the resources it needed, but reversed this policy after it was devastated in World War II. Currently, it imports most of the natural resources it consumes, but it still maintains an overall trade surplus.

17 If you don't know about Commodore Matthew Perry, eliminate answer choices that are inconsistent with your general knowledge of Japan or that are inconsistent with the idea of a foreigner visiting Japan.

1   Japan and Russia have often fought, but they haven't been allies. Also, you might know that Commodore Matthew Perry was from the United States, so an alliance between Japan and Russia wouldn't have resulted from his visit.

2   This is the best answer. Commodore Matthew Perry was sent to Japan from the United States to secure and ratify a trade treaty, which he did. You might also know that Japan reversed its isolationist policies in the nineteenth century, so this answer choice is consistent with that trend.

3   The only time Japan and the United States went to war was during World War II, which was nearly a century after Perry's visit.

4   This answer choice doesn't make much sense. If Japan were isolated, then what was a foreigner doing visiting Japan?

18 First, focus on the word "finally" in the cartoon. This means that previously, Japan was not importing U.S. rice. Then, notice that the people on the assembly line are literally counting grains of rice, which means that they are only importing a very small amount. What do you think is going on here? Make sure that you eliminate answer choices that refer to things that aren't even mentioned in the cartoon.

1 This cartoon doesn't attempt to predict the future. Besides, the guys on the assembly line are counting the rice one grain at a time, so that means there can't be very much rice.

2 Not only is this answer choice too extreme, it doesn't follow from the information in the cartoon. Japanese farmers are not referred to at all in the cartoon, but we know that Japan isn't importing very much rice from the United States. Therefore, it's likely that Japanese farmers still have some influence.

3 **This is the best answer. Even though the heading of the cartoon announces that Japan has finally allowed U.S. rice into the country, the heading is sarcastic, since in reality there really isn't very much rice coming in. The point is that Japan is continuing to protect its own industries and farms. Japan must import some of its food, but it protects the agricultural industries which are strong, including the rice industry and the fishing industry.**

4 This cartoon isn't about the technology in the factory, it's about the food coming in on the conveyer belt. Plus, you should already know that Japanese factories are very technologically advanced due to their own focus on technology.

19 Eliminate answer choices that do not apply to Latin America in the first place. If you're guessing, choose the answer choice that applies to almost any region of the world.

1 **This is the best answer. Latin America is a huge area of land and is geographically extremely diverse. Mountains, rain forests, and distance have isolated groups of people.**

2 Since colonization, Latin America has been overwhelmingly Christian—specifically Catholic. If anything, this has served to bring the people of Latin America together, not keep them apart.

3 The Dutch colonized some islands in the West Indies, but this is only a very small fraction of the land in Latin America. Almost the entire region was colonized by Spain, with the rather large exception of Brazil, which was colonized by Portugal.

4 During the colonial history of Latin America, no political parties existed because the European powers ran the show. Since independence, most nations have had dictatorships or one-party systems. Only recently have many different political parties developed, but this has not affected regionalism.

20 Focus on the words "broken the chains laid upon us by Spain." You want to find a person that would be angry about Spanish control.

1 Latin American nationalists fought against Spanish colonialism and succeeded in winning independence, thereby breaking the chains laid upon them by Spain.

2 Portuguese explorers would not have had chains laid upon them by Spain. They had nothing to do with Spain. That's why they're Portuguese.

3 Spain promoted the expansion of Catholicism into Latin America. Roman Catholic Bishops were not chained by Spain.

4 Spanish conquistadors conquered Latin America for Spain. They were rewarded by Spain, not chained by Spain.

21 You should be able to answer this question correctly if you know a little about colonial Latin America and if you realize that social classes are referred to in the graph. Alternatively, if you know why pyramid diagrams are used but don't know much about colonial Latin America, you can also answer this question correctly. If you know about both, of course, you're jammin'. If you don't know the definitions of the words in the answer choices, look them up in the glossary. All of them are important.

1 Colonial Latin American society did not encourage social mobility. The pyramid diagram is used not to show that people can move up and down the pyramid, but to show that the divisions between groups of people were very definite and secure.

2 This is the best answer. Colonial Latin American society was a rigid class system. The pyramid diagram illustrates this point. The slaves were the most numerous and were also at the bottom of the class system. The Peninsulares were the least numerous and at the top. The lines in between each class of people demonstrate that movement between the classes did not occur.

3 A pyramid diagram does not demonstrate interdependence between groups of people. Colonial Latin American culture was dependent on Spain and Spain was dependent on its colonies for raw materials, but this diagram doesn't illustrate that.

4 This diagram shows groups of people who are clearly separated from one another. While cultural diffusion occurred in Latin America, both from Europe and from Africa, nothing about this diagram or a listing of social classes illustrates that.

22　The native populations of Mexico dropped by over 23 million people between 1492 and 1608. Eliminate answer choices that probably wouldn't account for such a dramatic decrease in the population.

　1　Poor weather conditions sometimes hurt crops prior to 1492 as well as after, and yet the native populations managed to grow to 25 million! If the crop failures were so significant that so many deaths resulted, then the Spanish who were colonizing Latin America would probably have died as well, since they would have needed to eat too.

　2　The natives did not emigrate to Europe and Africa. America was their home.

　3　Native groups mostly stopped fighting with each other after the Spanish arrived because they couldn't fight both each other and Spain.

　4　This is the best answer. The Spanish brought with them diseases from Europe that the Native American population had never been exposed to. Because of the lack of exposure, they hadn't built up an immunity to the disease and were wiped out by the millions.

23　Eliminate answer choices that you know are not true, based on your knowledge of the region. Also, eliminate answer choices that wouldn't affect the development of a civilization, even if they were true. Finally, focus on an answer choice that gives a rational explanation for the development of a civilization.

　1　The location does not protect people from land invasion. (It can be attacked from almost every direction.) Even if it did, however, look for an answer choice that gives an affirmative reason that a civilization would develop in the first place, not an answer choice that merely gives a reason that the civilization would not be attacked once it already had developed.

　2　This is it. The question tells you that you're dealing with river valleys. River valleys sometimes flood, leaving behind rich soil once the river recedes into its banks. This was true of the Tigris-Euphrates river valley as well as the Nile river valley. Both river valleys were home to some of the earliest civilizations precisely for this reason.

　3　These rivers don't provide a direct trade route between Europe and Asia. Also, these civilizations developed early. Transcontinental trading hadn't yet developed. There just weren't very many other civilizations around yet.

　4　These rivers flow in the Persian Gulf. Even if they did flow in the Mediterranean Sea, it wouldn't be a reason for the development of early civilizations along the rivers' banks.

24   Even if you're not sure which answer choice refers to Islam, you should eliminate answer choices that refer to other religions that you might know about, since they probably don't share many of the same practices with Islam. Nevertheless, you need to educate yourself about major world religions, because they show up frequently.

1   Islam doesn't have bishops, but many Christian denominations do. Islam also doesn't use churches, but Christians do.

2   This is it. From their location in the mosques, Muezzins cry out the call to prayer five times a day. The Islamic faithful bow toward Mecca when they hear the call.

3   Islam doesn't have rabbis, but Judaism does. Islam also doesn't follow the teachings of the Torah, but Judaism does.

4   This answer choice probably refers to Buddhism, since Buddhism has both monks and temples. However, the point is that Islam does not have monks, nor does it have temples. Instead of temples, it has mosques.

25   Eliminate answer choices that do not apply to Egypt. If you're left with more than one answer, select the answer choice that best describes why two very powerful nations with plenty of other colonies would be particularly interested in Egypt.

1   Egypt doesn't produce spices. India does, however, and that was a reason for British colonization there.

2   Egypt did not have an industrial-based economy. Besides, Britain and France already had industrial-based economies. They were interested in Egypt because it would give them something that they needed.

3   Egypt does not have vital mineral resources. What resources it does have could be received from Britain's and France's other colonies.

4   Yes! Egypt is located in northeastern Africa and is bounded by the Mediterranean Sea and the Red Sea. It was the ideal location for the building of a canal that would link the two seas. The canal, later built by a French company and known as the Suez Canal, was important because it ended the need for ships to travel around the tip of Africa in their journeys between Europe and Asia. The canal opened up an alternative and much shorter route.

26 If you've never heard of any of these men before, eliminate answer choices that seem too specific to apply to all three men. You want a more general answer choice. If you know one or two of them, you should be able to eliminate at least a few answer choices.

1 Only Gamal Nasser of Egypt tried to achieve Arab unity.

2 None of these men founded OPEC. In fact, Turkey and Egypt aren't even members of OPEC, so if you know that Kemal Ataturk was a leader of Turkey and that Gamal Nasser was a leader of Egypt, you should have eliminated this answer choice immediately.

3 **All three men attempted to modernize their nations. Ataturk founded modern Turkey as a secular modern state and enforced westernization of dress and customs. Shah Pahlavi of Iran attempted to modernize Iran's economy and westernize some of its customs before the Islamic Revolution ousted both him and his ideas. Gamal Nasser of Egypt tried to unify the Arabs against Israel, as well as against the influence of the United States and Europe. Even though he was opposed to Western culture, he tried to modernize his nation's military and economy.**

4 None of these three men were Islamic fundamentalists. Nasser definitely aroused many causes dear to Muslims, but he would probably not be described as a fundamentalist. In any case, the other two men clearly were not fundamentalists.

27 If you're not familiar with the basics of the Renaissance and the Enlightenment, you need to be. Eliminate answer choices that are characteristic of other time periods. Also, consider eliminating answer choices that sound too much alike, especially if you're having difficulty choosing an answer.

1 No. By the time of the Renaissance, feudalism was on the way out. By the time of the Enlightenment, feudalism was dead or almost dead in most of Europe.

2 No. The use of reason and logic was encouraged. During the Renaissance, the use of reason and logic was applied to the sciences and the arts. During the Enlightenment, the use of reason and logic was extended further to the role of governments and of individuals in society.

3 No. Technology and science were considered important. Since both science and technology rely on reason and logic, this answer choice is also too similar to answer choice number two.

4 **This is it. With the Renaissance, Europe emerged from the Middle Ages with a new questioning spirit and attitude. People sought to understand their world rationally and to improve it, rather than simply accept it. During the Enlightenment, people began to question the role of government and sought greater control over their own destinies.**

28 Read this quote carefully. Most of the quote refers to the power of
    God. Then, the last six words suddenly compare the power of God to
    the power of kings. You need to determine which answer choice refers
    to the concept that kings have the powers of God.

    **1 This is the best answer. The theory of divine right holds that
        kings are given their power by God and therefore act as
        God's representative. This theory was challenged during the
        Renaissance and Enlightenment.**

    2 A despot is a leader who rules with unlimited authority. An
       enlightened despot is a leader who rules absolutely, but who makes
       rational decisions that are believed to truly benefit the people. The
       quote does not demonstrate an enlightened view of the world,
       since the person believes that kings have the power to create,
       destroy, give life, or death, all at their discretion.

    3 Social Darwinism is an application of Darwin's theories to the
       social sciences. It suggests that the social classes that happen to be
       at the top are there because they are superior to the lower classes.
       Some people have used this theory to justify a host of atrocities.
       While the quote certainly contends that the king is better than
       everybody else, it does so by claiming the power of the king is given
       by God, not that the king was elevated to his position because he
       was socially superior to everyone else.

    4 There is nothing constitutional about the monarchy described in
       the quote. A constitution limits the power of the king. This quote
       refers to an absolute monarchy and rationalizes it by claiming that
       the king gets his power directly from God.

29 You want an answer choice that describes a way that nations can
    expand, specifically so that they can get their hands on natural
    resources that they lack and have places to sell the stuff that they
    make. If you don't know the definitions of all the words in the answer
    choices, you need to, because they show up frequently.

    **1 This is the best answer. Many European nations established
        colonies in order to gain access to the resources in those
        colonies. They used the resources to make finished products
        in Europe and then turned around and sold the finished
        products back to the colonies. This policy is specifically
        known as mercantilism, which is a word that describes the
        economic reasons for imperialism.**

    2 Socialism does not necessarily involve the establishment of new
       markets or the search for raw materials. It is an economic structure
       that promotes government regulation and ownership of business, as

well as extensive welfare programs, but it can apply to an isolation-ist nation as well as to an imperialist one.

3   Isolationism is the practice of staying out of everyone's business and hoping they'll stay out of yours. It is a refusal to get involved in the world community. Isolationist nations most certainly aren't imperialistic.

4   Communism is similar to socialism economically, but it is also a political philosophy. Basically, it is the practice of establishing a classless society. The people own all the means of production. Imperialist nations may be communist or capitalist, but the ones described in this question were of a capitalist bent.

30   This test is just full of chains falling off! Question number four had chains falling off. Question number twenty referred to breaking the chains of Spain. And now this! This speaker is telling the workers of the world (the proletarians) to lose their chains and unite. You can pretty much bet that if you ever see the word "proletarians" in a quote on the test, it is either Karl Marx or a Marxist speaking. Which answer choice put a lot of people to work in the first place? Which answer choice created the situation where workers were exploited?

1   The Protestant Reformation didn't put people to work. It marked the split of groups of Christians (Protestants) away from the Catholic Church.

2   The Counter-Reformation didn't put people to work. It was the Catholic response to the Protestant Reformation.

3   The Commercial Revolution put a lot of people to work, but it didn't create a situation of widespread exploitation. Instead, the Commer-cial Revolution established monetary units, investment, and banking and pretty much restructured how business was financed. This is the revolution that essentially created white-collar jobs.

4   **This is it. The Industrial Revolution put the masses to work in factories, often under filthy and dangerous working conditions, for extremely long hours at very little pay. This is the revolution that created blue-collar jobs. Karl Marx urged the workers of the world to unite against the exploita-tion of the capitalists who owned the factories. He believed that their lives would only improve if the workers collec-tively owned the means of production.**

31 If you know any of the details of the Treaty of Versailles, you're done. The correct answer should be obvious. If you don't, eliminate answer choices that don't "punish" anyone.

1   How do open covenants of peace "punish" anyone? They don't. That's why you need to find a better answer.

2   Freedom doesn't "punish." Somebody's got to be paying a price.

3   This is it. The Treaty of Versailles made Germany accept full responsibility for World War I. It was downright humiliating for the Germans, who had to give up a lot of territory, pay reparations, and downsize their military. Now that's punishment!

4   No. This isn't it. Many Germans were included within the boundaries of nations other than Germany (especially in Poland, where the lines were drawn to give Poland access to the sea directly over former German lands). The Treaty of Versailles attempted to draw some lines according to nationality, but it fell far short, and all sorts of minority groups were embedded in nations where they just didn't seem to fit.

32 The cartoon depicts Hitler (the guy with the swastikas on his lapel) and Stalin (the guy with the hammer and sickles on his veil). You don't have to know that they are Hitler and Stalin. You do have to know that they represent Nazi Germany and the Soviet Union. The cartoon figuratively shows them getting married (or joining forces), but then the caption questions how long their alliance would last. Eliminate answer choices that either have nothing to do with the cartoon or that you know are historically incorrect.

1   The Soviet Union was communist. Nazi Germany was fascist. Even if you didn't know this, you still can't pick this answer, because their similarities wouldn't explain why Western Europe was surprised.

2   This is it. The Soviet Union was really far to the left (communist). Nazi Germany was really far to the right (fascist). Their temporary alliance surprised Western Europe because the nations were so different. They had cooperated to divide Poland between them. Germany did it because it was planning on expanding in that direction anyway. The Soviet Union agreed in order to appease Hitler and prevent him from attacking further east (plus, they also didn't mind expanding their territory). When Hitler did, in fact, attack the Soviet Union, their short honeymoon was over.

3   The Soviet Union and Great Britain do not have a long history of close relationships. Even during World War II, they were allies

because they had to be. You should eliminate this answer choice even if you didn't know this, because it has nothing to do with cartoon. There is no mention of Great Britain at all.

4 The Soviet Union was not an isolationist nation. Nor does a cartoon that shows a marriage between two countries in any way relate to isolationism, in which case both people would have stayed single.

33 Think of fascist Germany. Or fascist Italy. Or even fascist Japan. If you don't know the definition of fascism, you need to. At the very least, eliminate answer choices that describe political, economic, or social philosophies that you know and that, therefore, describe something other than fascism.

1 Fascism does not allow free enterprise. It does not take a laissez-faire approach to society, but rather a totalitarian approach to society.

2 This is it. Fascists were concerned with only one thing: their own goals and obtaining the power to achieve those goals. Everything else was treated as a means to achieving those goals.

3 This is communism, at least in theory.

4 This is humanism. Fascists were definitely not humanists. Individuals were treated as disposable commodities.

34 You want to find a geographic feature that not only describes Russia, but that would help explain its foreign policy and economic development. You probably know that Russia's foreign policy has traditionally been expansionist. Therefore, think of a geographic feature that would explain Russia's desire to expand.

1 If Russia lacked natural resources, this fact would certainly influence Russia's foreign policy and economic development. But it doesn't. Russia is an enormous piece of land with a variety of natural resources including copper, coal, lead, and forests.

2 Russia has deserts in the southeast, but they are not vast, nor have they significantly affected foreign policy or economic development.

3 This is it. Much of Russia is either land-locked or enclosed by frozen seas on the north. Its economic development has been hindered by this fact. Therefore, its foreign policy has attempted to gain access to warm water ports, especially to the west along the Baltic Sea and to the south along the Black Sea.

4 Russia has extensive mountain ranges in the east. However, these areas are sparsely populated and have not significantly affected the foreign policy or economic development of the nation.

35 You should be aware that the Soviet Union was a one-party communist nation that was extremely centralized and government-controlled. You should also know that under Stalin, the nation's economy was focused on the build-up of heavy industry.

1 No. The Soviet Union has never been a nation that has experienced an abundance of consumer goods. The government owned the means of production and determined how much, as well as what kinds of, goods would be available (a command economy). Since the government was focused on the build-up of heavy industry, it did not provide a surplus of consumer goods.

2 The Soviet Union was remarkably stable under Stalin, most probably because he was tremendously powerful and tremendously feared. He ruled absolutely, so few insurrections occurred. If they did, they were dealt with swiftly and brutally.

3 This is entirely inconsistent with Communism in general, and the Soviet Union in particular. Stalin collectivized the farms, which means that the government took ownership of the farm lands and directed the farm workers.

4 This is the best answer. Stalin's Soviet Union did not tolerate insurrection or alternative ideas. The secret police was used to quiet any insurrections or opinions contrary to those of the government.

36 Eliminate answer choices that are not related to self-determination or that are not related to the former Soviet Union or the former Yugoslavia.

1 The desire for self-determination does not result in collectivization; government policies do. Besides, communism fell apart in Eastern Europe, so it doesn't make sense to say that collectivization is increasing.

2 This is the best answer. Self-determination is often associated with ethnic conflict. In the former Soviet Union and the former Yugoslavia, various ethnic groups want to establish their own nations, and many have succeeded. Their desire for self-determination has brought them into conflict with other ethnic groups who also want their own nations, but who disagree on where the lines should be drawn and on who should be in control.

3 Self-determination is not necessarily related to economic equality. Nor has increased economic equality resulted in the former Yugoslavia and the former Soviet Union.

4   The desire for self-determination has not resulted in an increase in educational opportunities. The priorities of the newly formed nations include political and economic restructuring, so an increase in educational opportunities probably won't occur until after other priorities have been taken care of.

37   Eliminate answer choices that do not describe communism in the first place.

1   This is the best answer. Under communism, private ownership of business, especially major businesses, is almost nonexistent. Therefore, individuals cannot make a profit from their labor. No matter how hard they work, or how much creativity they bring to a job, they will still get paid the same salary. Without financial incentives, many people perform their job functions satisfactorily, but sometimes do not put forth extra effort. Since technologically advanced societies are dependent upon constant innovation and diligence, communist economies fell behind the economies of the Western world which reward individual excellence and competition.

2   Communism did not use the principles of mercantilism. Mercantilism is an economic policy of imperialist nations. Communism spread in Eastern Europe, and the Soviet Union was behind it, but not in the same sense that the Western European powers colonized much of the rest of the world. Besides, mercantilism is economically profitable for the colonizing nation, so even if the Soviet Union were mercantilist, it wouldn't be a reason for the collapse of the communist system.

3   Communist nations do not encourage laissez-faire practices and policies. Capitalist nations do.

4   Communist nations do not rely on any concept of the law of supply and demand, outdated or not. Capitalist nations rely on the law of supply and demand. Plus, the law of supply and demand isn't something that changes over time. It doesn't have an outdated version and then a modern version.

38   Think of the results of using wood, charcoal, and dung as sources of energy. At the very least, it's going to smell. In fact, the consequences are much worse than that. What do you think would increase as a result?

1   No. Developing countries are using wood, charcoal, and dung as sources of energy because they don't want to buy (or can't afford to buy) cleaner sources of energy from industrialized nations.

2   They're not using oil. They're using wood, charcoal, and dung.

3   This is it. The use of wood leads to deforestation (that's how they get the wood!). The use of dung and charcoal, you can imagine, leads to air, water, and soil pollution.

4   They're not using nuclear energy. They're using wood, charcoal, and dung.

39   If you don't know the definitions of the words in the answer choices, look them up now. They show up on the test over and over again.

1   This is the best answer. Cities provide more educational opportunities than rural areas do. They increase air pollution because they often create industrial output, burn fossil fuels, and have a lack of trees and other vegetation that would help absorb the effects of pollution. Finally, urbanization often results in the loss of traditional beliefs as individuals are exposed to new ideas and new lifestyles.

2   None of these three things occurs because of nationalism, although they may occur in nationalist societies as well as in those that are not nationalistic.

3   None of these three things is associated with cultural diffusion. Cultural diffusion is the movement of cultural characteristics from one culture to another. Air pollution moves from one society to another, but not because of cultural diffusion!

4   None of these three things are associated with colonialism. They occur in societies that have colonized, in the colonies themselves, and in nations that have never had colonies.

40   If you don't know anything about animism, look it up in the glossary. You really need to know world religions. If you just can't remember, eliminate answer choices that don't sound like they would be part of a religious belief system.

1   Most religions do not base their religions on a desire for wealth. Certainly, animist religions don't.

2   Most religions began as oral traditions and were later written down. Animism is very much an oral religion.

3   This is the best answer. Animist religions are based on the spirituality of the forces of nature. Followers of these religions believe that all natural objects are alive and contain spirits.

4   Get rid of this answer immediately. If any religion was based on a willingness to accept any other religion, the religion would simply dissolve and join the religions it was so willing to accept!

41 The Soviet Union was a communist nation, so even if you're not sure when the Five-Year Plans occurred, you can be sure they were consistent with communism. The Great Leap Forward occurred in China while it, too, was a strict communist nation. If you don't know this, then focus on the Soviet Union. Eliminate answer choices that don't fit with communist systems.

1 Neither attempted to increase private investment capital. Private investment capital is characteristic of capitalist economies.

2 Neither attempted to increase religious tolerance. Religious practice is not characteristic of communism. Religious tolerance is characteristic of constitutional democracies.

3 Neither attempted to increase individual ownership. Private ownership is characteristic of capitalism.

4 **This is it. The Great Leap Forward and the Five-Year Plans were attempts to increase industrial productivity. The Great Leap Forward resulted in the establishment of huge communes where people worked, but were not as productive as the government had anticipated. The Five-Year Plans were successful in the production of heavy industry, but at the expense of virtually everything else, except the military. Both nations instituted these plans to try to make their economies competitive and less reliant on other nations.**

42 You only need to know about either the accusations of witchcraft in seventeenth-century England or the practice of foot-binding in nineteenth-century China to get this one right.

1 **This is the best answer choice. Both situations describe discrimination against women. In England, accusations of witchcraft often led to ridiculous trials in which it was impossible to prove innocence. In China, foot-binding was a practice in which women were made to bind their feet to keep them small.**

2 China is not a matriarchal society. England has had its share of queens, but in the seventeenth century, it had kings.

3 "Accusations" is definitely is not consistent with a gradual improvement of women's rights around the world.

4 "Accusations" is definitely not consistent with respect, nor is foot-binding.

43　"Increased contact" means colonization. The nations of Europe colonized Africa, Asia, and South America during the eighteenth and nineteenth centuries. You should know at least a little about the colonial practices of the Europeans. If you don't, review them. If you do, start eliminating answer choices.

1　There was no cooperation. Europe swept in and took over.

2　Bingo! The European powers exploited the people and resources of these continents. They took the resources, sent them back to Europe, made products, and then sold them back to the colonists. In doing so, they became very, very rich and even more powerful. This economic policy is known as mercantilism.

3　No. Feudal Europe was very isolationist. The European imperialists established worldwide empires!

4　No. The rights of the indigenous peoples were at best disregarded, and at worst, brutally violated. Unlike the ancient Roman Empire, the empires of eighteenth and nineteenth century Europe made few attempts to respect the rights and cultures of the people whom they conquered, and when they did, it was often after violence had occurred. They believed that the conquered peoples were inferior to themselves and that as colonists, it was their job to bring "civilization" to these "barbarian" peoples.

44　Eliminate answer choices that are out of the time frame of either or both of these revolutions. Focus on answer choices that are very difficult to argue with. You should be able to narrow the answer choices down to two. Then, of those two, select the answer choice that actually applies to either or both of these revolutions.

1　It is true that people often rebel when they are governed by a foreign power. In fact, it's so true that it is hard to argue with. However, neither of these nations was governed by foreign powers when the people revolted. The revolutions were against the existing governments of their own sovereign nations, not against foreign powers.

2　Cuba was not a monarchy. France was, but France's population was not particularly culturally diverse, nor was this the complaint of the revolutionaries.

3　Karl Marx wrote after the French Revolution, not before it. Many in Cuba were inspired by Marx, but the revolution actually started as a democratic movement to overthrow the Batista dictatorship. It was only after the revolution was successful that Castro moved the nation closer and closer to a perversion of Marxism.

4 This is the best answer. The statement in the answer choice is very difficult to argue with. Virtually every revolution has been at least partly due to the inadequate economic policies of the existing government. In Cuba, the Batista dictatorship had created, impoverished, and exploited an enormous lower class. In France, the monarchy's favor of the rich led to insurrections and eventually revolution.

45 You only need to know about one or two of these groups in order to answer this question correctly. Also, focus on answer choices that reflect world trends.

    1 All three groups are trying to win independence for themselves. They haven't even established self-determination, so they are hardly in a position to establish colonies.

    2 No. All three groups are actively attempting to gain independence. The Sikhs, especially, have been very aggressive and often violent.

    3 This is the best answer. All three groups want to separate from their countries and establish their own nation. This should not be surprising, given world trends.

    4 Mercantilism is an economic policy of colonialist nations. These groups don't have colonies in the first place.

46 You only need to know about one of these groups in order to answer this question correctly.

    1 This is the best answer. All three groups tried to drive the Europeans out of their countries. All three groups also used violence in their attempts. The Sepoy Mutiny in India involved a rebellion against British ships. The Mau Mau in Kenya led extremely violent revolts against the British and won independence within about five years. The Boxer Movement in China involved the murders of European missionaries and mercantilists who had established spheres of influence.

    2 No. These movements were against Western aggression, not supported by it.

    3 None of these groups were Marxist. All three groups were traditionalists in the sense that they wanted to return their nations to the way they were before colonial intervention.

    4 No. All three groups used violence.

47 Look at the information in the chart carefully. The birthrates and infant mortality rates of twelve nations are compared. Notice that in both columns, the numbers get smaller as you go down the list. If you know which nations are developing and which ones are already developed, you just need to read the answer choices carefully. If you don't, pick an answer choice that is consistent with your knowledge of the world, without the aid of the chart.

1 No. For every nation on the chart, as the infant mortality rate decreases, so does the birthrate.

2 Yes. The nations at the bottom of the chart (Canada, France, Denmark, Italy, Germany, and Japan) are all developed. They also all have the lowest birthrates and infant mortality rates. The other nations, however, are all developing and they all have higher birthrates and infant mortality rates. Even without the aid of the chart, however, you might have known this already.

3 This doesn't make sense. If the infant mortality rate decreases, then that means more babies are surviving, and therefore the population will increase.

4 Nothing in the chart gives us information about population densities.

48 If you don't know the continents that *all* of the nations in the chart are located on, that's okay. Just look at the nations with the lowest birthrates. Most of the nations with the lowest birthrates are located on one continent.

1 Four of the five nations with the lowest birthrates are in Western Europe—France, Denmark, Italy, and Germany.

2 Japan, Pakistan, and Cambodia are in Asia, but only Cambodia is in Southeast Asia, and it doesn't have the lowest birthrate.

3 Only Canada is in North America, and while it has a relatively low birthrate, the nations of Western Europe have lower birthrates.

4 Uganda, Somalia, Angola, and Ethiopia are in Africa, and none of them have low birthrates.

PART II

1. ECONOMIC CHARACTERISTICS INFLUENCED BY GEOGRAPHY
Choice and use of building material—Middle East

Sumerian civilization began in the Tigris-Euphrates river valley in the fourth millennium B.C. Over the following three millennia, the Sumerians built towns, such as Ur and Eridu, that eventually grew into major city-states. While many other civilizations have used lumber and stone as primary building materials, for the most part, the cities of Sumer were built of clay removed from the river beds. Stone, wood, and other building materials are simply unavailable in many parts of the Middle East. Nevertheless, the Sumerians very capably used the materials they had. The clay was mixed with straw, shaped into bricks, and set out in the sun to dry. The Sumerians accomplished incredible feats with the clay bricks, including the construction of entire walled cities that served as commercial centers for the region.

Dependence on staple grains—South Asia

In Vietnam, the agricultural economy is dependent on the production of rice, a grain that originated in South Asia and is mostly grown in paddy fields. For over four thousand years, the people of the region have taken advantage of seasonal flooding caused by monsoons, which creates the ideal conditions for successful rice paddies. It shouldn't be surprising, then, that rice has been a major part of the regular diet of virtually everyone in Vietnam. In addition, because rice has a high yield per acre, the Vietnamese are able to grow not only enough for their own population, but enough to export as well, especially from the rice paddies of the Mekong river delta in South Vietnam. Therefore, both the internal food supply and the economy of Vietnam are dependent on the production of rice.

Industrialization—Europe

England is a European nation that was geographically well equipped for the Industrial Revolution. First, its harbors made trade with other nations easy. Ships carried raw materials and finished products to and from England and its colonies. Second, its close proximity to mainland Europe allowed it to easily trade with the other industrial giants of the time. Third, its natural resources of coal and iron were perfect complements to industrialization, providing both the energy source and the raw material necessary for the development of factories. It's no surprise that England emerged as an industrial and colonial giant and remained so until the middle of the twentieth century.

Intensive farming—East Asia

Intensive farming methods have become increasingly important in East Asian nations like Japan, which has a growing population and an insufficient acreage of farm and grazing land. Intensive farming often utilizes a controlled indoor environment to raise livestock or poultry, where feeding is regulated to maximize the growth of the animals as quickly as possible. Growth hormones are often injected into the animals to accomplish this goal. Intensive farming allows Japan to reduce the amount of food that it must import from other nations. Although the Japanese diet is mostly reliant on grains and fish, intensive farming methods have allowed the Japanese to enjoy a wider variety of foods.

Nomadic herding—Africa

Nomadic herding groups are common south of the Sahara. One group is the North Sahel, who raise cattle for food. A variety of factors require the North Sahel to move their cattle to lands where they can graze. In a typical year, the cattle have to be herded to new pastures when the old ones are depleted, but they periodically return to a central location where other members of the group farm the land. However, when unfavorable weather conditions affect the grazing land, the North Sahel have to travel even farther, and may be gone from the farming members of the group for an extended period of time. In the early 1970's, almost no rain fell in the region for a period of about four years. The cattle were moved, but soon all the grazing lands were dry. The governments of the region did very little to aid the nomads and as a result, thousands of cattle died, followed by thousands of people who depended on the cattle for food. Historically, nomadic groups such as the North Sahel have contributed to the region's lack of long-term economic development because they do not stay in one place long enough for economic activity to take root. Therefore, it is not surprising that during the drought, the economy of the region was even more unstable, and long-term economic growth seemed even more far fetched.

Single-crop economy—Latin America

In the Dominican Republic, sugar is the dominant crop. The nation also grows some coffee, tobacco, and rice, but not enough to offset the importance of sugar to the Dominican Republic's economy, especially since most of the production of sugar is intended for export. Without diversification, the nation's economy has become too dependent on the world's price for sugar, which in recent years has been depressed. The economic downturn is especially difficult for the nation, since the production of sugar not only dominates the nation's agricultural industry, but its manufacturing industry as well (in the form of sugar processing plants). The Dominican Republic is an unfortunate example of an unstable economy that relies too heavily on the production of a single crop. It is hoped that attempts to diversify the economy will reduce the nation's dependence on sugar.

2. ORGANIZATIONS

Amnesty International

Amnesty International was created in 1961 as an organization intent on freeing political prisoners who were arrested because they spoke their conscience. The group also works to bring an end to capital punishment, torture, and other penalties the members believe are excessive. The group has become particularly important in nations whose governments do not readily protect human rights on their own and who inaccurately report the human rights violations within their own borders. In 1977, Amnesty International was instrumental in the release of more than 10,000 political prisoners. For its efforts, the group received the Noble Peace Prize. Perhaps more importantly, however, the group has raised awareness of human rights abuses in nations that much of the industrialized world has traditionally ignored. This awareness has prompted the governments of nations with good human rights records to influence changes in nations with poor records.

European Union (EU)

With the signing of the Maastricht Treaty by fifteen European nations in 1993, the European Union took on its present form, though its beginnings stem all the way back to the 1950's. The EU is an economic and political alliance that works toward continued integration of the economies and, to a lesser extent, the political institutions of the member nations. It was formed primarily in response to the economic success of the United States and Japan, and the rise of manufacturing competition from developing nations. The biggest success has been the establishment of the Common Market, which established free trade between the member nations, and has helped Europe reassert itself in the global marketplace. Although each nation retains its own sovereignty and laws, one of the major goals of the European Union is to establish a common monetary system that will allow business transactions to flow unimpeded within the union.

Greenpeace

Greenpeace was formed in 1971 as an organization intent on raising worldwide awareness of environmental abuses such as the deliberate killing of wildlife, air pollution, and nuclear testing. The group has traditionally used nonviolent confrontations and media exposure to take stands against environmental endangerment, but increasingly some members are becoming extremely bold in their pursuit of environmental abusers, to the point of physically putting themselves between the abusers and the natural environment that is being abused. In 1985, a group of Greenpeace members protested French atmospheric nuclear testing in the South Pacific by taking their boat, Rainbow Warrior, to the site. Their protest was not well-received by the French, who sunk their boat, killing one of the crew members. Although Greenpeace was not immediately successful in stopping the harm to the environment, it did successfully raise public awareness of the environmental hazards. The public, in turn, has been able to change policy through the use of the political processes already in place.

North Atlantic Treaty Organization (NATO)

NATO was formed shortly after World War II in response to Soviet aggression in Europe. Many Western European nations, Greece, Turkey, the United States, and Canada formed the organization as a military alliance. Military aggression against one would be treated as aggression against all member nations. Troops and military hardware have been placed in strategic locations (West Germany, Turkey), but the troops from individual countries have remained under the control of each country that has sent them. Before the collapse of the Soviet Union, NATO was a key force against further Soviet expansion into Europe. Therefore, NATO's greatest success is not what it affirmatively accomplished, but what it prevented from occurring. NATO's goals were accomplished when the Soviet Union disbanded and communism died in Eastern Europe. Today, the future of NATO is in question. Many say that NATO is no longer necessary since the Soviet threat has been lifted. Nevertheless, NATO continues to expand, uniting much of Europe, both east and west, under a common military alliance with the United States and Canada. Over the course of the next decade, world political developments may make NATO obsolete, or may unite it against a common threat.

Organization of Petroleum Exporting Countries (OPEC)

OPEC nations control about three-fourths of the world's oil reserves. Most of the member nations are in the Middle East, but a few, like Venezuela and Nigeria, are elsewhere. These nations formed OPEC in order to gain more power in the world economy. Slowly, they realized that they could control the world's oil prices by collectively deciding to make less oil available. As the supply of oil fell, the price per barrel rose. OPEC was extremely successful in its efforts to produce a limited amount of oil in the 1970's. The other nations of the world had to compete with each other to purchase the petroleum, and prices more than tripled. Since then, the OPEC nations have remained loosely aligned, but individual member nations have been trying to outsell one another, thereby making more oil available on the market. But when OPEC was strongly united, it successfully controlled the world's supply of petroleum.

Palestine Liberation Organization (PLO)

The PLO formed in 1964 as a response to the creation of Israel. Many Muslim Palestinians want to establish a Palestinian state in the same location as present-day Israel, and have consequently endorsed terrorist attacks against the Israelis. For years, the region was embroiled in disputes and occupations of particular parts of Palestine that each group has laid claim to, like the West Bank, the Gaza Strip, East Jerusalem, and the Golan Heights. Then, in 1993 and 1994, peace talks were held between the PLO's Yasir Arafat and Israel's Yitzhak Rabin. In exchange for recognition by the PLO, Israel made concessions to the Palestinians in the Gaza Strip and Jericho, a city in the West Bank. The goals of the peace talks, however, have yet to be realized. Hard-line members of both sides were angered by their leader's moderation. Rabin was assassinated in 1995, Israel has continued to settle parts of the West Bank for itself, and terrorist attacks continue, though not necessarily as part of an organized PLO effort. Therefore, although the PLO has attempted to gain support for the creation of a Palestinian State, both through violence and negotiation, it has not been successful in achieving either its stated goals, or even a modification of its goals in the interest of peace.

United Nations

After World War II resulted in the deaths of millions and rearranged the political landscape of the globe, the United Nations was formed as an organization where conflicts could be settled peacefully and nations could work together to solve common problems. As time passed, the United Nations expanded beyond the realm of political conflicts and increasingly involved itself in the monitoring of human rights violations and other social problems, such as overpopulation, pollution, and substandard living and working conditions. Recently, the United Nations took action in Somalia, where famine and political instability were resulting in the starvation of millions of people. The UN humanitarian effort was one of its largest. Unprecedented amounts of food and medical supplies came pouring in from around the world. However, the effort was not as successful as the UN had hoped. Much of the food and many of the supplies never reached the people who needed them. Instead, warring tribes took control of the aid and used it for themselves. The UN troops lacked the authority and numbers to solve the political and military chaos in the nation and were eventually withdrawn. Meanwhile, the innocent people of Somalia continued to suffer. The UN effort in Somalia, therefore, is just one example of the difficulty of solving regional problems that stem from a complex interaction of political, economic, militaristic, social, and environmental causes.

3. FORCES CAUSING GROUPS TO MOVE
Crusaders (1096–1204)

The motivation behind the Crusades was primarily religious, but also involved a desire for power. Pope Urban began the campaign in 1096 in response to the success of the Seljuk Turks, who took control of the Holy Land. The Pope wanted Jerusalem, the most important city in Christianity, to be in the hands of Christians. He was also hoping that the efforts would help reunite the Roman Catholic Church with the Eastern Orthodox Church in Constantinople, which had split apart fifty years prior to the start of the Crusades. The Crusaders immediately set out to conquer the Holy Land, and initially captured several cities, including Antioch and most importantly Jerusalem. However, both cities quickly fell back into the hands of the Arabs. Through the year 1204, a total of four Crusades failed to produce the desired results, and the Eastern Orthodox Church and Roman Catholic Church separated even further (five more Crusades also followed, but were not successful in achieving the major goals). Most of the Crusaders either died or returned to Europe. The impact on the Holy Land was a series of violence and uncertainty. Since most of the region remained in the hands of the Muslim Arabs, the series of Crusades led to centuries of mistrust and intolerance between Christians and Muslims.

Africans (1500s–1800s)

The main motivation behind the move of Africans during the sixteenth through the nineteen centuries was economic. The Americans needed slave labor and the European colonial powers found it in Africa. The Africans were captured on the continent's interior and traded to the Americas like commodities. African slaves were in great demand because the plantation systems required thousands of hard laborers and yet, at the same time, the native populations of the American continents were dwindling due to exposure to European diseases and military conquest. The impact on the Americas was enormous, especially in parts of Central America, where African cultural traditions took root. As a result, the ethnic demographics of the Americas became more diverse.

Jews (1930's–1940's)

Jews were on the move in the 1930's and 1940's primarily for religious and social reasons. In Germany, Hitler's anti-Semitic policies grew more and more horrible, causing thousands of Jews to flee to more tolerant nations. Most, however, did not manage to escape in time and became victims of the Holocaust. Those who moved away from German-occupied lands in time, however, had a significant impact on the establishment of Israel. After World War II, nationalism within the Jewish population rose dramatically, and hundreds of thousands moved to the newly created nation of Israel, joining the Jews who had already begun to resettle in the area since the Balfour Declaration in 1917. The creation and maintenance of Israel, of course, has impacted the events and security of the Middle East, and the rest of the world, ever since.

Hindus and Muslims in South Asia (1947)

While Britain controlled the Indian subcontinent in the nineteenth and early twentieth centuries, two separate independence movements developed. The first was a movement by Mohandas Gandhi to gain independence through civil disobedience and then establish a united India where both Hindus and Muslims could practice their religions. The second was a movement by Muhammed Ali Jinnah to form a separate Muslim nation in the northern part of the Indian subcontinent, where Islam had become the dominant religion. After World War II, Britain granted independence to the Indian subcontinent, but separated it into thirds: India in the south, and Pakistan in two parts, one to the northwest of India and the other to the east. Both parts of Pakistan were Muslim, while India was predominantly Hindu, although officially secular. The result was chaotic. Millions of people moved or were forced to flee due to religiously motivated violence. Essentially, India and Pakistan exchanged millions of citizens, with practitioners of each religion moving to the nation where their religion was dominant. Eventually, East Pakistan became Bangladesh, but remained primarily a Muslim nation. But the move of so many people along religious lines only served to fuel the conflict between Pakistan and India. Today, the two nations are still fighting, especially in Kashmir along their borders, where religious self-determination still remains the big issue.

Chinese (1949)

In 1949, nearly two million Chinese nationalists moved from mainland China to Taiwan for political reasons. In the years prior to the move, Sun Yat-sen had revolutionized China as a more liberal-minded nation and had created a representative political party in South China known as the Koumintang. His successor, Chiang Kai-shek, unified the northern part of China with the southern part, and kept the nation on track to become a liberal democracy. However, during this time, Imperialist Japan attacked Manchuria in northern China and while the government of Chiang Kai-shek dealt with the invasion, the Communist Party under Mao Zedong gained support. After building up a rural peasant force of over one million soldiers, Mao Zedong swept through China and drove the Koumintang off mainland China and over to the nearby island of Taiwan, where the Koumintang created the Republic of China. The impact for mainland China was enormous. It became the largest communist nation in the world under the leadership of Mao Zedong. As for Taiwan, it remained separate from communist mainland China. Taiwan has rejected China's efforts toward reunification, but the two nations have grown close together, especially as the economies of both nations have grown stronger and stronger.

Peasants in Latin America (1980's–1990's)

In the 1980's and 1990's, large groups of peasants in Latin America, particularly Central America, left their countries en route to safety, particularly to the United States. In 1980, for example, a large group of Cubans (known as Marielitos) escaped poverty and the inhumanities of the Castro regime by fleeing on boats. Most of them ended up in Florida. Also in the early 1980's, thousands of Nicaraguans were given refugee status in the United States when they fled their country due to the horrors of the nation's civil war. In the late 1980's and early 1990's, the civil war in El Salvador also resulted in waves of refugees, many of whom were also given refugee status in the United States. The effect on the United States has been an influx of immigrants, especially in the Southern states of Florida and Texas. This has led to political and cultural debates concerning immigration policies and whether or not immigration hurts or helps the economy. In any case, the influx of immigrants has contributed to ethnic diversity in many areas of the United States, although in many areas, especially south Florida, the immigrants settle in neighborhoods dominated by members of their own nationality.

4. ART/ARCHITECTURE

Gothic cathedrals

Gothic cathedrals were built in Europe in the twelfth through seventeenth centuries. They were larger and more detailed than most of the cathedrals that came before them, and were unique in their use of pointed arches, flying buttresses and enormous, detailed stained glass windows. As the style became more popular, the windows became even more elaborate, dominating entire walls. The gothic cathedrals represented the power of the Church in Medieval Europe. They were centrally located in the cities, often on a high point dominating the skyline, representing the central and high position of religion in the lives of the masses. Increasingly, the scenes from the Bible were depicted in the stained glass windows, indicative of the role of religion in artistic expression. Many gothic cathedrals are still in use today, and remain the most prominent symbols of the Medieval history of Europe.

Tea ceremony (cha-no-ya)

The tea ceremony developed when a meditative form of Buddhism known as Zen made its way to Japan via a group of Buddhist monks from China. Tea drinking had already been popular in Japan, but combined with the ceremonies of Zen Buddhism, it became a ritual. The preparation of the tea is slowly and thoughtfully done. It is itself a form of meditation and connection with the natural world. The tea is then slowly consumed as the individual meditates on the simplicity of the task. The tea ceremony is just one ceremony by which Zen Buddhists make themselves one with nature. Together with flower arranging, painting, and poetry, the tea ceremony allows the Buddhist to contemplate while performing very basic but beautiful tasks.

Roman roads

The ancient Romans are credited with building the first network of paved roads, not just within cities, but between them. One such road, the Appian Way, was built from Rome all the way to Brindisi in southeastern Italy. The Romans first compacted the earth along the roadbed, making sure that the foundation was well-settled and firm. To ensure that the ground could support the pavement, they mixed in small stones and sand and leveled it completely. Then, slabs of masonry were placed on top of the foundation. Each slab had raised edges which served as curbs, allowing for easy drainage into the ditches dug along the side of the road. The slabs were fitted neatly together, forming roads that stretched for hundreds of miles. The completion of the road system illustrates not only the Roman interest in technology and practicality, but in travel as well. The Roman culture spread and stayed together for as long as it did in part because of the system of roads. Though much more technologically advanced, today road building involves the same general procedure.

Palace at Versailles

The baroque Palace at Versailles was built by Louis XIV, a long-reigning king of France whose power went virtually unchallenged. It seemed that no expense was spared. Not only was the palace enormous, but it was decorated elaborately with fine art and furnishings like no other palace in France. The excessive size and expense of the palace was characteristic of Louis XIV's monarchy specifically, and the nobility of France more generally. Power was measured in displays of wealth, usually at the expense of the peasant class, who labored to build the palace under the king's strict command. Only a century later, the great-grandchildren of those peasants would revolt, and the days of unlimited power would eventually be brought to an end.

Oral literature of Africa

Traditionally, literature in Africa has been passed along orally from one generation to the next. Individuals, usually elders of a tribe, became known as great storytellers who could simultaneously thrill and educate their listeners. In turn, the listeners would tell the stories to others. Some stories reflected the history of the region, others the natural environment or religion, but all the stories involved the values of the society and the character of the individuals involved. Furthermore, the intimate process of storytelling kept communities and families close together. Individuals did not learn by themselves, but together in groups, and their mutual reactions bound them together. Often, music was added to the stories for effect, and popular stories typically involved group responses and singing. Therefore, both the content of the stories and the process of storytelling reflected and contributed to the sense of community in African society.

Orthodox icons

During the Middle Ages, icons became a very important part of Orthodox Christian worship in the Byzantine Empire. Many of the icons included beautiful pictures and statues of the Saints, which increasingly became venerated. For example, when the Arabs attempted to take control of Constantinople in 717, huge crowds formed a procession around a sacred icon of the Virgin Hodegetria, which was then carried along the Theodosian Walls to protect the city. When the Arabs were driven back, the crowds worshipped the icon as their savior from the Arabs.

The veneration of icons led to the Iconoclastic Crisis when Leo attempted to remove religious icons from churches and public buildings because he believed that they were a form of idolatry. The iconodules—those who venerated the icons—revolted and the Byzantine Empire was thrust into an internal religious conflict that lasted for over one hundred years. It was finally ended in 845 when Theodora, an iconodule, repealed iconoclastic rules and reaffirmed the rules of the Seventh Ecumenical Council of 787, which allowed veneration of icons. A ceremony was held in Constantinople to mark the event, and continues to be celebrated each year as the Feast of Orthodoxy in the Greek Orthodox Church.

Mayan calendar

The Mayan calendar involved two distinct systems: the Long Count and the Calendar Round. The Long Count measures the number of days that have elapsed since the day that the Mayans believed that the earth was created (for the third time) in 3114 B.C. The Calendar Round involved two interlocking cogwheels, one as a numbered day, the other as a named day. The Mayan calendar is an excellent example of the way in which Mayan mythology interacted with Mayan technology. The technology of the clock system rivaled any other clock technology in the world at the time. The meaning of the days and years that were being counted, however, reflected the particular beliefs of the Mayan civilization.

5. CHANGES IN TRADITIONAL FAMILIES
India

Traditional families in India were typical of rural religious societies. The family was the basic and most important social unit. Each individual was surrounded not only by his parents and siblings, but also his grandparents, cousins, and other relations. Because of the dominance of the Hindu religion and caste system, family relations were truly a source of identity. Under the caste system, an individual is born into a caste and is expected to marry and socialize within that caste, keeping the individual surrounded by those similar to his own family. In addition, the dowry system in India requires the family of the bride to make a gift to the groom (the dowry) in exchange for the responsibility of providing for the woman, making an individual woman's desirability dependent on her family's ability to provide an acceptable dowry and, in the view of many, making daughters less desirable than sons.

The family dynamics are beginning to change in India, however. When India became independent, the government outlawed the caste system and provided for equality under the law. The traditional social society has not changed as quickly as the government policy, but as millions move to the cities and away from their families, attitudes are beginning to change. Families remain extremely important, but recent attempts to reform or eliminate the dowry system and to broaden individuals' exposure to groups beyond the caste of a particular family have resulted in a reduction of the influence of the family.

China

Traditional families in China followed the teachings of Confucius. The family was the basic and most important social unit, and included not just the immediate nuclear family but the extended family as well. The elderly were greatly respected and the decisions were made by the men. Children were expected to do as they were told with great reverence and courtesy, while their parents were expected to be just and caring providers who taught their children strong personal codes of behavior. Marriages were arranged by the parents as well.

The family dynamics have changed dramatically in China, however. In 1949, men and women were made legally equal and just one year later, individuals were granted the right to choose their marriage partner. These changes occurred when China became a communist nation. In addition, because the Communist Party wants the government to be perceived as the provider, loyalty to the state over the family is expected, with the government providing many of the services that were previously provided by parents. More recently, China has implemented a one-child-per-family policy. This policy was adopted in response to the overpopulation crisis and the inability for the economy to feed a population that exceeds one billion. The government has affected not only the rights and roles of individual family members, but the role of the family unit in the larger society.

Japan

Traditional Japanese families were "continuing." In other words, the family name, known as the *ie*, determined the family's status and even their taxation. The *ie* would continue from one generation to the next, binding the family together under a common reputation. The oldest son in the family would inherit the house and family *ie*, while the other children were expected to leave. Daughters would often marry and would become incorporated into their husband's family while younger sons would either be "adopted" by other families who didn't have sons or else leave to find work in the cities. The fact that younger brothers and sisters were expected to leave fit nicely with the process of industrialization. Millions left their families as expected and found work in the cities. As Japan modernized, the traditional family structure changed. The government officially abolished the *ie* in 1947 and individuals were encouraged to choose their occupations and spouses freely. Many of the oldest sons no longer stay home to run the family, and instead often move to the cities where lucrative jobs await them. Nevertheless, many family traditions remain strong in modern Japan. Children are expected to revere their ancestors and parents, and loyalty within the family unit remains strong.

Sub-Saharan Africa

The traditional families of sub-Saharan Africa are patriarchal. Marriages are arranged, after which the wife lives with the husband and his extended family. Under the bridewealth system, young men are expected to make a payment to a young woman's father (usually in the form of cattle or sheep) as compensation for the bride's family's loss of a worker. Extended families live together, share responsibilities for the functioning of the family, and share in any wealth that the family creates. Traditional family dynamics are changing, however, as African society urbanizes. In cities, the average family size is much smaller, as are the living conditions in tiny apartments. Increasingly, individuals are distancing themselves from their traditional pasts by choosing their own mates and ignoring the bridewealth system. As extended families split apart, factors other than family traditions become influential in the lives of those who have moved to the cities. The result has been an increase in opportunity and social mobility, but a decline in the stability and self-sufficiency of traditional rural areas.

Latin America

Most traditional families in Latin America are patriarchal and very large. Extended families live and work together. Businesses often stay in the family, passed from father to son. Even if the father works for the government, he often works hard to ensure that his family members also find jobs with the government. Most families are very loyal to the whole group, and individual members often return to the home during lunch to eat as a united family. Dating is strictly regulated and chaperoned, and the parents are often influential in the choice of a spouse. However, as Latin America has urbanized and developed, the younger generations feel less obliged to follow the traditions of their families. Many have left the family line of work to seek other opportunities in the city. In many cases, fathers do not make enough money to support their many children, and as a result, parents have actually encouraged their children to leave home to find work. Many poor youths also have chosen to live together rather than to officially marry, since traditional weddings cost money. As Latin America continues to urbanize and experience a population explosion, traditional family practices will likely continue to decline.

Middle East

Traditional family practices in most nations of the Middle East are based on the dictates of Islamic law. Under the Koran, a man may marry up to four wives, but women are punished severely if they marry more than one man. Actually, the men are favored over the women in a variety of ways. Daughters are only entitled to half the inheritance that their brothers are entitled to. In addition, women are expected to live in separate quarters and must expose any part of their body only to their husband. Many of the men in the Middle East claim that the laws help protect women, but recently many women have protested their treatment within the family structure. Many Middle Eastern nations, such as Iran under Shah Pahlavi, passed laws to increase the rights of women within the family structure, including giving women the right to divorce in certain situations. However, Islamic fundamentalist movements of the 1980's and 1990's have reversed many of the trends, and Islamic law has been reasserted as the authority of family life.

6. EVENTS THAT SHAPE THE LIVES OF PEOPLE

Moors conquer Spain (early 700's)

As Islam spread across North Africa, the Moors became increasingly convinced that they had a divine calling to conquer other lands in the name of Allah, much like the European Crusaders believed centuries later. When they crossed the Mediterranean to the Iberian Peninsula, they easily swept through Spain, which was ill-prepared for an invasion. The immediate impact was the introduction of the Islamic faith and Islamic culture to Western Europe. Because the Moors controlled much of the peninsula for nearly seven hundred years, the long-range impacts were substantial. Cultural influences remain even today. The Moors affected the art, architecture, and education on the Iberian peninsula, and some of these influences were spread even further when Spain and Portugal conquered Latin America.

Aztecs lose control of capital, Tenochtitlan (1520)

Aztecs lose control of capital, Tenochtitlan (1520)

The circumstances leading up to the Aztecs' loss of their capital were clearly against any Aztec success from the beginning. The Spanish, who had grand colonization plans for the region, were militarily superior to the Aztecs. They fought with horses, steel swords, and artillery. At first, the Aztecs didn't even fight against the Spanish, since they believed that Cortes, the Spanish explorer who first made contact with the Aztecs, might be a god. This allowed the Spanish to build up their forces with little opposition. When the Spanish began their attack, virtually everything went their way. European diseases, such as smallpox, were introduced to the Aztec population, which dwindled dramatically as a result. Furthermore, the Spaniards used other native groups whom they had previously conquered to help them unravel the huge Aztec Empire. The immediate impact was the defeat of the Aztec Empire. The long-range result was the establishment of Spain as the dominant empire on the continent. Eventually, the entire region was remade by the influx of Spanish culture, religion, politics, and art.

Glorious Revolution occurs (1688)

When King James of England wanted to establish an absolute monarchy, which would have eliminated any need for a British parliament, and reassert the Roman Catholic Church as the state religion, the British parliament supported the forces of William of the Netherlands who fought against the Catholic Irish forces supported by James. James eventually fled and his daughter, Mary, took over the throne with her new husband, William. The event is known as the Glorious Revolution because it resulted in the formation of a limited monarchy with considerable power granted to the parliament and in increased rights for the general citizenry. The long-term impact was even more considerable. It began a European movement against absolute monarchies and increased representation by the people. In addition, the English Bill of Rights, which was signed by the new monarchy and Parliament in 1689, served as a basis for the United States Bill of Rights and the wave of constitutional limitations on power that has swept the world ever since.

Archduke Franz Ferdinand is assassinated (1914)

Archduke Franz Ferdinand of Austria was assassinated while visiting Sarajevo by nationalist Slavic Bosnians. Bosnia was under the control of the Austrian-Hungary Empire, but many Slavic Bosnians wanted their own nation with other Slavs. As Austria-Hungary annexed more Slavic areas, Slavic nationalism grew more intense, and finally Slav's anger resulted in the assassination, which they hoped would provoke a war between Austria-Hungary and Serbia (with the help of Russia, they hoped). The immediate result was just that: War. Austria-Hungary made demands on Serbia, which complied with most of them. Nevertheless, Austria-Hungary declared war on Serbia, the Russians moved in to help Serbia, and Germany, Austria-Hungary's ally, declared war on Russia. This sparked a chain of war declarations involving most of the nations of Europe, igniting World War I. The long-term consequences of the war involved a peace treaty that punished Germany harshly. The German humiliation and ruined economy resulted in a situation ripe for the rise of a fascist, Hitler, who later provoked Europe, and the rest of the world, into an even bigger and deadlier war.

Berlin Wall is taken down (1989)

The Berlin Wall was taken down as the result of many factors converging at once. First, Communism was collapsing in the Soviet Bloc in general, and in East Germany in particular. Second, the wall was not serving its purpose of preventing East German emigration into West Germany, since tens of thousands of East Germans were managing to escape through Czechoslovakia and Hungary. Third, the prosperity of the West and the economic hardships of the East led to massive internal revolts against the very idea of separation. When the wall was finally torn down, the immediate impacts were the reunification of Germany, a mass exodus of people from the East to the West, the failure of businesses in the East, high unemployment on both sides, and an absolutely enormous reconstruction program. Long-range impacts, however, include the emergence of the united Germany as perhaps the major European economic power and an increase in German nationalism.

Iraq invades Kuwait (1990)

Iraq invaded Kuwait in 1990 because under the leadership of Saddam Hussein, Iraq wanted to gain control of a greater percentage of the world's oil reserves. Iraqi control of Kuwait would have nearly doubled Iraq's oil reserves to 20 percent of the world's total, and would have put it in a good position to take Saudi Arabia and United Arab Emerites, an action which would have given Iraq control of over half of the world's oil reserves. The world, especially the industrialized West, reacted immediately. The United Nations, and particularly the United States, sent forces to drive the Iraqis out of Kuwait. The immediate impact of their success was the liberation of Kuwait and the humiliation of Iraq, which was subjected to UN monitoring, severe limitations on its military activities, and economic sanctions. Nevertheless, Hussein has remained in power. The long-range impact has been the continued stability of oil prices and the continued security of the Persian Gulf nations south of Iraq. Yet the people of Iraq have also been affected long-term, since many of them are not getting the food and supplies that they need due to economic sanctions imposed by other nations and the militaristic priorities of their leader.

7. LEADERSHIP AND GOVERNING STYLES OF INDIVIDUALS

Ayatollah Khomeini

Ayatollah Khomeini of Iran was a theocratic leader. He believed that the goals of religion and the goals of government are inseparable. Khomeini would advise that the government can and should be used to enforce the practice of the state religion (Islam, in the case of Iran) and to restrict the practice of any other religion. Khomeini believed that he had a divine right to rule. Since he believed his actions were justified as the will of God, any dissent from government practices regarding virtually any matter could be regarded as heresy. This governing style maintains order well, as long as the state religion remains overwhelmingly dominant. Over a long period of time, it can lead to a stable government and society.

Catherine the Great

Catherine the Great, empress of Russia for over thirty years in the late eighteenth century, aggressively used her authority to westernize and expand her empire. She attacked the declining Ottoman Empire to the south and secured access to the Black Sea for Russia. She successfully fought wars and negotiated agreements to win parts of Poland, the Ukraine and Lithuania for the Russian Empire. Domestically, Catherine supported education and development of the arts and granted freedom of religion. She decentralized the power that Peter the Great had worked to amass, returning a considerable amount of power to the landlords. Catherine the Great would advise that leaders should focus on major national issues and territorial expansion, forcibly if necessary, while leaving local policies in the hands of the local leaders.

V.I. Lenin

Vladimir Lenin, the leader of the Bolshevik Revolution and the first dictator of the Soviet Union, believed that a strong central government with absolute power was necessary until capitalism, organized religion and any other force that he thought threatened the people were eliminated from Soviet society. He believed that the officials of the Communist Party knew what was best for the people, and opposition was not tolerated. In an effort to achieve his goal of a perfect communist society, Lenin engaged in practices inconsistent with communist philosophy. This included exercising strong central authority and allowing for limited capitalism to spark the economy. Lenin would advise a leader to engage in means that are temporarily inconsistent with the overall goal in an effort to put the nation in a position to eventually achieve the primary goal.

John Locke

John Locke believed that the natural rights of man are best protected in representative governments. He wrote that the power of government should be limited by the will of the people. If the people are dissatisfied with the decisions and policies of their leaders, they should be able to elect new ones. This philosophy represented a change in political thought. Before Locke and the other Enlightenment writers, monarchies claimed that their power came directly from God, and that the purpose of the citizenry was to accomplish the will of God as expressed by the monarchy. Locke challenged this justification for power and argued that the government is granted its right to govern from the governed. Therefore, it is the will of the people that the government must accomplish. However, not even the majority of people can act through the government to deny an individual his basic rights to life, liberty and property. Locke would advise that leaders represent the will of the people and subject themselves to limitations on their authority.

Niccolò Machiavelli

Machiavelli wrote that leaders are most successful when they are feared rather than loved. Leaders should assert themselves as the absolute authority, clearly define their goals and do whatever is necessary to achieve those goals. The leader should not create a situation in which the citizenry hates him, or else they might revolt. Instead, the citizenry should fear and be awed by the leader. This governing style allows the goals of the government to be swiftly accomplished.

Nelson Mandela

Nelson Mandela led the anti-apartheid movement in South Africa. Apartheid was established in South Africa in 1948 as a policy intent on not only separating black and white South Africans, but also denying blacks the same civil rights and opportunities that the white minority enjoyed. Mandela became leader of the African National Congress in the 1950s. At first, he advocated peaceful protest. But after the Sharpeville demonstrations resulted in the massacre of black protesters, the African National Congress supported guerrilla warfare. Mandela was arrested in 1964 for his role in anti-apartheid violence, and sentenced to life imprisonment. After decades of increasing pressure from the black majority and the international community, South Africa finally released Mandela in 1990 and agreed to negotiate on the policy of apartheid. In 1994, after apartheid was abolished, Mandela was elected president in the first free and open elections in South African history.

All of these experiences influenced the leadership style of Mandela. Mandela would advise that leaders should clearly define important goals, attempt peaceful means of achieving those goals, but if the goal is important enough, consider the use of other means to achieve it.

A MODERN INTERNATIONAL CRISIS

Under the direct orders of Fidel Castro, Cuba shot down two airplanes piloted by civilian Cuban Americans after those airplanes violated Cuban airspace in 1996. Controversy and tension resulted between the United States and Cuba, whose relations already were strained. Catherine the Great likely would have supported the action by Castro. Strong leadership is necessary, especially when it comes to the security of a nation's borders. She would argue that the action makes it clear to all of Cuba's neighbors that violation of the nation's airspace would not be tolerated. Catherine would also agree that a swift and centralized decision is necessary in such a case, and that Castro was justified in acting unilaterally as the leader of his nation.

EXAMINATION
JUNE 1997

Part I (55 credits): Answer all 49 questions in this part.

Directions (1–49): For each statement or question, write on the separate answer sheet the *number* of the word or expression that, of those given, best completes the statement or answers the question.

---

1 Revolutions have most often occurred in nations in which

  1 the majority of the people are economically prosperous
  2 social mobility is encouraged
  3 citizens can participate in the political process
  4 social, political, or economic dissatisfaction exists

2 "This was the last morning he would have to light the fire . . . Now father and son could rest. There was a woman coming to the house. Never again would Wang Lung have to rise summer and winter at dawn to light the fire. He could lie in his bed and wait, and he also would have a bowl of water brought to him...."

            —Pearl Buck, *The Good Earth*

Which type of society is portrayed in this reading?

  1 ethnocentric   3 monotheistic
  2 matriarchal   4 patriarchal

3 Take up the White Man's burden —
       Send forth the best ye breed —
    Go bind your sons to exile
       To serve your captives' need;
    To wait, in heavy harness,
       On fluttered folk and wild —
    Your new-caught, sullen peoples,
       Half-devil and half-child.

>   —Rudyard Kipling
>   "The White Man's Burden"

The phrase "White Man's burden" in this excerpt refers to the

1 negative attitude of Europeans toward peoples of the non-Western world
2 advantages Europeans would gain by colonizing Africa, Asia, and Latin America
3 positive role of the roman Catholic Church in Africa and Asia
4 challenges non-Europeans faced when trading with the Europeans

4 Which situation best illustrates a traditional practice of women in Masia society?

1 a young woman leaving her village to attend a university in the capital city
2 an educated woman returning to her village to become leader of her tribe
3 a young woman marrying and her husband giving cattle to her family as a wedding gift
4 a young mother discouraging her children from practicing animism

Base your answer to question 5 on the cartoon below and on your knowledge of social studies.

5 This 1994 cartoon suggests that in South Africa
1 both the black majority and the white minority have been denied the right to vote
2 inefficient voting methods lead to lengthy delays at election time
3 only the black majority should now enjoy the full privileges of citizenship
4 recent political changes have given the black majority the right to vote

6 "The Very First Thing You Should Know About South African Stocks and Bonds"

"Two Leading Financial Institutions Show You Around South Africa's Banking World"

"Amalgamated Banks of South Africa: Everything You'd Expect From An International Banking Partner"

The titles of these pamphlets, available in 1994 from an American business and financial publication, reflect

1 a continuation of the international trade sanctions imposed on South Africa in 1985
2 a renewed interest in investing in South Africa's economy
3 the hazards associated with overseas economic investment
4 a belief that the banks and the bond market in South Africa are inferior to those in Europe

7 A study of the Maya, Aztec, and Inca civilizations of Latin America would show that these civilizations

1 developed advanced and complex societies before the arrival of the Europeans
2 established extensive trade with Pacific Rim nations
3 were strongly influenced by their contact with Asian and African civilizations
4 were relatively large, but not well organized

8   In Latin America during the early period of Spanish colonialism, the deaths of large numbers of the native people led to

1   a decline in Spanish immigration to the Americas
2   the removal of most Spanish troops from the Americas
3   the importation of slaves from Africa
4   improved health care in the colonies

9   One similarity in the leadership of Latin Americans José de San Martín, Toussaint l'Ouverture, Bernardo O'Higgins, and Pedro I was that each leader

1   opposed United States intervention in Haiti
2   led a struggle to gain freedom for the people of his nation
3   opposed membership of his nation in the League of Nations
4   established an absolute monarchy in his nation

10   Which statement best reflects the effect of mercantilism on the colonies in Latin America?

1   Markets in the colonies were closed to manufactured goods from the mother country.
2   Land was distributed equally between the social classes.
3   Industries in the colonies manufactured the majority of finished goods for the mother country.
4   The wealth of the colonial power increased at the expense of the colony.

Base your answer to question 11 on the graph below and on your knowledge of social studies.

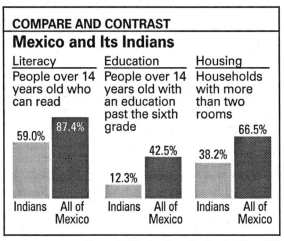

COMPARE AND CONTRAST
Mexico and Its Indians

Literacy	Education	Housing
People over 14 years old who can read	People over 14 years old with an education past the sixth grade	Households with more than two rooms

Literacy: Indians 59.0%, All of Mexico 87.4%

Education: Indians 12.3%, All of Mexico 42.5%

Housing: Indians 38.2%, All of Mexico 66.5%

Source: 1990 Mexican Census, The New York Times, 6/94
(adapted)

11 According to the graph, a major problem facing Mexico is the

1 increasing infant mortality rate
2 increasing rate of homelessness
3 inequality in educational and economic opportunities
4 lack of foreign investment capital available to Indians

_____

12 Which factor is most directly responsible for the decline in the importance of the caste system in India?

1 India's membership in the United Nations
2 disputes between Hindus and Muslims
3 India's relations with China
4 rapid urbanization

Base your answer to question 13 on the graph below and on your knowledge of social studies

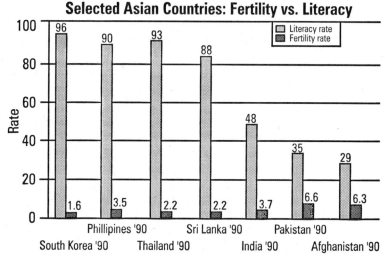

Selected Asian Countries: Fertility vs. Literacy

Source: Statistical Brief, U.S. Department of the Census, SB/93-18, November 1993

13 What is a valid conclusion based on the information provided in the graph?

1 The Philippines had a higher fertility rate than Afghanistan did.

2 In most instances, nations with higher literacy rates tend to have lower fertility rates.

3 The literacy rates for South Asian nations are higher than the literacy rates for Southeast Asian nations.

4 Southeast Asian nations have a higher rate of population growth than any other region in the world.

14 During India's independence movement, Mohandas Gandhi's boycott of British-made products was effective because the British considered India a major

1 shipping center
2 industrial center
3 market for manufactured goods
4 source of mineral resources

15 Disputes over India's control of Kashmir, Jammu, and Punjab are examples of the continuing problem of

1 territorial claims based on religion
2 Chinese claims to this region
3 terrorist actions by Serbian refugees
4 the policy of nonalignment

16 One similarity between the cultures of traditional China and traditional Japan was that

1 the educated class was held in high esteem
2 religion played a minor role in society
3 social mobility was encouraged
4 the people elected the political leaders

17 The arrival of Commodore Matthew Perry in Japan in 1853 signaled the end of Japanese

1 cultural contacts with the West
2 policies of isolationism
3 militarism in Southeast Asia
4 trade relations with the United States

Base your answer to question 18 on the map below and on your knowledge of social studies.

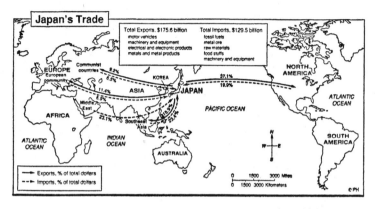

Source: Pageant of World History, 1990

18 Based on the information provided by this map, what is a valid conclusion about Japanese trade?

1 Japan had a favorable balance of trade.
2 Japan imported more goods than it exported.
3 Japan exported more fossil fuels than any other nation.
4 Japan traded more goods with Europe than with any other region.

---

19 Both Japan and China decided to limit trade with Europe during much of the 16th and 17th centuries because the Japanese and the Chinese

1 had few products to sell to the Europeans
2 held religious beliefs that prohibited contact with foreigners
3 thought European technology would hinder any effort to modernize
4 believed they would receive no benefit from increased contact with the Europeans

20 A major reason for the success of the Communist revolution in China was that the Communists

1 stressed Buddhism in their military training
2 included important businessmen in their ranks
3 promised land and power to the peasant class
4 fought successfully against the United States during World War II

21 In China, the Great Leap Forward and the Cultural Revolution promoted by Mao Zedong were similar in that both plans

1 ended dynastic rule
2 disrupted industrial development
3 encouraged capitalism
4 guaranteed human rights

22 One reason North Korea has been the focus of worldwide attention in the mid-1990's is because of its

1 nuclear weapons development programs
2 commitment to increasing political freedoms
3 development of a strong and expanding economy
4 efforts to revive communism in Eastern Europe

Base your answer to question 23 on the cartoon below and on your knowledge of social studies.

Mike Luckovich
Atlanta Constitution

23 What is the main idea of this political cartoon about the Middle East?

1 Peace between Israelis and Palestinians has little chance of succeeding.
2 Israeli and Palestinian leaders strongly oppose peace talks.
3 Israeli and Palestinian extremists have joined forces to bring peace to the Middle East.
4 The peace efforts of Middle Eastern leaders are hindered by radical groups on each side.

24 "If a seignior (noble) has knocked out the tooth of a seignior of his own rank, they shall knock out his tooth. But if he has knocked out a commoner's tooth, he shall pay one-third mina of silver."

—Code of Hammurabi

Which idea of Babylonian society does this portion of the Hammurabi code of law reflect?

1 All men were equal under the law.
2 Fines were preferable to corporal punishment.
3 Divisions existed between social classes.
4 Violence was always punished with violence.

25 Which type of government was established by Ayatollah Khomeini as a result of the Iranian Revolution in 1979?

1 constitutional monarchy
2 fundamentalist Islamic state
3 democratic republic
4 radical Marxist regime

26 One similarity in the leaderships of Kemal Atatürk, Gamal Nasser, and Shah Reza Pahlavi is that all these leaders

1 sought to modernize their nations
2 came to power as a result of democratic elections
3 encouraged their people to convert to Hinduism
4 led invasions into Israel

27 The Middle East is of global importance today because it

1 has become a model of economic and political equality
2 allows major European powers to retain their spheres of influence
3 provides much of the petroleum used by industrial nations
4 remains a primary source of uranium

Base your answers to questions 28 and 29 on the map below and on your knowledge of social studies.

Trade Routes (13th – 15th centuries)

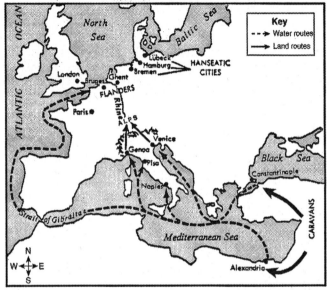

28 One reason Italian city-states were able to dominate the trade pattern shown on the map was that they were

1 centrally located on the Mediterranean Sea
2 situated north of the Alps
3 unified by the Hanseatic League
4 located on the trade routes of the North Sea

29 The development of trade along the routes shown on the map led to the

1 decline of the Greek city-states
2 start of the Renaissance in Italy
3 beginning of the Crusades to the Middle East
4 first religious wars in Europe

30 In European feudal society, an individual's social status was generally determined by

1 birth
2 education and training
3 individual abilities
4 marriage

31 After the fall of Rome, the eastern portion of the Roman Empire became known as the

| 1 Persian Empire | 3 Mongol Empire |
| 2 Byzantine Empire | 4 Gupta Empire |

32 Buildings such as the Gothic cathedrals in western Europe and the Parthenon in ancient Greece reflect each society's

1 imperialist attitudes
2 cultural values
3 belief in democracy
4 rigid social structure

33 "Christians should be taught that he who gives to a poor man or lends to a needy man does better than if he used the money to buy an indulgence."

Which major movement in European history started with the idea expressed in this statement?

1 Commercial Revolution
2 Industrial Revolution
3 Renaissance
4 Protestant Reformation

Base your answers to questions 34 and 35 on the quotation below and on your knowledge of social studies.

"Power tends to corrupt; absolute power corrupts absolutely."

—Lord Acton,
British historian

34 Based on this quotation, which type of government would Lord Acton most likely support?

1 dictatorship
2 absolute monarchy
3 totalitarian state
4 representative democracy

35 Which individual would most likely agree with this quotation?

1 Louis XIV
2 Niccold Machiavelli
3 John Locke
4 Joseph Stalin

36 The harsh conditions imposed by the Treaty of Versailles after World War I helped lay the foundation for the

1 rise of fascism in Germany
2 uprising during the French Revolution
3 division of Korea along the 38th parallel
4 Bolshevik Revolution in Russia

37 One similarity between V.I. Lenin's New Economic Policy of the early 1920's and Mikhail Gorbachev's perestroika policy of the late 1980's was that they both

1 stimulated agricultural and industrial production by implementing some elements of capitalism
2 reduced Russia's trade deficit by importing more grain from Canada
3 prevented foreign economic competition by imposing high tariffs
4 expanded trade into newly acquired colonies

Base your answer to question 38 on the graph below and on your knowledge of social studies.

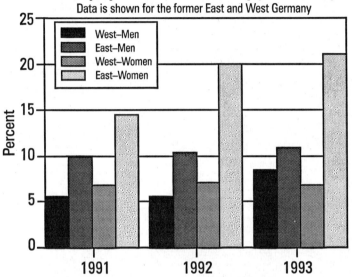

Unemployment Rate in Germany (1991–1993)

Data is shown for the former East and West Germany

Legend:
- West–Men
- East–Men
- West–Women
- East–Women

Source: *The Week in Germany* - September 10, 1993
(adapted)

38 This graph shows data on unemployment in Germany after reunification in 1990. Which conclusion can be reached, based on this information?

1 Prior to reunification, East Germany was economically stronger than West Germany.
2 Women in East Germany were poor workers.
3 A reunified Germany has had problems with steadily increasing unemployment rates.
4 The unemployment rate for women was declining in West Germany.

39 Before a nation can begin to industrialize, that nation must first develop

1 a democratic government
2 a rigid class structure
3 a strong religious foundation
4 an adequate food supply

Base your answer to question 40 on the cartoon below and on your knowledge of social studies.

(adapted)

40 In this cartoon, the cartoonist expresses his view of the United Nations policy on the situation in Serbia in 1994 and 1995. Which foreign policy would the cartoonist most likely have represented in a similar way?

1 mercantilism in the late 1700's
2 appeasement in the late 1930's
3 nonalignment in the 1960's
4 détente in the 1970's

41 One similarity between the actions of Mao Zedong, Adolf Hitler, and Pol Pot was that they all used

1 military force to build colonial empires
2 free and open elections to gain power
3 communism as a basis for their governments
4 intimidation and terror to control people

42 The Sepoy Rebellion, the Boxer Rebellion, and The Mau Mau uprising were reactions to

1 rapid industrialization
2 European imperialism
3 Mongol domination
4 World War I

43 A major purpose of the Organization of African Unity (OAU), the Organization of American States (OAS), and the European Union (EU) is to

1 encourage political and economic cooperation between member nations
2 end colonialism in member nations
3 control overpopulation in member nations
4 provide military assistance to member nations

44 Many scientists believe that the "greenhouse effect" is the result of

1 overgrazing on land in developing nations
2 using large amounts of gasoline, oil, and coal in developed nations
3 testing nuclear weapons in violation of the Nuclear Test Ban Treaty
4 using natural fertilizers to increase crop production

45 The Treaty of Tordesillas (1494), concerning Latin America, and the Berlin Conference (1884–1885), concerning Africa were similar in that each agreement

1 provided for self-government by the native peoples
2 declared that in these areas monarchs rule by divine right
3 divided each area into European-controlled segments
4 suppressed revolts by native peoples against European imperialists

Base your answer to question 46 on the graph below and your knowledge of social studies.

Military Spending

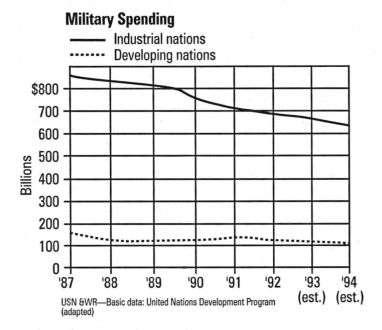

―――― Industrial nations
······· Developing nations

USN &WR—Basic data: United Nations Development Program (adapted)

46 Which statement is a valid conclusion based on the information provided in the graph?

1 Industrial nations increased military spending by $100 billion from 1992 to 1994.

2 Industrial nations sold $100 billion in weapons and military goods to developing nations in 1993.

3 Developing nations decreased military spending by $100 billion between 1987 and 1989.

4 Military spending in industrial nations decreased more than in developing nations from 1987 to 1994.

47 "United States Adopts Economic Sanctions Against South Africa"

"Chinese Dissidents Imprisoned After Student Protest"

"Kurds Forced to Flee Northern Iraq"

These headlines are similar in that each refers to the issue of

1 imperialist expansion
2 peasant revolts
3 human rights violations
4 isolationist policies

48 Which religious belief is shared by the followers of Shinto in Japan and of an animism in Africa?

1 Only one universal, all-powerful God exists.
2 Social status in a subsequent life depends on behavior in this life.
3 Spirits are found in all natural things.
4 Waging holy wars is an appropriate way to spread religious beliefs.

Base your answer to question 49 on the cartoon below and on your knowledge of social studies.

Dilemma
Edmund Valtman. © Hartford Times.

49 After 1956, strained relations between the Soviet Union and the People's Republic of China were often caused by

1 disagreements over the meaning and goals of communism
2 difficulties encountered in constructing the trans-Siberian railroad
3 technological differences between the two nations
4 China's reluctance to admit Russian workers into Manchuria

Answers to the following questions are to be written on paper provided by the school.

Students Please Note:

In developing your answers to Part II, be sure to

(1) include specific factual information and evidence whenever possible

(2) keep to the questions asked; do not go off on tangents

(3) avoid overgeneralizations or sweeping statements without sufficient proof; do not overstate your case

(4) keep these general definitions in mind:

    (a) <u>discuss</u> means "to make observations about something using facts, reasoning, and argument; to present in some detail"

    (b) <u>describe</u> means "to illustrate something in words or tell about it"

    (c) <u>show</u> means "to point out; to set forth clearly a position or idea by stating it and giving data which support it"

    (d) <u>explain</u> means "to make plain or understandable; to give reasons for or causes of; to show the logical development or relationships of"

Part II

ANSWER THREE QUESTIONS FROM THIS PART [45]

1 Nations often seek economic assistance from the International Bank for Reconstruction and Development (World Bank). Several nations which may seek assistance are listed below.

Nations

Albania
Bangladesh
Brazil
Haiti
Russia
Somalia
Vietnam

Select *one* nation from the list. Assume that you are a representative from that nation and your task is to write a proposal to the World Bank for economic aid.

Write a proposal that includes:

a a discussion of a specific economic or social problem faced by your nation   [3]
b a description of the current political conditions, economic conditions, and/or social conditions that affect the problem   [9]
c an explanation of how economic aid from the World Bank would solve the specific problem you identified in part *a*   [3]

2　Throughout history, citizen protests have led to change in specific nations.

Citizen Protests

Storming of the Bastille — France (1789)
Bread Riots — Russia (1917)
Amritsar Revolt — India (1919)
Sharpeville demonstrations — South Africa (1960)
Irish Republican Army insurrections — Northern Ireland (1969–1990's)
Intifada uprisings — Israel (1987–1997)
Tiananmen Square demonstrations — China (1989)

Select *three* of the citizen protests from the list and for *each* one selected:

- Explain the historical circumstances that led to this protest
- Describe the extent to which the protest led to change in the nation with which it is paired [5,5,5]

3　Nations have specific reasons for entering wars. These wars often have various results.

Wars — Nations

Russo-Japanese War — Russia
World War I — Austria-Hungary
World War II — Japan
Six-Day War — Israel
Vietnam War — South Vietnam
Persian Gulf War — Iraq

Select *three* wars from the list and for *each* one selected:

- Discuss *one* specific reason the nation with which it is paired entered the war
- Explain *one* specific result of the war on that nation [5,5,5]

4 Cultural diffusion often takes place as empires conquer and establish contact with other areas or people.

Empires (centuries)

Ancient Roman (1st–3rd)
Islamic (7th–12th)
Mongol (13th)
Mali (14th)
Spanish (15th–17th)
Manchu (17th–20th)
Russian (18th–19th)

Select *three* empires from the list and for *each* one selected:

- Identify *one* area or people the empire conquered
- Identify *one* specific example of cultural diffusion that resulted from this contact
- Discuss the impact of this contact on the people or areas affected   [5,5,5]

5 Geographic factors are often an important influence on specific events.

Events

Industrial Revolution in England
Catherine the Great's decision to conquer the Ukraine
Napoleon's invasion of Russia
Bolívar's attempt to create a United Grand Colombia
Building the Suez Canal in Egypt
European efforts to colonize Africa
Japan's decision to invade Manchuria

Select *three* events from the list and for *each* one selected:

- Identify *one* or more geographic factors related to the event
- Explain how that geographic factor or factors influenced that event   [5,5,5]

6

| UNIVERSAL DECLARATION OF HUMAN RIGHTS |

Article 2: Everyone is entitled to all the rights and freedoms set forth in this declaration, without distinction of any kind, such as . . . colour, sex, language, . . . national or social origin, property, birth or other status.

Article 5: No one shall be subjected to torture or to cruel, inhuman or degrading treatment or punishment.

Article 9: No one shall be subjected to arbitrary arrest, detention or exile.

Article 13: Everyone has the right to leave any country, including his own, and to return to his country.

Article 18: Everyone has the right to freedom of thought, conscience and religion.

Article 20: Everyone has a right to freedom of peaceful assembly and association.

Article 21: Everyone has the right to take part in the government of his country, directly or through freely chosen representatives.

— United Nations
December 10, 1948

Since the proclamation of the *Universal Declaration of Human Rights* in 1948, violations of these stated rights have occurred in several nations.

Nations

Bosnia
Cambodia
Cuba
India
Iran
Rwanda/Burundi
Soviet Union/Russia

Select *three* of the nations from the list and for *each* one selected:

- Describe a specific example of the way in which *one* article of the *Universal Declaration of Human Rights* has been violated since 1948 in that nation [Use a different article for each nation selected.]

- Discuss *one* action that has been taken by a specific group, government, or organization to correct this human rights violation   [5,5,5]

7 Religion and philosophy have played important roles in the development of a nation or region.

Religions/Philosophies — Nations/Regions

Buddhism — Southeast Asia
Confucianism — China
Hinduism — India
Islam — Middle East
Protestantism — Western Europe
Roman Catholicism — Latin America
Russian Orthodoxy — Russia

Select *three* of the religions or philosophies from the list and for *each* one selected:

• Describe *one* major belief or practice of the religion or philosophy [You must use a different belief or practice for each religion.]
• Explain how this belief or practice has affected the social, economic, or political development of the nation or region with which the religion or philosophy is paired   [5,5,5]

ANSWER KEY
JUNE 1997—PART I

1	4	26	1
2	4	27	3
3	1	28	1
4	3	29	2
5	4	30	1
6	2	31	2
7	1	32	2
8	3	33	4
9	2	34	4
10	4	35	3
11	3	36	1
12	4	37	1
13	2	38	3
14	3	39	4
15	1	40	2
16	1	41	4
17	2	42	2
18	1	43	1
19	4	44	2
20	3	45	3
21	2	46	4
22	1	47	3
23	4	48	3
24	3	49	1
25	2		

ANSWERS AND EXPLANATIONS
JUNE 1997—PART I

1   Why do people revolt? They revolt because they are unhappy. Which answer choice best represents this concept?
    1   If they're prosperous, why would they want to revolt?
    2   If they're able to climb the ladder, why would they revolt?
    3   If they can vote and affect the political decisions of the nation, why would they revolt?
    4   If they're dissatisfied, they might revolt.

2   In the reading, the father and the son get to rest because a woman is coming to the house. Instead, the woman will do the chores. Which word describes a society in which men are in control?
    1   People in an ethnocentric society generally believe that their society is superior to other societies. Nothing in this reading, however, describes one person's evaluation of another society.
    2   Matriarchal societies are those in which women are in control. But according to the reading, the woman is going to be the one who lights the fire and gets the water!
    3   A monotheistic society is one that worships only one god. The reading does not tell us anything about the dominant religion of a society.
    4   This is the best answer. The reading describes men getting to rest and women doing the work. In a patriarchal society, men are in control.

3   "White Man's Burden" was a justification for imperialism. Many Europeans thought that they had a moral duty to colonize lands where people were "half-devil and half-child" so that these "barbarians" could be helped. Which answer choice describes this attitude?
    1   This is the best answer. Thinking that non-Westerners are half-devil and half-child is a pretty negative attitude.
    2   This excerpt does not refer to the advantages of colonization, but rather the "burden" of colonization. Colonization was criticized by many people who believed that the Europeans were overrunning other cultures simply for financial gain. Justifications like "White Man's Burden" were put forth to suggest alternative reasons for colonization—namely, that the white man has a moral obligation to

overrun the natives of Africa, Asia, and the Americas! It's a pretty ethnocentric attitude, isn't it?

3   This excerpt does not discuss the role of the Roman Catholic Church. You also might know that the Roman Catholic Church has not been nearly as influential in Africa and Asia as it has in Latin America.

4   This excerpt is not written from the non-European perspective, but from the European perspective.

4   You don't need to know anything about the Masai society to answer this question correctly. Focus on the words "traditional practice." Eliminate answer choices that are not true of traditional cultures.

1   In traditional societies, women do not leave their villages to attend the university in the capital city. In fact, hardly anybody leaves their villages at all, and if they do, it's usually not to go to a university!

2   In traditional societies, few people are educated. Women usually don't leave their village in the first place, so there's no need for them to "return." They also don't become leaders of the tribe, unless it's a matriarchal society, but the Masai society is not. But you should have eliminated this answer choice by now anyway.

3   **This is the best answer. A man in Masai society essentially buys his wife from her family. He exchanges goods such as cattle for the woman. You don't need to know about the Masai society, however. You only need to know that this kind of practice is consistent with a traditional culture.**

4   No. Religion is usually very important in traditional societies. In many of the traditional societies of Africa, that religion is animism.

5   In the cartoon, a white guy is claiming he's been waiting too long on that particular election day. A black guy responds that *he* and his people have been waiting for three hundred years just for this day to come. What does this situation suggest? If you're not sure, eliminate answer choices that you know are not true, even without the aid of the cartoon. Concentrate on answer choices that you know are true based on your knowledge of recent history.

1   If everybody has been denied the right to vote, why are there so many people standing in line to cast a ballot?

2   This is a literal translation of the cartoon. There's got to be more meaning to this cartoon than just that. Plus, if this were the point, then the black guy would have responded, "I know! It *is* intolerable!"

3   The black guy isn't telling the white guy he shouldn't vote, he's just telling the white guy he shouldn't complain. Plus, this answer

choice uses extreme language, so you should be super-suspicious (but not necessarily superstitious!).

4 This is it. There must have been recent political changes, or else the black guy wouldn't be saying that they've been waiting 300 years to vote. In fact, of course, you should know that apartheid was abolished in South Africa in 1991.

6   The examples are titles of three pamphlets that apparently tell American investors how to invest and run a bank in South Africa. If American financial publishers are taking the time to write these pamphlets, then what can we conclude?

1   If the international trade sanctions were continued, then the American investors wouldn't be able to invest in South Africa and there would be no need for the pamphlets.

2   How can you disagree with this answer? You can't! There must be a renewed interest in investing in South Africa's economy, or else these pamphlets would not have been written.

3   There might be some hazards in overseas economic investment, but we don't know this from the existence of these pamphlets. The existence of the pamphlets seems to suggest that it might be a good idea to invest in South Africa.

4   Nothing in the titles of the pamphlets compares South African banks and bond markets to those of any other nation.

7   You only need to know about one of these societies in order to answer this question correctly. You should be attracted to a general answer choice that is hard to argue with.

1   This is it. All three civilizations developed advanced and complex societies before the arrival of the Europeans. Think about it; if they hadn't, they probably wouldn't be on the test. Also, there's no way the Regents are going to suggest that the development of an advanced and complex society is dependent on the Europeans!

2   These civilizations didn't trade with the Pacific Rim nations. They didn't even know the Pacific Rim nations existed.

3   These civilizations did not have contact with Asia and Africa. They didn't even know Asia and Africa existed.

4   These civilizations were well-organized. That's how they were able to become so large!

8 Choose the answer choice that is the most difficult to argue with. You should know that the Native Americans were treated poorly and many of them were enslaved by the European colonialists. A lot of them died, however, due to diseases which were brought over by the Europeans. Since a lot of them died, what do you think happened next?

1 No. More Spaniards came to the Americas. It doesn't follow that the deaths of Native Americans would lead to a decrease in Spanish immigration.

2 No. Spanish troops remained. It's true that there weren't as many Native Americans around, but there was an increase in the number of other people that the troops felt they needed to control. Namely, African slaves.

3 **This is it. When so many Native Americans died, the colonialists needed to find people to do the hard labor in the fields that the Native Americans had done. Therefore, they imported slaves from Africa who could easily adapt to the climate of Latin America.**

4 No. Health care remained inadequate through colonization. To this day, it is still inadequate in many regions.

9 Even if you only know one or two of these men, you should be able to answer this question correctly. Focus on a general answer choice that you think the test writers would actually ask a question about. In other words, focus on an answer choice that realistically would be a similarity among four different men.

1 The only man in the group of four who lived in Haiti was Toussaint L'Ouverture. He was opposed to British, Spanish, and French intervention in Haiti.

2 **Yes! San Martin led the struggle in Argentina, Chile, and Peru, Toussaint L'Ouverture in Haiti, O'Higgins in Chile, and Pedro I in Brazil. This answer choice also just makes sense. The test writers like asking questions about people who gained freedom for their nation. Do you really think they're going to ask about a list of four men whose one similarity was one of the other answer choices?**

3 All four men lived and died before the League of Nations was even established. Even if you know just one of these men, you should eliminate this answer choice.

4 Pedro I was the closest to establishing an absolute monarchy in Brazil and O'Higgins was known as "supreme dictator" in Chile (though it wasn't a monarchy). Toussaint L'Ouverture and San Martin didn't even come close to establishing monarchies.

10 You need to know the definition of "mercantilism." It shows up on the test a lot. Look it up in the glossary if you need to. Go ahead—no time like the present.

    1   No. This would defeat the point of mercantilism. The mother country wants to make money, not lose money!

    2   The only political or economic philosophy which even suggests equal distribution of land is communism, and under communist philosophy there are no social classes in the first place. Think about it. Even if you're not sure what mercantilism was all about, you should be aware that no society has successfully distributed land equally among all of its people.

    3   This answer choice has things turned around. Industries in the mother country, not the colonies, manufactured finished goods that were then sold to the colonies. This is what mercantilism was all about. The mother country would take the raw materials from its colonies without compensating the native people, then manufacture goods out of those raw materials, and sell them back to the same people in the colonies who got the raw materials out of the ground in the first place. It's a pretty profitable scheme!

    4   Yes! This is it! The colony made no money from the sale of its resources to the mother country, and then it had to pay for the goods that the mother country sold back to it. The mother country made money at the expense of its own colonies.

11 The graph compares Indians in Mexico to the overall population of Mexico. In each of the three categories, the Indians are not doing as well as the overall population of Mexico. Therefore, what's the problem facing the country?

    1   Nothing in the graph refers to the infant mortality rate.

    2   The graph tells us the percentage of people who have houses with more than two rooms, but it does not give us any information about people who have no house at all.

    3   This is it. The three categories deal with educational and economic opportunity. The bar graphs clearly demonstrate that there is not equality in literacy, education, and housing. No doubt about it—this is the best answer.

    4   Nothing in the graph refers to foreign investment capital. The cause of the inequality is due to a number of factors, including historical discrimination and current domestic policies.

12 You definitely need to know about the caste system in India because it shows up a lot. The caste system is a Hindu-based social class structure that is a part of traditional Indian culture. You need to figure out why something that is part of the tradition of India would begin to decline.

1 Membership in the United Nations is not dependent on the removal of traditional customs. To be sure, the government of India outlawed the caste system, but it was still practiced anyway due to the traditional beliefs of the people.

2 The Muslim population of India doesn't practice the caste system, so any disputes between Hindus and Muslims would have no bearing on the practice of the caste system.

3 India's relation with China has no effect on an individual's decision to continue to practice his or her own traditions.

4 This is the best answer. As people move from the traditional rural areas to the cities, they often are exposed to new ideas and new ways of living. As a result, they often modify their traditional beliefs and sometimes even reject them entirely. In India, most people who live in the traditional rural areas still adhere to the caste system. However, many of those who have moved to the cities have downplayed the importance of caste.

13 Look at the graph carefully. It compares literacy rates and fertility rates for *some* Asian countries. The light gray lines represent the literacy rates for each of seven nations; the dark gray lines represent the fertility rates. Go through the answer choices one by one and eliminate the ones that are not supported by the graph.

1 No. The Philippines had a fertility rate of 3.5 percent. Afghanistan had a fertility rate of 6.3 percent. Afghanistan's rate is higher, not lower.

2 This is the best answer. In general, as the literacy rates decrease (the light gray lines get shorter), the fertility rates increase (the dark gray lines get longer).

3 No. The literacy rates for the Southeast Asian nations (Philippines, Thailand) are higher than the literacy rates for the South Asian nations (Sri Lanka, India, Pakistan, Afghanistan). Plus, we only have information for *some* nations, so we can't make a generalization about the literacy rates for all Southeast Asian nations and all South Asian nations.

4 Nothing in the chart gives us information about population. Eliminate this one immediately.

14 If people boycott products, it means they used to buy those products, but they're not going to anymore, at least for the duration of the boycott. The question tells you that Gandhi's boycott of British-made products was effective. Therefore, what can we logically conclude?

1 We can't conclude that India is a major shipping center. The fact that items are shipped to and from India does not directly tell us why the boycott was effective. After all, it could be raw materials that are being shipped.

2 Whether or not items are produced in India has no direct impact on the success of a boycott. A boycott is a refusal to purchase certain products, not a refusal to produce them.

3 This is it. The fact that India is a major market for manufactured goods is a reason that Gandhi's boycott was so successful. If India was not a major market for manufactured goods, then that means Indians weren't buying many British products in the first place. Therefore, a boycott wouldn't have much impact because it wouldn't result in economic harm for Britain. It is because the Indians bought so many products before the boycott that economic harm resulted to Great Britain when the Indians refused to buy the goods.

4 The fact that India is a source of mineral resources has no effect on the boycott, since a boycott involves the refusal to purchase goods.

15 You only need to know about one of these regions in order to answer this question correctly. If you don't know about any, choose the answer choice that is hardest to argue with based on your general knowledge of the history of India.

1 This is the best answer choice. Disputes over these three regions are based on religion. In Punjab, the Sikhs want their own nation, separate from the Hindu majority of India. In Jammu and Kashmir, Pakistan and India have been fighting for control of a region part Hindu, part Islamic (with some Christians and Buddhists thrown in, just to complicate things even more). In all three cases, the territorial claims have not been settled and have led to violence.

2 China does not claim any of these regions. Exact boundaries are often in dispute, but there is no significant territorial dispute with China.

3 Terrorist actions by Serbian refugees do not affect India. The Serbian problem is much further to the west in the former Yugoslavia. Terrorist actions in general, however, are a problem, especially in Punjab. Sikh terrorists were responsible for the assassination of

Indira Gandhi after the Indian government raided the Golden Temple of Armitsar.

4 India's general policy of nonalignment is not a reason for the continuing problems in Kashmir, Jammu, and Punjab. However, India's desire to solve its own problems and keep the international community out of its internal affairs has resulted in some tension. Many in the international community believe that the people of these regions should choose their own destinies, and that makes India angry.

16 Think about traditional societies in general. Then try to think specifically about traditional Japan and traditional China.

1 This is the best answer. Although the educated class was not very large, it was held in high esteem in both nations. Think about Confucius, for example, who was educated and greatly respected.

2 Religion plays a major role in virtually every traditional society. In Japan, it was Shinto. In China, it was Buddhism and Taoism.

3 Social mobility was not encouraged in either society, nor is social mobility encouraged in any traditional society. Instead, individuals were expected to accept the roles that society had assigned them due to the circumstances of their birth. Confucius, for example, taught that the rulers owed fairness and kindness to those they ruled, but he never suggested that any of the peasants could ever rise to become one of the rulers. Instead, he suggested that peasants should respect their rulers and do as they are told.

4 Absolutely not. Traditional societies are not democracies. In both China and Japan, the ruling class was determined by birth (or conquest), not by free and open elections.

17 Focus on the phrase "signaled the end of." Eliminate answer choices that could not have "ended" in 1853, based on what you know about modern Japan. Of course, if you're familiar with Matthew Perry, then the correct answer choice should jump out at you.

1 Has Japan not had any cultural contacts with the West since 1853? Of course it has. Americans eat at Japanese steak houses and sushi bars; Japanese eat at American burger joints. All sorts of things have been exchanged. Baseball, movies, religions, you name it.

2 This is it. The arrival of Commodore Matthew Perry of the United States signaled the end of Japanese isolationism. He was sent to sign a trade treaty with Japan, and that's exactly what he did. You should realize that Japan has not been isolated for over a century.

3   Has Japan not been militaristic since 1853? Of course it has. Does World War II ring any bells?

4   Has there been no trade between the United States and Japan since 1853? Of course there has! You probably own several products made in Japan. And if you're still not sure, then look at the map for question number eighteen! Clearly, trade relations with the United States didn't end in 1853! In fact, that's when trade relations began.

18 Look at the map carefully. The map is centered on Japan and shows its trading patterns. The solid dark lines show the percentage of exports leaving Japan and going to each region of the world. The dotted lines show the percentage of imports coming into Japan from each region of the world. Finally, the box at the top of the page gives the total dollar amount of Japan's exports and imports, and then lists some of the major products and materials that it imports and exports. Go through the answer choices one by one and eliminate answer choices that are not supported by the information on the map.

1   **This is the best answer choice. By using the term "favorable balance of trade," the Regents mean a trade surplus, or a situation in which the dollar value of all exports exceeds the dollar value of all imports. Since total exports brought Japan $175.6 billion and imports cost Japan $129.5 billion, Japan made a profit of $46.1 billion. That's pretty favorable!**

2   We can't be sure of the *number* of goods that were imported and exported because we only have the dollar value of those goods. For example, $100 worth of imports might be one item, or one hundred $1 items. Therefore, we should eliminate this answer both because the information in the graph doesn't give us the number of goods, and because the dollar amounts support the idea that there were more exports than imports.

3   According to the chart, Japan didn't export any fossil fuels, although the chart only lists some of the major exports, not all of them. Even if the chart said that Japan *did* export a lot of fossil fuels, we wouldn't know how that compares with the exports of other nations. Finally, the chart tells us that Japan imports a lot of fossil fuels, so that must mean it doesn't have many fossil fuels of its own.

4   Japan sends 11.4 percent of its exports to Europe and receives 6.9 percent of its imports from Europe. Those two numbers average out to about 9.2 percent of its trade. However, it sends 37.1 percent of its exports to North America and receives 19.9 percent of its imports

from there. Those two number average out to about 28.5 percent of its trade! Therefore, Japan doesn't trade with Europe more than it trades with any other region.

19 Eliminate answer choices that are not consistent with your general knowledge of Japan and China, even if you're not sure why they didn't want to trade with Europe.
   1 Both nations have natural resources, especially China. If they didn't have anything to sell, then why would the Europeans want to trade with them in the first place?
   2 Shintoism, Buddhism, Taoism, and Confucianism do not prohibit contact with foreigners. No major religion does.
   3 Japan and China knew that European technology would modernize their nations, but they didn't want to modernize.
   4 Both Japan and China were isolationist during this time period. Neither nation believed that the Europeans had anything worthy to offer them. They believed the Europeans were just as barbaric as the Europeans thought they were, so since they hadn't yet commercialized, they had no need for the Europeans at all.

20 If you're not sure of the answer, think of a major reason behind the success of most revolutions. Also, eliminate answer choices that are inconsistent with communism.
   1 Communist China is officially atheist. Communist philosophy teaches that religion is a tool of exploitation.
   2 Communist nations do not promote private business. The Communist Revolution in China did not involve "important businessmen." The Communist Revolution did not establish businesses. It established collectivization, government ownership and government distribution of services.
   3 This is it. Most revolutions are successful because they have the support of the masses. There would be no need for a revolution unless the masses in China were suffering. Communism offered the peasants hope for an improved standard of living.
   4 China did not fight against the United States during World War II. If you're not sure of China's role in World War II, you should eliminate this answer because, logically, *no* nation could have fought successfully against any nation that won the war.

21 Eliminate answer choices that are inconsistent with communism in general (since you should know that Mao Zedong was the communist leader of China). You only need to know about one of these events in order to answer this question correctly.

1   Dynastic rule ended in China when it became a republic in 1912. When Mao Zedong came to power in 1949, China became a communist nation. Both the Great Leap Forward and the Cultural Revolution were promoted under his leadership.

2   **This is the best answer. Both programs were focused on rural areas, and millions of people were sent to farming communes as a way of recommitting the nation to communist philosophy. Neither policy was successful in expanding the economy, because large-scale industrial development was hindered due to a focus on small-scale rural industry and agriculture. Yet, the farming communes lacked incentives for productivity and involved forced labor, which eventually led to food shortages rather than food surpluses, especially during a time of severe drought. As a result, China was forced to import grain from the West and was behind the West in two areas (agricultural development and industrial development) instead of just one.**

3   Communism does not encourage capitalism. Both the Great Leap Forward and the Cultural Revolution were extremely anti-capitalist. In fact, the two programs were arguably more faithful to pure communist philosophy than any program initiated in the former Soviet Union.

4   No. Communist philosophy does not guarantee human rights because it does not promote individuality. Both programs forced millions of people into situations designed by the government, not designed by individual initiative.

22 If you're not sure of the answer, focus on an answer choice that would truly attract worldwide attention. Eliminate answer choices that you know are not true of North Korea, or that you suspect would not be true of a relatively small, really poor, communist Asian nation.

1   **North Korea has attracted worldwide attention because of its nuclear weapons development programs. Even though the superpowers have reduced their stockpile of nuclear weapons, many smaller nations, including North Korea, have continued production. In 1993, North Korea formally withdrew from the Nuclear Nonproliferation Treaty, an-**

nouncing to the world its intention to continue production. Since then, the issue has been sticky.

2   No. North Korea has not increased political freedoms, but continues to deny its citizens many basic rights. This fact should not be too surprising, given that North Korea is a centralized, communist nation. It also shouldn't be too surprising if you know anything about the new leader, Kim Jong II, who has actually sent people out of the capital city because of the way they look (Kim Jong II is a very eccentric man, to say the least).

3   The economy of North Korea is a disaster. Industrial output and agricultural output are down and a very poor population is getting even poorer as a result.

4   North Korea has not made efforts to revive communism in Eastern Europe. This answer choice just doesn't make sense. North Korea is a small nation in Asia. It does not have the capability to influence the political systems of nations in other regions of the world, nor is communism working well there in the first place.

23   Look carefully at the cartoon. Two groups of extremists are trying to separate two men who have reached agreement. Therefore, we can conclude that the extremists don't want the agreement that the more moderate leaders have shaken hands on. Eliminate answer choices that don't describe the scene in the cartoon.

1   The cartoon doesn't predict the chances of what is going to happen in the future. Instead, it merely makes an observation about the current situation.

2   No. The leaders want peace. It's the extremists who are trying to prevent them from reaching it.

3   The extremists haven't joined forces. They're not walking toward each other—they're walking away from each other.

4   **This is the best answer. Efforts to achieve peace in the Middle East have been hindered by extremists who do not want to compromise with the other side.**

24   Read the quote carefully. If one noble knocks out another noble's tooth, he's going to lose his own tooth as well. But if the noble knocks out the tooth of a commoner, he pays a small fine. What can we conclude?

1   All men were not equal under this law. The noble's tooth is more valuable than the commoner's tooth. Why would the code even bother to distinguish between two different groups (commoners and nobles) if these groups had equal rights?

2　Fines were apparently preferable to corporal punishment when it came to hurting a commoner, but not when it came to hurting a noble. It would appear that the worse the deed (in the minds of the lawmakers), the worse the punishment.

3　Yes! You just can't argue with this answer choice. There must have been a division between the social classes, or else the law would not have bothered to distinguish between commoners and nobles.

4　This answer choice uses extreme language, and is simply not true. First, we know from this particular part of the code that violence is punished with a fine if it is directed against a commoner. Second, we only have one portion of the code, and therefore we can't make any generalizations about punishments for other types of violence.

25　If you don't know anything about Ayatollah Khomeini or the Iranian Revolution of 1979, you're going to have a difficult time eliminating answer choices. Still, though, try to eliminate answer choices that do not reflect that region of the world.

1　Iran's constitution changed in 1979, but it did not establish a constitutional monarchy.

2　This is it. The Iranian Revolution of 1979 established the Islamic Republic of Iran. Ayatollah Khomeini assumed power after Shah Pahlavi fled. Islamic fundamentalists thereafter reversed the former Shah's attempts to westernize the nation.

3　The Iranian Revolution did not establish a democratic republic. The government was formed as an Islamic state with no toleration for opposing religions or political philosophies.

4　Iran has never been Marxist, before or since the Iranian Revolution in 1979. The traditions and social structures of Islam are not compatible with communist philosophy.

26　If you only know about one or two of these men, you should be able to eliminate at least a couple of answer choices. If you're guessing, choose the most general answer choice.

1　This is the best answer. Atatürk, Nasser, and Pahlavi all tried to modernize their nations. Atatürk modernized and westernized Turkey, transforming it into a secular state. Pahlavi sought to modernize Iran, especially its economy, schools and courts. Finally, Nasser sought to modernize the military and economy of Egypt, but remained very anti-Western throughout the changes.

2 No. Ataturk came to power through an election of the Turkish Assembly, not through a general popular election. Nasser was the leader of a military junta who eventually won the presidency through a referendum. Shah Pahlavi assumed the throne of Iran after his father abdicated it.

3 All of these men were Muslim.

4 Only Nasser fought head-to-head with Israel.

27 Think of everything you know about the Middle East during the modern era. Think of Iraq, Iran, Saudi Arabia, Syria or whatever countries you might be familiar with in the region. Eliminate answer choices that are inconsistent with the region as a whole.

1 The Middle East is not a model of economic and political equality. With the exception of Israel, the nations of the Middle East are mostly Muslim. The traditions of the religion have prevented broad reforms that otherwise might have occurred. And the recent uprisings of Islamic fundamentalists after the success of the Iranian Revolution in 1979 indicate that many in the region actually want to eliminate some of the reforms that *have* occurred.

2 The European spheres of influence are no longer in existence in the Middle East. When Nasser of Egypt nationalized the Suez Canal, the Europeans had pretty much been kicked out of the region entirely.

3 **Bingo! The Middle East contains roughly two-thirds of the world's petroleum reserves. Any instability in the region sends shock waves throughout the industrialized, gas-guzzling world. Remember the Persian Gulf War?**

4 No. The region is a primary source of petroleum, not uranium.

28 If you know your geography, this question is easy. Just eliminate answer choices that are way off the target. If you have no idea where Italy is on the map, you're going to have some problems. Still, try to think of the answer choice that describes a location that would dominate a trade pattern.

1 **This is it. Italy is the long peninsula that is sticking out into the Mediterranean Sea. The Italian city-states included Venice, Genoa, Pisa, and Naples. It's centrally located on the map! Even if you weren't sure which part of the map is Italy, you should still guess this answer because it just makes sense that a central location would dominate trade patterns.**

2 Italy is not situated north of the Alps. Flanders is.

3 Lubeck, Hamburg, and Bremen were unified by the Hanseatic League, but none of them are in Italy!

4 This map doesn't give us any trade routes through the North Sea, so definitely eliminate this one. (There were trade routes in the North Sea; however, it's just not the point of *this* map).

29 Look at the map carefully. The title informs us that the time period is from the thirteenth to the fifteenth centuries. The arrows on the dotted lines and solid lines inform us that stuff is moving from the Middle East and Africa to Europe (almost all the lines are moving north, northwest). Therefore, we want an answer choice that describes a situation that would have resulted from the movement of this stuff.

1 No. The Greek city-states declined long before the time period of this map. This map shows us Italian city-states, but no Greek city-states (like Sparta, Corinth) are anywhere on the map.

2 This is the best answer. You should be aware that the Renaissance occurred in the fifteenth and sixteenth centuries, so it just makes sense that the centuries just prior to the Renaissance would have led to the Renaissance. Also, you should be aware that the Renaissance was, in part, a rediscovery of the culture of the ancient world. The lines on the map show information and goods flowing to Europe from places like Alexandria and Constantinople (the holding places for many of the ancient documents and ideas). It was Europe's increased communication with these places that enabled it to rediscover its lost past.

3 No. The Crusades were during the eleventh, twelfth, and thirteenth centuries. In other words, the Crusades are significant to developments that led to this map, not the other way around. Even if you're not sure of the dates of the Crusades, you should be aware that the Crusades were launched from Europe into the Middle East, in which case the arrows on the map would have to be pointing in the other direction.

4 No. Religious wars in Europe occurred well before the thirteenth century.

30 Feudal societies are traditional societies. Think of how an individual's social status is determined in a society that doesn't encourage education, that doesn't permit social mobility, and that provides few avenues for people to even consider doing something other than what their parents have done.

1 **This is the best answer. Birth determined a person's status. If a person was born to parents who were peasants, he was a peasant himself. If a person was born to parents who were part of the ruling class, he became part of the ruling class himself.**

2 Education and training were not vehicles for social mobility. Only the ruling class were educated. The peasants received one-on-one training from their parents so that they could perform the same jobs.

3 Abilities were not related to social status. Peasants had few opportunities to demonstrate their abilities in the first place. And even if they did, their abilities would not have improved their social standing.

4 Peasants married peasants. Rulers married family members of other rulers. Enough said.

31 If you don't know the name of the eastern portion of the Roman Empire, at least try to eliminate empires that you know *weren't* the eastern portion.

1 The Persian Empire preceded Christianity entirely.

2 **This is it. The Byzantine Empire was the eastern portion of the Roman Empire, centered in Constantinople.**

3 The Mongol Empire was established in China and eventually in parts of Persia in the thirteenth and fourteenth centuries.

4 The Gupta Empire was all the rage in India in the fourth through the sixth centuries.

32 Okay. Let's think about this one if you missed it. First of all, you should know that the Regents like to test the ideas that religion affects a society's cultural values and that art and architecture then reflect those same values. This is especially true in traditional societies. Even if you don't remember that, you should look at all four answer choices and realize that the three wrong answer choices are all cultural values. Therefore, if you like answer choice number one (imperialist attitudes) then you also have to like cultural values. If you like number three (belief in democracy) then you also have to like... guess what... cultural values. If three answer choices are a subcategory of the fourth

general answer choice, choose the general answer choice! Keep in mind that you shouldn't have liked the three wrong answer choices in the first place, because they're wrong. The point, however, is that even if you went temporarily astray, you should have come around and picked the hard-to-argue-with "cultural values."

1 Western Europe did not have imperialistic attitudes during the time it built the Gothic cathedrals. The cathedrals were built in the Middle Ages, a time of isolationism.

2 Yes! Art and architecture reflect the cultural values of the society in which they were created. Remember it. The Regents test this concept a lot.

3 Europe during the Middle Ages was not full of fledgling democracies.

4 The social structure in both places was rigid, especially in Western Europe during the Middle Ages, but the cathedrals and the Parthenon don't represent this idea.

33 If you don't understand the reference to the word "indulgence," at the very least focus on the word "Christian." You want an answer choice that describes a religious movement.

1 The Commercial Revolution wasn't a religious movement, but rather a... well... a commercial one!

2 The Industrial Revolution wasn't a religious movement, but rather... how shall we put this... an industrial one.

3 The Renaissance wasn't a religious movement, but a cultural one.

4 Yes! The Protestant Reformation was a religious movement against the practices of the Catholic Church. This quotation refers to just one of those practices. The Catholic Church was selling paper indulgences in order to raise money. The Church claimed that by purchasing an indulgence, the Church would speak to God on the individual's behalf and reduce the time that he or she had to spend in purgatory. Many believed that if they bought enough indulgences, they could do as they pleased and still be granted immediate salvation with no layover in purgatory... no questions asked. Of course, this raised a lot of eyebrows, including Martin Luther's, who objected that salvation is granted by God and only by God, not by papers sold by the Church. Thus, Luther argued, individuals should use their money to do the will of God as they best understand that will to be.

34 Lord Acton doesn't like power. Since somebody has to have some power, however, if anything is going to get done, he would favor a government that at least spreads the power out among a bunch of people, since "absolute power corrupts absolutely." Which answer choice describes a government arrangement that doesn't concentrate power in one person?

1 A dictatorship has a dictator. His word is final. Absolute power. Corrupt.

2 An absolute monarchy has absolute power. Absolute power corrupts absolutely. Look for something a little more inclusive.

3 Totalitarian regimes have total power, usually within one person or a small group. "Total" means "absolute." Lord Acton wants total power divided into parts.

4 Yes! Representative democracies have a lot of people with power. Each representative represents the views of his or her constituency (the people who elected him or her). Since there are usually a lot of representatives standing for a lot of different views, power is spread out. In addition, the people themselves retain some power, because they can elect a new representative if they don't like their current one.

35 You want to find a person who dislikes absolute power. Alternatively, you can eliminate the three people who do, in fact, like absolute power. You should at least know Machiavelli, Locke, and Stalin, since these three show up on the test frequently.

1 Louis XIV of France definitely exercised absolute authority. He would not tolerate any challenges to his authority. This shouldn't be too surprising, if you know that his nickname was the "Sun King." Talk about putting yourself at the center of attention!

2 Machiavelli, you should know, argued that a prince should do just about anything within his power to keep it. He believed that power in itself is not a bad thing. While he did not advocate one type of government over another type, he most certainly did not believe that absolute power corrupts absolutely.

3 John Locke was an Enlightenment writer who argued against the absolute power of monarchies. He believed that individuals have rights that government cannot take away and that the government stems from the people, not the other way around. John Locke's writing inspired many of the revolutionaries in the American and French Revolutions.

4 Stalin was a dictator of the Soviet Union. He ruled absolutely, and often ruthlessly.

36 Eliminate answer choices that describe an event that occurred before World War I or that are entirely unrelated to the events in Europe during World War I. If you know the basics of the Treaty of Versailles, this question should not be a problem.

1 This is the best answer. The Treaty of Versailles severely punished Germany, which lost World War I. Germany's territory was reduced, its military was weakened, and it was forced to pay war reparations to the nations it attacked. As a result, Germany was humiliated and its economy was devastated, especially during a time when most of the industrialized world was experiencing a depression. This bleak state of affairs allowed a fascist by the name of Hitler to arouse the nationalistic spirit of Germans and unite them in a quest to reassert themselves as a world power.

2 The French Revolution occurred over a century before World War I.

3 The Treaty of Versailles had nothing to do with the Korean War or Korea in general. Korea was divided along the 38th Parallel in 1953 as a result of a stalemate in the war, not as a result of a World War I treaty.

4 The Bolshevik Revolution in Russia occurred in 1917. The Treaty of Versailles was signed in 1919. Therefore, the Treaty couldn't have laid the foundations for the revolution. Even if you're not sure of the dates, however, you should know that the treaty punished Germany to the advantage of Russia, not to the disadvantage of Russia.

37 You only need to know about one of these policies to answer the question correctly. If you're uncertain of the details of either of these policies, choose an answer choice that uses broad language as opposed to specific language. Also, eliminate answer choices that either don't make sense at all, or are inconsistent with the general policies of the Soviet Union during these time periods.

1 This is the best answer. Lenin's New Economic Policy was just that—new. In other words, it introduced some elements of capitalism to spark a stalling communist economy. The same goes for *perestroika* (which literally means "restructuring"). Gorbachev introduced elements of capitalism for the same reasons Lenin had.

2 This answer choice doesn't make sense. Nations don't reduce trade deficits by importing more; they reduce deficits by importing less, or exporting more, or both.

3 Neither Lenin nor Gorbachev imposed high tariffs as a part of these economic policies.

4 This answer choice doesn't fit with the time period. The Soviet Union did not acquire new colonies in the 1920's or the 1980's.

38 Look at the chart carefully. Choose an answer that is clearly represented by the information in the graph. Don't make conclusions about anything that occurred before 1991 or after 1993, since the graph only gives us unemployment rates for a three-year period and nothing more.

1 This graph doesn't give us any information about Germany prior to reunification. Eliminate it. You might know, however, that prior to reunification, East Germany was economically *weaker* than West Germany.

2 The graph doesn't give us any information about the characteristics of the women in East Germany. We only know that the unemployment rate among East German women increased from about 14% to 21% during this time period. We don't know anything about the majority of East German women, however.

3 **Bingo! The graph clearly shows that the unemployment rate rose from 1991 to 1993. When West Germany absorbed East Germany, it was very expensive for the West German economy. The unemployment rate rose on both sides of the newly unified nation.**

4 Absolutely not. West German women are represented by the solid gray lines. In 1991, the unemployment rate among West German women was about 6% or 7%. By 1993, the unemployment rate rose to about 9%. It increased, not decreased!

39 Choose the answer choice that is almost impossible to argue with. If you're still not sure, think of all of the industrial nations that you can, and then eliminate answer choices that are not consistent with all of them.

1 The former Soviet Union industrialized, but it was not a democracy. Democracy is not necessary for industrialization.

2 The United States has industrialized, but it does not have a rigid class structure. Rigid class structures are not necessary for industrialization.

3 The Soviet Union industrialized, but it did not have a strong religious foundation. In fact, it was officially atheist.

4 This answer choice is virtually impossible to argue with. If a society doesn't have food, whether it be an industrial society or some other type of society, it will die. In the case of industrial societies, it's especially important to insure in advance that an adequate food supply exists, since a significant percentage of the population will work in factories instead of on the farms.

40 The cartoon shows the United Nations building bent over, a symbolic way of showing that no one in the United Nations seems willing to take a stand on the war in Serbia. In other words, the cartoonist believes that the world community is willing to allow atrocities to occur in Serbia in the hopes that once the former Yugoslavia solves its own problems, the situation will get better. You need to find another time when the world community allowed atrocities to occur in the hopes that the situation would solve itself. Make sure you focus on the particular words used in the answer choices.

1 Mercantilism is the practice of being very involved in other nations. In fact, the mercantilist nations are so involved in other nations, they actually colonize them!

2 Appeasement is the practice of allowing aggression or other questionable activities to occur in the hopes that the aggressive nation will eventually cooperate if you give it what it wants. Europe appeased Hitler in the 1930s, but Hitler wasn't satisfied and eventually war broke out.

3 Nonalignment means not taking sides. Nonaligned nations usually just want to stay uninvolved. It's different from appeasement in the 1930's or the world reaction to Serbia in the 1990's. In those two situations, much of the world community was outraged, but not willing to stand up for their beliefs. Nonaligned nations, however, usually aren't outraged in the first place. They're simply not taking sides.

4 Détente is a situation in which two nations try to lessen the conflicts between them. In the 1970's, the Soviet Union and the United States experienced a détente, in which they were still opposed to one another, but tried to reduce tensions between them. Détente does not involve appeasement like the German situation in the 1930's or the Serbia situation in the 1990's.

41 Even if you know about only one of these men, eliminate answer choices that don't apply and then choose the most general answer choice.
    1   None of these men built colonial empires. Hitler conquered foreign lands, but he never established a colonial empire.
    2   None of these men came to power through the means of a free and open election.
    3   Hitler did not use communism as the basis for his government.
    4   All three men used intimidation and terror to control people. Millions died under the orders of all three men, and millions more were terrorized and made to suffer severe hardships. All three men attempted to eliminate people who held views dissimilar to their own.

42 You only need to know about one of these rebellions in order to answer this question correctly.
    1   None of these rebellions was a reaction to rapid industrialization. If you're guessing, look for an answer that you can be certain caused rebellions.
    2   This is the best answer. All three rebellions were motivated by a desire to drive the Europeans out of their colonies. The Sepoy Mutiny in India involved a rebellion against British ships. The Mau Mau in Kenya led very violent revolts against the British in Kenya, and won independence within about five years. The Boxer Movement in China was also very violent and involved the murders of European mission-aries and mercantilists who had established spheres of influence.
    3   None of these rebellions was a reaction to Mongol domination.
    4   The Sepoy Mutiny and Boxer Rebellion were prior to World War I. The Mau Mau uprising occurred in Kenya in the 1950's.

43 The three organizations affect four continents. The OAU involves Africa, the OAS affects both North and South America, and the EU involves Europe. Even if you're not sure about the details of these three organizations, you should focus on an answer choice that makes sense on all four continents.
    1   This is the best answer. All three organizations encourage political and economic cooperation between member nations. It just makes sense that regions of the world can become more stable if the nations in those regions cooper-ate on general economic and political goals. Of the three,

the European Union is the most organized and integrated. The other two are cooperative endeavors, but member nations make their decisions independently.

2 Notice that the verb in the question is in the present tense ("is"), not in the past tense ("was"). That means that these organizations are still in existence, just in case you didn't know that already. Most nations do not still have colonies. A few do, but their role in those colonies has been reduced. Also, Africa and the Americas didn't colonize, but were colonized by others.

3 Overpopulation is certainly a major world issue, and is a concern of international bodies, but it is not a "major" purpose of these organizations, especially in Europe, where the population is growing very slowly.

4 These organizations were developed to address common problems and to strengthen the regional economies. Military assistance is common among nations with strong political ties (NATO, for example) but is not part of the agenda of regional organizations that are merely intended to foster cooperation.

44 If you're not sure of the causes of the greenhouse effect, at least eliminate answer choices that don't sound like they would have a significant impact on the earth's atmosphere.

1 Overgrazing is an environmental problem because it leads to soil erosion, but it does not contribute to the greenhouse effect in any significant way.

2 This is the best answer. One cause of the greenhouse effect is the increase in the amount of fossil fuel billowing into the atmosphere from factories and automobiles. The fossil fuels let sunlight through to the earth, but then bounce it back down to the earth, just like a greenhouse does.

3 Nuclear radiation is an environmental threat, but it does not specifically contribute to the greenhouse effect.

4 Natural fertilizers do not pose an environmental threat, so long as they are appropriately used. Chemical fertilizers, however, can lead to soil and water pollution. In any case, fertilizers are not a cause of the greenhouse effect.

45 You only need to know about either the Treaty of Tordesillas or the Berlin Conference to answer this question correctly. If you're not sure about either of them, focus on the dates (1494, 1884-85) and the locations involved (Latin America, Africa). You should remember that during these time periods, Europe was colonizing the locations

involved. Choose the answer choice that is hardest to argue with, given that Europe was colonizing Latin America and Africa.

1 Europe was colonizing during these time periods. Neither the Treaty of Tordesillas nor the Berlin Conference provided for self-government by the native peoples. Think about it—in 1494, the colonizing nations themselves didn't have self-government by their own people, so do you really think they would have granted self-government to their colonies?

2 No. Neither the Treaty of Tordesillas nor the Berlin Conference provided for rule by divine right. You should eliminate this anyway, since divine right justifications for absolute monarchies were abandoned by the nineteenth century—well before the Berlin Conference.

3 This is the best answer. The Treaty of Tordesillas divided Latin America between Spain and Portugal. The Berlin Conference carved Africa up between several European powers. Even if you didn't know this, you should pick this answer because you should know that both regions were colonized by Europe during these approximate time periods.

4 Europe was certainly interested in suppressing revolts by the natives, but neither the Treaty of Tordesillas nor the Berlin Conference was about revolts. Revolts were generally suppressed by force, not by treaties.

46 Look at the graph carefully. The graph shows military spending over an eight-year period by two groups of nations—industrial nations and developing nations. Now look at the answer choices. Eliminate answer choices that are inconsistent with the information in the graph, or that refer to information not found in the graph.

1 This statement is not supported by the graph. Look at the solid black line between 1992 and 1994. It's going down, not up. That means that industrial nations *decreased* military spending.

2 Nothing in the graph refers to the dollar value of weapons *sold* by one group of nations to another group of nations. This graph only shows us the amount that the two groups of nations spent on their military programs. The graph, however, gives us no indication of what was bought with the money or whom it was bought from.

3 According to the graph, developing nations (the dotted line) decreased military spending between 1987 and 1989, but by less than $100 billion. The space between two horizontal lines repre-sents $100 billion. From 1987 to 1989, however, the dotted line stays between $100 billion and $200 billion.

4 This is the best answer. From 1987 to 1994, industrial nations decreased military spending from about $850 billion to about $650 billion (a decrease of about $200 billion). Developing nations, however, decreased military spending from about $150 billion to about $100 billion (a decrease of about $50 billion). Therefore, military spending in industrial nations decreased more than in developing nations from 1987 to 1994.

47 You only need to know about one or two of these incidents in order to answer this question correctly. Even if you're not sure of the details of the incidents, focus on the words used in the headlines ("dissidents imprisoned" and "forced to flee," for example).

1 None of these headlines refers to imperialist expansion. The United States did not expand its role in South Africa, but rather reduced it. As for the other two headlines, the Chinese and the Iraqi governments were responding to situations within their own borders, not within other nations.

2 The United States is not a peasant, nor are economic sanctions usually called "revolts." The students in China were not peasants. The students were educated and on their way to careers in fields such as business, industry, education, and science. The Kurdish situation might possibly be described as a peasant revolt, but it is more properly described as an ethnic revolt, and besides, the Kurds were forced to flee northern Iraq because Iraq was using chemical weapons against them, not simply because many of them protested against the government.

3 This is the best answer. The United States adopted economic sanctions against South Africa because of its policy of apartheid, a policy that violated the human rights of blacks in South Africa. The Chinese government violated the human rights of students who peacefully demonstrated against government policies by imprisoning many of them (and actually injuring and killing others). Finally, the Iraqi government physically forced the Kurds out of Northern Iraq, injuring and killing thousands, and causing a major refugee crisis at the Turkish border.

4 None of these headlines refers to isolationist policies. The United States adopted economic sanctions against South Africa in order to influence it, not in order to isolate itself. The Chinese and Iraqi governments were responding to situations within their own nations, not withdrawing from the world community.

48 You only need to know about either animism or the Shinto religion in order to answer this question correctly. Eliminate answer choices that refer to other religions that you know about, since the correct answer will likely be something that is unique about these religions.

1 Monotheism is central to Islam, Christianity, and Judaism, but not to animism and Shintoism.

2 The belief in reincarnation is central to Hinduism, but not to animism and Shintoism.

3 **This is it. Both religions focus on the interconnectedness of human spirits and spirits in the natural world. The followers of these religions believe there are spirits not just in plants and animals, but in stones, in water, and in storms.**

4 The followers of neither religion have engaged in holy wars. Muslims and Christians are two groups that have engaged in holy wars.

49 Look at the cartoon carefully. Two trains are headed directly toward each other. One is on the Chinese Party Line, the other is on the Soviet Party Line. The two tracks, however, don't quite meet. They're not connected, nor can they be connected because one of them is wider than the other. And based on the expressions on the faces, it doesn't look like either the Soviets or the Chinese want to be the ones to change the type of track they're on. Also, look at the caption. It simply says, "Dilemma." Also, look at the question. It tells you that relations between the Soviet Union and China have been strained since 1956. Finally, remember that the correct answer choice will not literally describe the picture, but instead will describe what is symbolically represented in the picture. Okay, now go through the answer choices one by one.

1 **This is the best answer. For over thirty years after 1956, both the Soviet Union and China were communist nations (China still is, of course). However, while both nations embraced communism and actively repressed alternative economic and political systems, they did not have similar goals, nor did they have similar domestic and foreign policies. This idea is well represented in the cartoon. A "party line" is an official position of a group. But the two party lines don't meet, nor are they built the same way (one is wider than the other). Therefore, although the two nations were the world's great defenders of communism, they're not philosophically connected.**

2 This is a literal interpretation of the cartoon. The railroad tracks

represent the "party lines" of the two nations, not the transportation lines. Also, the trans-Siberian railroad is entirely within the former Soviet Union.

3   This cartoon doesn't represent the technological differences between the two nations, but rather the philosophical differences. In the cartoon, both sides have trains, both sides have tracks, and both sides have guys with hammers. If the cartoon had focused on technological differences, it might have focused on the difference between the two nations' nuclear capacities, for example, or the differences in their space programs.

4   This answer choice is totally unrelated to the cartoon. Nothing in the cartoon specifically or symbolically refers to Manchuria, or policies against the admission of workers, or why this would be a "dilemma."

PART II

1. ECONOMIC ASSISTANCE FROM THE INTERNATIONAL BANK FOR RECONSTRUCTION AND DEVELOPMENT

Albania

Albania is one of the poorest nations in Europe. Its trade deficit is staggering (in recent years it has imported as much as six times the dollar value that it has exported). Its inflation rate and unemployment are among the highest in Europe. Much of the problem stems from a lack of quality public education (over one-fourth of the adult population is illiterate) and from instability in the government. In 1991 and 1992, public outrage with lack of government and economic reform led to a general strike. The unemployment rate was over 50 percent, the inflation rate exceeded 100 percent and virtually all of the food consumed was imported from foreign countries. The social and economic situation in Albania reached a crisis level. As a result, the communist majority was defeated in the 1992 elections, and the Democratic Alliance Party took over.

Albania has never recovered from its economic woes, however. Continued economic problems have led to constant shifts in government alliances. Ethnic and religious unrest add to the problems. World Bank assistance is needed to stabilize the economy and add legitimacy to a government that has never quite been able to turn things around on its own. Money can be used for education and diversification of the economy, and to offset the trade imbalance that has plagued Albania for decades. Albania simply does not have the resources, the educational system or the popular unity to emerge on its own as a prosperous, self-sufficient nation.

Bangladesh

Already one of the world's poorest nations, Bangladesh has suffered from severe natural disasters during the last decade. Monsoons and cyclones have devastated the nation, leaving millions homeless and causing billions of dollars in damage. To make matters worse, the economy has been struggling because of a decline in the world demand for jute, an agricultural product harvested almost exclusively in Bangladesh. Severe overcrowding in the cities has resulted in unsanitary conditions and the spread of disease.

World Bank assistance is desperately needed to build safe and sanitary housing that can withstand at least some of the natural disasters that continually haunt the area. Investment capital is also needed to diversify the economy, which at the present time is over three-quarters agricultural. Without aid, the situation in Bangladesh will likely continue to degenerate.

Brazil

The biggest problem in Brazil is the size of its foreign debt. It's among the highest in the world. As a result, a large proportion of government expenditures are being used to pay the interest and principal on this debt, and therefore an insufficient proportion of government expenditures is flowing back into the Brazilian economy. The high debt makes foreign investors wary of the stability of the economy. An extremely high inflation rate and school drop-out rate also contribute to the problem.

Economic aid from the World Bank would help the nation pay back its enormous loans and reinvest in its own economy. Brazil is a nation rich with resources and potential, but the government needs money to invest in its own people before these resources can be maximized. Job training, education, and inflation control all can be made possible if the foreign debt problem is brought under control.

Haiti

Haiti is experiencing problems that unfortunately are not uncommon in the developing world: severe unemployment and high inflation. The fact that it has a large trade deficit doesn't help matters. The economic problems stem, in part, from political instability. After free elections in 1990 led to increased relations with the rest of the democratic world, the military took control of the government in 1991. The result was devastating for Haiti's already struggling economy. The OAS initiated an economic blockade against Haiti. Since then, attempts to reestablish democracy in Haiti have been shaky, but in 1994 the president returned to Haiti and vowed to make the economic situation his number one priority.

Economic aid from the World Bank is crucial for two reasons. First, it will enable the government of Haiti to create jobs, educate the masses, and bring the inflation rate under control. Second, it will help stabilize the political situation, instill confidence in the government's ability to meet the economic needs of its people, and eventually create a stable environment attractive to private investment.

Russia

One of the most significant problems facing Russia since the Soviet Union disbanded is that the economy has had difficulty adjusting from a command economy to a free-market economy. There are not enough free-market industries to employ the millions of people in need of jobs. Furthermore, the industries that do exist are technologically inferior to similar industries in the West. Therefore, many Soviet industries are not able to compete in the world marketplace. The government does not have enough money to aid in the adjustment to a free-market economy, or to modernize the industries to make them competitive. The result is high unemployment, high crime, an increasing inflation rate, and an unstable political environment.

Economic aid from the World Bank would help the government modernize the nation's industries and stabilize the currency. Once the nation has been modernized, the nation could compete in the world marketplace, increase exports and decrease the unemployment and inflation rates. A better economy would help to stabilize the government, which currently is being challenged by communists, and would lead to a reduction is crime, which currently is increasing due to unemployment and general uncertainty about the future. Money, if well invested in the Soviet economy, could serve as a significant stabilizing force in a nation on the brink of chaos.

Somalia

In 1991, a severe drought hit Somalia, leading to widespread famine. Such a natural disaster would severely impact most nations, but in Somalia it was worse because only a year earlier, the central government had broken down and Somalia was in the midst of civil war. Various clans were rivaling for power and the people of Somalia had no organized way of getting food. When the world community responded to the crisis with an outpouring of food, the situation only worsened when various clans prevented the food from being delivered to the people who needed it. The United Nations sent nearly 30,000 troops to distribute the food, but the political chaos continued during the UN presence, as well as after the troops pulled out.

Enormous economic aid is needed to stabilize the political situation in Somalia and meet the basic needs of the citizens. If a centralized and free government can be established in Somalia, and if it is given humanitarian aid, it can then go about the business of rebuilding a divided nation, taking care of the basic needs of its citizens, and putting long-term economic plans into action.

Vietnam

In recent years, Vietnam's economy has grown significantly. Although it remains a communist nation, capitalist reforms, like those in China, have encouraged foreign investment and private enterprise. The centralized command economy has been loosened. Land reform was recently initiated in the agricultural sector, and the banking system has been modernized for easy transactions with the West. Nevertheless, even with all of this economic growth, the unemployment rate remains high, and the education levels remain low.

Economic aid can help Vietnam gain a foothold as a free-market nation. Since the government has a large foreign debt, limited funds are available for the education system. If education and job training can be administered on a large scale, Vietnam will not only improve its unemployment rate, but will create a demand for higher paying jobs. If a significant middle class can develop as a result, Vietnam will not only have become a stable economy, but political reform may follow.

2. CITIZEN PROTESTS LEADING TO CHANGE

Storming of the Bastille—France (1789)

The Storming of the Bastille, which set the French Revolution in motion, occurred because of middle class and lower class anger with the French nobility. The middle class (bourgeoisie) consisted of merchants and professionals who were experiencing an increase in wealth but also were paying increasing taxes. Together with the peasant class, who were not experiencing an increase in wealth but who were also paying excessive taxes, they wanted to increase their political power in the Estates General, a parliamentary body comprised mostly of the nobility. They were motivated by the ideas of representative government and the rights of man expressed by the Enlightenment writers and by the events in the American Revolution. Basically, they wanted one-man, one-vote. When they didn't get it, a riot broke out and a group of peasants stormed the Bastille, a political prison, and let the prisoners out. The French Revolution had begun and the rioting quickly swept the nation.

The storming of the Bastille did not directly solve any of the problems that the peasants and bourgeoisie were experiencing, but it did set the Revolution in motion. Eventually, after an extremely bloody revolution, a Reign of Terror imposed by the Jacobin republic which replaced the monarchy, and a sweep through Europe under Napoleon, France settled down into a modern republic, complete with a constitution and the economic, political, and social change that the original rioters wanted so badly.

Bread Riots—Russia

Food shortages in an era of excessive taxes, high unemployment, and a crumbling, exhausted government led to riots in the streets of Russia. World War I was actually at the root of the problems, since an increasingly frustrated Russian public was being denied basic needs like bread, while the czarist government was spending millions on pursuing the war. The rioting eventually led to the czar's abdication of the throne, which led to the temporary installment of a democratic government. The events quickly took an even more radical turn, however. Lenin and the Bolshevik Party quickly overtook the government and ignited the revolution with hundreds of thousands of proletarian followers, a group of armed revolutionaries intent on creating a communist state in the Marxian ideal, where the workers were a powerful group intent on creating equality. What had started as a series of riots led to the establishment of the first communist state, an event that would eventually lead to a worldwide showdown of the competing economic and political philosophies of communism and capitalism.

Amritsar Revolt—India

The Amritsar Revolt was an Indian response to British fears of conspiracy. After the success of the Bolshevik Revolution in Russia, Europe was alarmed. Britain became suspicious of any nationalistic tendencies within its colonies, most especially its crown jewel of India. Britain instituted tough new laws against Indian conspiracy for nationalism and this, of course, only provoked more nationalism. It was at this point that Gandhi first encouraged a change in British policy through peaceful civil disobedience, but some of his countrymen were more violent. They attacked and killed a few Englishmen in Amritsar in 1919. A British general reacted against the crowd, not just against the individual aggressors, and killed nearly four hundred Indians, injuring hundreds more.

The consequences of the Amritsar revolt and massacre were not immediate, but they were significant. Many British officials defended the general, while Indians rallied behind the nationalistic cause. Through it all, Gandhi maintained his practice of peaceful resistance in the aftermath of this violence, which allowed him to gain worldwide legitimacy and support. The British were reluctant to pursue violent suppression of nationalism against a well-maintained nonviolent opposition, and eventually India won its independence in 1947.

Sharpeville Demonstrations—South Africa

The Sharpeville demonstrations were staged as a protest against the policy of apartheid in South Africa. Apartheid (separation and inequality of blacks and whites) became law in 1948. While much of the world was racist in practice, South Africa was one of the few places that was actually legally establishing and expanding racially motivated laws. The African National

Congress was formed by many native South Africans to combat the policy of apartheid, and they chose Nelson Mandela as their leader. The Sharpeville demonstration was a part of their effort to gain support for the anti-apartheid cause.

It was disaster. The police opened fire on the demonstrators in Johannesburg, killing seventy-two. A state of emergency was declared, over 20,000 blacks were arrested, and the African National Congress was banned. The massacre only fueled the anti-apartheid cause, however. Mandela continued his resistance and was arrested himself just a few years later, remaining in prison until 1990. The massacre also enraged much of the Western world. While the Western powers were reluctant to intervene in South Africa on behalf of the black natives, clearly world opinion was turning against the South African government after the massacre. Eventually, the goal of the Sharpeville demonstrations was realized when the South African government abolished apartheid in 1991.

Irish Republican Army Insurrections—Northern Ireland

The Irish Republican Army is a group of Catholics in Northern Ireland, a part of Great Britain that is predominantly Protestant. When Britain granted Ireland independence, it maintained control of six northern provinces known as Northern Ireland. This seemed to be a good idea at the time, because Ireland was predominantly Catholic while Northern Ireland was predominantly Protestant, just like Britain. However, the government of Northern Ireland discriminated against the Catholic minority, and eventually the IRA was created to combat the discrimination. The IRA wants to join Ireland, while the Protestant majority want to remain as a part of the United Kingdom. The protests quickly led to violence, including bombings, and soon both sides inflicted violence against each other.

The consequence of the IRA insurrections is not yet known. We do know that the conflict has raged for decades and that thousands have died. We also know that both sides have been willing to enter into peaceful negotiations in recent years. But since the dispute remains unsettled, and since the Catholic population of Northern Ireland is quickly increasing in proportion to the Protestant population, the future of Ireland and the success or failure of the IRA are still in question.

Intifada Uprisings—Israel

The intifada uprisings are part of an ongoing dispute between Israel and Islamic Palestinians. Both want Palestine as their homeland. The source of the conflict goes back to the creation of Israel as a Jewish homeland in

1948. The Jews have claimed Palestine as their homeland since Biblical times. The Muslims claim Palestine as rightfully theirs, since they lived in the land during the time that most of the people in the region converted to the Islamic faith. The two groups have fought ever since, including the Six-Day War in 1967 and the Yom Kippur War in 1973. Most recently, there have been groups of young fundamentalists who have sponsored terrorism against Israel. These radical groups are known as the Intifada. The Intifada has even killed many within its own ranks who have been suspected of dealing with Israel.

The intifada uprisings have been a setback to the peace process in Palestine. While more moderate leaders of the Palestine Liberation Organization try to deal with Israel, the intifada threatens extremist action. The full consequences of the uprisings are not yet known. However, as long as they remain committed to their cause, they can delay the peace process, even if they represent a minority opinion.

Tiananmen Square Demonstrations—China

In 1989, thousands of Chinese students demonstrated in Tiananmen Square for social and political reforms in the Western fashion. They were encouraged by two things. First, the government of China under Deng had instituted many Western economic reforms that seemed to relax the overall governmental stance on communism. Second, the increased trade with the West exposed Chinese students to Western ideas and the successes of previous peaceful demonstrations. However, the demonstrators were not met with open ears from the Chinese government. Instead, the government reacted militarily, killing, injuring, and imprisoning hundreds of unarmed students.

The event sent a shockwave through the nation of China and the entire world. The government's reaction indicated that while China has been willing to make economic reforms, it is not yet ready to make political or social reforms. While much of the rest of the world strongly condemned the actions of the Chinese government, they continued to trade and increase business with China. Therefore, the demonstrations did not succeed in bringing about the desired social and political changes. The Chinese economy continues to boom, despite the government crackdown on free expression.

3. WARS

Russo-Japanese War—Russia

Russia was thrust into war with Japan when Japan attacked the Russian fleet at Port Arthur in Manchuria. Both Russia and Japan had been vying for control of Manchuria, which was rich with natural resources that the industrializing nations craved. Russia's loss to Japan was humiliating. For the first time, a major European power had lost a war to an Asian power, and as an added insult, it had been defeated with Western weaponry and technology. This not only sent a wake-up call to Moscow, but to the entire world. Japan was emerging as a world power. As for Russia, it lost land and fishing rights to Japan, but internally, the government lost much more. The czar lost legitimacy, setting the stage for insurrections and eventually revolution.

World War I—Austria-Hungary

Austria-Hungary didn't simply join the fighting of World War I; World War I started with Austria-Hungary. When Archduke Ferdinand was assassinated by Serbian nationalists in Sarajevo, Austria-Hungary made demands on the Serbian government. Although the Serbian government complied with most of the demands, Austria-Hungary was not satisfied. It wanted absolute control over the Balkans. So, it joined forces with Germany and together they attacked Serbia, setting off World War I. Russia sided with Serbia, Germany then attacked France, France sided with Russia, Turkey sided with Austria-Hungary, Great Britain sided with France and Russia, and millions of Europeans lost their lives.

The consequences for Austria-Hungary were devastating, so devastating that Austria-Hungary ceased to exist. Instead, it split into three nations— Austria, Hungary, and Czechoslovakia. As in many other European nations, millions of lives were lost, especially men in their teens and twenties. Austria-Hungary's aggressive response to the assassination cost it its existence.

World War II—Japan

Already in a war with China, Japan entered World War II on December 7, 1941 when it attacked the United States at Pearl Harbor. World War II had already consumed Europe by this time, and Japan had allied itself with Germany and Italy, but it was Japan's interest in China that brought it into the war. Japan wanted to overrun China and gain access to its resources. The United States made it clear that it would not allow that to occur, and imposed an economic embargo on Japan. In response, Japan attacked Pearl Harbor and declared war on the United States. When Germany, Japan's ally, also declared war on the United States, Japan became part of a much larger war than just its war with the United States and China.

The consequences of the war transformed Japan. Japan was militarily destroyed, and in the end, two of its cities, Nagasaki and Hiroshima, were obliterated by atomic bombs. Its imperial empire was stripped away, its military was reduced to almost nothing, and its government system was transformed into a parliamentary democracy. After a crushing defeat, Japan recreated itself in the political and economic mold of the West.

Six-Day War—Israel

After Egyptian President Nasser Arafat denied Israeli access to the Gulf of Aqaba, Israel attacked Egypt, Jordan, and Syria, sparking the Six-Day War. Israel took control of the Sinai Peninsula from Egypt, the West Bank from Jordan (as well as the Jordanian portion of Jerusalem), and the Golan Heights from Syria. Israel claimed that occupation of these lands was necessary for its protection. In 1982, Israel returned the Sinai Peninsula to Egypt. In 1993, some progress was made on the return of part of the West Bank to the Palestinians, but today, the future of most of the West Bank, East Jerusalem, and the Golan Heights remains unsettled.

The consequences for Israel were two-fold. First, it established itself as a military power that was not only willing to protect itself, but also to expand its territory. In other words, it established itself as an aggressor. Second, because it inflamed an already intense situation, it exposed itself to conflict and terrorism attacks that would continue for the next three decades, and quite possibly into the future. The territories in question have not been peacefully integrated into Israeli society. Instead, the territories gained by means of the Six-Day War remain disputed. The Six-Day War, then, helped to feed lasting conflict, rather than lasting peace.

Vietnam War—South Vietnam

Pro-Western South Vietnam entered the Vietnam War against the communist forces of North Vietnam in the hope of suppressing the spread of Communism, and creating a democratic state. With the help of the United States, the war escalated in the 1960's and continued into the 1970's, when the tide turned against South Vietnam. South Vietnam fell to the North in 1975, at which time Vietnam was unified as a communist state. Therefore, the result of the Vietnam War on South Vietnam was simply that the nation ceased to exist.

Persian Gulf War—Iraq

When Iraq invaded Kuwait in 1990 in order to gain control of Kuwait's oil reserves, the Persian Gulf War began. The imperialist motivations of Iraq were of tremendous concern to the other nations of the Persian Gulf region, especially Saudi Arabia, who assumed it was next in line for attack from Iraq. Since Iraq would have controlled nearly half of the world's oil reserves if it invaded Saudi Arabia, the industrialized world panicked and came to the immediate aid of the Kuwaiti government, driving the Iraqi military well back into its own territory.

The consequences of the war were devastating for Iraq. Not only was the military soundly defeated, but the United Nations continued to patrol Iraqi airspace. Economic sanctions imposed against Iraq resulted in widespread hunger and poverty. Nevertheless, Saddam Hussein, the leader of Iraq and instigator of the war, has remained in power and has threatened aggression again.

4. CULTURAL DIFFUSION

Ancient Roman Empire (first to third centuries)

During the first and second centuries AD, the Roman Empire reached its greatest extent, stretching from Britain in the northwest all the way to the Middle East and around the Mediterranean through northern Africa. One of the remarkable characteristics of the Roman Empire was that, in general, it allowed the customs of its conquered regions to remain intact. Therefore, Christianity spread in the Middle East even as the Romans ruled it. The Romans, as a consequence, were exposed to Christianity. This caused a reaction against Christianity, which some in Rome saw as a threat to traditional Roman values (others tried to integrate traditional Roman values with Christianity). Persecution of Christianity followed, but Christianity continued to spread. The Christian movement was gaining momentum not only in the Middle East and northern Africa, but in areas further west and north. Eventually, the Roman Empire embraced Christianity with the rise of Constantine. The religious culture of the Eastern provinces thereafter diffused into the entire Roman Empire.

Islamic Empire (seventh to twelfth centuries)

The Islamic Empire reached its greatest extent during the Abbasid Dynasty in the seventh to twelfth centuries. During this time, the Empire translated many ancient Greek and Roman texts, and expanded on mathematical and scientific knowledge gained from both the West and East. While knowledge in Europe was being lost during the Middle Ages, the Islamic Empire kept much of ancient Europe's past alive. But the Islamic Empire not only was affected by other cultures, it effected those cultures as well. During this time, the Moors conquered much of Spain. With them, they brought knowledge of math, science, architecture, and literature to Europe. The lasting impact of the Islamic culture of Spain can still be seen today in its architecture.

Mongol Empire (thirteenth century)

The Mongol Empire stretched from China all the way to Moscow. Described by many as barbarian, Mongol culture did not enhance the arts, science, or the economies of the regions it conquered, one of which was Russia. This is not to say, however, that it did not affect the culture of Russia tremendously. It did. It brought it to a standstill. Individuality was not recognized. Instead, loyalty to authority was expected. Basic subsistence farming was practiced and the general economic and social progress of Russia was slowed, even while the rest of Europe was emerging from the Middle Ages. Russia has been trying to catch up to the West's economic, social, and political reforms ever since.

Mali Empire (fourteenth century)

During the fourteenth century, the Mali Empire in western Africa was at its height. A nation of traders, people from Mali traveled throughout northern Africa on their way to the Middle East. The original leader of Mali, Sundiata, converted to the Islamic faith and with him all of Mali. Since they traveled so extensively throughout northern Africa, the Mali introduced Islam to much of the region, converting small kingdoms as they passed through. The Emperor Musa even visited Mecca and Cairo, taking with him caravans of gold. The Mali brought back ideas and learning from the Middle East and Egypt and established Timbuktu as a major cultural destination where people could learn not just about Mali culture, but all the cultures that the Mali had contact with. But it was the cultural diffusion of the Islamic faith that probably had the most lasting impact on the region.

Spanish (fifteenth to seventeenth centuries)

During the fifteenth, sixteenth, and seventeenth centuries, Spain conquered Latin America. The Spaniards destroyed the native Inca culture and replaced it with their own. Roman Catholicism became the dominant religion, Spanish became the dominant language, and even European diseases became the dominant killers. The entire region would never be the same. Even plants and animals from Spain were introduced to the region, and most certainly Spanish architecture was transplanted as well. Even after independence was won by the Latin American nations, the dominance of the Spanish influence remained. The region still practices Catholicism, still speaks Spanish, and although attempts have been made to revive some aspects of its ancient past, the region is still known as "Latin" America.

Manchu Empire (seventeenth to twentieth centuries)

The Manchu Empire was the last dynasty of China. It actually was an empire known more for the fact that it was conquered and divided up by European powers and Japan than for the fact that it conquered Tibet and Mongolia. Nevertheless, before the Europeans carved China up into spheres of influence, the Manchu Empire was highly organized and very stable. Its land redistribution programs in the conquered areas of Tibet and Mongolia changed the lives of the peasants. In addition, the Manchu introduced their art and porcelain into the conquered areas. When the European powers finally came to China, at first welcomed for their knowledge, but later resented for their pursuit of power in the region, the conquered areas of the Manchu Empire changed along with China itself. The entire region was overrun by the Europeans, and the ways of the West diffused in.

Russian (eighteenth to nineteenth centuries)

Early eighteenth century Russia was dominated by the expansion and westernization of Peter the Great. He took the Baltic region from Sweden, where he built his "window to the West," St. Petersburg, as the new capital of Russia. The most amazing thing about the culture that diffused into the conquered region is that Peter the Great served as a conduit for double cultural diffusion. Specifically, Peter the Great brought in Western scientists, architects, designers and businessmen, learned about the West and then transferred this new knowledge directly to the newly conquered region. In other words, it was not the traditional Russian culture that diffused into the conquered region, but rather the newly acquired western knowledge. Perhaps even more importantly, the newly acquired Western practices didn't merely *diffuse* into the new region, but were forcibly directed at it. The whole city of St. Petersburg was built specifically as a Western city! The impact on the Baltic region was enormous. Suddenly, it was at the center of activity in the Russian Empire. While the rest of Russia essentially dragged its feet in Peter the Great's Westernization attempt, the Baltic region became the symbol of the new Russia.

5. GEOGRAPHIC FACTORS INFLUENCING EVENTS

Industrial Revolution in England

England was geographically well equipped for the Industrial Revolution. First, its harbors made trade with other nations easy. Ships carried raw materials and finished products to and from England and its colonies. Second, its close proximity to mainland Europe allowed it to easily trade with the other industrial giants of the time. Third, its natural resources of coal and iron were perfect complements to industrialization. It's no surprise that England emerged as an industrial giant.

Catherine the Great's decision to conquer the Ukraine

During Catherine the Great's reign, Russia had access to the Baltic Sea, but lacked a warm-water port to the south. The Ukraine was conveniently located just south of Russia and along the shores of the Black Sea. By way of the Bosphorus, the Black Sea is connected to the Aegean Sea, which is connected to the Mediterranean Sea and thereby the rest of the world. Therefore, Catherine the Great conquered the Ukraine for Russia and embarked on building transportation networks to the Black Sea ports. The Ottoman Empire eventually fell and Russia thereafter had warm-water ports with access to the Mediterranean.

Napoleon's invasion of Russia

Napoleon was able to sweep through much of Western Europe swiftly, but when he reached Russia, he met his greatest enemies: the size of the land and the harshness of the winter. Russia is a massive expanse of land. Napoleon could not keep his troops well supplied as they traveled further into the interior of Russia, and further away from Western Europe. Exhausted and defeated, Napoleon was unsuccessful in his attempts to conquer Russia.

Bolívar's attempt to create a United Gran Colombia

After independence movements swept through Latin America, Bolívar envisioned the creation of a United Gran Colombia, unifying South America into a single nation. The region was already united under a common religion and all of the nations except Brazil were Spanish-speaking, but political and geographic forces stood in the way. South America is extremely diverse geographically. From the Andes mountains, to the Amazon rain forests, to the pampas, cross-continental transportation and communication were difficult, especially given the technology available at the time. People in different regions of South America had been isolated from one another due to these geographic features. This isolation allowed different subcultures to develop, inhibiting the possibility of unification. Therefore, even though geography did not necessarily directly result in a failed attempt at unification, it indirectly did in the sense that isolation led to the development of cultural differences.

Building of the Suez Canal in Egypt

The geography of the entire continents of Europe, Asia, and Africa played a role in the desire to build the Suez Canal in Egypt. The three continents are connected. Therefore, prior to the building of the Suez Canal, if a ship needed to travel from Britain to India, it had to go all the way around the tip of Africa and then back northeast again to reach India. Western Europe could reach the Middle East by way of the Mediterranean Sea, but it could go no further. However, a small strip of land between the Mediterranean Sea and the Red Sea changed all that. The geographic significance of this strip of land was enormous. It was the narrowest piece of land between the Mediterranean Sea and a string of waterways leading to India and the Pacific. It was here that the French and British logically built a canal. Travel time between Europe and Asia was reduced dramatically, and Egypt suddenly became strategically important.

European efforts to colonize Africa

Except for a small tip of Egypt which is connected to the Middle East, Africa is entirely surrounded by water. The Mediterranean Sea lies to the north, the Atlantic to the west and the Indian Ocean and the Red Sea to the east. Therefore, Europeans had easy naval access to Africa, especially given their superior naval technology. Nevertheless, Africa had remained largely unknown to the Europeans prior to their imperialistic successes in the Americas. Because of their knowledge of the coastal areas from trade voyages, the Europeans started on the periphery and slowly moved to the interior. The deserts, jungles, and weather patterns slowed the colonization process, but they still managed to colonize the entire continent. Soon Britain linked north and south with a huge railway, the Suez Canal was built, and Europe was exploiting all of Africa on a regular basis. Nevertheless, because of the difficulty of transportation over rough terrain, the European powers focused on settling the coastal regions. Even to this day, the interior regions remain more "unsettled" than many of the coastal regions.

Japan's decision to invade Manchuria

As Japan industrialized, it faced a major problem. It did not have natural resources such as coal and iron, and, unlike the European powers, it lacked a colonial empire from which it could supply its factories. It was at this point that Japan became imperialistic. Japan decided to invade Manchuria, which was loaded with coal and iron and located nearby. With its newly acquired Western technology, Japan was easily able to invade Manchuria.

6. UNIVERSAL DECLARATION OF HUMAN RIGHTS

Bosnia

Human rights violations have been common in Bosnia ever since independence was declared in 1992. Specifically, Article 5 has been violated repeatedly. The civil war in the region has involved murder, rape, and violent torture. Bosnian Serbs have attempted to "cleanse" the region of Muslims, slaughtering them on sight and burning their homes and mosques. After the United Nations supported the Dayton Conference for peace in the region in 1995, it sent peacekeeping forces to enforce the terms. Sporadic violence has continued, but it is hoped that the groups can live together in one nation, although in separate regions.

Cuba

Ever since Fidel Castro took control of Cuba, his regime has violated Article 21 of the Declaration of Human Rights. He has not tolerated political opposition or sought to establish a representative government. Instead, Castro stands as a dictator, even as his own people face economic hardships. The United States has reacted by imposing economic sanctions, which have become particularly effective since the fall of communism in Europe. The Soviet Union no longer supports the Castro regime, and without trade and cooperation with that industrialized nation, Cuba's future seems bleak. Unfortunately, if tradition holds, it will be the people of Cuba, rather than Castro himself, who will suffer the consequences.

India

The caste system in India has led to many violations of human rights, especially against members of the lowest caste, the "untouchables." Members of the lowest caste cannot associate with the members of higher castes, neither in social situations nor in business partnerships. The untouchables are prevented from marrying, befriending, or even talking to people of higher castes, in definite violation of Article 20.

The government of India has tried to alleviate the situation by outlawing the caste system. However, because the caste system is part of the traditional culture and dominant religion of India, the government's efforts have always been unsuccessful, especially in rural areas. In a further effort, the government has taken it upon itself to hire many untouchables for government jobs. Nevertheless, because the human rights violations of untouchables are culturally sanctioned by millions of Indians and by the dominant religion, the government can only do so much. If the untouchables are truly to gain human rights in India, a change in culture at a fundamental level will need to occur.

Iran

After the success of the Islamic Revolution in Iran in 1979, the new fundamentalist government reversed the human rights progress made by Shah Pahlavi and strictly monitored those with views opposed to the goals of the new regime. In direct violation of Article 18, the new government arrested, tortured, and killed people who it believed represented a threat to the social, political, and religious goals of the government. Much of the world was stunned by the success of a religiously motivated revolution, but the world has not been quick to act on behalf of the people whose religious and political rights are being violated. The United States enacted a trade embargo against Iran, but its decision was due to Iran's support of terrorism, not to Iran's suppression of freedoms within its own country. Instead, reform in Iran has come from within. Many Iranians have become increasingly dissatisfied with the state of the economy and general society since the Islamic Revolution. They are arguing, sometimes successfully, for a more open society.

Rwanda/Burundi

Human rights violations in Rwanda and Burundi stem from conflicts between two groups: the Tutsi (10 percent of the population in Rwanda and 15 percent of the population in Burundi) who traditionally have governed the Hutu (90 percent of Rwanda, 85 percent of Burundi). Hutu revolts against Tutsi leadership left hundreds of thousands dead. The Hutu eventually gained control in the 1970s. However, in 1994, the Hutu leaders of Rwanda and Burundi were killed in an airline crash, and thereafter the Tutsi swept through the nations and declared civil war, creating a refugee problem of nearly two million Hutu.

Many articles of the Universal Declaration of Human Rights have been violated by both sides of this ongoing problem, but most recently the problem has involved Article 9. The crisis has sent millions of refugees into Zaire. The Hutu are trying to escape torture and death and believe that they cannot safely return to their own country. The United Nations has intervened to aid Zaire in dealing with the onslaught of refugees and has sent a multinational force to restore order to the region. The goal of the UN effort is to create a stable situation in which the Hutu people can safely return to their countries. The problem remains unsettled, however.

Soviet Union/Russia

The former Soviet Union, and Russia before it, consistently violated Article 18 of the Declaration of Human Rights. In czarist Russia, Jews were discriminated against openly, segregated into walled ghettos and denied basic services. As the discrimination became more entrenched in Russian society, the czars even ordered the murder of innocent Jews and the ransacking of their homes and villages. Later, after the formation of the Soviet Union, the government continued its tradition of religious intolerance, especially since the Soviet Union was officially an atheist state. Citizens who openly practiced their religions were discriminated against, especially Muslims in the southern part of the Soviet Union. The international community has spoken out against religious discrimination, but it has not interfered in the internal religious struggles of Russia or the former Soviet Union.

7. RELIGION AND PHILOSOPHY

Buddhism—Southeast Asia

Central to Buddhism are the Four Noble Truths: life in this world involves unhappiness; unhappiness is caused by the desire for worldly things; happiness can be achieved by detaching oneself from these worldly things; nirvana can be reached by those who follow the Eightfold Path (which consists of basic rules of conduct and thought). This belief system based on a detachment from worldly desires has greatly affected the development of Southeast Asia. For centuries, the region remained relatively isolationist, content with subsistence farming methods and limited material wealth. Its wars were about control over land and people, but not about control of natural resources and industry. The region was dragged into the Industrial Revolution by European imperialists, but not after putting up a fight. Even today, as the region's economies are expanding rapidly, the typical person lives without attachment to material things, unlike many of his or her Western counterparts.

Confucianism—China

Confucianism is a life philosophy more than a religion because it is concerned with daily conduct in the here and now, not with salvation or the afterlife. Confucius focused on individual relationships—the duties that individuals owe to one another within their families, and their relationships with superiors and inferiors. Confucian philosophy assumes a class society wherein inferior classes owe respect to superior classes and superior classes (and most importantly the ruling class) owe fairness and kindness to the inferior classes. The same is true in family relationships. The younger generations must be respectful and dutiful to the older generations, including generations that have already passed away.

Confucianism has affected Chinese culture enormously. For centuries, it reinforced the class system and repressed new ideas from the younger generations. It also contributed to internal order within the society. As long as everyone played out the role expected of him or her, society was orderly and predictable. Today, Confucianism affects the social relationships of hundreds of millions of Chinese, even though Communist China is officially atheist and officially classless.

Hinduism—India

Hinduism is a traditional religion in the strictest definition. In other words, it has been passed down from generation to generation, not through an all-important written text or by a central religious authority, but simply as a matter of custom and tradition. Hindus believe that who you are in this life was determined by who you were in a past life. And how you conduct yourself in your assigned role in this life will determine the role (caste) you get in a future life. This belief has affected the social, political, and economic situation in India enormously.

The caste system in India is based on the Hindu religion. It was outlawed when India became an independent nation, but millions still practice it as part of their religion. The people of the lowest caste (the untouchables) cannot socially mingle or even work side by side with the people of the highest caste. This has led not only to widespread social discrimination, but widespread employment discrimination as well. The untouchables do all the dirty jobs that nobody else will do. Many Hindus do not challenge discrimination because they want to be rewarded with a higher caste in a later life. Social mobility is therefore greatly hindered. Nevertheless, as more people have moved to the cities, they have begun to disassociate themselves from the caste system. In fact, recently, untouchables have risen to positions of political authority. However, Hinduism remains a tremendous influence in the lives of millions of Indians.

Islam—Middle East

Islam is a monotheistic faith. Muslims do not worship Muhammed as God, but worship God through the message brought to them by Muhammed. Muslims believe that salvation is won through submission to the will of God, and that this can be accomplished by means of the Five Pillars of Islam. These five pillars include a confession of faith, prayer five times a day while bowing toward Mecca, charity to the needy, fasting during the month of Ramadan, and a pilgrimage to Mecca at least once during one's life. But there is much more to the Islamic faith than just the five Pillars.

Islam has affected the social and political development of the Middle East enormously. Since many nations are Islamic states, as opposed to secular states, the tenets of Islam serve as the official law of the land. Everything from women's rights to clothing is dictated by the Islamic faith and enforced by the law. In nations with a strong Islamic fundamentalist presence, attempts to modernize or westernize the economy and social customs of the nation often have been denounced as heresy. This has led to strained relations with the West. And although many Middle Eastern countries have had moderate leaders, as long as the majority of people want Islam to be entrenched in the political system, the Islamic faith will continue to dominate the political and social developments in the region.

Protestantism—Western Europe

Protestantism is a subdivision of Christianity that was created when people within the Roman Catholic Church, most notably Martin Luther, wanted to reform the Church's positions and interpretations of the Bible. When the Catholic Church resisted, the idea of reform led to the idea of actually breaking away from the Catholic Church, and thereby Protestant denominations were born. Like Catholics, Protestants believe in the divinity of Christ and the sanctity of the Bible, but they believe that individuals can interpret the Bible for themselves. They believe in salvation through faith in Christ, not simply through good deeds or the purchase of indulgences (a practice common in the Catholic Church during the time of the Reformation).

Protestantism affected Western Europe enormously. Not only did it destroy the religious unity of the region, but it invited people to think for themselves against authority. This attitude helped spark the Renaissance and the Enlightenment, which led to philosophies advocating individuality and denouncing absolute authority of government. In addition, the social unrest caused by a division in religious philosophy led to warfare based in part on these religious differences. This division is still seen today in the terrorist attacks common in Northern Ireland. Protestantism, therefore, changed not only the religious face of Europe, but the political and social faces as well.

Roman Catholicism—Latin America

Roman Catholicism has been the dominant religion of Latin America ever since Europe, most notably Spain, conquered the region. Roman Catholics are Christian, but can be distinguished from Protestants. Roman Catholics believe in the divinity of Christ and the Virgin Mary, and believe that the Church hierarchy of priests, Pope, and Saints serve as intermediaries between the faithful and God. Unlike most Protestants, Roman Catholics believe in the authority of their local priest to interpret the Bible for them and are much less likely to challenge Church doctrines.

Because it is the dominant religion of Latin America, Catholicism has affected the region enormously. It has served as a dominant unifying force, linking the cultures of Latin America by a common thread. Family life and social life have been greatly affected by the policies of the Church, but this is not to say that all Catholics agree. Liberal Catholic priests have attempted to raise the standard of living of the poor for moral reasons, while conservative Catholic priests have argued that individuals should remain faithful to the policies of their authorities. This dispute, however, only serves to show that the Catholic religion is an extremely important force in the social and political lives of Latin Americans.

Russian Orthodoxy

Russian Orthodoxy stemmed from the Eastern Christian Church (the Byzantine Empire of Constantinople), as opposed to the Western Christian Church (the Roman Empire). Like the Roman Catholics, the Orthodox share a belief in the divinity of Jesus Christ and believe in redemption through faith, but they reject many of the doctrines that have been added to Roman Catholicism since the seventh Ecumenical Council in 787, and do not look to the Pope as their leader. When Vladimir converted to Christianity in the late tenth century—and thereby imposed the religion on all of Russia—the effect on Russia for the remainder of the Middle Ages was remarkable. Russia was now decidedly culturally allied with the East, as opposed to the West. Cathedrals were built in the Byzantine tradition; Kiev was modeled in many ways after Constantinople. When Western Europe emerged from the Middle Ages, Russia lagged behind. It was not part of the Reformation movement in the West, and therefore was not part of the societal and cultural changes that occurred there. Vladimir's decision to become Orthodox rather than Roman Catholic was, therefore, extremely significant to the later development of Russia.

EXAMINATION
AUGUST 1997

Part I (55 credits): Answer all 48 questions in this part.

Directions (1–48): For each statement or question, write on the separate answer sheet the *number* of the word or expression that, of those given, best completes the statement or answers the question.

---

1 Social mobility would most likely occur in a society that has a

1 slow rate of economic growth
2 low per-capita income
3 traditional class structure
4 variety of educational opportunities

2 Which factor is a common characteristic of a subsistence economy?

1 a barely adequate supply of food
2 a highly skilled labor force
3 high levels of capital investment
4 dependence on the export of goods

3 Which statement can best be supported by the existence of the African kingdoms of the Songhai, Mali, Kush, and Nubia?

  1 Natural geographic barriers prevented major cultural development in these civilizations.
  2 Africans established thriving civilizations long before European colonization.
  3 These societies were so involved with violent civil wars that there was little time for cultural development.
  4 These African civilizations were entirely self-sufficient and discouraged trade with other areas.

4 A major reason for the recent increase in African urbanization is the

  1 reemphasis on the extended family in many cities in the region
  2 increasing job opportunities in industrial centers
  3 increasing famine relief efforts of the United Nations
  4 growth of political unrest in rural areas

5 Africa's rivers are often of little help in transporting large quantities of goods and people because they

  1 flow toward the mountains
  2 run only north and south
  3 are not long enough
  4 have many falls and rapids

6 A lasting influence of British colonialism on India is most evident in India's

  1 commitment to parliamentary democracy
  2 continuation of the caste system
  3 development of a policy of nonalignment
  4 establishment of a command economy

7 "Your words are wise, Arjuna, but your sorrow is for nothing. The truly wise mourn neither for the living nor the dead. There nerve was a time when I did not exist, nor you, nor any of these kings. Nor is there any future in which we shall cease to be. . . ."

  This passage best reflects a belief in

  1 ancestor worship
  2 the Eightfold Path
  3 reincarnation
  4 nirvana

8 In 1947, the subcontinent of India became independent and was divided into India and Pakistan. This division recognized the

  1 rivalries between religious groups
  2 strength of fascism in certain regions
  3 natural geographic boundaries of the region
  4 colonial boundaries established by the British

9 In the late 1980's and early 1990's, the improvement in the economies of most Pacific Rim countries could be attributed to

  1 greater industrialization
  2 a total reliance on cash crops
  3 continuing civil wars
  4 the oil crisis in the Middle East

10 What effect did the Opium War and the Treaty of Nanjing have on China?

    1 Chinese Nationalists increased their influence in rural areas.

    2 The Manchu government expelled the Western powers.

    3 China was divided into spheres of influence.

    4 China adopted a democratic system of government.

11 Which change occurred in China's economy in the 1980's and 1990's under the leadership of Deng Xiaoping?

    1 Economic policies were based on the ideas of the Cultural Revolution.

    2 Collectivization of agriculture was introduced into the economy.

    3 Foreign investment in the economy was encouraged.

    4 Privatization of industry was outlawed.

12 Which action by the Chinese Government since 1949 best reflects the influence of Confucianism?

    1 Dissidents have been allowed to criticize the government.

    2 Education has been discouraged at all levels of society.

    3 Democratic policies have been encouraged.

    4 Respect for and allegiance to rulers has been promoted.

13 "... the Japanese people forever renounce war as a sovereign right of the nation and the threat or use of force as a means of settling international disputes. ... In order to accomplish the aim. . . land, sea, and air forces. . . will never be maintained."

Which event is directly responsible for the inclusion of this statement in Japan's current Constitution?

1 Japan's defeat in World War II
2 Japan's involvement in the Persian Gulf War
3 United Nations sanctions against Japan
4 Japan's emergence as an economic superpower

Base your answer to question 14 on the diagram below and on your knowledge of social studies.

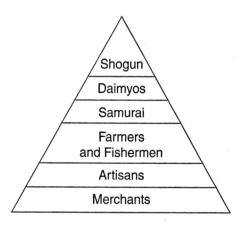

14 Merchants are shown at the bottom of this social pyramid of feudal Japan because they

1 comprised the largest percentage of Japan's population at that time
2 were viewed as having little status in the society
3 were unable to read or write
4 did not believe in the Shinto religion

15 The tea ceremony, Kabuki theater, and writing haiku poetry remain important in Japan today. What do these activities suggest about Japanese culture?

1 Western culture influences contemporary Japanese life
2 The ideas of Confucianism continue to dominate Japanese life
3 The Japanese continue to value traditional customs and practices
4 Social change remains a goal of Japanese society

16 Which statement provides the best evidence that Spain was the dominant colonial power in Latin America?

1 Spain and Mexico continue to use the same currency
2 Spain continues to provide military support for Latin America
3 Spanish is the principal language spoken in most of Latin America
4 Argentina elects representatives to the legislature of Spain

Base your answer to question 17 on the graph below and on your knowledge of social studies.

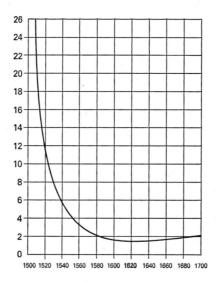

17 Which statement can best be supported by the information provided by this graph?

1 The Indian population in Mexico steadily increased between 1500 and 1700

2 The effects of the Spanish conquest on the Indian population in Mexico were most severe between 1500 and 1540

3 The Spanish conquest of Mexico improved the standard of living for the Indian population in Mexico

4 Spanish influence in Mexico had ended by 1700

18 For many Latin American nations, the reliance on single cash-crop economies has led to

1 unstable economies as world market prices rise and fall
2 long-term economic progress as exports continue to increase
3 an increased standard of living for the majority of farmers
4 increased agricultural surpluses as production of food exceeds demand

19 Which conclusion about Latin American political history could be reached after a study of the rise to power of Juan Perón in Argentina and Augusto Pinochet in Chile?

1 The strongest leaders are those who are elected democratically
2 Spain generally supported independence movements in Latin America
3 Latin America has a strong tradition of monarchy
4 People will often support dictators who promise to restore stability

Base your answers to questions 20 and 21 on the passage below and on your knowledge of social studies.

> **IN THE NAME OF ALLAH**
> **THE COMPASSIONATE**
> **THE MERCIFUL**
> Praise be to Allah, Lord of the creation,
> The compassionate, the merciful,
> King of the last judgement!
> You alone we worship,
> and to you alone we pray for help.

20 People who accept the beliefs stated in this passage believe in

1 polytheism 3 emperor worship
2 monotheism 4 papal authority

21 In which book can this passage be found?

1 old Testament of the Bible
2 Analects of Confucius
3 Talmud
4 Koran

22 Since 1948, the main disagreement between the Arabs and the Israelis has revolved around

1 Israel's isolationist policies
2 the interpretation of monotheism
3 territorial claims
4 the possession of oilfields

Base your answers to question 23 on the cartoon below and on your knowledge of social studies.

23 What is the main idea of this 1994 cartoon?

1 Israelis have become poorer because of their struggle with the Palestinians.
2 Various economic problems continue despite Palestinian autonomy in the Gaza region.
3 Israel is willing to invest large amounts of money in developing Gaza.
4 Peace has finally come to the Gaza region.

24 One similarity in the leadership of Mustafa Kemal Atatürk in Turkey and that of Shah Reza Pahlavi in Iran was that both leaders

1 conquered neighboring countries
2 began the process of westernization in their nations
3 promoted traditional Islamic practices
4 supported the establishment of communes

25 The issues of the sale of indulgences and of the worldly lives of the clergy were addressed by

1 Adam Smith in *The Wealth of Nations*
2 John Locke in his treatises on government
3 Martin Luther in his ninety-five theses
4 Karl Marx in *The Communist Manifesto*

26 The Renaissance, the French Revolution, and the European Industrial Revolution have all contributed to the development of

1 utopian societies
2 a powerful Roman Catholic Church
3 divine right monarchies
4 a growing and influential middle class

27 "Kings sit upon God's throne and rule according to God's law."

This statement would most likely have been made by a person who believed in

1 oligarchy
2 absolutism
3 democracy
4 glasnost

28 Which statement best describes a major reason that the Industrial Revolution began in Great Britain?

1 Sufficient coal and iron ore reserves and a good transportation system were available.
2 Industries were owned by the national government.
3 A strong union movement was able to secure good working conditions and high wages for factory workers.
4 Cities could easily accommodate the migration of people from rural to urban areas.

29 Which factor contributed most to the rise of totalitarian governments in Europe before World War II?

1 improved educational systems
2 expanding democratic reforms
3 increasing political stability
4 worsening economic conditions

30 Which term is used to identify the Soviet programs that established production goals for agriculture and industry under the leadership of Joseph Stalin?

1 Great Leap Forward   3 five-year plans
2 Four Modernizations   4 perestroika

31 The 1956 invasion of Hungary and the 1968 invasion of Czechoslovakia by the Soviet Union were attempts to

1 keep Communist governments in power in Eastern Europe

2 decrease Cold War tensions between Eastern Europe and the United States

3 prevent German militarism from spreading throughout Europe

4 provide humanitarian aid to the ethnic minorities of these nations

32 Which concept is best illustrated by the formation of new nations from the areas of the former Soviet Union?

1 self-determination 3 imperialism
2 nonalignment 4 utopianism

33 In the early 1990's, Czechoslovakia drew the attention of the world when it

1 expanded its territory south into Bosnia-Herzegovina

2 divided into two independent nations in a peaceful manner

3 became the first nation to rejoin the Warsaw Pact

4 resisted a United Nations invasion of Slovakia

Base your answer to question 34 on the cartoon below and on your knowledge of social studies.

34 This 1992 cartoon refers to Russia's
1 constant fear of invasion from the West
2 tendency to establish totalitarian rule during a crisis
3 attempts to settle foreign policy disputes
4 current difficulty in establishing economic reforms

35 "Let me say that our system of government does not copy the institutions of our neighbors. It is more the case of our being a model to others than of our imitating anyone else. Our constitution is called a democracy because power is in the hands, not of a minority, but of the whole people."

Which early society is most likely described in this quotation?

1 Spartan   3 Athenian
2 Babylonian   4 Egyptian

Base your answer to question 36 on the cartoon below and on your knowledge of social studies.

36 The cartoonist is suggesting that forgetting the past has resulted in

    1 tragic consequences for Bosnia's people
    2 an effective solution for Bosnia's problems
    3 independence for Bosnia
    4 fewer Bosnian problems in the 1990's than in previous decades

37 "The relationship between demographic growth and environmental degradation has been clearly established, but reducing birthrates will not, by itself, solve the planet's evironmental and human problems. Equally important is lowering consumption rates in industrial countries."

—Alan Durning

Which statement best reflects the meaning of the passage?

1 industrial societies and developing nations experience different problems.
2 Lifestyles in many nations are depleting the Earth's resources.
3 Technology alone can solve the world's environmental problems.
4 Consumption rates have little relationship to environmental problems.

38 A major goal of the Green Revolution was to

1 limit environmental pollution
2 prevent global warfare
3 increase agricultural production
4 decrease population growth

39 As global interdependence spreads, it increases the need for

1 trade restrictions between nations
2 the resumption of colonialism
3 economic cooperation between nations
4 a self-sufficient national economy

40 Which environmental problem affects large areas in both the Amazon Basin and Central Africa?

1 deforestation   3 acid rain
2 nuclear waste   4 air pollution

Base your answer to the question 41 on the chart below and on your knowledge of social studies.

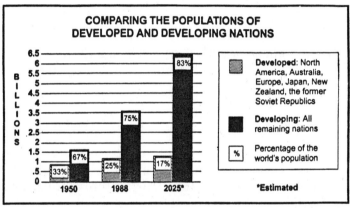

COMPARING THE POPULATIONS OF
DEVELOPED AND DEVELOPING NATIONS

Developed: North America, Australia, Europe, Japan, New Zealand, the former Soviet Republics

Developing: All remaining nations

% Percentage of the world's population

*Estimated

Source: UNESCO

41 Which statement is best supported by the information in the chart?

1 The population of Kenya is greater than the population of Japan.
2 The population in developed nations is expected to double by 2025.
3 The population in developed nations is increasing faster than it is in developed nations.
4 The percentage of the world's population living in developed nations is increasing.

42 "Asian Tiger Habitat Diminished by 50%"
    "Oil Spill Threatens Ecology of the North Sea"
    "Overcropping Limits Agricultural Production in Sudan"

These three newspaper headlines are most directly concerned with the

1 lack of pollution controls around the world
2 effect of humans on the environment
3 role of science in limiting environmental problems
4 need for fewer government regulations

43 One similarity in the unification of Italy, the Arab-Israeli conflict, and the breakup of Yugoslavia is that all were fueled by

1 imperialism   3 Marxism
2 terrorism   4 nationalism

44 Which factor explains the difficulty of achieving political stability in many of the nations of Southeast Asia?

1 degree of cultural diversity
2 rapid economic growth
3 lack of natural resources
4 geographic location

45 The divine right theory believed in by several European monarchs is most similar to the concept of

1 the Mandate of Heaven in imperial China
2 humanism during the Enlightenment
3 civil disobedience promoted by Mohandas Gandhi
4 the White Man's Burden

Base your answer to question 46 on the cartoon below and on your knowledge of social studies.

46 The main idea of this 1992 cartoon is that

    1 communism continues to threaten Western democratic nations

    2 communism is losing its influence throughout the world

    3 communist governments succeed best in nations with high standards of living

    4 most nations in Asia still follow the ideas of Marx and Lenin

47 Which factor has been most important in discouraging economic investment in many Latin American and African nations?

1 abundance of natural resources
2 historic dependence on Europe
3 stable birthrates
4 political unrest

48 The dominance of Christianity in Latin America and of Buddhism in Southeast Asia is a direct result of

1 racial intolerance
2 cultural diffusion
3 urbanization
4 militarism

Answers to the following questions are to be written on paper provided by the school.

Students Please Note:

In developing your answers to Parts II and III, be sure to

(1) include specific factual information and evidence whenever possible

(2) keep to the questions asked; do not go off on tangents

(3) avoid overgeneralizations or sweeping statements without sufficient proof; do not overstate your case

(4) keep these general definitions in mind:

   (a) <u>discuss</u> means "to make observations about something using facts, reasoning, and argument; to present in some detail"

   (b) <u>describe</u> means "to illustrate something in words or tell about it"

   (c) <u>show</u> means "to point out; to set forth clearly a position or idea by stating it and giving data which support it"

   (d) <u>explain</u> means "to make plain or understandable; to give reasons for or causes of; to show the logical development or relationships of"

Part II

ANSWER ONE QUESTION FROM THIS PART. [45]

1 Throughout history, societies have formulated sets of rules and have established practices that have influenced the political, economic, and social development of nations or regions.

Rules/Practices

Code of Hammurabi
Magna Carta
Five Basic Relationships of Confucianism
Five Pillars of Islam
Encomienda system
Apartheid system
United Nations Universal Declaration of
Human Rights

Choose *three* sets of rules or established practices and for *each* one chosen:

- Explain *one* major idea associated with this set of rules or practices

- Discuss how this idea influenced the political, economic, *or* social development of a specific nation or region [Use a different nation or region for each rule or practice chosen. Do *not* use the United States in your answer.] [5,5,5]

2   The historical development of civilizations and cultures is often influenced by geographic factors.

Civilizations/Cultures

Ancient Rome
Early Russia
Pre-Columbian Latin America
Ancient Middle East
Byzantine Empire
West African Kingdoms
Dynastic China

Choose *three* civilizations or cultures from the list and for *each* one chosen:

- Identify *one* specific geographic factor that has influenced that civilization or culture
- Discuss how the specific geographic factor influenced the historical development of that civilization or culture [5,5,5]

3   Throughout history, groups and organizations have been formed to meet the needs and interests of society.

Groups/Organizations

Amnesty International
North Atlantic Treaty Organization (NATO)
European Union (European Community)
Organization of Petroleum Exporting Countries (OPEC)
Zapatistas
Vietcong
Hamas

Choose *three* groups or organizations from the list and for *each* one chosen:

- Discuss a historical circumstance that led to the formation of the group or organization
- Identify *one* major goal of the group or organization
- Explain *one* action that the group or organization has taken to accomplish its goals [5,5,5]

4 Throughout the 20th century, nationalism has been a major force for change. Several nationalist groups are listed below.

Nationalist Groups

Khmer Rouge in Cambodia
Nazis in Germany
Solidarity in Poland
Boxers in China
Mau Mau in Kenya
Sandinistas in Nicaragua
Kurds in Iraq

Choose *three* of the nationalist groups and for *each* one chosen:

- State *one* specific goal of the nationalist group
- Explain *one* specific action taken by the group to achieve that goal of nationalism
- Discuss the extent to which the group was successful or unsuccessful in achieving that nationalistic goal [5,5,5]

5 The quotations below express the ideas of several individuals.

Quotations — Individuals

> "Life is not worth living unless it is lived for others."
> — Mother Teresa

> "I have cherished the ideal of a democratic and free society in which all persons live together in harmony and with equal opportunities."
> — Nelson Mandela

> "Political power grows out of the barrel of a gun"
> "I am the State."
> — Louis XIV

> "It is not by speeches and resolutions that the great questions are decided ... but by iron and blood."
> — Otto von Bismark

> "Peace, Land and Bread"
> — V.I. Lenin

> "The pursuit of truth does not permit the use of violence being inflicted on one's opponent."
> — Mohandas Gandhi

Choose *three* of the quotations and for *each* one chosen:

- Explain the idea expressed in the quotation
- Discuss *one* specific action this individual took to carry out the idea expressed in the quotation [5,5,5]

6 Newspaper headlines often provide a means to understanding important historical events or situations. If newspapers had existed throughout history, the following headlines might have appeared when these events occurred.

Headlines

Ottomans Conquer Constantinople
Pizarro Destroys Inca Capital
Catherine the Great Encourages Westernization
Manchester Textile Factory Hires Many Women
Committee of Public Safety Executes
    Robespierre
Emperor Meiji Given Authority To Rule
New constitution Ends Caste System

Choose *three* headlines from the list and for *each* one chosen:

- Identify the nation or region that is referred to in the headline
- Explain *one* cause of the event or situation associated with this headline
- Discuss *one* effect of that event or situation on the identified nation or region [5,5,5]

7 Throughout world history, many political, economic, and social connections have existed between global regions. Several pairs of regions are listed below.

Pairs of Regions

Western Europe — Latin America
Western Europe — Africa
East Asia — Southeast Asia
Middle East — East Asia
Middle East — Western Europe
Eastern Europe — Western Europe
Latin America — Africa

Chose *three* pairs of regions from the list and for *each* pair chosen:

- Identify *one* specific political, economic, or social connection between the two regions
- Discuss one important effect of this global connection [5,5,5]

ANSWER KEY
AUGUST 1997—PART I

1	4		25	3
2	1		26	4
3	2		27	2
4	2		28	1
5	4		29	4
6	1		30	3
7	3		31	1
8	1		32	1
9	1		33	2
10	3		34	4
11	3		35	3
12	4		36	1
13	1		37	2
14	2		38	3
15	3		39	3
16	3		40	1
17	2		41	3
18	1		42	2
19	4		43	4
20	2		44	1
21	4		45	1
22	3		46	2
23	2		47	4
24	2		48	2

ANSWERS AND EXPLANATIONS
AUGUST 1997—PART I

1. If you don't know what *social mobility* is, you need to look it up in the Hit Parade right away. It shows up in one form or another on every test. Look it up, memorize it, understand it, and earn yourself a point.

   1 A slow rate of economic growth has a detrimental effect on social mobility. Think about it this way: If there isn't much economic growth, then there aren't very many new opportunities being created. But for people to move from one social situation to another social situation, new opportunities are essential.

   2 In societies with a low per-capita income, society as a whole is poor. As such, there are only limited opportunities for people to move up the social ladder. (And, of course, there isn't much room for them to move *down* the social ladder either, since they're already at the bottom.)

   3 Social mobility is not characteristic of traditional class structures. In traditional societies, each generation adopts the occupation and social status of its predecessors. Review *traditional society* and *social mobility* in the Hit Parade if you picked this answer.

   4 Social mobility occurs in societies that give individuals a wide range of opportunities to succeed. In societies that provide a variety of educational opportunities, individuals can tailor their education to meet their career and personal goals, and thereby change their social status.

2. If you don't know what a *subsistence economy* is, you need to look it up in the Hit Parade. In the Hit Parade, it's listed under *subsistence farming*, which is pretty much the same thing. The bottom line is that the society is only producing enough to meet its basic needs, with nothing left over to sell to others or to stockpile for emergencies or for the maintenance of luxuries.

   1 This is it. Subsistence economies grow just enough food to feed the population. There is nothing left over for profit.

   2 Since subsistence economies grow just enough food to feed the population, most of the people are engaged in farming. Since the society doesn't produce a surplus, it can't accumulate wealth or support a large population that isn't involved in the production of food. Wealth and an agricultural surplus are essential for the creation of universities and businesses in which individuals can become highly skilled.

3 Subsistence economies don't create surpluses. Surpluses are needed to make money. Capital investment *is* money. Therefore, there is not a high level of capital investment in subsistence economies.

4 Subsistence economies don't have a surplus to export in the first place. Instead, they eat what they grow and use what they make. There isn't anything left over to export.

3. This question has shown up on several tests in one form or another. The Regents has traditionally loved to ask questions about the Songhai, Mali, and Kush, and this time around they threw in Nubia for good measure. You only need to know about one of these civilizations to answer this question correctly. If you don't know about *any* of them, you should, because they're all fascinating civilizations. In the meantime, don't fret. Instead, remember to pick an answer that is consistent with the goals of the Regents.

1 All of these civilizations had major cultural development. Do you really think the Regents would bother asking about civilizations that weren't significant?

2 This is the best answer. All of these civilizations thrived long before the Europeans colonized the African continent. One of the goals of the Regents is to instill an appreciation for cultures apart from those in Europe and North America. This answer choice screams, "pick me!"

3 All of these civilizations nurtured significant cultural development. If they hadn't, why would the Regents be asking about them?

4 This answer choice uses an extreme word, *entirely* , and therefore is an unlikely choice even if you're not sure of the trading practices of these civilizations. (In fact, these civilizations grew wealthy due to trade with the civilizations of the Middle East and beyond.)

4. If you know the definition and significance of *urbanization* as outlined in the Hit Parade, the right answer should be evident. At the very least, you should be able to eliminate answer choices 1 and 3, because they are inconsistent with urbanization in general.

1 Urbanization tends to break apart extended families, since typically only some members of an extended family move to the cities while the rest stay behind on the farms. Often, those who find work in the cities intend to send money and goods back to those on the farms, but they either can't find work in the overcrowded cities or they make only enough money to take care of themselves.

2   Why would a bunch of people move to a city? Because that's where the jobs are. Unfortunately, in many cities of the developing world, urbanization is occurring so rapidly that there are far more people looking for jobs than there are jobs to be filled.

3   The United Nations' efforts to relieve the effects of famine has not increased urbanization, but rather has allowed people to stay on the farms. It's when there *isn't* any intervention during times of famine that people feel compelled to leave farms in order to find work (and hence money and a method of survival) in the cities.

4   Political unrest can certainly result in a mass migration of people, whether from one country to another, or from one part of a country to another part of the same country. However, job opportunities have been the most significant reason that individuals have moved specifically to the cities. Typically, when a nation is enveloped in political unrest, neither the cities nor the rural areas escape the consequences. Therefore, in most cases, political unrest wouldn't result in people moving from rural areas to urban areas. (Instead, it would most likely result in people moving from conflicted areas to more peaceful areas.)

5. Okay. This one is an easy point if you just take the time to think about it. Eliminate answer choices that are inconsistent with any of the rivers you know about on the continent of Africa. If you don't remember anything about any African rivers, eliminate answer choices that are inconsistent with anything that you know about *any* river. If you're still left with more than one answer choice, think about this question logically: What would conceivably prevent the transportation of goods and people on a river?

1   Rivers don't flow toward the mountains—in Africa or anywhere else! Rivers flow downhill, not uphill. The downhill motion is what gets the water flowing!

2   You might be thinking about the Nile River if you picked this answer. And to be sure, the Nile River does, in fact, flow *primarily* from the south to the north, but even the Nile doesn't flow *only* north and south! (Can you imagine a river that flows in a straight line, mile after mile, *only* north and south? These are rivers, not interstate highways!) Rivers tend to meander. And then there are all those rivers in Africa that flow east and west, like the Zambezi, or that flow in very roundabout ways, like the giant horseshoe

created by the Niger river valley. Still not convinced? Well then, answer this question: Why in the world would the north-south flow of a river prevent large quantities of goods and people to be transported? It wouldn't.

3   Rivers tend to be pretty long. That's why we call them rivers instead of creeks or drainage ditches. If the tiny man-made rivers that dot America's amusement parks are long enough to transport people, then surely nature's rivers are long enough to do the job. Of course, if you've ever heard of the Nile River, and if you remember that the Nile is in Africa, then you have to eliminate this answer choice immediately, because the Nile River just happens to be the longest river in the world (4,180 miles, —1,300 more miles than the distance from New York City to Los Angeles!)

4   This answer choice just makes sense. Falls and rapids are most definitely barriers to the safe transport of goods and people, and most of Africa's principal rivers are not navigable for great distances precisely for this reason (although the Nile is navigable all the way through Egypt). The lack of navigable rivers in Africa has been a significant detriment to reliable and consistent communication and transportation efforts into the continent's vast interior.

6.   The question asks for a lasting influence of Britain on India. Eliminate answer choices that you know are either not true of Britain (in which case Britain couldn't have been the influence), not true of India (in which case India wasn't influenced in this way), or both.

1   Both India and Britain are parliamentary democracies. If you didn't know this, it isn't the end of the world (since lists of parliamentary democracies aren't tested with a great amount of frequency), but at the very least you should not have eliminated this answer choice. If you don't have a reason to eliminate an answer, hang on to it while you evaluate the other answer choices.

2   The caste system stems from India's centuries-old religious customs, not from British colonialism. The caste system existed before the British set foot in India, and has remained well after Britain pulled out.

3   India has generally tried to remain nonaligned in world affairs. (Don't know what *nonaligned* means? Look it up in the Hit Parade!) But India's policy of nonalignment is not due to the influences of British colonialism. Britain most certainly has been

aligned (ever hear of World War I? World War II? NATO?). If India were to follow Britain's lead, it would have been aligned with other nations as well.

4   Neither Britain nor India operate under a command economy. Free enterprise constitutes a significant percentage of economic activity in both countries. Look up *command economy* in the Hit Parade if you're not sure what it is.

7. There are two ways to approach this question. The first is to read the passage carefully, looking for key words that are part of the definition of one of the beliefs in the answer choices. The second way is to realize that this question is about India, because the Regents tends to group questions about the same country together. Therefore, when evaluating the answer choices, you should choose a belief that is common in India.

1   It's easy to tell that this passage is not about ancestor worship, because the passage explicitly states that "the truly wise mourn neither for the living nor for the dead." If you were worshipping your ancestors, you'd be thinking about dead people all the time.

2   Following the Eightfold Path is a practice of Buddhism, not of Hinduism, India's dominant religion. The Eightfold Path lists the basic rules of Buddhist conduct and thought. But this passage isn't about conduct; it's about the nature of existence.

3   **This is the best answer. If "there never was a time when I did not exist, nor you, nor any of these kings," then that means everyone exists forever. But yet we know from experience that individuals die. So what we have here is a paradox. The way out of this paradox? Reincarnation. An individual life is just a link in the chain of an everlasting soul, which is reborn again and again. Reincarnation is a central belief of Hinduism, and one that helps make the caste system possible.**

4   *Nirvana* is the state of complete bliss, which Hindus hope to achieve by properly following the Four Noble Truths, and Buddhists the Eightfold Path. This passage is not about the state of complete happiness and peace. It's about reincarnation. And according to the Hindu religion, sometimes people are reincarnated into very unhappy lives.

8. If you don't know the basics about the quest for independence on the Indian sub-continent—and the consequences—then you need to review your Global Studies materials a bit. The independence movement in India is a favorite topic of the Regents. Prior to 1947, the entire Indian subcontinent was known as India. After independence from Britain was granted in 1947, the subcontinent was divided between India and Pakistan. All you have to do is remember the primary reason for the division.

    1 **The subcontinent was divided because of rivalries between Muslims and Hindus. Pakistan became a Muslim country, while India officially became a secular country (but yet is dominated by Hindus).**

    2 Fascism was all but dead after World War II. Neither India nor Pakistan is, or ever was, a fascist country.

    3 The division had little to do with natural geography (like rivers and mountains) and everything to do with cultural geography (the dominant religion of people in certain areas). Areas that were predominately Muslim became the country of Pakistan, which was actually divided into two predominately Muslim areas: Pakistan to the north and west of India, and East Pakistan (now Bangladesh) to the east of India. In the middle, present-day India was carved out of an area dominated by Hindus. What happened if you were a Muslim in India or a Hindu is Pakistan? Most likely, you moved.

    4 The British colonial boundaries didn't recognize Pakistan and India as separate areas. Pakistan and present-day India were created after colonialism fell.

9. If you're not sure of the answer, choose an answer choice that (a) is true of some or most of the countries that you know about on the Pacific Rim, or (b) was true of much of the developing world in the late 1980s and early 1990, or (c) would logically result in an improvement in the economies of the countries of the Pacific Rim, even if you're not sure about the facts.

    1 **Greater industrialization has been occurring in virtually every country on the Pacific Rim (Japan, China, Korea, The Philippines, Indonesia, Australia, and New Zealand). It just makes sense that the economies of these countries would improve due to industrialization, since industrialization generally results in surpluses that can be sold for more than their cost to produce, allowing a consumption-based middle class to develop.**

2   A total reliance on cash crops is economically risky. Diversification, not total reliance on cash crops, generally results in economic improvement. Industrialization is the primary way in which many nations, especially those along the Pacific Rim, have substantially diversified their economies in recent decades. Look up *cash-crop economy* and *diversification* in the Hit Parade if you picked this answer choice.

3   This just doesn't make sense. Most Pacific Rim countries were not engaged in Civil Wars during the late 1980s and early 1990s, but even if they were, it doesn't make sense that such wars would result in an improvement to the economy. Civil wars result in widespread destruction, tremendous uncertainty, and a halt in investment. Political stability, on the other hand, results in a feeling of security that encourages investment in industry and infrastructure.

4   There wasn't an oil crisis in the Middle East in the late 1980s and early 1990s, except to the extent that OPEC members were in conflict with one another. Even if there were an oil crisis, it wouldn't improve the economies of most Pacific Rim countries. Pacific Rim countries have to import oil, so anything that would increase the cost of oil would negatively affect the economy.

10. If you know about the Opium War, then good for you, because the Regents tend to ask questions about it. If not, you can at least eliminate answer choices that are not true of China in the first place, and therefore couldn't have been an effect of the Opium War and the Treaty of Nanjing. If you're still not sure, choose an answer choice that you know was true of China at some point in its history, even if you don't know the cause.

1   The Opium War and the Treaty of Nanjing resulted in greater European and Japanese domination of China. It was the Europeans and the Japanese, not the Chinese nationalists, who increased their influence.

2   The Western powers increased their control of China as a result of the Opium War.

3   **This is it. Look up *spheres of influence* in the Hit Parade if you missed this question.**

4   China was not a democracy, and the European countries and Japan were not creating democracies in their spheres of influence.

11. You don't know anything about Deng Xiaoping? Well why not? He's in the Hit Parade for a reason, you know. Look him up and improve your score.

   1 No. This was Mao Zedong's influence, not Deng Xiaoping's. Mao, by the way, is also in the Hit Parade. Look him up if he's slipped your mind.

   2 No. This was Mao Zedong's influence, not Deng Xiaoping's.

   3 Deng Xiaoping introduced significant elements of capitalism into the Chinese economy, including foreign investment. Today, China's economy is swiftly becoming more westernized, although China has resisted change in the political and social realms.

   4 First of all, this answer choice is too extreme, so you should be highly suspicious of it. Second, it goes in the wrong direction. Privatization was actually allowed, and in some cases even encouraged, under Deng Xiaoping.

12. If you know the basics about China since 1949, then only one answer choice applies. If you know the basics of Confucianism, then only one answer choice applies. If you don't know about either—and you should if you expect to do well on this test—then at least think through the answer choices logically and pay attention to extreme language. By the way, Confucius is in the Hit Parade. Isn't that convenient?

   1 Confucius urged people to respect authority, not challenge it.

   2 Confucius encouraged education, for the elite class at least. Even if you didn't remember that, however, you still should have been suspicious of this answer choice because of the use of the extreme word *all*.

   3 Confucius promoted a class-based system, not a democratic system. He argued for mutual respect, but he certainly did not urge equality of rights or equality of votes.

   4 Confucius believed that the masses owed respect and allegiance to their rulers, while the rulers owed fairness and protection to the masses. Even to this day, respect for authority is an important part of the national character of China. If you don't remember much about Confucius, look him up in the Hit Parade. He's pretty important.

13. Here's what you should have gleaned from the quotation: The Japanese will no longer engage in war. Why would this statement be included in the country's current Constitution?

    1 This is it. After Japan was defeated in World War II, the victorious allies forced Japan to demilitarize itself. It actually turned out kind of well for Japan, because Japan could then focus its national budget on education and industry, rather than spending billions of dollars on national defense.

    2 Japan wasn't involved in the Persian Gulf War. Even if Japan were involved, it doesn't make sense that such involvement would result in the inclusion of this statement in Japan's Constitution.

    3 It was the victorious allies, not the United Nations, who drafted the proposal.

    4 Japan was certainly emerging as an economic superpower, but this didn't make it a less militaristic nation. Indeed, it's the other way around. Japan could no longer use its military to gain access to raw materials, so it had to rely on ingenuity and trade, which in turn have fueled the economy.

14. If you know the purpose of social pyramids, then this question answers itself. If you don't, then at least pick an answer choice that makes sense.

    1 Actually, farmers and fishermen comprised the largest percentage of Japan's population at the time. But even if you didn't know this, you should be suspicious of this answer because the question refers to the pyramid as a *social* pyramid, not a *population* pyramid.

    2 Social pyramids rank the different social classes according to status. The Shogun was the highest rank. The merchants were the lowest. Why were the merchants ranked below the farmers? Because the cultivation of food is pretty important. Even the Shogun has to eat!

    3 Most people in China were unable to read and write at that time. Even if you didn't know this, think through this answer choice logically. It's not likely that most of the farmers and fishermen knew how to read and write, while none of the merchants did.

    4 The Shinto religion was an integral part of feudal Japanese society. It penetrated all classes of people.

15. This question is a gift! You don't have to know about the tea ceremony, Kabuki theater, or haiku poetry to answer this question correctly, although it's great if you do know about them, since in past tests, these terms have shown up a few times on the essay portion. Still, for this particular question, you only need to know how to read carefully in order to gain a point. Look closely at the words in the question. The test-writers tell you that these activities *remain important in Japan today*. If they *remain* important, then that must mean that these customs were important in the past. And if you understand that, then all you have to do is pick the answer that you just can't argue with!

1 All of these cultural practices originated in Japan, not in the West. Even if they did originate in the West, that still wouldn't explain why they *remain* important in Japanese culture.

2 Confucius taught about proper conduct, not about cultural practices involving theater and poetry. What's more, the words used in this answer choice seem out of place and too extreme. Even if you don't know how these practices originated, you should realize that they don't *dominate* Japanese life. Japanese life is dominated by work, education, and obligations to family. It is *influenced* by cultural practices such as the tea ceremony, Kabuki theater, and haiku poetry, but not dominated by them.

3 This answer choice is almost impossible to argue with, given the wording in the question. These three social practices *remain* important because the Japanese *continue* to value *traditional* customs and practices.

4 If change is a goal, then why would anything *remain* important? If social change is important, then it is likely that social customs would change accordingly.

16 The question asks you to find the best evidence that Spain was the dominant colonial power in Latin America. In order to do this, you should focus on something that is (or was) true of Spain *and* Latin America.

1 Spain's monetary unit is the peseta. Mexico's is the peso. Even if you haven't devoted your life to the memorization of monetary units, you should still raise your eyebrows at this answer choice. Spain and Mexico are sovereign nations, after all. Traditionally, sovereign nations have had their own currencies. (Interestingly, developments in modern Europe are changing all of this, since most of the countries in the European Union are moving toward the use of a common currency while retaining their own sovereignty, but this is a radical departure from the past.)

2   Spain has not been militarily involved in Latin America since its independence.

3   **In Spain, the official language is Spanish (no surprise there). And in Latin America, most people also speak Spanish (except in Brazil, where most people speak Portuguese). How is it that Spanish came to be the dominant language of Latin America? Easy. Because Spain was the dominant colonial power in Latin America. You can bark orders at the people in the colonies a lot more easily if they speak the same language as you.**

4   Argentina and Spain are sovereign countries. The citizens of one sovereign country do not elect representatives to the legislatures of other sovereign countries.

17.   Look at the graph carefully. The horizontal lines represent millions of people. The vertical lines represent twenty-year increments. The graph is titled "Indian Population in Mexico," so the black line represents the number of Indians living in Mexico from the year 1500 through the year 1700. Notice that the black line drops sharply (meaning that the population of Indians dropped sharply) during the first few decades of the time period. What can we conclude with certainty?

1   No! The population decreased, not increased. If it increased, the black line would be rising as time passed, not falling.

2   **According to the graph, the most severe drop in the Indian population of Mexico occurred from 1500 to about 1540. In 1500, the population was somewhere near 26 million. By 1540, it dropped to about 6 million. That's a loss of 20 million Indians in 40 years. That's pretty severe!**

3   This graph doesn't tell us anything about the standard of living of the Indian population; it only tells us how many Indians were living there in the first place. As for the 2 million Indians that were still living in Mexico in 1700, we have no idea, based on the information in the graph, whether their standard of living increased. (Just in case you're wondering, unfortunately the standard of living of the Indians didn't improve in any significant way during this time period.)

4   First of all, this graph only gives us information through 1700, so we have no idea what happened after 1700. Second, we don't know if what did or didn't happen after 1700 was due to the influence of the Spanish. Third, you should already be aware that the Spanish influence didn't end by 1700, especially if you got question number 16 correct. To this day, the Spanish influence can most readily be seen in Mexico's language (Spanish), dominant religion (Catholicism), and architecture.

18. If you don't know the definition of a cash-crop economy, now would be an excellent time to look it up in the Hit Parade. Then think through the answer choices. Eliminate answer choices that aren't true of most Latin American nations. Note also that the use of the term *reliance* usually indicates that something bad will result—when the test writers want to emphasize a good result, they'll refer to the cause as an *opportunity;* when they want to emphasize a bad result, they'll use words like *reliance.* Therefore, given the test writers' choice of words, you can pretty much bet that the answer choice will describe something bad.

1 **Reliance on single cash-crop economies invariably leads to an unstable economy as world market prices rise and fall. The Dominican Republic, for example, has traditionally relied on the harvesting of sugar cane to fuel its agricultural sector and the processing of sugar to fuel its manufacturing sector. When the world's price for sugar went down, the Dominican Republic's economy went down with it. Most countries attempt to avoid this problem by stabilizing their economies through diversification.**

2 You might be aware that most Latin American countries have *not* experienced long-term economic progress. Recent developments have been encouraging, though, mostly due to diversification efforts. Still, most Latin American countries import far more than they export (Chile and Brazil are two exceptions, however).

3 Reliance on a single cash crop leads to more money when demand for the crop is high and less money when demand is low. Even when demand is high, and even when the weather is cooperating enough to allow a high crop yield, it is usually not the farmers whose standard of living increase, but the wealthy landowners. In most Latin American countries, only a very small percentage of the population actually owns most of the land (and in many cases, those owners are foreign corporations).

4 The problem with reliance on a single cash crop is that sometimes there's a surplus and sometimes there's a shortfall. In other words, there isn't always an increased agricultural surplus in the first place. That's why answer choice 1 is so much better.

19. If you don't know about either man in the question, then eliminate answer choices that aren't true in the first place (based on your general knowledge of global studies) or that just don't make sense. In the end, focus on the answer choice that is really hard to argue with.

1 Juan Perón was democratically elected, but then he assumed total power and acted like a dictator. And Augusto Pinochet wasn't democratically elected in the first place. Besides, even if everyone agreed on one definition of a strong leader, it's unlikely that we'd come to the conclusion that the strongest leaders are those who are elected democratically. Since the fall of Ancient Greece, democracy has only been practiced for the last few hundred years, and only widely practiced for the past fifty years or so. Were there no strong leaders during the Middle Ages? During the Renaissance? In China? In the former Soviet Union? Have there been no strong military leaders (who are not elected democratically) in the United States?

2 This answer choice doesn't make sense. First of all, Perón and Pinochet came to power long after independence was won. Second, if it were true that Spain generally supported independence movements, then no independence movement would have been necessary in the first place—independence simply would have been granted.

3 Pinochet and Perón were military dictators, not monarchs. Even if you didn't know this, you should question this answer choice if you realize that Latin America as a whole doesn't have a strong tradition of monarchy.

4 **This answer choice makes sense even if you haven't read the question. It just makes sense that people will often support *any* leader—dictator or otherwise—if that leader promises to restore stability during times of turmoil. Both Pinochet and Perón quickly rose to power precisely because they understood what the people wanted to hear.**

20. To answer this question correctly, you need to focus on just four words: *You alone we worship*. If you know the definitions of *polytheism* and *monotheism*, then you're set. If you don't, then you've been neglecting your Hit Parade. It's feeling lonely. Why don't you take some time and visit it?

   1 *Polytheism* is the worship of many gods. "You *alone* we worship is not a polytheistic statement.

   2 Bingo! *Monotheism* is the worship of one god. "You alone we worship" is a very monotheistic thing to say.

   3 Allah is not an emperor—Allah is the "Lord of the creation." Therefore, Allah must have existed before creation. Any emperor that you can name, however, came into being after the world was already here.

   4 *Papal authority* refers to the authority of the Pope. Is the "Lord of the creation" and the "King of the last judgment" the Pope? Nope.

21. Allah is the Supreme Being of Islam—in other words, God. If you know this already, then you just need to find the holy book of Islam in the answer choices. If you don't know this, then this question is pretty hard. But you can at least eliminate the non-monotheistic answer choice.

   1 The Old Testament is part of the Christian Bible. Judaism also incorporates the writings of the Old Testament, but doesn't refer to it as such. In part, the teachings of Islam also stem from the Old Testament, but the Old Testament is not the sacred book of Islam.

   2 Confucianism isn't a monotheistic religion, so this answer choice doesn't make much sense. Confucianism is more of a life philosophy than a religion that reveres a god.

   3 The Talmud is a collection of Jewish canons, or laws. The passage in the question is a song of praise, not a description of law.

   4 The Koran is the holy book of Islam.

22. If you know about the formation of modern-day Israel, or if you've been reviewing the Hit Parade, which includes such terms as *Zionism*, the *PLO* and *Judaism*, you have sufficient knowledge to get this question right. If not, review your global studies materials with regard to the Middle East, since this general topic shows up quite a bit. Also, think about all of the wars and conflicts throughout history. Of the four answer choices, which one describes something that people have consistently fought over?

   1 Israel has expansionist policies, not isolationist policies. Isolationist policies tend not to infuriate other people and so likely would not be the cause of a major disagreement.

2   Both the Arabs (mostly Muslim) and the Israelis (mostly Jewish) are monotheistic, but they're not arguing over the interpretation of monotheism. While the two groups practice very different religions, they both agree on what monotheism means. (It means that you worship only one god.)

3   **Throughout history, groups of people have fought over land, and the dispute between the Arabs and the Israelis is no exception. At a minimum, the Arabs don't want Israel to expand. Ideally, they want Israel to disband altogether, allowing the creation of a Palestinian (Muslim) state in its place. Currently, territorial disputes in the Golan Heights, West Bank, and Gaza threaten hopes for peace in the region.**

4   The disagreement is not over oil, since no major deposits of petroleum exist in the disputed regions. But even if you liked this answer choice, you should have liked answer choice 3 better, since any territorial claims would include control over oil within those territories. As such, you'd still have to pick answer choice 3, since it's more general and therefore harder to argue with.

23. First, eliminate answer choices that are totally inconsistent with the scene depicted in the cartoon. Notice the woman: She's not very happy. Her house is dilapidated. Notice the sign: The location is Gaza, which, according to the sign, is "under new management," meaning new leadership. If you know anything about the Gaza Strip in 1994, you're finished. If you don't, you can at least rely on the clues in the cartoon to help you eliminate answer choices. Remember to focus on answer choices that are hard to argue with.

1   The woman definitely looks like she's poor, but she's not Israeli, she's Palestinian. In 1994, Israel pulled out of part of Gaza as part of the peace process. Autonomous regions were established in that part of the Gaza region, which means that the area was under the control of the people who actually lived there (that's why we know that this woman in the cartoon is Palestinian and not Israeli). Yasir Arafat even relocated to Gaza. However, self-rule did not bring with it the desired economic benefits, and poverty actually increased.

2   **This is the best answer. The scene in the cartoon definitely depicts economic hardship. The reason is that even though the Palestinians gained autonomy in part of the Gaza in 1994, terrorism and poor economic planning continued. Even if you don't know anything about Gaza or the Palestinians, this answer choice would be almost impossible to argue**

with. For this answer choice to be incorrect, there would have to be no economic problems in the Gaza region. But every region of the world has at least *some* economic problems. And certainly the woman in the cartoon has economic problems. How can you argue with this answer choice?

3   All you have to do is look at the picture to realize that this isn't the answer. Where are the large amounts of money? Where's the development?

4   If peace had finally come to the Gaza region, the woman would probably seem more excited. (That's the point of the dove carrying the olive branch saying, "You don't seem very excited about it.") The dove and olive branch are symbols of peace, but the dove's comment implies that peace really hasn't been established. Unfortunately, peace has yet to be realized in the Gaza region.

24. You only need to know about one of these men to answer this question correctly. If you don't know about either, you should. Both show up occasionally on the test, and Atatürk has shown up enough to earn a spot on the Hit Parade. Look him up now—If you do, you'll have yourself an answer.

1   Shah Pahlavi didn't conquer or even invade neighboring countries. Atatürk was definitely militaristic, but he didn't conquer neighboring countries, he merely fought against them for control over disputed land (most notably against the Greeks, driving them out of Smyrna.)

2   This is the best answer. Both men began the process of westernization in their nations. Atatürk introduced western customs, dress, and political reforms to Turkey. To this day, Turkey remains the most western of the predominately Muslim nations, although a growing fundamentalist movement within Turkey—particularly eastern Turkey— threatens the further westernization of the country. Shah Pahlavi westernized Iran during the 1970s, permitting western influences in social customs and economic reform. In Iran, however, the fundamentalists were successful in toppling the Shah, and in 1979 Iran became a theocracy under Khomeini, who revitalized Islamic traditions and attempted to purge Iranian society of western influence.

3   Both men promoted westernization of their countries at the expense of traditional Islamic practices.

4   Neither man supported the established of communes. (Neither man was a communist.)

25. If you've been reviewing the Hit Parade, you're in luck. All four men in the answer choices are located on that list—and the sale of indulgences is discussed in reference to one of them. If you haven't reviewed the Hit Parade yet, then focus on the words *worldly lives of the clergy*. It just makes sense that you would want to choose a person who is associated with religion.

1 Adam Smith was an economic thinker. He didn't write about indulgences and the clergy, he wrote about the advantages of competition and the specialization of labor.

2 John Locke is the Regents' favorite Enlightenment writer. He didn't write about the sale of indulgences or the worldly lives of the clergy, though. He wrote about natural rights and limited government. Some general ideas in Locke's writings vaguely intersect with some general ideas in Luther's writings, but from a political and philosophical standpoint, not from a theological standpoint.

3 In his ninety-five theses, Martin Luther challenged the established Catholic Church by protesting the sale of indulgences and the worldly lives of the clergy. His original motivation was to reform the Church from within, but his writings and ideas quickly took on a life of their own and sparked what is now referred to as the *Protestant Reformation*.

4 Like Smith, Marx wrote primarily about economic matters, not the sale of indulgences or the worldly lives of the clergy.

26. You only have to know about one of the three events in the question to answer it correctly. (All three of the events, by the way, just happen to be located in that marvel of test preparation known as the Hit Parade.)

1 To our knowledge, and more importantly to the Regents' knowledge, no utopian society has ever existed. Have you visited a perfect society lately? We didn't think so.

2 All three of these events diluted the power of the Catholic Church because all three resulted in the distribution of power to people outside the Church.

3 Divine right monarchies didn't outlast the Renaissance. (Just so you know, *divine right* is in the Hit Parade.)

4 This is the best answer. All three events redistributed wealth and power and contributed to the growth of middle class workers and consumers.

27. The statement tells you that "kings sit upon God's throne." In other words, this person believes that kings are acting on behalf of God. And not just any god, but God. In all monotheistic religions, there is no power equal to or greater than God, so if you are acting on behalf of God, you have ultimate authority.

1 An *oligarchy* (a term that hardly ever shows up on the test) is simply a political system in which power is held by a very small group of people. In the society described in the question, power is held by God—and only the king (as opposed to a small group of people) is acting on behalf of God.

2 **This is the best answer. If the king is acting on behalf of God, and if God has absolute power, then this person definitely believes in absolutism. The divine right theory was often used as a justification for absolutist monarchies. Look up both *absolutism* and *divine right theory* in the Hit Parade if you missed this question.**

3 This statement doesn't describe a democracy because power is vested only in kings (who are supposedly acting on behalf of God). Democracies distribute power among the citizens, either directly or through representatives.

4 Glasnost was a policy of social and political reform in the former Soviet Union. Glasnost resulted in a more open society in which citizens gained more rights and representation. The passage, on the other hand, describes a very closed system in which power is concentrated in kings.

28. If you don't know what the Industrial Revolution was, you need to. Okay, now let's think about this question for a minute. It's asking you to determine why the Industrial Revolution began in Great Britain. Therefore, the right answer has to be something that was true of Great Britain *before* the establishment of large industries, or else those industries would not have developed in Great Britain in the first place. So you want to pick an answer choice that describes something that would attract the development of industry, as opposed to an answer choice that merely describes something that *results* from the building of industry. In other words, you're looking for a *cause* of the Industrial Revolution in Great Britain, not an *effect*.

1 **This is the best answer. The Industrial Revolution was sparked by the invention of the steam engine, and coal is needed for the steam engine to work. The steam engine was the catalyst of the factory system, which needed good transportation systems to transport raw materials to the**

factories and finished products away from the factories. **The Industrial Revolution itself also improved transportation systems dramatically through the creation of the steam-powered locomotive, which, of course, ran on iron rails. But even before the development of the railroad, Great Britain had relatively good transportation systems in place.**

2   Industries in Great Britain were generally private enterprises. Even if you didn't know that, you should have eliminated this answer choice anyway, because the question is asking you to locate something that would result in the development of industries in the first place, not something that describes who owned the industries once they were developed!

3   The development of unions occurred after the Industrial Revolution resulted in hundreds of thousands of low-paying and dangerous jobs in the factory system. This can't be the answer because the question is asking you to find a *cause* of the development of the factory system in Great Britain, not an *effect* of the factory system.

4   Actually, cities were overwhelmed with the influx of new residents during the Industrial Revolution. Multiple families crammed into single residences, and city services were severely strained. But you don't have to know about the development of cities to eliminate this answer choice. You only have to wonder about one thing: Why would British cities be different from cities in other countries in terms of the ability to accommodate new immigrants? Almost all cities are bustling and crowded, that's what makes them cities. If cities could easily accommodate migration, then that would be true of Japanese, Italian, and South American cities as well. So then why did the Industrial Revolution begin in Great Britain as opposed to these other locations? Lots of reasons, and answer choice 1 gives you three of them.

29. If you missed this question, you first should look up *totalitarianism* in the Hit Parade. Now that you know what a totalitarian government is, you can eliminate answer choices that logically would not contribute to the rise of such governments.

1   Educational systems did improve in Europe prior to World War II, but this did not contribute to the rise of totalitarian governments. While both educated and relatively uneducated people supported government reforms and even revolutions, the primary catalyst of change was working class discontent.

2 Had the nations of Europe expanded democratic reforms, individuals within these nations might have had a greater voice in their nation's affairs. But many of the people of Europe did not feel empowered in the years before World War II. Instead, they felt helpless, and as a result, the promises of order and prosperity from the future totalitarian leaders sounded very appealing.

3 You should know that the years before World War II were marked by increasing political instability, not stability. That's why there was a war!

4 This answer choice just makes sense. When economic conditions worsen, people demand change. The economies of Europe during the 1930s were most certainly affected by the global depression, and were exacerbated in Germany because of the penalties imposed by the Treaty of Versailles. Fascist dictators, particularly in Germany and Italy, tapped into the people's discontent and appealed to the citizens' nationalistic tendencies, promising a rebirth of their countries' militaries and economies. The promise of prosperity during difficult times is almost universally appealing. So is the promise of stability during uncertain times. If you understand this concept, you should have gotten question 19 correct as well.

30. First eliminate answer choices that you know had something to do with someplace other than the Soviet Union. Then, eliminate answer choices that were initiated by someone other than Joseph Stalin. If you're still not sure, look up Stalin in the Hit Parade and your answer will be apparent.

1 The Great Leap Forward didn't occur in the Soviet Union. Rather, it was undertaken in China under the leadership of Mao Zedong. Essentially, the plan involved organizing peasants into communes, where it was hoped modernity could be achieved more quickly. It is almost universally described (and remembered) as a disaster.

2 The Four Modernizations program didn't occur in the Soviet Union. Rather, it was devised in China by Mao's most-trusted advisor, Zhou Enlai. After the disaster of the Great Leap Forward, the Four Modernizations program attempted to modernize the country without relegating the peasants to communes.

3 This is the best answer. The five-year plans were instituted by Stalin in an effort to build up the Soviet Union's heavy industry while also increasing agricultural production. The five-year plans were rather successful in achieving these

goals, but at the expense of the production of consumer products, decreasing the daily standard of living for the citizens of the Soviet Union.

4 Perestroika was a reform plan instituted in the Soviet Union, but under Gorbachev, not Stalin. Perestroika involved loosening the grip of the government's control on industry, not tightening it.

31. If you don't know much about the 1956 and 1968 invasions, you can still eliminate answer choices by paying close attention to the time period and remembering the Soviet Union's general goals. Look up *Cold War Era* in the Hit Parade if you missed this question.

1 **You should already know that the former Soviet Union was a Communist country, and you might be aware that Communist governments were established in Hungary and Czechoslovakia in the years following World War II. These two invasions were carried out by Soviet armed forces in order to quell anti-Communist uprisings in Hungary and Czechoslovakia, thereby keeping Eastern Europe under Soviet domination.**

2 Does the word *invasion* sound like it would involve a decrease in Cold War tensions? No. An invasion was necessary because many of the people in Hungary and Czechoslovakia were demanding reform. The invasion actually increased Cold War tensions, since the United States wanted the Soviet Union to loosen its grip on Eastern Europe.

3 The invasions were not carried out in order to quell German aggression. They were carried out in order to quell internal uprisings. The Germans invaded Hungary and Czechoslovakia during World War II.

4 Focus on the word *invasion*. Rarely is an invasion necessary in order to provide humanitarian aid. This certainly was not the case during the Soviet invasions of Hungary and Czechoslovakia.

32. Three of the answer choices contain terms that are in the Hit Parade, including the one that's the right answer. Learn the Hit Parade! Love the Hit Parade! Live the Hit Parade!

1 **Even if you didn't already know that the former Soviet Union broke apart into smaller countries in 1991, you should have been able to glean it from the question. The question tells you that new nations were formed from the areas of just one nation, the Soviet Union. The Soviet Union was an amalgamation of a lot of different ethnic groups and**

religious groups. The new nations were formed in part so that these individual groups could establish a national identity for themselves.

2   The question refers to one big country breaking apart into smaller countries. Nonalignment is the policy of an individual country to not join forces with other countries or take sides in a dispute between other countries. It has nothing to do with a single country breaking apart into smaller countries.

3   Imperialism is the practice of establishing and maintaining colonies. When it broke apart, the Soviet Union no longer existed, and smaller countries were established in its place. That's hardly the establishment of colonies!

4   Utopianism is the belief and attempt to enact idealistic social policies in an effort to create the perfect society, or utopia. While there is little doubt that the people of these new countries hoped to create as good a country as possible, it is unlikely that any of them were expecting to create the perfect utopia.

33.   If you don't know the answer based on your knowledge of the former Czechoslovakia, at the very least eliminate answer choices that describe something that you know never happened or that is inconsistent with your knowledge of other world events going on in the early 1990's.

1   This never happened. Czechoslovakia never expanded its territory south into Bosnia-Herzegovina.

2   **In a remarkable decision in 1992, Czech and Slovak political leaders agreed to disband their federation in the united Czechoslovakia, thereby creating two independent countries. This was part of trend in Eastern Europe toward nationalistic self-determination. In other countries, however, such as in the former Soviet Union and Yugoslavia, the consensus was not as wide and the division therefore not as peaceful.**

3   The Warsaw Pact dissolved in the early 1990s, so it doesn't make sense that Czechoslovakia, united or divided, would have rejoined it.

4   There was no United Nations invasion of Slovakia.

34. The cartoon signifies Russia attempting to get capitalism off the ground. The problem is that the flag of capitalism will only fly if the plane speeds up. Yet, the guy in the back seat is telling Boris Yeltsin to slow down, as if that's going help. Capitalism is stalled, and the only thing that will get it moving—according to the cartoon at least— isn't even being considered. Now, all you have to do is find the answer choice that describes this situation.

1   There's no invasion in the cartoon, from the West or anywhere else.

2   First, Boris Yeltsin wasn't a totalitarian leader. Second, totalitarian rule has nothing to do with this cartoon. There is a crisis in the cartoon, but if totalitarian rule were the point, Boris would be telling the guy in the back seat to shut up and would be doing what he wanted.

3   This cartoon has absolutely nothing to do with a foreign policy dispute. Nothing in the cartoon even remotely symbolizes a foreign country, much less a dispute with that country.

4   Capitalism is an economic system. The plane is definitely having difficulty getting capitalism off the ground. Therefore, the cartoon refers to Russia's current difficulties in establishing economic reforms. Done.

35. Focus on the quotation carefully. We know the society in question was a democracy, and only one answer choice was a democracy. We also know from the words in the quotation that it was the *first* democracy, because it did not "copy" but instead served as a "model to others." Still not sure of the answer? Look up *democracy* in the Hit Parade.

1   Spartan civilization was not a democracy.

2   Babylonian society was not a democracy.

3   This is it. Ancient Athens was the first democracy. What's more, it was the only democracy in the world until after the European Enlightenment.

4   Egyptian society was not a democracy.

36. If you're familiar with what's been going on in Bosnia, you can probably guess the right answer without the aid of the cartoon. If you're shaky on Bosnia, this question will be a bit harder, but you can still utilize the clues in the cartoon. The four men represent Europe (that's why EUROPE is written in big letters over their chairs). One of the men is reading about Bosnia and comes across the term *ethnic cleansing* (that means that ethnic cleansing is occurring in Bosnia—or in other words, people are being killed simply because of their ethnicity). The four men are trying to remember where they've heard about ethnic cleansing before, when in fact they should remember that ethnic cleansing has been a part of Europe's past again and again, perhaps most notably during World War II. The question then asks about the result of "forgetting the past." Let's start evaluating the answer choices.

1 **This is the best answer. While Bosnia is in crisis, the rest of Europe is sitting on its collective butt, wondering whether ethnic cleansing in Bosnia has any relevance on the rest of Europe. They apparently have forgotten that ethnic wars and acts of mass genocide have torn Europe apart in the past, and while they wait, tragic consequences continue in Bosnia.**

2 If Bosnia doesn't have problems, then why is the man who is reading about Bosnia also reading about ethnic cleansing? What's more, why would Europe forgetting the past be an effective solution for anything?

3 The cartoon doesn't refer to independence or dependence, it refers to "ethnic cleansing." Besides, how would Europe forgetting the past result in independence for Bosnia?

4 The cartoon doesn't give us any dates to compare. Even if there were only a few problems in Bosnia in the 1990s, how would we know if that meant that there are fewer problems than before? What's more, the cartoon specifically refers to "ethnic cleansing," which can most certainly be described as a problem. Finally, how in the world would Europe forgetting about the past result in fewer problems? Instead of forgetting the past, why not just forget this answer choice.

37. First, eliminate answer choices that just aren't true (you should be able to eliminate two of them this way). Then, read Durning's statement very carefully. What does Durning believe will solve the planet's environmental problems? Not the reduction of birthrates by itself, but also the reduction of consumption rates.

   1 Industrial nations and developing nations might experience some different problems, but this has nothing to do with Durning's statement. All he suggests is that consumption rates be lowered in industrial countries, as well as population growth in the world as a whole.

   2 This is the best answer. Durning obviously believes that lifestyles in many nations are depleting the earth's resources, or else he wouldn't suggest that people in industrial countries lower their consumption rates.

   3 You should know that this answer choice is way too extreme even without reading Durning's statement. There's no way that the Regents are going to suggest that technology alone will solve the world's environmental problems.

   4 This answer choice is just plain false, with or without Durning's statement. For this answer choice to be true, it wouldn't matter how much exhaust was emitted from our cars, for example, because the air quality would be unchanged. We know that our consumption rates do have an effect on our environment. (And even if you happen to not agree, you better drill it into your head that the Regents think so, and never pick an answer choice that is inconsistent with that.)

38. You missed this question? You shouldn't have, because the Green Revolution is in the Hit Parade. Look at it. Memorize it. Understand its significance.

   1 The Green Revolution was an agricultural revolution, not an environmental revolution. In some cases Green Revolution techniques have actually contributed to environmental problems.

   2 The Green Revolution was an agricultural revolution, not a diplomatic or military revolution.

   3 Yes! Look at the definition in the Hit Parade if you don't understand why this answer choice is the best one. Increased agricultural production was the whole point of the Green Revolution.

   4 The Green Revolution was successful because it enabled farmers to increase their yield per acre, thereby allowing nations to grow enough food to feed their expanding populations. If anything, the Green Revolution has resulted in an increase in population growth.

39. If you don't understand the significance of *global interdependence*, look the term up in the Hit Parade. The right answer just happens to be the last line of the definition in the Hit Parade. (Hmmm. Do you think the Hit Parade might be useful?)

1   If nations are dependent on each other, then to a certain extent they need each other's goods and services. Trade restrictions are barriers to an exchange of goods and services.

2   Interdependence suggests that at least two groups are dependent on each other. There is a certain element of equality in interdependence. In other words, one group cannot survive without the other group, so therefore both groups are partners in mutual survival. Colonialism, however, is not necessary in a system of interdependence. The establishment and maintenance of colonies might lead to interdependence between the colonizing nation and the colonies, but in today's world, interdependence exists between independent and sovereign nations. Nothing inherent to interdependence suggests colonialism.

3   **This is the best answer. If nations aren't cooperating, then it is difficult for them to exchange goods and services. And if they can't exchange goods and services, then they likely aren't interdependent on each other in the first place.**

4   Self-sufficiency is the opposite of interdependence. A self-sufficient nation is one that doesn't need anybody else. It can do everything for itself. There is no nation in the world that is entirely self-contained. Every single nation trades goods, services, and information with other nations. Some are more self-sufficient than others, but in any case, global interdependence definitely does not increase the need for self-sufficiency.

40. All of the answer choices are environmental problems. So there are two ways to narrow down the possibilities: The first is to think about the topographies and cultures of the Amazon Basin and Central Africa and pick an answer that describes a likely problem. The second is to think about the Hit Parade, focusing on environmental problems that the Regents often test.

1   **Large areas of Central Africa and the Amazon Basin in South America contain some of the densest forests in the world. As towns and cities grow and highways are built, the logging industry fells trees. Perhaps most significantly of all, slash-and-burn farmers clear huge swaths of land, shrinking the forests. Yet, these large forests have a significant impact on our climate and atmosphere, and they also contain unique**

plant and animal life that is threatened to extinction. Deforestation is a significant environmental problem in these regions of the world.

2   Nuclear waste is an environmental problem in the developed countries of the northern hemisphere and in some of the urban centers of the southern hemisphere. Nuclear waste is not an immediate threat in the forested regions of South America and Africa.

3   Acid rain occurs when pollution rises from the earth into the atmosphere, gets carried along with the weather patterns, and then combines with raindrops and falls back down to earth. Acid rain is an immediate problem in regions that lie down-wind of major industrial centers, since a tremendous amount of pollution is created in those centers. The majority of the forested areas of South America and Central Africa, however, do not lie down-wind of major industrial centers.

4   The forested areas of Central Africa and South America are generally not amidst large industrial centers, so air pollution is not a significant problem. As the forests are cleared, however, air pollution tends to increase, because the act of clearing the forests often puts pollutants into the air (slashing and burning) and because in some cases the land is being cleared for the construction of highways and industrial-commercial-residential sprawl. However, in such cases, the main problem is the deforestation in the first place, with air pollution as a secondary consequence. Therefore, answer choice 1 is a much better answer.

41.   Look at the chart carefully. There are two separate bars for each of the years 1950, 1988, and 2025. Each dark bar represents the population in each of the three years for developed nations. Each shaded bar represents the population in each of the three years for developing nations. Each horizontal line represents a half billion people. Finally, the percentage within each white box represents the percentage of the world's population that the nations contain in a particular year. Eliminate answer choices that are not represented by the information in the graph or that are inconsistent with your general knowledge of world trends.

1   This graph gives us the total populations for groups of nations (developed and developing), but not the populations for individual countries. It's true that Kenya is a developing nation and that Japan is a developed nation, and it's also true that the developing nations

have a combined population that is greater than that of the developed nations, but that's all the information the graph gives us. We can't presume that every developing nation has more people than every developed nation—we only know about the *combined* populations. Indeed, if you were to look up the populations of the two nations in this answer choice, you would find that Kenya (a developing nation) has a population of about 28 million (a mid-1990s estimate), while Japan has a population of nearly 125 million (a mid-1990s estimate). Therefore, this answer choice is just plain wrong.

2 Look closely at the graph. One of the problems with this answer choice is that it doesn't give us a starting date. It just says the population is "expected to double by 2025." Does the answer choice mean it's expected to double between today's date and the year 2025? Between 1950 and the year 2025? We don't know. Nevertheless, this answer choice is definitely incorrect because no matter what combination of years we use, in no combination does the population in developed nations double. In 1950, the population of developed nations was about .8 billion people. If it were to double by the year 2025, the shaded bar would have to reach up to about 1.6 billion people. Instead the bar is well below the 1.5 billion line.

3 **This is the best answer. The population in developing nations is increasing much faster than the population in developed nations. From 1950 to 1988, the population in developing nations rose by nearly 2 billion people, while in developed nations it rose by less than a half billion. From 1988 to 2025, the population of developing nations is expected to rise by another 3 billion, while in developed nations it is only expected to rise by a couple hundred million.**

4 No. In 1950, the percentage of the population living in developed nations was 33 percent. By 1988, the percentage fell to 25 percent. By the year 2025, the percentage is expected to fall to 17 percent. At first, it might seem a bit strange that even though the population in the developed nations is growing, the percentage of people living in those developed nations is actually decreasing. But it's not that strange when you think about it. The reason is that the population in the developing nations is growing much faster than in the developed nations, so as a result, the developing nations have a higher and higher percentage of the total world population.

42. You need to find an answer choice that describes all three newspaper headlines. Eliminate answer choices that don't have anything to do with at least one headline. And remember, the more general the answer choice, the harder it is to argue with, and therefore the more likely that it's the answer.

1 Do we know that the Asian Tiger Habitat is being diminished because of pollution? Could it be diminishing because of urban sprawl? Logging? Roadway construction? Slashing and burning? Golf course development? Is overcropping in Sudan the result of a lack of pollution controls? Probably not.

2 **For this answer choice to be correct, we have to make a few assumptions, but they're all reasonable assumptions to make. Based on the information in the headlines, we don't know the cause of the diminishing of the Asian Tiger Habitat, but most likely, it's due to something human beings are doing. We don't know the cause of the oil spill, but for it to spill, it most likely was being carried by some human contraption in the first place (whales and dolphins don't typically carry barrels of oil). Finally, overcropping is most definitely a human endeavor, since no other species is known to farm. Therefore, it's a pretty safe bet that all of these headlines are concerned with the effects of humans on the environment.**

3 These headlines describe environmental problems—they don't describe the limitation of environmental problems. What's more, they don't directly involve science's role.

4 Nothing in the headlines tells us whether the environmental problems are due to government regulations (or a lack of government regulations) or something else entirely. It might be that the oil spill occurred because of an unavoidable accident that would have occurred even with greater regulations or fewer regulations. Is overcropping in Sudan due to government regulations? Is it due to a lack of government regulations? Beats us. Even if you believe that the government is involved in these headlines, you've got to believe that humans are involved in these headlines. Therefore, you've got to like answer choice 2 no matter what.

43. Eliminate answer choices that have nothing to do with even one of the examples in the question. Eliminate answer choices that don't make sense. And, as always, focus on themes that the Regents love to test.

1 Imperialism is the desire to extend the power or territory of a country into new lands. It doesn't make sense that the breakup of a country like Yugoslavia would be due to imperialism.

2 How in the world would terrorism cause a country like Italy to unify?

3 The countries of the Middle East are not, nor have ever been, Marxist. So this couldn't even possibly apply to the Arab-Israeli conflict.

4 **This is the best answer. There's a reason that the word** *nationalism* **appears in the Hit Parade. It's because the Regents think it's an extremely important concept to learn. Nationalism has resulted in similar regions unifying into one big country (Italy), and big countries with dissimilar nationalities to break apart into smaller countries (Yugoslavia). Nationalism is also at the heart of many conflicts and wars between existing countries (Arab-Israeli conflict).**

44. Southeast Asia includes Cambodia, Laos, Myanmar, Thailand, Vietnam, Indonesia, the Philippines, Malaysia, Singapore, Brunei, Micronesia, and Papua New Guinea. If you're not sure of the answer based on your knowledge of Southeast Asia, focus on an answer choice that logically would lead to political instability. Also, focus on the word *political* instability, as opposed to economic instability.

1 **The nations of Southeast Asia are extremely diverse. Differences in religious practices, ethnic customs, and political philosophies, as well as lifestyle differences between those who are moving to the cities and those who remain on farms and in villages, are characteristics of a dynamic social geography. All of this stands as a barrier to political stability, both within the countries themselves and between the countries in the region. These differences have led to nearly continuous warfare in the region, most notably in Vietnam, Laos, and Cambodia. Even if you're unaware of the social and cultural dynamics of Southeast Asian countries, you should be attracted to this answer choice because it makes sense that a high degree of cultural diversity would lead to differing, and sometimes combative, political philosophies, sparking ethnic clashes as well.**

2   It doesn't make sense that rapid economic growth would lead to political instability. When a country as a whole is making money, that country tends to settle its political differences in a peaceful and orderly fashion so that the economy isn't disrupted. In any case, the countries in Southeast Asia that have experienced the most political instability (Vietnam, Laos, and Cambodia) have not had thriving economies.

3   The question refers to political stability, not economic stability. In any case, Southeast Asia doesn't lack natural resources. The problem is that its population is growing too fast for the amount of resources that the region contains. In addition to a variety of agricultural resources such as rice, coconut oil, rubber, and abaca, the region also contains a large share of the world's tin and a significant amount of petroleum. These resources (or the lack of other resources), however, are not at the heart of the political stability in the region.

4   Political instability knows no geographic location. It doesn't make sense that political stability would be difficult to achieve merely because the nations are located on the Southeast corner of the Asian continent.

45. You need to know the definition of *divine right theory* if you don't already—it shows up fairly frequently (which is why the definition is located in the Hit Parade hint, hint). If you do know the definition, then all you have to do is find an answer choice that is similar to the divine right theory. Even if you're not sure of the answer, try to eliminate answer choices that definitely are *not* similar to divine right theory (answer choices 2 and 3).

1   The Mandate of Heaven in imperial China was extremely similar to the divine right theory. Both gave justifications for the rulers to rule with absolute authority. The emperor of China claimed he had Mandate from Heaven to rule as he pleased. Therefore, everything he said and did was on behalf of heaven. Similarly, the monarchs of Europe justified their absolute authority by claiming that their right to rule was granted to them by God (divine right).

2   Humanists during the Enlightenment opposed the divine right justification for authority. Look up *humanism* and *Enlightenment* in the Hit Parade if you picked this answer.

3   Monarchs who believed that they ruled according to divine right did not tolerate disobedience. In effect, they claimed that disobedience toward them was disobedience toward God. Mohandas

Gandhi, however, believed that sometimes rulers are misguided and that in such cases, peaceful disobedience is justified. Therefore, civil disobedience is contrary to the goals of divine right theory.

4   The *White Man's Burden* was used as a justification for improper power, but not in the same way that the divine right theory was used. The *White Man's Burden* was used as a way to promote European imperialism in the colonies, especially in Africa and Asia. The theory was that it was the white man's duty to invade these continents and change what they referred to as the "half-devils and half-children" into civilized, christian Europeans. In other words, the *White Man's Burden* was a justification for European expansion. Divine right theory, however, was a justification for a monarch's absolute rule over his or her subjects. Stated another way, divine right theory was a justification for a ruler's power over all people within its territory; the *White Man's Burden* was a justification for one race's power in a territory.

46.   You don't even need to look at this cartoon to get this question right. Three of the answer choices simply aren't true, with or without the aid of the cartoon. Therefore, if you've been keeping up with world political trends, you've got yourself an answer. If you haven't been keeping up with trends, however, then look closely at the cartoon. You'll notice that there are a lot of empty seats at the annual meeting of Amalgamated Evil Empires. You might also notice that the hammer and sickle, the symbol of the former Soviet Union, is used on the sign, but yet the Soviet Union doesn't have a representative attending the meeting. Why's that? Notice also that this is a 1992 cartoon. You might remember that something really big was going on in the early 1990s with regard to communism.

1   The annual meeting in the cartoon depicts a gathering of communist nations, but most of the chairs are empty. Do these guys look threatening? No. They look bored. They looked disappointed. They may even look a bit miffed. But as a group, they certainly don't look threatening. A room full of mostly empty chairs doesn't threaten anybody.

2   This is the best answer. Even without the aid of the cartoon, you should know that over the past decade, communism has been losing its influence on the world. In the cartoon, you can see that the only communist countries that showed up at the meeting are Cuba, North Korea, Vietnam, and China. Before the downfall of communism in Eastern Europe in the early 1990s, there used to be a lot more communist countries. That's why there are so many empty chairs. The empty

chairs represent all the countries that were once communist, but are no longer.

3 Communism gained legitimacy in regions of the world where standards of living were low. In any case, this can't be the point of the cartoon because only Cuba, North Korea, Vietnam, and China are present at the meeting, and none of these nations enjoy high standards of living when compared with other nations.

4 It's not true that most nations in Asia follow the ideas of Marx and Lenin. But even if you don't know this, you still can rely on the cartoon. The cartoon shows that only four countries are present at the meeting. And the countries who have representatives at the meeting are the ones who revere Marx. Yet there are all those empty chairs. North Korea, Vietnam, and China are the only Asian nations attending the meeting, and you should know that there are a whole lot of Asian countries (over two dozen), so it doesn't make sense that the point of the cartoon would be that most nations *in Asia* still follow the ideas of Marx and Lenin.

47. Use your common sense on this one. The question specifically refers to Latin America and Africa, but the right answer choice applies anywhere in the world. Just ask yourself which answer choice gives you something that would discourage people from investing in a country.

1 An abundance of natural resources encourages, not discourages, investment. Lots of money can be made by exploiting resources for financial gain.

2 Historic dependence on Europe wouldn't discourage economic investment in these regions, since the dependence is part of the regions' history but the investment would be happening in the present and the future. If anything, the historic dependence on Europe would actually encourage investment, since a significant amount of the money would be coming from Europe and from North America.

3 Africa and Latin America are not experiencing stable birthrates in the first place. Africa is the fastest growing continent on the globe due to a significant increase in the birth rate coupled with a significant decrease in the infant mortality rate.

4 **This answer choice just makes sense. Political unrest leads to uncertainty about the future. Which political group is going to win out? What's going to happen to the government and to its relationship with business enterprises? Investment in factories and infrastructure and general construction declines when the investors are relatively uncertain about the future.**

48. You need to know the basics of Christianity and Buddhism (as well as the basics of all major religions). But to answer this question correctly, you only need to know about one of them. You should also be aware that two of the answer choices contain words that are frequently tested (1 and 3), and that only one of them makes sense in regard to the dominance of religion in certain regions of the world.

1 We want an answer choice that describes the direct cause of the dominance of religions in certain regions of the world. While religious beliefs are sometimes used and abused to exercise racial intolerance against certain groups, the dominance of these two religions is not a direct result of racial intolerance.

2 This is by far the best answer. Why are these religions dominant in places where these religions did not originate? Because these religions spread to new areas. How did they spread? Through cultural diffusion. Christianity started in the Middle East, gained steam in Europe and then spread to Latin America through cultural diffusion associated with European colonization of the region. Buddhism started in Northern India and centuries later, spread to Southeast Asia when Asoka, a powerful emperor who extended his influence throughout the region, sent missionaries into the surrounding regions. Later, the spread of Buddhism was aided by merchants along the trade routes between India, China, and Southeast Asia, who, along with their goods, took their religion with them.

3 Christianity and Buddhism are practiced in rural communities as well as in urban communities. If anything, urbanization has led to a decline in the influence of Christianity and Buddhism.

4 While Christianity was enforced to some degree in Latin America by European militarists, it also spread by those who did not use force. And Buddhism definitely can't be classified as a militaristic religion; It generally spread not by force, but through missionaries and cultural diffusion.

PART II

1. RULES AND PRACTICES

Code of Hammurabi

The Code of Hammurabi was a Babylonian legal code developed by Hammurabi, a king of Babylon who ruled for forty-two years in the eighteenth century BC. It affected the development of law throughout the Middle East and, later, much of the Western world. The code was significant not just because of its reach (it extended beyond criminal law into areas of family law and economics), but because of its system of retribution. "An eye for an eye, a tooth for a tooth" is perhaps its most well known principle. The influence of the Code has been far-reaching. It deeply impacted the development of Jewish law and gives context to many of the writings in the Old Testament of the Bible. Further, since Jewish law later affected Roman law, and since ancient Roman law is the basis of modern western law, the impact of the Code of Hammurabi can still be seen today.

Magna Carta

As the first document to limit the power of a monarchy, the Magna Carta served as the first step toward modern representative government and constitutional rights. It was signed by King John of England in 1215, though he didn't sign it willingly. For years, he had ruled as a ruthless, self-serving tyrant, raising taxes on the nobility while restricting their privileges. The nobility organized against him, and King John fled to Runnymede, where the nobility caught up with him and made him sign the Magna Carta. Although it did not establish representative government or guarantee rights to the peasants, the document revolutionized the monarchy by limiting it. It established rule of law and the beginnings of due process. Eventually, English society built on the ideas of the Magna Carta and established a Bill of Rights and a representative parliament. Moreover, the Magna Carta served as the basis for the U.S. Constitution as well as hundreds of other national documents that impose limitations on the power of the government.

Five Basic Relationships of Confucianism

The five basic relationships of Confucianism not only established the societal framework of ancient China, but has affected societal development in China to this day. Confucius focused on five individual relationships: ruler/subject, parent/child, older brother/younger brother, husband/wife and friend/friend. Confucian society assumes a class society wherein inferior classes owe respect to superior classes, and superior classes (most importantly the ruling class) owe fairness and kindness to the inferior classes. The same is expected in family relationships. The younger generations must be respectful and dutiful to the older generations, including generations that have already passed away.

The five basic relationships of Confucianism have affected Chinese culture enormously. For centuries, it reinforced the class system and repressed new ideas from younger generations. It also contributed to internal order within the society. As long as everyone played out the role expected of him, society was orderly and predictable. Today, the basics of Confucianism continue to affect the social relationships of hundreds of millions of Chinese, even though Communist China is officially atheist and classless.

Five Pillars of Islam

Muslims are expected to carry out the Five Pillars of Islam in reverence and submission to God. These Pillars require all able Muslims to bear witness to God (shahadah), pray five times daily (salat), fast during the month of Ramadan (sawm), make a pilgrimage to Mecca (hajj), and finally, help the community by giving alms to those in need (zakat). This final Pillar has greatly affected social conditions in many Muslim nations. Those who can afford it are expected to give one-fortieth of their income to the poor each year. In wealthy countries such as Kuwait, one-fortieth adds up quickly. Although various economic classes exist within Kuwait, poverty has been reduced significantly. Due to the almsgiving, even those least able to provide for themselves have enough to meet their needs.

Encomienda System

As the Spaniards colonized Latin America, they planned to exploit the tremendous agricultural and mining potential of the region. Indeed, these opportunities for wealth were some of the main reasons for the colonization effort in the first place. Not wanting to do the hard labor themselves, and yet needing a large number of workers to complete the tasks of farming and mining, the Spaniards devised a system known as *encomienda*, by which they forced the natives to do the work. Most of the Spanish landlords treated the natives as slaves. As a result of the rigors of the system and the spread of European diseases within the exhausted slave community, the Native American population dropped sharply. Faced with a shortage of labor, the Spaniards turned eastward to Africa for replacements, ushering in the era of African slavery. Therefore, the impact of the encomienda system was far-reaching. The ethnic landscape of Latin America was forever changed—one ethnic group was virtually destroyed, and another replaced it.

Apartheid System

Apartheid was a racial policy in South Africa under which members of the major racial groups were separated from each other in order to ensure the dominance of the white minority. The white-controlled government first separated the racial groups' residences within each community, and then actually established homelands for the blacks. Lacking natural resources, these homelands were not economically viable. In addition, the races were separated in terms of educational opportunities, jobs, and the use of public facilities. As a result of this policy, the whites maintained control of all of the good land and good jobs in South Africa's rich economy, while most blacks not only lived in poverty, but had no legal opportunity to rise out of poverty. Further, most of the blacks worked the menial and sometimes dangerous jobs necessary to the white-owned industry, thus making the profitable white-owned businesses possible in the first place. The policy of apartheid, therefore, greatly influenced the social and economic development of South Africa, but due to internal uprisings and international pressure, was finally disbanded in the early 1990's.

United Nations Universal Declaration of Human Rights

The United Nations Universal Declaration of Human Rights represents a significant step toward global recognition of human rights that are not to be violated by any government under any circumstances. Among these rights are freedom of assembly and association; freedom of thought, conscience, and religion; and freedom from discrimination. The major idea behind these and other rights is that individuals should be able to participate as free, full, and equal members in their communities and as individuals in pursuit of their own goals.

The Declaration has not been adopted by the Chinese government, but it has still managed to affect the social development within the country. A growing number of individuals within China have asserted their rights under the Declaration, most notably during the Tiannenman Square uprising in 1989, when thousands of demonstrators urged social and political reform. Heavily armed government troops, however, dispersed the crowds with open fire. Thousands of Chinese were killed, injured, or arrested. Today the government policies that deny many the basic rights asserted in the United Nations Declaration are still enforced, but it is likely that the ideas within the Declaration continue to simmer within the minds of the Chinese population itself.

2. GEOGRAPHICAL INFLUENCE ON CIVILIZATIONS AND CULTURES

Ancient Rome

The Mediterranean Sea was at the heart of ancient Roman civilization, so much so that it is difficult to imagine the Roman Empire without it. Prior to the rise of the Roman Empire, Carthage controlled the Sea. But the Romans, who were conquering parts of central Italy, substantially expanded their fleet and fought a series of wars against Carthage for control of the vast body of water. These wars later became known as the Punic Wars, which lasted from approximately 264 BC to 146 BC. By the end of the Second Punic War, Rome controlled the western Mediterranean. In the decades that followed, Rome expanded its dominion over the entire region, its influence extending in a great swath around the perimeter of the sea. What's more, the city of Rome itself was located 15 miles inland, and therefore was protected from an invasion by sea. As a result, Rome was able to maintain a relatively stable empire for centuries. It used the Mediterranean as the centerpiece for not only military conquests, but commerce and trade. Indeed, one of the major functions of the Roman Navy was to protect travelers and merchants, ensuring a safe flow of goods. The impact was enormous, since for centuries Roman ideas spread across the sea to two other continents, and three continents worth of ideas and products flowed into Rome. The Mediterranean Sea, therefore, was one of the first major avenues of widespread cultural diffusion.

Early Russia

For centuries, Russia's only coastline ran along the Arctic Ocean in the north and then cut south in the east along the Bering Sea. The southern and western borders were landlocked. Since the Arctic Ocean is almost entirely covered in ice year round, Russia was not able to establish port cities throughout much of its history, except in the east, where the population is sparse and thousands of miles away from the population centers of the west. Then, in the eighteenth century, Peter the Great drove the Swedes out of part of the Baltic region and established his new capital city on the Baltic Sea. In addition, both he and, later, Catherine the Great fought wars against the Ottoman Empire in the south in order to gain access to the Black Sea. Thereafter, Russia's coastline included warm-water ports that it had previously lacked. As a result, Russia's international trade increased dramatically, as did its naval capacity. The limited warm-water coastline of Russia, therefore, dramatically affected its territorial expansion policy for most of its history.

Pre-Columbian Latin America

Latin America is rich with a diverse geography that has both blessed and haunted the region's development. It is hard to ignore the particular impact of the Andes Mountains, especially in Pre-Columbian Latin America. The mountains are located near the coast of western South America, creating a very narrow coastal plain that is virtually unusable for farming. Yet, the Incas were able to develop a thriving, advanced civilization throughout this mountainous region. Simply put, the geographical challenge led to agricultural innovation. The Incas used methods of irrigation and terrace farming to cultivate the slopes and highlands, and successfully farmed corn and potatoes to feed their growing population. Eventually, the Incan Empire extended all along the western slopes of the mountain range, creating a very narrow but long Empire united under a common geography and way of life.

Ancient Middle East

The Middle East is dominated by desert regions, which extend from the Sahara in North Africa across the Red Sea and throughout the Arabian Peninsula. Tucked within these giant parched regions, however, are two river valleys that greatly affected the development of the region—the Nile River Valley in Egypt and the Tigris/Euphrates River Valley in Mesopotamia. The seasonal flooding of these river valleys provided rich farmland and a predictable agricultural cycle. The ancient Egyptians and Mesopotamians learned to exploit the rich farmland, resulting in a regular food surplus capable of sustaining large populations. Valley villages grew into cities, the population increased along with the food supply, and two of the world's great early civilizations emerged.

Byzantine Empire

The most significant geographic feature of the Byzantine Empire was the location of its capital, Constantinople. Built in 330 BC on the site of a small Greek seaport town known as Byzantium, Constantinople became the hub of the Eastern Roman Empire, and, after the fall of Rome, carried on Roman traditions throughout the Eastern Mediterranean for another thousand years. Constantinople owed its success in large part to the wealth it obtained through its location at the continental crossroads, where the Black Sea meets the Mediterranean Sea and where the Asian land mass meets the European land mass. Goods from Scandinavia and Russia generally traveled across the Black Sea, through Constantinople, and on to Asia or across the Mediterranean Sea to Africa or Western Europe. Likewise, goods flowing from Western Europe and Africa were sent by sea through Constantinople on their way northward. What's more, major land routes also went through Constantinople, since it was built on a very narrow band of water, known as the Bosporus, separating the two great land masses. Goods flowing overland from as far away as China in the East and the Iberian Peninsula in the West went through Constantinople. As a consequence, whether by land or by sea, goods and people intended for transcontinental voyages almost always managed to make their way through the city. The emperors of the Byzantine Empire used this location both to spread their influence outward along the trade routes as well as to bring in wealth from around the world. By AD 1000, Constantinople was the largest and arguably most influential city on earth, with a population of nearly half a million and an empire at the center of cultural diffusion between three continents.

West African Kingdoms

The Sahara Desert dominates northern Africa, stretching in a thousand-mile-wide path from Western Sahara and Mauritania on the Atlantic Ocean, to Egypt and northern Sudan on the Red Sea. With the exception of the coastal communities along the Mediterranean Sea and along the Nile River, North Africa is virtually swallowed by the ever-expanding desert. Traditionally, the desert served as a barrier between the Mediterranean, Middle Eastern, and Egyptian Empires on one side, and those of sub-Saharan Africa on the other. The West African empires of Mali and Ghana sent traders on caravans through the desert to trade with the Middle East, and successfully exchanged ideas and resources like gold. Yet, overall, the desert had a negative impact on cultural diffusion and trade. For the most part, sub-Saharan Africa—specifically the West African Kingdoms—remained largely unknown to the Middle East and Europe (and thereby the rest of the world) for most of its history. During the Age of European Exploration, European ships became familiar with the coastal regions of sub-Saharan Africa, but the interior remained a mystery. It was not until the African slave trade, and then later during the extensive European colonization of the continent, that much of the rest of the world learned of the accomplishments of the West African Kingdoms. And by then, the industrialized world was more interested in conquering the region than in learning from it. Therefore, the past greatness of West African Kingdoms was protected and isolated due to the Sahara Desert, and as a result modern day scholars are only beginning to learn of their accomplishments.

Dynastic China

China is a geographically isolated country surrounded by mountains, deserts, and water. The Himalayas to the south and the Gobi Desert to the north are just two examples of geographic barriers to travel, and hence cultural diffusion, in and out of the ancient country. Consequently, dynastic China developed independently for centuries. Oblivious to much of the rest of the world, China grew as an ethnocentric empire, thinking of itself as the center of civilization. When the rest of the world finally came to China, China's lack of experience in world affairs worked to a great disadvantage. China was carved up into European and Japanese spheres of influence. Therefore, dynastic China's geographic and cultural isolation resulted in the formation of a unique but largely ill prepared society.

3. GROUPS AND ORGANIZATIONS

Amnesty International

Amnesty International was created in 1961 in response to increasing worldwide awareness of political prisoners. Members of the organization keep track of the number of political prisoners around the world and develop methods by which to attempt to negotiate a prisoner's release. The group also works to bring an end to capital punishment, torture, and other excessive penalties. Amnesty International has become a particularly important influence in nations whose governments do not readily protect human rights and who inaccurately report human rights violations within their own borders. In 1977, Amnesty International was instrumental in the release of more than 10,000 political prisoners. For its efforts, the group received the Noble Peace Prize. Just as importantly, however, Amnesty International has raised awareness of human rights abuses in nations that much of the industrialized world has traditionally ignored. This awareness has prompted the governments of nations with relatively good human rights records to influence changes in nations with poor records.

North Atlantic Treaty Organization (NATO)

NATO was formed shortly after World War II in response to Soviet aggression in Europe. Many Western European nations, Greece, Turkey, the United States, and Canada formed the organization as a military alliance. Military aggression against one member nation of NATO would be treated as aggression against all member nations. Troops and military hardware have been placed in strategic locations (such as West Germany and Turkey), but the troops from individual countries remain under the control of that country. Before the collapse of the Soviet Union, NATO was a key force against further Soviet expansion into Europe. Therefore, according to its defenders, NATO's greatest success is not what it has affirmatively accomplished, but what it has prevented from occurring. NATO's original goals were accomplished when the Soviet Union disbanded and communism fell from power in Eastern Europe. Today, the future of NATO is in question. Many say that NATO is no longer necessary, since the Soviet threat has been lifted. Nevertheless, NATO continues to expand, uniting much of Europe under a common military alliance with the United States and Canada. Over the course of the next decade, world political developments may make NATO obsolete, or may unite it against a new common threat.

European Union (European Community)

With the signing of the Maastricht Treaty by fifteen European nations in 1993, the European Union took on its present form, though its beginnings stem all the way back to the 1950s. The EU is an economic and political alliance that works toward continued integration of the economies and, to a lesser extent, the political institutions of the member nations. It was formed primarily in response to the economic success of the United States and Japan, as well as a rise in the level of manufacturing competition in developing nations. The biggest EU success has been the establishment of the Common Market, which established free trade among member nations and has helped Europe reassert itself in the global marketplace. Although each nation retains its own sovereignty and laws, one of the major goals of the European Union is to establish a common monetary unit, to be known as the Euro, that will allow business transactions to flow unimpeded within the union. In the coming years, the implementation of the Euro is expected to transform the European marketplace.

Organization of Petroleum Exporting Countries (OPEC)

OPEC nations control about three-fourths of the world's oil reserves. Most of the member nations are in the Middle East, but a few, like Venezuela and Nigeria, are elsewhere. These nations formed OPEC in order to gain more power in the world economic community. They realized that by uniting, they could control the world's oil prices by collectively deciding to make less oil available. As the supply of oil fell, the demand for oil remained consistent, and in some cases even grew. Thus, the price of oil per barrel rose. OPEC was extremely successful in its efforts to produce a limited amount of oil in the 1970s. The other nations of the world had to compete with each other to purchase petroleum, and as a result, prices more than tripled. Since then, the OPEC nations have remained loosely aligned, but individual member nations have been trying to outsell one another, thereby making more oil available on the market. But when OPEC was strongly united, it successfully controlled the world's supply, and price, of petroleum.

Zapatistas

Emiliano Zapata was largely responsible for toppling the dictatorship of Porfirio Díaz in 1911. He and his followers (Zapatistas) demanded the return of large portions of Mexican land to Native Americans who throughout the 1800s and early 1900s had been robbed of their land by wealthy landowners, government action, and government inaction. By the beginning of the twentieth century, the vast majority of Mexican farmers didn't own the land they were farming, and were not given the income or the means to rise above the poverty level. A major goal of the Zapatistas was to regain control of the land and redistribute it to the Native Americans, who were farming the land for the wealthy landowners and whose ancestors had owned and cared for the land. The new government did not oblige, so the Zapatistas rebelled against the landlords and the government soldiers in an effort to seize control of large plots of land. After a decade of fighting, a new constitution was adopted in 1917 that granted limited land rights to the peasants.

Vietcong

In 1954, the country of Vietnam was split into two halves. Ho Chi Minh ruled the northern half of the country under the communist flag; Ngo Dinh Diem ruled the southern half of the country under a pro-democratic flag. In 1956, the fate of the entire country was to be decided by a general election, but fearing communist success, Ngo Dinh Diem blocked the election and maintained southern separation. At this point, the Vietcong gained momentum as an organization intent on ousting Ngo Dinh Diem and thereby reuniting Vietnam under communist rule. The Vietcong launched a guerrilla war against South Vietnam from the countryside's small farming villages, contributing to South Vietnam's eventual defeat in 1975.

Hamas

The Islamic Resistance Movement, or *hamas*, was organized in response to the general Palestinian failure to achieve its goal of an independent Palestinian state in present-day Israel. As an offshoot of the intifada uprising of the late 1980s and 1990s in the West Bank and Gaza Strip, hamas hopes to win a no-compromise victory over Israel. Unlike most Palestinians in the region, hamas uses violence and terrorism to achieve its goals, not only against Israelis, but also against Arabs suspected of cooperating with Israelis. To date, hamas has not succeeded in achieving its goal of an independent Palestinian state, and many moderate Palestinians have distanced themselves from the organization, partially blaming hamas for an inability to achieve lasting peace in the region.

4. NATIONALIST GROUPS

Khmer Rouge in Cambodia

The initial goal of the Khmer Rouge, originally a coalition of communist-trained Cambodians and various ethnic groups opposed to the establishment of the right-wing Khmer Republic, was to take control of Cambodia and establish a Marxist state. The Khmer Rouge achieved this goal in 1975 by gaining control of nearly two-thirds of Cambodia, including Phnom Penh. Under Pol Pot, the Khmer Rouge undertook its own cultural revolution reminiscent of the one in China. The Khmer Rouge began a program of ethnic and intellectual cleansing, forcing all intellectuals and professionals to collectives in the countryside and undertaking a mass extermination of ethnic minorities and religious followers such as Buddhists and Muslims. In the process, an estimated 3 million people were slaughtered. Pol Pot was overthrown in 1979 by invading forces from Vietnam, but he continued his guerrilla war tactics against the Vietnam-backed People's Republic of Kampuchea for years. Neither side can claim long-term success, and the people of Cambodia, caught in the crossfire, continue to suffer.

Nazis in Germany

Mein Kampf, Adolf Hitler's account of his struggle, is the definitive statement of the goals of the Nazi Party. In the 1930s, the Nazis became the largest political party in Germany by supporting the claims in Hitler's book. The most notable of these claims were that Germany had been wrongly victimized by the Treaty of Versailles, that the Jews and other "undesirables" were behind many of Germany's problems, and that the Aryan Race was destined to rule the world. The goal of the Nazi party, therefore, was to gain control of Germany and establish an Aryan Superpower. Under the leadership of Hitler, who was sworn in as Chancellor in 1933 and then shortly thereafter assumed the title and authority of *fuhrer*, the Nazis swiftly created a new political and social order. They utilized a secret police force, the Gestapo, to quash dissent. They built concentration camps to carry out the mass genocide of Jews, gypsies, and homosexuals. And all the while they united Aryan Germany by feeding the flames of Aryan nationalism. Ultimately, however, the Nazi defeat served as a lesson to the world on the dangers of ethnocentric nationalism that seeks to elevate itself at the expense of others.

Solidarity in Poland

Solidarity formed in Poland in 1980 with a shipyard strike with the simple goals of improving working conditions and employee compensation. Under the leadership and negotiation strategy of Lech Walesa, the strike was successful, leading to other Polish workers wanting the same results. These other workers urged Walesa to continue striking in a show of *solidarity*, or unity. He did, and within just a year, Solidarity represented 10 million Polish workers and was registered with the Polish government. In 1981, however, the military government banned Solidarity, which only enlarged Solidarity's demands to encompass major political and economic goals. By 1989, after Solidarity was once again made legal, the government was dominated by members of the Solidarity movement, as opposed to members of the Communist party. In 1990, Walesa was elected President of Poland, and the free-market economic and political goals of Solidarity had the force of the government behind them.

Boxers in China

The Society of Righteous and Harmonious Fists, or Boxers, was organized in response to the Manchu government's defeats and concessions to the western powers and Japan. The concessions of China were highlighted by two major events: first, the Treaty of Nanjing, which involved China's release of Hong Kong to Great Britain, and second, the Treaty of Shimonoseki, which involved Japan's acquisition of Taiwan. Infuriated, the Boxers led an uprising in the 1890s in an effort to drive the Europeans and Japanese out of China. Adopting guerrilla warfare tactics, the Boxers slaughtered Christian missionaries and seized control of foreign embassies. Ultimately, however, they were not successful in achieving their goals. Instead, their uprising resulted in the dispatching of foreign reinforcements, who quickly put down the rebellion. The Manchu government, already having made great concessions to the Europeans and Japanese, was even further humiliated. As a result of the rebellion, China was forced to sign the Boxer Protocol, which demanded indemnities to the Europeans and Japanese for costs associated with the rebellion. Thus, the Boxers were not only unsuccessful in reclaiming China under nationalistic control, but inadvertently increased the foreign presence in China.

Mau Mau in Kenya

After World War II, nationalism swept much of Africa, including Kenya, which had long wanted independence from the British colonialists. Jomo Kenyatta encouraged feelings of nationalism and led protests against the whites and the Asians who had settled in Kenya. At the same time, guerrilla groups known as the Mau Mau began to instigate violence against the white settlers, which resulted in thousands of deaths. Kenyatta was accused by the British of leading the group and was sentenced to seven years of hard labor, but the violent uprisings continued. The British finally abandoned their attempts to suppress the uprisings and granted independence in 1963, at which point Jomo Kenyatta became president of the new nation of Kenya. Therefore, the Mau Mau's goals were ultimately achieved. Kenyatta ordered the removal of whites and Asians, which had an immediate adverse impact on the economy. Kenyatta persisted in his reforms, however, and eventually Kenya's economy grew.

Sandanistas in Nicaragua

Between 1936 and 1979, the Somoza family ruled Nicaragua ruthlessly, recognizing virtually no civil rights in the peasant class. In 1977, a guerrilla group known as the Sandinista National Liberation Front began a bloody campaign against the Somoza family with the goal of returning land, and therefore economic power, to the peasants. By 1979, the Sandinistas overthrew the Somoza government. However, once in power, they didn't embrace a redistribution of land as much as they embraced government collectives. They established ties with the Soviet Union and Cuba and nationalized banks, mines, and plantations. Although the living standards of many Nicaraguan peasants improved, civil rights were severely limited under Sandanista control. The Sandanistas, therefore, did not achieve a goal consistent with that of Augusto Sandino, for whom they named their movement. (Augusto Sandino was a revolutionary leader of the 1920s and 1930s who sought to change the policies of the corrupt Nicaraguan government in favor of the peasant class.)

Kurds in Iraq

The Kurds are a distinct nation of people with their own language and traditions, and yet no place to call home. In addition to Iraq, millions of Kurds are located in Southeastern Turkey and Northern Iran, but most hope to one day live in a country of their own. Their goal of self-determination has withstood the worst of circumstances. After World War II, Britain promised to establish the independent nation of Kurdistan in the Treaty of Sevres, but it was never ratified. Since then, the governments of the region have tried to force the Kurds to renounce their identity by prohibiting the use of the Kurdish language, restricting Kurdish literature, and closing Kurdish schools. More recently, the Iraqi government used the Kurds in its war against Iran and then, after the war ended, turned on them. Tens of thousands of Kurds fled to Turkey when Saddam Hussein's government chased them out with chemical weapons. Since Turkey has also violated the rights of the Kurds, they feel as though they have no place to go. But Kurdish resistance is largely unorganized because subgroups of Kurds have different goals. The Kurds do have one goal in common: representation in government. Currently, however, they enjoy no meaningful representation in any national government and hopes of the establishment of an independent nation are dim.

5. INDIVIDUAL IDEAS

Mother Teresa

Mother Teresa, a Christian missionary in India, truly believed that "life is not worth living unless it is lived for others." She lived her life as an example of her statement. In 1928, Mother Teresa moved to India to teach at a convent, but in the 1940s left the convent to work alone among the destitute in the slums of Calcutta, devoting her heart, mind, and hands to those most in need. As word of her generosity spread, she inspired others to join her efforts in India, and with the gain in momentum was able to open schools and a house for the dying. Eventually Mother Teresa helped found an entire international organization known as the Missionaries of Charity. For her efforts, Mother Theresa was awarded the Nobel Peace Prize in 1979. She died in 1997, having lived her entire adult life in service to others.

Nelson Mandela

For decades, Nelson Mandela's goal has been the establishment of a democratic and free South Africa in which all persons—black, white, and Asian—could live together in harmony and with equal opportunities. Nelson Mandela's goal seemed nearly impossible to achieve during the height of the apartheid era in South Africa. Under apartheid, the minority whites controlled the economy and political system of South Africa, while enforcing strict laws against blacks and Asians. In 1964, Mandela was imprisoned for leading the African National Congress, an anti-apartheid organization, in a national strike and other forms of boycotts, which sometimes led to violence. Mandela was released from prison in 1990 with the end of apartheid in sight. In 1991, Mandela was elected president of South Africa and thereby gained the opportunity to establish a democracy consistent with his statement of peace and equal opportunity.

Mao Zedong

Mao Zedong made the statement "political power grows out of the barrel of a gun" to underscore his belief that only through force would the peasants gain power for themselves. Prior to making this statement, Mao had come to believe that the Chinese government was ignoring the most basic needs of its people. After building up a rural force of over 1 million peasant soldiers, Mao swept through China and drove the Nationalists off the mainland and over to the nearby island of Taiwan. Throughout his life, Mao not only held fast to his communist beliefs, but also to his belief that power was gained and maintained "through the barrel of a gun." He forced millions to work side-by-side in collectives, kept strict control of all means of production, remained intolerant of dissent, and ruled as dictator over virtually every aspect of Chinese life. With the force of the military, he managed to keep power even when his policies failed on their merits.

Louis XIV

Louis XIV, known as "the Sun King," ruled France during the late seventeenth and early eighteenth centuries. Believing he had a divine right, he ruled with absolute authority, often boasting, "I am the state" when his authority was questioned. His main goal was to increase the wealth and territory of his beloved France, which was the same as increasing his own wealth and territory, since he considered himself the state. This worried the rest of Europe. At one point, his grandson was in a position to inherit the Spanish throne, and Louis XIV became ecstatic about the size of the kingdom that would result. When much of the rest of Europe, most notably Great Britain, reacted by declaring war, the limited power of France was revealed. The Treaty of Utrecht brought peace to Europe, prohibiting the combination of France and Spain under a single monarchy and maintaining the relative balance of power. As a result, Britain—a rival of both Spain and France—continued in its effort to build itself as the emerging world power of the following century. The reign of Louis XIV brought much glory and cultural development to France, such as the building of the incredibly excessive Palace of Versailles. However, Louis XIV's boldness and anxiousness to expand his territory led to a treaty that secured the balance of power long enough for Britain, not France, to emerge as the world power. Less than eighty years later, the monarchy in France would be dead.

Otto von Bismarck

Otto von Bismarck believed in taking whatever measures necessary to make Germany a great nation. In the nineteenth century, Germany was still a loose collection of city-states, while much of Europe (France, Britain, and Spain, for example) had long been unified under a single government. Bismarck became chief minister of Prussia, the largest of the German states, in 1862 and began his quest for unification through "iron and blood." He first enlisted the support of Austria in a war against Denmark in order to gain control of two small German states under Denmark's control. After succeeding at this, Bismarck turned against Austria and defeated it soundly, winning control of the German states that were under Austria's control. The rest of Europe, especially France, was nervous about the prospect of a united Germany, so Bismarck provoked France into declaring war on Prussia (Germany) so that the rest of Europe wouldn't think that Prussia was aggressive. Bismarck easily crushed France in the Franco-Prussian War, unified Germany, and became the leader of the newly united country. The result of all these Bismarck-led wars was not only the restructuring of the balance of power in Europe, but the development of a strong sense of nationalism in Germany, which proved to be a very dangerous force just decades later in both World Wars. Through constant warfare, therefore, Bismarck transformed the fate of Germany, not merely "by speeches and resolutions but by iron and blood."

V.I. Lenin

Vladimir I. Lenin rose to power in Russia by promising "Peace, Land, and Bread" to the beaten and battered populace at the height of World War I. By promising to bring a close to the war, Lenin promised peace. By promising to redistribute the farms so that they would be under the control of the peasants, Lenin promised land. And, by promising that peace and land would bring prosperity, Lenin promised bread. To achieve this, Lenin signed the Treaty of Brest-Litovsk, which brought an end to the war with Germany. Then, he enacted the New Economic Policy of 1921 to institute land reform. By fulfilling his promise to bring "Peace, Land, and Bread," Lenin gained legitimacy and raised the hopes of the Russian population, if only for a time.

6. HEADLINES OF HISTORICAL EVENTS

Ottomans Conquer Constantinople

This headline refers to present-day Turkey, and more specifically to present-day Istanbul. The reason the Ottomans were able to conquer Constantinople was two-fold. First, the city, while well defended, was exhausted by a relentless barrage of attacks. Second, the sheer determination of Sultan Mehmet II to wage any war necessary into order to win control of Constantinople gained momentum as time passed. Once conquered, Constantinople became the new seat of the Ottoman Empire, thus marking the downfall of the Christian Byzantine Empire and the rise of Islam in the region.

Pizarro Destroys Inca Capital

This headline refers to a narrow band of land on the western edge of the Andes Mountains, extending from present-day Ecuador through the southern end of present-day Chile. Pizarro was successful against the Incas primarily because he was able to militarily out-maneuver the Incas, and because he was ruthless. By convincing one of the enemies of the Incan ruler to join forces with the Spaniards, Pizarro was able to use his ally's knowledge to quickly gain access to the heart of the Incan capital. Once there, Pizarro captured Atahualpa, the Incan Emperor, turned on his ally, and within a matter of three years, destroyed the entire Empire.

The significance of the resounding defeat was dramatic. The Spaniards became the dominant power in Latin America and transformed the region with their language, customs, religion, and intolerance for native cultures. Today, while the Incan civilization has largely been erased from the landscape, evidence of the Spanish conquest can be seen everywhere.

Catherine the Great Encourages Westernization

The nation referred to in this headline is eighteenth century Russia. Catherine the Great, empress of Russia for over thirty years, continued the westernization efforts of Peter the Great in hopes of modernizing the country's economy and social structure. These steps were necessary in order to assert Russia as a major world power, given that power had so dramatically shifted toward the West. As examples of her westernizing influence, Catherine the Great supported educational reform, development of the arts, and freedom of religion. However, she decentralized power in favor of the landlords, who were still operating under the feudal system, which had died long ago in the West. Therefore, although Catherine was successful in implementing significant western reforms, her failure to truly unify the country under her control undermined her ultimate goal of creating a Russian world power in the western image.

Manchester Textile Factory Hires Many Women

This headline refers to Great Britain during the Industrial Revolution. Due to the sweeping success of the factory system in Britain, families moved from the countryside, where they were farmers, to the cities, where they were expected to work in factories, in droves. Simply put, it was where the jobs were. Although women were accustomed to hard labor on farms and in their homes, the factory system exposed them to a different kind of labor, and more significantly, a different kind of lifestyle. Men, women, and children all worked in the factories, but they did not work side-by-side as they had done on the farms. As a result, family dynamics changed dramatically. Women were exposed to air pollution, hazardous materials, and dangerous machinery, most of them for the first time. The eventual consequence not only changed the woman's role with regard to her family, but inspired women in Great Britain to become socially active in pushing for workplace reform. Therefore, the factory system's employment of women contributed to their eventual emergence in the public sphere.

Committee of Public Safety Executes Robespierre

This headline refers to France during and after the French Revolution. Robespierre was a leader of the Revolution in 1792 and for his efforts was soon elected to the Committee of Public Safety, which, under his direction, unleashed the famous Reign of Terror on its enemies, sending hundreds to die at the guillotine. His ruthlessness did not result in widespread respect and admiration. Instead, it resulted in his own execution when the Committee's fanaticism with destroying the people it feared turned on him. In the confusion and uncertainty that was characteristic of France during this time period, Napoleon managed to gain control of the emerging Directoire, ushering in the Napoleonic Era in France. Robespierre's execution was one step in the consolidation of France's power in one man: Napoleon.

Emperor Meiji Given Authority to Rule

This headline refers to nineteenth century Japan, a time when western spheres of influence were dominating nearby China and much of the rest of the world. During this time, the United States was exerting pressure on Japan to open its ports of trade through various treaties such as the Treaty of Kanagawa. These treaties grossly favored the United States and other countries, while giving Japan little in return. As in China, the nationalists grew resentful, but unlike the Chinese, the Japanese were organized. Through the leadership of the samurai, they revolted against the Shogun, who had ratified these treaties, and restored Emperor Meiji to power.

The Meiji Restoration ushered in an era of Japanese westernization from which Japan emerged as an aggressor. Rather than falling victim to the colonization plans of the Western powers, Japan joined in the game, and soon colonized parts of Asia for access to raw materials needed for its own developing industrial base.

New Constitution Ends Caste System

The headline refers to India in the 1940's. The caste system, intricately woven into the essence of the Hindu religion, has been a part of India's social fabric from nearly its beginning. Traditionally, members of the lowest caste, the untouchables, could not associate with members of higher castes, neither in social situations nor in business partnerships. The untouchables are prevented from marrying, befriending, and initiating conversations with people in the higher castes. When India won its independence and wrote its own constitution, reformists won out. The new government outlawed the caste system and attempted to make everyone equal under the law. However, because the caste system is part of the traditional culture and dominant religion of India, the government's efforts have been largely unsuccessful, especially in rural areas. In a further effort, the government has taken upon itself to hire many untouchables. Nevertheless, because the human rights violations of untouchables are culturally sanctioned by millions of Indians and by the dominant religion, the government is capable of only so much. If the lives of the untouchables are to truly improve on a widespread scale, a change in culture at a fundamental level will need to occur.

7. POLITICAL, ECONOMIC, AND SOCIAL CONNECTIONS BETWEEN REGIONS

Western Europe—Latin America

Western Europe, specifically Spain and Portugal, financed explorations of the open seas in order to find the shortest possible path to Asia, where they hoped to gain access to Asian resources. Spain sponsored the voyage of Christopher Columbus, for example, in an attempt to find a route by sailing west across the Atlantic (but of course he ended up in Latin America instead). When it was later realized that Columbus had not arrived in Asia, both Spain and Portugal funded expeditions to explore, and then conquer, the vast and unknown continent. When the Europeans began their attack, virtually everything went their way. European diseases such as smallpox were introduced to the native population, which dwindled dramatically as a result. Furthermore, the Spaniards' superior military weapons and use of horses enabled them to inflict devastating assaults on the Incan and Aztec Empires. Spain became the dominant culture on the continent while Portugal took control of present-day Brazil. Eventually, the entire region was remade by the influx of European culture, religion, politics, and art.

Western Europe—Africa

Western Europeans initially became interested in Africa not because Africa offered something they wanted, but because the continent of Africa was an obstacle between Europe and its colonies in Asia. Before the construction of the Suez Canal, ships traveling between Europe and Asia had to go around the tip of Africa, a journey so long that the Europeans established "way stations" along the African coast. These way stations were to ships what rest stops are to present-day interstate trucks. Ships would stop to replenish their food and water supply, rest, and gain protection from storms. As ship traffic increased, these way stations became permanent European settlements, which later served as bases of operation for the slave trade. The Europeans eventually pushed into the interior of the continent, carving the great land mass into colonies for their own purposes, just as they had done in Asia. To this day, the effect of European colonialism can be seen in the continent's political system, religion, language, and architecture.

East Asia—Southeast Asia

Soon after World War II began in 1939, Japan made its move on Southeast Asia. Japan needed access to a greater and greater supply of raw materials as well as markets for its manufacturing base. As the Europeans had done before them, Imperial Japan operated under a mercantilist policy by which it intended to use the entire region for its own purposes. The impact of Japan's short-lived colonization effort in Southeast Asia was tremendous. While in control of the region, Japan nurtured the populations' distrust of the West. This distrust increased Southeast Asian nationalism, which in turn worked against foreign interference in Southeast affairs. After Japan was defeated, the Southeast Asian countries declared their independence from both Japanese and Western control. Thereafter, East Asia and Southeast Asia shared a common political connection: Both regions were filled with fledgling governments.

Middle East—East Asia

In recent decades, one of the most dramatic examples of regional interdependence has developed between the Middle East and East Asia. Specifically, East Asia has become dependent on the Middle East for much of its petroleum supply. Although China has large petroleum reserves, Japan and Korea do not. Yet Japan and Korea consume tremendous quantities of petroleum and have built their economies in large part on petroleum consumption. Of the 11 billion barrels of petroleum that are carried from one country to another each year, nearly one and a half billion barrels flow from the Middle East to East Asia (not including South and Southeast Asia, both of which also import substantial amounts). As a consequence, these two regions of the world have become economically interdependent. Although Middle Eastern nations export petroleum worldwide, East Asia constitutes nearly one quarter of that market. As for East Asia, although it imports some of its petroleum from Southeast Asia, over 75 percent of its petroleum needs are met by the nations of the Middle East. The overall effect has been an increase in economic consultation between these two regions of the world, as well as a heightened interest in the domestic political and economic situations within the nations on which this interdependence rests.

Middle East—Western Europe

As Islam spread across North Africa, the Moors became increasingly convinced that they had a divine calling to conquer other lands in the name of Allah, much like the European Crusaders believed centuries later. When they crossed the Mediterranean to the Iberian Peninsula of Europe, they easily swept through Spain, which was ill prepared for the invasion. The immediate impact was the introduction of the Islamic faith and Islamic culture to Western Europe. Because the Moors controlled much of the peninsula until 1492, when they lost control of Granada, the long-range impacts were substantial. The Moors affected the art, architecture, and educational system of the Iberian peninsula, and some of these influences, particularly in architecture, were spread even further when Spain and Portugal conquered Latin America.

Eastern Europe—Western Europe

Since the end of World War II, Eastern Europe and Western Europe developed not only in two *different* directions, but also in two *opposing* directions. The nations of Eastern Europe were militarily organized under the Warsaw Pact, led by the Soviet Union, and their economies and political institutions were modeled after the Soviet example. Western European nations, in addition to being militarily allied with the United States under NATO, were also economically and increasingly politically allied with each other under the European Economic Community, which later matured into the modern European Union. For forty years the two regions developed as separate worlds, true to their separate economic and political philosophies. However, since the fall of the Soviet Union and the Warsaw Pact, interaction between Eastern and Western Europe has increased dramatically. Economically, the regions have grown much closer together. East Germany was absorbed by West Germany into a united Germany under a capitalist/socialist economy. The other nations of Eastern Europe retained their sovereignty but westernized their economies as well. Today, western investment capital is pouring into Eastern Europe, especially Poland, the Czech Republic, and Russia. What's more, several Eastern European nations want to join the European Union, further integrating the two regions. And although enormous economic and political challenges remain in Eastern Europe, the overall effect of the recent interaction between the two regions has been great. If the progress continues into the next decade, the significant movement toward truly compatible economic philosophies may bind Europe together like never before.

Latin America—Africa

In the sixteenth century, Latin America was faced with a labor shortage. European diseases, combined with the hard labor of the ecomienda system, drained the continent of its Native American population, the very people whom the Europeans had forced to work in the fields and mines. If its grand mercantilist plan were to work, the Europeans needed to find a new source of slave labor, so they turned to Africa. Africans were plucked from villages and towns and traded to the Americas like commodities. Because Africa and Latin America share a similar climate in many ways, many African slaves managed to survive in their new environment, thereby encouraging the colonists to seek out even more African slaves. The impact on the Americas was enormous, especially in parts of Central America, where African cultural traditions took root. Therefore, due to the forced migration of millions of slaves, the ethnic demographics of America became more diverse, enriching its overall culture.

EXAMINATION
JANUARY 1998

Part I (55 credits): Answer all 48 questions in this part.

Directions (1–48): For *each* statement or question, write on the separate answer sheet the *number* of the word or expression that, of those given, best completes the statement or answers the question.

---

1 Which aspect of a nation's culture is most directly influenced by the physical geography of that nation?

   1 form of government
   2 religious beliefs
   3 population distribution
   4 social class system

2 Before towns and cities can develop in a society, the society needs to establish

   1 an educational system
   2 an agricultural surplus
   3 a writing system
   4 a democratic government

3 Which idea was shared by the ancient Maya, Aztec, and Inca civilizations?

1 practicing rituals to please the gods
2 equality among the social classes
3 direct democracy
4 monotheism

4 One effect that mountain ranges, rain forests, and river systems have had on Latin America has been to

1 encourage cultural diffusion
2 limit the development of transportation and communication systems
3 permit the nations of the area to use a single form of government
4 allow the development of large amounts of arable land

5 In many Latin American nations, the leadership roles assumed by the military and by the Roman Catholic Church evolved from

1 Native American beliefs
2 the development of the triangular trade
3 the effects of matriarchal societies
4 Spanish colonial rule

[OVER]

6 Which statement best illustrates the contradictory actions of the Catholic Church in colonial Latin America?

1 The Jesuits destroyed the temples of the Native Americans, but allowed them to continue their religious rituals.
2 The Church expressed concern over the mistreatment of Native Americans, but supported the encomienda system.
3 The Church moved many Native Americans from Spanish territory to Portuguese territory, but encouraged the importation of African slaves.
4 The Pope endorsed the Treaty of Tordesillas, but outlawed further exploration.

7 In Japan, the period of the Meiji Restoration was primarily characterized by

1 strict isolation
2 feudal government
3 religious revival
4 reform and modernization

8 In the 1930's, the Japanese Government followed a policy of imperialism primarily to

1 acquire new sources of raw materials
2 spread Zen Buddhism throughout Asia
3 sell more consumer goods to European nations
4 spread the ideas of bushido

9 What is a result of the trade imbalance in recent decades between Japan and the United States?

 1 Japan has limited its manufacturing because of declining markets in the United States.
 2 Japan has stopped advertising Japanese-made goods in the United States.
 3 The United States has threatened to raise tariffs and establish quotas on products from Japan.
 4 The United States has prohibited the importation of products from Japan.

10 Which statement about Japanese society today is most accurate?

 1 Japan continues a commitment to military rule.
 2 Within Japanese society, individual achievement has become more important than group effort.
 3 Little racial or ethnic diversity exists within Japanese society.
 4 The power of the Emperor is still based on the concept of divine right.

11 The main reason the United Nations sent troops to Korea in 1950 was to

 1 ensure that food reached areas of the Korean Peninsula affected by famine
 2 prevent North Korea from conquering the people of South Korea
 3 force the inspection of nuclear weapons plants in North Korea
 4 restore peace between warring factions of Buddhism and Shinto

[OVER]

12 The main reason the Chinese Communists gained control of mainland China in 1949 was that

  1 they were supported by many warlords and upper class Chinese
  2 the United States had supported the Chinese Communist Party during World War II
  3 the dynamic leadership of Mao Zedong had the support of the peasant class
  4 they had superior financial resources and were supported by Japan

13 Which statement best describes a result of the student demonstrations in Beijing's Tiananmen Square in 1989?

  1 Prodemocracy protestors were successful in achieving their goals.
  2 A state-controlled education program was begun.
  3 The government further restricted freedom of expression in China.
  4 Collectivization programs were started in China.

14 During the 1980's and 1990's, the economic policies of China, supported by Deng Xiaoping, have led directly to

  1 an expansion of China's colonial empire
  2 an increase in trade with the West
  3 a return to a strict command economy
  4 the success of the commune system

15 Since India's independence in 1947, the government has had the greatest success in

1 increasing overall food production
2 reducing the population
3 eliminating religious conflict
4 controlling industrial pollution

16 Which statement best reflects a belief of Mohandas
Gandhi?

1 Muslims and Hindus must be separated if true
peace is to come to India.
2 India must adopt the British factory system.
3 The caste system must remain an important
cornerstone of Hindu society.
4 India must achieve independence, but not at
the expense of further dividing the Indian
people.

17 In addition to providing water for Indian agriculture, the Ganges River remains important to India because it is

1 the only source of Indian hydroelectric power
2 a sacred river for the Hindu population
3 the birthplace of Hindu civilization
4 an unofficial boundary between the Hindus and
Muslims

[OVER]

18 Which statement best supports the idea that cultural diffusion has greatly affected Southeast Asia?

1 The population of Southeast Asia is concentrated in rural areas.

2 Monsoon climates affect food production in Indonesia.

3 A reliance on subsistence agriculture remains a problem for many Southeast Asian economies.

4 Buddhism, Hinduism, and Islam are practiced throughout Southeast Asia.

Base your answer to question 19 on the cartoon below and on your knowledge of social studies.

19 Which conclusion is best supported by this cartoon?

1 Imprisonment of political dissidents rarely ends opposition to the government.
2 The United Nations supports punishment for acts of civil disobedience.
3 Better media coverage would prevent the imprisonment of protesters.
4 Mistreatment of political prisoners often results in their acceptance of government policies.

[OVER]

20 The West African kingdoms of Ghana, Mali, and Songhai flourished between A.D. 700 and 1600 mainly because they

1 controlled the trade routes across the Sahara
2 developed self-sufficient economies
3 became religious centers considered sacred to Africans
4 received support from European colonial governments

21 Which statement best characterizes the period of apartheid in South Africa?

1 The majority of the population had the right to vote.
2 The Boers attempted to conquer Nigeria.
3 Many racist ideas of the ruling minority were adopted into laws.
4 French was declared the official language of the nation.

22 Which statement is most accurate about many African societies today?

1 Modern medicines have been ineffective in decreasing infant mortality throughout Africa.
2 New attitudes and values often clash with traditional tribal practices.
3 Agriculture is no longer the most important economic activity in Africa.
4 European influence no longer exists in the former colonial territories.

23 Which factor helps explain the scientific and literary achievements of the Muslims during their Golden Age (A.D. 800–1300)?

1 expansion of trans-Atlantic trade
2 innovations introduced by the Europeans during the Renaissance
3 cultural diversity accepted by many Islamic governments
4 legal equality of all people in the Islamic empire

24 In Iran, the Revolution of 1979 and the rise of Islamic fundamentalism have resulted in

1 an increase in women's rights
2 the westernization and modernization of the nation
3 a return to many traditional customs
4 the introduction of a democratic form of government

25 The conflict between Israel and the Arab nations since 1948 was often considered part of the Cold War primarily because

1 the policy of détente evolved from this conflict
2 communist governments were established in many Arab nations
3 the leadership of Joseph Stalin strongly influenced the policies of Saddam Hussein
4 the United States supported Israel and the Soviet Union supported several Arab nations

[OVER]

26 The Mongols played a significant role in Russian history by

1 supporting Czar Nicholas II during the Russian Revolution
2 supporting the rule of Ivan the Terrible
3 ending the reign of Catherine the Great
4 isolating Russia from western Europe during the early Renaissance

27 Which slogan expressed the ideals of the Bolshevik Revolution of 1917?

1 Liberty, Equality, and Fraternity
2 Bread, Land, and Peace
3 Land and Liberty
4 Nationalism, Democracy, and the People's Livelihood

28 One reason the Soviet Union formed the Warsaw Pact was to

1 ease the transition to democracy
2 help institute capitalism in Eastern Europe
3 limit the threat of invasion from Western Europe
4 challenge the economic successes of the Common Market

29 The initial reaction of the Russian Government to the fighting that broke out in Chechnya in the 1990's demonstrated that Russia

1 is unwilling to grant independence to dissenting ethnic groups
2 has little control over its arsenal of nuclear weapons
3 will defend its remaining republics against foreign invasion
4 favors reestablishing communism

30 Which economic system existed in Europe during the early Middle Ages?

1 free market   3 manorialism
2 socialism   4 command

31 One factor that enabled the Renaissance to flourish in Northern Italy was that the region had

1 a wealthy class that invested in the arts
2 a socialist form of government
3 limited contact with the Byzantine Empire
4 a shrinking middle class

32 John Locke and Jean Jacques Rousseau would be most likely to support

1 a return to feudalism in Europe
2 a government ruled by a divine right monarchy
3 a society ruled by the Catholic Church
4 the right of citizens to decide the best form of government

33 During the 18th and 19th centuries, Europeans improved roads and bridges and built railroads in their colonies primarily to

1 provide jobs for the colonists
2 obtain raw materials needed for industrialization
3 impress the colonists with their technological knowledge
4 help missionaries spread Christianity

34 A major cause of World War I was

1 a decline in the policy of imperialism
2 the existence of opposing alliances
3 an increase in acts of aggression by England
4 the spread of communism throughout Europe

35 What was one reason the Nazi programs and policies of the early 1930's appealed to many people in Germany?

1 The people were frustrated with their current economic and political situation.
2 Germany had been denied membership in the United Nations.
3 A coup d'etat had forced communism on the German people.
4 The German people feared that the French or the British would soon gain control of the Polish corridor.

36 In recent years, a major success of the European Union (EU) has been the

1 creation of a single military force
2 rejection of national sovereignty
3 adoption of a single language
4 elimination of trade barriers

37 Which statement describes a characteristic of the British parliamentary system today?

1 The Prime Minister is elected by the majority party in Parliament.
2 The monarch serves as a strong head of state.
3 The members of the House of Commons are appointed for life.
4 The minority party has no vote in the Parliament.

38 An effect of a mountainous topography on Inca and Chinese civilizations was the development of

1 industrialization
2 single-crop economy
3 desalinization projects
4 terrace farming

39 The Japanese feudal system and the Hindu caste system are similar in that both systems

1 promoted social mobility
2 developed a rigid class structure
3 encouraged the people to take part in government
4 resulted in economic opportunties for the lower classes

[OVER]

40 A major factor in the economic recoveries of Japan and West Germany after World War II was their

1 desire to avoid an invasion from China
2 acceptance into the United Nations
3 ability to produce nuclear weapons
4 need to replace destroyed factories

41 One way in which Eastern Orthodoxy, Roman Catholicism, and Protestantism are similar is that each

1 accepts the supreme authority of the Pope
2 rejects the Old Testament as part of the Bible
3 is a branch of Christianity
4 was once the official religion of the Byzantine Empire

42 One similarity in the leadership of Peter the Great of Russia, Kemal Atatürk of Turkey, and Jawaharlal Nehru of India is that each leader

1 expanded his territory by invading Greece
2 borrowed ideas and technology from western Europe
3 supported equal rights for women
4 increased the power of religious groups in his nation

43 "Compared to other peoples of the world we have the greatest [largest] population and our civilization is four thousand years old, . . . Today we are the poorest and weakest nation in the world and occupy the lowest position in international affairs. Other men are the carving knife and serving dish, we are the fish and the meat. As a consequence . . . we are being transformed everywhere into a colony of the foreign powers."

Which events formed the basis for the ideas expressed in this early 1900's passage?

1 Opium War and Boxer Rebellion
2 Mau Mau uprising and adoption of apartheid
3 Sepoy Mutiny and the Salt March
4 Haitian Revolution and Cortés' march on Mexico City

44 The Koran, jihad, and the hegira are most closely associated with the practice of

1 Islam
2 Judaism
3 Shinto
4 Buddhism

[OVER]

Base your answer to question 45 on the graph below and on your knowledge of social studies.

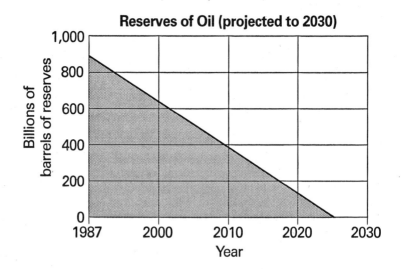

Reserves of Oil (projected to 2030)

45 Which action will help slow the trend indicated by the graph?

1 expanding Green Revolution technology
2 increasing industrialization in developing nations
3 using alternative energy sources
4 lowering worldwide oil prices

Base your answer to question 46 on the cartoon below and on your knowledge of social studies.

46 Which conclusion about the North Atlantic Treaty Organization (NATO) can be drawn from this 1994 cartoon?

1 NATO did not react quickly enough to the crisis in Bosnia.
2 Bosnia and NATO continue to disagree about the causes of the civil war.
3 NATO's actions have allowed communism to take advantage of the destruction of Bosnia.
4 The United States will probably withdraw from NATO as a result of the Bosnian crisis.

[OVER]

47 "Cuba today is a land of impossible contradictions, a utopia with beggars, a so-called puppet still dancing after the puppet master's death."

In this 1993 newspaper quotation, which nation is referred to as the "puppet master"?

1 Haiti
2 Soviet Union
3 Spain
4 United States

48 "What harms the victim most is not the cruelty of the oppressor, but the silence of the bystander."

—Elie Wiesel

In this quotation, the author is suggesting that

1 totalitarian governments generally support civil liberties
2 nations of the world must always condemn human rights violations whenever they occur
3 ethnic cleansing is not an issue to be addressed by the United Nations
4 demonstrations against human rights violations are of limited value

Answers to the following questions are to be written on paper provided by the school.

Students Please Note:

In developing your answers to Part II, be sure to

(1) include specific factual information and evidence whenever possible

(2) keep to the questions asked; do not go off on tangents

(3) avoid overgeneralizations or sweeping statements without sufficient proof; do not overstate your case

(4) keep these general definitions in mind:

    (a) <u>discuss</u> means "to make observations about something using facts, reasoning, and argument; to present in some detail"

    (b) <u>describe</u> means "to illustrate something in words or tell about it"

    (c) <u>show</u> means "to point out; to set forth clearly a position or idea by stating it and giving data which support it"

    (d) <u>explain</u> means "to make plain or understandable; to give reasons for or causes of; to show the logical development or relationships of"

[OVER]

PART II

ANSWER THREE QUESTIONS FROM THIS PART.
[45]

1 Individuals have often expressed similar or different points of view on a specific issue.

Pairs of Individuals	Issues
Confucius – Niccolò Machiavelli	Power of the ruler
Napoléon Bonaparte – Catherine the Great	Expansion
John Calvin – Martin Luther	Attitudes toward Catholic Church
Simón Bolívar – Jomo Keyatta	Independence movements
Mohandas Gandhi – Adolph Hitler	Use of force
Louis XIV – Baron de Montesquieu	Forms of government

Choose *three* pairs of individuals and for *each* pair chosen:

- Explain how the points of view of these two individuals are similar *or* different on the issue that is listed with these individuals
- Explain *one* specific way *each* individual acted on his or her point of view on the issue [5,5,5]

2 Throughout history, nations and regions have experienced barriers to development as a result of geographic factors.

Nations/Regions

Greece
India
Japan
Middle East/North Africa
Russia
Southeast Asia
Switzerland

Choose *three* of the nations or regions listed and for *each* one chosen:

- Describe a geographic factor and show how it was a barrier to development [You must use a different factor for each nation or region chosen.]
- Discuss how the people of this nation or region attempted to adapt to the barrier to development [5,5,5]

3 Religions greatly affect the way in which people live their lives.

Religions

Buddhism
Christianity
Hinduism
Islam
Judaism

Choose *three* of the religions and for *each* one chosen, explain *two* teachings of the religion that answer the question "How should a person live his or her life?" [You must use different teachings for each religion chosen.] [5,5,5] [OVER]

4 The artistic creations of different cultures reflect the values and goals of the people. These works are created in a variety of artistic mediums.

List A	List B
Cultures	*Artistic Medium*
Traditional Chinese	Architecture
Traditional African	Dance
Ancient Egyptian	Drama
Ancient Greek	Music
Medieval European	Painting
Traditional Japanese	Pottery
Traditional South Asian	Sculpture

Choose *three* cultures from list *A* and match each culture with an artistic medium from list *B*. [You may use an artistic medium more than once.] For *each* culture chosen:

- Describe an example of an artistic creation in the chosen medium
- Explain the beliefs or goals of the culture that are reflected in this artistic creation [5,5,5]

5 Major conflicts in various regions have often developed over a particular factor.

Factors — Regions

Land — Middle East
Natural resources — Latin America
Religion — Western Europe
Political beliefs — East Asia
Imperialism — Africa
Ethnic differences — Eastern Europe

Choose *three* factors and the region with which each is paired. For *each* factor chosen:

- Identify a specific conflict that was a result of that factor and explain the historical circumstances surrounding the conflict [You may *not* use a specific conflict more than once.]
- Discuss either an effect of this conflict on the region *or* the current status of this conflict in the region   [5,5,5]

6 Scientific ideas and inventions have led to many changes in the world.

Scientific Ideas and Inventions

Compass/Astrolabe
Heliocentric theory
Printing press
Steam engine
Nuclear energy
Green Revolution
Computers

Choose *three* scientific ideas or inventions and for *each* one chosen:

- Identify a nation or region in which the scientific idea or invention has had an impact [Do *not* use the United States in your answer.]
- Explain how the scientific idea or invention was used in or by that nation or region
- Discuss how the scientific idea or invention has changed life in that specific nation or region [5,5,5]

[OVER]

7 Throughout the world, people have developed a variety of social customs.

Social Customs

Dowry/bride price
Polygamy
Filial piety
Primogeniture
Extended family
Footbinding

Choose *three* social customs and for *each* one chosen:

- Identify a specific nation or region associated with this custom [Do *not* use the United States in your answer. You may *not* use the same nation or region more than once.]
- Show how the custom has traditionally been practiced in that nation or region
- Explain an advantage *or* a disadvantage of this social custom for the society   [5,5,5]

ANSWER KEY
JANUARY 1998–PART I

1	3		25	4
2	2		26	4
3	1		27	2
4	2		28	3
5	4		29	1
6	2		30	3
7	4		31	1
8	1		32	4
9	3		33	2
10	3		34	2
11	2		35	1
12	3		36	4
13	3		37	1
14	2		38	4
15	1		39	2
16	4		40	4
17	2		41	3
18	4		42	2
19	1		43	1
20	1		44	1
21	3		45	3
22	2		46	1
23	3		47	2
24	3		48	2

[OVER]

ANSWERS AND EXPLANATIONS
JANUARY 1998—PART I

1   The key words in this question are *physical geography*. You probably remember that the Regents often asks questions about the impact of religion on various cultures of the world, but in this question the test writers are focusing on the influence of geography. Use logical reasoning and think through the answer choices.

    1   A nation's physical geography generally doesn't influence the form of government. China and Cuba are communist, yet very different geographically. While Japan and Cuba are geographically similar (they're both small island nations) their governments are very different (Japan is a constitutional monarchy; Cuba is a communist state). Moreover, there are tons of examples of nations that have experienced changes in their type of government, without any corresponding change in their physical geography. When Chile went from a military regime to a democracy and then back to a military regime and then back to a democracy, did the physical geography of the nation change as well? Of course not.

    2   Religious beliefs definitely influence a nation's culture, but the question is asking which aspect of a nation's culture is affected by its physical geography.

    3   This is the best answer. The population distribution of a nation is greatly affected by the physical geography of that nation. Traditionally, cities have flourished along major waterways. Deserts, dense rain forests, and mountainous regions are typically sparsely populated. As technology brings irrigation to deserts, air conditioning and heat to intemperate climates, transportation, and a steady food supply to all parts of a nation, the population distribution of some developed nations has become less dependent on physical geography. Even in developed nations, however, geography still has a significant impact on where people choose to live.

    4   Social class systems are typically not affected by physical geography. It's true that many rural areas have more rigid social class systems than their urban counterparts, but rural areas can be found in the mountains, on the plains, and even along the sea. And so can urban areas. Isn't answer choice 3 a much better answer?

2   Use your common sense. Pick the thing that you absolutely, positively need in order to build yourself a city. If a city can be built and maintained without the item in the answer choice, throw it out.

1   You don't need an educational system to build a city. It's nice to have one as it will lead to a diversified work force, but thousands of towns and cities have been built and maintained without a system of education in place. Even today, people flock to cities in the developing world to find work, though in some places many people are illiterate. Yet, the cities continue to grow. Why is that? Because growth doesn't absolutely, positively depend on an educational system.

2   **An agricultural surplus is absolutely necessary for the development of a city. You probably don't know too many city dwellers that work on farms, do you? Yet all those people who aren't working on the farms still have to eat, right? Therefore, the people who do, in fact, work on the farms have to grow enough food for both themselves and the people in the cities, or else the people in the cities would starve. If there isn't an agricultural surplus, there isn't going to be a significant urban population, and what you have is an agrarian society characterized by subsistence farming.**

3   A writing system isn't necessary to a city in development. In the developing world, many people don't use writing systems because they are illiterate. Yet the cities continue to grow. Historically, the Incas and the Aztecs built extremely impressive cities despite the fact that they never developed writing systems. Instead, these two empires relied on an oral tradition not only to transmit information to one another, but also to pass along stories and customs from one generation to the next.

4   A democratic government definitely isn't needed to build cities. Other than in ancient Greece, democracy didn't become commonplace until the last three centuries. You should be well aware that impressive cities have been built throughout the world for thousands of years.

3 You only need to know about one of these civilizations in order to answer this question correctly, because the three wrong answer choices don't apply to any of the civilizations.

   1 This is it. All three civilizations were polytheistic and all three engaged in elaborate rituals in an attempt to please their gods. Also, notice that this answer choice is the opposite of answer choice 4; *the gods* means there is more than one god, which means the culture can't be monotheistic. It's a good idea to remember that if two opposites appear in the answer choices, one of them is usually the right answer.

   2 This answer choice is way too extreme. Equality among the social classes has never been achieved anywhere, although some societies have certainly tried harder than others to achieve it. None of these three civilizations, though, were even remotely interested in the idea of equality. Rigid social structures were in place and extreme inequality (in the form of slavery) was all too common.

   3 None of these civilizations were democracies, much less direct democracies. A direct democracy has never existed in any major civilization. If you know your general time periods, you have to eliminate this answer. Democracy developed in ancient Greece, disappeared for nearly 2,000 years, and then resurfaced during the Enlightenment. These three civilizations prospered well before the Enlightenment, and well after ancient Greece.

   4 All three were polytheistic, not monotheistic. Look these words up in the Hit Parade if you don't know them. The three major monotheistic religions in the world are Judaism, Christianity, and Islam. If a civilization does not adhere to one of these three religions, it most likely will *not* be described by the Regents as monotheistic.

4 Here's the deal: Latin America has mountain ranges, rain forests, and river systems. We didn't have to figure that out; the test writers told us. By the way, it doesn't matter that the question refers to Latin America. The only thing you have to do is figure out the logical result of a region with mountain ranges, rain forests, and river systems, no matter where that geographic combination exists.

   1 If you don't know what *cultural diffusion* is, you better look it up in the Hit Parade, because the Regents love to ask questions about it. In this case, though, it's the wrong answer. Cultural characteristics spread from one culture to another more easily when there aren't geographical boundaries like mountain ranges and rain forests standing in the way.

2 **Bingo!** If people manage to traverse mountain ranges, rivers, and rain forests, we slap them on the back and tell them how tough and amazing they are. For the rest of us, we look at places like mountain ranges and rain forests and say to ourselves, "Hmmm. . . those look kind of hard to get around. Let's just stay where we are, why don't we." So, it would be fair to say that these types of geographical features limit communication and transportation, wouldn't it? In fact, in Latin America (as well as in many other parts of the world), these types of geographical features kept cultures separated from each other for centuries.

3 Geographical barriers such as mountains and rain forests keep people separated, which in turn makes it hard for them to unify under a single government. The test writers typically don't try to show a cause and effect relationship between geography and political systems. (See the explanation for question 1)

4 Absolutely not. How in the world do mountain ranges and rain forests allow for the development of *large* amounts of arable land? They don't. There are too many mountains and trees in the way. (See question 38 for a way that some cultures have managed to create a *limited* amount of arable land in the mountains.)

5 Get rid of answer choices that are inconsistent with the Roman Catholic Church or the military, even if you don't know much about the specific history of Latin America. Then, go with the most general answer choice. Think about it from this perspective: From which institution or occurrence has virtually everything in present-day Latin America evolved?

1 When the Europeans came barging into Latin America, Native American beliefs were nearly wiped out right along with the Native Americans themselves. To be sure, in recent years there has been a resurgence in Native American art and culture in Latin America (due to a conscious effort to renew aspects of the cultural heritage of the region). However, Native American beliefs have not been the basis for the leadership roles assumed by the military and the Roman Catholic Church.

2 Does the leadership role of the Church stem from triangular trade? Does the leadership role of the military? Even if you don't know much about triangular trade, you should determine that it is some sort of trading practice and then have doubts that it would be the basis for the leadership roles of the church and military. Trading is a basis for the leadership roles of business and political entities.

3 Is the Catholic Church based on a matriarchal society? Is the military? Have you ever heard of a female Pope? Can you name some female generals, please?

4 This is it! Like almost everything else in modern Latin America, the leadership roles assumed by the military and by the Roman Catholic Church stem from Spanish colonial rule. The Spanish colonists were intensely militaristic and intensely Catholic. Latin America today is still relatively militaristic (although not as much as it used to be) and remains overwhelmingly Catholic.

6 Try to think of everything that you know about the Catholic Church, specifically in Latin America. Then focus on the words in the question. The correct answer must state two things that (a) are contradictory and (b) actually occurred. Eliminate answer choices that either don't state a contradiction or never even happened in the first place.

1 The Jesuits tried to convert the Native Americans. They didn't allow them to continue their religious rituals. Therefore this answer choice does, in fact, state a contradiction, but the second statement never happened.

2 This is the best answer. If you don't know about the encomienda system, you should read about it in your global studies materials because it's been showing up on the test quite a bit lately. The Church was ideologically tied (and indebted to) the political and practical justifications for imperialism, and therefore supported the encomienda system, which ultimately enslaved much of the Native American population in colonial Latin America. Despite the fact that the Church had little respect for Native American cultures and beliefs, many people in the Church believed it was their moral duty to protect their fellow human beings from blatant mistreatment. Yet, the encomienda system was one of the major causes of the mistreatment.

3 The Church didn't move Native Americans from Spanish to Portuguese territory, although the Church did play a major role in drawing the lines between Spanish and Portuguese territory in the first place. Also, the Church didn't encourage the importation of African slaves, although they didn't make any significant attempt to stop.

4   The Treaty of Tordesillas was an agreement between Spain and Portugal made in 1494 regarding the division of Latin America. Nothing about a boundary agreement between two nations is contradictory with the outlaw of further exploration. Of course, you might already know (or have reasoned) that further exploration *wasn't* outlawed. Therefore, this answer choice is wrong for two reasons: it states something that never occurred, and also something that wouldn't be contradictory even if it *had* occurred.

7   Look up *Meiji Restoration* in the Hit Parade if you need to. It's on the list because it keeps showing up on the test.
   1   No. The Meiji Restoration was important because centuries of isolationism finally gave way to an increase in foreign contact.
   2   No. Feudalism was characteristic of Japanese society prior to the Meiji Restoration, not during or after it.
   3   No. The Meiji Restoration had impact on the political and economic situation in Japan, not the religious culture of Japan. Religion was important in Japan before, during, and after the Meiji Restoration.
   4   Yes. The Meiji Restoration was a period of extensive change in Japan. Japan saw what happened to China during the nineteenth century, and rather than fall victim to the Western powers itself, the country decided to compete with the West at its own game. To do so, it had to reform and modernize.

8   If you're having difficulty with this question, think about the reasons behind imperialism in general, whether it be in Japan or anywhere else on the globe.
   1   This is it. Japan was imperialistic for the primary reason that it was mercantilist. It had developed a system of factories and needed the raw materials and sources of energy that the relatively small island nation lacked. So, it embarked on a quest to colonize other parts of Asia in order to gain cheap access to those materials.
   2   Like all other major world religions, Buddhism is not confined to its place of origin, but rather has spread to many other parts of the globe. The spread of Buddhism, however, has been the result of relatively haphazard cultural diffusion as opposed to a concerted and determined effort by particular governments. Zen Buddhism is not what is known as an evangelical religion. In other words, Zen

Buddhists do not believe that they are called upon to make all nations Buddhists. Christians and Muslims are typically the most evangelical, and therefore members of both religions have vigorously attempted to spread their religions to other nations, and sometimes have supported imperialist efforts as a way of accomplishing that end. Imperialism in Japan, however, was not connected to the idea of spreading a particular religion.

3   Imperialism in Japan had little to do with Europe and a lot to do with the rest of Asia. In the 1930s, Japan conducted most of its trade with Asia, and concentrated all of its colonizing efforts in Asia.

4   While the samurai code of bushido has had a lasting impact on Japan, even as recently as World War II, it is not a code that the Japanese government has attempted to spread to other countries. Look it up in the Hit Parade if you need to.

9   Use your common sense on this one. You should be aware that the trade imbalance between the United States and Japan favors the Japanese. In other words, Japan sells more stuff to the United States than the United States sells to Japan.

1   No. Japan has found a huge and consistent market in the United States.

2   You'll know that this answer choice is incorrect if you've been watching TV instead of studying for the test. Seen any commercials for Toyota lately? Or Fuji? Or Nintendo? Yes? Well then you know that Japan has not stopped advertising Japanese-made goods in the United States.

3   **This is the best answer. Japan doesn't allow free trade with the United States, but rather sets high tariffs and sets quotas that favor Japanese-made goods. In response, the United States has threatened to do the same to Japan, unless Japan opens up its markets.**

4   The word *prohibited* is way too strong, so this answer choice is way too wrong. Know anybody who owns a Sony Playstation? Did they smuggle it in? Of course not. They probably just drove to an electronics superstore in their Honda Civic and bought it straight off the shelf.

10   This one might be a little tough to answer if you don't know much about Japan. Still, eliminate answer choices that are inconsistent with any information that you *do* know about Japan. And then go review your materials on Japan.

  1   No. Japan's military has been very limited since the end of World War II. The victors of World War II enforced significant limitations on Japan's ability to establish a strong military.

  2   No. While individual achievement is important in Japanese society, it is not generally accomplished at the expense of the group. The well-being of the group to which one belongs, whether it is one's family or one's employer, is a central concern of most Japanese.

  3   This is the best answer. Japan is one of the most homogeneous nations on Earth. This allows most Japanese to maintain a strong sense of identity, but also places a tremendous amount of pressure on individuals to conform to that singular identity, even when their individual talents, beliefs, tastes, or personalities conflict with the group identity.

  4   No. At the end of World War II, the Emperor was forced to publicly deny that he was a deity. Modern Japan is a constitutional monarchy, but the monarch is pretty much just a figurehead.

11   If you know anything about Korea in the 1950s, you probably got this one right. If not, you should be attracted to the most general answer choice, since *main reasons* are typically stated in a very generalized way.

  1   Oftentimes the United Nations is involved in humanitarian relief efforts, but in the 1950s on the Korean Peninsula, the UN was involved for political reasons, not humanitarian ones.

  2   This is the most general, and correct, answer choice. You should definitely know that Korea was in the midst of a violent civil war in the 1950s. The UN sent troops in a successful attempt to prevent communist North Korea from conquering democratic South Korea. Ever since, Korea has remained split into two.

  3   Full-fledged war had broken out. There was no inspection of nuclear weapons plants because there had been no agreement to limit weapons production. Also, you might be aware that in the 1950s, North Korea didn't have nuclear capability.

  4   Factions of Buddhism and Shinto were not at war. Plus, Shinto is not a significant religion in Korea, but rather in Japan.

12 Get rid of answer choices that don't make logical sense. Also, get rid of answer choices that attempt to associate Communists with nations that you know are not Communist. When you're done eliminating, you should be left with only one answer.

    1 Why would the upper class of a nation support communism, an economic system that supports the abolition of the upper class in favor of a classless society? They probably wouldn't, because they'd lose a lot of power and money. In China's case, they definitely didn't. It was the peasant class that supported the Communists, not the wealthy class.

    2 The United States has never supported communism, in China or anywhere else. Often, it has actively fought against it.

    3 This is it. In 1949, the peasant class in China was both enormous and extremely impoverished. Mao Zedong offered them hope.

    4 The communists were not backed by Japan, which has never been a communist nation and has always been extremely class-based.

13 Get rid of answer choices that were true of China before 1989 and thus could not have been a result of the demonstrations in Tiananmen Square. Also, remember that if you see two opposites in the answer choices, one of them is usually correct.

    1 This answer choice is just plain false. In fact, the direct opposite happens to be true.

    2 State-controlled education began in China after the Communists took over in 1949.

    3 This is it. Pro-democracy protesters were not successful in achieving their goals. Instead, their demonstration backfired, resulting in a government crackdown on demonstrations and other forms of expression.

    4 No. Collectivization programs were popular in the 1960s and 1970s in China. In the 1990s, however, China has made many capitalist reforms and has therefore allowed limited private ownership of farms (as opposed to collectivizing the farms). Yet, despite these economic reforms, Chinese leadership has resisted democratic reform. Look up *collectivization* in the Hit Parade if you need to refresh your memory.

14 Eliminate answer choices that refer to China *prior* to the 1980s. Also, eliminate answer choices that just plain don't apply to China.

    1 China doesn't have, nor has it ever had, a significant colonial empire.

    2 This is it. Deng Xiaoping introduced elements of capitalism into the Chinese economy, leading to an increase in trade with the West.

    3 No. Deng Xiaoping moved away from the strict command economy that characterized the nation under Mao Zedong.

    4 No. The failure of the commune system led to Deng's introduction of some elements of capitalism into the Chinese economy.

15 Beware of extreme language. Try to remember everything you know about India and then go with the answer choice that is hardest to argue with.

    1 You should know that India keeps getting bigger and bigger, growing at a faster rate than even China, which is the only nation with more people than India. If India's population keeps increasing, there must be ways that all these new people are being fed, or else they'd die, in which case India's population wouldn't be increasing as fast as it is. In fact, India's government has been very proactive about increasing overall food production. The government has strongly embraced Green Revolution techniques, but it has had some difficulty in convincing rural farmers to change their traditional farming practices.

    2 No, no, no! India's population is going up, not down.

    3 *Eliminating* is much too strong a word. India's government has not eliminated religious conflict. In fact, some would argue that it hasn't reduced religious conflict. Today, conflicts between Hindus and Muslims and between Hindus and Sikhs remain both common and violent.

    4 India has certainly been industrializing successfully, but unfortunately it has not been keeping tabs on the consequences. Pollution is unfortunately on the rise, not the decline, throughout the Indian subcontinent.

16 You've just gotta know about Gandhi. He's been reincarnated on this test again and again. You've seen him before, you'll see him again, probably until the end of time (or until you graduate, whichever comes first).

1   Gandhi wanted the entire Indian subcontinent to be united as a whole nation, despite its religious diversity. But Gandhi's dream didn't materialize. Instead, the subcontinent was divided between Muslim Pakistan and secular, but predominately Hindu, India.

2   Gandhi was not concerned with industrialization, but rather with independence and morality. However, the first prime minister of India, Jawaharlal Nehru, was an industrialist and sparked the economy of modern India by westernizing India's industry. Even if you don't know this, though, you should be suspicious of this answer because of the use of the extreme word *must*.

3   Gandhi was against the caste system, and worked hard to abolish discrimination against India's lowest caste, the *untouchables*.

4 This is the best answer. Gandhi gave much of his life to the cause of Indian independence. But he did so in an attempt to unite India as a complete nation. Therefore, the division of the Indian subcontinent between Muslim Pakistan and predominately Hindu India was a great disappointment. This also happens to be one of the few times that the extreme word *must* appears in a correct answer choice. Usually, you should be very suspicious of answer choices that have extreme language. In this case it's okay though, because the word *must* was moderated with a *but*. In other words, Gandhi didn't believe that India must achieve independence at any cost, but instead strongly believed that independence should be achieved only under certain conditions.

17 If you missed this one, think about the goals of the Regents. In other words, why would the Regents even be asking this question?

1   This answer choice is much too extreme because of the word *only*. You don't have to know anything about the Ganges River or hydroelectric power in India to eliminate this answer. Do you really think that the Regents are going to expect you to know which rivers in which nations are the sources of hydroelectric power? Let's hope not.

2   The Ganges River is sacred to Hindus because they believe
    that it springs from the hair of Shiva, one of the main Hindu
    gods. Hindus believe that if they bathe in the Ganges, they will
    achieve purification. Even if you didn't know this, you should
    have been attracted to this answer because the Regents love
    asking questions about world religions. (Knowing about world
    religions will help you on the essay portion as well. Duh.)

3   The birthplace of Hindu civilization was in the Indus River Valley,
    not the Ganges River Valley. Those tricky test writers!

4   The Ganges flows through northern India, where it is bound on both
    sides by a predominately Hindu population. It then flows southeastward
    through Bangladesh, where it is bound on both sides by a predominately
    Muslim population. Therefore, it couldn't be the official, or even the
    unofficial, boundary between the two religions, because at different
    points in its stream, people of the same religion live on both sides of its
    banks! You can also think of this answer choice from another perspec-
    tive: India is predominately Hindu, while both Pakistan and Bangladesh
    are predominately Muslim. Since Pakistan is to the west of India and
    Bangladesh is to the east of India, the Ganges couldn't be the unofficial
    boundary between Muslims and Hindus unless it somehow managed to
    surround India. But if it surrounded India, it wouldn't be a river at all,
    but rather a sea! Look at a map and you'll see what we mean.

18 Okay, we want an answer choice that suggests that the cultural
    characteristics of one area have spread from their place of origin and
    mixed in with the cultural characteristics of another area.

    1   Simple geographic distribution doesn't tell us if cultural diffusion
        has occurred. It tells us where people live, but not where they
        came from and what they brought with them.

    2   We want an answer choice that tells us about cultural characteris-
        tics that are on the move, not winds that are on the move.

    3   If there's a reliance on subsistence agriculture, then people
        probably aren't moving around a whole lot. Instead, they're staying
        where they are, farming just enough food for themselves with no
        room for outsiders. Isn't there a better answer?

    4   None of these three religions got their start in Southeast
        Asia. Buddhism and Hinduism originated in South Asia
        (namely India) and then spread to Southeast Asia. Islam
        originated in the Middle East and managed to make the
        even longer journey to Southeast Asia. All three are part of
        the religious melting pot we now call Southeast Asia.

19 Look at the cartoon carefully. In the first box, we see an itty-bitty Mandela being shoved into the jail by two faceless brutes. In the last box, a huge Mandela emerges from the jail. He went in small; he came out tall. As long as you already know that Mandela opposed the government policy of apartheid (if you don't, you need to review the basics about him because he's a regular cast member on the test), you should get this one right. If you're still having difficulty, eliminate answer choices that you know are just plain wrong, even without the aid of the cartoon, or that aren't consistent with the goals of the test writers.

1 This answer choice makes sense, even without the aid of the cartoon. Mandela was imprisoned by the South African government, but opposition to apartheid continued to grow. His prison sentence only served to make him stronger. He is now president of South Africa.

2 This answer choice is false. The United Nations does not support punishment for acts of civil disobedience.

3 Better media coverage doesn't prevent imprisonment of protesters or anyone else. Better media coverage simply means that we get to watch the cops put the cuffs on without having to leave our living room sofa. Anyway, you should hate this answer choice because there's no media in this cartoon! (How do the Regents come up with some of these answer choices, anyway?)

4 Mandela didn't get out of jail because he accepted government policy. He got out because the government had started to change. This answer choice should also violate your common sense. When the government mistreats you, does it make you want to accept its policies?

20 Even if you only know about one of these civilizations, you should be able to get this one right. If you don't know about any of them you should review your materials on Africa, because it's been showing up on the test a lot lately. In the meantime, focus on the word *flourished* and start eliminating answer choices that don't make sense.

1 This is the best answer. These three kingdoms controlled major trade routes across the Sahara Desert and into the Nile River valley and beyond. They made tremendous profits from trade with the Middle East. Even if you didn't know this, however, you should have liked this answer because it makes sense that a kingdom would *flourish* due to trade.

2 To an extent, these kingdoms were self-sufficient in that they had the means of meeting most of their own needs. However, this doesn't explain why these kingdoms *flourished*. Instead, it would only explain how these kingdoms managed to get by. These kingdoms flourished, however, because they gained tremendous wealth through trade.

3 These three kingdoms were not religious centers considered sacred to Africans, but even if they were, these kingdoms wouldn't necessarily *flourish*. You need to find an answer choice that more clearly describes a strong economic base, not necessarily a strong spiritual base.

4 This answer choice doesn't make sense. If they *flourished*, why would they need support from Europe? They didn't, in fact, need support, and they certainly didn't get it from Europe. When Europe finally *did* arrive on the African scene, it wasn't motivated by generosity.

21 *Apartheid* is in the Hit Parade for a reason. Haven't you read the Hit Parade yet?

1 The majority of the population is (and was) black. Only the minority white population had the right to vote.

2 This question is specifically about South Africa, not Nigeria. That's why the test writers use the words *South Africa* in the question. Plus, this answer choice is just plain wrong. The Boers never attempted to conquer Nigeria; they had too much trouble as it was hanging on to South Africa.

3 **If you know that apartheid was a racist policy, you're finished with this question.**

4 The Dutch and then the British colonized South Africa, not the French. English was declared the official language during apartheid.

22 This question is a gift. It's great if you know a lot about what's going on in Africa, but you don't need to in order to answer this particular question. Instead, all you have to do is choose the answer choice that you just can't argue with.

1 Actually, modern medicines have been extremely effective in decreasing the infant mortality rate in Africa. There are problems, however, in delivering medical treatment to the people who need it. Still, infant mortality rates are way down throughout the continent.

2   **This is the best answer. How can you argue with this sentence, whether you're talking about Africa or anywhere else? It just makes sense that new attitudes often clash with traditional practices. In Africa, new attitudes are clashing big time with the old ones because rapid urbanization is bringing millions of Africans in contact with new ideas and alternative ways of living.**

3   This answer choice is false. Despite a dramatic increase in the rate of urbanization, agriculture remains the most important economic activity in Africa. And with good reason. Africa's population is booming. In fact, Africa has the highest growth rate of any continent. With all the new mouths to feed, it's a good thing that food production is the number one economic activity. It is hoped that Green Revolution techniques will dramatically increase the efficiency of farms in Africa.

4   This statement is too strong because of the words *no longer exists*. To be sure, European influence has declined in Africa, but European influence still remains. Economically, the two continents are strongly tied. And in many nations such as South Africa, significant cultural ties remain.

23   Eliminate answer choices that have nothing to do with the time period or with the region. Also, eliminate answer choices with extreme wording. Finally, look up the term *Golden Age* in the Hit Parade if you need to.

1   There was no trans-Atlantic trade during the Islamic Golden Age.

2   The Renaissance occurred in Europe from approximately the middle of the fourteenth century to the middle of the seventeenth century, so it couldn't have played a role in the Islamic Golden Age. The Islamic Golden Age certainly played a role in the achievements of the European Renaissance, however. Since many ancient European texts were in the hands of the Muslims during their Golden Age and toward the end of the Islamic Golden Age, they made their way back to Europe, thus helping to spark the European Renaissance.

3 **This is the best answer. Cultural diversity contributed greatly to the Islamic Golden Age. The Muslims were concerned with learning, but they didn't really care where the lessons came from. Therefore, they welcomed knowledge and trade with all parts of the known world, obtaining information and literature from Europe, Africa, and other parts of Asia. This type of activity is characteristic of most Golden Ages: The society is focused on art and science, and since art and science know no national boundaries, tremendous diversity often results.**

4 No way. First, this answer choice is much too extreme. Legal equality of all people has never existed anywhere. Think about it. Even in the United States, are twelve-year-olds the legal equals of adults? Do prisoners have the same rights as the free? Of course not. Legal equality of *all* people in a particular nation or empire has never existed. In the Islamic Empire, women were legally subservient to men (and in many nations, they still are).

24 If you know the definition of the term *fundamentalism*, this question almost answers itself. If you don't, look the word up right now in the Hit Parade. What are you waiting for?

1 Nope. Islamic fundamentalists definitely don't want to increase the rights of women.

2 Nope. Islamic fundamentalists are opposed to westernization and modernization, which they claim compete with the teachings of the Koran.

3 **Yes! Fundamentalists are traditionalists. In Iran, Shah Pahlavi attempted to westernize Iran during the 1970's with some success. The fundamentalist-led Iranian Revolution brought an end to the Shah's reign, however. It reinstituted Iran as a theocracy, with the goal of returning Iranian culture to many of its traditional customs.**

4 Nope. The Iranian Revolution resulted in the creation of a theocracy, severely reversing the trends toward democracy that occurred under Shah Pahlavi.

25   The Cold War was waged between the United States and the former
     Soviet Union. With this in mind, you can better sort through the
     answer choices: First, eliminate answer choices that never occurred.
     Then, find an answer choice that mentions something about the
     United States and the former Soviet Union, and when you find one
     that does, to make sure that it logically ties together the Israeli-Arab
     conflict with the Cold War.
     1   Détente between the United States and the Soviet Union had
         nothing to do with the Israeli-Arab conflict.
     2   Communist governments were not established in Arab nations.
         Arab nations have no desire to build a classless society.
     3   No matter what Hussein thinks of Stalin, it hardly has an impact on
         the Cold War or the conflict between Israel and Arab nations or
         how those two conflicts are interrelated.
     **4   This answer choice mentions the United States and the
         former Soviet Union. It also logically explains how the
         Israeli-Arab conflict could have been part of the Cold War.
         Done.**

26   If you know about the Mongols in Russia, good for you, because it will
     help you to piece together Russian history and will enable you to
     understand the reason traditional Russia was considered more a part
     of Asia than a part of Europe. If you're uncertain about the role of the
     Mongols in Russia, you need to at least learn general time frames. The
     Mongols ruled Russia for about 200 years, from the thirteenth to the
     fifteenth century. Eliminate answer choices that are inconsistent with
     the time frame.
     1   The Russian Revolution occurred in 1917. Enough said.
     2   Ivan the Terrible was the grandson of Ivan the Great. Ivan the
         Great was the one who broke Russia free from Mongol domination.
         Therefore, the Mongols were history by the time Ivan the Terrible
         terrorized the Russian people.
     3   Catherine the Great ruled Russia in the late eighteenth century,
         long after Mongol domination.
     **4   The Mongols significantly impacted the history of Russia by
         isolating it from Western Europe during the early Renais-
         sance. While Europe was turning to art and science, logic
         and learning, Russia remained under the domination of the
         Mongols, who didn't want anything to do with art and
         learning. As Europe progressed economically, technologi-
         cally, and culturally, Russia remained stuck in the Middle**

Ages. **If you understand all of this, then you'll probably understand why Peter the Great and Catherine the Great are so significant to Russian history. They tried to westernize Russia in the centuries following Mongol rule.**

27　If you don't know the answer to this one, don't sweat it. You definitely shouldn't be intimidated by this question and think that you need to spend your time memorizing slogans. Nevertheless, you obviously shouldn't leave this question blank. Think of everything you know about Russia during the time of the Bolshevik Revolution. Why were the people revolting? What did they want?

　1　People were starving and tired of war. Liberty and equality would have been nice, but they needed other stuff first. Plus, you probably know that this was the slogan of the French Revolution.

　2　This is it. The people needed basic necessities (bread), they wanted security (land) and they most definitely wanted peace. Bread! Land! Peace!

　3　Liberty is obviously a key word in the American Revolution, but in the Russian Revolution, the people weren't demanding freedom from anyone. Instead, they desired a system in which their needs could be met in a peaceful environment.

　4　This is another historically significant slogan, but in China.

28　Even if you don't know much about the Warsaw Pact, if you know anything about the former Soviet Union, you can eliminate two answer choices easily. If you know the approximate time period when the Warsaw Pact was formed, you can eliminate a third answer choice. Remember, you don't have to know exact dates, but if you know which events occurred in approximately the same general time period, you'll do very well.

　1　During the formation of the Warsaw Pact, the Soviet Union wasn't moving toward democracy. The Soviet Union was a communist nation, both economically and politically, and was trying to expand that philosophy to other nations.

　2　The Soviet Union most certainly didn't want capitalism in Eastern Europe. Instead, it wanted to spread communism.

　3　This is the best answer. The Soviet Union formed the Warsaw Pact after World War II to solidify Eastern Europe behind the "Iron Curtain" and counterbalance the alliance forming in Western Europe and North America known as NATO.

4   The Common Market wasn't formed until well after the formation
    of the Warsaw Pact. In addition, the Warsaw Pact was not an
    economic arrangement as much as it was a political and military
    arrangement.

29 You don't have to know very much about Chechnya in order to answer
    this question correctly. If you are aware that Chechnya was fighting
    against Russia, you can choose the best answer choice.
    **1   This is the best answer. Many people in Chechnya wanted
        independence from Russia. When Russia reacted violently, it
        was obvious that Russia was not willing to grant it indepen-
        dence.**
    2   Nuclear weapons were not used in this conflict, nor were nuclear
        weapons floating around Europe and Asia as a result of this
        conflict. Had they been, you can be sure that you would have
        learned a lot more about Chechnya in your Global Studies class!
    3   Chechnya wasn't being invaded by foreigners. It was fighting
        against Russia for independence.
    4   The conflict in Chechnya had little to do with communism and
        everything to do with self-determination.

30 If you didn't get this question correct, you need to review major
    economic systems as well as the philosophies behind them. If you
    don't know the terms in the answer choices and the approximate time
    periods in which they were developed, it'll come back to haunt you
    again and again. All of them are in the Hit Parade.
    1   Free market capitalism didn't develop until after the Middle Ages.
    2   Socialism didn't gain a lot of steam until the nineteenth and
        twentieth centuries.
    **3   Manorialism, also known as *feudalism*, is so closely tied to
        the Middle Ages that you should think about it as soon as
        you see the words *Middle Ages*. Look *feudalism* up in the Hit
        Parade if you don't know what it means.**
    4   Command economies, such as communist economies, were
        developed in response to the exploitation occurring in nineteenth
        century capitalist economies.

31   If you know anything about the Renaissance, you probably know that it
     was a time of great achievement in the arts. With this in mind, choose
     the answer choice that makes the most sense.
     **1   Bingo! Italy's wealthy class (including the Catholic Church)
         poured tons of money into the arts.**
     2   Italy didn't have a socialist form of government during the Renais-
         sance.
     3   The Byzantine Empire was dead by the fifteenth century. The
         Renaissance in Northern Italy was all the rage from the fourteenth
         to the seventeenth centuries. Therefore, it's true that Northern
         Italy had limited contact with the Byzantine Empire, but this had
         nothing to do with the success of the Renaissance.
     4   Actually, a middle class of merchants was beginning to emerge in
         Italy during the Renaissance. But the middle class, no matter how
         large or small, had little to do with the success of the Renaissance.
         Instead, the success was due to major centers of learning and
         people with a lot of money.

32   You only need to know about one of these men to answer this question
     correctly. Look up *John Locke* in the Hit Parade if you've forgotten
     who he is. Also, since both men were Enlightenment writers, look
     Enlightenment up in the Hit Parade as well.
     1   Neither man supported feudalism. They both supported democracy.
     2   Neither man supported Divine Right theory. In fact, they actively
         argued against it. (Look up *Divine Right* in the Hit Parade. It's
         there for a reason.)
     3   Neither man supported a *theocracy*, which is a society ruled by a
         church (also in the Hit Parade).
     **4   This is the best answer. Both men believed in the right of
         self-determination.**

33   Choose the answer choice that would best describe the *primary* reason
     the Europeans would have improved roads and bridges and built
     railroads in their colonies. To accomplish this task, you should focus on
     the primary reason the Europeans established colonies in the first
     place. The answer to that question is a favorite word of the Regents.
     It's in the Hit Parade. And it begins with an *M*. Need any more clues?
     1   Undoubtedly, the building of roads, bridges and railroads provided
         jobs for many of the colonists, but this wasn't the primary motiva-
         tion behind these endeavors. If they simply wanted to provide jobs,
         they could have required the colonists to do all sorts of things. Why
         specifically roads, bridges and railroads?

2 **During the eighteenth and nineteenth centuries, the Europeans established colonies primarily because of their economic policy of mercantilism. The colonies provided the mother countries with the raw materials that they lacked in their own countries. To get to these raw materials (often located well into the interior of the colonies), and to transport them back to the harbors where their ships were docked, they needed an extensive network of roads, bridges, and railroads. Look up** *mercantilism* **in the Hit Parade, because you definitely need to know how this system worked.**

3 We can't be sure if the colonists were impressed, but it's safe to say that if the Europeans were primarily concerned with impressing the colonists, they could have done it for a lot less money than they spent building thousands of miles of roads, railroads, and bridges. Surely the Europeans had a more significant reason behind this enormous expenditure of time and money.

4 Certainly some Europeans supported imperialism because of a personal evangelical goal to spread Christianity, and certainly roads and railroads contributed to the missionary effort, but it was not the *primary* motivation behind the enormous road and railroad building effort. Instead, European governments and industries were primarily motivated by their mercantilist policies.

34 World War I started in Europe in 1914. The rest of the world was dragged in because Europe had colonies all over the globe. If you don't remember the cause of the war, choose an answer choice that makes sense, or at least eliminate answer choices that are out of the time period.

1 Imperialism was still hot. Africa and Asia were practically owned by Europe.

2 **This answer choice makes a lot of sense. Wars tend to start when people oppose one another. In this case, it was Germany and Austria-Hungary against Britain, France, and Russia (before everybody else was pulled in, that is). It started with Austria declaring war on Serbia and Russia backing Serbia. With Austria and Russia at war, they dragged in their alliances, and the alliances dragged in their colonies and friends. Ka-boom!**

3 England was focusing all of its acts of aggression on its colonies in Africa and Asia during this time period. England very reluctantly joined this particular war, and it was only after German aggression got way out of hand.

4 Communism didn't spread in Europe until after World War I, more so after World War II. It never spread "throughout" Europe, though, since Western Europe never adopted the system.

35 You should know about the rise of the Nazi party in Germany not only because it sometimes shows up on the test, but also because it will help you understand a lot about people and history in general. Nevertheless, if you're not sure about the answer, choose the most general answer choice. In what kinds of general circumstances are people willing to give new leadership a chance?

1 When people are frustrated with their current economic and political situation, they are attracted to new ways of doing things. Germany was never able to recover, economically or politically, from World War I because the Treaty of Versailles was very punitive. When the world suffered an economic depression in the 1930s, it was felt especially hard in Germany. Adolf Hitler and the Nazi Party told the Germans that they deserved more than they were getting. The Nazis aroused public support by appealing to both the nationalism and the frustrations of the Germans.

2 The United Nations didn't exist in the 1930s. It came along after World War II.

3 East Germany wasn't communist until after World War II.

4 The French and the British were not threatening the region in the 1930s.

36 If you don't know much about the European Union, you should read up on it a little, especially if you missed this question. You need to understand that first and foremost, the EU is an *economic* union.

1 The EU is not a military union. NATO is the dominant military alliance in the region, but even NATO didn't create a single military force. Instead, it merely created an alliance. Each individual nation retains control over its own military.

2 This answer choice is way too extreme. The EU didn't create one gigantic European nation with no national sovereignty. It certainly weakens national sovereignty to a degree, but each member nation retains control of most of its own affairs.

3 The EU definitely hasn't adopted a single language. Many people in Europe are multilingual, with English, German, and French being the most popular languages. Still, though, the French predominately speak French, the Germans German, and the English English, and nations such as France are pushing legislation to protect their national languages.

4 **Even though this answer choice uses the word *elimination*, it is not too extreme, because the elimination of trade barriers was one of the major reasons for the creation of the EU in the first place. Remember that the EU is, first and foremost, an economic union.**

37 If you know that Britain's government is considered a friend of democracy, you might be able to guess the answer without knowing the details of the British Parliament. And remember, be suspicious of extreme language.

1 **The Prime Minister is elected by the majority party in Parliament. Unlike the President of the United States or leaders of some other democracies, the Prime Minister is not elected by a majority of electoral votes or by a majority of the population. Still, the members of Parliament are elected by the people, and the majority in Parliament determines the leader, so you should be attracted to this answer choice because it's consistent with majority rule.**

2 The monarch no longer serves as a strong head of state in Britain. The Prime Minister is the strong head of state; the monarch has been reduced to a ceremonial figurehead.

3 The members of the House of Commons are elected for five-year terms. The members of the House of Lords are there for life.

4 This is much too strong. Of course the members of the minority party have a vote. If they had no vote at all, why would they bother sticking around?

38 If you know a lot about Incan and Chinese civilization and the role
    that topography played in those civilizations, good for you. If not, don't
    fret. It doesn't matter that the Regents refer to the Chinese and the
    Incas, it only matters that they told you about the mountainous
    topography. Which answer choice seems a logical development in a
    civilization built in the mountains?

    1 Nothing about mountains makes people want to industrialize.
       Mountains make it hard to get raw materials to the factories and
       hard to get finished products away from the factories. Also, you
       should be aware that the Inca Empire flourished well before
       industrialization swept the globe. You might also know that China
       has traditionally lagged behind much of the rest of the world in
       terms of industrialization, although it is rapidly gaining ground.

    2 Mountainous regions make it difficult to grow most kinds of crops,
       unless you do something else first (and that something happens to
       be the right answer choice). Even though some crops do grow in
       mountainous regions, those crops wouldn't be the basis of a single-
       crop economy, since most of the farming is done in the valleys and
       on the plains.

    3 Desalinization means to take the salt out of something (namely
       water). Desalinization projects are typically used in areas that have
       lots of salt water and very little fresh water for drinking or for
       agriculture. The process of removing the salt from water is a
       relatively modern and extremely expensive technique. So it doesn't
       make sense that the Incas would have used it. It also has nothing to
       do with mountainous regions. Desert areas near bodies of salt
       water have the most use for desalinization projects.

    4 **This is the best answer, hands down. Terrace farming sounds
       like exactly what it is—farming on terraces. The Incas and
       the Chinese successfully transformed mountain slopes into a
       series of terraces—long, narrow, flat areas rising one above
       the next—in the same way an outdoor amphitheater might
       be built into the side of a hill. In this way they were able to
       create rows of flat land suitable for farming.**

39 You only need to know about one of these systems to answer this question correctly. The three incorrect answer choices are really bad.
1 Neither system promoted social mobility. Look *social mobility* up in the Hit Parade if you need to. Both of these systems were class-based systems and therefore social mobility was virtually nonexistent.
2 This is by far the best answer choice. Both systems developed rigid class structures, and just happen to be two of the Regents' favorite examples of class-based systems. Read about both of these systems in your Global Studies materials because they come up often, especially the Hindu caste system.
3 Both systems left decision-making to the people in the upper class.
4 No way. Both systems were structured to keep people in the economic and social class to which they were born. Social and economic mobility was forbidden.

40 Focus on the words *economic recoveries* and *after World War II*. You really don't have to know very much about World War II history in order to answer this question correctly. You only need to know that in the war, a lot of cities were destroyed, and then you need to use logical reasoning to determine which answer choice would be a factor in the economic recovery of those cities.
1 Neither West Germany nor Japan was concerned about an invasion from China. But even if you didn't know this, why would concern over an invasion be a major factor in economic recovery? It wouldn't. That's why this is a bad answer.
2 Certainly Japan and West Germany wanted acceptance into the United Nations, but we want an answer choice that tells us about a *major* factor in their *economic* recovery. Look for something better.
3 We want an answer choice that describes something important to the economic recovery of these nations, not to their military recovery. You might also be aware that Japan's military has been very insignificant since the end of World War II, yet its economy has grown dramatically.
4 This is the best answer. All those bombs that were dropped during World War II destroyed thousands of factories in both nations. In order for the nations to recover economically, Japan and West Germany needed to focus their attention on rebuilding the factories.

41 You only need to know about one of these religious denominations in order to narrow the answer choices down to two. If you are able to narrow the choices down to two, choose the most general answer choice. If you aren't able to narrow the answer choices down to two, still choose the most general answer choice, since you're just guessing (and you're not even going to *think* about leaving any questions blank).

1 Only Roman Catholicism accepts the supreme authority of the Pope. If you know about Roman Catholicism but not about the other two branches, you might like this answer choice, but then you should also like answer choice number 3, since Roman Catholicism is a branch of Christianity. Therefore, in the end, you should have chosen choice 3 since it is the more general answer choice.

2 None of these three denominations reject the Old Testament as part of the Bible. They are all Christian denominations that accept both the Old and the New Testament.

3 **This is the best answer choice. Eastern Orthodoxy, Roman Catholicism, and Protestantism are all major branches of Christianity.**

4 Eastern Orthodoxy was once the official religion of the Byzantine Empire, but if you know about Eastern Orthodoxy, then you probably also know that it is a branch of Christianity, which means that you should have also liked answer choice number 3.

42 You only need to know about one of these men in order to start narrowing the choices down. If you know even a little bit about two or three of them, you should be able to choose the best answer. Remember to always keep in mind the goals of the test. What is one of the biggest world trends that the Regents consistently test? The answer to that is revealed in the explanation for the correct answer.

1 Turkey is near Greece, and Russia isn't extremely far away, but even if you don't know anything about any of these three men, you should probably guess that India didn't expand its territory by invading Greece. For the record, Peter the Great, while an expansionist, didn't expand Russia into Greece. Kemal Atatürk was involved in territorial skirmishes with Greece, however.

2 **This is the best answer. Westernization is a key Regents concept. It's happening in most parts of the globe this century, but it started happening a few centuries ago. Peter the Great and Kemal Atatürk are two of the Regents' favorite examples of men who westernized their nations'**

customs, dress, technology and, to some degree, their nations' attitudes and government policies. Jawaharlal Nehru, the first Prime Minister of modern India, also borrowed significantly from the West, especially in his effort to industrialize India and in his support of certain fundamental rights.

3 Atatürk and Nehru certainly made significant changes that benefited women, but to say that they supported equal rights would be a significant overstatement. As for Peter the Great, he didn't concern himself with civil rights.

4 Atatürk and Nehru intentionally and significantly limited the institutional power of their nations' predominant religions, Islam and Hinduism respectively. Peter the Great didn't directly limit the power of the Orthodox Church within Russia, but his tremendous westernizing efforts brought his country in much more regular contact with the Western European branches of Christianity. As a result, the hold of the Orthodox Church within Russia was weakened, although not to any tremendous degree.

43 The Regents tell you that this passage is from the early 1900s. From the passage you should glean that some country had the largest population, was 4,000 years old at the time, was weak and poor, and was being carved up by foreign powers. Hopefully, you know that this country is China. So, eliminate answer choices that don't have anything to do with China.

1 This is the best answer. The Opium War and the Boxer Rebellion occurred in China as a result of Chinese opposition to European imperialism and the creation of European spheres of influence.

2 The Mau Mau uprising and the adoption of apartheid have a lot to do with European imperialism, but in Africa, not in China. And they both occurred much later than the early 1900s.

3 The Sepoy Mutiny and the Salt March have a lot to do with opposition to European imperialism, but in India, not in China. And the Salt March occurred later than the early 1900s.

4 The Haitian Revolution and Cortés' march on Mexico City have a lot to do with European imperialism, but in Latin America, not in China.

44 You only need to know about one of the items on the list in order to
    answer this question correctly (and you definitely should know about
    the Koran, even if you don't know about the other two items).
    1 **All three are associated with Islam. The Koran is the sacred
       text of Islam, composed of writings accepted by Muslims as
       the revelations Allah made to Mohammed through the angel
       Gabriel. The hegira was the flight of Mohammed from Mecca
       to Medina in 622 AD, marking the beginning of Islam and
       celebrated by millions of Muslims who make a similar pil-
       grimage each year. A jihad is a holy war waged against the
       enemies of Islam. All three are central to the Islamic faith.**
    2 None of these three things have anything to do with Judaism.
    3 Sorry, not Shinto. If you picked this answer, you need to consider
       spending some more time reviewing major world religions. The
       knowledge, once acquired, will earn you a lot of points.
    4 Nope. Buddhism is entirely unrelated to the Koran, the hegira, and
       jihad. Study those major world religions!

45 Look at the graph carefully. It suggests that as time passes, the number
    of barrels of oil reserves will decrease dramatically, eventually hitting
    zero. Yet, you probably already know that much of the world is
    dependent on oil as a source of fuel. The question asks us how to slow
    the trend shown in the graph. In other words, we need an answer
    choice that will explain how our world's oil reserves can last longer
    than the time period shown in the graph.
    1 Look up *Green Revolution* in the Hit Parade if you're not familiar
       with the term. Nothing about Green Revolution technology will
       slow the trend shown in the graph. If anything it will expand it,
       since Green Revolution technology depends, in part, on agricul-
       tural techniques dependent on fuel.
    2 An increase in industrialization will result in an increase in the
       consumption of fuel, thus speeding up the trend indicated in the
       graph, not slowing it.
    3 **Bingo! If we utilize sources of energy other than oil (such as
       solar, water, wind, and nuclear) we can still increase our
       energy output, but not at the expense of the oil reserves,
       thereby slowing the trend indicated in the graph.**
    4 If the worldwide price of oil drops, the consumption of oil will
       increase. Such is the law of supply and demand. Therefore, the
       trend will likely speed up, not slow down. It is when the price of oil
       increases that nations more vigorously search for alternative
       sources of energy in the hope of decreasing their reliance on oil.

46   The cartoon shows us a burned up landscape labeled *Bosnia* and a
     NATO official talking to an American about how shameful it is that the
     smoke detectors weren't better. What's the purpose of a smoke
     detector? It's to warn that there is a fire. In this case, the NATO
     official apparently believes that they didn't have enough warning to
     prevent a crisis before it engulfed the nation. Which answer choice
     describes this scenario?
   **1   This is the best answer. The NATO guy is saying that they
       didn't have enough time to avert the crisis. Critics of NATO
       claim that NATO and others did, in fact, have enough time,
       but waited too long before reacting.**
   2   Nothing in the cartoon suggests a conversation between Bosnia and
       NATO, much less a disagreement about the cause of the war.
   3   Nothing in the cartoon suggests that communism played a role.
       Nothing in the cartoon suggests anyone taking advantage of
       anything. There's just a whole lot of destruction.
   4   Nothing in the cartoon suggests that the United States is withdrawing
       from anything. Plus, this answer choice doesn't make sense. If NATO
       eventually disbands, it won't be because of the Bosnian crisis. Crises
       suggest that international organizations are necessary. It is the *absence*
       of a need for international organizations, not the need, which could
       eventually lead to the disbandment of those organizations.

47   If you know about Cuba's relationship with other nations, this question
     is easy. But even if you're not sure which nation was Cuba's former
     puppet master, you can still get this question right. How? Focus on the
     words *still dancing after the puppet master's death*. Simply look for a
     country that is now "dead." The three wrong answer choices are
     nations that are still alive and kicking. The right answer choice,
     however, is the only nation that no longer exists.
   1   Haiti is still a nation.
   **2   The Soviet Union no longer exists. It broke apart into
       smaller nations such as Russia and Ukraine. If you know the
       history of Cuba, of course, you would have picked this
       answer anyway, because the former Soviet Union strongly
       supported Cuba in its establishment of a communist society.**
   3   Spain is still with us. If you picked this answer, you're going to
       have to explain to millions of Spaniards why you thought their
       country was dead. They probably wouldn't like that very much.
   4   Last time we checked, the United States was still in existence. Also,
       the United States, of course, can hardly be described as the puppet
       master of Cuba. Cuba and the United States are not allies.

48 The quote is telling us that the silence of a bystander harms a victim more than the cruelty of the oppressor. In other words, people who watch cruelty done to another person and refuse to do anything about it are, according to the quote, more harmful to victims than the people performing the cruelty. Which answer choice suggests that people, therefore, shouldn't ignore the suffering of others but rather do something about it?

1   This answer choice has nothing to do with the quote. Even if you didn't understand the quote, though, you still should have eliminated this answer choice, because it's false. Totalitarian governments typically suppress civil liberties, and often grossly violate civil liberties.

2   **This is the best answer. It suggests that people shouldn't stand idly by and watch the violation of human rights, but instead actively condemn violations in an effort to help the victims.**

3   This answer is inconsistent with the quote. Elie Wiesel wants the people of the world to address problems such as ethnic cleansing, not ignore them. According to Elie Wiesel, ignoring problems such as ethnic cleansing contributes to the problem!

4   This answer choice is both inconsistent with the quote and inconsistent with the Regents. There is no way that the Regents are going to suggest that demonstrations against human rights violations won't work!

PART II

1. INDIVIDUALS WITH SIMILAR OR DIFFERENT POINTS OF VIEW

Confucius and Machiavelli—Power of the Ruler

Confucius and Machiavelli were worlds apart, not only because they lived in different centuries and cultures, but also because of their profound differences regarding the appropriate characteristics of a good ruler. Confucius believed that a good ruler had the responsibility to set an example for those that were ruled; all relationships had corresponding responsibilities. The higher rungs in society (rulers and parents, for example) owed fairness, justice, and, in some cases, kindness to the lower rungs (peasants and children). In return, the lower rungs owed respect to the higher rungs and were expected to do as they were told with quiet acceptance. Confucius stressed that authority was not a license to do as one pleased, but rather a responsibility to do as one should. The goal was the maintenance of justice, fairness, and order. Confucius traveled throughout China, counseling rulers and peasants about their corresponding responsibilities. Eventually he gained an enormous following, and for centuries after his death, millions of Chinese continued to strive to live according to his ideals.

In contrast, Machiavelli believed that a good ruler should use any means available, including deceit, to achieve his goals. While subjects were supposed to do as they were told and to live in fear, rulers did not necessarily have any responsibilities to those they governed. Machiavelli argued that such a ruler would actually be serving the interests of the governed by achieving societal goals swiftly and effectively. Of course, this is only true if the goals are "good" goals in the first place. Even if they are, the means to achieve them, according to Machiavelli, are unlimited, and therefore fraud, suffering, and even murder are justifiable (though his actual beliefs might have been somewhat tamer than some of the ideas he formally expressed). Machiavelli publicized the full range of his ideas in *The Prince*, which he dedicated to Lorenzo de Medici, the ruler of Florence whose favor Machiavelli desperately wanted. Rather than impressing Medici, however, *The Prince* was ignored by him. It was not ignored by the printing presses, however. Today, Machiavelli is still recalled when someone argues that *the ends justify the means* and his name has even led to the use of the adjective *Machiavellian*.

Clearly, Machiavellian rulers did not feel that they owed justice, fairness, and kindness in the same way that Confucian rulers did. Simply put, Confucius believed that the characteristics of a good ruler are mostly a product of his behavior and understanding of his role. Machiavelli believed that the characteristics of a good ruler are mostly a product of his accomplishments, with little regard for the manner in which those accomplishments are achieved.

Napoleon Bonaparte and Catherine the Great—Expansion

Napoleon of France and Catherine the Great of Russia both used their highly concentrated authority to expand the geographic boundaries of their empires. Both leaders had wide-ranging goals for their empires, from social reforms to economic reforms, but both leaders put territorial conquest at the top of the list and, in an effort to reach their goals as swiftly and completely as possible, assumed absolute authority to personally direct the conquests.

There were differences, however, in their approaches to expansion. Although both leaders had large appetites for ever-increasing empires, Catherine the Great's pursuits were geographically targeted to specific areas for specific reasons. For example, she pursued and won former Ottoman Empire lands along the Black Sea to the south of Russia as part of her goal to gain access to warm-water ports. On the other hand, Napoleon seemed to seize territory for the simple reason of gaining more territory (he once said, "Conquest has made me what I am and only conquest can enable me to hold my position."). His conquests were directed against everything that wasn't under his control, and thereby lacked the focus and purpose of Catherine's. He continuously pushed forward in his aim to control all of continental Europe, and consequently stretched his resources. Napoleon decided to push forward into the interior of Russia when he shouldn't have, and although he seized temporary control of Moscow, he was eventually defeated and pushed back. Napolean later gave his dreams of conquest one last try, but was defeated once and for all at Waterloo.

Ironically, although Catherine the Great's conquests actually resulted in territorial gains for Russia, her impact on Europe was arguably not as significant as Napoleon's. Napoleon, who in the end managed to shrink the territorial size of France rather than enlarge it, left many of the marks of the French Revolution throughout much of Europe. Although Napoleon didn't personally practice many of the ideas behind the French Revolution, his temporary conquests carried these more permanent ideas to new lands, including the ideas of constitutional government, rule of law, abolishment of the feudal system, and nationalism. Therefore, it could be said that while Catherine the Great intentionally expanded the territory of Russia, Napoleon unintentionally expanded the ideas of France.

John Calvin and Martin Luther—Attitudes toward Catholic Church

Although John Calvin and Martin Luther had very different theological beliefs, they were both similar in their frustration with the Catholic Church. Martin Luther, an Augustinian friar in Germany, originally did not intend to break away from the Catholic Church. Instead, he hoped to reform it from within. Luther posted ninety-five theses on a church door in Wittenberg to protest the Catholic Church's selling of *indulgences*, pieces of paper that the Church claimed would reduce the amount of time the seller would have to stay in purgatory. As his reform movement gained momentum, however, Luther questioned more and more of the Church's practices and positions. He questioned papal authority, rejected strict transubstantiation, and most importantly, professed that people are justified by faith, not merely by their deeds or observance of sacraments. In all his efforts, Luther tried to individualize people's relationship with God, lessening their reliance on the Church hierarchy to act as an intermediary between God and man. He even translated the Bible into German so that individuals could read and interpret it for themselves.

John Calvin, a Frenchman who found a following in Geneva, rejected many of the same Catholic principles, but had a profoundly different theology from Luther's. Calvin believed that the absolute depravity of man after the fall of Adam made salvation impossible except for a select few whom were predestined by God. These few were known as The Elect. According to Calvin, only God knew who The Elect were, but Calvinists strove to live a godly life in the hope that they were among the chosen. In many senses, Calvin individualized Christianity by focusing on each individual's deeds and their relationship with God. He set up a theocratic state in Geneva, but his movement was hardly limited to Switzerland; it spread throughout much of Europe, challenging Catholicism and even Lutheranism.

In summary, both John Calvin and Martin Luther, while enormously different from one another, challenged the authority of the Catholic Church and succeeded in establishing new denominations of Christianity. They refocused Christians in Europe on the words of the Bible, and on the importance of their individual conduct not as an end in itself but as a sign of something else (either faith, for Lutherans, or as membership in The Elect, for Calvinists). They both also stressed the individual's personal relationship with God without the aid of intermediaries.

Simón Bolívar and Jomo Keyatta—Independence Movements

Although they lived in different centuries and on different continents, both Simón Bolívar and Jomo Kenyatta were similar in many of their beliefs and actions regarding the struggles for independence from European imperialists. Both men were strongly motivated by the writings and the actions of enlightened thinkers who came before them. Bolívar was influenced by the ideas generated before and during the American and French Revolutions. The actions and ideas of Bolívar himself influenced the later revolutions in Africa led by Jomo Kenyatta, who was also influenced by many of his contemporaries. Both men strongly believed in the right of self-determination for their people, and found similar strands of European resistance standing in their way.

Bolívar successfully liberated present-day Bolivia, Colombia, Ecuador, Peru, and Venezuela from Spain. He personally led armies of men, freeing the slaves and declaring victory as he went. Kenyatta was somewhat influenced by many of the nonviolent activities of his contemporaries, such as Gandhi, but, like Bolívar, Kenyatta was not opposed to fighting for freedom. He was accused by the British of organizing and leading the ultra-violent Mau Mau and was jailed, but eventually released. He ultimately became the first president of Kenya, just as Bolívar became the first president of Colombia. Both men, therefore, were successful in accomplishing their goals of independence.

Mohandas Gandhi and Adolph Hitler—Use of Force

With regard to the appropriate use of force, Mohandas Gandhi of India and Adolph Hitler of Germany are at opposite ends of the spectrum. Gandhi is one of the clearest examples of nonviolent activities the world has ever known; Hitler is one of the clearest examples of violence. Gandhi refused to react violently against oppression even as imperialist oppressors enacted violence against his people; Hitler willingly and methodically murdered millions of people even though those people had engaged in no violence against him. Gandhi gained power the more he stood up to force; Hitler was powerless without force.

In his effort to win independence from Britain for the Indian subcontinent through the use of nonviolence, Gandhi initiated strikes, boycotts, and marches. His efforts won the sympathy of much of the rest of the world, and he and other Indian leaders were ultimately successful in negotiating independence for the subcontinent (although violence between Hindus and Muslims prevented the region from experiencing peace). In contrast, Hitler ordered the execution of millions of Jews, homosexuals, and other "undesirables" in an atrocious campaign known as the Holocaust. His efforts won the hatred of much of the rest of the world, and Germany was ultimately defeated in World War II. The two opposing methods of the two men, therefore, led to two opposing outcomes.

Louis XIV and Baron de Montesquieu—Forms of Government

Louis XIV and Montesquieu did not share a common political philosophy. Louis XIV, also known as the Sun King, was precisely the kind of leader that Montesquieu, one of the famed Enlightenment writers, argued so strongly against. Louis XIV was an absolute monarch, which meant that his word was the final authority on virtually every national policy, foreign or domestic. He never called an Estates-General, the traditional ruling body of noblemen, and thereby eliminated any competition with his authority. He spent enormous sums of money and cost thousands of lives in personally directed military campaigns, acts of persecution, and internal building projects, such as his palace at Versailles.

In his book *The Spirit of the Laws,* Montesquieu argued for separation of powers within government in order to prevent absolute monarchs like Louis XIV from seizing control of an entire nation. In concert with the works of other Enlightenment writers, he greatly influenced the popular opinion regarding the best form of government, thereby weakening the arguments of monarchs who claimed they had a divine right to absolute rule. In the centuries since, constitutional monarchies and democracies, both of which separate powers within the government, have become the most common forms of government in the world.

2. GEOGRAPHIC BARRIERS TO NATIONAL DEVELOPMENT

Greece

Greece is mountainous. It also contains thousands of tiny islands. These two features made Ancient Greece a difficult place to control from a central location. Nevertheless, Greece thrived, mostly because of the way it organized itself.

Ancient Greece was really a collection of much smaller city-states. Each one governed itself and developed its own culture. The geographic barriers greatly contributed to this separation of culture. The more the city-states remained separated, the more they developed into unique cultures— different from each other, and often even against one another. Athens and Sparta, for example, were continuously in competition. Nevertheless, the people of ancient Greece overcame their geographic barriers. They remained united in their common language, and they developed the tradition of the Olympic games, which brought them together at regular intervals and helped them to create a unique Greek identity. They were also bound together in mutual defense against non-Greeks, namely Persians. Eventually, the city-states were unified under the Macedonians. Throughout what became known as the Hellenistic Age, ancient Greece was united despite the geographic barriers, partly due to a tremendous increase in the use of boats for travel, commerce, and military pursuits.

India

The Himalayas have played an important role in the development of the Indian subcontinent, which lies to the south of the mountain range. Geologists believe that the Himalayas were created when India drifted into Asia about forty million years ago. The result was the creation of the highest mountain range in the world. Like most mountain ranges, the Himalayas create a barrier between the lands on either side. The mountains stretch from just northeast of Burma all the way to the northeast corner of Pakistan, isolating the Indian peninsula from central Asia and from the Middle East. Therefore, the mountains acted as a barrier to trade, inhibiting the development of major trades to the rest of Asia and to the Middle East. India's relative isolation meant that it could not economically develop as it might have had it not been for the mountains.

The people of India adapted to the barrier, however, and made use of the benefits of the mountain range. For example, the Himalayas prevent heavy monsoon rains from crossing into central Asia, allowing the clouds to empty over the subcontinent, thereby benefiting the rice paddies. The Himalayas also protect the subcontinent from cold blasts of air that sweep across northern and central Asia. Therefore, the climate created as a result of the mountain range provided an ideal environment for the growth of a stable agrarian culture. The Indians took advantage of the climate and built a tremendous civilization, despite the fact that for centuries it was relatively isolated and lacked money from international trade. Its isolation, however, eventually got the best of India when it was overrun by British imperialists. Since independence, however, India has entered the global economy with new hope, this time with technological ways of getting around the Himalayas, mostly by air and sea. What's more, the barrier of the mountains is on the verge of becoming a blessing. If peace in the region can be maintained, the Himalayas may become one of the world's great tourist destinations.

Japan

Japan is a small, mountainous island nation with relatively few natural resources. At the same time, it has a growing population and a growing economy. Japan has managed to overcome its geographic barrier to development by importing raw materials from other nations. Since the Meiji Restoration in the late nineteenth century, Japan has been a major player in the world economy by effectively managing its imports and exports. In the early twentieth century, Japan invaded other parts of Asia in order to gain inexpensive access to the raw materials it needed. The Japanese followed the trend of mercantilism established by European imperialists centuries before. They robbed their colonies of their plentiful resources and shipped them back to Japan, where they were made into finished products. Japan then sent these finished products abroad (as well as back to the colonies), where they were sold for a profit. Since the end of World War II, Japan has continued to manage its imports and exports well, despite the fact that it no longer has colonial holdings. Japan still imports most of its raw materials from other nations, but turns the relatively inexpensive raw materials into much more expensive high-tech finished products. Combined with protectionist trade barriers against other nations, Japan has consistently managed to overcome its geographic barriers by making a profit from other nations' natural resources.

Middle East/North Africa

In the Middle East and North Africa, deserts are the primary geographical barrier to development. The Sahara Desert dominates northern Africa, stretching in a 1,000-mile wide path from Western Sahara and Mauritania on the Atlantic Ocean to Egypt and northern Sudan on the Red Sea. With the exception of the coastal communities along the Mediterranean Sea and along the Nile River, North Africa has been virtually swallowed by the ever-expanding desert. In the Middle East, the landscape is also dominated by deserts, with the exception of the lands of the Fertile Crescent in the Tigris-Euphrates River Valley, which are the source of significant vegetation.

In recent decades, the nations of this region of the world have transformed their economies despite the desert, mostly because of the vast supply of petroleum that lies beneath the sands. As the world has industrialized, it has become increasingly dependent on petroleum for fuel. As a result, the region has become more and more wealthy, supplying as much as two-thirds of the world's petroleum. With all this new-found money, many nations, such as Saudi Arabia, are spending billions on attempts to improve their agricultural sectors. In this way, the nations of the region have not simply adapted to the deserts, but are beginning to overcome and transform them.

Russia

Russia's greatest geographical barrier to development has been its location. For centuries, Russia's only coastline ran along the Arctic Ocean in the north and then cut south in the east along the Bering Sea. The southern and western borders were landlocked. Since the Arctic Ocean is almost entirely covered in ice year-round, Russia was not able to establish port cities throughout much of its history, except in the east where the population is sparse and thousands of miles away from the population centers of the west. In short, Russia was too big and yet too confined by its landlocked and ice-locked borders to get its economy jump-started in any meaningful way.

Russia overcame its barrier to development by expanding to the west and to the south. In the eighteenth century, Peter the Great drove the Swedes out of part of the Baltic region and established his new capital city on the Baltic Sea. In addition, both he and, later, Catherine the Great fought wars against the Ottoman Empire in the south to gain access to the Black Sea. Thereafter, Russia's coastline included warm-water ports. As a result, Russia's international trade increased dramatically, as did its naval capacity. Today, Russia continues to rely heavily on its warm-water ports.

Southeast Asia

In Southeast Asia, one of the greatest geographical barriers to development has been flooding due to monsoon rains. The floods have destroyed homes and villages, and have traditionally made it difficult to create permanent industry. Yet the region has taken advantage of this "problem" by increasing its production of rice, a grain that originated in South Asia and is mostly grown in paddy fields. It so happens that the monsoon pattern of heavy rains followed by long dry spells creates the ideal conditions for successful rice paddies. It shouldn't be surprising, then, that rice has been a major part of the regular diet of virtually everyone in Southeast Asia. But more important to the economic development of the region, rice has a high yield per acre. Consequently, Southeast Asia is not only able to grow enough rice for its own exploding population, but enough for export as well, especially from the rice paddies of the Mekong River Delta in South Vietnam. Therefore, both the internal food supply and the trade balance of the region have benefited from the region's adaptation to its geographical challenge.

Switzerland

Switzerland is nestled in the midst of the Alps mountain range. Nearly half of Switzerland's land area is over 3,300 feet above sea level, and because the highlands are steep and difficult to traverse, only about 5 percent of Switzerland's population lives in the mountains. The rest of the population lives in the valleys, and are also relatively isolated because their towns and farms are surrounded by the mountains. Due to the relative isolation, different cultures have developed within Switzerland. To add to the complexity, each of these cultures speaks its own language. While the German language dominates central Switzerland, a French-speaking majority exists in western Switzerland. In eastern Switzerland, Italian and Romansh are the dominant languages. Yet all of these cultures coexist in one country relatively peacefully, in large part because the government is decentralized, allowing each region of the country to control most of its own affairs. Interestingly, while decentralization and multiculturalism are in many ways positive factors, they also make it difficult for the country to have consistent and unifying political and economic policies. As such, national development is often sacrificed for local development, which further contributes to the regional detachment that was initially caused by the mountainous terrain.

3. RELIGIONS AND HOW PEOPLE SHOULD LIVE THEIR LIVES

Buddhism

Although there are hundreds of branches of Buddhism, in general most Buddhists believe that it is up to oneself to acquire wisdom and peace, and that the effort to do so will allow one to break free of materialism and worldly pain.

Buddhism is based on Four Noble Truths: (1) all life is suffering, (2) this suffering is due to selfish desire that is based on an attachment to the material world, (3) it is possible to overcome selfish desire by overcoming one's attachment to the material world, and (4) following the Eightfold Path will enable one to attain wisdom and inner-peace, thereby eliminating selfish desire from one's life. The Eightfold Path more specifically outlines the way Buddhists should live their lives. They should make every attempt to have Right Views, Right Intentions, Right Speech, Right Conduct, Right Livelihood, Right Effort, Right Mindfulness, and Right Contemplation. In addition to the Eightfold Path, the various branches of Buddhism teach that life should be lived according to the *Precepts*. Buddha taught Ten Precepts, but certain sects teach as many as 250 Precepts. Included in these Precepts are standards of morality common to many organized religions, including abstinence from stealing, lying and consuming alcohol. However, in some sects, the Precepts micro-manage daily life to a much greater degree, literally down to the size of bed one should sleep on. In general, though, the Four Noble Truths, the Eightfold Path and the Precepts all lead to one goal: the attainment of inner-peace and wisdom. Ultimately, Buddhists hope to reach *nirvana*, which means *extinguished*, or the elimination of selfish desire.

Christianity

There are many divisions of Christianity, but in general, Christians are called upon to live their lives according to two prescriptions: First, Christians believe that they are saved through faith in Jesus Christ and that God will forgive them their sins. Christians do not believe that they can release themselves from the bondage of sin (unlike Buddhists, who believe they can release themselves to a desire-free life), but instead need forgiveness from God, who will readily grant forgiveness to those who have faith in him. Second, Christians believe that they should live their lives according to God's will. It is not enough that they confess their past sins, they must genuinely try to improve their lives and refrain from repeating those sins. Christians believe that the Bible (both the Old and the New Testaments) gives the fundamental will of God regarding how Christians should live their lives. Often, Christians interpret the Bible differently, but even when they agree on an interpretation, it is not always easy for them to live life accordingly. For example, the law of the Bible is very explicit in many places, particularly in the Old Testament with the enumeration of laws such as the Ten Commandments. Yet the Bible also calls upon Christians to love their neighbors as themselves and reserve the final judgment to God. This is particularly true in the New Testament, where the Gospel seems to elevate the importance of compassion, restraint, and humility. Many Christians have difficulty loving their neighbor in the same spirit of Jesus Christ while also following the law of God as outlined in the Old Testament, and the way in which each Christian resolves this problem (or whether they see this as a problem at all), is at the heart of many of the various divisions within Christianity today.

Hinduism

Hindus believe that life is a series of births. One's lot in life is the result of how one behaved in a previous life; one's future lot in life will be the result of how one behaved in the present life. With this in mind, how one lives one's life is critical. It determines the caste into which one is born and, in turn, one's caste determines everything else about one's life. It is the goal of all Hindus to break the cycle of rebirths entirely, reaching the state of *Moksha,* which is essentially like the Buddhist state of *nirvana,* a state of peace free from suffering.

In order to reach Moksha, Hindus believe they must live their lives according to the Vedas, the sacred text of Hinduism. As such, they must follow strict guidelines with regard to the major elements of life: birth, marriage, and death. They must make offerings and pilgrimages, follow the rules of their caste, and pay proper respect to the Hindu gods. Hindus also believe that they must show regard for their ancestors and for all of life, since all parts of nature, both past and present, are part of the cycle of rebirth. One way in which they can show such respect is by having children themselves, thereby contributing to the cycle. Therefore, in virtually every aspect of their lives, Hindus are consciously aware of the effects of their thoughts and deeds on the cycle of life.

Islam

First and foremost, Muslims believe that they should submit to the will of God. They also believe that His will is made explicitly clear in the Koran, the most sacred text of Islam. There are essentially two categories of behavior which govern the life of the typical Muslim. The first is strict adherence to the Five Pillars of Islam: (1) There is no god but God, and Mohammed is his messenger; (2) prayer is required five times a day; (3) almsgiving equal to one-fortieth of one's moveable possessions must be given to the poor; (4) fasting is required during Ramadan; and (5) one must make a pilgrimage to Mecca at least once, if possible. The second category is adherence to the details of the daily routine as outlined in the Koran. The more fundamentalist the Muslim, the more strict the adherence to the details. The Koran is very specific regarding what should be eaten, what should be worn, how one should behave, and even how one should pray. All of this is done in an effort to submit as best as one can to the will of God.

Judaism

Judaism has many divisions, but all of them agree that Jews should do their best to emulate God. There are two different ways in which the Jews attempt to do so.

Jews believe that there is but one God, and He is to be at the center of one's life. Therefore, all conduct should be consistent with the will of God. In other words, Jews believe that people should be merciful, just, compassionate, and tolerant, since those are the qualities they associate with God. In general, they believe that the worship of God, whether it is in a synagogue or in all aspects of daily life, should be grounded in love as opposed to fear. To help them in this quest, Jews follow the teachings of the Torah, the sacred book of Judaism. The Torah outlines God's commandments and establishes rites and ceremonies, including circumcision and observance of the Sabbath. The divisions within Judaism, of course, center around how strictly and literally the Torah should be followed and how many accommodations should be made for the changing world.

Jews also believe that life should be a constant pursuit of knowledge, since the very essence of God is knowledge—knowledge of truth. Education has traditionally been extremely important in Jewish communities. The word *rabbi* means teacher, for example. In ancient times, Jewish children were given cakes and breads in the shape of letters of the alphabet, helping them to understand that learning is just as much a fundamental part of life as eating. The love of learning, Jews believe, does not at all interfere with the worship of God, but rather *is* the worship of God, since it is the only way to achieve an understanding of truth. In summary, Jews believe that they not only achieve the will of God by following the specific mandates of the Torah, but also by keeping oneself occupied in a constant pursuit of truth.

4. ARTISTIC CREATIONS OF DIFFERENT CULTURES

Traditional Chinese—Painting

Traditional Chinese paintings typically focus on the natural world. People are often present, but they are diminished in comparison to huge landscapes of mountains, lakes, and trees. The paintings utilize multiple focal points, allowing the viewer's eyes to wander across the landscape rather than to become isolated and directed on a singular image.

One of the best examples of this type of flowing natural landscape is Li Cheng's *A Solitary Temple Amid Clearing Peaks*. The peaks dominate the landscape, yet they don't diminish the buildings and foliage in the foreground. Instead, the entire landscape blends together, all parts fitting together to make a complete whole. The effect on the viewer is one of peace and tranquillity, as if the viewer himself is part of the landscape. Indeed, the painting seems to lead the viewer from the bottom left corner through the valley, past the temple and on toward the mountaintops, ultimately toward heaven. The result is that the viewer is treated as a traveler on a spiritual journey instead of a mere observer.

Li Cheng's painting, and so many others like it, reflect China's traditional concern with blending the natural world with the spiritual world. A multitude of Chinese painters have succeeded in their attempt to make art a spiritual experience, rather than merely a sensory experience. In this way, the paintings helped promote Buddhism within the Chinese culture.

Traditional African—Sculpture

Some of the most significant African sculptures are those created in Benin from the eleventh through the fifteenth centuries. Mostly made of bronze and copper, the sculptures were not only linked with the religious practices of the people of Benin, but were also made to honor rulers. Interestingly, early Benin sculptures are far more realistic than contemporary sculptures made in other parts of the world. However, as the culture continued to grow, the sculptures, especially those of rulers, became increasingly more idealistic and ornate, perhaps suggesting a change in the culture's reverence for its rulers. The bronze sculptures are significant not just as astounding pieces of art, but because they give us an understanding of Benin culture itself. The Benin culture even developed the bronze-making techniques that they used. Therefore, the sculptures not only give us clues about the dress, customs, and traditions of Benin but also about the level of technology. These clues are especially important since there is no written record of the kingdom. Archeologists, therefore, analyze the sculptures in great detail, also hoping to achieve greater insight into the rich history of Benin civilization.

Ancient Egyptian—Architecture

Perhaps the most significant examples of ancient Egyptian architecture are the pyramids. The three Great Pyramids were built around 2500 BC as tombs for three kings. Each of the pyramids was built with blocks of limestone and granite. The largest of the pyramids, the Great Pyramid of Cheops, stands 480 feet high. It was believed that the shape of the pyramids would attract Ra, the sun god, since the sides of the pyramids represent the rays of the sun. The kings were mummified inside the pyramids and placed with many of their belongings, which according to Egyptian religion, they would need in the afterlife. Moreover, the interior of the tombs serves as a wonderful display for other types of Egyptian art, especially sculptures and paintings. Sculptures of the dead king served as potential resting places for his *ka* (soul) should something happen to his mummy, while paintings of everyday objects were placed on the walls because the objects depicted were believed to be accessible to the *ka* as if they were the objects themselves. The pyramids and their contents, therefore, are not only architectural and artistic wonders, but also serve as present day reminders of the importance of the afterlife in Egyptian religion.

Ancient Greek—Drama

The ancient Greeks used drama, specifically tragedy, to not only tell the story of their history and mythology, but also to instill a humanistic philosophy in their culture. The plays of Aeschylus, Sophocles, and Euripedes each introduce the audience to a hero who has a fatal character flaw that inevitably does him in, despite his other outstanding features. Even the Greek gods were often portrayed in a humanistic way. Sometimes the writers used drama as a commentary against certain Greek policies. For example, *The Trojan Women* by Euripides dramatized the emptiness of the Greek victory over Troy, suggesting that it was the women of Troy as opposed to the men of Greece who were the real victors, because they managed to retain their humanity while the men of Greece succumbed to savagery. The Greek dramatists were masters of the art form, utilizing masks, music, scenery, and, of course, wonderful poetry. But it was the message of their plays, not the medium, which truly influenced the beliefs and goals of Ancient Greek culture as much as it reflected it. In the end, the dramatists' focus on humanism and tragic destiny affected the moral and philosophical development of ancient Greece more than perhaps any other single force.

Medieval European—Architecture

Gothic cathedrals were built in Europe in the twelfth through seventeenth centuries. They were larger and more detailed than most of the cathedrals that came before them, and were unique in their use of pointed arches, flying buttresses, and enormous, detailed stained glass windows. Chartres Cathedral stands as one of the greatest examples of the High Gothic style in Europe and as an excellent reflection of Medieval Christianity. After the first attempt to build the cathedral ended in a fire, it was finally completed in 1220, twenty-six years after the second attempt began. Three features of the tremendous Cathedral combined architecture with Christian theology. First, the altar rests at the intersection of a long nave and two side galleries. In other words, the floor plan is in the shape of the cross, the most important symbol of Christianity. Second, the ceiling of the nave rises to nearly 120 feet, and the towers outside rise much higher than that, focusing the eyes and the spirit upward toward heaven. Third, the walls are dominated by enormous stained glass windows, larger and more intricate than anything that had come before them. Christian symbolism and Biblical stories are represented within the designs of the windows. Therefore, the architectural style of Chartres Cathedral reflected and reinforced the values of Christian Medieval Europe.

Traditional Japanese—Drama

Kabuki, a traditional form of drama combined with elements of music and dance, stands out as one of the most unique forms of artistic expression in Japan. In the seventeenth century, *kabuki* was an extremely popular form of entertainment, appealing to a wide variety of people. The actors did whatever they could to please the crowd, even to the point of combining historical drama with provocative dance styles that served as a way for actress-prostitutes to solicit customers from the audience. Hoping to put a stop to some of the more questionable *kabuki* practices, the Shogunate in 1629 banned all females from performing. In 1652, the Shogunate went further, removing young boys from performances, leaving the theatre companies with only adult males. *Kabuki* adapted brilliantly, staging elaborate battles and dances with their all-male casts, even using male cast members in female roles. The crowds loved it, and *kabuki* became increasingly profit-motivated and commercialized, helping to set the stage for the consumer revolution that would take place in Japan after the Meiji Restoration. Yet, interestingly, during the Meiji Restoration, *kabuki* became more refined and "European," submitting to the goals of a Japanese government intent on bringing Japan in line with many of the western conventions of the day. *Kabuki*, therefore, is a wonderful example of a Japanese art form that has reflected the values and conflicts within Japanese society throughout several centuries.

Traditional South Asian—Sculpture

Traditional Indian sculpture was primarily religiously motivated, and often made to pay homage to a god, (a god associated with Buddhism, Hinduism, or Jainism). Indian sculptors believed that their work should shed light on the spiritual world, inviting people to use their artwork as a passageway to contemplation. Buddhist statues, for example, were often made to look calm and serene, so that when an observer would look upon the statue, he or she would feel the same way. During the Gupta Dynasty, the statues, often made of bronze, further reflected the values of Buddhism in that they were intentionally idealized, elevating the Buddha above the imperfect human form. Hindu statues were similarly religiously motivated. *Siva Nataraja* (Lord of dance) portrays the goddess Siva spinning inside a wheel, her arms seemingly moving the wheel in the eternal dance of destruction and reconstruction that is central to the Hindu perception of the cycle of life. In addition, since Hindus believe the Ganges River flows from the hair of Siva, the statue depicts her hair flowing forth as the river's source. Therefore, as these examples suggest, in many ways sculptures in traditional India were explicitly made to reinforce Buddhist and Hindu values and beliefs.

5. CONFLICTS DUE TO A PARTICULAR FACTOR

Land—Middle East

The intifada uprisings are part of an ongoing dispute between Israelis and Islamic Palestinians. Both want Palestine, a small region along the eastern edge of the Mediterranean Sea, as their homeland. The source of the conflict goes back to the creation of Israel as a Jewish homeland in 1948. The Jews have claimed Palestine as their homeland since Biblical times. For decades prior to the creation of Israel, thousands of Jews had already been moving to the region as part of the Zionist movement, an organized effort by Jews to settle the land that was promised them by God to Moses. The Muslims claim Palestine as rightfully theirs, since they lived in the land during the time that most of the people in the region converted to the Islamic faith. The two groups have fought ever since, including the Six Day War in 1967 and the Yom Kippur War in 1973. Most recently, however, there have been groups of young fundamentalists who have sponsored terrorism against Israel. The uprisings of these radical groups are known as the intifada. They have even killed many within their own ranks that have been suspected of dealing with Israel.

The intifada uprisings have been a setback to the peace process in Palestine. While more moderate leaders of the Palestine Liberation Organization try to deal with Israel, the intifada threatens extremist action. Recently, the Oslo accords have offered the hope of peace by giving autonomy to the Palestinians in the Gaza and West Bank, while giving Israel autonomy in the rest of Palestine. It has been an uneasy peace, however, since both sides claim the other is violating the agreement and since Israel seems intent to expand its settlements in areas claimed by the Palestinians. Therefore, the full consequences of the intifada uprisings and of the Oslo accords remain unknown.

Natural Resources—Latin America

Two groups oppose each other in Brazil: those who want to cut down parts of the rain forests for lumber, farming and development and those who want to protect the rain forests from further destruction. In the north and western parts of the nation, the Amazon basin dominates the landscape. Its tropical rain forests support incredibly diverse species of plants and animals. This area has traditionally been sparsely populated, mostly by tribes, and the rain that falls in the region feeds the great and powerful Amazon River, a vital source of transportation and water downstream. The vegetation of the rain forest comprises Brazil's greatest natural resource, yet when it tries to exploit its resources like other nation's have done, the world community reacts in nearly unanimous opposition, as do environmental groups within Brazil. The Brazilian government is allowing the rain forests to be cut down at a rate that many claim will have an irreversible environmental impact. The land is being cleared mostly by logging companies, but as the government has expanded the Trans-Amazon highway, the land is increasingly becoming developed with housing and industry. The destruction of the rain forest may have a significant global impact because it could upset the balance between carbon dioxide and oxygen in the earth's atmosphere, potentially leading to global warming. In 1989, the government unveiled a comprehensive environmental program to limit the destruction of the rain forest. In addition, the nation hosted the 1992 Earth Summit to improve its public image as an environmentally conscious nation. Despite these efforts, the rain forest continues to be chopped down and the Brazilian debate continues.

Religion—Western Europe

The Irish Republican Army is a group of Catholics in Northern Ireland, a part of Great Britain that is predominately Protestant. When Britain granted Ireland independence, it maintained control of six northern provinces known as Northern Ireland. This seemed to be a good idea at the time, because Ireland was predominately Catholic while Northern Ireland, like England, was predominately Protestant. However, the government of Northern Ireland discriminated against the Catholic minority, and eventually the IRA was created to combat the discrimination. The IRA wants Northern Ireland to join Ireland, while the Protestant majority wants to remain a part of the United Kingdom. These protests have led to violence on both sides, including bombings. The consequence of the IRA insurrections is not yet known. We do know that the conflict has raged on for decades and that thousands have died. We also know that both sides have been willing to enter into peaceful negotiations in recent years. But since the dispute remains unsettled, and since the Catholic population of Northern Ireland is quickly increasing in proportion to the Protestant population, the future of Ireland and the success or failure of the IRA insurrections are still in question.

Political Beliefs—East Asia

Although the communist government of China has initiated significant economic reforms, the government has been challenged by an increasing number of reformists, including many university students, who want both political and social reform. In 1989, the Chinese government reacted violently against over 100,000 peaceful demonstrators in Beijing's

Tiananmen Square. University students and others had gathered in the square to push for democratic reforms. Heavily armed government troops converged on the square and dispersed the crowds with open fire. Thousands of people were killed, injured, or arrested. Although the world community condemned the action, it has continued to increase trade relations with China. Today, the government policies that deny freedom of expression are still in place, and demonstrators continue to wait for reform.

Imperialism—Africa

European imperialism in Africa during the nineteenth and twentieth centuries was not accepted willingly by most native Africans, and, as a result, conflicts between African nationalists and colonial rulers became increasingly common. There was much to be resented in the way the Europeans had imposed themselves on Africa. The European nations of Belgium, Britain, France, Germany, Spain, Portugal, and Italy carved up the entire continent of Africa into colonies, without respecting original tribal lines. Instead, they agreed on boundary lines between their colonies at a conference in Berlin in 1845 and drew the lines based on political and economic bargaining. The results led to chaos; in some situations, tribal lands were cut in half, while in other situations two rival tribes were unwillingly brought together under the same colonial rule. For a time, the disruption of the traditional tribal boundary lines worked to the Europeans' advantage, since it was difficult for the native Africans to organize an opposition within each colony. Nevertheless, by the beginning of the twentieth century, nationalism among the native Africans grew intensely. The Africans resented the way in which the Europeans had imposed their own culture, language, and religion on them. They resented the fact that they were treated as second-class citizens at best, and slaves at worst. They resented that they were not represented in the colonial governments. Yet, since most of the resistance was relatively peaceful, it became more and more difficult for European governments to ignore the calls for independence, and increasing international pressure insisted that Africans have the right to self-determination, especially in the years during and immediately following World War II. By 1945, South Africa and Egypt were granted independence. By the early 1960s, most of the rest of the African colonies had also achieved independence, and in most cases without warfare. Today, there are no remaining European colonial holdings in Africa.

Nonetheless, the effect of imperialism on the continent of Africa remains enormous. Most African nations have structured their governments on the European models, have adopted their colonial languages as an official language, and have in most cases retained the colonial boundary lines. In addition, the prevalence of Christianity in sub-Saharan Africa also stems from the colonial period. Nevertheless, nationalism in African continues to grow, as Africans rediscover their ancient pasts while also preparing for the future as independent, sovereign nations with a voice in the world community.

Ethnic Differences—Eastern Europe

Bosnia was created in 1992 after the downfall of communism in Eastern Europe and the rise of movements aimed at self-determination led to the dismemberment of the former Yugoslavia. However, the problems between Christian Serbs and Muslims are centuries old. In the former Yugoslavia, the ethnic hatred between the two groups was overshadowed by a totalitarian government that limited expression and the practice of religion in the first place. Once Yugoslavia disbanded, however, the ethnic hatred was renewed. Muslims are the majority in Serbia and believe that they have the right to determine the future of the nation, especially since Christian Serbs were much more powerful in the former Yugoslavia despite the fact that they represented a minority of the population. The Serbs, however, refuse to be ruled by the Muslims and want either their own nation or to be annexed by Serbia. Horrendous acts of violence have resulted. Thousands upon thousands of people have been killed, raped, and beaten. Entire villages were destroyed as the world community looked on, unwilling to become too involved in a war so tied to ethnic differences. Temporary cease-fires brought short-term peace to the region, but the fighting resumed in 1995. More recently, the United Nations has sent peacekeeping forces to the region, but true peace and respect has yet to materialize.

6. SCIENTIFIC IDEAS AND INVENTIONS LEADING TO CHANGE

Compass/Astrolabe

The consequences of the development of the astrolabe and compass are so far-reaching that it seems safe to say that every nation on every continent has been affected. In some cases, nations owe their very existence to these two devices. The astrolabe, which measures the altitude of celestial bodies, and the compass, which utilizes the Earth's magnetic field to give direction parallel to the Earth's surface, were essential navigational aids that made the Age of Exploration and the subsequent Age of Imperialism possible. Used by the navies of the European powers, these instruments made possible the destruction of native civilizations in the Americas, Africa, Asia, and Australia by allowing hundreds of ships to successfully make repeated voyages to the exact same destination. This led to the indisputable military and commercial supremacy of Europe for centuries, and changed the political and cultural landscape of everywhere else. Isolationism, therefore, became almost impossible after these two instruments were perfected.

Heliocentric Theory

Nicolas Copernicus was a sixteenth century Polish astronomer who believed that the sun, not the Earth, was at the center of the known universe. This view was in sharp contrast to the Ptolemaic model that had dominated the western world's understanding of the universe. Ptolemy, an ancient Greek astronomer, believed that the earth was at the center of the universe. Science and philosophy had developed for 1,500 years under this assumption, as had the Catholic Church for thirteen centuries. The Church challenged Copernicus, claiming his theory reduced the role of man as the center of God's creation. The Catholic Church insisted that since man was made in the image of God, the sun was made to serve the interests of man, and this meant that the sun must revolve around the Earth. Nevertheless, Copernicus continued to study the solar system. Those who followed him, including Galileo, proved Copernican theories, revolutionized the way we look at the universe, and damaged the credibility of the Catholic Church, which eventually accepted the Copernican model. The momentum pushed forward, ushering in an entire era of skepticism regarding not only science and philosophy, but also politics and social science. The political underpinnings of the Enlightenment and the scientific underpinnings of the Industrial Revolution all were built upon the change in attitudes due to Copernicus and his theories. The contribution of Copernicus is so significant to our understanding of our universe that it is now known as the Copernican Revolution.

Printing Press

In the 1588, Guttenberg invented movable type and the printing press was born. The consequences were profound in Europe. Because of the printing press, the ideas of Luther's Reformation spread rapidly, leading to the reorganization of Europe along religious lines. The Bible was printed in popular languages, allowing people to read and interpret it for themselves, rather than relying on the Church hierarchy, thus contributing to individualism. This individualism led to the Enlightenment, which questioned the role of government authority and consequently changed man's relationship with man. All the while, literacy increased dramatically, books became much less expensive, and education became an important goal for millions. In short, the printing press revolutionized Europe and the rest of the world because it brought information to the masses. If knowledge is power, the printing press resulted in a redistribution of power.

Steam Engine

The steam engine made the Industrial Revolution in Europe possible by becoming the principal power source for industry and transport. Steam-powered railroads brought tons of raw materials to steam-powered factories and then took finished products back to the communities that were developing along the rail lines. In the European colonies, the colonists built thousands of miles of railroad lines straight into the heart of areas rich in natural resources, robbing the natives of them. Through the use of steam-powered ships, the Europeans more efficiently carried out their mercantilist policies in the colonies, enabling the powers to control greater and greater expanses of land with ease. Within Europe, the factory system changed daily life, characterized by health hazards, long work hours, child labor, and mindless repetition. As a result, new political philosophies such as communism became attractive to large numbers of exploited factory workers, while unrestrained capitalism became attractive to many factory owners. Thus, while the steam engine was the catalyst of the Industrial Revolution, it was the engine of social, philosophical, political, and cultural change as well.

Nuclear Energy

Nuclear energy relies on the power contained within every atom. Heavy atoms are split into smaller atoms in a process known as nuclear fission. Light atoms are joined together into one heavier atom in a process known as nuclear fusion. Fission is the process that is used in nuclear bombs and nuclear power plants. Nuclear power plants offer a potentially unlimited amount of energy and are vitally important in areas that lack other consistent sources of energy. In the former Soviet Union, for example, nuclear energy became common in the middle and late twentieth century. Despite the advantages of the energy source, however, there are disadvantages so overwhelming that many people want the process banned entirely. In 1986, an explosion at a nuclear reactor in Chernobyl in the former Soviet Union sent tons of radioactive debris into the atmosphere. The land around the nuclear reactor was severely affected. Thousands of people were evacuated and their crops and livestock were ruined by contact with radioactive particles. Much of the land in the immediate area still cannot be farmed today, and access to the region has been restricted because the overall effects of the explosion are still being monitored. Since the Soviet Union tended to downplay incidents within its own nation, they attempted to solve the problem on their own. The reactor was immediately shut down and an investigation was conducted. It was determined that the reactor's design was flawed. Therefore, the government has inspected its other reactors and planned to shut down those with similar flaws. The land around Chernobyl remains contaminated and cleanup has been slow. Still, despite these horrible consequences, many look to nuclear energy as a way of bringing much needed energy to the developing world.

Green Revolution

Since the end of World War II, the population of India has exploded to nearly one billion people. During this same time period, the Green Revolution has swept through much of the developing world, offering innovative ways to increase agricultural yield per acre. In India, the results have been dramatic, but ultimately insufficient to keep up with the rate of population growth. Irrigation systems have been installed to bring water to farms during the dry season. Increased use of farm machinery and fertilizers has also helped to maximize yield. Yet, the rural farming communities of India remain very traditional in both their beliefs and practices. Many people have resisted the changes imposed on them by the government. Using the tools and methods of their parents, they want to continue to follow the traditional patterns of wet and dry seasons created by the monsoons. Therefore, although the government and urban population of India have pushed for agricultural reform and have succeeded to some degree, the reforms will not lead to a widespread agricultural revolution unless the people who actually have to carry out the reforms on the farms can find a way to reconcile their traditional beliefs with agricultural change.

Computers

In their most simple form, computers are devices used to calculate, or compute. When transistors, which are devices used to control electric currents, were applied to computers, scientists could make computers that were both smaller and faster. In the 1960's, the invention of the integrated circuit, also known as the *chip*, further revolutionized computer technology. Computers could now compute thousands of times faster than their predecessors, store an unprecedented amount of information, and occupy only a limited amount of space. The computer revolution changed the world. Computers impacted the global community by making worldwide transportation feasible (computers are used to route airplanes, for example) and worldwide communication commonplace through the use of computer-controlled satellites and networks.

Computers have revolutionized life in Japan. A populous but geographically small, island nation, Japan is dependent on computer technology in its industrial sector. Computer technology and efficiency allows Japan to manufacture high technology products and process billions of calculations in a very small amount of space (especially when compared to the amount of space needed in the industrial and information sectors prior to the computer revolution). In a very practical way, then, computer technology has helped shrink the amount of space needed for industrialization, while expanding industrial output. Since in Japan extra space is literally a luxury, the computer revolution has not only provided well-paying jobs, but has contributed to the quality of life.

7. SOCIAL CUSTOMS

Dowry/Bride Price

In sub-Saharan Africa, traditional marriages are arranged by the parents of both the bride and the groom. Since the wife is expected to leave her family in order to live with her husband and his extended family, the bride's family loses an important member when a marriage occurs. Every person in the traditional African family has an important role to play, and often the new bride was a valued worker in her own family's house. Under the bridewealth system, young men are expected to make a payment to a young woman's father (usually in the form of cattle or sheep) as compensation for the bride's family's loss of a worker.

Although the dowry system helps compensate the bride's family, there are many unfortunate consequences. Families who need cattle or sheep more than an extra worker sometimes rush their daughters into marriage. As for the groom's family, if they are poor, they sometimes have a difficult time marrying off their sons, since they may not have much to give away as a bride price, and they may have difficulty feeding yet another adult. The danger of the bride price, then, is that rather than being a way to show that a woman is worthy, it sometimes can lead to viewing a woman as merely a possession.

Polygamy

In traditional Islamic cultures, polygamy is not only allowed, but sometimes even encouraged. According to the Koran, the sacred book of Islam, a man may marry up to four wives, but only if he can treat them all equally. Otherwise, a man is advised to marry only once. Most men in traditional Islamic cultures have only one wife. However, in the upper classes polygamy is more common, and in the past it was very common.

Although there are obvious drawbacks to polygamy, especially when compared to the value system of most western nations, there are several important advantages. The system allows women who might have otherwise gone unmarried to be provided for. Perhaps even more importantly, it allows an already married man to take in single or widowed women with children and provide a family environment for them.

Filial Piety

In traditional Confucian society, filial piety (behavior that is befitting a child who respects elders and legitimate authority) was a cornerstone of the social structure. Filial piety was seen as the practical way in which an orderly and harmonious society was maintained. Children were told that obedience should be their primary goal, and that if they were obedient, they would grow up to be well-respected parents. Confucian society was replete with stories about obedient children, which of course were told over and over again in the family setting. One story, for example, was about a dutiful boy who slept naked and without covers to encourage the mosquitoes to feed on him rather than on his parents, who were sleeping nearby. Such stories reminded children that it was not merely their duty to listen to their parents and legitimate authority, but also their duty to put their parents well-being and the well-being of the family above their own.

Filial piety was encouraged in order to maintain an orderly society, but the tradition had disadvantages as well. For one thing, some parents and authorities ruthlessly or carelessly put children in danger, but the children could not object because to do so would be to show disrespect. Therefore, filial piety sometimes led to unfortunate outcomes, especially when parents and authorities were not as true to their obligations under Confucian philosophy as the children were to theirs.

Primogeniture

Traditional Japanese families were known as continuing. In other words, the family name, known as the *ie*, determined the family's status and even their taxation. The *ie* would continue from one generation to the next, binding the family together under a common reputation. The oldest son in the family would inherit the house and family *ie*, while the other children were expected to leave. Traditional Japanese culture, however, was structured in such a way that it could absorb the children who were not fortunate enough to be the oldest male. Daughters would often marry and become incorporated into their husband's families, while younger sons would either be "adopted" by other families who didn't have sons or else leave to find work in the cities.

One advantage of primogeniture is that it gave children very clearly defined roles from an early age. There was little use fighting over the family name or inheritance. Unfair as it might have been, the system allowed children who were not the first born to prepare themselves earlier in their lives than perhaps children from other cultures. What's more, the fact that younger brothers and sisters were expected to leave fit nicely with the process of industrialization. Millions of young Japanese left their families to find work in the cities. Therefore, in one sense primogeniture actually encouraged the younger siblings to make a better life for themselves. They were so successful that in many ways their lives brought them more material gain than had they inherited the family *ie*.

On a side note, the government of Japan officially abolished the *ie* in 1947 and since then, children have been encouraged to choose their occupations and spouses freely. Many of the oldest sons no longer stay home to run the family, and instead often move to the cities where lucrative jobs await them. Nevertheless, many family traditions remain intact in modern Japan. Children are expected to revere their ancestors and parents, and loyalty within the family unit remains strong.

Extended Family

Traditional Chinese society valued large families, both because children were able to help with the chores in the house and on the farm and because Confucian philosophy gave identity to people based on their relationship— the parent/child relationship being one of the most important. The home was the most basic social enterprise, and those who lived under one roof included not just the immediate family of parents and siblings, but the extended family as well. The elderly were greatly respected and listened to. Children were expected to do as they were told with great reverence and courtesy, while their parents were expected to be just and caring providers and grandparents were expected to teach the children strong personal codes of behavior. Even ancestors were considered part of the extended family, and were remembered during family rituals. Marriages were arranged by the families, with the bride moving into the home of the husband's family.

One of the great advantages of the extended family system is that it provides social stability and gives a useful identity to each member. In China, this system is beginning to fall apart, as the communist government not only competes with the family for authority, but also has instituted strict population control measures. Nevertheless, the family remains the chief source of identity and stability in the fast-changing world of modern China.

Footbinding

Footbinding began in around the tenth century during China's T'ang Dynasty. Girls as young as five years old were selected for the excruciating process. The top toe was bent backward while the other toes were tucked underneath the foot, thereby breaking the arch and inhibiting the growth of the feet. Then, the entire foot was wrapped tightly in linens, holding the disfigurement in place. Originally, feet were bound because men found them erotic, but soon the bound feet became a status symbol for the young girls themselves. Despite the excruciating pain, young girls understood that without bound feet, they could not be expected to receive a good offer of marriage. By the time the process reached its height in the fourteenth and fifteenth centuries, only the poor refrained from the ritual, mostly because they couldn't afford to lose a worker.

The cultural ritual, of course, had many disadvantages. Those who could not afford to have the process done correctly nearly killed their daughters trying. And even for those whose feet were bound "the right way," the results were nearly useless feet that inhibited everyday activities. So horrendous were the health consequences that the Manchu rulers finally banned the process in 1912. Fortunately, the ritual has virtually vanished from the Chinese culture.

EXAMINATION
JUNE 1998

Part I (55 credits): Answer all 48 questions in this part.

Directions (1–48): For each statement or question, write on the separate answer sheet the *number* of the word or expression that, of those given, best completes the statement or answers the question.

---

1 One result of the Neolithic Revolution was
    1 an increase in the number of nomadic tribes
    2 a reliance on hunting and gathering for food
    3 the establishment of villages and the rise of governments
    4 a decrease in trade between cultural groups

2 One reason the cultures of North Africa developed differently from the cultures of the rest of Africa was that these areas of Africa were separated by the
    1 Congo River Basin   3 Sahara Desert
    2 Great Rift Valley   4 Arabian Sea

Base your answers to questions 3 and 4 on the poem below and on your knowledge of social studies.

> . . ., you, African, suffered like a beast
> Your ashes strewn to the wind that roams the desert,
> Your tyrants built the lustrous, magic temples
> To preserve your soul, preserve your suffering.
> Barbaric right of fist and the white right to whip,
> You had the right to die, you could also weep.
>
> —Patrice Lumumba, "Dawn of the Heart of Africa"

3 This African poem is discussing the evils of

   1 imperialism   3 nationalism

   2 communism   4 regionalism

4 The tyrants referred to in the poem were

   1 communist revolutionaries who took over the newly independent African governments

   2 the European governments that had divided the continent of Africa into colonies

   3 tribal chieftains who fought each other to control African lands

   4 merchants who sought to expand the drug trade in colonial Africa

[OVER]

5 Mansa Musa's journey to Mecca in the 1300's is evidence that

1 the Crusades had a great influence on western Africa
2 most African leaders were educated in the Middle East
3 European culture was superior to the cultures of western Africa
4 Islam had a major influence on the Mali Empire

6 • Rebellion in the Congo during the 1960's
  • Civil war in Nigeria from 1967–1970
  • Fighting in the Sudan in the 1980's
  • Massacres in Rwanda in the 1990's

Which factor was the main reason for these conflicts?

1 poor food distribution systems
2 communist interference
3 demands for land reform
4 ethnic rivalries

7 In which way has the end of apartheid had a positive economic effect on South Africa?

1 Black South African managers have increased industrial productivity throughout the nation.
2 The introduction of communism has led to a more equal distribution of income.
3 Many foreign companies have resumed trading and investing in South Africa.
4 All profits of South Africa's industries are now reinvested out of the country.

8 In China, the development of ethnocentrism was most influenced by

1 its historic reliance on foreign nations
2 a long history of democratic government
3 a strong belief in Christianity
4 its geographic isolation

[OVER]

Base your answer to question 9 on the cartoon below and on your knowledge of social studies.

9 What is the main idea of the cartoon?

1 Labor camps remain China's primary method of punishing political prisoners.

2 The Chinese consider the United States an imperialistic power.

3 Economic development in modern China has sometimes been achieved by ignoring human rights issues.

4 The Chinese believe that human rights abuses are also an issue in the United States.

10 The Confucian view of government and the Chinese Communist view of government were similar in that both stressed

1 loyalty to the government
2 the need for filial piety
3 a civil service system
4 equality of men and women

11 The results of the Opium War (1839–1842) indicate that China was

1 still a major military power
2 not strong enough to resist Western demands
3 rapidly building a modern industrial economy
4 accepting Western nations as equal trading partners

12 The Tiananmen Square massacre in China was a reaction to

1 Deng Xiaoping's plan to revive the Cultural Revolution
2 students' demands for greater individual rights and freedom of expression
3 China's decision to seek Western investors
4 Great Britain's decision to return Hong Kong to China

13 Taoism and Shintoism are similar in that both religions stress

1 adhering to the five Confucian relationships
2 following the Eightfold Path
3 developing harmony between humans and nature
4 believing in one God

[OVER]

14 In Japan between 1603 and 1868, the most notable action taken by the Tokugawa Shogunate was the

1 military conquest of China
2 development of extensive trade with the Americas
3 formation of cultural links with Europe
4 virtual isolation of the country from the outside world

15 Between the Meiji Restoration and World War II, Japan tried to solve the problem of its scarcity of natural resources by

1 exporting agricultural products in exchange for new technology
2 establishing a policy of imperialism
3 building nuclear power plants
4 cooperating with the Soviet Union to gain needed resources

16 In the past decade, Japanese automobile manufacturers have sought to improve Japanese-American trade relations by

1 drastically lowering the price of Japanese automobiles for American customers
2 allowing an unlimited number of American automobiles to be sold in Japan
3 importing most spare parts from Mexico
4 building an increasing number of Japanese automobiles in the United States

17 Which of these nations is located closest to the Philippines, Malaysia, and Indonesia?

1 Korea 3 Somalia
2 Vietnam 4 Pakistan

18 In India, which aspect of society has been most heavily influenced by religious beliefs, tradition, and the division of labor?

1 caste system
2 policy of neutrality
3 urbanization
4 parliamentary government

19 The "homespun movement" and the Salt March promoted by Mohandas Gandhi in India are examples of his policy of

1 industrialization 3 nonalignment
2 isolationism 4 nonviolent protest

20 Which statement best explains why India was partitioned in1947?

1 The British feared a united India.
2 One region wanted to remain under British control.
3 Religious differences led to political division.
4 Communist supporters wanted a separate state.

[OVER]

21 From the perspective of the North Vietnamese, the war in Vietnam in the 1960's was a battle between

1 fascism and liberalism
2 nationalism and imperialism
3 republicanism and totalitarianism
4 theocracy and monarchy

22 One similarity between the Five Pillars of Islam and the Ten Commandments is that both

1 support a belief in reincarnation
2 promote learning as a means to salvation
3 encourage the use of statues to symbolize God
4 provide a guide to proper ethical and moral behavior

Base your answer to questions 23 on the cartoon below and on you knowledge of social studies.

23 This 1994 cartoon suggests that peace in the Middle East will

1 never be achieved
2 put a stranglehold on region's politics
3 occur only with the assistance of the United States
4 be accomplished only through negotiation and compromise

[OVER]

Base your answer to question 24 on the map below and on your knowledge of social studies.

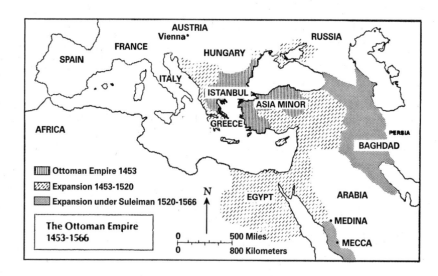

24 An observation about the Ottoman Empire in the 15th and 16th centuries is that the Empire

1 originated in Hungary
2 had a strategic location between Europe and Asia
3 was totally landlocked
4 had control over most of western Europe

25 One major result of the Crusades was the

1 permanent occupation of the Holy Land by the Europeans
2 long-term decrease in European trade
3 conversion of most Muslims to Christianity
4 spread of Middle Eastern cultures and technology to Europe

26 One way in which the civilizations of the Sumerians, the Phoenicians, and the Mayas were similar is that each

1 developed extensive writing systems
2 emphasized equality in education
3 established monotheistic religions
4 encouraged democratic participation in government

27 One reason the Spanish conquistadors were able to conquer the Aztec and Inca Empires rapidly is that

1 these empires had no standing armies
2 the Spanish had better weapons than the Aztecs and Incas did
3 the Spanish greatly outnumbered the Aztecs and Incas
4 the Aztecs and Incas joined together to fight the Spanish

[OVER]

28 Which type of government has resulted from the changing political trends in much of Latin America during the 1990's?

1 monarchy 3 democracy
2 military junta 4 fascism

Base your answer to question 29 on the cartoon below and on your knowledge of social studies.

29 What is the main idea of this cartoon?

1 Ancient ruins and artifacts are often destroyed by modern technology.
2 Trade agreements are sometimes used to reestablish direct colonial rule.
3 Trade agreements sometimes have negative consequences.
4 The civil rights of native peoples are usually recognized by industrialized nations.

[OVER]

30 A major contribution of the Roman Empire to Western society was the development of

1 gunpowder
2 the principles of revolutionary socialism
3 monotheism
4 an effective legal system

31 • Man is born free and everywhere he is in chains.
   • Everyone has the natural right to life, liberty, and property.
   • Slavery, torture, and religious persecution are wrong.

During which period in European history would the ideas in these statements have been expressed?

1 Pax Romana   3 Enlightenment
2 Age of Exploration 4 Age of Imperialism

32 The growth of feudalism in Europe during the Middle Ages was primarily caused by the

1 rivalry between the colonial empires
2 suppression of internationalism
3 decline of the Roman Catholic Church
4 collapse of a strong central government

33 Which idea about leadership would Niccolò Machiavelli most likely support?

   1 Leaders should do whatever is necessary to achieve their goals.

   2 Leaders should fight against discrimination and intolerance.

   3 Leaders should listen to the desires of the people.

   4 Elected leaders should be fair and good.

34 European society during the Renaissance differed from European society during the Middle Ages in that during the Renaissance

   1 the Church was no longer influential

   2 the emphasis on individual worth increased

   3 economic activity declined

   4 art no longer contained religious themes

35 A major result of the Industrial Revolution was the

   1 concentration of workers in urban areas

   2 increased desire of the wealthy class to share its power

   3 formation of powerful craft guilds

   4 control of agricultural production by governments

[OVER]

36 According to the theories of Karl Marx, history can be viewed as a

1 succession of famines that result in the destruction of civilizations
2 repeating cycle of imperialism and colonialism
3 listing of the accomplishments of the ruling classes
4 continuous struggle between economic classes

37 • Congress of Vienna redraws map of Europe.
• Triple Entente is formed to combat the Triple Alliance.
• Treaty of Versailles calls for the creation of the League of Nations.

These events are similar in that each reflects

1 the aggressiveness of dictators
2 an effort to establish a balance of power
3 the rivalry between France, Germany, and Greece
4 the concept of mercantilism

38 After the breakup of the Austro-Hungarian Empire and the Soviet Union, new nations were formed. Which generalization accurately reflects the effect of the breakup on these new nations?

1 New nations are generally too poor and weak to become active members of the United Nations.

2 New nations rarely use their limited resources to wage war.

3 National and ethnic differences often lead to instability and violence in new nations.

4 Self-determination generally leads to democratic forms of government in new nations.

39 Which series of events is arranged in the correct chronological order?

1
The Treaty of Versailles is signed.
Adolf Hitler becomes Chancellor of Germany.
German troops invade Poland.

2
German troops invade Poland.
The Treaty of Versailles is signed.
Adolf Hitler becomes Chancellor of Germany.

3
Adolf Hitler becomes Chancellor of Germany.
The Treaty of Versailles is signed.
German troops invade Poland.

4
The Treaty of Versailles is signed.
German troops invade Poland.
Adolf Hitler becomes Chancellor of Germany.

[OVER]

Base your answer to question 40 on the cartoon below and on your knowledge of social studies.

Palma/Expresso/Lisbon

40 Which conclusion can be drawn from this cartoon?

   1 Many nations are interested in buying nuclear technology from the former Soviet Union.
   2 Developing countries are looking to the former Soviet Union for investment capital.
   3 Soviet nuclear scientists are looking for jobs in the Middle East.
   4 The nations of the Middle East are spending millions of dollars on nuclear disarmament.

Base your answers to questions 41 and 42 on the map below and on your knowledge of social studies.

Eastern Europe in 1960

41 Which symbol is used on this map to identify nations that were considered satellites of the Soviet Union?

(1)    (3)

(2)   (4)

[OVER]

42 The reason that Ukraine, Lithuania, and Belarus are not included on this map is that they were

1 located outside the geographic area shown
2 republics of the Soviet Union and not considered independent nations
3 provinces in Poland and Rumania
4 members of the North Atlantic Treaty Organization (NATO)

---

43 When Russia was under Mongol domination, the effect on Russia was to

1 end feudalism
2 convert the Russian people to Hinduism
3 keep Russia isolated from western Europe
4 reunite the Eastern Orthodox Church with the Roman Catholic Church

44 Which headline concerning the Soviet Union refers to a Cold War event?

1 "Yeltsin Assumes Power"
2 "Trotsky Forms Red Army"
3 "Germany Invades USSR"
4 "Warsaw Pact Formed"

45 In the 1980's, the governments of both Brazil and Malaysia supported the cutting of timber in their rain forests as a means of

1 achieving economic prosperity
2 increasing the national debt
3 controlling rebellions of indigenous peoples
4 preventing exploitation by imperialist nations

46 **"Germany Will Make Reparations For WWI"**

"OPEC Supports Oil Embargo Against Western Nations"

"UN Imposes Sanctions on Iraq"

Which conclusion can be drawn from these headlines?

1 Economic measures are often designed to achieve political goals.
2 Communism as an economic system has failed.
3 Economic policies are often formulated to encourage investment.
4 Nationalism plays a small role in economic decisionmaking.

47 The code of bushido of the Japanese samurai is most similar to the

1 belief in reincarnation and karma of Hindus
2 practice of chivalry by European knights
3 teachings of Judaism
4 theory of natural rights of the Enlightenment writers

48 One similarity between the leadership of the Meiji emperors of Japan, Peter the Great of Russia, and Shah Reza Pahlavi of Iran was that they all supported policies that

1 increased the power of the aristocracy
2 introduced new religious beliefs
3 kept their nations from industrial expansion
4 westernized their nations

[OVER]

Answers to the following questions are to be written on paper provided by the school.

Students Please Note:

In developing your answers to Part II, be sure to

(1) include specific factual information and evidence whenever possible

(2) keep to the questions asked; do not go off on tangents

(3) avoid overgeneralizations or sweeping statements without sufficient proof; do not overstate your case

(4) keep these general definitions in mind:

    (a) <u>discuss</u> means "to make observations about something using facts, reasoning, and argument; to present in some detail"

    (b) <u>describe</u> means "to illustrate something in words or tell about it"

    (c) <u>show</u> means "to point out; to set forth clearly a position or idea by stating it and giving data which support it"

    (d) <u>explain</u> means "to make plain or understandable; to give reasons for or causes of; to show the logical development or relationships of"

PART II

ANSWER THREE QUESTIONS FROM THIS PART. [45]

1 Geographic features have influenced the historical, economic, political, and social development of many nations and regions of the world. Several of these nations and regions and a geographic feature in that area are listed below.

Nations/Regions — Geographic Features
Egypt — Nile River
Japan — Island location
Poland — Northern European Plain
Roman Empire — Mediterranean Sea
Russia — Frozen rivers
South Africa — Gold and diamond mines

Select *three* nations or regions and the geographic feature with which each is paired. For *each* one selected, discuss several specific ways that this feature has influenced the historical, economic, political, or social development of the nation or region. [5,5,5]

[OVER]

2 Throughout history, the ideas of leaders have affected historical events within their own nation or region. The ideas of some leaders are reflected in the quotations below.

> I cannot and will not recant anything, for to go against conscience is neither right nor safe . . . . Here I stand. I cannot do otherwise.
> **Martin Luther**

> The position of the inhabitants of the American hemisphere has been for centuries purely passive. Politically they were nonexistent. We have been molested by a system which has not only deprived us of our rights but has kept us in a state of permanent childhood with regard to public affairs.
> **Simón Bolívar**

> Dear comrades, soldiers, sailors and workers, I am happy to greet in you the victorious Russian revolution, to greet you as the advance guard of the international proletarian army. . . .
> **V.I. Lenin**

> Extremes must be fought by extremes. Against the infection of [Marxism], against the Jewish pestilence, we must hold aloft a flaming ideal. And if others speak of the World and Humanity, we must say the Fatherland—and only the Fatherland!
> **Adolf Hitler**

> [British rule] has impoverished the dumb millions by a system of progressive exploitation . . . . It has reduced us politically to serfdom. It has sapped the foundations of our culture . . .and degraded us spiritually.
> **Mohandas Gandhi**

> A revolution is not a dinner party, or writing an essay, or painting a picture or doing embroidery; it cannot be so refined, so leisurely and gentle, so . . . kind, courteous, restrained, and generous. A revolution is an insurrection, an act of violence by which one class overthrows another.
> **Mao Zedong**

> . . . did the former regime not use the radio and television to render religious beliefs valueless and ignore national traditions and customs? In any case, . . . courage, patience, virtue, . . . avoiding dependence on the powers, and . . . sensing responsibility toward the masses, have revived the [leaders] and rendered them steadfast and popular.
> **Ayatollah Khomeini**

Select *three* of the quotations above and for each one selected:

- Explain the main idea of the quotation
- Describe the historical circumstances related to the quotation
- Explain the role or the action of the leader in the historical event [5,5,5]

3 Turning points are events or key developments that change a nation's history.

Nations

Cuba
Egypt
France
Ireland
Kenya
Korea
Turkey

Select *three* nations from the list and for *each* one selected:

- Identify and describe a turning point in that nation's history
- Explain why that event or development was a turning point in that nation's history [5,5,5]

4 Religion often has significant effects on different aspects of culture.

Aspects of Culture

Architecture
Dietary laws
Dress
Justice

[OVER]

Painting and sculpture
Social relationships

Select *three* of these aspects of culture and for *each* one selected:

- Identify a specific religion that has influenced that aspect of culture [You must use a different religion for each aspect of culture selected.]
- Discuss how the religion's teachings or beliefs have influenced that aspect of culture [5,5,5]

5 Throughout history, technological developments have had a major impact on the global community and on specific nations. Several technological developments are listed below.

Technological Developments

Atomic energy
Chemical fertilizer
Computer
Genetic engineering
Gunpowder
Printing press
Steam engine

Select *three* of the technological developments and for *each* one selected:

- Discuss one specific positive *or* one specific negative impact of the technological development on the global community or on a specific nation [Do *not* use the United States in your answer.]
- Discuss why the technological development had a positive *or* a negative impact   [5,5,5]

6 Swedish inventor Alfred Nobel established a peace prize to be awarded annually ". . . to the person [or group] who shall have done the most or the best work for fraternity [brotherhood] between nations . . . and promotion of peace . . . ." In some years, the award has been shared by several individuals or groups who have worked toward a common goal.

Nobel Peace Prize Winners

Amnesty International (1977)
Mother Teresa (1979)
Lech Walesa (1983)
Elie Wiesel (1986)
Mikhail Gorbachev (1990)
Rigoberta Menchú (1992)
Nelson Mandela and F.W. de Klerk (1993)
Yasir Arafat, Yitzhak Rabin, and Shimon Peres (1994)

Select *three* winners (or group of winners) from the list and for *each* one selected:

- Identify and describe the issue for which the Nobel Peace Prize was given that year

- Discuss the specific contributions or actions of the winners in dealing with this issue   [5,5,5]

7 Every society must answer basic economic questions in order to survive.

Nations

France (1200–1500)
Belgian Congo (1890–1960)
Soviet Union (1917–1985)

[OVER]

Israel (1949–present)
Japan (1950–present)
Brazil (1950–present)

Select *three* nations from the list and for *each* one selected:

- Explain how these basic economic questions have been answered during the time period given:
  –What shall be produced?
  –How shall goods be produced?
  –Who will use the goods produced?
- Discuss the nation's economic system in that time period [In your discussion, identify who controls the resources and who makes the major economic decisions.] [5,5,5]

ANSWER KEY
JUNE 1998—PART I

1	3		25	4
2	3		26	1
3	1		27	2
4	2		28	3
5	4		29	3
6	4		30	4
7	3		31	3
8	4		32	4
9	3		33	1
10	1		34	2
11	2		35	1
12	2		36	4
13	3		37	2
14	4		38	3
15	2		39	1
16	4		40	1
17	2		41	3
18	1		42	2
19	4		43	3
20	3		44	1
21	2		45	1
22	4		46	1
23	4		47	2
24	2		48	4

[OVER]

ANSWERS AND EXPLANATIONS
JUNE 1998—PART I

1. The Neolithic Revolution doesn't show up on every test, but it has made a guest appearance a couple of times in the past few years. If you're guessing, remember to focus on the goals of the test. In other words, there must be something significant about the Neolithic Revolution, or else the Regents wouldn't ask you about it. That said, pick an answer choice that describes something significant!

   1 The Neolithic Revolution resulted in the cultivation of crops. There was actually a decrease in the number of nomadic tribes because people no longer needed to wander around in constant search of food.

   2 Prior to the Neolithic Revolution, tribes relied on hunting and gathering. The whole point of calling the Neolithic Revolution a "revolution" is that it changed things significantly. Namely, hunting and gathering was out and farming was in. With farming, food surpluses were made possible. This is essential to the establishment of towns and cities since in a society with a food surplus, not everybody has to be a farmer.

   3 Bingo. The Neolithic Revolution marked the beginning of the development of villages and the establishment of organized governments. You should have guessed this, since the answer choice describes something that would have a "revolutionary" effect on the development of global civilizations, which is the whole point of the question!

   4 The Neolithic Revolution actually increased trade; because of agricultural surpluses and the creation of villages, people had a lot more stuff to trade. Plus, with villages and towns firmly established in permanent locations, regular trade routes could be established between them.

2. Your review for this test should include a world map. While looking at it, think about this: What separates North Africa from the rest of Africa?

   1 The Congo River Basin is in Central Africa. It does not separate North Africa from the rest of Africa.

   2 The Great Rift Valley runs down the spine of central Africa, separating the great forests of the Congo Basin and Zambezi River

Valley from the east African nations of Mozambique, Tanzania, Kenya and Uganda. It's nowhere near North Africa.

3 **This is the best answer. The Sahara Desert dominates the landscape of North Africa, separating it geographically, and therefore culturally, from the rest of Africa. The difference is so dramatic that the rest of Africa is simply referred to as *sub-Saharan Africa*, meaning the part of Africa below the great desert. Although several West African kingdoms established regular Saharan trade routes through which they amassed tremendous wealth, for the most part, the desert served to culturally separate North Africa from the rest of Africa. As a result, North African kingdoms developed cultural links with the Middle East while the rest of Africa developed more independently.**

4 So you say you don't even see the Arabian Sea on your map of Africa? Don't blame the mapmakers—they did their job. The Arabian Sea is way off to the east of Africa between Saudi Arabia and India.

3. Okay, so the passage from the poem isn't so straightforward. But hey, that's kind of the point of poetry! Fortunately, however, you don't have to be a literary genius to answer this question. What's more, you really don't even have to read the passage in the first place if you've become test-wise. All you have to do is read the question carefully. The question definitely refers to Africa and it specifically refers to something evil that happened in Africa. Only one answer choice describes something that Africans would describe as evil, and it should be readily apparent if you've been reviewing your materials and the Hit Parade.

1 **The poem discusses the suffering of the Africans at the hand of the European imperialists. You don't understand the poem? Big deal. With all due respect to Patrice Lumumba, the poem isn't nearly as important as your understanding of general concepts. If you realize that European imperialism was evil from the African perspective, you not only realize something very important, but you also earn yourself a point.**

2 Africa is not, nor has it ever been, dominated by communists. Communism made short-lived gains in some African nations, but not at such a grand scale that the Regents would include a poem about it.

3   Nationalism has been a source of African pride and therefore is not typically considered evil. The aim of poems such as this one was to increase nationalism so that the people would rise against imperialism. The poem considers nationalism a method of eliminating the evil, not the evil itself.

4   Regionalism has been a detriment to African unity, but it is not something that would likely be called evil. And of course, this poem doesn't even refer to regionalism in the first place.

4.   There are two ways to approach this question. The first is to read the poem carefully. Who were the tyrants? Who had the "right to whip"? The whites, or, in other words, the Europeans. The second way to approach this question is to ask yourself what themes the Regents repeatedly test. If you've been reviewing the practice tests you already know. One answer choice stands out as a Regents favorite.

1   First, this poem refers to Africa before independence, not after. Second, while a few African governments were controlled by communists for short periods of time, the communist influence in Africa was not so substantial that the Regents would ask you about it.

2   The tyrants are the whites who are doing the whipping—the Europeans. You should remember from your studies that the Europeans began dividing coastal Africa into colonies in the seventeenth and eighteenth centuries and then worked their way into the interior of Africa all the way through World War II. The European colonists didn't have the greatest amount of respect for those they were colonizing (Kipling refers to them as "half-devil and half-child" in his poem "White Man's Burden"). Not only were the natives treated harshly within the new colonies, but they were also shipped off by the hundreds of thousands for use as slaves. That's pretty evil, wouldn't you say?

3   Tribal chieftains have most certainly fought each other in Africa, but this poem has nothing to do with those wars. What's more, with the exception of very recent history, African tribal fighting is not something that the Regents have traditionally felt globally significant enough to include on the test. That's why *colonialism* is in the Hit Parade and *tribal chieftain infighting* is not.

4   In this case, it's not the merchants who are the tyrants, but the European governments (which, to be sure, were in part representing the interests of the merchants). Nevertheless, if a question asks you about tyrants, focus on government authorities.

5. If you don't remember Mansa Musa, you can still answer this question correctly as long as you realize that Mansa Musa was an African. You should be able to glean that Mansa Musa was an African in two ways. First, the answer choices refer to Africa. Second, question 4 refers to Africa, and question 6 also refers to Africa. Since the Regents group questions about the same country together, it follows the Regents pattern that question 5 is about Africa as well. That said, you also need to remember at least a little bit about Mecca, specifically that it is the holiest city in Islam.

1 First of all, the Crusades were undertaken by European Christians in the Middle East, not in western Africa. You've forgotten this? Look up Crusades in the Hit Parade. In the meantime, you should eliminate this answer choice anyway because it doesn't have anything to do with Mecca.

2 Some African leaders were educated in the Middle East. "Most," however, is taking it too far. What's more, even if you don't know about the educational backgrounds of African leaders, you still can't pick this answer choice because the question only refers to one person. It doesn't make sense that one man's journey would be sufficient evidence that most African leaders were educated in the Middle East.

3 There is *no way* that the Regents are going to suggest that European cultures are superior to African cultures. That said, you have another reason to get rid of this answer choice: Mecca is in Saudi Arabia, so why would someone's trip to Mecca have something to do with a comparison between Europe and western Africa? It wouldn't.

4 **Mecca should make you think about *Islam*. Mansa Musa, who had amassed great wealth and traded frequently with the kingdoms of the Middle East, was an Islamic leader of the Mali Empire. Even if you don't recall Mansa Musa from your studies, you should pick this answer choice because it's the only one that logically connects Africa to Mecca. By the way, the Regents like to ask questions about the west African kingdoms of Mali, Songhai, and Kush.**

6. Even if you only know the details behind a couple of these headlines you should be able to answer this question correctly. If you're guessing, pick an answer choice that explains a whole lot of conflicts, no matter where they occur in the world.

   1 Poor food distribution systems most certainly exacerbated these conflicts because people who needed food where not able to get it, but the distribution systems were not the *cause* of the conflicts in the first place.

   2 Of the four conflicts mentioned in the question, the communists played a role only in the Congo.

   3 Demands for land reform were behind many conflicts in Latin America, but not so much in Africa.

   4 Ethnic rivalries are behind all of these conflicts. The Regents sometimes likes to ask questions about Rwanda so you should be aware that the conflict there is between the Tutsi and the Hutu. This is a good choice because it applies to so many of the world's conflicts.

7. Eliminate answer choices that aren't true of South Africa in the first place. Also, eliminate answer choices that, if true, would not have a positive economic effect.

   1 Blacks have yet to become managers on a broad scale within South Africa. Positive steps have been taken to open management opportunities to all citizens, but it will likely be years before blacks will truly be integrated into South African industrial management.

   2 South Africa is not, nor has it ever been, communist.

   3 This is the best answer. During apartheid, many nations adopted economic sanctions against South Africa, while some companies pulled out of South Africa on their own. When apartheid ended, the sanctions were lifted and companies no longer had a moral or public relations reason to avoid doing business with South Africa. Currently, there is a flood of foreign investment pouring into the resource-rich country.

   4 This answer choice is too extreme (note the use of the word *all*.) Second, even if it were true (it's not), it wouldn't have a positive economic impact on South Africa, but a negative one.

8. Eliminate answer choices that aren't true of China. That should leave you with one. If you're not sure what's true of China, get rid of answer choices that wouldn't logically result in ethnocentrism even if they were true. (Find *ethnocentrism* in the Hit Parade if you missed this question.)

   1 China has not historically relied on foreign nations. Foreign nations forced themselves on China during the European Age of Imperialism, but China did not "rely" on them even then. What's more, reliance wouldn't result in ethnocentrism.

   2 China does not have a long history of democratic government. Ever hear of Tiananmen Square?

   3 Christianity is not the dominant religion of China, nor has it ever been the dominant religion of China. Confucianism and Buddhism are the major religious influences in China.

   4 Geographic isolation often leads to ethnocentrism for the simple reason that the region is not exposed to other regions. In China, isolation over many centuries led to ethnocentric attitudes within both the population and the government. China referred to itself for many years as the Middle Kingdom, as if it were the center of the universe.

9. There are lots of things to focus on in this cartoon, like the harsh labor conditions, Uncle Sam peeping through the doorway, and the military guards. But the most important thing to focus on is the message: *Forget human rights, enjoy our cheap prices.* You need to pick an answer choice that connects human rights violations to cheap prices.

   1 What does punishing political prisoners have to do with cheap prices? This can't be the point of the cartoon.

   2 This answer choice doesn't have anything to do with cheap prices, so it can't be the point of the cartoon.

   3 "Ignoring human rights issues" should remind you of "forget human rights" in the cartoon. "Economic development" would be achieved if China could undercut the competition by selling its goods cheaply abroad. This is the point of the cartoon. As China has reformed its economy to compete with the rest of the world, it has not reformed its social and political cultures. Some people are urging the United States government to cease trading with China until its human rights record improves, but the United States government isn't willing to cross that line. That's why the person outside the door is urging Uncle Sam to forget about the human rights violations and instead enjoy the economic advantages.

4 This answer choice has nothing to do with cheap prices, so it can't be the answer.

10. First, focus on the words *view of government*. Then, look up *Confucianism* and *Mao Zedong* in the Hit Parade if you don't know the Confucian or the Chinese Communist views of government. Eliminate answer choices that apply only to the Communists or to the Confucianists and/or those that apply to views other than governmental views.

1 Loyalty to the government (and to authority in general) was stressed by both Confucius and the Chinese Communists. Again, review both *Confucius* and *Mao Zedong*, the most significant Chinese Communist leader, in the Hit Parade if you missed this question.

2 The need for filial piety is a Confucian view, not a Chinese Communist view.

3 A civil service system is a communist view, not a Confucianist view.

4 Equality of men and women is a Chinese Communist view, not a Confucian one.

11. The Opium War and the Boxer Rebellion are the Regents' two favorite conflicts between China and the West. Make sure you review both in your global studies materials. In the meantime, at least eliminate answer choice 3 because it is inconsistent with the time period.

1 The Chinese lost the Opium War so it's not appropriate to say that they were still a major military power. And besides, compared to the Europeans, they weren't that much of a military power in the first place, so it doesn't make much sense to use the word *still*.

2 This is the best answer. The West got just about everything it wanted as out of the Opium War. As a result of the Treaty of Nanjing, which ended the war, Britain gained unrestricted access to a whole slew of Chinese ports, it gained Hong Kong as a colony, and to add insult to the Chinese injury, it got war indemnities from China. China was most definitely not strong enough to resist Western demands!

3 This is the wrong time period. Even if you just know the basics of Chinese history, you should realize that China was not industrializing during the early-to-mid-nineteenth century. In fact, China didn't start industrializing on any large scale until well into the twentieth century.

4 No! China and the West were not equal trading partners before or after the Opium War.

12. If you don't know about the Tiananmen Square massacre, you need to review your global studies materials and commit it to memory. It shows up on the test a lot. In the meantime, focus on the word *massacre* and at least try to eliminate a few answer choices that way.

1 This statement isn't true in the first place, so it couldn't have been a precipitating force in the Tiananmen Square massacre. Deng Xiaoping didn't plan to revive the Cultural Revolution. To be sure, the Cultural Revolution did, in fact, result in the massacre of people, but over two decades before the Tiananmen Square incident (and under Mao, not Deng). Look up *Cultural Revolution* and *Deng Xiaoping* in the Hit Parade if you chose this answer.

2 In response to a mass student demonstration for greater individual rights and freedom of expression the Chinese government opened fire in Tiananmen Square. The massacre was an enormous setback for social and political reform within China. If you were guessing, this would have been a good one to pick, since throughout history people have been killed for asserting their rights (or for desiring additional rights).

3 The decision to seek Western investors was a decision that was made by the Chinese government. The massacre occurred during the same time period that China was seeking Western investors, but the massacre was not a reaction to this decision.

4 Great Britain's decision to return Hong Kong to China was a cause for celebration in China, not a cause for a massacre.

13. Although Shintoism is in the Hit Parade, Taoism isn't since it rarely shows up on the test. Fortunately, though, you only need to know about Shintoism to answer this question correctly. If you're guessing, eliminate answer choices that clearly refer to other religions that you *do* know about and that likely wouldn't apply to other religions.

1 Confucianism stresses adherence to the five Confucian relationships, not Taoism or Shintoism. (That's why it's called Confucianism!)

2 Buddhism is the only religion that stresses adherence to the Eightfold Path.

3 This is the best answer. Both religions focus on the natural world and the pursuit of harmony within it. If you missed this question, you need to look up *Shintoism* in the Hit Parade. It's very likely that you'll have multiple questions about world religions on your test.

4 Neither Taoism nor Shintoism are monotheistic. Judaism, Christianity, and Islam are the world's three major monotheistic religions.

14. Think about Japan prior to 1868, which means prior to the Meiji Restoration. If you don't know about the Meiji Restoration, you should, because it tends to show up a lot on the test (including in the next question!). The Meiji Restoration was an enormous turning point in Japanese history. You need to find the answer choice that describes Japan prior to this major turning point, so avoid answer choices that describe modern Japan.

   1 Japan never achieved a military *conquest* of China. It did establish a sphere of influence in China, but not until the nineteenth century (after the Meiji Restoration).

   2 During this time period, Japan wasn't really trading with anybody. Extensive trade with the Americas better describes modern Japan.

   3 Cultural links with Europe came during and after the Meiji Restoration.

   4 Prior to Meiji Restoration, Japan was virtually isolated from the outside world. This isolation affected the development of Japanese society enormously. Even today, Japan remains one of the world's most homogeneous societies—not because it is still isolated, but because of a strong national identity.

15. Remember to thoroughly review the Meiji Restoration in your materials because it tends to show up on the test quite frequently. In the meantime, eliminate answer choices that don't fit the time period. Also, eliminate answer choices that describe something that isn't true about Japan in the first place, even if you're fuzzy on the Meiji Restoration.

   1 Japan doesn't have a large agricultural sector. It's a small island nation packed with mountains and people. There isn't a whole lot of room for rolling waves of grain or any other agricultural product. Plus, the question asks how the Japanese solved their natural resource problem. New technology is great, but it doesn't solve the problem of scarcity. Even with new technology, Japan would still lack the resources.

   2 In order to gain access to raw materials, Japan established a policy of imperialism, just like Europeans did centuries before. Japan invaded regions in East and Southeast Asia, took the resources that it needed without compensating the countries it colonized, and quickly built an empire.

   3 Nuclear power plants didn't come along until after World War II. This is totally out of the time period.

   4 Japan didn't cooperate with the Soviet Union at all. In fact, Japan invaded eastern parts of the Soviet Union for access to raw materials!

16. If you're not sure of the answer, first eliminate answer choices that you know aren't true. Then eliminate answer choices that wouldn't logically result in an improvement in Japanese-American trade relations (even if they're true). Of course, it helps if you understand why trade relations between Japan and America are strained in the first place.

1 The Japanese have not drastically lowered automobile prices for American consumers over the past decade. In fact, Japanese automobiles have always been priced competitively against American automobiles. Also, many higher-end Japanese automobile lines have been introduced to Americans over the past decade. However, even if you didn't know all of this, you should have still eliminated this answer choice because even if it were true, it wouldn't logically result in an improvement in Japanese-American trade relations. It would instead result in the Japanese selling even more automobiles in America, thus further straining the relationship between Japan and America.

2 Be wary of extreme words like *unlimited*. But even without the extreme language, this answer choice is just plain false. The reason trade relations are so strained in the first place is that Japan has protectionist trade policies against foreign-made goods while the United States espouses a free trade environment. Japan has saturated the American marketplace, but won't allow America to saturate *its* marketplace, at least with regard to automobiles.

3 This is not only false, it's irrelevant. The "America" in the question refers to the United States, not the continent of North America.

4 This is the best answer. While Japanese companies continue to sell millions of automobiles in the United States each year, they are building an increasing number of cars in automobile plants within the United States, particularly in the Ohio River valley. This eases the strain on trade relations between the two countries since this action by the Japanese gives Americans high-paying, highly skilled jobs. In this way, both Americans and Japanese can benefit from the sale of Japanese automobiles within the United States.

17. Go grab your map if you missed this question. Increasingly, the Regents test writers have enjoyed asking plain, old geography questions, so it's a good idea to keep a map handy throughout your studies. If you know that the Philippines, Malaysia, and Indonesia are in Southeast Asia, you're doing well. If you at least remember that they're in the eastern part of Asia you can eliminate a couple of answer choices.

   1 Korea is the second closest, but it is in East Asia, not Southeast Asia. See it on the map? Korea is sort of between China and Japan.

   2 This is the best answer. These countries are near Vietnam and, together with a few other countries, comprise a region referred to as Southeast Asia.

   3 Somalia is in Africa.

   4 Pakistan is in central Asia.

18. As soon as you see the nation of India paired up with *tradition* and/or *religious beliefs*, you should automatically think of two things: Hinduism and the caste system. If you're not automatically thinking of these two things, you need to review the Hit Parade and your global studies materials until you do. If you're a fan of the Hit Parade, this question is a gift!

   1 The caste system is a byproduct of Indian traditions, specifically the Hindu religion. If you don't know what the caste system is you need to look it up immediately in the Hit Parade. Never think about India without also thinking about the caste system. It gives context to all questions about India.

   2 India is fairly neutral, but not because of its religious beliefs, tradition, and the division of labor. It's neutral because of its political policies.

   3 Urbanization most definitely does not stem from religious beliefs and tradition. If you look it up in the Hit Parade you will learn that urbanization often results in the weakening of traditional values.

   4 India does have a parliamentary government, but not because of its religious beliefs, tradition, and division of labor. Instead, it has a parliamentary government because of the British influence during colonization. When India won independence it established itself under a constitutional, parliamentary government in stark *contrast* to its traditions.

19. As soon as you see Mohandas Gandhi you should know the answer. Look him up in the Hit Parade immediately if you missed this question. You don't even have to know about the "homespun movement" or the Salt March. All you have to know is the general policy that Gandhi advocated.

   1 Gandhi was not an industrialist.
   2 Gandhi was not an isolationist.
   3 Gandhi was not particularly aligned, but there is a much better answer.
   4 Gandhi's policy was one of nonviolent protest. Sometimes the Regents use the term *civil disobedience*, but typically they stress the nonviolent nature of his attempts to achieve Indian independence. As soon as you see the name Gandhi your brain should be trained to think of the words *nonviolent protest*. You'll never miss a Gandhi question again.

20. The Regents love to ask questions about the history of India, particularly the independence movement of Gandhi and the consequences of that movement. If you missed this question, you really need to review India's independence movement in your global studies materials. It shows up on the test all the time.

   1 If the British feared a united India and yet Indians wanted to be united, they would have united. In 1947, independence was granted, so Britain no longer had any say. In reality, India divided because Indians wanted to separate.
   2 All of India gained independence. Both regions wanted self-determination. . . from Britain and from each other!
   3 The Indian subcontinent was divided between Muslim Pakistan and secular, but overwhelmingly Hindu, India in 1947 due to differences between these two major religions. Gandhi wanted one huge, united India, but lost out to those who advocated separation. Today, Pakistan and India remain at odds. If you need to, review the religious and political background of modern India and Pakistan in your global studies materials.
   4 Communists never gained a foothold on the Indian subcontinent. Both Hinduism and Islam are extremely class-based.

21. There are eight terms in the answer choices. Six of them are in the Hit Parade. So if you missed this question because you didn't know the terms in the answer choices, you have no excuse. On the other hand, if you missed this question because you couldn't determine the perspective of the North Vietnamese during the Vietnam War, then you need to review your global studies materials. In the meantime, eliminate answer choices that don't describe Vietnam in the first place.

1 The North Vietnamese didn't see themselves as fascists and the South Vietnamese as liberals. Nor did they see themselves as liberals and the South Vietnamese as fascists.

2 This is the best answer. The North Vietnamese perceived themselves as nationalists who wanted a united Vietnam. They perceived South Vietnam as imperialist controlled (namely the French and then the Americans) who were preventing Vietnam from uniting under communist rule. Review *nationalism* and *imperialism* in the Hit Parade and then review your global studies materials on the Vietnam War.

3 The North Vietnamese didn't perceive either side as totalitarian. Nor did they contrast totalitarianism with republicanism.

4 The war in Vietnam had nothing to do with a ruling church pitted against a ruling family.

22. You should be familiar with the Five Pillars of Islam and the Ten Commandments. You should know the basics of the world's major religions. That said, you don't have to know the Five Pillars and the Ten Commandments word for word. Instead, you just have to know what they are in general. If you're uncertain, focus on an answer choice that describes something that you think the Regents would want you to know.

1 Reincarnation is associated with Hinduism. The Five Pillars are associated with Islam and the Ten Commandments are associated with Judaism and Christianity.

2 The Five Pillars and the Ten Commandments do not suggest that if a person learns, he will be saved. Learning is important to most religions, but not as a means (in and of itself) to salvation.

3 Don't be fooled by those crafty test writers! The Regents wants to trick you into associating the word *Pillars* with the words *statues* in this answer choice. But the Five Pillars of Islam are not five statues! In fact, representations of the human body and of God have traditionally been forbidden in Islam.

4 Both the Five Pillars and the Ten Commandments are guides to proper ethical and moral conduct. Even if you don't remember the details of either, you should have

guessed this answer, since every major world religion hopes to guide its followers through difficult ethical and moral decision-making. Review the Five Pillars and the Ten Commandments in your global studies materials. (The Five Pillars, in particular, show up on the essay portion of the test quite frequently.)

23. The cartoon shows two men (can you name them?) engaged in a peace process in which one man loosens his grip on the other man a little bit, and then expects the same in return. Remember to eliminate answer choices that describe a literal translation of the cartoon. Also, be wary of extreme language.

    1 This answer choice is way too strong. Plus, the men are loosening their grips, not tightening them.

    2 Each man appears to be strangling the other man. The test writers are hoping you'll see the strangling in the cartoon and be attracted to the word *stranglehold* in this answer choice, but the correct answer to cartoon questions will never be this literal. Plus, this answer choice doesn't make sense. How is it possible to put a stranglehold on a region's politics? There can be a stranglehold on a region's governments, but not on its politics. Even when governments are destroyed, politics is still going on.

    3 The United States isn't even in the cartoon. Plus, this answer choice is way too extreme. The Regents wouldn't suggest that positive results would occur in the world *only* with the assistance of the United States. The United States is often an engine of positive change, but there are a whole lot of influential countries and groups who are capable of bringing about good results.

    4 This is the best answer. In the cartoon, one man (Rabin) loosened his grip on the other man (Arafat) and expected the same in return. That's negotiation. That's compromise.

24. Look at the map carefully. The solid vertical lines show the area of the Ottoman Empire in 1453. The dotted slanted lines show the area into which the Ottoman Empire had expanded by 1520. And finally, the shaded area is the area into which the Ottoman Empire had expanded yet again by 1566. Although it isn't labeled, the Mediterranean Sea is between Africa (on the south) and Asia Minor and Europe (on the north). The Black Sea is to the north of Asia Minor and to the south of Russia.

    1 The Ottoman Empire couldn't have originated in Hungary because, according to the map, the Empire expanded into Hungary from lands previously occupied to the south.

2 Europe is to the north and the west. Asia to is to the east and southeast. The Empire was also located on major waterways. That's a pretty strategic location between Europe and Asia!

3 The Empire was definitely not landlocked. In fact, its location on the seas was one of its greatest assets.

4 Even at its greatest extent, the Ottoman Empire did not control western Europe. That's why France, Italy, and Spain aren't shaded on the map.

25. Look up the *Crusades* in the Hit Parade if you missed this question and—presto—the right answer will be evident. If you refuse to use the Hit Parade, we'll weep for you, but in the meantime, eliminate answer choices that describe something that never happened at all, regardless of your knowledge of the impact of the Crusades.

1 The Holy Land was never permanently occupied by the Europeans. If it were permanently occupied by the Europeans, then the Europeans would still occupy it today. But they don't. What's more, the Crusades generally failed to result in much European occupation of the Holy Land at all—temporary or permanent.

2 European trade has increased, not decreased, since the time of the Crusades. Since the Europeans didn't trade much during the Middle Ages trade had nowhere to go but up. And due to cultural diffusion associated with the Crusades, it most certainly went up. . . and has been going up ever since.

3 Most Muslims have never converted to Christianity. Islam is one of the fastest growing religions in the world. What's more, Islam has spread into previously Christian regions of the world, most notably the old Byzantine Empire.

4 **The Crusades led to widespread cultural diffusion in both directions between Europe and the Middle East. European crusaders brought Middle Eastern culture and technology back to Europe when they returned. Over the course of centuries, this exposure to Middle Eastern culture eventually influenced the European emergence from the Middle Ages and into the age of the Renaissance.**

26. If you only know about one of these civilizations, you can answer this question correctly. If you at least remember that they were ancient civilizations you can probably eliminate at least a couple answer choices.

1 **The Phoenicians, the Sumerians and the Mayas all developed extensive writing systems. The Phoenicians laid the groundwork for the alphabet later used by the Greeks, the Sumerians used cuneiform, and the Mayas used hieroglyphics.**

2 None of these civilizations emphasized equality in anything.

3 All of these civilizations were polytheistic.

4 None of these civilizations encouraged democratic participation in government. Democracy was tried for a while in ancient Greece and then didn't reemerge until the European Enlightenment.

27. If you remember the basics about either the Aztecs or the Incas you should be able to get the right answer. If not, review the basics in your materials, but also think through the answer choices carefully.

1 Both the Aztecs and the Incas had standing armies, though the Aztecs were better known as warriors than the Incas. In any case, armies were extremely important to both Empires. That's how they became Empires in the first place!

2 **This is the best answer. The relatively primitive weapons of the Aztecs and the Incas were no match for the weapons (or the diseases) of the Europeans, who have almost always used new technologies to devise weapons before nearly anything else. The Spaniards were able to blow their way through the two Empires (whose populations were already ravaged by diseases such as smallpox) in short order.**

3 The Spaniards did not outnumber the Aztecs and the Incas. Remember, the Spaniards came over on boats. They came over by the hundreds and the thousands, not by the millions. The Spaniards were greatly outnumbered, but their weapons were superior and more destructive.

4 The Aztecs and the Incas did not join together, Even if they *had* joined together, it wouldn't explain why the Spanish conquistadors were able to conquer them.

28. Think of a few Latin American countries. Do you know what type of government they currently have? If you do, then look for the answer. If you don't, then do two things: First, get rid of answer choices that you're pretty sure don't apply to Latin American countries. Second, think about general world trends during the 1990s.

1 Monarchies aren't the new trend in Latin America or anywhere else.

2 Military juntas were very common in Latin America since independence from Spain. Military juntas were even common as recently as the 1980s. But the 1990s have seen the growth of another type of government, which just happens to be the right answer choice.

3 **This is the best answer. Democracy is sweeping through Latin America. One nation after another has ousted its dictator and replaced him with democratically elected leaders. It happened in Nicaragua, Chile, and Paraguay.**

4 Fascism is a form of dictatorship. Look it up in the Hit Parade if you've forgotten it. Fascism saw its main growth in the 1930s and 1940s.

29. If you don't know what NAFTA is, it'll be hard to get this question correct. Yet, you should know what it is because it's in the Hit Parade. Notice that the word NAFTA is drawn as if it's part of some ancient ruins. Yet, it doesn't make any sense that it would be part of ancient ruins since it was formed in the 1990s. Now notice that the guys are talking about the Mayas, who were finished off by the Europeans centuries ago. Interestingly, though, they attribute Mayan decline to free trade with Spain. What does all this mean?

1 Modern technology isn't the enemy in this cartoon. The enemy is free trade. That's what the cartoon claims destroyed the Mayas.

2 NAFTA is a trade agreement, but nothing in this cartoon refers to colonial rule.

3 **This is the point of the cartoon. In reality, the Mayas were not destroyed by free trade with Spain, but the cartoonist is of the opinion that the negative consequences of NAFTA will be so great that Mexico will be destroyed—just like the Mayas were destroyed by the Europeans.**

4 Nothing about this cartoon refers to civil rights. What's more, the cartoon refers to destruction (*Whatever happened to the Mayas?*), not something positive.

30. Eliminate answer choices that don't describe something common in Western society. Eliminate answer choices that were developed well before or well after the rise and fall of the Roman Empire. Eliminate! Eliminate! Eliminate!

    1 Do you really think the Regents are going to ask you a question about gunpowder? Its development was most certainly significant, but the Regents generally won't ask questions about inventions other than the steam engine or the printing press. Besides, gunpowder was developed long after the fall of the Roman Empire.

    2 Socialism developed long after the fall of the Roman Empire. As for *revolutionary* socialism, we're not even sure what that is!

    3 Monotheism was developed long before the rise of the Roman Empire. And besides, the Romans were polytheistic. Ever hear of the term Roman gods? If you believe in more than one god, you're polytheistic, not monotheistic.

    4 The Romans codified law. Their system (actually borrowed from civilizations in the Middle East) has served as a basis for much of modern-day Western law.

31. Eliminate answer choices that describe a period in time in which slavery, religious persecution, and severe inequalities were rampant. You should be left with only one answer, which just happens to be located in the Hit Parade.

    1 The Pax Romana was a period of Roman peace. But the Romans had slaves. And people were most certainly tortured.

    2 During the Age of Exploration, the natives of the regions being explored by the Europeans were tortured, persecuted against, and killed.

    3 The Enlightenment marked the beginning of a philosophy that elevates the worth of individuals and stresses a nurturing environment in which people are encouraged to meet their potential. Look up *Enlightenment* in the Hit Parade if you missed this question. These days, the meaning is so ingrained in our language that we refer to leaders who recognize the value, rights and individuality of those they lead as enlightened.

    4 The Age of Imperialism was an age during which millions were enslaved, untold numbers were tortured, and people operated under a system of gross inequalities.

32. Eliminate answer choices that do not describe Europe during the Middle Ages. Eliminate answer choices that are inconsistent with *feudalism*, which is located in the Hit Parade. Eliminate answer choices that are nothing but gobbledygook. You should be left with just one answer.

  1 Colonial empires developed after Europe emerged from the Middle Ages. Colonial empires were the result of strong central governments. Feudalism thrives in the absence of strong central governments.

  2 This answer choice is gobbledygook. Internationalism means cooperation between nations. Suppression of internationalism means (we suppose) keeping countries from cooperating with each other. That's a pretty hard thing to do, especially if countries want to cooperate. Basically, *suppression of internationalism* is a phrase that sounds like it means a lot more than it does. In any case, feudalism didn't result from the suppression of internationalism because internationalism wasn't very popular during the Middle Ages in the first place.

  3 The Roman Catholic Church was all the rage in Europe during the Middle Ages.

  4 This is the best answer. Feudalism puts power in the hands of local landlords. And the only way the feudal lords could gain and keep their power was to somehow limit the power of the central authorities (the monarchs). After the fall of the biggest central government of them all (the Roman Empire), Europe was divided into scores of smaller kingdoms and thousands of local manors. Look up *feudalism* in the Hit Parade if you missed this question.

33. If you missed this question, then you haven't been reviewing the Hit Parade. Question after question after question involves the people and terms on that list. In the meantime, if you're guessing, choose the answer choice that seems to be the opposite of the others.

  1 In *The Prince*, Machiavelli asserted that leaders can and should do whatever is necessary to achieve their goals. "The ends justify the means" is a very Machiavellian thing to say.

  2 Machiavelli did not believe leaders should fight against discrimination and intolerance. This answer choice better describes Regents' favorites, Gandhi and Mandela.

  3 This answer choice describes the Enlightenment writers, but not Machiavelli.

  4 First, Machiavelli did not write about *elected* leaders. Second, he did not write about fairness and goodness. This answer choice might best describe Confucius, but even that's a bit of a stretch, since *fair* and *good* are so general as to be hard to define.

34. If you missed this question, look up the *Renaissance* and *humanism* in the Hit Parade.

    1 This answer choice is too extreme. The Church was still extremely influential during the Renaissance, just not *quite* as influential as it was during the Middle Ages (when it was pretty much the only show in town). Of course, the Church remains influential even today, so when you think about it, this answer choice doesn't make much sense.

    2 This is the best answer. During the Renaissance, a philosophy known as humanism developed. This philosophy focused on the potential to improve human life.

    3 Economic activity increased, not decreased, during the Renaissance. Look up the *Commercial Revolution,* which occurred at the tail end of the Middle Ages and into the Renaissance, in the Hit Parade if you don't understand why.

    4 This answer choice is also too extreme. Art contained religious themes during both the Middle Ages and the Renaissance. In fact, the Church was one of the biggest patrons of the arts during the Renaissance. The difference is that during the Middle Ages, art was almost exclusively religiously oriented while during the Renaissance, artistic expression broadened to include both religious representations and more humanist ones.

35. Look up the *Industrial Revolution* and *urbanization* in the Hit Parade if you missed this question. You should remember that the Industrial Revolution resulted in the development of thousands of factories. Which answer choice is consistent with everything you know about factories?

    1 This is the best answer. Hundreds of thousands of people left the country in search of work in the factories of the cities during the Industrial Revolution. You probably already know that factories tend to be built in cities (and that cities tend to be built around factories) since factories need a lot of workers and need to be near transportation hubs. During the Industrial Revolution, city growth exploded.

    2 The Industrial Revolution created an incredibly small, wealthy upper class and an incredibly huge impoverished class. To be sure, prior to the Industrial Revolution, most people were relatively impoverished, but at least most people had land to farm. During the Industrial Revolution, many people no longer had any land to

farm. While extremely generous philanthropists have shared their wealth and power throughout history, these individuals were certainly the exception during the Industrial Revolution. For the most part, the wealthy class concentrated power within itself, challenging the Church and everyone else in terms of supremacy over political, social, and economic life.

3   Craft guilds thrived *prior* to the Industrial Revolution. The factory system brought about the decline of individual craftsmanship and with it the guilds that bound them together.

4   The government didn't control agricultural production until well after the Industrial Revolution. During the Industrial Revolution, agricultural production was generally determined on the local level by farmers, feudal lords, or businesses.

36.   If you don't know much about Karl Marx you need to look him up in the Hit Parade and read about him in your global studies materials. He's that important. Don't take this test without knowing the basics of the Regents' regular cast of characters. They're the people with one, two, or three asterisks next to their names in the Hit Parade. In the meantime, eliminate answer choices that just plain don't make sense.

1   Civilizations are destroyed by a lot of things, not the least or greatest of which are famines. Famines are tragic, of course, but you won't be able to explain much of history if you only concentrate on famines and the consequences of famines.

2   Imperialism and colonialism are pretty much the same thing. So it doesn't make much sense to talk about a repeating cycle of imperialism and colonialism. It wouldn't be a cycle at all—it would be just one long period of time. Plus, it wouldn't explain the periods of history when there wasn't much imperialism or colonialism to talk about. (Do isolationist countries not have a history?)

3   Many people view history as a listing of accomplishments of the ruling classes, but not Karl Marx.

4   There have always been different classes of people. History, according to Marx, is the story of the continuous struggle between these classes. Marx believed that since class struggles always result in winners and losers (and sometimes just losers), the best way to get around the despair of history is to eliminate the class struggle. And the best way to eliminate the class struggle is to eliminate classes. Hence, communism. Again, make sure you review Marx in your materials. There's a good chance you'll see him on your test.

37. If you missed this question, review the Treaty of Versailles. It shows up a lot on the test, either explicitly or implicitly through the impact it had on Europe, especially Germany. In the meantime, though, focus on the words in the question, specifically on *Triple Entente is formed to combat the Triple Alliance*. Then, notice the reference to the League of Nations, which was an organization intended to prevent wars through diplomatic solutions. What could these two things possibly have in common?

1   The League of Nations was not formed at the hands of aggressive dictators.

2   This is the best answer. In all three cases, the events involved an attempt to establish a balance of power. Look up *balance of power* in the Hit Parade if you missed this question. The example of the Triple Entente and Triple Alliance is part of the definition! In order to establish a balance of power within a region (or the world), sometimes organizations are formed to balance out other organizations (i.e., Triple Entente/Triple Alliance, Warsaw Pact/NATO). And sometimes worldwide organizations are called into play (i.e., League of Nations, United Nations).

3   France and Germany most certainly have been rivals, but France, Germany, and Greece don't share any special rivalries. Nor do any of the events in the question specifically involve France, Germany, and Greece as the main players of a rivalry.

4   None of these events reflect the concept of mercantilism.

38. If you know about the new nations formed from the breakup of the Austro-Hungarian Empire and the breakup of the Soviet Union, good for you. But you can probably answer this question even if you don't, as long as you have a general understanding of the Regents. Pick an answer choice that repeats a recurring theme on this test.

1   No, no, no. Nations don't need a lot of money to become members of the United Nations. Almost all countries are members, and most of them are relatively poor. (The new nations formed from the breakup of the Soviet Union are all members, by the way.)

2   New nations wage war. Old nations wage war. New and old nations use whatever resources they have or they can borrow or steal to wage war! If a nation could avoid war by breaking apart and becoming "new," nations would be breaking apart all over the place!

3 This answer choice is almost impossible to argue with. Of course national and ethnic differences often lead to instability and violence. Certainly the new nations formed from the breakup of the Austro-Hungarian Empire and the breakup of the Soviet Union didn't avoid violence.

4 Self-determination sometimes leads to democratic forms of government, and sometimes not. In the case of the breakup of the Austro-Hungarian Empire, it didn't. In the case of the breakup of the Soviet Union, it did.

39. Hitler shows up on the test a lot; make sure you review him in your materials. You should review the Treaty of Versailles as well, specifically with regard to its impact on Germany. Even if you simply remember that the Treaty of Versailles was signed after World War I, you should be able to put these events in order.

1 **The Treaty of Versailles was signed at the end of World War I. It blamed Germany for the war and punished it harshly—so harshly that Germany was humiliated and thrown into economic crisis. Years later, Adolf Hitler rose to power in part by blaming the Treaty of Versailles for the crisis in Germany. He incited the masses to assert themselves as a powerful German nation. After becoming the Chancellor of Germany (and then the totalitarian *fuhrer*), German troops invaded Poland, marking the beginning of World War II.**

2 It was Hitler who ordered the invasion of Poland, and he wasn't able to do that until after he became Chancellor.

3 Adolf Hitler became Chancellor of Germany after the signing of the Treaty of Versailles. In fact, his frustration over the Treaty of Versailles helped to shape his political philosophy, which in turn partly facilitated his rise to power.

4 It was Hitler who ordered the invasion of Poland, and he wasn't able to do that until after he became Chancellor.

40. Look at the cartoon carefully. Japan, Iran, and Libya are handing over wads of money to an unemployed nuclear scientist who happens to be leaning against a nuclear warhead. Even if this is all you understand of the cartoon you can answer this question correctly. Of course, if you've been following recent developments in global studies, you can answer this question even without the aid of the cartoon.

1 **This is the best answer. Not only is it a true statement, but it also describes the scene in the cartoon. Three countries are handing over money to an unemployed Soviet nuclear scientist. Just by looking at the expressions on the faces of the people in the cartoon it's safe to conclude that the big-money guys are really interested in buying something from the nuclear guy.**

2 This statement really isn't true in the first place, since the former Soviet Union is not economically viable enough to be investing large sums of money elsewhere. This statement also has nothing to do with the cartoon, since it isn't the Soviet guy who's handing out the money, but the guys from the other countries. What's more, Japan is a developed country, not a developing one. Need any more reasons to scratch this answer?

3 Japan isn't a Middle Eastern country. What's more, the Soviet nuclear scientist isn't the one searching out the jobs. Instead, the job offers are coming to him. It's quite possible that some former Soviet nuclear scientists are searching for jobs in the Middle East, but that's not the point of this particular cartoon.

4 First, this is not a true statement. Many nations in the Middle East are arming, not disarming. What's more, this statement doesn't describe what's going on in the cartoon. Three guys are trying to buy weapons technology. Nobody's disarming.

41. Focus on 1960, the date of the map. In 1960, the Warsaw Pact was alive and well. Look up *Warsaw Pact* in the Hit Parade if you missed this question. From the Hit Parade definition you will know that the Soviet Union's satellites were in Eastern Europe. If you're still confused, then it probably makes sense to pick the countries that are geographically closest to the Soviet Union, wouldn't you say?

1 The USSR is the Soviet Union. The USSR is marked with the horizontal lines. It doesn't make sense that the USSR would be its own satellite.

2 These countries were allied against the Soviet Union and its satellites in an organization known as NATO.

3 **This is the answer. These nations, known as satellites of the Soviet Union, were all a part of the Warsaw Pact in 1960. As you can see on the map, they formed a barrier between the Soviet Union and the rest of Europe.**

4 Only one country, Yugoslavia, is marked by the slanted lines. Yugoslavia was not a satellite of the Soviet Union in 1960. You could have figured this out, though, since the question asks you for "nations" and there is only one nation with slanted lines.

42. You might know the answer to this question even without the aid of the map, but if you don't, think through the answer choices logically. Why would the Regents be asking this question?

1 Ukraine, Lithuania, and Belarus are not located outside the geographic area shown. Lithuania is to the northwest of Minsk, Belarus is located in the western portion of the former USSR in and around the city of Lvov, and Ukraine is located in the south-western portion of the former Soviet Union in and around the city of Kiev. So you say you didn't know this? Well, you should still eliminate this answer choice because it doesn't make much sense that the Regents would give you a map and then ask you about what's not on it.

2 **This is the best answer. All three of these places, now independent countries, were republics of the Soviet Union in 1960. See the explanation to answer choice 1 for the locations.**

3 It's highly unlikely that the Regents will expect you to know the provinces of Poland or Rumania, so don't get all wigged out over this answer choice. The reason that the former republics of the USSR are so important is that they are now independent nations.

4 This answer choice doesn't make sense. Lots of members of NATO, such as West Germany and Italy, are on the map. So this can't be the reason that the Ukraine, Lithuania, and Belarus are not in the map. In fact, since the Ukraine, Lithuania, and Belarus were republics of the Soviet Union in 1960 they most certainly were not members of NATO.

43. Eliminate answer choices that never happened, even if you have no idea what specifically happened as a result of Mongol domination. You should be left with two answer choices. If you don't know much about Russian history you might have some difficulty at this point, but try to pick the one that describes the greatest global significance. If you're suspicious of extreme wording, you'll pick the right one as well.

1 Feudalism didn't end in Russia until the last half of the nineteenth century, significantly later than in the rest of Europe.

2 The people of Russia are not, nor have they ever been, primarily Hindu. The only nation that is predominately Hindu is India.

3 **This is the answer. Under the Mongols, Russia was in extreme isolation. While western Europe emerged from the Middle Ages and made tremendous advancements in technology, the arts, and philosophy, Russia did not. It wasn't until the rise of Peter the Great and then later Catherine the Great that Russia began to catch up with the rest of Europe.**

4 The Eastern Orthodox Church was never reunited with the Roman Catholic Church, under the Mongols or anyone else.

44. Get rid of answer choices that occurred before the Cold War. Get rid of answer choices that occurred after the Cold War. You should be left with one. Don't remember what the Cold War was and/or when it was? Look it up in the Hit Parade.

1 **Yeltsin rose to power *after* the Cold War.**

2 Trotsky formed the Red Army *before* the Cold War.

3 Germany invaded the USSR *before* the Cold War.

4 The formation of the Warsaw Pact marked the beginning of the Cold War.

45. If you don't know the specifics about the cutting of timber in Brazil and Malaysia, don't fret. First, look at the time period. It's the 1980's. Second, focus on the general answer choices. In other words, what's a basic reason that a country would cut down its forests for timber? (Oh, and by the way, it would be a really good idea to look up *deforestation* in the Hit Parade when you have a chance.)

1 **Sure! Brazil and Malaysia are cutting down their forests for timber in order to make some bucks. Imagine that! Most nations exploit their resources for economic prosperity. Nations with oil drill. Nations will coal mine. Nations with farmland grow stuff. Nations with forests cut them down.**

2 Who in the world would cut down trees for the purpose of owing more money?

3 Cutting down rain forests typically doesn't make indigenous people happy. In fact, since it often ruins their homeland and way of life, they usually get really upset. Cutting down the rain forests actually increases rebellions, not decreases them.

4 The question refers to the 1980s. The imperialist nations pulled out of Brazil and Malaysia long before then. But even if they hadn't, it doesn't make sense that cutting down trees would prevent exploitation by imperialists.

46. If you know the story behind just one of these headlines you have enough information to answer this question correctly. If not, at least eliminate answer choices that don't generally describe Germany, OPEC, western nations, and Iraq. Or, looked at in a slightly different way; which answer choice describes something that Germany, OPEC, and the UN could possibly have in common?

1 This is the best answer. In fact, it's almost impossible to disagree with. Of course economic measures are often designed to achieve political goals! Germany was blamed for World War I (a political determination) and was made to pay war reparations to the victors (an economic measure). OPEC was politically allied against western nations (a political determination) and used an oil embargo (an economic measure) to advance its political position. And the United Nations is fairly politically united against Iraq, imposing economic sanctions to compel Iraq to comply with the UN's political determinations.

2 Germany, OPEC, western nations, the UN, and Iraq are not, nor have they ever been, communist. (Okay. . . *East* Germany was, but not during or immediately following World War I) As such, this can't possibly be the answer.

3 This is a true statement, but unfortunately it has absolutely nothing to do with these headlines. What do reparations, an embargo, and sanctions have to do with encouraging investment? Absolutely nothing. In fact, they discourage investment and ruin economies.

4 Was Germany nationalistic? Sure! Was Iraq nationalistic? Sure! Are OPEC nations nationalistic? Sure! Nationalism actually plays a large role in economic decision-making, not a small one. In the case of Germany and Iraq, nationalism has actually worked against their economies.

47. The code of bushido and samurai are in the Hit Parade precisely because of these kinds of questions. The Hit Parade is your friend. Treat it like one: Visit it often.
    1 The samurai were not Hindu. Nor did they believe in reincarnation.
    2 Like the samurai under the code of bushido, the European knights under the practice of chivalry expressed tremendous loyalty to their country.
    3. The samurai were not Jewish.
    4. Compare *Enlightenment writers* (found in the Hit Parade under *Enlightenment*) with samurai (also in the Hit Parade). See any similarities? Neither do we.

48. You only have to know about one of these men in order to answer this question correctly. Peter the Great is in the Hit Parade, and since the Regents keep asking the same question about him, if you look him up, the correct answer will be evident.
    1 Of the men in the question, only Peter the Great increased the power of the aristocracy. (The Meiji Restoration marked the end of feudalism in Japan.)
    2 None of these men truly introduced new religious beliefs, although to a certain extent they had a religious impact on their countries. After the Meiji Restoration in Japan, for example, Buddhism and Confucianism were viewed as "foreign influences," and the country focused on the state Shinto religion. And under Shah Pahlavi, strict adherence to literal interpretations of the Koran was relaxed. But still, it cannot be said that these men "introduced new religious beliefs." They simply refocused the national attention on certain religious beliefs that already existed.
    3 Japan, Russia, and Iran all expanded their industrial base under the leadership of these men.
    4 This is the best answer. All three are among the Regents' favorite examples of westernization. The Regents also like using Catherine the Great, Mikhail Gorbachev and Kemal Atatürk in questions about westernization. Look up *westernization* in the Hit Parade and earn points!

PART II

1. GEOGRAPHIC FEATURES

Egypt—Nile River

The Nile River has been the lifeblood of Egypt since ancient times. Floodwater from the river creates a narrow band of excellent farmland stretching for nearly 1,000 miles from its mouth on the Mediterranean Sea. Although the river sometimes brings exceptionally high floodwaters, the soil is replenished when the floodwaters recede. Long ago, this process brought about the development of a self-sustaining empire that dominated the region for centuries. The ancient Egyptians maintained a prosperous kingdom for centuries along its banks. The river provided them not only with food, but with transportation between the villages and cities, all of which were built close to the river bank.

Japan—Island Location

Japan is a nation of islands off the coast of mainland Asia. The water surrounding the nation has provided it with security from both military invasions and cultural diffusion. The result has been the development of a society with a very strong identity and a strong sense of purpose, although its isolation has led to an ethnocentric attitude. Nevertheless, the fact that Japan is an island nation has generally had a positive impact on its culture. Japan has experienced longer periods of peace than a vast majority of nations, and has developed a fishing industry second to none. Fishing is a very cost-effective way to feed a growing population since the oceans provide the fish for free, and since Japan's mountainous topography permits only limited farming.

Poland—Northern European Plain

Except along the mountainous southern border, Poland is a large, flat plain. Economically, Poland has benefited from the land, which not only is agriculturally rich but is also rich in resources such as coal, copper, natural gas, and sulfur. However, politically, Poland has been cursed by the land, which does not offer many natural barriers against invasion, especially from the west, east, and southeast. Poland has been carved into pieces as a result of invasions from Prussia, Austria, and Russia. In 1918, independence was achieved and it looked like Poland might actually develop peacefully. But in

1939 the Germans swept through Poland sparking World War II. When the war finally ended Poland was left devastated, and the Soviets swept in and took it over. Eventually, in 1990, Poland split from the Soviet Bloc and, under the leadership of Lech Walesa, has developed its economy. Poland now relies on its alliances with the West, most notably with NATO, to give it the protection that its topography and location cannot.

Roman Empire—Mediterranean Sea

The Mediterranean Sea was at the heart of the Roman Empire, so much so that it is difficult to imagine the Roman Empire without it. Prior to the rise of the Roman Empire Carthage controlled the Sea. But the Romans, who were conquering parts of central Italy, substantially expanded their fleet and fought in a series of wars against Carthage for control of the vast body of water. These wars later became known as the Punic Wars which lasted from approximately 264 BC to 146 BC. By the end of the Second Punic War Rome controlled the western portion of the Mediterranean Sea. In the decades that followed, Rome expanded its dominion over the entire region, its influence extending in a great swath around the perimeter of the sea. What's more, the city of Rome itself was located fifteen miles inland, and therefore was protected from an invasion by sea. As a result, Rome was able to maintain a relatively stable empire for centuries. It used the Mediterranean as the centerpiece for not only military conquests, but also commerce and trade. Indeed, one of the major functions of the Roman Navy was the protection of travelers and merchants, ensuring a safe flow of goods. The impact was enormous, since for centuries Roman ideas spread across the sea to two other continents, while three continents worth of ideas and products flowed into Rome. The Mediterranean Sea, therefore, was one of the first major avenues of widespread cultural diffusion.

Russia—Frozen Rivers

For centuries, Russia's only coastline ran along the Arctic Ocean in the north and then cut south in the east along the Bering Sea. The southern and western borders were landlocked. Since the Arctic Ocean is almost entirely covered in ice year round, and since most of the rivers are frozen for several months each year, Russia was not able to establish port cities throughout much of its history except in the east, where the population is sparse and thousands of miles away from the major cities of the west. Then, in the eighteenth century, Peter the Great drove the Swedes out of part of the Baltic region and established his new capital city on the Baltic Sea. In addition, both he and, later, Catherine the Great fought wars against the Ottoman Empire in the south to gain access to the Black Sea. Thereafter,

Russia's coastline included warm-water ports that it previously lacked. As a result, Russia's international trade increased dramatically, as did its naval capacity. The limited warm-water coastline of Russia, once acquired, dramatically affected its economy and territorial expansion policy for most of its history.

South Africa—Gold and Diamond Mines

Prior to the discovery of gold and diamonds in South Africa in the 1860s and 1880's, South Africa was valuable to the Europeans only for shipping and military reasons. The Dutch arrived first and founded Cape Town as a stopping point for ships on the way from Europe to India. In 1795 the British seized Cape Town for themselves, and the South African Dutch (now known as *Boers* or *Afrikaners*) trekked northeast into the interior of South Africa, finally settling in a region known as the Transvaal. When the Boers later discovered diamonds and gold in the Transvaal, the British followed the Boers into the interior and fought a series of wars against them for rights to the resources. After years of bloody battles, the British reigned supreme and all of South Africa was annexed as part of the ever-expanding British Empire. Thus the discovery of valuable gold and diamond mines greatly affected the European conquest of the region. Throughout this entire process, the natives were allowed no claims to the gold and diamonds, and were made to work in the mines as their natural resources were sent abroad. To this day, South Africa remains a country rich in resources and economic potential.

2. IDEAS OF LEADERS

Martin Luther

When Martin Luther stated that he could not nor would not recant anything, he was referring to the theological positions that he took against the Roman Catholic Church, which was engaging in practices he found objectionable. For centuries, the Roman Catholic Church had controlled all religious worship and expression in Western Europe. The Church had been engaging in a number of activities that raised the eyebrows of some of the monks and priests for some time, but when the Church hierarchy began to sell indulgences, Martin Luther, an Augustinian friar in Germany, could no longer contain his anger. *Indulgences* were pieces of paper that the Church sold to raise funds for its ambitious construction projects. The Church claimed that the purchase of an indulgence would result in a reduction in the amount of time that the purchaser would stay in purgatory. In response to this practice and others, Martin Luther nailed ninety-five theses to a church door in Wittenberg, Germany, in 1517, pointing out the theological flaws in the Church's practices. Luther's ideas spread quickly, especially with the aid of the printing press. By the time Church authorities excommunicated him—an action they took after he refused to recant—northern Europe had already turned against the Catholic Church. These dissenters referred to themselves as *Protestants*. Other Protestant movements gained steam under the direction of John Calvin, Huldrych Zwingli, and others. The consequences were enormous. Europe was no longer unified under the Catholic Church, but the Catholic Church that remained became stronger, even more centralized, and re-energized. Today, there are millions of Catholics and Protestants throughout the world who peacefully coexist side-by-side, but unfortunately, the unresolved divisions between them can still be seen in places like Northern Ireland.

Simón Bolívar

Statements such as this one by Simón Bolívar were intended to motivate the peasant masses in Latin America against the oppression and domination of the Europeans. Inspired by Bolívar as well as by developments in France and the United States, the people of Latin America began their revolt against Spanish rule in 1810. Bolívar served competently not only as the military and emotional leader of the revolution, but also as an intelligent and thoughtful strategist. After years of struggle, independence was finally won in 1824 for parts of South America, including Venezuela, Colombia, Ecuador, Peru, and, of course, Bolivia, which was named in his honor. Bolívar wanted to establish a United Grand Colombia, essentially a "United States of South America," but a conference with Jose San Martin, the leader of the revolution in Argentina, failed miserably. Other movements eventually led to the establishment and maintenance of the individual Latin American nations that still exist today. Bolívar died unhappily due to his failure to unite the continent, but his success as a revolutionary is undisputed.

V. I. Lenin

With these words, Lenin marked the beginning of a new era in Russian history. The October Revolution of 1917 culminated in Lenin's ascension to the leadership of the new Soviet Union. Lenin's long-term goal was to establish a communist state, but his immediate goal concerned meeting the basic needs of the Soviet population who had been battered by years of warfare and neglect. Lenin redistributed the farms so that they were under the control of the peasants, or at least under the control of the state but in the interests of the peasants. More immediately, however, Lenin was concerned with the maintenance of peace and order, and so he signed the Treaty of Brest-Litovsk which brought an end to the war with Germany. With peace realized, he then enacted the New Economic Policy of 1921 in an effort to spark economic prosperity in the new nation.

Adolf Hitler

Adolf Hitler was a man of very dramatic speech. Statements such as this one were made to appeal to German nationalism which Hitler brought to a boiling point by not only reminding Germans of how they had been wronged by other nations, but also by advancing the idea that Germans were superior to all other races. These ideas were first stated by Hitler in *Mein Kampf*, his personal account of struggle that later became the definitive statement of the Nazi Party. In the 1930s the Nazis became the largest political party in Germany by asserting the claims in Hitler's book—most notably that Germany had been wrongly victimized by the Treaty of Versailles after World War I, that the Jews and other "undesirables" were behind many of Germany's problems, and that the Aryan race was capable and destined to rule Germany and the world. The ultimate goal of the Nazi party, therefore, was to gain control of Germany and establish an Aryan superpower. Under the leadership of Hitler, who managed to be sworn in as Chancellor in 1933 and then shortly thereafter assumed the title and authority of *fuhrer*, the Nazis acted on their goals by swiftly creating a new political and social order. They utilized a secret police force, the Gestapo, to quash dissent. They built concentration camps to carry out the mass genocide of Jews, Gypsies, and homosexuals. And all the while, they united Aryan Germany by feeding the flames of Aryan nationalism. Ultimately, however, the Nazi defeat served as a lesson to the world on the dangers of ethnocentric nationalism.

Mohandas Gandhi

When Gandhi spoke of the consequences of British imperialism he not only spoke from a nationalist perspective with regard to his native India but also from a global perspective. Born in India, Gandhi was educated in Britain and spent several years in British South Africa where he saw firsthand the consequences of institutionalized racism. Outraged, he became an advocate for Indian nationals in South Africa and then returned to India, where in the 1920s and 1930s he embarked on a large-scale resistance against British rule, leading such efforts as the Salt March and the Quit India Movement. Even though Gandhi spoke with great determination and refused to back away from his goals, he was strongly opposed to the use of violence.

Instead, his approach is one of history's clearest examples of civil disobedience. He opposed British imperialism, transformed rural education, improved the rights of members of India's lowest caste, and encouraged Hindu-Muslim unity, all through peaceful measures. Although Gandhi's goal of Indian self-determination was finally achieved in 1947, it was not a unified peace. Instead, animosity between Hindus and Muslims led to the establishment of separate nations for each group, who were increasingly violent toward one another. Gandhi's nonviolent approach came to an ironic end when he was assassinated in 1948, proving that although many of his goals had been achieved, the message of his nonviolent methods in some cases fell on deaf ears.

Mao Zedong

Mao Zedong made this statement about violence to underscore his belief that only through force would the peasants successfully defeat the Nationalists. Prior to making this statement, Mao had come to believe that the government was ignoring the most basic needs of its people. After building up a rural force of over one million peasant soldiers, Mao swept through China and drove the Nationalists off the mainland and the nearby island of Taiwan. Throughout his life, Mao not only held fast to his communist beliefs, but also to his belief that power was gained and maintained "through the barrel of a gun." He forced millions to work side-by-side in collectives, kept strict control of all means of production, remained intolerant of dissent, and ruled as dictator over virtually every aspect of Chinese life. With the force of the military, he managed to keep power even when his policies failed.

Ayatollah Khomeini

Ayatollah Khomeini made statements such as this one to bolster the support of his countrymen for the drastic reforms initiated in the years following the Islamic Revolution in Iran. Khomeini was the ruler of the new Islamic Republic in the years following the 1979 overthrow of Shah Pahlavi. A strict advocate of Shiite Islamic fundamentalism, Khomeini opposed the earlier westernization efforts of the Shah, which he quickly reversed. By pitting western values against Islamic traditions, Khomeini essentially told his countrymen that a proper Muslim could not be both western and Islamic. To be true to their religion, Iranians were encouraged to resist "dependence on the powers" and to focus their lives according to the laws of the Koran. With nationalism running high, Khomeini declared April 1, 1979, as "the first day of a government of God."

3. TURNING POINTS

Cuba

In 1959, the dictatorship of Fulgencio Batista was overthrown by democratic revolutionaries led by Fidel Castro. Instead of implementing a democratic system, however, Fidel Castro acted as dictator himself, nationalizing industries and plantations, both domestically and foreign owned. Within two years, Castro established a Communist dictatorship that not only failed to put democratic reforms into place, but also committed atrocious abuses of basic human rights. Although the Cuban Revolution changed the leadership and government philosophy of the nation, the daily lives of most Cubans did not take a turn for the better.

Egypt

In 1952, a group of young army officers overthrew the Egyptian King and declared the nation a republic under the leadership of Gamal Abdel Nasser. During the nineteenth century until 1922, Egypt had been a British protectorate. During this period the Suez Canal was built under British and French direction. Between 1922 and 1952 Egypt was officially independent, but the King cooperated very closely with Britain, and it was this cooperation that the revolutionaries resented. In 1956 Nasser moved to nationalize the Suez Canal, which was still controlled by British and French interests. Although initial attempts to nationalize the canal were unsuccessful, the canal eventually came under Egyptian control. As Egypt's most important resource, the canal generates billions of dollars in fees that are now spent within Egypt rather than in Britain and France.

France

The storming of the Bastille, which set the French Revolution in motion, was one of the most important turning points in the nation's history. It occurred because of middle class and lower class anger with the French nobility. The middle class consisted of merchants and professionals who were experiencing an increase in wealth and paying an increase in taxes. Together with the peasant class, who were not experiencing an increase in wealth but who were also paying excessive taxes, the middle class wanted to increase their political power in the Estates General, a parliamentary body composed mostly of the nobility. They were motivated by the ideas of representative government and the rights of man expressed by the Enlightenment writers and by the American Revolution. Basically, they wanted a system of one-man, one-vote. When they didn't get it, they stormed the Bastille, a political prison, and set the prisoners free. The French Revolution had begun and rioting quickly swept the nation. The storming of the Bastille did not directly solve any of the problems of the lower classes, but it did set unstoppable reforms into motion that would eventually help the lower classes. After an extremely bloody revolution, a Reign of Terror imposed by the Jacobin republic that replaced the monarchy, and a sweep through Europe under Napoleon, France settled down into a modern republic, complete with a constitution and the economic, political, and social change that the original rioters wanted.

Ireland

In 1845 potato crops, the main source of food for most Irish, were destroyed by a deadly fungus. As a result of its sudden and far-reaching impact, as well as a reluctance of the British government to do anything about it, the fungus led to the deaths of over 20,000 people from starvation and the deaths of a million more from disease. Millions more picked up and left the country entirely, many immigrating to the United States.

The famine, and more specifically the British non-reaction to it, fanned the flames of revolution within Ireland. The revolutionaries wanted the right to self-determination and demanded homerule, but the British were not anxious to give up control of the region. Although the revolutionaries received some concessions over the following decades, their self-determination did not pay off until 1921 when Ireland was split between British-controlled Northern Ireland and the independent Irish Republic.

Kenya

After World War II, nationalism swept much of Africa, including Kenya, which had long wanted independence from the British colonists. Jomo Kenyatta encouraged these feelings of nationalism and led protests against the whites and the Asians who had settled in Kenya. At the same time, guerrilla groups known as the Mau Mau began to instigate violence against white settlers. Kenyatta was accused by the British of leading the group and was sentenced to seven years of hard labor, but the violent uprisings continued. The British finally abandoned their attempts to suppress the uprisings and granted independence in 1963, at which point Jomo Kenyatta became president of the new nation of Kenya. Kenyatta did not look to reunite the different ethnic and racial groups of Kenya. Instead, he ordered the removal of whites and Asians, which had an immediate adverse impact on the economy. Kenyatta persisted in his reforms, however, and eventually Kenya's economy grew.

Korea

Prior to World War II, Korea was invaded by Japan and annexed as part of the expanding Japanese Empire. After Japan was defeated in World War II Korea was supposed to be reestablished as an independent nation, but until stability could be achieved and elections held, it was occupied by the Soviet Union and the United States in two separate pieces—the Soviet Union north of the 38th parallel and the United States south of it. As the Cold War developed between the two superpowers, they couldn't agree on the terms of a united Korea. In the meantime, each continued to exert its own influence over the political and cultural developments within the territory it occupied. In 1948, two separate governments were established: a Soviet-backed communist regime in North Korea and a United States-backed democracy in South Korea. Both the Soviet Union and the United States withdrew their troops in 1949, but in 1950, North Korea attacked South Korea in an attempt to unite the two nations under a single communist government. The United Nations condemned the action and soon a multinational force, largely consisting of U.S. and British troops, went to the aid of the South Koreans. The UN forces made tremendous headway under General MacArthur, but when it looked as if the North Koreans would be defeated, China entered the war on behalf of the Communist North. The two sides battled it out along the 38th parallel, eventually leading to an armistice in 1953. Today, the two nations remain separate and true to the political philosophies under which they were created.

Turkey

In 1922, a group of Turkish nationalists led by Mustafa Kemal Atatürk overthrew the last Ottoman emperor. In 1923, the nationalists established the republic of Turkey, the first republic in the Middle East. Atatürk's main goal was to establish Turkey as a modern nation more in line with the European tradition as opposed to the Middle Eastern tradition. Among the hundreds of changes that he implemented, Atatürk severed the close connection between church and state by establishing secular laws independent of the law of Islam. He replaced religious courts with secular courts and expanded the rights of the citizens, especially those of women, who under Islamic law did not have legal and political rights equal to those of men. Atatürk even dressed in the European style and enforced that dress code on others. In the new secular schools, children were taught the Roman alphabet, not the Arabic script, and in the workplace, the economy was quickly industrialized. Ever since this major turning point in its history, Turkey arguably has been the most western-oriented of all the Islamic nations.

4. IMPACT OF RELIGION ON CULTURE

Architecture—Christianity

Gothic cathedrals were built in Europe in the twelfth through seventeenth centuries. They were larger and more detailed than most of the cathedrals that came before them, and were unique in their use of pointed arches, flying buttresses, and enormous, detailed stain glass windows. Chartres Cathedral stands as one of the greatest examples of the High Gothic style in Europe and as an excellent reflection of Medieval Christianity. After the first attempt to build the cathedral ended in a fire, it was finally completed in 1220, twenty-six years after the second attempt began. Three features of the tremendous Cathedral combined architecture with Christian theology. First, the altar rests at the intersection of a long nave and two side galleries. In other words, the floor plan is in the shape of the cross, the most important symbol of Christianity. Second, the ceiling of the nave rises to nearly 120 feet, and the towers outside rise much higher than that, focusing the eyes and the spirit upward toward heaven. Third, the walls are dominated by enormous stain glass windows, larger and more intricate than anything that had come before them. Christian symbolism and Biblical stories are represented within the designs of the windows. Therefore, the architectural style of Chartres Cathedral reflected and reinforced the values of Christian Medieval Europe.

Dietary Laws—Judaism

The dietary laws of Judaism are as ancient as the religion itself, extending from the written law of the Torah as well as from rabbinic tradition, legislation, and local custom. These rules determine what is *kosher*, or in other words, what is acceptable for consumption. The dietary laws are quite extensive, including rules regarding which animals are fit for consumption, forbidden parts of otherwise permitted animals, methods of slaughtering, methods of meat preparation, and even proper proportions of food when different foods are mixed. These dietary laws have of course had an enormous impact on Jewish culture, but just as dramatically it has had an effect on the economy and the geography of predominately Jewish areas. The agricultural economy of Jewish regions and neighborhoods has developed over centuries in such a way as to favor kosher foods.

Dress—Islam

The Koran, the most important text of Islamic law and tradition, stipulates the basic forms of dress to which Muslims are expected to adhere, especially women. Women are expected to cover their hair and body, leaving only the face exposed. Their garments cover their arms and legs all the way to the hands and feet, and are not tight fitting or revealing in any way. In some Islamic countries, women might wear a *niqaba*, a veil worn over the face, as a way of emulating some of Muhammad's wives—but these are generally only worn in countries such as Saudi Arabia and Iran, where the rules of proper Islamic dress are strictly enforced. In other Islamic countries, western influences have moderately and, in some cases, greatly altered the traditional fashion customs. But in most Islamic countries there is a considerable amount of social pressure to at least partially conform to Islamic tradition. Proper dress remains important to many Muslims because it is an outward expression of faithfulness to Islamic law.

Justice—Judaism

The Code of Hammurabi was a Babylonian legal code developed by Hammurabi, a king of Babylon who ruled for forty-two years in the eighteenth century BC. The Code of Hammurabi affected the development of law throughout the Middle East and, later, much of the western world. The Code was significant not just because of its reach (it extended beyond criminal law into areas of family law and economics), but because of its system of retribution. "An eye for an eye, a tooth for a tooth" is perhaps its most well known principle. The influence of the Code has been far-reaching. It deeply impacted the development of Jewish law and gives context to many of the writings in the Old Testament of the Bible. Further, since Jewish law later affected Roman law, and since ancient Roman law is the basis of modern western law, the impact of the Code of Hammurabi can still be seen today.

Painting and Sculpture—Buddhism/Hinduism/Jainism

Traditional Indian sculpture was primarily religiously motivated and often made to pay homage to a god (a god associated with Buddhism, Hinduism, or Jainism). Indian sculptors believed that their work should shed light on the spiritual world, inviting people to use their artwork as a passageway to contemplation. Buddhist statues, for example, were often made to look calm and serene, so that when an observer would look upon the statue, he or she would feel the same way. During the Gupta Dynasty, the statues, often made of bronze, further reflected the values of Buddhism in that they were intentionally idealized, elevating the Buddha above the imperfect human form. Hindu statues were similarly religiously motivated. *Siva Nataraja* (Lord of dance) portrays the god Siva spinning inside a wheel, his arms seemingly moving the wheel in the eternal dance of destruction and reconstruction that is so central to the Hindu perception of the cycle of life.

In addition, since Hindus believe the Ganges River flows from the hair of Siva, the statue depicts his hair flowing forth as the river's source. Therefore, as these examples suggest, in many ways sculptures in traditional India were explicitly made to reinforce Buddhist and Hindu values and beliefs.

Social Relationships—Islam

In traditional Islamic cultures, polygamy is not only allowed, but sometimes even encouraged. According to the Koran, the sacred book of Islam, a man may marry up to four wives, but only if he can treat them all equally. Otherwise, a man is advised to marry only once. Most men in traditional Islamic cultures have only one wife. However, in the upper classes polygamy is more common, and in the past it was very common. Although there are obvious drawbacks to polygamy, especially when compared to the value system of most western nations, there are several important advantages. The system allows women who might have otherwise gone unmarried to be provided for. Perhaps even more importantly, it allows an already married man to take in single or widowed women with children and provide a family environment for them.

5. TECHNOLOGICAL DEVELOPMENTS

Atomic Energy

Atomic energy relies on the power contained within every atom. Heavy atoms are split into smaller atoms in a process known as nuclear fission. Light atoms are joined together into one heavier atom in a process known as nuclear fusion. Fission is the process that is used in nuclear bombs and nuclear power plants. Nuclear power plants offer a potentially unlimited amount of energy and are vitally important in areas that lack other consistent sources of energy. In the former Soviet Union, for example, nuclear energy became common in the middle and late twentieth century. Despite the advantages of the energy source, however, there are disadvantages so overwhelming that many people want the process banned entirely. In 1986, an explosion at a nuclear reactor in Chernobyl in the former Soviet Union sent tons of radioactive debris into the atmosphere. The land around the nuclear reactor was severely affected. Thousands of people were evacuated and their crops and livestock were ruined by contact with radioactive particles. Much of the land in the immediate area still cannot be farmed today, and access to the region has been restricted because the overall effects of the explosion are still being monitored. Since the Soviet Union tended to downplay incidents within its own nation, they attempted to solve the problem on their own. The reactor was immediately shut down and an investigation was conducted. It was determined that the reactor's design was flawed. Therefore, the government inspected its other reactors and planned to shut down those with similar flaws. The land around Chernobyl remains contaminated and cleanup has been slow. Still, despite these horrible consequences, many look to nuclear energy as a way of bringing much needed energy to the developing world.

Chemical Fertilizer

Due to the spread of Green Revolution techniques to less developed regions of the world, the use of chemical fertilizers has become increasingly common. And while these fertilizers has had their intended effect—global food production has risen dramatically, as has agricultural yield per acre—these fertilizers have also had many unintended consequences that may cause long-term damage to the environment. For example, chemical fertilizers are not properly absorbed back into the land. Instead, in many cases, chemical fertilizers drain into streams and rivers, contaminating the water and threatening aquatic wildlife and the drinking supply for land-based animals, including humans. Ironically, the regions of the world who need to increase their food production the most, and which therefore have the most to gain from chemical fertilizers, are the same regions of the world that generally lack high environmental standards and enforcement of those standards. As a result, widespread use of chemical fertilizers has arguably caused a significant amount of damage to the environment in a matter of just a few decades.

Computer

In their most simple form, computers are devices used to calculate, or compute. The first, large, digital computer that served as the basis for our modern home and business computers was developed at the University of Pennsylvania in the 1940s and 1950s. When transistors, which are devices used to control electric currents, were applied to computers, scientists could make computers that were both smaller and faster than the first computer. In the 1960s, the invention of the integrated circuit, also known as the chip, further revolutionized computer technology. Computers could now compute thousands of times faster than their predecessors, store an unprecedented amount of information, and occupy only a limited amount of space. This computer revolution changed the world. Computers impacted the global community by making worldwide transportation feasible (computers are used to route airplanes, for example) and worldwide communication commonplace through the use of computer-controlled satellites and networks. The global community has been transformed in what is now known as the Information Age, a time in which our world is growing ever inter-connected through the instant exchange of communication and information from one side of Earth to the other.

Genetic Engineering

Genetics is the study of the hereditary properties of a living organism's cells, and *genetic engineering* is the manipulation of those properties. By manipulating the genes within an organism's cells, scientists have successfully inserted new characteristics into cells that otherwise would not have had these characteristics naturally. For example, transferring genes from hearty plants into frail plants has made those plants more productive and resistant to disease. As a result, thousands of new genetically mutated super-crops have been devised. The implications for food production have been enormous. In addition, genetic engineering has resulted in mass production of insulin for diabetics and will potentially lead to finding cures or ways to avoid genetically caused diseases. Although tremendous ethical and moral issues have plagued the debate concerning the ultimate uses of genetic engineering, when used responsibly, genetic engineering promises new methods of solving age-old problems.

Gunpowder

Invented in China in the ninth century, gunpowder is the oldest known explosive. When the Europeans started using gunpowder in the fourteenth century, they immediately began using it for military purposes. By combining gunpowder with the latest metal technology, they were able to create the most sophisticated guns and cannons of the time period. In the years to follow, Europe began a centuries-long imperialism effort by establishing colonies first in the Americas, and then in Africa and Asia. Since most of the rest of the world had not invested heavily in gunpowder and military technology, in some cases because of a lack of knowledge and in other cases because of a lack of resources, the European military powers were able to conquer much of the world. Therefore, for the Europeans, gunpowder had a positive impact to the extent that it played a significant role in the expansion of European empires. For much of the rest of the world, however, gunpowder had a negative impact for precisely the same reason. From either perspective, however, it is indisputable that gunpowder and the military technology it spawned served to increase the rate and intensity of European cultural diffusion throughout the world.

Printing Press

In the sixteenth century, Guttenberg invented movable type and the printing press was born. The consequences were profound in Europe. Because of the printing press, the ideas of Luther's Reformation spread rapidly, leading to the reorganization of Europe along religious lines. The Bible was printed in popular languages, allowing people to read and interpret it for themselves, rather than relying on the Church hierarchy, thus contributing to individualism. This individualism led to the Enlightenment, which questioned the role of government authority and consequently changed man's relationship with man. All the while, literacy increased dramatically, books became much less expensive, and education became an important goal for millions. In short, the printing press revolutionized Europe and the rest of the world because it brought information to the masses. If knowledge is power, the printing press resulted in a redistribution of power.

Steam Engine

The steam engine made the Industrial Revolution in Europe possible by becoming the principal power source for industry and transport. Steam-powered railroads brought tons of raw materials to steam-powered factories and then took finished products back to the communities that were developing along the rail lines. In the European colonies, the colonists built thousands of miles of railroad lines straight into the heart of areas rich in natural resources, robbing the natives of them. Through the use of steam-powered ships, the Europeans more efficiently carried out their mercantilist policies in the colonies, enabling the powers to control greater and greater expanses of land with ease. Within Europe, the factory system changed daily life, characterized by health hazards, long work, child labor, and mindless repetition. As a result, new political philosophies such as communism became attractive to large numbers of exploited factory workers, while unrestrained capitalism became attractive to many factory owners. Thus, while the steam engine was the catalyst of the Industrial Revolution, it was the engine of social, philosophical, political, and cultural change as well.

6. NOBLE PEACE PRIZE WINNERS

Amnesty International (1977)

Amnesty International was created in 1961 as an organization intent on freeing political prisoners who were arrested because they spoke their conscience. The group also works to bring an end to capital punishment, torture, and other penalties the members believe are excessive. Amnesty International has become particularly important in nations whose governments do not readily protect human rights on their own and who inaccurately report human rights violations within their own borders. In 1977, Amnesty International was instrumental in the release of more than 10,000 political prisoners. For its efforts, the group won the Nobel Peace Prize. Perhaps most importantly, however, the group has raised awareness of human rights abuses in nations that much of the industrialized world has traditionally ignored. This awareness has prompted the governments of nations with good human rights records to influence changes in nations with poor records.

Mother Teresa (1979)

Mother Teresa, a Christian Missionary in India, dedicated her life to helping others. In 1925, she moved to India to teach at a convent, but in the1940s left the convent to work among the destitute, devoting her heart, mind, and hands to those in need. As word of her compassion and generosity spread, she served as a model for others. With the gain in momentum, Mother Teresa was able to secure the funds to open schools, a house for the dying, and eventually founded an international organization known as the Missionaries of Charity. For her efforts, she was awarded the Nobel Peace Prize in 1979. She died in 1997, having spent virtually her entire adult life in service to others.

Lech Walesa (1983)

Lech Walesa received the Nobel Peace Prize in 1983 in recognition for his efforts to improve the plight of his fellow Polish workers. Under the leadership of Lech Walesa, the organization know as Solidarity began in Poland in 1980. It began as a shipyard strike with the simple goal of improving working conditions and employee compensation. Walesa's negotiation abilities won a quick decisive victory for the strikers, and soon other workers in Poland wanted the same results. These other workers urged Walesa to continue striking in a show of *solidarity*, or unity. He did, and within just one year, Solidarity represented ten million workers and was registered with the Polish government. In 1981, the military government banned Solidarity, and Walesa was imprisoned. This resulted in a new agenda for the organization: political reform. Even with Walesa in prison, Solidarity continued to strike against the government-run industries in an effort to force political change. By 1989, after Solidarity was re-legalized, the government was dominated by members of Solidarity, as opposed to members of the Communist party who had previously dominated the government. In 1990, Walesa became the president of Poland. The economic and political goals of Solidarity, therefore, now had the force of the government behind them.

Elie Wiesel (1986)

Elie Wiesel won the Nobel Peace Prize in 1986 in recognition for his lifelong efforts to eradicate the causes and consequences of institutionalized hatred. As a Jewish man whose family was killed in Aushwitz during World War II, Wiesel was all too familiar with the horrors of institutionalized racism taken to its most brutal extremes. His haunting memories of the Holocaust found expression through his writings. His books, both fictional and non-fictional, are among the world's starkest reminders of man's destructive potential. Wiesel has not written such powerful words simply to express sorrow, however. Rather, his main goal has been to educate future generations of the importance of mutual respect and understanding, and it is for this effort that he won the Nobel Peace Prize.

Mikhail Gorbachev (1990)

Mikhail Gorbachev received the Nobel Peace Prize in recognition of his efforts to end the Cold War. Gorbachev reversed the Brezhnev Doctrine that had served as the justification for Soviet military and political involvement in Eastern Europe and beyond, he reduced the Soviet's military capacity by signing arms control agreements with the United States, and he relaxed political and social control over the citizens of the Soviet Union, who in turn were able to more freely choose their own destiny. For all of these reasons, Mikhail Gorbachev is viewed as a man who changed his country's path from destructive policies toward more peaceful policies.

Rigoberta Menchu (1992)

Rigoberta Menchu received the Nobel Peace Prize in 1992 for her ceaseless efforts against the Guatemalan government's inhumane campaign against the native Indian peasant population. A Mayan Indian, Menchu lost most of her family to atrocities carried out by the Guatemalan government. Her father was killed in the 1970's while protesting the policies of the government. In 1979, her brother was tortured and burned by the military and killed. The following year, Menchu's mother was raped and mutilated by Guatemalan soldiers. Although she fled to Mexico in 1981, Menchu did not put her past behind her. Instead, she worked tirelessly to organize an international effort against the human rights abuses of the Guatemalan government. The publication in 1983 of her book *I, Rigoberta Menchu* soon led to worldwide recognition of a previously ignored problem in Guatemala. Today, Rigoberta Menchu is a leading public speaker against human rights violations.

Nelson Mandela and F.W. de Klerk (1993)

Nelson Mandela and F.W. de Klerk jointly received the Nobel Peace Prize in 1993 for their efforts to transform South Africa from a nation divided due to racial apartheid laws, to a nation in which all citizens are given equal fundamental rights. For decades, Mandela had been working for the abolishment of the apartheid system, which segregated blacks from whites and severely limited basic opportunities for blacks. He headed the some-times-violent African National Congress, an organization dedicated to the abolishment of apartheid, and was jailed by South Africa's government. In 1989, South African President de Klerk bowed to international and domes-tic pressure to move away from complete apartheid by calling for the rights of minorities to control their own affairs. He legalized mass demonstrations and released political prisoners, including Mandela. In response, the African National Congress agreed to curb violence. De Klerk then began the process of integration by agreeing to phase out specific homelands for blacks and by granting all citizens the right to vote. This sweeping change of events in South Africa led to Mandela's election as president in 1994, but not before he jointly accepted the Nobel Peace Prize with de Klerk. It is difficult to imagine that apartheid would have been abolished without Mandela's persistence and de Klerk's willingness to compromise.

Yasir Arafat, Yitzhak Rabin, and Shimon Peres (1994)

Yasir Arafat, Yitzhak Rabin and Shimon Peres were jointly given the Nobel Peace Prize in 1994 for their movement toward peace in the Middle East. The three men signed a 1994 agreement that gave Palestinians in Gaza and the West Bank limited self-rule, signaling a new era of cooperation between Israelis and Palestinians. Although peace in the Middle East has not been secured in the years since, the agreement still stands as a significant move toward mutual recognition between Palestinians and Israelis.

7. ECONOMIC POLICIES

France (1200–1500)

In the early Middle Ages, France's feudal manors were at the heart of its agricultural economy. Peasants lived in small villages on the manor, farming the land in part for themselves and in part for their lord. By 1200, improvements in agricultural technology led to an increase in food production, and as a direct consequence, the population increased. Soon the small farming villages became crowded. Since only a fraction of the population was now needed to farm the fields, an increasing percentage of the population had opportunities to engage in other kinds of economic activities. This new group of people became known as the *burghers*, since they lived in burgs (or villages), which later became the *bourgeoisie*. As years passed, the bourgeoisie manufactured an increasing number of consumer goods such as shoes and glassware, and provided services such as tailoring. Most significantly of all, they invented the *guild system*. Trade guilds were formed by merchants who wanted to establish a set of rules. Eventually, the guilds controlled all trade within their town of operation. They fixed prices, supply, and even a system of standard weights and measures for each product sold, such as the appropriate size for a loaf of bread. At first, the goods were sold to those within the town and the surrounding farmland. However, as time went by, the villagers increasingly relied on trade, especially as the commercial revolution transformed local economies into regional banking and investment endeavors.

Belgian Congo (1890–1960)

Prior to independence in 1960, the Congo's resources and native population were exploited by the mercantilist policies of Belgium. King Leopold II of Belgium seized control of the Congo's natural resources such as copper, rubber, and ivory. While the natives of the Congo endured the hard labor of the fields and mines, the King and the wealthy landowners became rich by exporting the resources to other European powers. Since these valuable resources were traded as if they belonged to Belgium and not to the Congo, the people of the Congo received nothing in return, even as the landscape was stripped of its economic value. This disastrous policy continued for multiple generations until the Congo finally gained its independence from Belgium in 1960.

Soviet Union (1917–1985)

After the Soviet Union was created in 1917, Lenin established a command economy that redistributed land and industries into collectives intended to benefit the entire population. Eventually, all major means of production were controlled by the government, and all economic policies were derived and carried out by a central authority. The government not only set prices and wages, but also determined the supply of all goods and services. Unfortunately for most Soviets, the government placed a high priority on heavy industry, so for nearly three generations machines, weapons, and steel were churned out with much greater frequency than were consumer products. Therefore, even though a great percentage of the manufacturing output was consumed within the country, the daily lives of the individual citizens didn't reflect this consumption. As such, the gap in the material quality of life between the average Soviet and his western counterpart widened with each passing year. This economic policy continued until the late 1980's when significant market forces were introduced into the economy, eventually leading to the downfall of the Soviet Union and a command economy.

Israel (1949–present)

When Israel was created in 1949, it quickly emerged as a modern "western" power. This emergence was due to the millions of Jews who poured into the new nation from all over the world, particularly Europe and the United States. Since throughout history, Jews were often denied the opportunity to own land, tens of thousands of Jews established their wealth through manufacturing and banking as opposed to farming. In recent centuries, the Jewish population as a whole economically benefited as a result, and so by the time the new nation of Israel was created, significant capital and know-how was already in place for the establishment of a modern economy. From the start, the new nation of Israel placed a premium on skilled workers, commerce, and trade. Isreal quickly achieved a relatively high standard of living. Although the nation is small in size, its economy is sound due to its diversity. Israel relies heavily on diverse industries such as diamond cutting, electronics, textiles, and public services, and also relies heavily on exports and trade with the United States, Europe, Japan, and South Africa.

Japan (1950–present)

At the close of World War II, which was economically devastating to Japan, the country lost its colonies and with them its access to the raw materials that are lacking within its own borders. As a result, the government of Japan quickly focused on the one resource it had plenty of: people. By spending billions on technical schools and infrastructure, Japan managed to establish a manufacturing base that added considerable value to the raw materials it imported. Products such as machine tools, autos, electronics, TVs, transistors, cameras, and computers poured off the assembly lines. All of these products had one thing in common: They were much more valuable than cost of the materials used to create them. As a result, from the 1950s to the 1970s, Japan had the highest economic growth rate in the world. What's more, since Japanese workers are employed for life, their loyalty to the companies for which they work is almost unparalleled in the world, thus contributing to an even more efficient economy since relatively little energy has to be spent on the training and hiring process. The products made by these knowledge-intensive industries were first intended for use within Japan, and the government policies contributed to this effort by establishing protectionist trading policies. Eventually, Japan dramatically increased its exports to offset the raw materials it was importing. Since the finished products are worth considerably more than the raw materials used in their creation, and since Japan's protectionist trade policies have continued into the present, Japan has been able to build up a sizable trade surplus.

Brazil (1950–present)

In the decades since World War II, Brazil's economy has been rocky, but has nevertheless ultimately moved toward the establishment of a relatively stable market economy. In the 1950s, foreign investment was encouraged, especially in the heavy industries such as transportation and steel. In addition, consumer goods became more abundant than ever before, their price and availability determined on the open market. In the 1960s, however, a military coup resulted in a reversion to a command economy wherein wages, prices, and supply were determined not by the marketplace, but by government decision-makers. Foreign investment was severely, although temporarily, curtailed. Since the mid-1980s, however, the new democratically elected government abandoned command economics and reinstituted market forces. Today, Brazil's emerging middle class is evidence that market economics, when applied to the country's vast resources, have allowed millions of Brazilians to improve their standard of living.

EXAMINATION
AUGUST 1998

Part I (55 credits): Answer all 48 questions in this part.

Directions (1–48): For each statement or question, write on the separate answer sheet the number of the word or expression that, of those given, best completes the statement or answers the question.

---

1 Which two nations are archipelagoes?

  1 Japan and the Philippines
  2 Egypt and Israel
  3 Spain and France
  4 Cuba and Mexico

2 Many Japanese industries use industrial diamonds from South Africa and oil from Indonesia to create consumer goods that are then exported to other nations. This situation demonstrates the concept of

  1 regionalism   3 interdependence
  2 social mobility   4 mercantilism

[OVER]

3 Which statement best describes an effect of the Opium War on China?

1 The British expelled all Chinese from Hong Kong.
2 The British victory led to spheres of influence in China.
3 The British ended the importing of opium into China.
4 The British established a parliamentary democracy in China.

4 Despite increasing contact with the Chinese prior to the 19th century, Europeans had little impact on China's culture mainly because

1 the Chinese viewed their culture as superior to that of the Europeans
2 the Europeans had forbidden their missionaries from going to China
3 Japanese culture had become the dominant culture in China
4 Confucian custom prohibited the Chinese from speaking to the Europeans

5 During the Communist-Nationalist civil war, Chiang Kai-shek lost the support of the Chinese people mainly because he

1 refused to accept support from foreign nations
2 defeated the forces of Deng Xiaoping
3 signed an alliance with Great Britain
4 ignored the needs of the peasant population

6 One aspect common to both Shinto and Taoism is a
   1 deep reverence and respect for nature
   2 belief in one God
   3 ban on the consumption of pork
   4 belief in the reincarnation of souls

   Base your answer to question 7 on the poem below and on your knowledge of social studies.

> May our country
> Taking what is good
> And rejecting what is bad
> Be not inferior
> to any other
>
> —Mutsuhito

7 According to this Japanese poem, Mutsuhito believed Japan should modernize by
   1 completely changing Japanese society
   2 borrowing selectively from other societies
   3 controlling other cultures that were superior
   4 rejecting foreign influences

8 Japanese imperialism increased in Southeast Asia
   during the first half of the 20th century as a result of Japan's
   1 decision to join the League of Nations
   2 desire to spread Shinto
   3 attempts to impose capitalism in the region
   4 efforts to become a political and economic power

[OVER]

9 Which statement is valid about modern Japan?

   1 Most Japanese continue to worship the Emperor as a god.

   2 Japan is a nation that includes many ethnic minority groups.

   3 As an urban, industrialized nation, Japan continues to preserve many elements of its traditional culture.

   4 Japan's isolationist policies continue to limit its influence in world affairs.

10 A negative effect of the partitioning of India in 1947 was that

   1 foreign rule was reestablished in India

   2 Hinduism became the only religion practiced in India

   3 the government policy of nonalignment further divided Indian society

   4 civil unrest, territorial disputes, and religious conflicts continued throughout the region

11 In India today, the caste system continues to have the most influence on Hindu people who

   1 live in rural areas

   2 have been educated in the West

   3 attend colleges in India

   4 have industrial jobs in urban areas

Base your answer to question 12 on the cartoon below and on your knowledge of social studies.

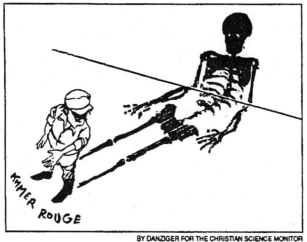

BY DANZIGER FOR THE CHRISTIAN SCIENCE MONITOR

12 The main idea of the cartoon is that the Khmer Rouge

1 is responsible for the genocide practiced in Cambodia in the past

2 is most responsible for the problem of over-population in Cambodia today

3 continues to force an agrarian economy on Cambodia

4 has widespread popular support

[OVER]

13 One way in which Singapore, Hong Kong, and Taiwan are similar is that each

1 is currently experiencing ethnic conflicts
2 was formerly controlled by the Soviet Union
3 has a free-market economy
4 is currently controlled by a communist goverment

14 One major effect of the European slave trade on Africa was that the slave trade

1 strengthened the traditional African Economic systems
2 led to a rapid decrease in tribal warfare
3 hastened the decline of African Kingdoms
4 increased the number of trade routes across the Sahara

15 Which statement about the European partitioning of Africa the 1800's is most accurate?

1 Europeans drew colonial borders based on African tribal boundaries.
2 The African Continent was divided equally among the colonial powers.
3 European control did much to improve the economies of most tribal groups.
4 African cultural and ethnic traditions were often ignored by colonial governments.

16 In the Republic of South Africa, pass laws were abolished in 1986, segregation in public places was ended in 1990, and the remaining apartheid laws were abolished in 1994. The events were partially the result of the

1 increasing influence of the white minority government
2 success of the economic sanctions placed on the South Africa by many foreign nations
3 defeat of Nelson Mandela in the 1994 South African election
4 United Nations expelling South Africa from the organization

17 Which characteristic is common to the Maya, Aztec, and Inca civilizations?

1 advancement of scientific knowledge
2 origin in the Andes Mountains
3 equality of all members of society
4 territorial expansion without warfare

18 Since the Cuban Revolution of 1959, a major goal of the government of Fidel Castro has been to

1 strengthen its political ties to the United States
2 convince Latin American nations to withdraw from the United Nations
3 encourage large United States corporations to invest in Cuba
4 reform Cuban society using socialist ideals

[OVER]

19 Economic development in Latin American nations has been hindered most by

1 a scarcity of goods produced for trade and a lack of natural resources.
2 governments that are primarily concerned with preserving the environment
3 problems of overpopulation, land distribution, and lack of investment capital
4 corporations that are not interested in the use of modern technology

20 Which statement is most accurate about Latin America today?

1 Elections in several Central and South American nations have brought communist governments to power.
2 Military governments or dictatorships have been replaced by democracies in many Latin American nations.
3 Most Latin American governments are encouraging subsistence agriculture.
4 Debts owed to most foreign nations have been paid.

21 An important achievement of the Golden Age of Muslim culture was the

1 preservation of ancient Greek and Roman ideas
2 development of gunpowder
3 establishment of trade with South America
4 emergence of feudalism as a unifying force

22 Which situation has limited economic development in much of the Middle East?

1 abundance of water resources
2 political instability
3 geographic isolation
4 lack of deep-water seaports

23 Which term refers to the Jewish movement to establish a homeland in Palestine?

1 Zionism   3 animism
2 secularism   4 Marxism

24 The 1979 signing of the Camp David accords led directly to

1 the assassination of Israeli Prime Minister Menachem Begin
2 Palestinian self-rule in the West Bank and Gaza Strip
3 a military alliance between Arab nations
4 a formal peace agreement between Egypt and Israel

25 A nation governed by Islamic fundamentalists would be most likely to

1 allow many different interpretations of the Koran
2 adopt the values and culture of the West
3 emphasize the traditional beliefs and values of the religion
4 promote active participation of women in government

[OVER]

26 All citizens in ancient Athens had the right to attend the Assembly, where they could meet in open discussion and cast votes. This situation is an example of

1 direct democracy
2 totalitarianism
3 parliamentary democracy
4 absolutism

27 Which statement about the social structure in Europe during the Middle Ages is most accurate?

1 The nobles encouraged social mobility.
2 The practices of the Catholic Church led to the development of a classless society.
3 Sharp class distinctions divided European society.
4 Industrialization led to the growth of socialism throughout Europe.

28 As the Middle Ages ended, the rise of a middle class in western Europe can be attributed to the

1 economic policies of the Roman Empire
2 increase in trade that resulted from the Crusades
3 strength of Christianity in medieval Europe
4 self-sufficiency of the manor system

29 In the 17th and 18th centuries, the theory of divine right was most often used to justify the

1 involvement of peasants in making political decisions
2 introduction of free trade policies
3 supreme power of the Catholic Church
4 establishment of an absolute monarchy

30 In western Europe, the Protestant Reformation brought an end to

1 the colonial period
2 strong central governments
3 religious unity
4 market economies

31 A primary cause of the French Revolution in 1789 was the

1 increasing dissatisfaction of the Third Estate
2 rise to power of Napoleon Bonaparte
3 actions of Prince Metternich
4 execution of Louis XVI

32 Karl Marx and Friedrich Engels encouraged workers to improve their economic conditions by

1 overthrowing the capitalist system
2 increasing the tax rate
3 supporting small regional governments
4 establishing tariffs

33 Which statement best explains why many Germans became discontented with the Weimar Republic in the early 1930's?

1 The failure to slow population growth in Germany had created shortages of basic necessities.
2 The leaders of the German Government were not elected by universal suffrage.
3 The German Government had refused to join the League of Nations.
4 Germany was experiencing widespread unemployment and other economic problems.

[OVER]

34 The formation of the North Atlantic Treaty Organization (NATO) and the European Union (EU) are examples of Western Europe's

1 responses to the oil embargo of 1974
2 attempts to solve mutual problems
3 efforts to maintain control of colonial empires
4 struggles for economic self-reliance

35 Which group had the greatest influence on early Russian culture?

1 Franks
2 Ottoman Turks
3 Byzantine Empire
4 Roman Catholic Church

36 One similarity between Russia under the czars and the Soviet Union under Joseph Stalin is that in both types of government these leaders

1 tried to reduce their nation's influence in world affairs
2 developed policies to limit industrial growth
3 supported the creation of a national church
4 established an authoritarian form of government

37 One similarity between V. I. Lenin's New Economic Policy and Mikhail Gorbachev's policy of perestroika is that both policies

1 supported collectivization of farms in the Soviet Union
2 allowed some aspects of capitalism in the Soviet economy
3 increased citizen participation in the Soviet Government
4 strengthened governmental control over the Soviet Republics

38 In the late 1980's, Mikhail Gorbachev's decision to stop interfering in the internal affairs of Eastern European nations led directly to

1 the collapse of the free-market economies in the region
2 an increase in Cold War tensions
3 a renewal of religious violence between Orthodox Christians and Russian Jews
4 the collapse of the communist governments in the region

39 In many developing nations, rising levels of pollution and continued housing shortages are a direct result of

1 increased urbanization
2 a reliance on single-crop economies
3 changing climatic conditions
4 increasing nationalism

[OVER]

Base your answer to question 40 on the chart below and on your knowledge of social studies.

World Oil Reserves by Region and Availability		
Region	**Oil Reserves (billion barrels)**	**Availability (number of years)**
Middle East	660	110
Latin America	125	51
Former Soviet Union & Eastern Europe	60	13
Africa	59	28
Asia, Australia, & New Zealand	47	20
North America	42	10
Western Europe	18	13
World	1,011	44

Source: *State of the World 1991*, W.W. Norton

40 Which conclusion about world oil reserves can best be drawn from the information in the chart?

1 Most of the people in Latin America are employed by the oil industry.
2 Searching for alternative fuel sources is no longer necessary.
3 The Middle East accounts for less than half the world's oil reserves.
4 The former Soviet Union and Eastern Europe have fewer years of oil reserves available than Africa does.

41 Genocide in Rwanda, apartheid in South Africa, and labor camps for dissidents in the Soviet Union are all examples of

1 war crimes
2 acts of international terrorism
3 violations of human rights
4 civil disobedience

42 Why are the Suez Canal, the strait of Hormuz, the Dardenelles, and the Bosporus strategic waterways?

1 The nation that controls these waterways can have economic control over other nations.
2 They are natural geographic boundaries and have often separated warring nations.
3 They are located along the Tropic of Cancer, the Equator, or the Tropic of Capricorn.
4 The nations that adjoin these waterways depend on them as a source of fresh water.

43 Economic sanctions were imposed against Saddam Hussein in Iraq and Fidel Castro in Cuba in an effort to

1 encourage exports to those nations by removing tariffs
2 force these leaders from power by isolating their nations from the world community
3 increase the power of the military forces of those nations
4 prevent smaller regional conflicts form turning into larger global conflicts

[OVER]

44 During the 1990's, the Chechens the Sikhs, and the Tibetans have all protested their lack of

1 membership in the European Union
2 economic stability
3 independent homelands
4 representation in the Arab League

45 The Dome of the Rock, Chichén Itzá, and the Hagia Sophia were built for the purpose of

1 religious worship
2 public punishment
3 trade
4 government

46 One difference between the war in Korea in the early 1950's and the war in Vietnam in the late 1960's is that

1 the United Nations played a major role in ending the war in Vietnam, but a minor role in ending the war in Korea
2 tactical nuclear weapons were used in Korea, but not in Vietnam
3 after the wars ended, Korea remained a divided nation, but Vietnam was reunited under a communist government
4 United States forces played a minor role in the war in Korea, but a major role in the war in Vietnam

47 "Take sides. Neutrality helps the oppressor, never the victim. Silence encourages the tormentor, never the tormented."

— Elie Wiesel, Holocaust survivor

Based on this quotation, which situation would have most concerned Elie Wiesel?

1 formation of the United Nations
2 the world's initial reaction to ethnic cleansing in Bosnia
3 Arab reaction to the creation of Israel in 1948
4 dismantling of the Berlin Wall

48 In the spring of 1998, which two nations caused world concern with their underground testing of nuclear weapons?

1 Japan and Egypt 　 3 Germany and Cuba
2 Mexico and Chile 　 4 India and Pakistan

[OVER]

Answers to the following questions are to be written on paper provided by the school.

Students Please Note:

In developing your answers to Part II, be sure to

(1) include specific factual information and evidence whenever possible

(2) keep to the questions asked; do not go off on tangents

(3) avoid overgeneralizations or sweeping statements without sufficient proof; do not overstate your case

(4) keep these general definitions in mind:

    (a) <u>discuss</u> means "to make observations about something using facts, reasoning, and argument; to present in some detail"

    (b) <u>describe</u> means "to illustrate something in words or tell about it"

    (c) <u>show</u> means "to point out; to set forth clearly a position or idea by stating it and giving data which support it"

    (d) <u>explain</u> means "to make plain or understandable; to give reasons for or causes of; to show the logical development or relationships of"

Part II

1 In the 20th century, many nations or regions have faced various crises that have led to international efforts to resolve those crises.

Nations/Regions in Crisis

Manchuria in 1931
Poland in 1939
South Korea in 1949
Egypt in 1956
Kuwait in 1991
Somalia in 1992
Bosnia in1995

Select *three* nations or regions in crisis and for *each* one selected:

- Explain why the situation in the nation or region was considered a crisis
- Identify an international group or organization that attempted to resolve the crisis and discuss the extent to which that international effort was successful [5,5,5]

2 Leaders must often deal with specific events or problems facing their nations.

Leaders — Nations

Queen Isabella I — Spain
Elizabeth I — England
Peter the Great — Russia
Maximilien Robespierre — France
Kemal Atatürk — Turkey

[OVER]

Joseph Stalin — Soviet Union
Mao Zedong — China

Select *three* of the leaders listed and for *each* one selected:

- Identify a specific event or problem the leader faced in his or her nation

- Discuss an action taken by the leader dealing with that event or problem

- Discuss *one* effect of that action on the leader's nation [5,5,5]

3 Religions and philosophies have influenced various cultures in many areas of the world.

Religions/Philosophies

Animism
Buddhism
Christianity
Confucianism
Islam
Judaism

Select *three* religions or philosophies listed and for *each* one selected:

- Identify a specific region or nation where that religion or philosophy has had a significant influence [Do *not* use the United States in your answer.]

- Describe *one* specific belief or practice of that religion or philosophy [You must use a different belief or practice for each religion selected.]

- Explain a lasting impact of that religion or philosophy on a culture in the nation or region. [5,5,5]

4   Geographic factors have often had a negative impact on the history and culture of many regions of the world.

Regions

Africa
Asia
Europe
Latin America
Middle East

a   Select *three* regions from the list and for *each* region selected:

* Identify *one* geographic factor that has had a *negative* impact on the region [You must use a different type of geographic factor for each region selected.]

* Identify *one* specific nation from the region affected by the geographic factor

* Discuss a specific problem related to the geographic factor in that nation [4,4,4]

b   For *one* nation selected in part *a*, discuss how that nation has tried to overcome the problem associated with the geographic factor you identified. [3]

5   Inventions and technological advances often lead to a major change in societies.

Societies

Ancient Egyptian (3500 – 1090 B.C)
Maya (300 – 900)
Islamic (600 – 1200)
Western European (1400 – 1700)
British (1700 – 1900)

[OVER]

Japanese (1853 – present)
South Asian (1970 – present)

Select *three* societies form the list and for *each* one selected:

- Identify and describe an invention or a specific technological advance associated with that society [You must use a different invention or technological advance for each society selected.]

- Discuss a social, political, or economic effect of that invention or technological advance on that society [5,5,5]

6 In the 20th century, many instances of human rights violations have occurred. Several groups whose human rights have been violated are listed below.

Groups

Chiapas Indians in Mexico
Women in China
Political dissidents in the Soviet Union
Jews in Europe
Indigenous peoples in Brazil
Kurds in Iraq
Untouchables in India

Select *three* groups from the list and for *each* one selected:

- Describe a specific way this group's human rights have been violated

- Explain a historical, political, economic, *or* cultural factor that led to this human rights violation [5,5,5]

7 Imperialism, colonialism, and independence movements are major forces that have changed the relationships between people in many different areas of the world.

  a Identify *one* imperialistic European nation and select *one* specific nation or region in Asia, Africa, Latin America, or the Middle East that was controlled by the European power you identified. [2]

  b Explain why that European nation chose to become imperialistic. [3]

  c Explain the impact of imperialism on the people and culture of the nation or region under European control. [5]

  d Describe the way the nation or region under European control became independent. [5]

[OVER]

ANSWER KEY
AUGUST 1998—PART I

1	1		25	3
2	3		26	1
3	2		27	3
4	1		28	2
5	4		29	4
6	1		30	3
7	2		31	1
8	4		32	1
9	3		33	4
10	4		34	2
11	1		35	3
12	1		36	4
13	3		37	2
14	3		38	4
15	4		39	1
16	2		40	4
17	1		41	3
18	4		42	1
19	3		43	2
20	2		44	3
21	1		45	1
22	2		46	3
23	1		47	2
24	4		48	4

ANSWERS AND EXPLANATIONS
AUGUST 1998—PART I

1. Archipelagoes are groups of islands. If you didn't know that, this question might have been difficult. But if you remembered that *archipelago* is a geographic term, you chose an answer choice with two nations that are similar in some geographic way.

    1 Both Japan and the Philippines are archipelagoes. Japan contains four main islands; the Philippines consists of eleven major islands and thousands of smaller islands.

    2 Neither Egypt nor Israel is an archipelago.

    3 Neither Spain nor France is an archipelago.

    4 Cuba is an island nation, but not an archipelago because it is comprised of a single island instead of a group of islands. Mexico isn't even a single island.

2. According to the question, Japan is importing raw materials from South Africa and Indonesia and transforming them into consumer goods, which are then exported to others. Three of the terms in the answer choices, including the correct answer, are in the Hit Parade.

    1 *Regionalism* is a commitment to other nations within your region (East Asian countries, for example). The question, however, refers to a global situation in which Japan is importing from other regions and then exporting to still other regions.

    2 Nothing in this question refers to social mobility. The situation described in the question refers to one nation interacting with other nations, not individuals within a nation interacting with other individuals. Review *social mobility* in the Hit Parade if you chose this answer.

    3 This is the best answer. Japan is dependent on other nations for the raw materials it needs to manufacture consumer goods. What's more, Japan is dependent on global markets to buy the consumer goods once it has manufactured them. Viewed from another perspective, South Africa and Indonesia are increasingly dependent on Japan to buy their resources, and the global community is increasingly dependent on Japan for its consumer goods. This is an example of interdependence. Review the term in the Hit Parade if you missed this question.

4 Mercantilism is somewhat similar to the situation described in the question, but it's not the same thing. Mercantilism is an economic policy adopted by an imperial nation as a way of exploiting its colonies. A mercantilist nation takes raw materials from its colonies, uses them in the manufacturing process, and then sells the finished products back to the colonies. The situation described in the question is not one between an imperial nation and its colonies, but between independent and sovereign nations who have become economically dependent on each other. Look up *mercantilism* in the Hit Parade if you picked this answer.

3. You should make sure you know about the Opium War in China, because it shows up on the test fairly frequently. Review it in your global studies materials if you need to. Nevertheless, don't forget to evaluate the answer choices wisely. Eliminate answer choices that describe things that never happened. Alternatively, focus on an answer choice that describes something important that you might remember from your Global Studies course.

1 This answer choice is much too extreme. The British did not expel all Chinese from Hong Kong. Rather, the British took control of Hong Kong. They wanted the Chinese there, however, because they wanted the Chinese to buy their products and work for them!

2 As a result of the Opium War, British spheres of influence were established in China. Look up *spheres of influence* in the Hit Parade if you missed this question. The opium situation just happens to be described in the explanation in the Hit Parade. Isn't that convenient?

3 No! The British *wanted* to import opium into China. The British were making a lot of money as a result of this trading.

4 The British did not establish a parliamentary democracy. Instead, it established spheres of influence. A parliamentary democracy would have been disastrous for the British, since in a parliamentary democracy the interests of citizens are represented, and the vast majority of Chinese citizens were resentful of the British influence in their country.

4. According the question, the situation is this: The Chinese were interacting with the Europeans, and yet the Europeans didn't have much impact on the Chinese. You want to find an answer choice that explains why this is. Don't forget to eliminate answer choices that never occurred in the first place, and therefore couldn't possibly be the right answer. Focus on an answer choice that describes a situation that the Regents think is important—in other words, an answer choice that describes a concept the Regents test frequently.

   1 **This answer choice just makes sense. If you think you're superior to someone else, then you can interact with him without being influenced by him. This was the attitude of the Chinese prior to the nineteenth century (it was also the attitude of the Europeans, so even though the Chinese and the British were in constant contact, they still pretty much stayed true to their own cultures). This type of attitude is known as *ethnocentrism*, which is a favorite concept of the Regents. Make sure you review it in the Hit Parade.**

   2 This isn't true. The Europeans encouraged their missionaries to go to China. When the Chinese finally revolted against European imperialism in the Boxer Rebellion, some of these missionaries lost their lives.

   3 Japanese culture has never been the dominant culture in China.

   4 Confucian custom did not prohibit the Chinese from speaking to the Europeans. If it had, how would there have been an increase in contact between the Europeans and Chinese in the first place? Mimes?

5. If you don't remember much about the Communist Revolution in China, you should take the time to study it, because it's tested frequently—and it's in the Hit Parade. In the meantime, focus on an answer choice that is almost impossible to disagree with. Why do most world leaders fall into disfavor with their own people?

   1 Chiang Kai-shek didn't refuse to accept support from foreign nations.

   2 Chiang Kai-shek didn't defeat the forces of Deng Xioping. Deng fought on the side of Mao's communists, who were ultimately victorious.

   3 Chiang Kai-shek didn't sign an alliance with Great Britain.

   4 **This is the best answer. Chiang Kai-shek ignored the needs of the peasant population, even as malnutrition and starvation became commonplace. Chiang's bad judgment led to the downfall of the nationalists, since the peasants looked to the communists to increase their standard of living.**

6. You need to know the basics about major world religions to do well on this test. If you're sketchy on Taoism and Shinto, at least eliminate answer choices that specifically refer to a religion that you *do* know about, since the test writers are banking on the idea that some students will get confused.

   1 This is the best answer. Both religions are centered on nature. Look up Shinto in the Hit Parade if you missed this question.

   2 Neither religion is monotheistic.

   3 Neither religion bans the consumption of pork. If you chose this answer, you're probably thinking of Islam or Judaism.

   4 Neither religion believes in the reincarnation of souls. That's Hinduism.

7. Mutsuhito suggests that Japan take what is good and reject what is bad. All you have to do is paraphrase this idea to get this question right.

   1 This answer choice uses extreme language, so be very skeptical. Mutsuhito is not suggesting a complete change, but rather a partial change (taking what is good and rejecting what is bad).

   2 This is the best answer. By taking what is good and rejecting what is bad, a country is borrowing selectively.

   3 The poem doesn't refer to controlling other countries. Mutsuhito talks about what Japan can do for itself.

   4 Mutsuhito most certainly doesn't suggest that Japan reject foreign influences, or else he wouldn't have suggested that Japan take "what is good."

8. If you're unfamiliar with Japanese history between the Meiji Restoration and World War II, review the basics, since it's a favorite time period of the Regents. As the question states, during this time Japanese imperialism in Southeast Asia increased. If you don't remember why imperialism increased, choose the most general, most difficult-to-argue-with answer choice. More generally, think of the reasons *any* imperialist nation was that way. Finally, as always, eliminate answer choices that don't make sense.

   1 Imperialism wasn't a requirement for membership in the League of Nations. In fact, since the League of Nations was a body of sovereign countries, to a certain degree, imperialism was inconsistent with the goals of the organization.

   2 The desire to spread Shinto was not a motivation behind Japanese imperialism. Shinto is not an evangelical, or universalizing, religion.

Rather, it is a religion so intertwined with the Japanese culture that it seems out of place outside of Japan. In any case, Japanese imperialism did not increase due to a desire to spread Shinto.

3 Japan did not have a desire to impose capitalism in the region. If that were the case, it would have been difficult for Japan to maintain its colonies, since as capitalists the colonies would treat Japan as a customer instead of as an authority.

4 Of course this is the answer! Why would a nation colonize other nations? To become powerful! In the specific case of Japan, it colonized other nations in order to gain inexpensive access to the raw materials it lacked.

9. If you're not sure of the answer, at least eliminate answer choices that seem inconsistent with anything you *do* know about modern Japan.

1 This is not true. After Japan was defeated in World War II, the Emperor of Japan was forced to publicly declare that he was not, in fact, a deity, as he had previously claimed. The public disavowal pretty much brought an end to emperor worship in Japan.

2 Japan is actually an extremely homogeneous country. In fact, it's one of the least ethnically diverse countries on the planet.

3 This is the best answer. Japan is modern and industrialized in an economic sense, and yet traditional in a social and cultural sense.

4 Japan is not isolationist at all. It is a main player in global interdependence.

10. You should definitely know about the partitioning of India in 1947, since the Regents ask a question about it almost every time. Remember, eliminate answer choices that are too extreme. And eliminate answer choices that do not describe a clear negative effect.

1 In 1947, the Indian subcontinent gained its independence from British rule. As such, foreign rule ended in 1947, so this can't be the answer.

2 This answer is too extreme. While it's true that Hinduism dominated India as a result of many Muslims moving to neighboring Pakistan, Hinduism was not the *only* religion practiced in India. What's more, it's not clear that even if this were true that it would be negative.

3 The government policy of nonalignment was not an effect of the partitioning of India in the first place. What's more, the policy of nonalignment was a unifying force, not a divisive force, since by staying neutral, the government refrained from favoring some citizens' policies over others.

4 The partitioning of India did not ease the civil unrest, territorial disputes, and religious conflicts in the region. Indeed, the partitioning of India might have contributed to this unrest since each of the disputing factions (Pakistan and India) now had an entire governmental framework on its side, as opposed to one government that was working to ease the tension between the warring factions. This unrest remains today, and has actually been exacerbated by recent developments (see question 48).

11. Look up *caste system* in the Hit Parade if you missed this question. If you're still not sure of the answer, you need to realize that the caste system is part of the Hindu religion in India, and is therefore part of the cultural tradition of the country. Which answer choice describes a group of people who are most likely to adhere to the cultural traditions of a country?

1 **This is the best answer. People who live in rural areas are much more likely to favor traditional customs than their urban counterparts. Look up *traditional society* in the Hit Parade for a detailed explanation.**

2 There are two reasons to strike this answer. First, formally educated people are less likely to continue cultural traditions than those who are not. Second, since these people were educated specifically in the West, there is even more reason to suspect that they would not adhere to the caste system, since the West not only does not practice the caste system, but in many cases speaks out against it.

3 College students in India are less likely to practice the caste system than those who do not attend college. College exposes students to new ideas, cultures, and people. As a result, many college students modify, and in some cases completely abandon, the traditions under which they were raised.

4 Urban dwellers are less likely to practice traditional customs than their rural counterparts. This is most definitely true in India, where the caste system remains the central social system in rural areas but has been greatly compromised in urban areas.

12. Even if you don't know much about the Khmer Rouge, you should be able to answer this question correctly simply by focusing on the skeleton and by knowing the definitions of the terms in the answer choices. Eliminate answer choices that are not consistent with death.

   1 Look up *genocide* in the Hit Parade if you missed this question. The Khmer Rouge is responsible for the deaths of several million Cambodians, which ranks as one of the world's worst acts of genocide. The skeleton in the cartoon indicates that "behind" the Khmer Rouge is a policy of death.

   2 If the Khmer Rouge were responsible for overpopulation, the shadow would be in the form of an infant, not a skeleton! The Khmer Rouge is responsible for ending life, not creating life.

   3 Nothing in the cartoon suggests an agrarian economy. To be sure, the Khmer Rouge enforced farm collectives, but this isn't the point of the cartoon. If an agrarian economy were the point of the cartoon, the shadow would be in the form of a rice paddy, not a skeleton! Look up *agrarian economy* in the Hit Parade if you've forgotten what it is.

   4 Nothing in the cartoon suggests widespread popular support. Generally speaking, people don't support organizations or policies that result in widespread death.

13. If you know about one of these locations, you should be able to eliminate at least a couple of answer choices. If you know about two, you should be able to eliminate all three wrong answer choices.

   1 Singapore, Hong Kong, and Taiwan are not currently experiencing significant ethnic conflicts.

   2 None of these locations were ever formally controlled by the Soviet Union.

   3 Each of these locations has a free-market economy. Hong Kong recently returned under the control of China, after 100 years as a colony of Britain, but yet still operates under a free-market system.

   4 Only Hong Kong is currently controlled by a communist government, namely China. Taiwan is claimed by China, but is not under China's control. Singapore is not claimed or controlled by any communist government.

14. Eliminate answer choices that don't make sense. Logically speaking, what sort of an effect would the European slave trade have on Africa?

1 Africans were being captured and taken from Africa by the hundreds of thousands. How in the world would this scenario have strengthened traditional African economic systems? It wouldn't. That's why it's not the answer.

2 The African slave trade actually led to an increase in tribal warfare, both because it contributed to general instability and because individual tribes hoped to capture members of other tribes and sell them to the Europeans.

3 As the Europeans descended on the African continent and forcibly captured Africans, it hastened the decline of the African kingdoms already in place. Part of the decline was due to the removal of a sizable portion of the population, and part of it was due to the European presence, which increasingly asserted more and more authority on the continent.

4 The European slave trade was a naval trade, not a land-based trade. The slaves were sent to Europe and especially to the Americas, not northeast across the Sahara.

15. Think of everything you know about European colonialism. Did the Europeans generally respect the people they conquered? No? Well, then, even if you don't remember much about the European partitioning of Africa, which answer choice makes the most sense?

1 Europeans did not draw colonial borders based on African tribal boundaries, and the results were disastrous. Cohesive tribes were often split between two or more colonies. What's more, rival tribes were sometimes combined within the same colony. Europeans drew colonial borders according to their own needs, without considering the needs of the tribes.

2 The African Continent was not divided equally among the colonial powers. Claims were made by the European powers, followed by negotiating and occasional fighting over these claims. When the dust settled, Britain and France emerged as the major colonial powers on the continent.

3 European control did much to improve European economies, not the economies of the tribal groups. Look up *mercantilism* in the Hit Parade for more details.

4 This is the best answer. Europeans considered themselves superior to the Africans, and as such ignored the cultural

and ethnic traditions of Africa. **The Europeans' attitude toward Africans is one of the clearest examples of ethnocentrism in history. Many Europeans believed that the Africans were barbarians and that they, the Europeans, had a duty to "civilize" the Africans in the European tradition, by force if necessary. Look up *ethnocentrism* in the Hit Parade.**

16. If you're unfamiliar with recent South African history, you should review the basics in your Global Studies materials, since the Regents like to ask questions about it. The question describes the timeline by which apartheid was abandoned. All you have to do is find an answer choice that describes one of the reasons that apartheid was abandoned in South Africa.

   1 No. The white minority government is the group that enacted apartheid in the first place.

   2 This is the best answer. While economic sanctions were by no means the only reason that apartheid was abandoned (look up *Nelson Mandela* in the Hit Parade), economic sanctions certainly influenced the South African government.

   3 Nelson Mandela won the 1994 election, so this can't be the answer. What's more, the question describes events that occurred prior to 1994! It doesn't make sense to claim that the abolishment of laws in 1986 came about as a result of an election in 1994!

   4 The United Nations did not expel South Africa.

17. If you're not certain of the answer, choose the answer that is the most difficult to argue with.

   1 This is the best answer. All three civilizations advanced in scientific knowledge. This is a pretty safe answer choice, since it's difficult to be a civilization without advancing in some sort of scientific knowledge, whether it's in architecture, medicine, or transportation. The Maya were masters of agricultural technology and calendar keeping, the Aztecs were masters of architecture, and the Incas were masters of stone-masonry.

   2 Only the Incas had their origins in the Andes.

   3 All of these civilizations were class-based. None of them upheld the equality of all members of society.

   4 Territorial expansion without warfare was not common to all three civilizations. The Aztecs in particular were warlike.

18. Look up *Fidel Castro* in the Hit Parade if you missed this question. If you do, the correct answer should be immediately evident.

1   Fidel Castro's government strengthened it ties to the Soviet Union, not the United States. Since the demise of the former Soviet Union, Cuba has been politically isolated, and remains politically and economically at odds with the United States.

2   Cuba has not attempted to convince Latin American nations to withdraw from the United Nations. Even if you didn't know this, you should be skeptical of this answer choice since, even if it were true, it's unlikely that it would be described as a *major* goal.

3   The United States has imposed economic sanctions against Cuba. Cuba and the United States are not economic partners in any sense of the phrase.

4   **This is the best answer. Since the Cuban Revolution, Fidel Castro has attempted to reform Cuban society through the use of socialist ideas. Look up *Fidel Castro* in the Hit Parade for details.**

19. If you're not sure of the right answer, focus on finding an answer choice that describes developing countries (as opposed to developed countries) in general. Also, focus on finding an answer choice that would logically hinder economic development.

1   Latin America not only produces more consumer goods than ever before, but also is rich in natural resources.

2   The governments of Latin America are not primarily concerned with preserving the environment. Indeed, it's unlikely that the government of any nation anywhere in the world is *primarily* concerned with preserving the environment. In Latin America, the policies of many governments have actually harmed the environment, especially in regard to rain forests in the Amazon River valley. Look up *deforestation* in the Hit Parade if you picked this answer.

3   **This is the best answer. Like other developing countries, the nations of Latin America are experiencing considerable problems with overpopulation, land distribution, and a lack of investment capital. These problems, in turn, have hindered economic development. Overpopulation strains limited resources; land distribution problems contribute to a large, landless peasant class that cannot accumulate wealth; and a lack of investment capital limits improvement and modernization of basic infrastructure and industries.**

4   Almost all corporations are very interested in using modern technology. The problem in Latin America is that there isn't enough investment in many cases for the corporations to use it.

20. If you're not sure of the answer, focus on general world trends.
   1   Elections have not brought communist governments to power. Cuba is the only communist government in Latin America. In terms of general world trends, communist governments are generally falling out of power, so you shouldn't have picked this answer choice.
   2   **This is the best answer. In most Latin American countries, democracies have replaced military governments and dictatorships.**
   3   Most Latin American governments are encouraging diversification of their economies, not subsistence agriculture. Look up *subsistence agriculture* and *diversification* in the Hit Parade if you picked this answer.
   4   Debts owed to foreign nations in many cases have not been paid. International debt plagues Latin America.

21. Look up *Golden Age* in the Hit Parade if you missed this question. Recall that a golden age usually refers to successes in arts and sciences.
   1   **This is the best answer. During the Golden Age of Muslim culture, important ideas from ancient Greece and Rome were preserved and built upon. Europe, however, was in the midst of cultural decline, and neglected and eventually forgot those ideas. The preservation of ancient Greek and Roman ideas was significant not only for Muslim culture, but also for Europe and the rest of the world, since these ideas were reintroduced to Europe during the European Renaissance, and through Europe to the rest of the world.**
   2   Gunpowder was invented in China, not in the Islamic Empire. What's more, the Regents like to focus on peaceful and positive events when they ask questions about golden ages, not harmful events.
   3   During the Golden Age of Muslim culture, the Islamic Empire didn't even know South America existed, nor did South America know that Muslim culture existed. The Golden Age of Muslim culture occurred well before the European discovery of the Americas, and the Middle East learned of the Americas through the Europeans.

4   Feudalism emerged before the Golden Age of Muslim culture, but not in the Islamic Empire. Rather, feudalism emerged in Europe, China, and Japan. What's more, the phrase *unifying force* is so ambiguous that it's difficult to determine whether the term would apply to feudalism.

22. Eliminate answer choices that don't apply to the Middle East, and you should be left with only one answer choice. If you're uncertain about the characteristics of the Middle East, then choose an answer choice that would logically result in limited economic development—and that way you'll be able to eliminate at least one answer choice. Finally, focus on an answer choice that describes a concept that the Regents test over and over again, which you should know if you've been doing practice tests.

1   The Middle East doesn't have an abundance of water resources. If it did, those water resources would aid economic development, not hinder it.

2   **When you take the test, arm yourself with this simple fact: political instability hinders economic development. It has in the Middle East. It has in Latin America. It has in Southeast Asia. It has in Eastern Europe. Wherever it takes hold on the globe, political instability harms economies, since long-term investment requires predictability, and political instability makes things extremely unpredictable.**

3   The Middle East is not geographically isolated. Rather, it's at the crossroads of three continents: Africa, Europe, and Asia. Just about everything from these three continents has traveled through the Middle East at some point or another.

4   The Middle East does not lack deep-water seaports, so this can't be the answer. Even if you weren't sure, however, you should still have chosen answer choice 2, since it describes a more pervasive problem.

23. Three out of the four terms in the answer choices are in the Hit Parade, including the right answer. Isn't it about time you sat down and familiarized yourself with the terms on that list?

1   ***Zionism* has traditionally referred to the Jewish movement to establish a homeland in Palestine, and ever since the nation of Israel was created, Zionism has referred to the movement to maintain it.**

2   *Secularism* is a term used to describe indifference to religion. The secular world doesn't have anything to do with religion. It's not

necessarily against religion, it's just apart from religion (mathematics is secular, for example). The Jewish movement to establish a homeland in Palestine was most definitely religiously motivated, and therefore cannot be described as secular.

3 *Animism* is a group of traditional African religions. Animism has nothing to do with the Jewish movement to establish a homeland in Palestine. Look up *animism* in the Hit Parade if you guessed this answer.

4 *Marxism* is the economic philosophy at the heart of socialism and communism. It has nothing to do with the Jewish movement to establish a homeland in Palestine. Look up *Marxism* in the Hit Parade if you picked this answer.

24. If you don't remember anything about the Camp David accords, this question might be a bit tricky, but you can still guess well. First, eliminate answer choices that describe something that never occurred. Then, focus on choices that name a major event you remember from class, even if you're not sure what the cause of the major event was. Also, focus on the words *signing* and *accords*. What sorts of things are *signed*? Treaties, agreements—those types of things.

1 Shortly after the signing of the accords, Egyptian President Anwar el Sadat was assassinated, but Israeli Prime Minister Menachem Begin was not.

2 Movement toward Palestinian self-rule in the West Bank and Gaza Strip occurred in the 1990s.

3 The Camp David accords were signed by Israel and Egypt, not by a group of Arab nations.

4 **This is it. Formal peace agreements are precisely the kinds of things that are *signed*. The Camp David accords marked a turning point in the previously volatile relations between Egypt and Israel.**

25. Look up *fundamentalism* in the Hit Parade if you missed this question. It really doesn't matter if your talking about Islamic fundamentalists or Christian fundamentalists or Hindu fundamentalists, in all cases the answer choice would be the same.

1 Fundamentalists believe in a literal interpretation of religious texts, so Islamic fundamentalists believe in a literal interpretation of the Koran, not many different interpretations.

2 Islamic fundamentalists do not adopt the values and cultures of the West, because the West is not Islamic.

3 This is it. Fundamentalists emphasize the traditional beliefs
of their religion. Fundamentalists do not favor a change of
interpretations, traditions, or values.

4 Fundamentalists do not promote active participation of women in
government, because women have not traditionally participated in
government. Fundamentalists favor traditional gender roles.

26. All of the words in the answer choices are in the Hit Parade. Ignore
the Hit Parade at your own peril!

1 **Ancient Athens is the only true example of a direct democracy. Currently, no direct democracies exist. Look up
democracy in the Hit Parade for a discussion of the various
kinds of democracies.**

2 Totalitarianism does not involve citizen participation in government. Look up *totalitarianism* in the Hit Parade.

3 A parliamentary democracy involves representatives who vote on
behalf of those who elect them. This is quite different from a
direct democracy, in which citizens vote on policy issues for
themselves.

4 Absolutism does not involve citizen participation in government.
Look up *absolutism* in the Hit Parade.

27. As discussed in chapter 2, you need to review major time periods in
world history, including the Middle Ages. It helps if you remember
that feudalism existed in Europe during the Middle Ages, since the
definition of *feudalism* includes the right answer to this particular
question. Alternatively, if you remember that during the Middle Ages
Europe was a *traditional society*, you'll get the right answer for the
same reason, because as you know the definition of a *traditional
society* according to the Hit Parade. The point? Learning the Hit
Parade helps you on questions that don't even directly ask you about
the terms on the Hit Parade!

1 The nobles had no reason to encourage social mobility because
they benefited if the serfs remained loyal to them.

2 The practices of the Catholic Church did not lead to the development of a classless society. The Catholic Church is hierarchical,
and supported a class-based society during the Middle Ages.

3 **This is the best answer. European feudalism was marked by
sharp class distinctions. Look up *feudalism* in the Hit Parade
if you missed this question.**

4   This answer choice describes a different time period. Industrialism occurred well after the European Middle Ages. Industrialization occurred after the Renaissance and Enlightenment. (Remember, you should be able to put major world time periods in sequence.) Review chapter 2. Look up *industrialization* in the Hit Parade if you chose this answer.

28.   There are two ways to answer this question. The first is to think about time periods: you want to pick an answer choice that describes Europe at the end of the Middle Ages as opposed to an answer choice that describes Europe at the height of the Middle Ages or before the Middle Ages. The second is to think about this question logically, especially if you're shaky on European history. Logically speaking, what sorts of events would result in the rise of a middle class? Probably something that would allow a large number of people to get their hands on a reasonable amount of money.

1   The Roman Empire existed before the Middle Ages even started. It was the fall of the Roman Empire that ushered in the Middle Ages.

2   This is the best answer. As trade increased, an increasing number of merchants were able to make money. Over generations, a reasonable amount of wealth was earned and then reinvested into merchant activities, which in turn led to the employment of even more people and the distribution of goods. This led to the emergence of a middle class, which was not part of the wealthy nobility or the poverty-stricken peasant class.

3   Christianity did not have a direct impact on the development of a middle class. For the most part, Christianity supported a strict class-based system that separated the Europeans into two classes: lord and servant. Plus, this answer choice describes medieval Europe, not Europe at the *end* of the Middle Ages.

4   Europe during the Middle Ages was characterized by self-sufficiency of the manor system. At the close of the Middle Ages, however, the manor system deteriorated as a middle class and guild system emerged. Look up *manorialism* in the Hit Parade if you picked this answer.

29. If you've been reviewing the Hit Parade, then you're probably not even reading this explanation. If you haven't been reviewing the Hit Parade, that explains why you're trying to figure out why you missed this question. Isn't it about time you made friends with the Hit Parade?

    1 The divine right theory put power in the hands of kings, not peasants.

    2 The divine right theory was a political and religious doctrine, not an economic policy. Even if you have no idea what divine right theory was, however, you should be skeptical of this answer, because free trade policies are a relatively recent development, not something that existed during the seventeenth and eighteenth centuries.

    3 The divine right theory didn't justify the supreme power of the Catholic Church. It justified the supreme power of monarchies who, by invoking the theory, claimed to have power on behalf of God.

    4 The divine right theory was used to justify the establishment of an absolute monarchy by asserting that monarchs were appointed by God to act on his behalf. As such, opposition to the monarchy was considered opposition to God.

30. If you don't remember anything about the Protestant Reformation, you should still be able to eliminate two answer choices by focusing on things that haven't *ended* in the first place. In other words, if any answer choice describes something that still occurs in the world, then it doesn't make sense to claim that the Protestant Reformation ended it! If you know that Protestantism is a religious denomination, then you should be able to guess the right answer. In any case, you actually don't have any excuse to miss this question, since *Protestant Reformation* is in the Hit Parade.

    1 The Protestant Reformation didn't bring about an end to the colonial period. In fact, the colonial period hadn't yet developed at the time of the Protestant Reformation.

    2 Strong central governments still exist in western Europe, as well as throughout much of the world, so how in the world could the Protestant Reformation have brought an end to them?

    3 The Protestant Reformation brought an end to religious unity in western Europe. Prior to the Reformation, western Europe was united under Roman Catholicism. After the Reformation, northern Europe and parts of central Europe

were Protestant, while southern Europe and parts of central Europe remained Catholic. Review *Protestant Reformation* in the Hit Parade for more details.

4 Market economies still exist in western Europe and much of the world, so this answer choice doesn't make much sense.

31. The French Revolution is in the Hit Parade, so make sure you review it. This question is quite detailed, however, so even if you remember the basics of the French Revolution, you might not remember all the people in the answer choices. As always, when you're guessing, it's important to pick an answer choice that describes something general and hard to argue with, since it's more likely that something general will be correct than something too specific.

1 **Why do revolutions occur? Because people are dissatisfied. The Regents have asked questions time and again about various revolutions, whether it be the Cuban Revolution, the Latin American Revolution, the Russian Revolution, the Communist Revolution in China, or, as here, the French Revolution. In all cases, revolutions have occurred because a large chunk of the population was frustrated with the status quo. *The Third Estate* was a name given to the middle class and peasants. It was their dissatisfaction that led to the revolution. Refresh your memory by looking up *French Revolution* in the Hit Parade.**

2 Napoleon rose to power as a *result* of the French Revolution. Review *Napoleon Bonaparte* in the Hit Parade, especially if you thought this was the right answer.

3 Metternich was an Austrian Prince who had nothing to do with the French Revolution, though he played an active role in France in the years following the Revolution. You don't remember who Metternich was? Don't worry about it. With all due respect to Metternich, it's hard to imagine that he'd ever show up in a correct answer choice, since it's unlikely that the Regents will determine that the actions of Metternich are one of the forty-eight most important things to test you on.

4 The execution of Louis XVI occurred well after the French Revolution began. Louis XVI's execution was a consequence of the revolution, not a cause of it.

32. Karl Marx is a regular cast member of the Regents exam, so you better know about him. He's in the Hit Parade, and if you read it, the correct answer will be obvious.

1 Karl Marx and Friedrich Engels wrote about the evils of capitalism and the exploitative consequences that capitalism had on the working class. They encouraged workers to overthrow the capitalist system and establish a classless society (communism).

2 Marx and Engels did not write about increasing the tax rate.

3 Marx and Engels were economic philosophers more than political philosophers. They did not write about the differences between small governments and large governments, but rather between capitalist, class-based systems and classless systems.

4 Marx and Engles did not encourage workers to improve their economic conditions by establishing tariffs. Trade policies were not a focus of either of the two writers. What's more, this answer choice doesn't make much sense, even if you don't recall the writings of Marx and Engles, since workers don't establish tariffs in the first place—governments do!

33. If you don't remember the term *Weimar Republic*, don't fret. The important part of the question is the location and the date: Germany in the early 1930s. The Regents love to ask about Germany in the 1930s, but they usually don't specifically refer to the *Weimar Republic*. If you don't know anything about Germany in the 1930s, review it in your Global Studies materials. While you're at it, review the Treaty of Versailles, since the Regents love to ask about that as well, and since the Treaty is at the root of Germany's problems in the early 1930s.

1 The problem was not population growth. When the Regents ask questions about the problems of population growth, they're usually referring to less developed countries.

2 Voting was not the problem.

3 Germany's relations with the world community was not the most immediate problem. Isn't there an answer choice that describes *a more severe problem*?

4 This is the best answer. During the early 1930s, a world-wide economic depression hit Germany especially hard. Naturally, many Germans were discontented with the government as a result. You definitely should review this part of German history in your global studies materials, especially since this discontent led to the rise of Hitler, which in turn changed the course of developments through-

out the globe. Even if you were just guessing, you should
have picked this answer because economic problems are
often at the heart of discontent and this fact is often tested
by the Regents.

34. NATO and the EU are both in the Hit Parade, so if you review them,
you won't have to miss questions like these. Both are major international organizations. Why would major international organizations
form? Choose the answer choice that is hardest to argue with.
1 NATO formed in the years following World War I, and the predeces-
sor of the modern EU formed in the 1950s. As such, neither could
have possibly formed as a response to the oil embargo of 1974.
2 **How can you argue with this answer? Individual countries
enter into international organizations for mutual gain.
NATO is a collection of nations that came together to solve
mutual military problems; the EU is a collection of nations
that came together primarily to solve mutual economic
problems. Review both organizations in the Hit Parade for
more details.**
3 Neither organization formed to maintain control of colonial
empires. Colonialism was collapsing during the years that these
organizations were formed.
4 NATO is a military alliance, not an economic alliance. The EU
formed because economic self-reliance wasn't working, and
member nations banded together to gain economic power.

35. If you don't remember much about early Russian history, at least try to
remember the geographic locations of the groups in the answer
choices. Focus on answer choices that describe groups that were
influential in the Black Sea region northward.
1 The Franks impacted western Europe, not early Russia.
2 The Ottoman Turks didn't make it as far north as Russia.
3 **The Byzantine Empire had an enormous impact on the
development of early Russian culture. As the eastern
counterpart to the western Roman Empire, the Byzantine
Empire extended well into the midst of Russia, greatly
affecting the religious and cultural development of the
region. The Russian Orthodox Church is an offshoot of
Byzantine Christianity.**
4 The Roman Catholic Church greatly influenced the cultural
development of western, northern, and southern Europe, but
Russia was culturally allied with the eastern Byzantine Church.

36. If you missed this question, you should review the basics of Russian history in your Global Studies materials, since there are typically two or three questions about Russian history on each test. Stalin, of course, is also in the Hit Parade. Only one answer choice is consistent with the Soviet Union under Stalin, so even if you only know about him, you should be able to answer this question correctly.

   1 While it's true that some of the Russian czars were relatively isolationist, Stalin most certainly wasn't. Stalin had a very aggressive military and political philosophy, as he hoped to influence his region of the world and beyond.

   2 Stalin enacted policies to encourage industrial growth, especially heavy industry.

   3 Stalin did not encourage the creation of a national church. To the contrary, Stalin enforced a ban on religious expression in the Soviet Union.

   4 Both Stalin and the Russian czars established an authoritarian form of government. The czars believed in a class-based feudal society in which they had ultimate authority. Stalin believed in the establishment of a classless society for the masses, but ran the country as an authoritarian dictator.

37. Look up both Lenin and Gorbachev in the Hit Parade if you missed this question. You also might want to review Lenin's New Economic Policy and Gorbachev's policy of perestroika in your global studies materials, since the Regents often ask questions about both policies.

   1 While Lenin did support collectivization, that wasn't the point of his New Economic Policy. Rather, the New Economic Policy was enacted to combat some of the problems of collectivization by allowing individuals to keep some of the fruits of their labor. Gorbachev's policy of perestroika didn't support collectivization.

   2 Both policies allowed some aspects of capitalism in the Soviet economy. Both Lenin and Gorbachev needed to spark their ailing economies. In the case of Gorbachev's policy of perestroika, however, once free market reforms were allowed, demands for even greater reforms led to the eventual downfall of communism in the Soviet Union.

   3 Stalin did not allow citizen participation in the Soviet Government, but rather ruled the country as a totalitarian dictator. Gorbachev increased citizen participation through the policy of glasnost, but not through the economic policy of perestroika.

   4 Both policies were aimed at economic reform, not at military or political control over the Soviet Republics.

38. If you missed this question, review your global studies materials concerning the former Soviet Union and, specifically, Mikhail Gorbachev. Even if you simply read about Gorbachev in the Hit Parade, however, you should be able to answer this question correctly.

  1 Gorbachev encouraged free-market reforms.

  2 Gorbachev's decision decreased Cold War tensions, since Eastern Europe reformed in ways more favorable to the West. Look up *Cold War* in the Hit Parade if you need to.

  3 Gorbachev's decision did not have a direct impact on religious violence. It was first and foremost a political and economic decision.

  4 When the Eastern European nations were given more autonomy, they abandoned their communist governments and initiated democratic and capitalist reforms. Within just a few short years, communism had collapsed in Eastern Europe.

39. This question is extremely generalized. As such, choose the answer choice that is most difficult to argue with. In any randomly selected country, what do you think would be the cause of rising levels of pollution and continued housing shortages?

  1 Whether in Africa, Asia, or South America (the developing world), urbanization is contributing to pollution and housing shortages. Unfortunately, pollution control measures have been lacking in most of these fast-growing cities. In addition, widespread housing shortages exist because the cities are growing too fast for adequate housing to be built, and because a tremendous number of people are working low-wage jobs and therefore often cannot afford to live in adequate housing.

  2 A reliance on single-crop economies generally does not, in itself, contribute to housing shortages and rising levels of pollution. What's more, many developing countries are diversifying their economies, and as a result cannot be classified as single-crop economies in the first place.

  3 To be sure, changing climatic conditions can affect pollution levels and, in the case of devastating floods and earthquakes, can most certainly contribute to housing shortages. But these conditions are not widespread throughout the developing world. What's more, changing climatic conditions affect both the developed world and the developing world. It doesn't make sense that the question would specifically refer to the developing world if this were the answer.

4 Rising levels of pollution and housing shortages exist in extremely nationalist countries as well as in countries that are not so nationalistic. Increasing nationalism impacts the political environment within a country and might have an effect on the economy of a country, but it is highly unlikely that it would affect pollution rates.

40. There's no reason to miss chart questions if you're careful. The chart lists regions of the world in the left-hand column, the number of barrels (in billions) of oil reserves within each region in the center column, and the availability of oil within each region in the right-hand column. *Availability* means the number of years the oil reserves will last in each region, but you don't even have to know this in order to answer the question correctly. Instead, simply compare the information in each answer choice with the information in the chart.

1 The chart doesn't give us *any* information about employment, so based on the information in the chart, there is no way we can determine the truth of this statement. It happens to be false, by the way, but the point is this statement can't be based on the information in the chart.

2 The chart doesn't make any value judgments concerning what is necessary. It just gives information. To be sure, many people might look at the information in the chart and make conclusions about what is necessary, but this is not something the Regents would expect from you. By the way, the search for alternative sources of fuel is more necessary than ever, since the availability of current world oil reserves will be depleted within forty-four years.

3 Look at the information in the chart very carefully. The Middle East has 660 billion barrels of oil reserves. The world total (at the bottom of the chart) is 1,011 billion barrels. Half of 1,011 billion is about 505 billion, but since the Middle East has 660 billion barrels, the Middle East has more than half of the world's oil reserves! What is this—the Global Studies test or the Math Sequential I test?

4 According to the information in the chart, the former Soviet Union and Eastern Europe have thirteen years of available oil reserves. Africa, however, has twenty-eight years of oil reserves available. Since thirteen is less than twenty-eight, we can conclude that the former Soviet Union and Eastern Europe have fewer years of oil reserves available than Africa does.

41. This question is an excellent example of how it's a good idea to choose a general answer choice that is difficult to argue with. Answer choices 1 and 2 are arguably subcategories of answer choice 3. Therefore, if you're attracted to answer choices 1 or 2, then you should also be attracted to answer choice number 3! What's more, as soon as you see the word genocide you should eliminate answer choice number 4. Look up *genocide* and *civil disobedience* in the Hit Parade if you need to refresh your memory. The bottom line is that if you don't remember the details of any of the examples in the question, you can still get the question correct if you use the right techniques!

1 Apartheid in South Africa and labor camps for dissidents in the Soviet Union are not examples of war crimes because they existed apart from wars.

2 None of these examples are acts of international terrorism, but even if you thought they were, wouldn't they still all be examples of violations of human rights? And isn't answer choice 3 a more general answer choice? (It's quite arguable that *all* acts of terrorism violate human rights, simply by their nature.)

3 **This is the best answer. In all of the examples in the question, violations of human rights occurred. Genocide is by its very nature a violation of human rights. Apartheid involved multiple violations of human rights, including the imprisonment of political dissenters and institutionalized racism, which dramatically favored whites over blacks. Finally, labor camps for dissidents also inherently violate human rights, by punishing people for their political beliefs.**

4 None of these examples are examples of civil disobedience. In the case of apartheid, Nelson Mandela and thousands of others undertook acts of civil disobedience to *combat* apartheid, but apartheid itself was not an example of civil disobedience. It was a policy enforced by the government.

42. Focus on the word *strategic*. Even if you don't know anything about **any** of these waterways, you should be able to eliminate two of the answer choices just by focusing on this word. Even if you only know about one of these waterways, you should be able to answer this question correctly. By the way, these waterways show up relatively frequently on both parts of the exam, so it would be a good idea to locate them on a map and to think about why they are so strategically important.

    1 This is the best answer. They are *strategically* important because they give power to the nations who control these waterways. The Suez Canal links the Mediterranean Sea to the Red Sea, saving ships traveling between Europe and Asia thousands of miles that they would otherwise travel. Egypt, which controls the Suez Canal, makes a tremendous amount of money charging fees to use the canal. Located in Turkey, the Dardenelles and the Bosporus connect the Black Sea to the Aegean Sea, which is connected to the Mediterranean Sea. Since Russia relies on its Black Sea ports, Turkey is the economic beneficiary of goods that must travel through the Dardenelles and the Bosporus en route to and from Russia. Finally, the Strait of Hormuz sits at the mouth of the Persian Gulf, and therefore is the waterway through which the Persian Gulf's oil is distributed to the rest of the world—that's pretty strategically important!

    2 The Suez Canal isn't a natural boundary in the first place—it's man-made. The other waterways are indeed natural, but they don't separate warring nations. They have played roles in wars, but they're most significant strategic importance, especially in recent decades, has been economic.

    3 None of these waterways are along the Tropic of Cancer, the Equator, or the Tropic of Capricorn. Even if they were, it wouldn't explain why these waterways are strategically important.

    4 All of these waterways consist of salt water.

43. Economic sanctions are bad, not good. Even if you don't remember the specifics concerning the economic sanctions imposed against Iraq and Cuba, you should focus on the intended impact of *any* economic sanction, no matter where or when it has occurred.

    1 Economic sanctions are used to discourage trade, not encourage it. Countries that impose sanctions against other countries do it in an effort to harm their economies.

2 This is the best answer. Economic sanctions are used as a way of influencing political developments in other countries. In these cases, economic sanctions were imposed against Iraq and Cuba in an effort to force these leaders from power. It was hoped that the sanctions would harm the economies of these nations, and thereby harm the political popularity of their leaders to the point that the people in these countries would rise up against their leaders. As of the date of this printing, economic sanctions have not been successful in achieving this goal, since both Castro and Hussein remain in power.

3 No! Economic sanctions are intended to harm a nation, not help it.

4 Actually, sanctions have contributed to the global significance of conflicts, as opposed to containing them. Both Cuba and Iraq are globally significant (especially Iraq in recent years). It is because they are globally significant that many in the world community, especially the United States, have chosen to impose economic sanctions.

44. If you only know about one of these groups, you should be able to eliminate the three incorrect answer choices. If you don't know much about the groups, but remember where they are located, you should still be able to eliminate answer choices. If you don't remember anything at all about any of these groups, pick an answer choice that is consistent with a major theme that the Regents like to test.

1 None of these groups are located in Europe. The Chechens are located near Europe, but they are in no position to protest their lack of membership in the European Union, since they don't have a sovereign country in the first place (the European Union is made up of sovereign countries).

2 Economic stability is a problem within all three of these groups, but it's not something that they are protesting.

3 This is the best answer. The Chechens, the Sikhs, and the Tibetans all want independent homelands, but currently they are under the control of Russia, India, and China, respectively. Self-determination is a theme that is often tested by the Regents. In addition to these three groups, the Regents often ask similar questions about the Kurds and the Tamils.

4 None of these groups are Arab, so none are concerned about representation in the Arab League.

45. Even if you only know about one of these three structures, you should
be able to answer this question correctly. If you don't know about any
of these three structures, then remember to focus on general themes
that the Regents like to test.

1 **This is the answer. The Dome of the Rock was built at the
location where Muhammad is believed to have ascended
into heaven, and therefore it is religiously significant to
Muslims. Chichén Itzá is a pyramid that was built by the
Mayas for religious worship. Hagia Sophia was built as a
Christian church in Constantinople, and then became an
Islamic mosque after the Ottomans captured the city in
1453. If you didn't know about any of these structures, you
should still have been attracted to this answer choice
because the Regents like to ask questions about religious
customs and structures on both parts of the exam.**

2 None of these structures were built for the purpose of public
punishment.

3 None of these structures were built for the purpose of trade.

4 None of these structures were built for the purpose of government.
Interestingly, the Regents do not typically ask questions about
structures of government.

46. If you don't remember much about the Korean War and the Vietnam
War, you should review your global studies materials. Still, as long as
you remember the general outcome of both wars, you should be able
to focus on the correct answer. Try to think about everything you know
about Korea and Vietnam, even as they exist today, and you should be
able to guess the right answer.

1 The United Nations played a major role in the ending the war in
Korea.

2 Nuclear weapons were not used in the Korean War, nor in any
other war other than World War II. Had they been used, it would
have been extremely significant, but they weren't. Commit this
simple piece of information to your memory if you guessed this
answer: *nuclear weapons were only used in World War II and only
by the United States against Japan.*

3 **This is the best answer. If you've ever heard of North Korea
and South Korea, then you should realize that Korea
remains a divided nation to this day. Vietnam, however, was
reunited after the Vietnam War and remains a single,
communist nation.**

4 United States forces played a major role in both wars.

47. Since Elie Wiesel believed that neutrality is bad, you want to pick an answer choice that describes a situation in which neutrality has resulted in negative consequences. And if an answer choice describes a situation in which people weren't neutral in the first place, then you have to eliminate it.

1 The United Nations isn't a neutral organization, it takes sides all the time. In fact, in many situations the United Nations has stepped in to help protect the tormented.

2 This is the best answer. The world's initial reaction to the crisis in Bosnia in the early 1990s was one of neutrality. Most of the world's powers justified their inaction by claiming that it was inappropriate to become involved in what is essentially a civil war, and that their objectives in becoming involved were too unclear. So, while world leaders hemmed and hawed, millions of lives were devastated, either through outright murder or displacement. The neutrality of the world community allowed the aggressors in the Bosnian crisis to continue their agendas, while the victims had no one to turn to for help.

3 Arab reaction to the creation of Israel was hardly neutral—they were decidedly against it! Even today, the Arab reaction to the creation of Israel (as well as the Israeli response to the Arab reaction) contributes significantly to instability in the Middle East.

4 The dismantling of the Berlin Wall was hardly an act of neutrality. It was dismantled because East Germany collapsed and then combined with West Germany into the single nation of Germany. This wasn't an act of neutrality, but a conscious choice.

48. Given that this test was administered in August 1998, this question represents an attempt by the Regents to be up-to-the-minute. Hopefully your teachers were up-to-the-minute as well, since most of the materials you use in class are not. In any case, if you don't know the answer based on your knowledge of recent events, choose two nations that have strained relations, and therefore would be more likely to use nuclear weapons once they have them, causing global concern.

1 Nope. Japan and Egypt do not have nuclear weapons.

2 Mexico and Chile do not have nuclear weapons.

3 Germany and Cuba do not have nuclear weapons.

4 This is it. When India and Pakistan tested nuclear weapons in 1998, it concerned the global community greatly, not only because it represented an expansion of nuclear armament, but because of the fear that India and Pakistan would actually use them against each other.

PART II

1. NATIONS/REGIONS IN CRISIS

Manchuria in 1931

During the first few decades of the 1900s, Japan embarked on building an imperial empire in East Asia. Three motivations drove Japan's endeavors. First, it wanted to gain access to raw materials. Second, it wanted to obtain new foreign markets. And third, it needed living space for its surplus population, especially since the Japanese were restricted from emigrating to the United States, Canada, and Australia.

By the 1930s, Japan turned its attention to Manchuria, a province of China located immediately north of Korea, a nation that Japan had already established as a protectorate in 1907. Manchuria was rich in iron and coal, two resources Japan needed for its expanding industrial economy. In 1930, Japan invaded Manchuria and established the Japanese-controlled state of Manchukuo in its place. The League of Nations condemned the action, but was unsuccessful in negotiating a Japanese withdrawal from Manchuria. Instead, Japan withdrew from the League of Nations, leaving the organization powerless against it. With the world community's main organization struggling to remain a cohesive group, and with many of the industrial nations preoccupied with their own economic depressions, Japan continued to build up its mercantilist empire, setting the stage for a showdown with the allied powers in World War II.

Poland in 1939

In the mid 1930s much of western Europe followed a policy of appeasement toward an increasingly aggressive Germany. Because of this, Germany was able to make sizable territorial gains in central Europe. In 1939, however, after Germany invaded Czechoslovakia, Hitler made claims on Polish territory that alarmed Britain and France, and both countries vowed to defend Poland against German aggression. Meanwhile, the Germans entered into a pact with the Soviet Union, allowing Germany to invade Poland without fear of an attack from the Soviet Union, which shared a border with Poland. Germany's invasion led Britain and France to declare war on Germany, thus beginning World War II. Although initially Britain, France, and the other allied powers were unsuccessful in containing German aggression, the entrance of the United States into the war in 1941 eventually led to Nazi Germany's collapse. Thus, the allied powers were successful in liberating Poland from German control. But because Poland became part of the Soviet Bloc in the decades following World War II, it would be nearly fifty years before Poland would become a truly sovereign and independent nation once again.

South Korea in 1949

Prior to World War II, Korea was invaded by Japan and annexed as part of the expanding Japanese Empire. After Japan was defeated in World War II, Korea was supposed to be reestablished as an independent nation. However, until stability could be achieved and elections held, it was occupied by the Soviet Union and the United States in two separate pieces—the Soviet Union north of the 38th parallel and the United States south of it. As the Cold War developed between the two superpowers, they couldn't agree on terms of a united Korea. In the meantime, each superpower continued to exert its own influence over the political and cultural developments within the territory it occupied. In 1948, two separate governments were established—a Soviet-backed communist regime in North Korea and a United States-backed democracy in South Korea. Both superpowers withdrew their troops in 1949, but this quickly led to crisis when North Korea attacked South Korea in an attempt to unite the two nations under a single communist government. The United Nations condemned the action and soon a multinational force, largely consisting of U.S. and British troops, was sent to the aid of the South Koreans. The UN forces made tremendous headway under General MacArthur, but when it looked as if the North Koreans would be defeated, China entered the war on behalf of the communist North. The two sides battled it out along the 38th parallel, eventually leading to an armistice in 1953. Today, the two nations remain separate and true to the political philosophies under which they were created.

Egypt in 1956

Like the rest of Africa, Egypt was subjected to European imperialism in the nineteenth and twentieth centuries. Great Britain and France completed the Suez Canal in 1869 and subsequently kept troops in Egypt to protect it. In 1956, however, Egypt, under the leadership of Gamal Abdel Nasser, joined the wave of nationalistic independence movements sweeping across Africa by announcing that it would assume control of the Suez Canal. This action infuriated Britain and France, and aggravated tensions between Israel and Egypt as well, since Arab nations refused to give Israel access to the Canal. Later in 1956, Britain, France, and Israel attacked Egypt, with Israeli forces advancing well into the Sinai Peninsula. In response, the

United Nations intervened on behalf of Egypt and ordered the complete withdrawal of the invading troops. UN forces were then sent to keep peace on the border. Egypt went through with its plan to nationalize the canal and subsequently built up its military power. Although significant wars followed, Israel and Egypt eventually reached a peace agreement in the Camp David accords in 1979. As for the European powers, they pulled out of Egypt entirely.

Kuwait in 1991

Iraq invaded Kuwait in 1990 under the leadership of Saddam Hussein, because Iraq wanted to gain control of a greater percentage of the world's oil reserves. Iraqi control of Kuwait would have nearly doubled Iraq's oil reserves to 20 percent of the world's total. This would have put Iraq in a good position to take Saudi Arabia and the United Arab Emirates, an action that would have given Iraq control of over half of the world's oil reserves. The world, especially the industrialized West, reacted immediately. The United Nations, particularly the United States, sent forces to drive the Iraqis out of Kuwait. The immediate impact of their success resulted in the liberation of Kuwait and the humiliation of Iraq, which was then subjected to UN monitoring, severe limitations on its military activities, and economic sanctions. Nevertheless, Hussein has remained in power. The long-range impact has been the continued stability of oil prices and the continued security of the Persian Gulf nations south of Iraq. Yet the people of Iraq have also been affected long-term, since many of them are not getting the food and supplies that they need due to economic sanctions imposed by other nations and the militaristic priorities of their leader.

Somalia in 1992

In 1992, a severe drought hit Somalia, leading to widespread famine. Such a natural disaster would severely impact most nations, but in Somalia the consequences were particularly tragic. Just a year earlier, the central government had broken down and by 1992 Somalia was in the midst of civil war. Various clans were vying for power and the people of Somalia had no organized way of getting food. When the world community responded with an outpouring of help, the situation only worsened. Much of the food and many of the supplies never reached the people who needed them. Instead, warring tribes took control of the aid and used it for themselves. UN troops lacked the authority and numbers to solve the political and military chaos in Somalia, and eventually withdrew. Meanwhile, the innocent people of Somalia continued to suffer. The UN effort in Somalia, therefore, is just one example of the difficulty of solving regional problems that stem from a complex interaction of political, economic, militaristic, social, and environmental causes.

Bosnia in 1995

Bosnia was created in 1992 after the downfall of communism in Eastern Europe and the rise of movements aimed at self-determination led to the dismemberment of the former Yugoslavia. However, the problems between Christian Serbs and Muslims, the two main religious groups in Bosnia, are centuries old. In the former Yugoslavia, the ethnic hatred between the two groups was overshadowed by a totalitarian government that limited expression and the practice of religion. Once Yugoslavia disbanded, however, ethnic hatred was renewed. Muslims are the majority in Serbia and believe that they have the right to determine the future of the nation, especially since Christian Serbs were much more powerful in the former Yugoslavia (despite the fact that they represented a minority of the population). The Serbs, however, refuse to be ruled by the Muslims and want their own nation or else to be annexed by Serbia. Horrendous acts of violence have resulted. Thousands upon thousands have been killed, raped, and beaten. Entire villages were destroyed even as the world community seemed to be merely watching, unwilling to become too involved in a war so tied to ethnic differences. Temporary cease-fires brought short-term peace to the region, but the fighting resumed in 1995. More recently, the United Nations has sent peacekeeping forces to the region, but true peace and respect have yet to materialize.

2. LEADERS DEALING WITH PROBLEMS

Queen Isabella I—Spain

In the mid-fifteenth century, Queen Isabella, the ruler of Castille (a kingdom in central, present-day Spain) faced the problem of fractured power. There were two reasons for this. First, Castille was one of three independent Spanish kingdoms, and therefore no single ruler controlled the region. Second, the peasants were split along religious lines (mostly Christian and Muslim) due to the remnants of the Muslim conquest of the Iberian peninsula during the Middle Ages. To solve both of these problems, Isabella married Ferdinand, heir to the Spanish kingdom of Aragon, in 1469, thus uniting most of Spain under a single monarchy. Then, Isabella and Ferdinand, both Christians, made the Catholic Church a strong ally, as opposed to competing with the Church for authority. This alliance increased Spanish nationalism under the new monarchy by tying it to Christianity, thus resulting in an end to religious toleration in the region.

The result was that Muslims and Jews were forced to convert to Christianity or leave, ushering in an era known as the Spanish Inquisition. Although the consequences for non-Christian Spaniards were tragic, the consequences for the Spanish monarchy were extraordinary. Newly unified and energized, Spain embarked on an imperial quest that brought it tremendous wealth and glory, eventually resulting in the spread of the Spanish language, Spanish customs, and Christianity to much of the New World.

Elizabeth I—England

At the same time that Shakespeare was securing Britain's position as a leader in world literature, Elizabeth I was securing Britain's position as a great world power. However, one major obstacle stood in her way. Spain, under the leadership of King Philip II, was threatening to invade England and establish it as a Catholic nation once again. Spain's naval capacity was growing with each passing year, and its increasing dominance of the seas made Elizabeth very nervous indeed. In quiet retaliation, she supported pirate ships, known as English Sea Dogs, which attacked and captured Spanish ships. This enraged Philip, who in turn assembled a huge fleet of ships, known as the Spanish Armada, and sent them across the English Channel toward England. Elizabeth ordered a counter-attack, and although the English had fewer and smaller ships, they were much faster and therefore were able to encircle the Armada before it reached England's shore. The English fleet forced the Armada into the North Sea, where violent weather finished the Armada off. Although Spain remained powerful after the defeat, England was emboldened. Under Elizabeth's leadership, England then focused its newfound security on building an empire of its own.

Peter the Great—Russia

In the early eighteenth century, Russia's only coastline ran along the Arctic Ocean in the north and then cut south in the east along the Bering Sea. The southern and western borders were landlocked. Since the Arctic Ocean is almost entirely covered in ice year around, Russia was unable to establish port cities throughout much of its history, except in the east, where the population is sparse and thousands of miles away from the population centers of the west. As a result, Russia was increasingly becoming isolated from the world community, and was not able to keep pace with Western European powers. In response to this problem, Peter the Great drove the Swedes out of part of the Baltic region to the west of Russia and established a new warm-water port city on the Baltic Sea. The new city, St. Petersburg, was built specifically as a "window to the west," and became Russia's new capital. The impact for the Baltic region was enormous. Suddenly, it was at the center of activity in the Russian empire. And although much of the rest of Russia dragged its feet in Peter the Great's westernization attempt, the new city of St. Petersburg allowed Russia to expand its naval capacity, its international trade, and perhaps most importantly of all, its presence on the world scene.

Maximilien Robespierre—France

Robespierre was a leader of the French Revolution in 1792, and for his efforts was soon elected to the Committee of Public Safety. Under Robespierre's direction, the Committee believed that France's greatest threat was the presence of traitors within its own borders. In response to this threat, the Committee initiated a campaign to root out traitors—a campaign so ruthless that it became known as the Reign of Terror. A Law of Suspects was enacted, which declared that individuals suspected of traitorous acts could be arrested for "their conduct, their relations, their remarks, or their writings." With little evidence of actual treason, thousands were arrested under this law and sent to the guillotine (including the former monarch, Marie Antoinette, and hundreds of nobles). However, Robespierre's ruthlessness did not result in widespread respect and admiration. Instead, the country became increasingly restless about the extent of the executions, and eventually Robespierre himself was arrested and, ironically, quickly executed. In the confusion and uncertainty that was so characteristic of France during this time period, Napoleon Bonaparte managed to gain control of the emerging Directorie, ushering in the Napoleonic Era. Therefore, Robespierre's execution was one step in the consolidation of France's power in one man: Napoleon.

Kemal Atatürk—Turkey

After World War I, in 1922, a group of Turkish nationalists led by Mustafa Kemal Atat rk overthrew the last Ottoman emperor. In 1923, the nationalists established the republic of Turkey, the first republic in the Middle East. During this time, Atatürk's main concern was that Turkey was not westernized enough. He believed that because of this, Turkey was ill equipped to take a leading position in the increasingly westernized world. As a result, he methodically and dictatorially set Turkey on a course of modernization more in line with the European tradition than with the Middle Eastern tradition. Among the hundreds of changes that he implemented, Atatürk severed the close connection between church and state by establishing secular laws independent of the law of Islam. He replaced religious courts with secular courts and expanded the rights of the citizens, especially those of women, who under Islamic law did not have legal and political rights equal to those of men. Atatürk even dressed in the European style and enforced that dress code on others. In the new secular schools, children were taught the Roman alphabet, not the Arabic script, and in the workplace, the economy was quickly industrialized. Ever since this major turning point in its history, Turkey arguably has been the most western-oriented of all the Islamic nations.

Joseph Stalin—Soviet Union

When Stalin rose to power in 1927, the Soviet Union lagged far behind Europe in terms of industrial and agricultural production. One of the main problems with the Soviet Union's primitive agricultural techniques was that it was incredibly inefficient. In other words, in order for the all the people to be fed, most of the people had to work on farms. Since most people were working on the farms, there weren't many people left to work in factories. So in order to industrialize, Stalin first decided to reform the agricultural sector by collectivizing the farms, an action he hoped would increase agricultural efficiency, thereby allowing more workers to be placed in the factories. In his process of collectivization, he ordered all farmers to give up their land to the state-owned collective farms, which were run in a centralized bureaucratic fashion. By 1930, over 90 percent of the peasants lived on collective farms. But many of the peasants resented the loss of their own land. An organized resistance resulted in the destruction of crops and livestock, and millions of Russians subsequently lost their lives as a result of Stalin's reaction to the resistance and to the food shortages that followed.

Mao Zedong—China

Mao Zedong was the leader of the Communist Revolution in China, and after its success, the leader of the Communist Republic of China. Mao collectivized agriculture and industry, instituted sweeping social reform, and, for a time, improved the lives of millions of peasants. However, by the 1960's, Mao believed that parts of Chinese society were straying from the goals of communism. He attributed this to the influence of the West and the revisionist forces within the university systems. In response, Mao embarked on his most famous domestic agenda, which was given the grand name "the Cultural Revolution." Culture was truly revolutionized: The universities were shut down for four years, and the students and faculty were sent to work in the fields in an effort to change their "elitist" attitudes. When the universities reopened, the curriculum was reorganized to include only communist studies and vocational training. After the Cultural Revolution and Mao's death in 1976, the new leadership quickly changed the education policy and began to focus on restructuring the economic policies. Nevertheless, Mao's Cultural Revolution succeeded in reaffirming communist philosophy at a time when the rest of the communist world was beginning to question itself.

3. RELIGIONS AND PHILOSOPHIES INFLUENCING CULTURE

Animism—Sub-Saharan Africa

Animism is not an organized, definable religion in the same way that Islam, Judaism, and Catholicism are. Instead, Animism is the label given to the hundreds of religions that have developed in sub-Saharan Africa. Animist religions do share some common bonds. They generally share a belief in a supreme being that regulates nature, but they also share a belief in thousands of lesser spirits found in all natural things. The religious leaders of the tribes in Africa communicate with the spirits in trees, rocks, water, and even storms, pleading with them to meet the needs of the tribes and listening to them for messages to give to their followers. The idea of the importance of nature has long made Africa more resistant to materialism and industrialization. The traditional African religions require people to love the positive forces of nature while fearing and respecting the negative forces. The predominant role of nature in Animist religions has affected the arts, rituals, and even the economic development of sub-Saharan Africa.

Buddhism—Southeast Asia

Buddhism might be better described as a life philosophy than a religion, since its practitioners do not believe in an all-powerful god or gods that can grant them salvation. Buddhists believe that it is up to the individual to acquire wisdom, and that the effort to do so will allow the individual to break free of materialism, eventually achieving the state of nirvana—a desire-free life. Buddhism is predominant in East and Southeast Asia, and has affected the cultural and social development of the region. Buddhism focuses on proper behavior, realized through the Four Noble Truths and the Eightfold Path. In general, this behavior is centered on meditation and a denial of materialism. These beliefs have contributed to the region's relative isolation and general subsistence living for centuries.

Christianity—Europe

Christians believe that Jesus Christ is the son of God and that forgiveness of sins, and ultimately everlasting life, is achievable only through belief in the divinity, death, and resurrection of Christ. Because Christianity is an evangelical religion, many Christians also believe that it is their duty to spread their message to the unconverted. After Constantine converted to Christianity, the Christian hierarchy dominated not only religious activity in Europe, but political and social activity as well. During the European Middle Ages, Christians were not tolerant of the practitioners of other religions, and embarked on the Crusades in order to convert the Muslims who had taken control of the Holy Land. Ultimately, they were not successful. Yet, even after the Reformation, both Protestants and Catholics remained committed to the conversion of others. This fit in nicely with the imperialistic plans of the European monarchies. The monarchies gained overwhelming public support for their invasions of established nations in the Americas, Africa, and Asia by justifying the actions as a way to convert the heathens to Christianity. Many Europeans supported imperialism as a moral and religious duty, in some cases supporting any means available to accomplish their end. Millions of Christians, of course, practiced their religion faithfully and genuinely, and consequently converted others to Christianity based on the strength of their faith and the merits of their religion. Nevertheless, imperialists and mercantilists were not above using the religion of the people to support their political and economic agendas. As Europe attempted to convert the world to Christianity, it transformed itself into the most dominant and powerful continent the world had ever seen.

Confucianism—China

Confucianism is a life philosophy more than a religion because it is concerned with daily conduct in the present, not with salvation or the afterlife. Confucius focused on individual relationships, including the duties that individuals owe to one another within their families and the relationships between superiors and inferiors. Confucian philosophy assumes a class society wherein inferior classes owe respect to superior classes and superior classes (most importantly the ruling class) owe fairness and kindness to the inferior classes. The same is true for family relationships: The younger generations must be respectful and dutiful to the older generations, including generations that have already passed away.

Confucianism has affected Chinese culture enormously. For centuries, it reinforced the class system and repressed new ideas from the younger generations. It also contributed to internal order within the society. As long as everyone played out the role expected of them, society was orderly and predictable. Today, Confucianism affects the social relationships of hundreds of millions of Chinese, even though Communist China is officially atheist and officially classless.

Islam—Middle East

Islam is a monotheistic faith. Muslims do not worship Muhammad as God, but worship God through the message brought to them by Muhammad. Muslims believe that salvation is won through submission to the will of God, and that this can be accomplished by means of the Five Pillars of Islam. These Five Pillars include a confession of faith, prayer five times a day while bowing toward Mecca, charity to the needy, fasting during the month of Ramadan, and a pilgrimage to Mecca at least once during one's life. But there is much more to the Islamic faith than just the Five Pillars.

Islam has affected the social and political development of the Middle East enormously. Since many nations are Islamic states as opposed to secular states, the tenets of Islam serve as the official law of the land. Everything from women's rights to clothing is dictated by the Islamic faith and enforced by the law. In nations with a strong Islamic fundamentalist presence, such as Iran, attempts to modernize or westernize the economy and social customs often have been denounced as heresy. This has led to strained relations with the West. And although many Middle Eastern countries have had moderate leaders, as long as the majority of people want Islam to be entrenched in the political system, the Islamic faith will likely continue to dominate the political and social developments of the region.

Judaism—Israel

Judaism is an ancient religion of the Middle East, specifically Palestine. Jews are monotheistic, and believe that life should be spent living the will of God as told to Moses. There are many subgroups within Judaism, but the belief that they are the chosen people of God is central to the faith. It is this belief that has bonded them together even as they were dispersed around the world during the Diaspora. Throughout the Middle Ages and since, Jews have been persecuted and separated from Christian groups in Europe, North America, and North Africa. Yet, many of them never lost touch with their faith. If anything, persecution and atrocities like the Holocaust made them stronger in their faith. The Zionist movement was built on the idea that Jews are the chosen people of God, and advocated the creation of a Jewish homeland in Palestine, the land that was promised to Moses by God. As a result, the modern nation of Israel was established in 1947 as a Jewish state, but it remains surrounded by hostile Muslim nations. Therefore, one lasting impact of the creation of the state of Israel as a Jewish homeland has unfortunately been persistent animosity and violence, which in turn has contributed to an unprecedented military build-up in the region.

4. NEGATIVE IMPACT OF GEOGRAPHIC FACTORS

Africa—the North Sahel

Nomadic herding groups are common south of the Sahara in Africa. One such group is the North Sahel, who raise cattle for food. A variety of factors require the North Sahel to move their cattle to lands where they can graze. In a typical year, the cattle have to be herded to new pastures when the old ones are depleted, but they periodically return to a central location where other members of the group farm the land. However, when unfavorable weather conditions affect the grazing land, the North Sahel have to travel even farther, and may be gone from the farming members of the group for an extended period of time. In the early 1970s, almost no rain fell in the region for about four years. The cattle were repeatedly moved, but soon all the grazing lands were dry. The governments of the region did very little to aid the nomads and, as a result, thousands of cattle died, followed by thousands of people who depended on the cattle for food. Historically, nomadic groups such as the North Sahel have contributed to the region's lack of long-term economic development because they do not stay in one place long enough for economic activity to take root. Therefore, it is not surprising that during the drought, the economy of the region was even more unstable, and long-term economic growth seemed even more farfetched.

To offset the problems in the Sahel region, which stretches south of the Sahara from Mauritania in the west to Ethiopia in the east, the governments of the region worked hard to attract foreign food and financial aid. This was very important, since the population growth in the region has strained their resources for several decades. While aid was relatively generous in the 1970s, most of the aid unfortunately did not actually reach those who needed it the most. Most of the aid from the United States, for example, was actually used to pay the salaries of the experts who were sent to help, rather than being used directly for food and agricultural technology.

Asia—Japan

Japan is a small, mountainous island nation with relatively few natural resources. At the same time, its population has grown dramatically for centuries. With little farmland and few natural resources, Japan's geographical size and topography have been tremendous barriers to development.

Japan has managed to overcome its geographic barrier to development by importing raw materials from other nations. Since the Meiji Restoration in the late nineteenth century, Japan has become a major player in the world economy by effectively managing its imports and exports. In the early twentieth century, Japan invaded other parts of Asia in order to gain inexpensive access to the raw materials it needed. The Japanese followed the trend of mercantilism established by European imperialists centuries before. They robbed their colonies of their plentiful resources, shipped them back to Japan where they were made into finished products, and then sent those finished products abroad (as well as back to the colonies), where they were sold for a profit. Since the end of World War II, Japan has continued to manage its imports and exports well, despite the fact that it no longer has colonial holdings. Japan still imports most of its raw materials from other nations, and it turns those relatively inexpensive raw materials into much more expensive high-tech finished products. Combined with protectionist trade barriers against other nations, Japan has consistently managed to overcome its geographic barriers by making a profit from other nations' natural resources.

Europe—Poland

Except along the mountainous southern border, Poland is a large, flat plain. Economically, Poland has benefited from the land, which not only is agriculturally rich, but also is rich in resources such as coal, copper, natural gas, and sulfur. However, politically and militarily, Poland has been cursed by the land, which does not offer many natural barriers against invasion, especially from the west, east, and southeast. Poland has been carved into pieces as a result of invasions from Prussia, Austria, and Russia. In 1918, independence was achieved, and it looked like Poland might actually develop peacefully and intact. But in 1939, the Germans swept through Poland, sparking World War II. When the terrible war finally ended, leaving Poland devastated, the Soviets took over. Eventually, in 1990, Poland split from the Soviet Bloc and, under the leadership of Lech Walesa, developed its economy.

Poland now relies on its alliances with the West, most notably with NATO, to give it the protection that its topography and location cannot. So long as Poland has friendly neighbors, its topography can actually serve as an economic benefit, since few geographic barriers stand in the way between the Polish economy and those of its neighbors.

Latin America—the Incan Nation

Latin America is a region with a diverse geography that has both blessed and haunted the development of the region. It is hard to ignore the particular impact of the Andes Mountains, especially in pre-Columbian Latin America. The mountains are located near the coast of western South

America, creating a very narrow coastal plain that is virtually unusable for farming. For the Incas, who built their empire in the Andes, the topography presented an agricultural challenge that had to be overcome in order for the empire to survive.

The Incas were able to develop a thriving, advanced civilization throughout this mountainous region. Simply put, the geographical challenge led to agricultural innovation. The Incas used methods of irrigation and terrace farming to farm the slopes and the highlands. They successfully farmed corn and potatoes to feed their growing population. Eventually, the Incan Empire extended all along the western slopes of the mountain range, creating a very narrow but very long empire united under a common geography and way of life.

Middle East—Saudi Arabia

In the Middle East and North Africa, deserts are the primary geographical barrier to development. The Sahara Desert dominates North Africa, and in the Middle East, the landscape is also dominated by deserts, with the exception of the lands of the Fertile Crescent in the Tigris-Euphrates River Valley, sources of significant vegetation. Saudi Arabia, for example, is nearly entirely a desert region. As such, fresh drinking water is in short supply, and agricultural development is severely impaired.

In recent decades, Saudi Arabia has transformed its economy—even its agricultural economy—despite the desert. This is mostly because of the vast supply of petroleum that lies beneath the sands. As the world has industrialized, it has become increasingly dependent on petroleum for fuel. As a result, Saudi Arabia has become more and more wealthy, supplying as much as one quarter of the world's petroleum. With all this newfound money, Saudi Arabia is spending billions on attempts to improve its agricultural sector through irrigation and desalinization processes. In this way, Saudi Arabia is not simply adapting to the desert, but is beginning to overcome and transform it.

5. INVENTIONS AND TECHNOLOGICAL ADVANCES

Ancient Egyptian (350–1090 BC)

The Ancient Egyptian kingdom thrived along the banks of the Nile River for two millennia, taking advantage of the constant water supply that the river provided. Seasonal flooding created rich farmland along the banks of the Nile, but some areas had too much water and other areas didn't get enough. To help solve this problem, the ancient Egyptians devised a system of draining and irrigation, which redistributed and balanced the water supply over a much greater land area than nature allowed. The effect was enormous. It allowed the empire to feed a growing population, and the growing population expanded the empire further and further away from the banks of the Nile.

Maya (300–900)

Among many innovations developed by Mayan civilization, the Mayan calendar is one of the most impressive. It involved two distinct systems: the Long Count and the Calendar Round. The Long Count measured the number of days that had elapsed since the day the Mayas believed the earth was created (for the third time) in 3114 BC. The Calendar Round involved two interlocking cogwheels, one as a numbered day and the other as a named day. The Mayan calendar is an excellent example of the way in which Mayan mythology interacted with Mayan technology. The technology of the Mayan clock system rivaled other clock technology in the world at the time. The meaning of the days and years that were being counted, however, reflected the particular beliefs of the Mayan civilization. In this way, the calendar not only kept track of Mayan progression, but actually contributed to it.

Islamic (600–1200)

The Golden Age of Islamic culture made great contributions to math, science, and the arts. In the process, Baghdad became a center of culture and knowledge. One of the most significant innovations was in medicine. Muslim doctors perfected techniques for both diagnosing diseases as well as for treating them. Muhammad al-Razi even published a medical encyclopedia known as *The Comprehensive Work in Medicine.* Building on this tradition, Muslims later set up medical schools and qualifying examinations for physicians. These innovations in medicine had an obvious impact on the health of the Islamic Empire, and influenced the world beyond as well. During the European Renaissance, European medical schools were inspired by the innovations that had been developed in the Islamic Empire and drew from them. And through Europe, the ideas spread to much of the world.

Western European (1400–1700)

In the fifteenth century, Guttenberg invented movable type, and the printing press was born. The consequences were profound in Europe. Because of the printing press, the ideas of Luther's Reformation spread rapidly, leading to the reorganization of Europe along religious lines. The

Bible was printed in popular languages (such as German), allowing people to read and interpret the Bible for themselves, rather than relying on the Church hierarchy. This individualism led to the Enlightenment, which questioned the role of government authority and consequently changed man's relationship with man. All the while, literacy increased dramatically, books became much less expensive, and education became an important goal for millions. In short, the printing press revolutionized Europe and the rest of the world because it brought information to the masses. If knowledge is power, then the printing press resulted in a redistribution of power.

British (1700–1900)

The steam engine made the Industrial Revolution in Europe, specifically in Britain, possible by becoming the principle power source for industry and transport. Steam-powered railroads brought tons of raw materials to steam-powered factories, and then took finished products back to communities that were developing along the rail lines. In the British colonies, the colonists built thousands of miles of railroad lines straight into the heart of areas rich in natural resources, robbing the natives. Through the use of steam-powered ships, the Europeans more efficiently carried out their mercantilist policies in the colonies, enabling the powers to control greater and greater expanses of land with relative ease. Within Britain, the factory system changed daily life, characterized by health hazards, long work hours uninterrupted by seasonal change, child labor, and mindless repetition. As a result, new political philosophies such as communism became attractive to large numbers of exploited factory workers, while unrestrained capitalism became attractive to many factory owners. Thus, while the steam engine was the catalyst of the Industrial Revolution, it was also the engine of social, philosophical, political, and cultural change.

Japanese (1853–present)

At the close of World War II, which was economically devastating to Japan, the country lost its colonies and with them, its access to the raw materials that are not within its own borders. As a result, the government of Japan quickly focused on the one resource it did have: people. By spending billions on technical schools and infrastructure, Japan managed to establish a manufacturing base that added considerable value to the raw materials it imported. Products such as machine tools, autos, electronics, TVs, transistors, cameras, and computers poured off the assembly lines. All of these products had one thing in common: They were much more valuable than the cost of the materials used to create them. As a result, from the 1950s to the 1970s, Japan had the highest economic growth rate in the world. What's more, since Japanese workers are employed for life, their loyalty to the companies for which they work is almost unparalleled. This contributes to an even more efficient economy, since relatively little energy has to be spent on the training and hiring process. The products made by these knowledge-intensive industries were first intended for use within Japan, and government policies contributed to this effort by establishing protectionist trading policies. Eventually, Japan dramatically increased its exports to offset the raw materials it was importing. Since the finished products are worth considerably more than the raw materials used in their creation, and since Japan's protectionist trade policies have continued into the present, Japan has been able to finish most years with a sizable trade surplus.

South Asian (1970–present)

Since the end of World War II, the population of India has exploded to nearly one billion people. In addition, the Green Revolution has swept through much of the developing world, offering innovative ways to increase agricultural yield per acre. In India, the results have been dramatic, but insufficient to keep up with the rate of population growth. Irrigation systems have been installed to bring water to farms during the dry season. Increased use of farm machinery and fertilizers have also helped to maximize yield. Yet, the rural farming communities of India remain very traditional in both their beliefs and practices. Many people have resisted the changes imposed on them by the government. Using the tools and methods of their parents, they want to continue to follow the traditional patterns of the wet and dry seasons created by monsoons. The government and urban population of India have pushed for agricultural reform, and have succeeded to some degree. However, the reforms will not lead to a widespread agricultural revolution unless the people on the farms can find a way to reconcile their traditional beliefs with agricultural change.

6. TWENTIETH CENTURY HUMAN RIGHTS VIOLATIONS

Chiapas Indians in Mexico

The Chiapas Indians in Mexico are of Mayan descent, and have been treated as lower class citizens since the European conquest of Latin America. The Chiapas have traditionally been forced to work the land, but they have not been permitted to own land themselves. Throughout the 1800s and early 1900s, the Chiapas joined other groups in protesting and even fighting for the right to own land, or at the very least the right to earn an income sufficient enough to give them the means to rise above the poverty level. Their cause was taken up in 1911 by Emiliano Zapata, who toppled the dictatorship of Porfirio Diaz and demanded the return of large portions of Mexican land to Native Americans. The new government did not oblige, so a group of Chiapas, calling themselves Zapatistas, rebelled against the landlords and the government soldiers in an effort to seize control of large plots of land. After a decade of fighting, a new constitution was adopted in 1917 that granted limited land rights to the peasants. However, because of racial prejudice, the Chiapas Indians have not been able to take advantage of the land rights that have been extended to other groups. In 1994, a group of Chiapas, once again calling themselves Zapatistas, renewed the century-old rebellion and actually captured the second largest city in the Chiapas region of Mexico. President Salinas sent troops to quell the rebellion, which is precisely what they did. In recent years, the Chiapas have been negotiating with the Mexican government for the basic rights to own land and to receive appropriate wages through which they can reasonably acquire land.

Women in China

In traditional China, women's rights were consistently and methodically violated by cultural and institutional practices that subjugated them to their husbands, restricted their rights of marriage and divorce, condoned their sale into slavery by their families, and imposed cruel expectations (such as footbinding). In the twentieth century, as a result of the Communist Revolution, these practices have been abandoned. However, a new type of human rights violation now threatens Chinese women—namely, the violation of their reproductive rights. Due to unprecedented population growth, during the 1980s the Chinese government enforced a one-child-per-family law that not only restricted women's choices, but led to government-encouraged sterilization and abortions, even in cases in which the woman would have preferred to have a second child. What's more, the policy increased female infanticide in the country, since most Chinese couples would rather have a son than a daughter. Since, under the policy, couples were limited to one child, they would sometimes kill their first-born if she were a female in the hope of getting a male the second time around. Fortunately, the Chinese government has recently relaxed its one-child policy.

Political Dissidents in the Soviet Union

Political dissidents are people who speak out against the policies of their government. In the case of the former Soviet Union, political dissidents were seen as threats to the stability of the communist regime, and were consequently sent to labor camps, mental hospitals, and/or to their deaths.

Most dissidents tried to bring national and international attention to human rights violations, censorship, and the use of the secret police. Typically they did not act in the form of public demonstrations, because to do so would have resulted in even harsher punishments. Rather, they used the *samizdat*, an underground press network that circulated writings throughout the Soviet Union and beyond. One of the best examples of this comes from Alexander Solzhenitsyn, who wrote three books about his prison and labor camp experiences and then distributed them via the samizdat. Eventually, the books made it out the country and were openly published abroad. The books so angered the Soviet authorities that they exiled Solzhenitsyn from the country. Andrei Sakharov, a prominent Soviet scientist, was a political dissident whose denunciation of Soviet human rights violations led the Nobel committee to award him the Nobel Peace Prize in 1975 (the Soviet Union would not allow him to leave the country to accept the award). These men are just two examples of thousands of political dissidents who, simply because they expressed their political views in a peaceful fashion, were subjected to severe human rights violations by their government.

Jews in Europe

Although many groups of people were denied basic human rights in Germany in the years prior to and during World War II, Jews were singled out and deliberately slaughtered. The rise of Adolf Hitler in post-World War I Germany led to an increase in anti-Semitic propaganda, since Hitler's brand of intense nationalism was based not merely on love of country, but love of race. Hitler's Nazi party did not attempt to unite all Germans, it sought to unite *Aryan* Germans against virtually everyone else. The millions of Jews who lived in Germany and German-occupied lands were rounded up, blamed for every conceivable problem in society, and methodically killed in gas chambers, firing lines, and ovens. When Nazi Germany was finally destroyed, Germany was split in half and tensions in the region remained high. Many of the surviving Jews fled to Israel and the United States. The Holocaust can never be undone; however, many survivors have made it their mission that the inhumanity never be forgotten so that it is never repeated.

Indigenous Peoples in Brazil

The Yanomami of northern Brazil have traditionally been one of South America's most secluded groups of indigenous people. They are a small, self-sufficient group of hunters and gatherers who live in small groups scattered throughout the rain forest. And although they engage in very little self-destructive behavior, they are on the verge of dying out. Since the

1960's, logging companies have slowly destroyed their homeland. To make the situation worse, for decades the government of Brazil not only politically and economically backed the logging companies, but also constructed highways and airstrips in the region occupied by the Yanomami, bringing ecological disruption and disease. By the late 1980s, the development in the region had reached fever pitch, and thousands of Brazilian prospectors rushed to the region in search of valuable resources rumored to be contained below the forests. All of this was being done in violation of the basic human rights of the Yanomami whose centuries-old homeland and way of life was being taken away from them without their consent. Fortunately, in 1991, the newly elected President Fernando Collor de Mello set aside a sizable chunk of land for the Yanomami. It is hoped that enough Yanomami have survived the human rights violations of this century that they can prosper once again in the next.

Kurds in Iraq

Iraq has consistently violated the human rights of one of its most unwanted minorities, the Kurds. The Kurds are a distinct nation of people with their own language and traditions, and yet no place to call home. In addition to Iraq, millions of Kurds are located in Southeastern Turkey and Northern Iran, but most hope to one day live in a country of their own. Their goal of self-determination has withstood the worst of circumstances. After World War II, Britain promised to establish the independent nation of Kurdistan in the Treaty of Sevres, but it was never ratified. Since then, the governments of the region have committed atrocious violations of human rights, in an attempt to force the Kurds to renounce their identity. They have prohibited the use of the Kurdish language, restricted Kurdish literature, and closed Kurdish schools. More recently, the Iraqi government used the Kurds in its war against Iran and then, after the war ended, turned on them. Tens of thousands of Kurds fled to Turkey when Saddam Hussein's government chased them out with chemical weapons. Since Turkey has also violated the rights of the Kurds, they feel as though they have no place to go. But Kurdish resistance is largely unorganized because subgroups of Kurds have different goals. The Kurds do have one goal in common: representation in government. Currently, however, they enjoy no meaningful representation in any national government and hopes of the establishment of an independent nation are dim.

Untouchables in India

The caste system in India has led to many violations of human rights, especially against members of the lowest caste, the *untouchables*. Members of the lowest caste cannot associate with members of higher castes, neither in social situations nor in business partnerships. The untouchables are prevented from marrying, befriending, or even talking to people of higher castes. The government of India has tried to alleviate the situation by outlawing the caste system. However, because the caste system is a part of the traditional culture and dominant religion of India, the government's efforts have not been successful, especially in rural areas. In a further effort, the government has taken it upon itself to hire many untouchables for government jobs. Nevertheless, because the human rights violations of untouchables are culturally sanctioned by millions of Indians and by the dominant religion, the government can only do so much. If the untouchables are truly to gain human rights in India, a change in culture at a fundamental level will need to occur.

7. IMPERIALISM AND INDEPENDENCE

Great Britain, perhaps the most powerful colonial power the world has ever known, became imperialistic for a variety of reasons, ranging from egoism to the need for strategically located military outposts. Most significantly, however, Great Britain became imperialistic for economic reasons. From the seventeenth to the twentieth centuries, Great Britain followed an imperialistic policy known as *mercantilism*. Specifically, Great Britain established colonies in order to gain unlimited and unrestricted access to raw materials, which were then shipped back to Great Britain. As Britain industrialized, these raw materials were used to make finished products, which in turn were shipped back to the colonies for sale at a profit. Since Britain did not allow its colonies to trade with any other nation, Britain guaranteed itself markets for its products.

Although no continent managed to escape British colonialism, the Indian subcontinent was perhaps Britain's greatest colonial holding. A nation blessed with rich resources, India also had an enormous population, which had the potential of developing into an enormous market for British-made goods. In 1600, the English East India Company set up shop in India, hoping to make money by selling Indian made goods in world markets. Throughout the eighteenth century, the East India Company methodically increased its influence over Indian affairs, eventually building forts, maintaining an army of sepoys (Indian soldiers who served in British armies), and exerting political influence in many parts of India. By the mid-1800s, many leaders in the British Parliament wanted the British government to assume responsibility for India, thereby taking authority away from the East India Company. After the Sepoy Rebellion against the British in 1858, Parliament finally took direct control of India by sending in its own troops. By 1858, India was a full-fledged colony of Britain.

The impact of British colonialism on India was enormous. First, the British shifted agricultural production in India away from growing food to growing cotton, which in turn was used in British factories. Although this policy was beneficial for the British, it was devastating for the Indians. Not only did the policy hurt Indian-owned hand-made industries, which could not compete with the price of mass-produced British goods, but it created a food shortage in India that resulted in the starvation of millions. Second, the British were intent on imposing their own culture onto India, and thereby attempted to Christianize the region by building schools in which the curriculum was equivalent to that of British schools. This policy led to the development of a western-educated middle class within India that eventually led to a nationalist movement against British control.

In 1885, several well-educated Indians formed the Indian National Congress. Initially, the group did not appeal for independence from Britain. Rather, it argued for greater rights for Indians and greater Indian representation in the government. British leaders did not take the formation of the Indian National Congress seriously, however, even after some members began calling for Indian independence. This lack of concern was based mostly on the realization that the native population was split between Hindus and Muslims, who often were pitted against each other. As a result of the religious split, British authorities assumed that the Indian population would never be organized enough to carry through with a united revolt.

Indian nationalism grew, however. Britain became increasingly nervous, especially after the surprising success of the Bolshevik Revolution in Russia, which sent a wake-up call to traditional European powers. Britain became suspicious of any nationalistic tendencies within its colonies and in the early twentieth century, instituted tough new laws against Indian conspiracy for nationalism. This act, of course, only served to encourage greater nationalistic tendencies. It was at this point that Gandhi, the leader of the Indian National Congress, called for a change in British policy through peaceful civil disobedience. Some of Gandhi's countrymen were more violent in their demands—they attacked and killed a few Englishmen in Amritsar in 1919. A British general reacted against the crowd (not just against the individual aggressors), and killed nearly 400 Indians, injuring hundreds more.

The consequences of the Amritsar revolt and massacre were not immediate, but they were significant. Many British officials defended the general, while Indians rallied behind the nationalistic cause. Through it all, Gandhi maintained his practice of peaceful resistance, which allowed him to gain worldwide legitimacy and support. After Gandhi successfully gained world sympathy by leading fasts and salt marches, international pressure came to bear on Britain. The British became increasingly reluctant to pursue violent suppression of nationalism in the face of well-maintained, nonviolent opposition, and as a consequence, India was finally granted its independence in 1947.

EXAMINATION
JANUARY 1999

Part I (55 credits): Answer all 48 questions in this part.

Directions (1–48): For each statement or question, write on the separate answer sheet the *number* of the word or expression that, of those given, best completes the statement or answers the question.

---

1 Most traditional societies maintain social control and group cooperation through the use of
1 subsistence farming
2 regional elections
3 democratic decisionmaking
4 the extended family

2 Which statement is most closely associated with the economic policy of mercantilism?
1 Colonies should exist for the benefit of the mother country.
2 Local authority should determine the type of goods to be produced.
3 Governments should not be involved in the economy.
4 Business and industry should be owned by the state.

3 India's earliest civilizations were located in
1 mountainous areas
2 river valleys
3 coastal regions
4 dry steppes

4 The *Upanishads,* the *Ramayan,* and the *Bhagavad Gita* are considered to be significant pieces of Indian literature because they

1 provide guidelines for Hindu living and behavior
2 identify basic Buddhist principles
3 show the constant class struggle in Indian life
4 reflect the similarities between the Hindu and Muslim religions

5 A newspaper published in India recently included these items.

- an article entitled "Toward Christian Unity in India"
- a picture of an Indian cricket team
- a review of an Elton John compact disc

Which is the most valid conclusion to be drawn from this information?

1 The Indian Government has abandoned its policy of nonalignment.
2 Cultural diffusion is a factor in Indian life.
3 The British still have control over Indian affairs.
4 The Indian people have abandoned their traditional religions.

6 The Meiji Restoration in Japan was characterized by a movement toward

1 feudalism   3 isolationism
2 modernization   4 socialism

[OVER]

Base your answer to question 7 on the cartoon below and on your knowledge of social studies.

7 In the 1930's, Japan decided that one way to solve its economic problems was by expanding its territory. Based on this cartoon, which statement reflects the result of this decision?

1 Japanese rule benefited many people in Asia.
2 Japan lost control of East Asia.
3 Imperialism can have unintended consequences.
4 Technological progress requires international cooperation.

8 "Under the weight of winter snow
   The pine tree's branches bend
   But do not break."

   —Emperor Hirohito

   In this poem, what message was the Japanese
   Emperor trying to communicate to his people at
   the end of 1945?

   1 As a victorious nation, Japan must treat those
      it conquered with kindness.
   2 As a result of its defeat, Japan must adopt Con-
      fucian ideals.
   3 Since Japan had been the strongest nation in
      Asia, the nation would try to defeat its enemies
      again.
   4 Although Japan had been defeated in war, the
      economy and the nation would recover.

9 The ethnocentric attitudes of various Chinese emperors can best be attributed to the

   1 cultural isolation of China
   2 failure of other nations to become interested
      in China
   3 interest of Chinese scholars in other civiliza-
      tions
   4 great cultural diversity within China's borders

[OVER]

10 In China, the terms "commune," "Great Leap Forward," and "Cultural Revolution" are associated
with the

1 economic success o the Manchu dynasty
2 Mandate of Heaven
3 Confucian emphasis on the five human relationships
4 leadership of Mao Zedong

Base your answer to question 11 on the quotation
below and on your knowledge of social studies.

"It doesn't matter if the cat is black or white as
long as it catches mice."
— Deng Xiaoping

11 In this quotation, Deng Xiaoping implies that to
achieve success, China should

1 adhere to strict Marxian socialism
2 continue Mao Zedong's elimination of Western
   cultural influences in China
3 establish a policy of mercantilism
4 use whatever means necessary to improve its
   economy

12 In the 17th and 18th centuries, the Dutch interest in the islands of Southeast Asia was mainly based
on the

1 spice trade
2 large numbers of Christian converts
3 rich deposits of gold and silver
4 development of manufacturing sites

13 Although many Southeast Asian nations have vecome independent, they have not been totally free of Western influence. One indication of this influence is that the governments in these nations have

1 joined the European Union
2 depended heavily on foreign capital for economic development
3 adopted Christianity as the official state religion
4 relied mainly on European nations for their food supply

14 In the 19th century, opposition to the encomienda system in Latin America demonstrated the need for

1 landholding reforms
2 trade restrictions
3 female suffrage
4 a minimum-wage law

15 In the 19th century, the independence movements in Latin America were greatly influenced by the

1 Glorious Revolution   3 Boer War
2 Hundred Years War   4 French Revolution

[OVER]

16 "North Americans are always among us, even when they ignore us or turn their back on us. Their shadow covers the whole hemisphere. It is the shadow of a giant."

— Octavio Paz

Which attitude is being summarized by this Latin American writer?

1 admiration for United States technology and wealth
2 desire for American cultural values and traditions
3 resentment of United States economic and political influence
4 envy of American democratic institutions

Base your answer to question 17 on the cartoon below and on your knowledge of social studies.

Gorrell, Richmond Times-Dispatch

17 What is the main idea of this 1994 cartoon?

1 Haiti's lack of industrialization has led to economic stagnation.

2 Haiti's limited experience with democracy has made it difficult to establish this form of government.

3 The desire for democracy has led Haiti to neglect its development of modern technology.

4 The presence of American industry has failed to improve Haiti's economy.

[OVER]

18 Archbishop Desmond Tutu and Nelson Mandela both won Nobel Peace Prizes for their opposition to
   1 the practice of apartheid in South Africa
   2 European imperialism in North Africa
   3 international sanctions against South Africa
   4 foreign religious influences in Africa

19 Since the African National Congress came to power in South Africa in 1994, its primary aim has been to
   1 establish one-party rule in South Africa
   2 unite the people of South Africa in a democratic republic
   3 restore Dutch influence on South African culture
   4 create a homeland for white separatists

Base your answer to question 20 on the map below and on your knowledge of social studies.

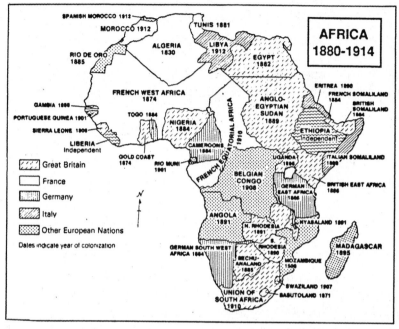

Source: *World History: Patterns of Civilization*

20 Which conclusion is valid, based on the information shown on this map of Africa in 1914?

1 All of North Africa was controlled by France.
2 Belgium was the last country to establish colonies in Africa.
3 The Union of South Africa was settled by the Spanish in the early 20th century.
4 Great Britain and France controlled most of Africa.

[OVER]

21 The Code of Hammurabi of Sumeria, the Twelve Tables of Rome, and the Justinian Code of the Byzantine Empire were similar in that they

1 provided a basis for behavior for medieval knights and Japanese samurai
2 are legal systems developed to create order for the society
3 are documents that maintained the position of the upper classes
4 became examples of religious doctrine for other societies

22 When Kemal Atatürk became the political leader of Turkey, his policies differed from those of the Ottoman Empire. One difference between these policies was that

1 Western ideas and practices were adopted
2 a limited monarchy was established
3 Islamic fundamentalism became a major political force
4 imperialism was used to gain territory in Europe

23 Great Britain's primary motivation for acquiring control of the Suez Canal in the late 19th century was to

1 protect British trade interests in Asia
2 introduce democratic principles in this region
3 make up for the loss of the Panama Canal
4 prohibit the movement of ships from Russia

24 In Iran under Ayatollah Khomeini and in Afghanistan throughout the 1990's, an effect of the Islamic
fundamentalist government has been to

1 produce an agrarian-based economy
2 eliminate anti-Israeli terrorist groups
3 create a strong military alliance with the United
States
4 limit rights for women

25 Which European historical periods are in the proper
chronological order?

1 Middle Ages → Renaissance →Ancient Greece
→ Roman Empire
2 Renaissance → Ancient Greece → Roman
Empire → Middle Ages
3 Ancient Greece → Roman Empire → Middle
Ages → Renaissance
4 Roman Empire → Middle Ages → Renaissance
→ Ancient Greece

[OVER]

Base your answer to question 26 on the quotations below and on your knowledge of social studies.

> "The pope is the only person whose feet are kissed by all princes. His title is unique in the world. He may depose [remove] emperors."
>
> — Pope Gregory VII
> (11th century)

> "An emperor is subject to no one but to God and justice."
>
> — Frederick Barbarossa, Holy Roman Emperor
> (12th century)

26 The ideas expressed in these quotations show that during the Middle Ages in Europe

1 popes gave little attention to political matters
2 monarchs dominated the Church's leaders
3 popes and monarchs sometimes challenged the other's authority
4 monarchs and popes strengthened the role of the Church

27 One similarity between the Renaissance and the Enlightenment is that both historic periods

1 produced major cultural changes
2 encouraged traditional values
3 limited technological advancements
4 ignored individual achievements

28 A major effect of the Reformation in Europe was the

1 decline of religious unity
2 increased use of the divine right theory
3 emergence of mercantilism
4 increase in military dictatorships

29 "I offer neither pay, nor quarters, nor provisions; I offer hunger, thirst, forced marches, battles, and death. Let him who loves his country in his heart, and not with his lips only, follow me."

—Giuseppe Garibaldi

Which concept is expressed by Garibaldi in this statement?

1 scarcity
2 nationalism
3 humanism
4 empathy

[OVER]

Base your answers to questions 30 and 31 on the quotation below and on your knowledge of social studies.

"No observer of Manchester [England] in the 1830's and 1840's dwelt on its happy, well-fed people. 'Wretched, defrauded, oppressed, crushed human nature lying in bleeding fragments all over the face of society,' wrote an American in 1845. . . . Can we be surprised that the first generation of the labouring poor in . . . Britain looked at the results of capitalism and found them wanting?"

—E.J Hobsbawm

30 This quotation describes some negative effects of the

1 Black Plague   3 Napoleonic Wars
2 Glorious Revolution   4 Industrial Revolution

31 The conditions in England described in this quotation encouraged the growth of

1 socialism   3 feudalism
2 Christianity   4 Zionism

Base your answer to question 32 on the map below and on your knowledge of social studies.

Mongol Empires, 1200–1350

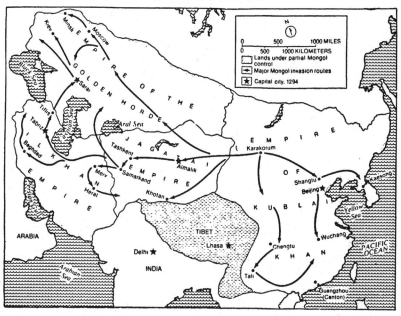

32 Which statement about the Mongol Empire is supported by information provided by the map?

1 Moscow became a capital city in 1294.
2 The Mongol Empire extended from the Pacific Ocean to the Atlantic Ocean.
3 Much of present-day Ukraine and Russia was under the rule of the Mongols.
4 The Mongol invasion routes passed through the city of Dehli.

[OVER]

33 A study of the Byzantine civilization would show that this civilization

1 collapsed as a result of the Germanic invasions of the early Middle Ages

2 preserved Greek and Roman learning and passed it on to western and eastern Europe

3 based its economy on subsistence farming and slash-and-burn agriculture.

4 reduced the influence of the Eastern Orthodox Church

34 Which practice was similar under the rule of the Bolsheviks in Russia and of the Nazi Party in Germany?

1 establishing communism in their respective nations

2 permitting a series of multiparty elections

3 increasing the power of the middle class

4 limiting government opposition through intimidation and fear

Base your answer to question 35 on the map below
and on your knowledge of social studies

35 Which event in the early 1990's resulted in the formation of the six new nations shown on the map?

1 unification of Eastern European ethnic groups
2 dismantling of the Berlin Wall
3 collapse of the Soviet Union
4 resolution of long-standing border disputes

[OVER]

36 Under both the czarist regime of Russia and the Communist government of the Soviet Union, artistic expression was censored primarily because

1 the arts were considered unimportant
2 no markets existed for artistic or literary works
3 criticism of the government was sometimes reflected in the arts
4 support of the arts was considered a waste of money

37 The strong showing by the Communist Party in the Russian Presidential election of 1996 suggests that large numbers of Russian people

1 favored a return to Stalin's policy of imprisoning dissidents
2 feared continuing economic instability and high inflation
3 wanted the Russian Orthodox Church to play a larger role in government
4 supported a return to isolationist policies

38 One similarity between the feudal manors of Europe and the traditional villages of India is that

1 peasants were seldom able to change their social status
2 women dominated the political decisions of the local councils
3 children could choose from a number of different occupations
4 monarchs exerted absolute power over local governments

39 • Aztec civilization
   • Roman Empire
   • Reign of the czars in Russia

During each of these historical periods, one similar development was the

1 expansion of civil rights for the individual
2 disruption of trade and commerce in that society
3 centralization of legal and economic authority
4 introduction of representative government

40 One way in which the European Crusades, the Age of Exploration, and the Islamic Revolution in Iran were similar is that during each period

1 religion played an important role in political events
2 imperialism led to an increase in traditional values
3 self-determination encouraged policies of home rule
4 weak central governments led to a return to feudalism

41 The creation of the United Nations, the expansion of the European Economic Community (European Union), and the signing of the North American Free Trade Agreement (NAFTA) resulted in an increase in

1 political revolutions
2 nonalignment policies
3 military alliances
4 international cooperation

[OVER]

Base your answer to question 42 on the chart below and on your knowledge of social studies.

Nation	GDP (Per Capita)	Secondary School Enrollment (Women)	Fertility Rate
Germany	$16,200	93%	1.5
Greece	5,340	93	1.7
Peru	1,090	61	3.6
Morocco	900	30	4.2
Zimbabwe	640	42	5.3
Pakistan	370	11	5.9

42 Which generalization about the impact of the gross domestic product (GDP) on a nation can be drawn from this chart?

1 The GDP has no relationship to the status of women.
2 Women in nations with a low GDP tend to have fewer children.
3 The percentage of women enrolled in secondary schools is higher in nations with a high GDP.
4 Nations with a high GDP usually try to increase their population.

43 Which action would best help developing nations improve their standard of living?

1 borrowing from the World Bank to purchase food for their citizens
2 relying on a few cash crops for export sale in the world market
3 encouraging an increase in the trade deficit
4 investing in the development of human resources

44 The violence and destruction that occurred during World War II led to the

1 expansion of colonial empires in Africa
2 formation of the United Nations
3 signing of the Versailles Treaty
4 unification of Germany

[OVER]

Base your answer to question 45 on the cartoon below and on your knowledge of social studies.

Bruce Shanks in The Buffalo Evening News, Sept. 30, 1968

45 Which statement best reflects the viewpoint of the cartoonist?

1 Organizations such as the League of Nations and the United Nations will continue to maintain world peace.
2 Violence and bloodshed will continue to plague the world, despite efforts to end war.
3 The economy of the world will improve if wars are ended.
4 War will be eliminated by the 21st century since the world has learned from past conflicts.

46 • Boxer Rebellion
   • Solidarity Movement
   • Intifada
   • Shining Path Movement

   One action that is common to the groups involved in these events is that each group
   1 strengthened its ties with former imperialistic powers
   2 established international terrorist organizations
   3 used political demonstrations or revolts to bring about change
   4 created religious unity in the group's nation

47 In the late 1990's, international demands to conduct trials for war crimes similar to those conducted at Nuremberg after World War II are responses to war crimes taking place in
   1 Bosnia   3 Poland
   2 the Czech Republic   4 Russia

48 Which nongovernmental organization has been most involved in the effort to achieve freedom for political prisoners throughout the world?
   1 Amnesty International
   2 Doctors without Borders
   3 Greenpeace
   4 Red Cross

[OVER]

Answers to the following questions are to be written on paper provided by the school.

Students Please Note:

In developing your answers to Part II, be sure to

(1) include specific factual information and evidence whenever possible

(2) keep to the questions asked; do not go off on tangents

(3) avoid overgeneralizations or sweeping statements without sufficient proof; do not overstate your case

(4) keep these general definitions in mind:

(a) <u>discuss</u> means "to make observations about something using facts, reasoning, and argument; to present in some detail"

(b) <u>describe</u> means "to illustrate something in words or tell about it"

(c) <u>show</u> means "to point out; to set forth clearly a position or idea by stating it and giving data which support it"

(d) <u>explain</u> means "to make plain or understandable; to give reasons for or causes of; to show the logical development or relationships of"

Part II

ANSWER THREE QUESTIONS FROM THIS PART. [45]

1 Geographic factors often have an important influence on the history, economy, and culture of regions and nations.

Geographic Factors

Amazon rain forest
Irregular coastlines
Island locations
Khyber Pass
Monsoons
Nile River Valley
Sahara Desert

Select *three* geographic factors from the list and for *each* one selected:

- Identify *one* specific region or nation affected by the factor

- Discuss *two* effects of the factor on the history, economy, and/or culture of the specific region or nation [5,5,5]

2 Throughout history, men and women have attempted to change their societies through reform or revolution.

Reformers/Revolutionaries

Catherine the Great
Simón Bolívar
Sun Yat-sen
Mohandas Gandhi
Jomo Kenyatta

[OVER]

Anwar Sadat
Rigoberta Menchú

Select *three* of the reformers or revolutionaries from the list and for *each* one selected:

- Discuss the historical circumstances that led to the need to reform the nation or society
- Identify *one* specific action taken by the individual to bring about this reform
- Evaluate how successful the individual's action was in carrying out this reform [5,5,5]

3   Religions have influenced the development of various societies.

Religions

Animism
Buddhism
Christianity
Taoism (Daoism)
Hinduism
Islam
Judaism

Select *three* religions form the list and for *each* one selected:

- Identify *one* area of the world where that religion has had an influence on a particular society [Do *not* use the United States in your answer]
- Discuss *one* major idea of the religion
- Explain *one* way that major idea influenced the society [5,5,5]

4 Historical concepts are often identified by descriptive titles. Several concepts with this type of title are listed below.

Concepts
> Divine right of monarchs
> Jihad
> Liberation theology
> Peristroika
> Spheres of influence
> The Four Modernizations
> White Man's Burden

Select *three* historical concepts form the list and for *each* one selected:

- Identify a nation or region affected by this concept
- Explain the major idea expressed by the concept
- Discuss *one* social, economic, *or* political effect of the concept on the identified nation or region [5,5,5]

5 Throughout history, a number of regions have experienced internal troubles, revolts, or wars.

Regions
> Central Africa
> Central America
> Eastern Europe
> Korean Peninsula
> Middle East
> Northern Ireland

Select *three* regions from the list and for *each* one selected:

[OVER]

- Discuss the historical background of the problem in that area [In your discussion, identify at least *two* of the major groups involved in the problem.]
- Discuss the extent to which the problem has been resolved. [5,5,5]

6 The ideas contained in written works have often influenced societies.

Written Works

The Analects
Magna Carta
Mein Kampf
Ninety-five theses
Communist Manifesto
Two Treatises on Government
Vedas

Select *three* works from the list and for *each* one selected:

- Describe a major idea discussed in the work
- Identify a specific society or nation affected by the work [Do *not* use the United States in your answer.]
- Explain *one* way the society or nation changed as a result of this written work [5,5,5]

7 Throughout history, inventions and technological changes have had both positive and negative impacts on nations and regions.

Inventions/ Technological Changes

Factory system
Steam engine
Computers
Hydroelectric power
Medical advances
New types of fertilizers
Nuclear power

a Select *three* inventions or technological changes from the list and for *each* one selected, discuss a positive *and* a negative impact of the invention or technological change on a specific nation or region. [Do not use the United States in your answer.] [4,4,4,]

b For *one* of the inventions or technological changes you selected in part *a*, discuss whether the invention or technological change has had a greater positive *or* a greater negative impact on the nation or region. [3]

[OVER]

ANSWER KEY
JANUARY 1999—PART I

1	4		25	3
2	1		26	3
3	2		27	1
4	1		28	1
5	2		29	2
6	2		30	4
7	3		31	1
8	4		32	3
9	1		33	2
10	4		34	4
11	4		35	3
12	1		36	3
13	2		37	2
14	1		38	1
15	4		39	3
16	3		40	1
17	2		41	4
18	1		42	3
19	2		43	4
20	4		44	2
21	2		45	2
22	1		46	3
23	1		47	1
24	4		48	1

GLOBAL STUDIES

ANSWER SHEET

☐ Male

Student . . . . Sex: ☐ Female

Teacher . . . .

School . . . .

Write your answers for Part I on this answer sheet, and write
your answers for Part II on the paper provided by the school.

FOR TEACHER USE ONLY		
Part I Score		
(Use table below)		
Part II Score		Rater's Initials:
Total		. . . .

PART I CREDITS

Directions to Teacher:

In the table below, draw a circle around the number of right answers and the
adjacent number of credits. Then write the number of credits (not the number
right) in the space provided above.

No. Right	Credits		No. Right	Credits
48	55		23	34
47	54		22	34
46	53		21	33
45	53		20	32
44	52		19	31
43	51		18	30
42	50		17	29
41	49		16	29
40	48		15	28
39	48		14	27
38	47		13	26
37	46		12	25
36	45		11	23
35	44		10	21
34	43		9	19
33	43		8	17
32	42		7	15
31	41		6	12
30	40		5	10
29	39		4	8
28	38		3	6
27	38		2	4
26	37		1	2
25	36		0	0
24	35			

1. . . . .   25 . . . .
2. . . . .   26 . . . .
3. . . . .   27 . . . .
4. . . . .   28 . . . .
5. . . . .   29 . . . .
6. . . . .   30 . . . .
7. . . . .   31 . . . .
8. . . . .   32 . . . .
9. . . . .   33 . . . .
10. . . . .   34 . . . .
11. . . . .   35 . . . .
12. . . . .   36 . . . .
13. . . . .   37 . . . .
14. . . . .   38 . . . .
15. . . . .   39 . . . .
16. . . . .   40 . . . .
17. . . . .   41 . . . .
18. . . . .   42 . . . .
19. . . . .   43 . . . .
20. . . . .   44 . . . .
21. . . . .   45 . . . .
22. . . . .   46 . . . .
23. . . . .   47 . . . .
24. . . . .   48 . . . .

No.
Right . . . .

The declaration below should be signed when you have completed the examination.

I do hereby affirm, at the close of this examination, that I had no unlawful knowledge of the questions or answers prior to the examination, and
that I have neither given nor received assistance in answering any of the questions during the examination.

_____

Signature

The University of the State of New York

GLOBAL STUDIES

ANSWER SHEET

Part I (55 credits)

☐ Male

Student .... Sex: ☐ Female

Teacher ....

School ....

Write your answers for Part I on this answer sheet, and write your answers for Part II on the paper provided by the school.

FOR TEACHER USE ONLY		
Part I Score		
(Use table below)		
Part II Score		Rater's Initials:
Total		....

PART I CREDITS

Directions to Teacher:

In the table below, draw a circle around the number of right answers and the adjacent number of credits. Then write the number of credits (not the number right) in the space provided above.

No. Right	Credits	No. Right	Credits
48	55	23	34
47	54	22	34
46	53	21	33
45	53	20	32
44	52	19	31
43	51	18	30
42	50	17	29
41	49	16	29
40	48	15	28
39	48	14	27
38	47	13	26
37	46	12	25
36	45	11	23
35	44	10	21
34	43	9	19
33	43	8	17
32	42	7	15
31	41	6	12
30	40	5	10
29	39	4	8
28	38	3	6
27	38	2	4
26	37	1	2
25	36	0	0
24	35		

1......... 25.........
2......... 26.........
3......... 27.........
4......... 28.........
5......... 29.........
6......... 30.........
7......... 31.........
8......... 32.........
9......... 33.........
10......... 34.........
11......... 35.........
12......... 36.........
13......... 37.........
14......... 38.........
15......... 39.........
16......... 40.........
17......... 41.........
18......... 42.........
19......... 43.........
20......... 44.........
21......... 45.........
22......... 46.........
23......... 47.........
24......... 48.........

No. Right ....

The declaration below should be signed when you have completed the examination.

_____
Signature

The University of the State of New York

REGENTS HIGH SCHOOL EXAMINATION

GLOBAL STUDIES

ANSWER SHEET

☐ Male

Student .... Sex: ☐ Female

Teacher ....

School ....

Write your answers for Part I on this answer sheet, and write
your answers for Part II on the paper provided by the school.

Part I (55 credits)

1.........	25.........
2.........	26.........
3.........	27.........
4.........	28.........
5.........	29.........
6.........	30.........
7.........	31.........
8.........	32.........
9.........	33.........
10.........	34.........
11.........	35.........
12.........	36.........
13.........	37.........
14.........	38.........
15.........	39.........
16.........	40.........
17.........	41.........
18.........	42.........
19.........	43.........
20.........	44.........
21.........	45.........
22.........	46.........
23.........	47.........
24.........	48.........

FOR TEACHER USE ONLY	
Part I Score .... (Use table below)	
Part II Score	Rater's Initials:
Total	....

PART I CREDITS

Directions to Teacher:

In the table below, draw a circle around the number of right answers and the
adjacent number of credits. Then write the number of credits (not the number
right) in the space provided above.

No. Right	Credits		No. Right	Credits
48	55		23	34
47	54		22	34
46	53		21	33
45	53		20	32
44	52		19	31
43	51		18	30
42	50		17	29
41	49		16	29
40	48		15	28
39	48		14	27
38	47		13	26
37	46		12	25
36	45		11	23
35	44		10	21
34	43		9	19
33	43		8	17
32	42		7	15
31	41		6	12
30	40		5	10
29	39		4	8
28	38		3	6
27	38		2	4
26	37		1	2
25	36		0	0
24	35			

No.
Right ....

The declaration below should be signed when you have completed the examination.

I do hereby affirm, at the close of this examination, that I had no unlawful knowledge of the questions or answers prior to the examination, and
that I have neither given nor received assistance in answering any of the questions during the examination.

_____

Signature

The University of the State of New York

REGENTS HIGH SCHOOL EXAMINATION

GLOBAL STUDIES

ANSWER SHEET

Sex: ☐ Male ☐ Female

Student ....

Teacher ....

School ....

Write your answers for Part I on this answer sheet, and write
your answers for Part II on the paper provided by the school.

FOR TEACHER USE ONLY		
Part I Score		
(Use table below)		
Part II Score		Rater's Initials:
Total		....

PART I CREDITS

Directions to Teacher:

In the table below, draw a circle around the number of right answers and the
adjacent number of credits. Then write the number of credits (not the number
right) in the space provided above.

No. Right	Credits		No. Right	Credits
48	55		23	34
47	54		22	34
46	53		21	33
45	53		20	32
44	52		19	31
43	51		18	30
42	50		17	29
41	49		16	29
40	48		15	28
39	48		14	27
38	47		13	26
37	46		12	25
36	45		11	23
35	44		10	21
34	43		9	19
33	43		8	17
32	42		7	15
31	41		6	12
30	40		5	10
29	39		4	8
28	38		3	6
27	38		2	4
26	37		1	2
25	36		0	0
24	35			

1......... 25.........
2......... 26.........
3......... 27.........
4......... 28.........
5......... 29.........
6......... 30.........
7......... 31.........
8......... 32.........
9......... 33.........
10......... 34.........
11......... 35.........
12......... 36.........
13......... 37.........
14......... 38.........
15......... 39.........
16......... 40.........
17......... 41.........
18......... 42.........
19......... 43.........
20......... 44.........
21......... 45.........
22......... 46.........
23......... 47.........
24......... 48.........

No.
Right ....

The declaration below should be signed when you have completed the examination.

I do hereby affirm, at the close of this examination, that I had no unlawful knowledge of the questions or answers prior to the examination, and
that I have neither given nor received assistance in answering any of the questions during the examination.

_____

Signature

The University of the State of New York

GLOBAL STUDIES

Part I (55 credits)

1.........		25.....	
2.........		26.....	
3.........		27.....	
4.........		28......	
5........		29.....	
6.........		30......	
7.........		31......	
8.........		32......	
9.........		33......	
10.........		34......	
11.........		35......	
12.........		36......	
13.........		37......	
14.........		38......	
15.........		39......	
16.........		40......	
17.........		41......	
18.........		42......	
19.........		43......	
20.........		44......	
21.........		45......	
22.........		46......	
23.........		47......	
24.........		48......	

ANSWER SHEET

☐ Male

Student .... Sex: ☐ Female

Teacher ....

School ....

Write your answers for Part I on this answer sheet, and write your answers for Part II on the paper provided by the school.

FOR TEACHER USE ONLY

Part I Score ....
  (Use table below)

Part II Score ....   **Rater's Initials:**

  Total ....

  ....

PART I CREDITS

Directions to Teacher:
In the table below, draw a circle around the number of right answers and the adjacent number of credits. Then write the number of credits (not the number right) in the space provided above.

No. Right	Credits		No. Right	Credits
48	55		23	34
47	54		22	34
46	53		21	33
45	53		20	32
44	52		19	31
43	51		18	30
42	50		17	29
41	49		16	29
40	48		15	28
39	48		14	27
38	47		13	26
37	46		12	25
36	45		11	23
35	44		10	21
34	43		9	19
33	43		8	17
32	42		7	15
31	41		6	12
30	40		5	10
29	39		4	8
28	38		3	6
27	38		2	4
26	37		1	2
25	36		0	0
24	35			

No. Right ....

The declaration below should be signed when you have completed the examination.

I do hereby affirm, at the close of this examination, that I had no unlawful knowledge of the questions or answers prior to the examination, and that I have neither given nor received assistance in answering any of the questions during the examination.

_____

Signature

The University of the State of New York

REGENTS HIGH SCHOOL EXAMINATION

GLOBAL STUDIES

ANSWER SHEET

☐ Male

Student .... Sex: ☐ Female

Teacher ....

School ....

Write your answers for Part I on this answer sheet, and write your answers for Part II on the paper provided by the school.

FOR TEACHER USE ONLY	
Part I Score	
(Use table below)	
Part II Score	Rater's Initials:
Total	....

PART I CREDITS

Directions to Teacher:

In the table below, draw a circle around the number of right answers and the adjacent number of credits. Then write the number of credits (not the number right) in the space provided above.

No. Right	Credits		No. Right	Credits
48	55		23	34
47	54		22	34
46	53		21	33
45	53		20	32
44	52		19	31
43	51		18	30
42	50		17	29
41	49		16	29
40	48		15	28
39	48		14	27
38	47		13	26
37	46		12	25
36	45		11	23
35	44		10	21
34	43		9	19
33	43		8	17
32	42		7	15
31	41		6	12
30	40		5	10
29	39		4	8
28	38		3	6
27	38		2	4
26	37		1	2
25	36		0	0
24	35			

The declaration below should be signed when you have completed the examination.

I do hereby affirm, at the close of this examination, that I had no unlawful knowledge of the questions or answers prior to the examination, and that I have neither given nor received assistance in answering any of the questions during the examination.

_____
Signature

1......... 25.........
2......... 26.........
3......... 27.........
4......... 28.........
5......... 29.........
6......... 30.........
7......... 31.........
8......... 32.........
9......... 33.........
10......... 34.........
11......... 35.........
12......... 36.........
13......... 37.........
14......... 38.........
15......... 39.........
16......... 40.........
17......... 41.........
18......... 42.........
19......... 43.........
20......... 44.........
21......... 45.........
22......... 46.........
23......... 47.........
24......... 48.........

No. Right ....

The University of the State of New York

REGENTS HIGH SCHOOL EXAMINATION

GLOBAL STUDIES

ANSWER SHEET

Sex: ☐ Male
☐ Female

Student . . . .

Teacher . . . .

School . . . .

Write your answers for Part I on this answer sheet, and write your answers for Part II on the paper provided by the school.

FOR TEACHER USE ONLY	
Part I Score . . . . (Use table below)	
Part II Score	**Rater's Initials:**
Total	. . . .

PART I CREDITS

Directions to Teacher:
In the table below, draw a circle around the number of right answers and the adjacent number of credits. Then write the number of credits (not the number right) in the space provided above.

No. Right	Credits		No. Right	Credits
48	55		23	34
47	54		22	34
46	53		21	33
45	53		20	32
44	52		19	31
43	51		18	30
42	50		17	29
41	49		16	29
40	48		15	28
39	48		14	27
38	47		13	26
37	46		12	25
36	45		11	23
35	44		10	21
34	43		9	19
33	43		8	17
32	42		7	15
31	41		6	12
30	40		5	10
29	39		4	8
28	38		3	6
27	38		2	4
26	37		1	2
25	36		0	0
24	35			

Part I (55 credits)

1.........   25.........
2.........   26.........
3.........   27.........
4.........   28.........
5.........   29.........
6.........   30.........
7.........   31.........
8.........   32.........
9.........   33.........
10.........   34.........
11.........   35.........
12.........   36.........
13.........   37.........
14.........   38.........
15.........   39.........
16.........   40.........
17.........   41.........
18.........   42.........
19.........   43.........
20.........   44.........
21.........   45.........
22.........   46.........
23.........   47.........
24.........   48.........

No.
Right . . . .

The declaration below should be signed when you have completed the examination.

The University of the State of New York

REGENTS HIGH SCHOOL EXAMINATION

GLOBAL STUDIES

ANSWER SHEET

☐ Male

Student . . . . Sex: ☐ Female

Teacher . . . .

School . . . .

Write your answers for Part I on this answer sheet, and write
your answers for Part II on the paper provided by the school.

FOR TEACHER USE ONLY		
Part I Score . . . . (Use table below)		
Part II Score		Rater's Initials:
Total		. . . .

PART I CREDITS

Directions to Teacher:

In the table below, draw a circle around the number of right answers and the
adjacent number of credits. Then write the number of credits (not the number
right) in the space provided above.

No. Right	Credits		No. Right	Credits
48	55		23	34
47	54		22	34
46	53		21	33
45	53		20	32
44	52		19	31
43	51		18	30
42	50		17	29
41	49		16	29
40	48		15	28
39	48		14	27
38	47		13	26
37	46		12	25
36	45		11	23
35	44		10	21
34	43		9	19
33	43		8	17
32	42		7	15
31	41		6	12
30	40		5	10
29	39		4	8
28	38		3	6
27	38		2	4
26	37		1	2
25	36		0	0
24	35			

Part I (55 credits)

1	25 . . . .
2	26 . . . .
3	27 . . . .
4	28 . . . .
5	29 . . . .
6	30 . . . .
7	31 . . . .
8	32 . . . .
9	33 . . . .
10	34 . . . .
11	35 . . . .
12	36 . . . .
13	37 . . . .
14	38 . . . .
15	39 . . . .
16	40 . . . .
17	41 . . . .
18	42 . . . .
19	43 . . . .
20	44 . . . .
21	45 . . . .
22	46 . . . .
23	47 . . . .
24	48 . . . .

No.
Right . . . .

The declaration below should be signed when you have completed the examination.

I do hereby affirm, at the close of this examination, that I had no unlawful knowledge of the questions or answers prior to the examination, and
that I have neither given nor received assistance in answering any of the questions during the examination.

_____

Signature

NOTES

www.review.com

Expert Advice

Counselor-O-Matic

Pop Surveys

www.review.com

Paying for It

www.review.com

THE
PRINCETON
REVIEW

Getting In

Word du Jour

www.review.com

www.review.com

College Talk

Find-O-Rama College Search

www.review.com

Best Schools

SAT Survival

www.review.com

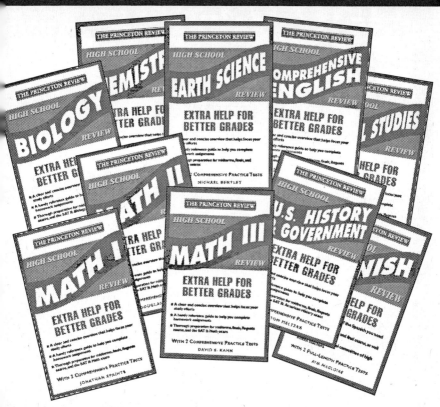

FIND US...

International

Hong Kong
4/F Sun Hung Kai Centre
30 Harbour Road, Wan Chai,
Hong Kong
Tel: (011)85-2-517-3016

Japan
Fuji Building 40, 15-14
Sakuragaokacho, Shibuya Ku,
Tokyo 150, Japan
Tel: (011)81-3-3463-1343

Korea
Tae Young Bldg, 944-24,
Daechi- Dong, Kangnam-Ku
The Princeton Review- ANC
Seoul, Korea 135-280,
South Korea
Tel: (011)82-2-554-7763

Mexico City
PR Mex S De RL De Cv
Guanajuato 228 Col. Roma
06700 Mexico D.F., Mexico
Tel: 525-564-9468

Montreal
666 Sherbrooke St.
West, Suite 202
Montreal, QC H3A 1E7 Canada
Tel: (514) 499-0870

Pakistan
1 Bawa Park - 90 Upper Mall
Lahore, Pakistan
Tel: (011)92-42-571-2315

Spain
Pza. Castilla, 3 - 5° A, 28046
Madrid, Spain
Tel: (011)341-323-4212

Taiwan
155 Chung Hsiao East Road
Section 4 - 4th Floor,
Taipei R.O.C., Taiwan
Tel: (011)886-2-751-1243

Thailand
Building One, 99 Wireless Road
Bangkok, Thailand 10330
Tel: (662) 256-7080

Toronto
1240 Bay Street, Suite 300
Toronto M5R 2A7 Canada
Tel: (800) 495-7737
Tel: (716) 839-4391

Vancouver
4212 University Way NE,
Suite 204
Seattle, WA 98105
Tel: (206) 548-1100

National (U.S.)

We have over 60 offices around the U.S. and
run courses in over 400 sites. For courses and locations
within the U.S. call 1 (800) 2/Review and you will be
routed to the nearest office.